Pre-Algebra
Mathematics

REVISED EDITION

HOLT, RINEHART AND WINSTON, INC.
NEW YORK, TORONTO, LONDON, SYDNEY

EUGENE D. NICHOLS

Pre-Algebra
Mathematics

REVISED EDITION

About the Author

Eugene D. Nichols is Professor and Head,
Department of Mathematics Education,
The Florida State University, Tallahassee, Florida

PHOTO CREDITS:

Pages xii; 160; 274; 320; 344; 410; Robert Bull
Page 30; A. Devaney, Inc., New York
Page 66; Adelaide DeMenil, Photo Researchers, Inc.
Pages 98; 188; Courtesy of Education Center, Newton, Massachusetts
Page 130; Peter Sahula, Photo Researchers, Inc.
Page 220; Russ Kinne, Photo Researchers, Inc.
Page 242; Courtesy of United Control Corporation, Redmond, Washington
Page 376; Ronny Jaques, Photo Researchers, Inc.

Preface

This textbook is a revision of *Pre-Algebra Mathematics*, 1965. The author is grateful to the many teachers and students who have made constructive suggestions for improving the original version of the book. In response to these suggestions, the chapters have been arranged in a more teachable order, and the work on numeration systems has been reduced by eliminating computations in bases other than ten.

The textbook has proved to be well suited for a modern general mathematics course or for a course to precede a modern course in algebra in junior or senior high school.

Throughout the entire text development, the student is made an active participant in the learning process by means of the consistent use of the discovery approach. Significant mathematical topics are presented so that students have the opportunity to develop the mathematical maturity necessary for the study of algebra.

While students pursue the study of structural characteristics of mathematics, constant attention is devoted to the development and maintenance of computational skills and the uses of mathematical concepts in solving problems. Arithmetic, algebra, geometry, and an introduction to coordinate geometry are balanced to provide a sound foundation for further study of mathematics or to serve as a terminal course in mathematics.

The labors of many colleagues — mathematicians, mathematics educators, and teachers — who explored new ideas and thereby made an impression upon the author, are hereby acknowledged.

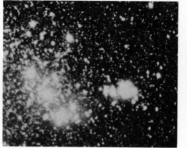

Contents

Symbols

$\{1, 2, 3\}$	the set consisting of the numbers 1, 2, and 3 (11)
$\in$	belongs to, is an element of, is a member of (12)
$\notin$	does not belong to, is not an element of, is not a member of (12)
$1, 2, 3, \ldots$	one, two, three, and so on [continues in the same pattern] (13)
ϕ	the empty set, the null set (15)
$\cup$	union (18)
$n(A)$	the number of elements in set A [Read: n of A] (19)
$\cap$	intersection (20)
G.C.F. $(35, 42)$	Greatest Common Factor of 35 and 42 (23)
L.C.M. $(2, 3)$	Least Common Multiple of 2 and 3 (24)
$\subseteq$	is a subset of (31)
$\nsubseteq$	is not a subset of (32)
$\neq$	is not equal to (32)
$<$	is less than (42)
$>$	is greater than (42)
10^4	ten to the fourth power, or ten to the fourth, or the fourth power of ten (69)
$.09\overline{09}$	the 09 repeats on and on (115)
$\sqrt{4}$	square root of four (131)
$\doteq$	is approximately equal to (132)
$\sqrt[3]{1,000}$	cube root of 1,000 (133)
$\overline{AB}$	segment with endpoints A and B (140)
U	universal set (149)
$\overline{A}$	complement of set A (150)

$a \leftrightarrow b$	a is matched with b (152)
%	per cent (161)
$^{+}5$	positive five (190)
$^{-}5$	negative five (190)
$\lvert^{-}3\rvert$	absolute value of negative three (200)
$-x$	opposite of x (244)
$\leq$	is less than or equal to (256)
$\geq$	is greater than or equal to (256)
$\nleq$	is not less than and is not equal to (256)
$\ngeq$	is not greater than and is not equal to (256)
$\{x \mid x > a\}$	the set of all numbers x such that x is greater than a (257)
$[a]$	greatest integer not greater than a (261)
aRb	a is related to b (268)
(a, b)	the ordered pair of numbers a and b (275)
$A(x, y)$	point A with first coordinate x and second coordinate y (287)
Q_1	first quadrant (293)
$\triangle ABC$	triangle ABC (322)
$\overleftrightarrow{AB}$	line with points A and B on it (324)
$\overset{\circ}{\overrightarrow{AB}}$	half-line starting after point A with point B on it (324)
$\overrightarrow{AB}$	ray with endpoint A and point B on it (324)
$\angle ABC$	angle ABC (326)
AB	measure of $\overline{AB}$ (327)
$m\angle A$	measure of angle A (327)
$35°$	35 degrees (327)
h_C	half-plane which contains point C (331)
$\square ABCD$	rectangle $ABCD$ (345)
$\text{Area}_{\square ABCD}$	area of rectangle $ABCD$ (345)
$\square ABCD$	parallelogram $ABCD$ (347)
$\perp$	is perpendicular to (348)
π	pi (359)
$\overset{\frown}{BC}$	arc from B to C (381)
$\sim$	is similar to (394)

CHAPTER ONE

Whole Numbers, Divisibility, and Factoring

DIVISIBILITY BY 2

When we speak of divisibility, we will be concerned with the *whole* numbers. To show the whole numbers, we write

$$0, 1, 2, 3, \ldots$$

The three dots mean that we continue on and on in the same pattern. The smallest whole number is 0. But there is no largest whole number.

$16 \div 2 = 8$. We say that 16 is divisible by 2, because when 16 is divided by 2, the quotient is a whole number, 8, and the remainder is 0. We call 2 a divisor of 16.

$15 \div 3 = 5$. Why is it true that 15 is divisible by 3? Is 3 a divisor of 15?

■ We say that a whole number x is *divisible* by a whole number y if the quotient, $x \div y$, is a whole number, and the remainder is 0. y is called a *divisor* of x.

1. $147 \div 7 = 21$. Why is 147 divisible by 7?

2. **a.** Is 64 divisible by 4? Why or why not?

   b. Is 64 divisible by 12? Why or why not?

   c. Is 64 divisible by 32? Why or why not?

3. Is 1001 divisible by 11? Why or why not?

4. Which of the following numbers are divisible by 2?

a. 20	**d.** 329	**g.** 114	**j.** 1,024
b. 11	**e.** 115	**h.** 584	**k.** 2,408
c. 32	**f.** 326	**i.** 37	**l.** 433

5. Put the numbers in exercise **4** into two groups: *even* numbers and *odd* numbers.

6. Are all even numbers divisible by 2?

7. Are any odd numbers divisible by 2?

8. What digits may be in the units' place of numbers divisible by 2?

Did you find the following to be true? Even numbers are divisible by 2. Odd numbers are not divisible by 2.

We say: 2 is a divisor of every even number because when dividing an even number by 2, the quotient is a whole number, and the remainder is 0.

DIVISIBILITY OF A NUMBER BY ITSELF AND ONE

1. Classify each of the following into two groups: even numbers and odd numbers.

   a. 1,378   **d.** 399   **g.** 4,011   **j.** 9,067

   b. 1,012   **e.** 204   **h.** 210   **k.** 2,323

   c. 3,763   **f.** 1,166   **i.** 965   **l.** 3,232

2. Give answers to the following:

   a. $56 \div 1$ **c.** $39 \div 1$ **e.** $904 \div 1$ **g.** $78 \div 1$

   b. $371 \div 1$ **d.** $143 \div 1$ **f.** $342 \div 1$ **h.** $90 \div 1$

3. Explain why the following statement is true.

   Every whole number is divisible by 1.

The following pattern is suggested by the examples in exercise **2**.

■ For every whole number n, $n \div 1 = n$.

4. Complete this sentence to describe the pattern above. Every whole number divided by ___ is equal to ___ .

5. Give answers to the following:

   a. $37 \div 37$ **c.** $41 \div 41$ **e.** $114 \div 114$ **g.** $76 \div 76$

   b. $142 \div 142$ **d.** $10 \div 10$ **f.** $89 \div 89$ **h.** $53 \div 53$

The following pattern is suggested by the examples in exercise **5**.

■ For every whole number n (except 0), $n \div n = 1$.

6. Complete this sentence to describe the pattern above. Every whole number (except zero) divided by ___ is equal to ___ .

We can draw two conclusions from the examples just given.

    1. Since every whole number is divisible by 1, 1 is a divisor of every whole number.
    2. Since every whole number (except zero) is divisible by itself, every whole number is a divisor of itself.

7. Why is every whole number (except zero) divisible by itself? (See the definition of divisibility on page 1.)

You have probably noticed that we avoided division by 0. Later you will see that there are some good reasons for this.

DIVISORS OF WHOLE NUMBERS

We can now conclude that every whole number (except zero) has itself and 1 as divisors.

1. Which number has exactly one divisor?

Some numbers have exactly two divisors. For example, 5 and 13 are such numbers.

The divisors of 5 are 1 and 5.
The divisors of 13 are 1 and 13.

2. Which of the following numbers have exactly two divisors?

a. 7	**d.** 11	**g.** 37
b. 9	**e.** 19	**h.** 21
c. 2	**f.** 15	**i.** 41

Some numbers have more than two divisors.

$$10 \div 1 = 10$$
$$10 \div 2 = 5$$
$$10 \div 5 = 2$$
$$10 \div 10 = 1$$

3. How many divisors does the number 10 have?

4. List the four divisors of 10.

5. List *all* divisors of each of the following numbers.

a. 12	**d.** 55	**g.** 36
b. 27	**e.** 49	**h.** 62
c. 17	**f.** 25	**i.** 43

6. List the five smallest numbers which have 3 as one of their divisors.

7. List the five smallest numbers which have 9 as one of their divisors.

8. List the five smallest numbers which have 5 as one of their divisors.

9. What digits are in the units' place if a number is divisible by 5?

10. If a number is divisible by 10, is it also divisible by 5?

11. If a number is divisible by 5, is it also divisible by 10?

12. If a number is divisible by 15, is it also divisible by 5?

Test Your Arithmetic Skills

If you make errors in any of the exercises, take the test keyed to that exercise. The table on the next page shows where to find the tests.

Add.

1.   575
    6,366
      144
    5,379
      986
13,450

2. 3,766
       25
    4,618
      339
    5,112
13,860

3. $12\frac{1}{2}$

$13\frac{1}{4}$

$5\frac{3}{4}$

$6\frac{1}{2}$

$19\frac{1}{4}$

$57\frac{1}{4}$

4. $3\frac{1}{2}$

$12\frac{5}{6}$

$1\frac{1}{3}$

$5\frac{1}{6}$

$17\frac{2}{3}$

$40\frac{1}{2}$

5. .56
     .49
     .36
     .79
     .68
2.88

6. 23.17
     5.25
     3.13
    17.12
    56.28
104.95

Subtract.

7. 17,365
     3,423
13,942

8. 117,365
     19,489
97,876

9. $17\frac{3}{4}$

$16\frac{1}{2}$

$1\frac{1}{4}$

10. $368\frac{2}{5}$

$69\frac{3}{5}$

$298\frac{4}{5}$

11. 36.27
     29.85
6.42

12. 172.162
      98.279
73.883

Multiply.

13. 236
      422
99,592

14. 1,376
       985
1,355,360

15. 2,481
      3,279
8,135,199

16. $\frac{5}{7} \times \frac{3}{4}$

17. $1\frac{3}{5} \times \frac{3}{4}$

18. $\frac{5}{6} \times 8$

19. $7 \times \frac{4}{9}$

20. $3\frac{4}{5} \times 6$

21. $3\frac{1}{2} \times 5\frac{1}{3}$

22. 17.23
       28

23. 12.3
      26.8

24. 6.58
      19.7

Divide.

25. $35\overline{)376,205}$ *$10748\frac{5}{7}$*

26. $198\overline{)209,397}$

27. $321\overline{)482,507}$

28. $12 \div \frac{4}{5} = $ *15*

29. $\frac{2}{9} \div \frac{4}{7} = $ *$\frac{7}{18}$*

30. $\frac{2}{7} \div 6 = $ *$\frac{1}{21}$*

31. $4\frac{1}{3} \div 7\frac{2}{7} = $ *$\frac{91}{153}$*

32. $25\overline{)1.25}$ *.05*

33. $.7\overline{)10.15}$ *14.5*

34. $.5\overline{)3.765}$ *7.53*

Where to Find the Tests

This table shows where to find the tests which you may need for additional practice.

| | | Fractional numbers | |
Operation	Whole numbers	Fractional form	Decimal form
Addition	5	35	71
Subtraction	7	42	76
Multiplication	9	46	84
Division	15	52	86

Test in Addition of Whole Numbers

1.
6	4	9
8	9	3
3	7	8
2	6	2
1	1	7
9	6	7

2.
7	2	6
9	8	3
8	7	9
4	4	4
1	9	1
9	9	7
6	5	6

44 *44* *36*

3.
36	11	27
25	37	36
13	84	72
87	72	85
91	45	46
46	56	39
53	39	18
84	68	91

4.
67	55	21
28	32	98
45	18	47
32	12	63
58	79	75
61	43	26

291 *239* *330*

5.
106	908	888
368	685	735
272	398	370
908	406	569
867	398	176
198	769	306
206	805	509

6.
809	1,695	2,366
38	98	1,703
3,782	389	9,507
466	74	3,506
9,008	8,003	4,007
1,762	689	1,776
84	365	5,365
369	88	1,837

16,318 *11,401* *30,067*

If you had fewer than two problems correct in any one group, turn to pages 423–424 for practice in adding whole numbers.

DIVISIBILITY BY 3

Many interesting things about divisibility of numbers can be learned from observing patterns. In this discussion and others like it, we will use "sum of the digits" to mean "sum of the numbers named by the digits."

Each number listed under *Number* in the table is divisible by 3. Note that the sum of the digits in each numeral is also divisible by 3.

1. Do you think you can find a number divisible by 3 in which the sum of the digits is not divisible by 3? Try!

   Test for Divisibility by 3
Add the digits. If the sum is divisible by 3, the number is divisible by 3. Otherwise, the number is not divisible by 3.

2. Use the Test for Divisibility by 3 and tell which of the following numbers are divisible by 3.

   a. 303   **f.** 56,322

   b. 112   **g.** 106,523

   c. 1,951   **h.** 471,862

   d. 20,361   **i.** 541,512

   e. 78,201   **j.** 919,191

3. Divide the numbers in exercise **2** by 3.

   a. In the case of numbers not divisible by 3, is the remainder ever greater than 2?

   b. Why do we never have a remainder of 4 when dividing a number by 3?

   c. What would be the greatest possible remainder when dividing a number by 5? 9? 25?

Number	Sum of the digits
3	3
6	6
9	9
12	$1+2=3$
15	$1+5=6$
18	$1+8=9$
21	$2+1=3$
24	$2+4=6$
27	$2+7=9$
30	$3+0=3$
33	$3+3=6$
36	$3+6=9$
39	$3+9=12$
42	$4+2=6$
45	$4+5=9$
48	$4+8=12$
.	
.	
.	
333	$3+3+3=9$
336	$3+3+6=12$
339	$3+3+9=15$
.	
.	
.	
987	$9+8+7=24$
990	$9+9+0=18$
	and so on

Test in Subtraction of Whole Numbers

1.	875	375	503	4.	3,506	33,675	90,305
	623	158	484		1,628	4,833	27,416

2.	211	507	685	5.	643,115	503,116	980,000
	184	398	599		512,004	424,115	891,111
	27	*109*	*86*		*131,111*	*79,001*	*88,889*

3.	1,120	3,765	2,063	6.	37,205	406,375	100,000
	865	98	907		307	8,499	9,806

If you had fewer than two problems correct in any one group, turn to page 424 for practice in subtracting whole numbers.

DIVISIBILITY BY 9

1. List the names for the first ten numbers divisible by 9.

2. Compute the sums of digits for the numbers in exercise 1.

   a. Are the sums divisible by 9?

   b. Is 42 divisible by 9?

   c. $4 + 2 = 6$. Is 6 divisible by 9?

3. Is every number which is divisible by 3 also divisible by 9? Give two examples to support your answer.

4. Is every number which is divisible by 9 also divisible by 3? Give two examples to support your answer.

Test for Divisibility by 9
Add the digits. If the sum is divisible by 9, the number is divisible by 9. Otherwise, the number is not divisible by 9.

5. Using the Test for Divisibility by 9, tell which of the following are divisible by 9.

   a. 909
   b. 22,221
   c. 1,008
   d. 7,899

   e. 9,919
   f. 12,348
   g. 10,017
   h. 88,884

   i. 5,454
   j. 17,235
   k. 10,343
   l. 123,453

6. Divide the numbers in exercise **5** by 9.

    a. In the case of numbers not divisible by 9, is the remainder ever greater than 8?

    b. Why do we not ever have a remainder of 10 when dividing by 9?

    c. What would be the meaning of remainder 9 when dividing by 9? Would it mean the same as remainder 0?

FACTORS AND PRIME NUMBERS

The number 24 is divisible by 1, 2, 3, 4, 6, 8, 12, and 24. Each of the eight divisors is called a *factor* of 24.

1. Give four pairs of factors, each pair having 24 for the product.

2. Every number except 1 has at least one pair of different factors. One of these factors is 1. What is the other factor?

■ Numbers which have only themselves and 1 as different whole number factors are called *prime numbers*.

3. The first 6 prime numbers are: 2, 3, 5, 7, 11, and 13. What are the next 5 prime numbers that follow 13?

■ Numbers which have more than two whole number factors are called *composite numbers*.

The number 1 is neither prime nor composite. Why?

    The number 4 has three factors: 1, 2, and 4. It is the smallest composite number.

4. Give the names for the other composite numbers less than 10. For each number, list all of its factors.

5. Classify each of the following as either a prime number or a composite number.

a. 27	**d.** 67	**g.** 81	**j.** 417
b. 17	**e.** 49	**h.** 547	**k.** 601
c. 109	**f.** 33	**i.** 205	**l.** 204

6. Give the least factor, different from 1, of each of the following numbers.

a. 14	**c.** 111	**e.** 49	**g.** 23
b. 35	**d.** 81	**f.** 121	**h.** 91

7. Give the greatest factor, different from the number itself, of each of the following numbers.

a. 14   **c.** 111   **e.** 49   **g.** 202

b. 35   **d.** 81   **f.** 121   **h.** 213

8. List all factors of each of the following numbers.

3, 35; 5, 21; 7, 15   2, 512, 4, 256; 8, 128;   3, 81; 9, 27

a. 22   **c.** 105   **e.** 1,024   **g.** 243

7, 13   *3, 147; 7, 63; 9, 49*   *3, 155; 5, 93; 15, 31;*

b. 33   **d.** 91   **f.** 441   **h.** 465

9. Classify each of the following numbers as either even or odd.

a. 1,013   **c.** 2,376   **e.** 23,765   **g.** 99,100

b. 17,108   **d.** 9,901   **f.** 17,009   **h.** 48,077

10. Which of the following numbers are divisible by 3?

a. 1,737   **b.** 2,005   **c.** 16,479   **d.** 3,143   **e.** 176,367

11. Which of the following numbers are divisible by 9?

a. 989   **b.** 3,078   **c.** 16,479   **d.** 96,307   **e.** 80,838

12. Write the greatest possible three-digit numeral using the digits 1, 3, and 5.

13. Write the least possible three-digit numeral using the digits 1, 3, and 5.

14. Tell why each of the numbers you gave as answers in exercises **12** and **13** is divisible by 9.

Test in Multiplication of Whole Numbers

1. 23	136	358	**4.** 709	830	907	
5	7	4	20	60	90	
115	*952*	*1,432*	*14,180*	*49,800*	*81,630*	
2. 467	899	189	**5.** 411	517	367	
8	8	7	312	411	156	
3,736	*7,192*	*1,323*	*128,232*	*212,487*	*57,252*	
3. 332	547	359	**6.** 709	1,105	9,007	
12	23	46	26	207	305	
3,984	*12,581*	*16,514*	*18,434*	*228,735*	*2,747,135*	

If you had fewer than two problems correct in any one group, turn to page 425 for practice in multiplying whole numbers.

COMPLETE FACTORIZATION

Every prime number has exactly two factors.

1. One of the two factors of a prime number is the number 1. What is the other factor?

It is easy to tell whether a small number is a prime number. But it is not always easy to tell whether a large number is a prime number.

■ A prime number which is a factor of some number is called a *prime factor* of that number.

2. 2 is a prime factor of 12. What is the other prime factor of 12?

3. 3 is a prime factor of 15. What is the other prime factor of 15?

4. Give all prime factors of these composite numbers.

a. 21	**c.** 18	**e.** 36	**g.** 51	**i.** 99
b. 22	**d.** 14	**f.** 49	**h.** 40	**j.** 112

Can every composite number be given as a product of only prime factors? The examples below suggest that the answer to this question may be "yes."

$$12 = 2 \times 2 \times 3 \qquad 25 = 5 \times 5 \qquad 620 = 2 \times 2 \times 5 \times 31$$

2 and 3	5	2, 5, and 31
are prime numbers.	is a prime number.	are prime numbers.

■ When a number is named as a product of prime numbers only, we say that the number is *completely factored.*

5. Give the *complete factorization* of the following numbers.

Example 1 $35 = 5 \times 7$

Since 5 and 7 are prime numbers, 5×7 is the complete factorization of 35.

Example 2 $64 = 2 \times 2 \times 2 \times 2 \times 2 \times 2$

Since 2 is a prime number, $2 \times 2 \times 2 \times 2 \times 2 \times 2$ is the complete factorization of 64.

a. 10	**e.** 52	**i.** 150	**m.** 1,000
b. 9	**f.** 66	**j.** 390	**n.** 3,000
c. 34	**g.** 96	**k.** 460	**o.** 1,024
d. 42	**h.** 125	**l.** 625	**p.** 2,048

6. For each pair of numbers, name the greatest number which is a common factor of both numbers.

   Example 8, 12

   4 is the greatest common factor of 8 and 12.

   a. 2, 4   **d.** 25, 35   **g.** 50, 70   **j.** 60, 75

   b. 5, 25   **e.** 14, 35   **h.** 48, 36   **k.** 51, 34

   c. 10, 15 **f.** 50, 100   **i.** 52, 39   **l.** 12, 60

7. It is claimed that perhaps every even number greater than 2 can be shown as the sum of a pair of primes. Show each of the following even numbers as the sum of a pair of primes.

   Examples $4 = 2 + 2$ $18 = 11 + 7$ $24 = 19 + 5$

   a. 6   **c.** 12   **e.** 42   **g.** 84   **i.** 100

   b. 10   **d.** 26   **f.** 36   **h.** 78   **j.** 200

8. Two prime numbers which differ by 2 are called *twin primes*. For example, 11 and 13 are twin primes because each of them is a prime number, and their difference is 2. Find 5 more pairs of twin primes.

SETS

■ A *set* is a collection of things. Objects which belong to a set are called *members*, or *elements*, of the set.

1. On the right is a picture of a set of dishes. How many members does this set have?

2. On the right is a picture of a set of golf clubs. How many members does this set have?

3. What are the two members of the set of prime factors of 12?

4. What are the elements of the set of prime factors of 15?

When discussing sets, we list the names of their members within braces { }. For example, the set of all factors of 6 is designated as

$$\{1, 2, 3, 6\}$$

5. How many members are there in the set of factors of 6?

6. Why does 4 not belong to the set of factors of 6?

7. Choose any whole number. Is it true that the number you have chosen either belongs to the set of factors of 6 or it does not belong to this set?

We use capital letters as short names for sets. Let A be the set of all factors of 12. Then $A = \{1, 2, 3, 4, 6, 12\}$.

8. How many elements belong to A?

9. B is the set of all factors of 21. List the elements of B.

10. Set X consists of numbers named inside the rectangle on the right. Arrange the elements of X in order from the smallest to the largest.

Set X

2	16	8
20	10	14
12	6	18	4

11. How many elements belong to X?

12. Is this a correct description of X: X is the set of all even numbers which are between 1 and 21?

To say that 6 belongs to the set X, we write $6 \in X$.

Read $6 \in X$ as *six belongs to set X*,
or *six is an element of set X*,
or *six is a member of set X*.

13. Write each of the following in words in three different ways as shown above.

    a. $12 \in M$ **b.** $4 \in H$ **c.** $0 \in T$

7 is not a member of the set X pictured above. We write $7 \notin X$ to mean *seven does not belong to set X*, or *seven is not a member of set X*.

14. Write each of the following in words in two different ways.

    a. $10 \notin Q$ **b.** $25 \notin R$ **c.** $15 \notin S$

15. Let E be the set of all even numbers. Which are true and which are false?

    a. $6 \in E$ **c.** $311 \in E$ **e.** $79 \notin E$ **g.** $300{,}208 \notin E$

    b. $128 \notin E$ **d.** $1{,}024 \notin E$ **f.** $10{,}300 \in E$ **h.** $500{,}000 \in E$

FINITE AND INFINITE SETS

Set C of all whole numbers greater than 2 and less than 10 is: $\{3, 4, 5, 6, 7, 8, 9\}$. Is it true that every member of set C is greater than 2 and less than 10? Set C consists of seven elements. It is a *finite set*. It is possible to count the elements of every finite set. It would not take you very long to count the elements of set C.

It probably would take quite a long time to count all the elements in a set which has 367,507 elements. But, given sufficient time, they can be counted. Therefore, such a set is a finite set.

1. Is the set consisting of students in this class a finite set? Why or why not?

2. Is the set consisting of students in this entire school a finite set? Why or why not?

3. Is the set of all human beings in this town a finite set? Why or why not?

4. Is the set of all human beings in the world a finite set? Why or why not?

5. a. List the elements of set M, where M is the set of all odd numbers less than 10.

   b. How many members does M have? Is M a finite set?

Let us start naming whole numbers in order.

$$0, 1, 2, 3, 4, 5, 6, 7, 8, 9, 10, \ldots$$

6. What do the three dots mean?

7. Can you complete counting *all* whole numbers? Why or why not?

■ The set of all whole numbers is an *infinite set*.

8. Name the first ten members of the set of even numbers.

9. Is the set of all even numbers a finite set? Why or why not?

10. Name the first ten members of the set of odd numbers.

11. Is the set of all odd numbers a finite set? Why or why not?

12. Name the first ten members of the set of numbers divisible by 5.

13. Is the set of all numbers divisible by 5 a finite set? Why or why not?

14. Is the set of all whole numbers greater than 10,000,000,000 a finite set? Why or why not?

15. Is the set of whole numbers less than 10,000,000,000 a finite set? Why? If it is a finite set, how many elements does it have?

It is impossible to list all members of an infinite set. To show that there are more elements in an infinite set, we list a few, then write three dots. By observing the pattern which is true for the listed elements, we decide what other elements belong to the set.

16. If $A = \{2, 4, 6, 8, 10, \ldots\}$, which are true and which are false?

a. $102 \in A$ **c.** $1630 \notin A$ **e.** $10,000 \in A$

b. $375 \in A$ **d.** $9031 \notin A$ **f.** $100,000 \notin A$

g. Every even number belongs to A.

h. No odd number belongs to A.

i. Some odd numbers belong to A.

17. If $M = \{3, 6, 9, 12, 15, \ldots\}$, which are true and which are false?

a. $12 \in M$ **d.** $33 \in M$ **g.** $1002 \in M$

b. $17 \in M$ **e.** $50 \in M$ **h.** $5001 \notin M$

c. $21 \in M$ **f.** $102 \notin M$ **i.** $10,005 \notin M$

j. Every odd number belongs to M.

k. Every even number belongs to M.

l. Some odd numbers belong to M.

m. Some even numbers belong to M.

n. All numbers divisible by 3 belong to M.

o. No numbers which are not divisible by 3 belong to M.

p. Some numbers divisible by 6 belong to M.

q. Some numbers divisible by 9 belong to M.

r. No numbers divisible by 100 belong to M.

18. $H = \{5, 10, 15, 20, 25, 30, \ldots\}$. Describe the elements of H by completing the following statement: Every number which belongs to H is divisible by ____.

THE EMPTY SET

There are no pink elephants in this room. The set of pink elephants in this room is the *empty set*.

■   A set which has no elements is called the *empty set*.

Which of the following describe the empty set? For non-empty sets, list their elements.

1. the set of whole numbers which are less than 11 and also greater than 10

2. the set of mathematics books on the "fiction shelf" in your library

3. the set of even numbers which are divisible by 3

4. the set of numbers which are less than 10 and also divisible by 5

5. the set of numbers which are less than 100 and also divisible by 100

6. the set of numbers which are less than 21 and also divisible by 20

7. the set of brooms in a closet filled to capacity with clothes

8. the set of polar bears whose natural habitat is Africa

9. the set of prime numbers which are divisible by 2

■   The symbol for the empty set is ϕ. The empty set is also called the *null set*.

10. Make up two descriptions of your own for ϕ.

Test in Division of Whole Numbers

1. $7)\overline{182}$ $5)\overline{1,255}$ $9)\overline{2,079}$ $2)\overline{11,007}$

     26   251   231   5503 r1

2. $4)\overline{2,205}$ $8)\overline{3,700}$ $36)\overline{4,392}$ $25)\overline{5,300}$

     551 r1   462 r4   122   212

3. $12)\overline{2,640}$ $63)\overline{1,268}$ $85)\overline{3,306}$ $17)\overline{9,007}$

     220   20 r 8   38 r76   529 r14

4. $25)\overline{789}$ $51)\overline{96,845}$ $110)\overline{119,206}$ $368)\overline{405,990}$

     31 r14   1898 r47   1083 r 76   1103 r 86

If you had fewer than three problems correct in any group, turn to pages 425–427 for practice in dividing whole numbers.

Checking Division by Multiplication

The operations of division and multiplication are related. As you work the exercises below, you will notice how they are related.

1. Replace the frames to obtain true statements.

   Example 1 $125 \div 5 = 25$ means $25 \times \square = 125$

   5 for $\square$ gives a true statement;
   $25 \times 5 = 125$

   a. $366 \div 2 = 183$ means $183 \times \square = 366$

   b. $576 \div 4 = 144$ means $\square \times 4 = 576$

   c. $121 \div 11 = 11$ means $\square \times \square = 121$

   d. $500 \div 25 = 20$ means $20 \times 25 = \square$

   Example 2 $36 \div 5 = 7$, R 1 means $(\square \times 5) + 1 = 36$

   7 for $\square$ gives a true statement;
   $(7 \times 5) + 1 = 36$

   e. $56 \div 5 = 11$, R 1 means $(\square \times 5) + 1 = 56$

   f. $210 \div 4 = 52$, R 2 means $(52 \times \square) + 2 = 210$

   g. $115 \div 50 = 2$, R 15 means $(\square \times 50) + 15 = 115$

   h. $200 \div 80 = 2$, R 40 means $(2 \times 80) + \square = 200$

2. Explain why the remainder is always less than the divisor.

Patterns in Mathematics

Watch for patterns in mathematics. Patterns save work! If you know that the following is true,

$$1.26 \times 1.35 = 1.701$$

then you know, without having to do any work, that the following two statements are also true.

$$1.701 \div 1.35 = 1.26$$
$$1.701 \div 1.26 = 1.35$$

1. For each multiplication statement, give two related division statements.

   a. $3.05 \times 3.7 = 11.285$ **c.** $56.1 \times 1.1 = 61.71$

   b. $12.1 \times .9 = 10.89$ **d.** $39.5 \times .5 = 19.75$

Addition and subtraction are related in a way similar to multiplication and division. For example, if

$$6.583 + .769 = 7.352$$

then the following statements are also true.

$$7.352 - .769 = 6.583$$
$$7.352 - 6.583 = .769$$

2. For each addition statement, give two related subtraction statements.

   a. $23.7 + 15.2 = 38.9$ c. $1.25 + 3.67 = 4.92$

   b. $15.6 + 19.7 = 35.3$ d. $.68 + .21 = .89$

THE FOUR BASIC OPERATIONS

The most commonly used operations with numbers are addition, subtraction, multiplication, and division. Each of these operations produces one number from a pair of numbers. Below we show a different way of writing addition.

$$3, 5 \xrightarrow{+} 8 \qquad 10, 1 \xrightarrow{+} 11$$
$$5, 3 \xrightarrow{+} 8 \qquad 1, 10 \xrightarrow{+} 11$$

1. Is it true that for any two whole numbers n and k, if $n, k \xrightarrow{+} t$, then $k, n \xrightarrow{+} t$? Why or why not?

Subtraction can be written in a similar way. For example,

$$9, 4 \xrightarrow{-} 5 \qquad 17, 2 \xrightarrow{-} 15$$

2. Replace each ☐ to obtain a true statement.

   a. $25, 6 \xrightarrow{-} ☐$ c. $32, 2 \xrightarrow{-} ☐$ e. $100, 25 \xrightarrow{-} ☐$

   b. $17, 9 \xrightarrow{-} ☐$ d. $45, 10 \xrightarrow{-} ☐$ f. $120, 40 \xrightarrow{-} ☐$

3. Explain why $3, 7 \xrightarrow{-} ☐$ has no answer among the whole numbers.

4. Give an example to show that if $a, b \xrightarrow{-} c$, then it does not follow that $b, a \xrightarrow{-} c$.

5. Replace each ☐ to obtain a true statement.

   a. $10, 10 \xrightarrow{-} ☐$ b. $137, 137 \xrightarrow{-} ☐$ c. $1262, 1262 \xrightarrow{-} ☐$

6. On the basis of your answers to exercise 5, replace the ☐ to make a true statement. For every whole number a: $a, a \xrightarrow{-} ☐$.

The following two statements are true.

$$3, 6 \xrightarrow{\times} 18 \qquad 10, 5 \xrightarrow{\div} 2$$

7. Replace each □ to obtain a true statement.

   a. $3, 4 \xrightarrow{\times} \square$ **d.** $7, 5 \xrightarrow{\times} \square$ **g.** $4, 4 \xrightarrow{\times} \square$

   b. $4, 3 \xrightarrow{\times} \square$ **e.** $10, 12 \xrightarrow{\times} \square$ **h.** $9, 0 \xrightarrow{\times} \square$

   c. $5, 7 \xrightarrow{\times} \square$ **f.** $12, 10 \xrightarrow{\times} \square$ **i.** $0, 9 \xrightarrow{\times} \square$

8. Is it true that for any two whole numbers a and b, if $a, b \xrightarrow{\times} c$, then $b, a \xrightarrow{\times} c$? Why or why not?

9. Replace each □ to obtain a true statement.

   a. $30, 10 \xrightarrow{\div} \square$ **d.** $10, 5 \xrightarrow{\div} \square$ **g.** $5, 5 \xrightarrow{\div} \square$

   b. $10, 30 \xrightarrow{\div} \square$ **e.** $12, 3 \xrightarrow{\div} \square$ **h.** $12, 12 \xrightarrow{\div} \square$

   c. $5, 10 \xrightarrow{\div} \square$ **f.** $3, 12 \xrightarrow{\div} \square$ **i.** $1, 1 \xrightarrow{\div} \square$

10. Is it true that for any two numbers x and y, if $x, y \xrightarrow{\div} z$, then $y, x \xrightarrow{\div} z$? If your answer is "no," give an example showing that it is not always true.

UNION

It is possible to have operations with sets just as it is possible to have operations with numbers.

Consider a pair of sets: $A = \{1, 2, 3, 4\}$; $B = \{4, 6, 8, 10\}$. We form a new set C by "combining" the elements of sets A and B.

$$C = \{1, 2, 3, 4, 6, 8, 10\}$$

■ The *union* of sets A and B is the set containing all the elements of set A and all the elements of set B. The symbol for union is ∪.

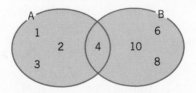

The union of sets A and B consists of the elements in the entire shaded area.

$$A \cup B = \{1, 2, 3, 4, 6, 8, 10\}$$

1. Of what letter does the symbol for union remind you?

2. Given $X = \{2, 4, 6\}$ and $Y = \{4, 6, 15\}$.

   a. Sets X and Y have two elements in common. Name them.

   b. Where do the elements common to both sets X and Y lie in the set diagram below?

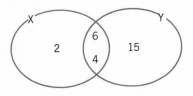

   c. List the elements of $X \cup Y$.

3. $R = \{1, 3, 5\}$ and $T = \{4, 6, 8, 12\}$

   a. What is $R \cup T$?

   b. How many elements are there in R? in T?

   c. How many elements are there in $R \cup T$?

   d. If $n(R)$ [Read: n of R] means the number of elements in set R, what does $n(T)$ mean?

   e. What does $n(R \cup T)$ mean?

   f. Is it true that $n(R) + n(T) = n(R \cup T)$? Why?

4. G = the set of all girl students in your school
   B = the set of all boy students in your school

   a. What is $G \cup B$?

   b. Is $n(G) + n(B) = n(G \cup B)$ true?

5. $D = \{2, 3, 4\}$ and $E = \{3, 4, 5, 6, 7\}$

   a. What is $D \cup E$?

   b. Is $n(D) + n(E) = n(D \cup E)$ true? If not, how do $n(D) + n(E)$ and $n(D \cup E)$ compare; that is, which is larger?

6. If finite sets A and B have no common elements, how do $n(A) + n(B)$ and $n(A \cup B)$ compare?

7. If finite sets A and B have at least one common element, how do $n(A) + n(B)$ and $n(A \cup B)$ compare?

INTERSECTION

$$A = \{10, 20, 30\} \qquad B = \{20, 30, 40, 50\}$$

Sets A and B have two elements in common. The common elements are the numbers 20 and 30.

$\{20, 30\}$ is the set of all elements common to A and B.

1. Give the set of all elements common to each pair of sets. One pair has no common elements.

   a. $\{1, 2\}$; $\{1, 5, 10\}$

   b. $\{0, 3, 6\}$; $\{0, 5, 10\}$

   c. $\left\{\dfrac{1}{2}, \dfrac{1}{3}, \dfrac{1}{4}\right\}$; $\left\{\dfrac{1}{2}, \dfrac{1}{3}, \dfrac{1}{4}, \dfrac{1}{5}, \dfrac{1}{6}\right\}$

   d. the set of all students in this school;   the set of all boy students in this school

   e. the set of all students in this school;   the set of all teachers in this school

■ The *intersection* of sets A and B is the set containing all those elements which are common to set A and set B. The symbol for intersection is ∩.

Consider sets A and B given at the top of the page.

$$A \cap B = \{20, 30\}$$

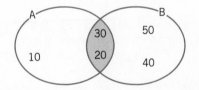

The elements of $A \cap B$ lie in the shaded area in the diagram.

2. What is the intersection of $\{2, 4, 6\}$ and $\{4, 6, 15\}$?

Sets $\{1, 2, 3\}$ and $\{4, 6, 8, 10\}$ have no common elements. Therefore, their intersection is the empty set: $\{1, 2, 3\} \cap \{4, 6, 8, 10\} = \phi$.

3. Give the intersections for the following pairs of sets.

   a. $\{1, 10\}$; $\{100, 10\}$ c. $\{0\}$; $\{0, 10, 20\}$

   b. $\left\{\dfrac{1}{2}, \dfrac{1}{3}, \dfrac{1}{4}\right\}$; $\left\{\dfrac{1}{4}, \dfrac{1}{5}\right\}$ d. $\{1, 5\}$; $\{11, 15\}$

4. Suppose A is any set.

   a. What is $A \cup A$?   **c.** What is $A \cup \phi$?

   b. What is $A \cap A$?   **d.** What is $A \cap \phi$?

■   Two sets which have no common elements are called *disjoint* sets.

5. What is the intersection of two disjoint sets?

6. Give the union and the intersection of each pair of sets.

   a. the set of states bordering on Lake Michigan;
      the set of states bordering on Lake Superior

   b. the set of United States presidents whose names begin with
      the letter M;
      the set of United States presidents whose names end with the
      letter N

   c. the set of United States presidents inaugurated after 1928;
      the set of United States presidents inaugurated after 1932

   d. $\{0, 2, 4, 6, 8, 10, 12, \ldots\}$; $\{1, 3, 5, 7, 9, 11, 13, \ldots\}$

   e. $\left\{\dfrac{1}{2}, \dfrac{1}{4}, \dfrac{1}{8}, \dfrac{1}{16}\right\}$; $\left\{\dfrac{1}{2}, \dfrac{1}{4}, \dfrac{1}{6}, \dfrac{1}{8}\right\}$

   f. the set of states bordering on the Pacific Ocean;
      {Nevada, California, Idaho}

   g. $\{3, 6, 9, 12, 15, 18, \ldots\}$; $\{9, 18, 27, 36, 45, 54, \ldots\}$

   h. $\{2, 4, 6, 8, 10, 12, \ldots\}$; $\{6, 12, 18, 24, 30, 36, \ldots\}$

   i. $\{5, 10, 15, 20, 25, \ldots\}$; $\{20, 40, 60, 80, 100, \ldots\}$

7. **a.** Give the set of all factors of 8.

   b. Give the set of all factors of 10.

   c. Give the set of all common factors of 8 and 10.

8. **a.** Give the set of all factors of 5.

   b. Give the set of all factors of 17.

   c. Give the set of the common factors of 5 and 17.

9. Why is $\{0\}$ not the empty set?

10. Why is $\{0, 5\} \cap \{0, 8\}$ not the empty set?

SETS OF FACTORS OF WHOLE NUMBERS

Every number multiplied by 1 is that number. Therefore, 1 is a factor of every number.

■   For every number n, $n \times 1 = n$.

1 is also a factor of 0, because $0 \times 1 = 0$.

> Let G be the set of all factors of 5. Then $G = \{1, 5\}$.
> Let H be the set of all factors of 11. Then $H = \{1, 11\}$.

1. What is $G \cap H$?

2. Is 5 a prime number? Why or why not?

3. Is 11 a prime number? Why or why not?

4. **a.** Give the set of all factors of 19.

    b. Give the set of all factors of 31.

    c. What is the intersection of the set of all factors of 19 and of 31?

    d. Are 19 and 31 prime numbers? Why or why not?

5. **a.** Give the set of all factors of 17; call this set A.

    b. Give the set of all factors of 37; call this set B.

    c. What is $A \cap B$?

    d. Are 17 and 37 prime numbers? Why or why not?

6. What common factor do any two prime numbers have?

7. Supply the missing part to make the following statement true. The intersection of the set of factors of each of two prime numbers is ——.

> 6 and 8 are even numbers.
>
> The set of factors of 6 is $\{1, 2, 3, 6\}$.
> The set of factors of 8 is $\{1, 2, 4, 8\}$.

8. What is the intersection of the set of factors of 6 and of 8?

9. **a.** Is 12 an even number? Why or why not?

    b. Is 26 an even number? Why or why not?

    c. Give the set of factors of 12.

d. Give the set of factors of 26.

e. What is the intersection of the set of factors of 12 and of 26?

10. What two numbers belong to the set which is the intersection of the set of factors of each of two even numbers?

GREATEST COMMON FACTOR

The set of factors of 35 is $\{1, 5, 7, 35\}$.
The set of factors of 42 is $\{1, 2, 3, 6, 7, 14, 21, 42\}$.
The set of common factors of 35 and 42 is $\{1, 7\}$.
The greatest number which is a common factor of 35 and 42 is 7.

7 is the Greatest Common Factor of 35 and 42.

A commonly used abbreviation for Greatest Common Factor is G.C.F. We shall abbreviate the statement, "The Greatest Common Factor of 35 and 42 is 7," as follows:

$$G.C.F. (35, 42) = 7$$

1. Give the G.C.F. of each pair of numbers.

a. 35, 42	**f.** 24, 36	**k.** 196, 32
b. 5, 11	**g.** 15, 33	**l.** 49, 196
c. 12, 18	**h.** 10, 50	**m.** 104, 125
d. 51, 48	**i.** 18, 24	**n.** 121, 289
e. 42, 43	**j.** 15, 15	**o.** 32, 32

2. If both members of a pair of numbers are the same number, what is the G.C.F. of this pair?

3. What is the G.C.F. of any two prime numbers?

4. Is 2 the G.C.F. of any two even numbers? If your answer is "no," give an example of two even numbers for which the G.C.F. is greater than 2.

5. Can 8 be the G.C.F. of two even numbers? If your answer is "yes," give an example of two such numbers.

6. Can 2 be the G.C.F. of two odd numbers?

7. Can 3 be the G.C.F. of two odd numbers? If your answer is "yes," give an example in support of your answer.

8. Can 5 be a factor of an even number? If your answer is "yes," give an example to support your answer.

9. Can 5 be the factor of an odd number? If your answer is "yes," give an example to support your answer.

10. Can 5 be the G.C.F. of two numbers, one of which is even and the other odd? If your answer is "yes," give an example to support it.

LEAST COMMON MULTIPLE

When adding fractional numbers, we use a common denominator. For example, when adding $\frac{1}{2}$ and $\frac{1}{3}$ we usually do the following:

$$\frac{1}{2} + \frac{1}{3} = \frac{3}{6} + \frac{2}{6}, \text{ or } \frac{5}{6}$$

The common denominator we chose for $\frac{1}{2}$ and $\frac{1}{3}$ was 6. Of course, 12 would also be a common denominator for $\frac{1}{2}$ and $\frac{1}{3}$. We could write

$$\frac{1}{2} + \frac{1}{3} = \frac{6}{12} + \frac{4}{12} = \frac{10}{12}, \text{ or } \frac{5}{6}$$

We prefer the smaller common denominator because it involves simpler computations.

Addition of fractions involves finding a *common multiple* of two or more numbers. Let us find a few more common multiples of 2 and 3. To do that let us find separately the set S of multiples of 2 and the set T of multiples of 3.

$$S = \{2, \quad 4, \; \textcircled{6}, \; 8, \; 10, \textcircled{12}, \; 14, \; 16, \textcircled{18}, \; 20, \; 22, \textcircled{24}, \ldots\}$$
$$T = \{3, \; \textcircled{6}, \; 9, \textcircled{12}, \; 15, \textcircled{18}, \; 21, \textcircled{24}, \ldots\}$$

The set of common multiples of 2 and of 3 is the intersection of S and T.

$$S \cap T = \{6, 12, 18, 24, \ldots\}$$

The smallest number in $S \cap T$ is 6.

6 is the Least Common Multiple of 2 and 3.

We shall abbreviate the statement, "The Least Common Multiple of 2 and 3 is 6," as follows:

$$\text{L.C.M. } (2, 3) = 6$$

Let F be the set of multiples of 4.

$$F = \{4, 8, 12, 16, 20, 24, 28, 32, 36, 40, 44, 48, \ldots\}$$

Let X be the set of multiples of 6.

$$X = \{6, 12, 18, 24, 30, 36, 42, 48, 54, \ldots\}$$

The set of common multiples of 4 and 6 is the intersection of F and X.

$$F \cap X = \{12, 24, 36, 48, \ldots\}$$

The smallest element of this set is 12. Therefore, L.C.M. $(4, 6) = 12$.

1. For each number, give the set of all multiples less than 100.

   Example 9 The set of all multiples of 9 less than 100 is $\{9, 18, 27, 36, 45, 54, 63, 72, 81, 90, 99\}$.

   a. 5 **b.** 7 **c.** 8 **d.** 10 **e.** 11 **f.** 14 **g.** 16 **h.** 18

2. Using the sets in exercise 1, give the set of common multiples less than 100 for each of the following pairs of numbers.

a. 5, 7	**e.** 10, 18	**i.** 8, 16	**m.** 5, 14
b. 5, 8	**f.** 7, 14	**j.** 7, 11	**n.** 5, 11
c. 7, 8	**g.** 5, 10	**k.** 10, 11	**o.** 5, 18
d. 8, 10	**h.** 5, 16	**l.** 16, 18	**p.** 14, 16

3. If you were asked to continue beyond 100, how many common multiples of 5 and 7 exist? of 5 and 8? of 16 and 18?

The sets of multiples of 2, of 3, and of 4 are given below.

$$A = \{2, 4, 6, 8, 10, 12, 14, 16, 18, 20, 22, 24, 26, 28, 30, 32, \ldots\}$$
$$B = \{3, 6, 9, 12, 15, 18, 21, 24, 27, 30, 33, 36, 39, \ldots\}$$
$$C = \{4, 8, 12, 16, 20, 24, 28, 32, 36, 40, \ldots\}$$

Now let's consider the set of elements which are common to sets A, B, and C. This set is the intersection of the three sets, or $A \cap B \cap C$.

$$A \cap B \cap C = \{12, 24, 36, \ldots\}$$

4. List four more elements in the set $A \cap B \cap C$ above.

5. What is the Least Common Multiple of 2, 3, and 4?

6. Find the L.C.M. of the following:

    a. 2, 4, 6   **b.** 2, 4, 5   **c.** 3, 4, 5   **d.** 4, 8, 10   **e.** 2, 4, 8

7. Find the L.C.M. of the following:

    a. 1, 3   **b.** 1, 15   **c.** 1, 36   **d.** 1, 100   **e.** 1, 795

8. What is the L.C.M. of 1 and n, where n is any number?

9. Find the L.C.M. of the following:

    a. 2, 3   **b.** 2, 5   **c.** 3, 5   **d.** 5, 7   **e.** 11, 13   **f.** 5, 17

10. What kind of numbers are 2, 3, 5, 7, 11, 13 and 17?

11. Give a rule for determining the L.C.M. of two prime numbers.

MORE ABOUT DIVISIBILITY

1. Each of the following numbers is divisible by 2 and by 3. Test each number to see whether it is divisible by 6.

    a. 6   **b.** 72   **c.** 294   **d.** 3,072   **e.** 55,872

2. Can you find a number which is divisible by both 2 and 3, but is not divisible by 6? Why or why not?

3. Each of the following numbers is divisible by 5 and by 6. Test each number to see whether it is divisible by 30.

    a. 60   **b.** 120   **c.** 600   **d.** 930   **e.** 33,030

4. Each of the following numbers is divisible by 4 and by 6. Test each number to see whether it is divisible by 24.

    a. 12   **b.** 24   **c.** 60   **d.** 48   **e.** 132

5. If a number is divisible by a and by b, is it always divisible by the product $a \times b$?

6. **a.** What number when multiplied by 1,001 will give 707,707 for the product?

    b. Is 707,707 divisible by 1,001?

7. **a.** What number when multiplied by 1,001 will give 917,917 for the product?

    b. Is 917,917 divisible by 1,001?

8. Show that each number is divisible by 1,001.

    a. 113,113   b. 507,507   c. 319,319   d. 569,569

9. Do you see that each of the numbers in exercise **8** has a name of the form *abc,abc*?

KEEPING ARITHMETICALLY FIT

For exercises **1–4**, numerals in parentheses refer to pages where you can find similar exercises.

1. Add. (423–424)

a.	b.	c.	d.
237	4,367	375	111
315	5,005	1,266	6,702
921	6,372	56,109	37
106	7,005	300	89,004
711	1,607	578	6
210	3,575	30,000	99
409	4,495	7,005	63,741
370	3,001	46	3,456
3279	*35427*	*95679*	*163156*

2. Subtract. (424)

a.	b.	c.	d.
4,062	135,367	10,004	10,000
389	8,409	5,999	9,009
3673	*126958*	*4005*	*991*

3. Multiply. (425)

a. 36	c. 207	e. 2,937	g. 1,006
5	35	26	375
180	*7245*	*76362*	*377,250*
b. 117	d. 3,766	f. 6,801	h. 2,075
9	8	99	803
1053	*30,128*	*673,299*	*1,666,225*

4. Divide. (425–427)

a. 2)2,308 *1154*   c. 12)2,005 *167 r1*   e. 93)106,395 *1144 r3*   g. 105)210,300 *2,002 r 90*

b. 2)4,407 *2,203 r1*   d. 45)46,109 *1024 r29*   f. 49)567,101 *11,573 r24*   h. 306)712,809 *2,329 r 135*

5. Compute to see if the following are true.

a. 3 × 49 = (3 × 50) − 3   *147* *147* *T*   c. 6 × 49 = (6 × 50) − 6   *294* *294* *T*

b. 5 × 49 = (5 × 50) − 5   *245* *245* *T*   d. 2 × 49 = (2 × 50) − 2   *98* *98* *T*

6. The pattern illustrated by the four examples in exercise **5** can be shown as

$$\square \times 49 = (\square \times 50) - \square$$

Replace $\square$ by each of the following and perform the necessary operations to see if the statements you obtain are true.

a. 1 **b.** 4 **c.** 15 **d.** 10 **e.** 20

VOCABULARY REVIEW

complete factorization (10)
composite number (8)
disjoint sets (21)
divisible (1)
divisor (1)
element (11)
empty set (15)
factor (10)
finite set (13)
Greatest Common Factor (23)

infinite set (13)
intersection (20)
Least Common Multiple (24)
member (11)
null set (15)
prime factor (10)
prime number (8)
set (11)
union (18)
whole numbers (1)

A CHALLENGE TO YOU

1. Show that 1,001 is a factor of every number whose name in base ten is of the form *abc,abc*.

2. How many years would it take to count 100 billion one-dollar bills by counting one every second?

3. In a barn there are some hens and pigs. There are 13 heads and 34 legs altogether. How many hens and how many pigs are there in the barn?

4. The number of bacteria enclosed in a bottle doubles each minute. If the bottle is completely filled with bacteria after 30 minutes, after how many minutes was the bottle half full?

5. A farmer carries a basket of eggs across three bridges. At each bridge he has to pay $\frac{1}{2}$ of his eggs plus $\frac{1}{2}$ egg. After he has crossed the three bridges, he has no eggs left. How many eggs did he have to start with?

CHAPTER TEST

1. Which numbers are divisible by 2?

   (a.) 102   (c.) 52   (e.) 0   (g.) 3,054   (i.) 37,332

   (b.) 18   (d.) 1,002   f. 87   h. 5,043   (j.) 430,044

2. Which numbers are divisible by 3?

   (a.) 102   c. 52   (e.) 0   (g.) 3,054   (i.) 37,332

   (b.) 18   (d.) 1,002   (f.) 87   (h.) 5,043   (j.) 430,044

3. Which numbers are divisible by 6?

   (a.) 102   c. 52   (e.) 0   (g.) 3,054   (i.) 37,332

   (b.) 18   (d.) 1,002   f. 87   h. 5,043   (j.) 430,044

4. Which numbers are divisible by 9?

   (a.) 1764   c. 4,013   e. 8,236   (g.) 1,008

   (b.) 909   d. 379   f. 1,365   h. 2,609

5. Which numbers are prime numbers?

   (a.) 17   b. 15   (c.) 31   d. 33   e. 49   (f.) 37   g. 77

6. Give the complete factorization of each number.

   5×7 $3 \times 2 \times 7$ $2 \times 2 \times 3$ 3×7 7×11 1×53 $3 \times 3 \times 11$

   a. 35   b. 42   c. 12   d. 21   e. 77   f. 53   g. 99

7. If $A = \{4, 8, 12, 16, \ldots\}$, which are true and which are false?

   a. $16 \in A$ T   b. $20 \notin A$ F   c. $1,000 \in A$ T   d. $26 \notin A$ T

8. Give the union and intersection of each pair of sets.

   a. $\{1, 5, 7\}; \{0, 5\}$ b. $\{0\}; \{0, 2\}$ c. $\{2, 4, 6, \ldots\}; \{1, 3, 5, \ldots\}$

9. Give the G.C.F. and the L.C.M. of each set of numbers.

   a. $\{4, 5\}$ 1, 20   b. $\{9, 12, 15\}$ 3, 180 c. $\{10, 15\}$ 5, 30   d. $\{7, 11\}$ 1, 77

10. Which of the following describe the empty set?

    a. $\{1, 2\} \cap \{1, 5\}$ (b.) $\{0, 1\} \cap \{2\}$ c. $\{0, 5\} \cap \{0\}$

11. Explain why a number which is divisible by 9 is also divisible by 3.

12. Is it true that the greater the number, the more divisors it has? If your answer is "no," give an example to support your answer.

CHAPTER TWO

Operations and
Their Properties

NATURAL NUMBERS AND WHOLE NUMBERS

In counting, we use the numbers $1, 2, 3, 4, 5, 6, \ldots$ The three dots mean that we continue on and on.

■ The set $\{1, 2, 3, 4, 5, 6, \ldots\}$ is called the set of *counting numbers*. Another name for counting numbers is *natural numbers*.

1. What is the least natural number?

2. Is there a greatest natural number?

Suppose Al claims that he knows the greatest natural number. We can prove that he is wrong as follows:

> We ask Al to add 1 to the number he claims to be the greatest natural number. Now Al has a number which is 1 greater. Therefore, the number he had previously was not the greatest natural number after all.

3. Jimmy claims he has the greatest even natural number. Prove that Jimmy is wrong.

4. Mary claims she has the greatest odd natural number. Prove that Mary is wrong.

The set of natural numbers

$$\{1, 2, 3, 4, 5, 6, 7, 8, 9, 10, 11, 12, \ldots\}$$

is an *infinite set*. There is no end to the natural numbers.

■ The set of *whole* numbers consists of all the natural numbers and 0. Every natural number, therefore, is a member of the set of whole numbers.

5. Is every whole number a member of the set of natural numbers? Why or why not?

SUBSETS

W = the set of whole numbers = $\{0, 1, 2, 3, 4, 5, 6, \ldots\}$

N = the set of natural numbers = $\{1, 2, 3, 4, 5, 6, \ldots\}$

The set of natural numbers N is a subset of the set of whole numbers W, because every element of N also belongs to W. $N \subseteq W$ means N *is a subset of* W.

Example 1 $A = \{1, 3, 5\}$; $B = \{10, 5, 6, 3, 1\}$. $A \subseteq B$, because every element of A also belongs to B.

Example 2 $C = \{2, 4, 9\}$; $D = \{2, 4, 9\}$. $C \subseteq D$, because every element of C also belongs to D. Note also that $D \subseteq C$, because every element of D is an element of C.

Example 3 $X = \{3, 5, 10\}$; $Y = \{5, 10, 15\}$. It is *not* true that $X \subseteq Y$ because not every element of X is an element of Y.

$X \not\subseteq Y$ [Read: X is *not* a subset of Y] means that at least one element of X is *not* an element of Y.

■   Two sets are *equal* whenever they have the same elements.

For example, if $A = \{0, 2, 4\}$ and $B = \{0, 3 + 1, 1 + 1\}$, then $A = B$, because $0 = 0$, $1 + 1 = 2$, and $3 + 1 = 4$. Thus, each set has the same elements, the numbers 0, 2, and 4. So, $\{0, 2, 4\}$ and $\{0, 3 + 1, 1 + 1\}$ are two names for the same set.

1. Write out an argument for the truth of the following statement. For any two sets A and B, if $A \subseteq B$ and $B \subseteq A$, then $A = B$.

2. What number should you "toss" into the set of natural numbers to obtain the set of whole numbers?

3. For each pair of sets A and B, tell if A is a subset of B.

   a. A = the set of thirteen original states
      B = the set of all present states

   b. A = {John Adams, James K. Polk, James Buchanan, John F. Kennedy, Lyndon B. Johnson, Richard M. Nixon}
      B = the set of all United States presidents

   c. A = the set of all students in this math class
      B = the set of all girls in this math class

   d. $A = \{1, 2, 3\}$; $B = \{1, 2\}$

   e. $A = \{0\}$; $B = \{0, 2, 4, 6, 8, 10, \ldots\}$

   f. $A = \{2, 4, 6\}$; $B = \{2, 4, 6\}$

Note that $\{0\}$ is a set consisting of one element, the number 0. Thus $\{0\}$ is not the empty set, because it has one element in it, whereas the empty set has no elements.

$$\{0\} \neq \phi$$

The set consisting of the number zero is not equal to the empty set.

4. Do you agree that the set of even whole numbers is a subset of the set of whole numbers?

5. Is 0 an even or an odd number?

Read thoughtfully the following mathematical argument, because it shows the way we can derive certain statements from other statements. We will show that 0 is an even number.

We agree that:
1. Every whole number is either even or odd (not both).
2. If two numbers differ by 2 and one of the numbers is even, then the other is also even.
3. 8 is an even number.

Now, $8 - 6 = 2$, so 6 is even. Why?
$6 - 4 = 2$, so 4 is even.
$4 - 2 = 2$, so 2 is even.
$2 - 0 = 2$, so 0 is even.

Here is another way to prove that 0 is an even number.

We agree that:
1. An even number + an even number = an even number. (For example, $8 + 6 = 14$.)
2. An odd number + an odd number = an even number. (For example, $5 + 7 = 12$.)
3. Every whole number is either odd or even (not both).
4. Any number added to 0 is that number. (Therefore, $0 + 0 = 0$.)

Now suppose 0 is an odd number. We know that $0 + 0 = 0$. And so we have that an odd number + an odd number = an odd number. But agreement 2 above states that an odd number + an odd number is an even number. So, 0 cannot be an odd number. Therefore, by agreement 3, 0 is an even number.

6. Is the set of even whole numbers a subset of the set of natural numbers?   Why or why not?

7. Is the set of prime numbers a subset of the set of natural numbers? Why or why not?

8. Is the set of students in this pre-algebra mathematics class a subset of the set of all students in this school?   Why or why not?

9. Is {5} a subset of the set of natural numbers between 1 and 10?

THE NUMBER ZERO

There are some special things which are true about the number zero. These properties are not true of other numbers.

1. Read the examples on the right. Complete the following statement: When the number zero is added to any number, the sum is ____.

$$1 + 0 = 1$$
$$5 + 0 = 5$$
$$98 + 0 = 98$$
$$590 + 0 = 590$$
$$\cdots$$
$$n + 0 = n$$

2. Is the *Property of Zero for Addition*, which you stated above, also true for zero? Verify your answer. [HINT: Is it true that $0 + 0 = 0$?]

3. Read the examples on the right. Complete the following statement: When any number is multiplied by zero, the product is ____.

$$1 \times 0 = 0$$
$$10 \times 0 = 0$$
$$25 \times 0 = 0$$
$$96 \times 0 = 0$$
$$\cdots$$
$$n \times 0 = 0$$

4. Is the *Property of Zero for Multiplication*, which you stated, also true for zero? Verify your answer. [HINT: Is it true that $0 \times 0 = 0$?]

5. Read the examples on the right. Complete the following statement: When the number zero is divided by any number except zero, the quotient is ____.

$$0 \div 3 = 0$$
$$0 \div 12 = 0$$
$$0 \div 125 = 0$$
$$0 \div 976 = 0$$
$$\cdots$$
$$0 \div n = 0$$

6. In each case, supply the missing number in place of □ to obtain a true statement.

a. $\square \div 367 = 0$ d. $67 \times \square = 0$ g. $3,001 \times \square = 0$

b. $59 + \square = 59$ e. $\square + 0 = 0$ h. $\square \div 5,000 = 0$

c. $37 + 0 = \square$ f. $\square + 0 = 69$ i. $17 \times \square = 0$

THE NUMBER ONE

The number one also has some properties which are not true of any other number. Examples below will help you discover these properties.

1. Read the examples on the right. Complete the following statement: When any number is multiplied by the number one, the product is ____.

$$3 \times 1 = 3$$
$$17 \times 1 = 17$$
$$92 \times 1 = 92$$
$$125 \times 1 = 125$$
$$\cdots$$
$$n \times 1 = n$$

2. Is the *Property of One for Multiplication* also true for the number one? Verify your answer.

3. Read the examples on the right. Complete the following statement: When any number is divided by 1, the quotient is ____.

$$17 \div 1 = 17$$
$$35 \div 1 = 35$$
$$40 \div 1 = 40$$
$$160 \div 1 = 160$$
$$\cdots$$
$$n \div 1 = n$$

4. Is the *Property of One for Division* also true for the number one? Verify your answer.

5. Read the examples on the right. Complete the following statement: When any natural number is divided by itself, the quotient is ____.

$$35 \div 35 = 1$$
$$99 \div 99 = 1$$
$$150 \div 150 = 1$$
$$738 \div 738 = 1$$
$$\cdots$$
$$n \div n = 1$$

6. Is the property you stated in exercise 5 also true for the number one? Verify your answer.

7. In each case, replace $\square$ to obtain a true statement.

a. $47 \div \square = 47$ d. $462 \div \square = 462$ g. $107 \times \square = 107$

b. $99 \div \square = 1$ e. $905 \times \square = 905$ h. $465 \div 465 = \square$

c. $\square \div 15 = 0$ f. $131 + 0 = \square$ i. $0 \times 1 = \square$

Test in Addition (Fractional Numerals)

Find the sums. Give the simplest name for each answer.

1. $\dfrac{1}{5} + \dfrac{2}{5}$ $\dfrac{2}{7} + \dfrac{3}{7}$ $\dfrac{2}{3} + \dfrac{2}{3}$ $\dfrac{4}{7} + \dfrac{5}{7}$ $\dfrac{5}{6} + \dfrac{7}{6}$

2. $\dfrac{1}{2} + \dfrac{3}{4}$ $\dfrac{2}{5} + \dfrac{3}{10}$ $\dfrac{4}{7} + \dfrac{3}{14}$ $\dfrac{5}{3} + \dfrac{7}{6}$ $\dfrac{3}{4} + \dfrac{5}{8}$

3. $1\dfrac{1}{2} + 5\dfrac{1}{2}$ $9\dfrac{1}{4} + 7\dfrac{3}{4}$ $2\dfrac{1}{5} + 6\dfrac{2}{5}$ $3\dfrac{1}{7} + 2\dfrac{6}{7}$ $1\dfrac{2}{5} + 4\dfrac{4}{5}$

4. $3\dfrac{1}{2} + 5\dfrac{1}{4}$ $3\dfrac{3}{5} + 4\dfrac{7}{10}$ $6\dfrac{1}{3} + 7\dfrac{5}{6}$ $2\dfrac{1}{4} + 7\dfrac{1}{2}$ $4\dfrac{1}{8} + 7\dfrac{3}{8}$

5. $\dfrac{1}{3} + \dfrac{1}{4}$ $\dfrac{2}{5} + \dfrac{3}{4}$ $\dfrac{1}{2} + \dfrac{2}{5}$ $\dfrac{3}{7} + \dfrac{4}{5}$ $\dfrac{1}{9} + \dfrac{3}{4}$

6. $1\dfrac{3}{4} + 2\dfrac{1}{3}$ $3\dfrac{7}{15} + 2\dfrac{1}{5}$ $9\dfrac{1}{7} + 3\dfrac{2}{5}$ $3\dfrac{6}{7} + 4\dfrac{1}{5}$ $9\dfrac{6}{7} + 10\dfrac{1}{5}$

7. $\dfrac{1}{2} + \dfrac{1}{3} + \dfrac{1}{4}$ $\dfrac{2}{3} + \dfrac{5}{6} + \dfrac{2}{9}$ $3\dfrac{1}{2} + 4\dfrac{1}{6} + 3\dfrac{3}{4}$ $5\dfrac{2}{5} + 3\dfrac{6}{15} + 9\dfrac{1}{10}$

If you had more than one problem incorrect in any group, turn to pages 428–430 for practice in addition (fractional numerals).

Patterns in Mathematics

1. $\dfrac{2}{3}+\dfrac{4}{5}=\dfrac{2\times5}{3\times5}+\dfrac{4\times3}{5\times3}=\dfrac{10}{15}+\dfrac{12}{15}=\dfrac{10+12}{15}=\dfrac{22}{15}=1\dfrac{7}{15}$

2. $\dfrac{4}{7}+\dfrac{5}{6}=\dfrac{4\times6}{7\times6}+\dfrac{5\times7}{6\times7}=\dfrac{24}{42}+\dfrac{35}{42}=\dfrac{24+35}{42}=\dfrac{59}{42}=1\dfrac{17}{42}$

3. $\dfrac{1}{2}+\dfrac{3}{7}=\dfrac{1\times7}{2\times7}+\dfrac{3\times2}{7\times2}=\dfrac{7}{14}+\dfrac{6}{14}=\dfrac{7+6}{14}=\dfrac{13}{14}$

Here is the pattern illustrated in the three exercises above. Two symbols are missing in this pattern. Copy the pattern and fill in the missing symbols.

$$\frac{\square}{\triangle}+\frac{\bigcirc}{\square}=\frac{\square\times\square}{\triangle\times\square}+\frac{\bigcirc\times\triangle}{\ }=\frac{(\square\times\square)+(\bigcirc\times\triangle)}{\triangle\times\square}$$

Make sure you know this important pattern in addition (fractional numerals).

THE COMMUTATIVE PROPERTIES

Each of the two statements below is true.

$$7+9=16$$
$$9+7=16$$

The statement $7+9=9+7$ follows from the two statements and is also true.

1. For each statement below, give its related statement as above. Then write the statement which follows from the two statements.

   Example $15+9=24$

   $9+15=24;\quad 15+9=9+15$

   a. $11+13=24$ **c.** $30+17=47$

   b. $12+36=48$ **d.** $45+10=55$

2. The pattern shown in such statements as $7+9=9+7$ can be shown for all whole numbers by writing $x+y=y+x$. Using u and w instead of x and y, write a statement showing the same pattern.

The property shown by this pattern is called the *Commutative Property of Addition.*

$$x+y=y+x$$

3. The example $5 + 8 = 8 + 5$ is a specific instance of the Commutative Property of Addition. Is this property true for any pair of numbers?

4. The statement $3 \times 7 = 7 \times 3$ is true because $3 \times 7 = 21$ and $7 \times 3 = 21$. Is the statement $4 \times 5 = 5 \times 4$ true?

5. Using x and y, write a statement about multiplication similar to the Commutative Property of Addition.

The property shown by this pattern is called the *Commutative Property of Multiplication.*

$$x \times y = y \times x$$

6. Using the numbers 2 and 5, write a statement which is a specific instance of the Commutative Property of Multiplication.

7. Using the numbers 2 and 5, show that the operation of division does not have the commutative property.

8. Using the numbers 2 and 5, show that the operation of subtraction does not have the commutative property.

We conclude:

Addition and multiplication are *commutative* operations.
Subtraction and division are *non-commutative* operations.

9. Change the order of the numbers in each exercise and tell whether the result is still the same. If you think that there is no answer among the whole numbers, write "no answer."

Example 1	5×11	$5 \times 11 = 55$; $11 \times 5 = 55$. The result is the same.
Example 2	$10 \div 5$	$10 \div 5 = 2$; $5 \div 10$, no answer. The results are different.
Example 3	$10 - 7$	$10 - 7 = 3$; $7 - 10$, no answer. The results are different.

a. $4 \div 2$	**f.** $125 + 15$	**k.** $5 \div 1$
b. $17 + 13$	**g.** $5 - 0$	**l.** $1 - 1$
c. $12 - 4$	**h.** $0 + 10$	**m.** 1×1
d. $5 - 5$	**i.** 3×17	**n.** $1 + 1$
e. $21 \div 21$	**j.** 0×12	**o.** $1 \div 1$

We will make up some new operations. Each operation is defined in terms of familiar operations.

10. T means add twice the second number to the first number. Compute the answers.

> *Example*   3 T 5 $3\ T\ 5 = 3 + (2 \times 5) = 3 + 10 = 13$
>
>> [NOTE: The parentheses in "$3 + (2 \times 5)$" mean to first find the product of 2 and 5, and then add this product to 3.]

   a. 10 T 7   c. 12 T 2   e. 11 T 13

   b. 7 T 10   d. 2 T 12   f. 13 T 11

   g. Examine the answers to these pairs of problems: **a** and **b**; **c** and **d**; **e** and **f**. Is T a commutative operation?

11. M means multiply twice the first number by the second number. Compute the answers.

> *Example*   5 M 9 $5\ M\ 9 = (2 \times 5) \times 9 = 90$

   a. 4 M 7   c. 2 M 5   e. 6 M 11

   b. 7 M 4   d. 5 M 2   f. 11 M 6

   g. Is M a commutative operation?

12. H means multiply 2 by the sum of the pair of numbers. Compute the answers.

> *Example*   9 H 6 $9\ H\ 6 = 2 \times (9 + 6) = 2 \times 15 = 30$

   a. 5 H 6   c. 3 H 15   e. 4 H 12

   b. 6 H 5   d. 15 H 3   f. 12 H 4

   g. Is H a commutative operation?

13. S means take the smaller of the pair of numbers. Compute the answers.

> *Example*   5 S 36 $5\ S\ 36 = 5$, because 5 is less than 36.

   a. 3 S 4   c. 5 S 120   e. 1 S 0

   b. 4 S 3   d. 120 S 5   f. 0 S 1

   g. Is S a commutative operation?

   h. Using the operation S, give an example which has no answer.

14. *G* means take the greater of the two numbers. Compute the answers.

a. 5 *G* 100

c. 1 *G* 0

e. 14 *G* 17

b. 100 *G* 5

d. 0 *G* 1

f. 17 *G* 14

g. Is *G* a commutative operation?

h. Using the operation *G*, give an example which has no answer.

15. *Q* means add three times the second number to twice the first number. Compute the answers.

Example   4 *Q* 9 $4 \, Q \, 9 = (2 \times 4) + (3 \times 9) = 8 + 27 = 35$

a. 1 *Q* 2

c. 5 *Q* 4

e. 10 *Q* 10

b. 2 *Q* 1

d. 4 *Q* 5

f. 4 *Q* 4

g. Is *Q* a commutative operation?

16. *R* means divide the product of the first and second numbers by the product of the second number and itself. Compute the answers.

Example   4 *R* 2 $4 \, R \, 2 = (4 \times 2) \div (2 \times 2) = 8 \div 4 = 2$

a. 8 *R* 4

c. 6 *R* 2

e. 10 *R* 10

b. 4 *R* 8

d. 2 *R* 6

f. 121 *R* 11

g. Is *R* a commutative operation?

17. *N* means multiply each of the pair of numbers by itself and add the results. Compute the answers.

Example   3 *N* 9 $3 \, N \, 9 = (3 \times 3) + (9 \times 9) = 9 + 81 = 90$

a. 1 *N* 6

c. 0 *N* 3

e. 0 *N* 0

b. 6 *N* 1

d. 3 *N* 0

f. 2 *N* 3

g. Is *N* a commutative operation?

18. *D* means take the first number as a factor in a product the number of times indicated by the second number. Compute the answers.

Example   5 *D* 4 $5 \, D \, 4 = 5 \times 5 \times 5 \times 5 = 625$

a. 9 *D* 2

c. 2 *D*

e. 6 *D* 4

b. 2 *D* 9

d. 3 *D*

f. 0 *D* 5

g. Is *D* a commutative operation?

THE ASSOCIATIVE PROPERTY OF ADDITION

Parentheses are important punctuation marks in mathematics. They help us to say clearly what we mean. For example, $3 + (4 \times 6)$ means multiply 4 and 6 first; then add this product to 3.

$$3 + (4 \times 6) = 3 + 24 = 27$$

$(3 + 4) \times 6$ means add 3 and 4; then multiply the sum of 3 and 4 by 6.

$$(3 + 4) \times 6 = 7 \times 6 = 42$$

1. Is the statement $3 + (4 \times 6) \neq (3 + 4) \times 6$ true? Why or why not? [NOTE: The symbol $\neq$ means *is not equal to*.]

2. Is the statement $(25 - 2) \times 12 \neq 25 - (2 \times 12)$ true? Why or why not?

3. Is the statement $(5 + 3) + 7 \neq 5 + (3 + 7)$ true? Why or why not?

4. Is the statement $(3 \times 2) \times 4 \neq 3 \times (2 \times 4)$ true? Why or why not?

5. In place of each $\square$, supply the correct missing number.

   a. $\left.\begin{array}{l} (3 + 4) + 1 = 7 + 1 = 8 \\ 3 + (4 + 1) = 3 + 5 = 8 \end{array}\right\}$ $(3 + 4) + 1 = 3 + (4 + \square)$

   b. $\left.\begin{array}{l} (7 + 5) + 6 = 12 + 6 = 18 \\ 7 + (5 + 6) = 7 + 11 = 18 \end{array}\right\}$ $(7 + 5) + 6 = 7 + (\square + 6)$

   c. $\left.\begin{array}{l} (10 + 3) + 7 = 13 + 7 = 20 \\ 10 + (3 + 7) = 10 + 10 = 20 \end{array}\right\}$ $(10 + 3) + 7 = \square + (3 + 7)$

   d. $\left.\begin{array}{l} (10 + 6) + 9 = 16 + 9 = 25 \\ 10 + (6 + 9) = 10 + 15 = 25 \end{array}\right\}$ $(10 + \square) + 9 = 10 + (\square + 9)$

   e. $\left.\begin{array}{l} (1 + 17) + 12 = 18 + 12 = 30 \\ 1 + (17 + 12) = 1 + 29 = 30 \end{array}\right\}$ $(1 + 17) + \square = 1 + (17 + \square)$

6. Fill in the two missing symbols to show the pattern displayed by the examples in exercise 5.

$$(\square + \triangle) + \bigcirc = \square + (\underline{\quad} + \underline{\quad})$$

The property shown by this pattern is called the *Associative Property of Addition*.

$$(x + y) + z = x + (y + z)$$

7. Replace x by 2, y by 3, and z by 4 in this pattern and compute the answer both ways.

THE ASSOCIATIVE PROPERTY OF MULTIPLICATION

1. In place of each $\square$, supply the correct missing number.

   a. $\left.\begin{array}{l}(5 \times 2) \times 7 = 10 \times 7 = 70 \\ 5 \times (2 \times 7) = 5 \times 14 = 70\end{array}\right\}$ $(5 \times 2) \times 7 = 5 \times (2 \times \square)$

   b. $\left.\begin{array}{l}(4 \times 1) \times 9 = 4 \times 9 = 36 \\ 4 \times (1 \times 9) = 4 \times 9 = 36\end{array}\right\}$ $(4 \times 1) \times 9 = \square \times (1 \times 9)$

   c. $\left.\begin{array}{l}(10 \times 5) \times 6 = 50 \times 6 = 300 \\ 10 \times (5 \times 6) = 10 \times 30 = 300\end{array}\right\}$ $(10 \times 5) \times 6 = 10 \times (\square \times 6)$

2. Fill in the two missing symbols to show the pattern displayed by the examples in exercise 1.

$$(\square \times \triangle) \times \bigcirc = \square \times (\underline{\hspace{1cm}} \times \underline{\hspace{1cm}})$$

The property shown by this pattern is called the *Associative Property of Multiplication*.

$$(x \times y) \times z = x \times (y \times z)$$

3. Replace x by 9, y by 1, and z by 4 in this pattern and compute the answer both ways.

4. Work each example in two ways as written.

   a. $(5 + 3) + 7; \quad 5 + (3 + 7)$

   b. $(99 + 1) + 48; \quad 99 + (1 + 48)$

   c. $(142 + 58) + 78; \quad 142 + (58 + 78)$

   d. $(5 \times 6) \times 12; \quad 5 \times (6 \times 12)$

   e. $(15 \times 6) \times 8; \quad 15 \times (6 \times 8)$

   f. $(20 \times 5) \times 15; \quad 20 \times (5 \times 15)$

5. Is it easier to do $(48 + 52) + 92$ or $48 + (52 + 92)$? Why?

6. Use the appropriate associative property to make the work easier in finding answers to the following:

   a. $73 + (27 + 48)$ 148   e. $(782 + 125) + 875$ 1782   i. $5 \times (6 \times 12)$ 360

   b. $(34 + 49) + 151$ 234   f. $1,136 + (864 + 785)$ 2785   j. $15 \times (6 \times 9)$ 810

   c. $488 + (12 + 99)$ 599   g. $25 \times (8 \times 13)$ 2600   k. $(9 \times 18) \times 5$ 810

   d. $(963 + 888) + 112$ 1963   h. $12 \times (5 \times 7)$ 420   l. $(3 \times 35) \times 2$ 210

7. Work each example in two ways as written.

   a. $(24 \div 4) \div 2$; $24 \div (4 \div 2)$ **b.** $(100 \div 10) \div 2$; $100 \div (10 \div 2)$

8. Does division have the associative property?

9. Work each example in two ways as written.

   a. $(15 - 10) - 4$; $15 - (10 - 4)$ **b.** $(25 - 12) - 1$; $25 - (12 - 1)$

10. Does subtraction have the associative property?

   $4 < 6$ means 4 is less than 6. $6 > 4$ means 6 is greater than 4.

11. Replace the blank with either $=$, $<$, or $>$ to make each of the following a true statement.

   a. $(32 \div 2) \div 2$ _____ $32 \div (2 \div 2)$

   b. $(75 \div 5) \div 5$ _____ $75 \div (5 \div 5)$

   c. $17 - (1 - 1)$ _____ $(17 - 1) - 1$

   d. $33 - (4 - 1)$ _____ $(33 - 4) - 1$

Test in Subtraction (Fractional Numerals)

Find the differences. Give the simplest name for each answer.

1. $\dfrac{5}{7} - \dfrac{2}{7}$ $\dfrac{4}{9} - \dfrac{2}{9}$ $5\dfrac{3}{4} - 2$ $7\dfrac{5}{7} - 2\dfrac{3}{7}$ $5\dfrac{5}{6} - 5\dfrac{1}{6}$

2. $\dfrac{5}{6} - \dfrac{1}{2}$ $\dfrac{7}{8} - \dfrac{3}{4}$ $2\dfrac{1}{2} - 1\dfrac{1}{6}$ $5\dfrac{3}{8} - 3\dfrac{1}{4}$ $1\dfrac{5}{12} - \dfrac{1}{4}$

3. $\dfrac{1}{3} - \dfrac{1}{4}$ $\dfrac{5}{8} - \dfrac{1}{3}$ $5\dfrac{5}{7} - 3\dfrac{1}{3}$ $3\dfrac{1}{2} - 1\dfrac{2}{5}$ $8\dfrac{3}{7} - 2\dfrac{1}{6}$ *6 11/42*

4. $\dfrac{7}{9} - \dfrac{1}{2}$ $\dfrac{4}{5} - \dfrac{1}{4}$ $3\dfrac{3}{7} - 1\dfrac{1}{8}$ *2 17/56* $4\dfrac{2}{9} - 2\dfrac{1}{11}$ *2 13/99* $6\dfrac{1}{10} - 5\dfrac{1}{12}$ *1 1/60*

5. $4 - \dfrac{7}{8}$ $1 - \dfrac{3}{11}$ $6 - 5\dfrac{9}{11}$ $9 - 6\dfrac{2}{7}$ $10 - 9\dfrac{19}{20}$

6. $5\dfrac{1}{4} - 3\dfrac{3}{4}$ *1½* $6\dfrac{3}{5} - 2\dfrac{4}{5}$ *3⅘* $7\dfrac{4}{9} - 2\dfrac{8}{9}$ *4 5/9* $2\dfrac{1}{3} - 1\dfrac{2}{3}$ *⅔* $5\dfrac{1}{6} - 3\dfrac{5}{6}$ *1⅓*

7. $3\dfrac{1}{6} - 1\dfrac{2}{3}$ *1½* $5\dfrac{2}{5} - 3\dfrac{7}{10}$ *1 7/10* $9\dfrac{3}{7} - 3\dfrac{1}{2}$ *5 13/14* $15\dfrac{1}{5} - 4\dfrac{1}{2}$ *10 7/10* $6\dfrac{3}{8} - 4\dfrac{6}{7}$ *1 29/56*

If you had fewer than four problems correct in any group, turn to pages 430–432 for practice in subtraction (fractional numerals).

Patterns in Mathematics

Use □, △, ○, and ▱ to write the pattern suggested by each pair of examples.

Example $\dfrac{5}{2} - \dfrac{1}{2} = \dfrac{5-1}{2}$; $\dfrac{11}{7} - \dfrac{3}{7} = \dfrac{11-3}{7}$

$$\dfrac{\square}{\triangle} - \dfrac{\bigcirc}{\triangle} = \dfrac{\square - \bigcirc}{\triangle}$$

1. $\dfrac{3}{4} - \dfrac{2}{5} = \dfrac{3 \times 5 - 2 \times 4}{4 \times 5}$; $\dfrac{5}{7} - \dfrac{1}{6} = \dfrac{5 \times 6 - 1 \times 7}{7 \times 6}$

2. $\dfrac{5}{6} \times \dfrac{7}{8} = \dfrac{5 \times 7}{6 \times 8}$; $\dfrac{2}{3} \times \dfrac{5}{9} = \dfrac{2 \times 5}{3 \times 9}$

3. $\left(2 + \dfrac{1}{3}\right) \times 5 = (2 \times 5) + \left(\dfrac{1}{3} \times 5\right)$; $\left(3 + \dfrac{2}{5}\right) \times 4 = (3 \times 4) + \left(\dfrac{2}{5} \times 4\right)$

4. $\dfrac{3}{4} \div \dfrac{2}{5} = \dfrac{3}{4} \times \dfrac{5}{2}$; $\dfrac{5}{9} \div \dfrac{3}{7} = \dfrac{5}{9} \times \dfrac{7}{3}$

5. $\left(7 + \dfrac{3}{5}\right) \div 2 = (7 \div 2) + \left(\dfrac{3}{5} \div 2\right)$; $\left(4 + \dfrac{3}{8}\right) \div 5 = (4 \div 5) + \left(\dfrac{3}{8} \div 5\right)$

THE LEFT-DISTRIBUTIVE PROPERTY

Are these two amounts of money the same?

"30 tickets and 70 tickets, each at 60¢"
"100 tickets at 60¢"

The answer to the question above is "yes." We shall use this fact to illustrate a very important mathematical property involving two operations. Consider the following:

Example   The Prudent Junior High had a two-day sale of tickets to a school play. The price of a ticket was 60¢. The first day 30 tickets were sold; the second day 70 tickets were sold. Find the total amount of money taken in from the sale of the tickets.

How to Solve   We compute the amount of money taken in the first day. 60 × 30 = 1,800. Answer: $18.00

We compute the amount of money taken in the second day. 60 × 70 = 4,200. Answer: $42.00

Total taken in: $60.00

The computations can be written in this way:

$$(60 \times 30) + (60 \times 70) = 1,800 + 4,200 = 6,000$$

Another Way to Solve   We compute the number of tickets sold during both days.
$30 + 70 = 100$

We compute the total amount of money taken in.
$60 \times 100 = 6,000$. Answer: $60.00

Each solution leads to the same answer. Thus, we can conclude the following:

$$60 \times (30 + 70) = (60 \times 30) + (60 \times 70)$$

1. Compute the answers to each pair of examples.

   a. $10 \times (5 + 15)$; $(10 \times 5) + (10 \times 15)$

   b. $4 \times (3 + 17)$; $(4 \times 3) + (4 \times 17)$

   c. $6 \times (2 + 3)$; $(6 \times 2) + (6 \times 3)$

   d. $7 \times (10 + 20)$; $(7 \times 10) + (7 \times 20)$

   e. $6 \times (27 + 3)$; $(6 \times 27) + (6 \times 3)$

Examples like

$$60 \times (30 + 70) = (60 \times 30) + (60 \times 70)$$

fit the following pattern.

$$\bigcirc \times (\square + \triangle) = (\bigcirc \times \square) + (\bigcirc \times \triangle)$$
$$\begin{array}{ccccccc} \uparrow & \uparrow & \uparrow & \uparrow & \uparrow & \uparrow & \uparrow \\ 60 & 30 & 70 & 60 & 30 & 60 & 70 \end{array}$$

2. In the example above, what numeral always fills

   a. $\bigcirc$?   **b.** $\square$?   **c.** $\triangle$?

3. Using a, b and c in place of $\bigcirc$, $\square$, and $\triangle$, respectively, rewrite the pattern above.

The property shown by this pattern is called the *Left-Distributive Property of Multiplication over Addition*.

$$x \times (y + z) = (x \times y) + (x \times z)$$

4. How many operations are involved in the Left-Distributive Property?

5. What operations are involved in the Left-Distributive Property?

THE RIGHT-DISTRIBUTIVE PROPERTY

Compute the answers to each pair of examples. Show each step, as in the example.

Example $(5 + 7) \times 3;$ $(5 \times 3) + (7 \times 3)$

$(5 + 7) \times 3 = 12 \times 3 = 36$
$(5 \times 3) + (7 \times 3) = 15 + 21 = 36$

1. $(6 + 4) \times 15;$ $(6 \times 15) + (4 \times 15)$

2. $(1 + 12) \times 5;$ $(1 \times 5) + (12 \times 5)$

3. $(17 + 3) \times 10;$ $(17 \times 10) + (3 \times 10)$

4. $(20 + 30) \times 10;$ $(20 \times 10) + (30 \times 10)$

5. $(15 + 15) \times 15;$ $(15 \times 15) + (15 \times 15)$

6. $(21 + 9) \times 7;$ $(21 \times 7) + (9 \times 7)$

7. $(85 + 15) \times 7;$ $(85 \times 7) + (15 \times 7)$

8. $(191 + 9) \times 9;$ $(191 \times 9) + (9 \times 9)$

Each of the examples above fits the following pattern.

$$(\bigcirc + \square) \times \triangle = (\bigcirc \times \triangle) + (\square \times \triangle)$$

The property shown by this pattern is called the *Right-Distributive Property of Multiplication over Addition*.

$$(x + y) \times z = (x \times z) + (y \times z)$$

9. Replace x by 4, y by 7, and z by 11 in this pattern and compute the answer both ways.

There are two ways of finding the number of squares in the large rectangle on the right:

First way: $(3 \times 4) + (5 \times 4) = 12 + 20$
                                                  $= 32$

Second way: $(3 + 5) \times 4 = 8 \times 4 = 32$

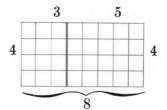

10. The two ways of finding the number of squares in the rectangle above involve the Right-Distributive Property. Explain how this property is involved.

11. a. Use two ways in finding the number of squares in the large rectangle below.

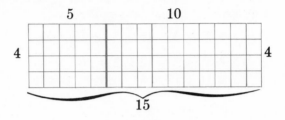

b. Show how one of the distributive properties is involved in this problem.

EXTENSION OF THE LEFT-DISTRIBUTIVE PROPERTY

Example $4 \times (2 + 3 + 5) = 4 \times 10 = 40$
$(4 \times 2) + (4 \times 3) + (4 \times 5) = 8 + 12 + 20 = 40$

Therefore,
$4 \times (2 + 3 + 5) = (4 \times 2) + (4 \times 3) + (4 \times 5)$

Compute the answers to each pair of examples.

1. $5 \times (1 + 2 + 3);$ $(5 \times 1) + (5 \times 2) + (5 \times 3)$

2. $7 \times (2 + 6 + 10);$ $(7 \times 2) + (7 \times 6) + (7 \times 10)$

3. $15 \times (9 + 3 + 3);$ $(15 \times 9) + (15 \times 3) + (15 \times 3)$

Test in Multiplication (Fractional Numerals)

Find the products. Give the simplest name for each answer.

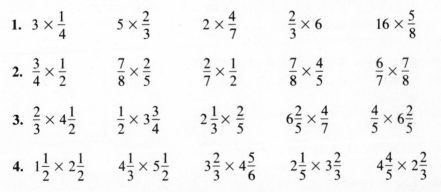

If you had less than four problems correct in any group, turn to pages 432–433 for practice in multiplication (fractional numerals).

Different Ways of Saying "Multiply"

We have been using the symbol "×" to mean "multiply." There are other symbols for multiplication. One of these is "·".

"5 · 6" means the same as "5 × 6"

1. Rewrite each multiplication example using "·".

    a. 35×17 **b.** $7 \times \frac{5}{8}$ **c.** $\frac{3}{5} \times \frac{1}{2}$ **d.** $2\frac{1}{5} \times 4\frac{7}{10}$

Another way to indicate multiplication is to enclose numerals in parentheses.

"(5)(6)" means the same as "5 × 6"

2. Rewrite each multiplication example using parentheses.

    a. 36×7 **b.** $\frac{3}{4} \times 7$ **c.** $\frac{4}{7} \times \frac{2}{9}$ **d.** $3\frac{1}{6} \times 15\frac{4}{13}$

When describing patterns, we used the symbols ○, □, and △ which can be replaced by numerals. When using such symbols, multiplication is indicated by writing these symbols next to each other.

The symbol "△□" means the same as "△ × □"

Sometimes in place of these frames we use letters, and so we agree that

"*ab*" means the same as "*a* × *b*"

"*a* · *b*" also means "multiply *a* by *b*"

"(*a*)(*b*)" also means "multiply *a* by *b*"

3. Why would it be wrong to abbreviate 2 × 3 as 23?

4. For each product, give two other ways of writing it. Whenever possible, give *three* other ways.

    Examples 1   5 · 6 may be shown as 5 × 6 or (5)(6).

    2   *m* × *t* may be shown as (*m*)(*t*), *m* · *t* or *mt*.

    3   5 × *s* may be shown as (5)(*s*), 5 · *s* or 5*s*.

    a. 3×7 **e.** $t \times u$ **i.** mx **m.** $n \times 5$

    b. $19 \cdot 5$ **f.** $5 \cdot n$ **j.** $(9)(25)$ **n.** $(7)(8)$

    c. $(20)(6)$ **g.** $a \cdot t$ **k.** $4 \times d$ **o.** $(a)(b)$

    d. $125 \cdot 0$ **h.** $2 \cdot d$ **l.** $u \times c$ **p.** st

ORDER OF OPERATIONS

Parentheses are used to make clear what is meant. For example, $3 \times (2 + 7)$ means:

Add 2 and 7 first, then multiply 3 by the sum of 2 and 7.

$$3 \times (2 + 7) = 3 \times 9 = 27$$

Sometimes, two or more operations are shown, but parentheses are omitted. What does the following mean?

$$3 + 5 \times 7$$

It may mean: add 3 to 5, and multiply the sum by 7.

$$3 + 5 \times 7 = 8 \times 7 = 56$$

or it may mean: add the product of 5 and 7 to 3.

$$3 + 5 \times 7 = 3 + 35 = 38$$

Certainly, these two meanings are different because 56 is not equal to 38.

We shall use the following agreement.

AGREEMENT   If parentheses are not included, multiplication and division are performed first, then addition and subtraction are performed in the order in which they appear. If only addition and subtraction are involved, perform the operations, one at a time, from left to right. If only multiplication and division are involved, perform the operations, one at a time, from left to right.

Study each example to see how these agreements are put to use.

Example 1 $3 + 6 \times 9 = 3 + 54 = 57$

Multiplication is performed first ($6 \times 9 = 54$),
then addition ($3 + 54 = 57$).

Example 2 $5 \times 7 + 16 \div 2 = 35 + 8 = 43$

Multiplication and division are performed first
($5 \times 7 = 35$, $16 \div 2 = 8$),
then addition ($35 + 8 = 43$).

Example 3 $3 \times 25 - 9 \div 3 + 2 \times 5$
$= 75 - 3 + 10 = 72 + 10 = 82$

Multiplication and division are performed first
($3 \times 25 = 75$; $2 \times 5 = 10$; $9 \div 3 = 3$),
then addition and subtraction from left to right
($75 - 3 = 72$; $72 + 10 = 82$).

Example 4 $12 \times 5 \div 3 = 60 \div 3 = 20$

Operations are performed from left to right.

In the three exercises below, explain in what order the operations were performed.

1. $36 + 4 - 10 \times 2 = 36 + 4 - 20 = 40 - 20 = 20$

2. $2 \times 10 \div 2 = 20 \div 2 = 10$

3. $2 + 25 - 7 + 3 - 4 = 27 - 7 + 3 - 4 = 20 + 3 - 4 = 23 - 4 = 19$

Compute the answers.

4. $15 + 2 \times 3$ 21
5. $7 \times 4 + 32$ 60
6. $2 \times 7 - 8$ 6
7. $12 - 3 \times 4$ 0
8. $50 \times 4 + 24 \div 6$ 204
9. $12 \div 6 - 32 \div 16$ 0
10. $3 \times 14 - 5 \times 2$ 32
11. $50 \times 2 - 200 \div 10$ 80
12. $78 - 10 + 22 \div 11$ 70
13. $30 \times 10 - 100 - 50$ 150
14. $3 \times 8 + 42 \div 6$ 31
15. $3 \times 10 \div 2$ 15
16. $100 \div 25 \times 5$ 20
17. $3 \times 17 + 35$ 86
18. $36 - 105 \div 5$ 15
19. $12 + 18 \div 3$ 18
20. $16 - 5 \times 2$ 6

21. $60 + 100 - 500 \div 50$ 150
22. $10 \times 5 - 3 + 2 \times 6 - 10 \div 2$ 54
23. $14 \times 2 + 2 \times 6 - 3 \times 4 - 20 \div 10$ 26
24. $7 \times 10 \div 2 \times 3 \div 5$ 21
25. $3 + 27 - 2 + 12 - 1 + 120$ 159
26. $7 - 5 - 2 + 20 - 13 + 18$ 25
27. $33 + 9 - 12 + 16 - 2 + 11$ 55
28. $3 \times 9 \times 2 + 16 \div 2 - 3 \times 4$ 50
29. $80 \div 4 \times 10 - 2 \times 7$ 186
30. $5 \times 3 \times 2 - 50 \div 2 \div 5 + 20 \times 2 \div 4$ 35
31. $18 \times 4 \div 12 \times 3 \div 2$ 9
32. $3 + 126 - 19 + 12 - 13$ 109
33. $3 \times 4 \times 5 + 12 \div 2 \times 3 - 12 \div 4$ 75
34. $12 \times 4 \div 3 - 12 \div 4 \div 3 + 28 \div 4$ 22
35. $22 \times 185 \times 0 + 0 \div 367 + 2 \times 6 \div 3$ 4
36. $16 \times 6 \div 3 + 1 - 12 \div 3 \times 4 + 0$ 17
37. $42 + 5 \div 5 - 2 \times 20 - 36 \div 12$ 0

SUMMARY OF PROPERTIES

We have introduced a number of properties of numbers and operations. These properties are listed below. Letters are used to indicate that the properties are true for all whole numbers.

- *Property of Zero for Addition*
  $n + 0 = n$

- *Property of Zero for Multiplication*
  $n \times 0 = 0$

- *Property of Zero for Division*
  $0 \div n = 0 \quad [n \neq 0]$

- *Property of One for Multiplication*
  $n \times 1 = n$

- *Property of One for Division*
  $n \div 1 = n$

- *Property of Number and Itself for Division*
  $n \div n = 1 \quad [n \neq 0]$

- *Commutative Property of Addition*
  $x + y = y + x$

- *Commutative Property of Multiplication*
  $xy = yx$

- *Associative Property of Addition*
  $(x + y) + z = x + (y + z)$

- *Associative Property of Multiplication*
  $(xy)z = x(yz)$

- *Left-Distributive Property of Multiplication over Addition*
  $x(y + z) = (xy) + (xz)$

- *Right-Distributive Property of Multiplication over Addition*
  $(x + y)z = (xz) + (yz)$

State the property or properties illustrated in each exercise below.

1. $3 + 7 = 7 + 3$

2. $127 + 0 = 127$

3. $(3 + 9)(2) = (3 \times 2) + (9 \times 2)$

4. $0 \div 67 = 0$

5. $53 \times 317 = 317 \times 53$

6. $(4 + 109) + 216 = 4 + (109 + 216)$

7. $(5 + 17) \times 9 = (9 \times 5) + (9 \times 17)$

8. $1 \times 138 = 138$

9. $(3 \times 9) \times 98 = 3 \times (9 \times 98)$

10. $(4 \times 15) \times 20 = 4 \times (20 \times 15)$

11. $60 \times 0 + 1 = 1 + 0$

12. $0 + 0 = 0$

13. $1 + 0 = 1$

14. $6(4 + 3) = (6 \times 4) + (6 \times 3)$

15. $1 \times 0 = 0$

16. $(1 + 1) \times 1 = 1 \times (1 + 1)$

17. $1{,}738 \div 1{,}738 = 1$

We can show that the properties for whole numbers listed on page 50 are also true for fractional numbers.

Make the necessary computations; then name the property which each exercise illustrates.

Example 1 $\dfrac{2}{3} \times \dfrac{4}{7}$; $\dfrac{4}{7} \times \dfrac{2}{3}$

$$\frac{2}{3} \times \frac{4}{7} = \frac{2 \times 4}{3 \times 7} = \frac{8}{21}$$

$$\frac{4}{7} \times \frac{2}{3} = \frac{4 \times 2}{7 \times 3} = \frac{8}{21}$$

The Commutative Property of Multiplication is illustrated.

Example 2 37.605×0

$37.605 \times 0 = 0$

The Property of Zero for Multiplication is illustrated.

18. $\dfrac{23}{47} \div \dfrac{23}{47}$ 19. 217.36×0 20. $0 \div \dfrac{12}{23}$ 21. $.762 \times 1$

22. $\frac{1}{2} \times \left(\frac{4}{5} + \frac{2}{3}\right)$; $\left(\frac{1}{2} \times \frac{4}{5}\right) + \left(\frac{1}{2} \times \frac{2}{3}\right)$

23. $(1.25 + 3.35) + 7.12$; $\quad 1.25 + (3.35 + 7.12)$

24. $(1.1 + 3.2) \times 3$; $\quad (1.1 \times 3) + (3.2 \times 3)$

25. $\left(\frac{2}{5} \times \frac{3}{7}\right) \times \frac{1}{2}$; $\frac{2}{5} \times \left(\frac{3}{7} \times \frac{1}{2}\right)$

26. $2.78 + 3.16$; $\quad 3.16 + 2.78$

27. $\frac{76}{19} \div 1$

28. $\frac{4}{7} \times \frac{5}{2}$; $\frac{5}{2} \times \frac{4}{7}$

Test in Division (Fractional Numerals)

Find the quotients. Give the simplest name for each answer.

1. $\frac{1}{2} \div 2$ $\qquad \frac{1}{3} \div 4 \qquad \frac{2}{3} \div 2 \qquad \frac{2}{5} \div 3 \qquad \frac{4}{5} \div 2$

2. $6 \div \frac{1}{2} \qquad 4 \div \frac{1}{3} \qquad 2 \div \frac{1}{4} \qquad 5 \div \frac{1}{6} \qquad 3 \div \frac{1}{4}$

3. $\frac{1}{2} \div \frac{1}{4} \qquad \frac{2}{3} \div \frac{1}{4} \qquad \frac{5}{6} \div \frac{2}{3} \qquad \frac{3}{7} \div \frac{4}{5} \qquad \frac{2}{3} \div \frac{2}{5}$

4. $\frac{2}{3} \div \frac{3}{7} \qquad \frac{4}{5} \div \frac{5}{6} \qquad \frac{1}{2} \div \frac{2}{5} \qquad \frac{4}{7} \div \frac{5}{6} \qquad \frac{1}{3} \div \frac{5}{9}$

5. $\frac{2}{9} \div \frac{4}{3} \qquad \frac{5}{6} \div \frac{5}{2} \qquad \frac{4}{3} \div \frac{3}{2} \qquad \frac{7}{4} \div \frac{5}{2} \qquad \frac{7}{2} \div \frac{3}{2}$

6. $\frac{1}{2} \div 2\frac{1}{2} \qquad \frac{2}{3} \div 3\frac{1}{3} \qquad \frac{4}{7} \div 4\frac{1}{2} \qquad \frac{4}{9} \div 1\frac{1}{2} \qquad \frac{1}{2} \div 5\frac{1}{3}$

7. $3\frac{1}{4} \div \frac{1}{2} \qquad 5\frac{1}{2} \div \frac{2}{3} \qquad 3\frac{1}{4} \div \frac{2}{5} \qquad 4\frac{3}{4} \div \frac{2}{5} \qquad 5\frac{1}{2} \div \frac{5}{7}$

8. $2\frac{1}{2} \div 3\frac{1}{2} \qquad 4\frac{1}{3} \div 5\frac{1}{2} \qquad 1\frac{3}{5} \div 2\frac{4}{5} \qquad 2\frac{1}{2} \div 7\frac{1}{2} \qquad 4\frac{1}{3} \div 5\frac{2}{7}$

If you had fewer than four problems correct in any group, turn to pages 434–436 for practice in division (fractional numerals).

Understanding Division (Fractional Numerals)

1. Give correct replacements of frames in the following:

a. $\dfrac{2}{3} = \dfrac{2 \times 4}{3 \times \square} = \dfrac{8}{\triangle}$

d. $\dfrac{4}{5} = \dfrac{4 \times 3}{5 \times \square} = \dfrac{12}{\triangle}$

b. $\dfrac{4}{7} = \dfrac{4 \times \square}{7 \times 2} = \dfrac{\triangle}{14}$

e. $\dfrac{2}{9} = \dfrac{2 \times \square}{9 \times 5} = \dfrac{\triangle}{45}$

c. $\dfrac{3}{8} = \dfrac{3 \times \square}{8 \times 4} = \dfrac{\triangle}{32}$

f. $\dfrac{4}{11} = \dfrac{4 \times 5}{11 \times \square} = \dfrac{20}{\triangle}$

2. Give correct replacements of frames in the following:

a. $\dfrac{1}{2} \div \dfrac{1}{3} = \dfrac{\frac{1}{2}}{\frac{1}{3}} = \dfrac{\frac{1}{2} \times 6}{\frac{1}{3} \times \square} = \dfrac{3}{\triangle}$

c. $\dfrac{4}{5} \div \dfrac{3}{7} = \dfrac{\frac{4}{5}}{\frac{3}{7}} = \dfrac{\frac{4}{5} \times 35}{\frac{3}{7} \times \square} = \dfrac{28}{\triangle}$

b. $\dfrac{3}{4} \div \dfrac{5}{6} = \dfrac{\frac{3}{4}}{\frac{5}{6}} = \dfrac{\frac{3}{4} \times 12}{\frac{5}{6} \times \square} = \dfrac{9}{\triangle}$

d. $\dfrac{5}{2} \div \dfrac{3}{4} = \dfrac{\frac{5}{2}}{\frac{3}{4}} = \dfrac{\frac{5}{2} \times 4}{\frac{3}{4} \times \square} = \dfrac{10}{\triangle}$

3. Compute the products and compare the results with the examples in exercise 2.

a. $\dfrac{1}{2} \times \dfrac{3}{1}$ b. $\dfrac{3}{4} \times \dfrac{6}{5}$ c. $\dfrac{4}{5} \times \dfrac{7}{3}$ d. $\dfrac{5}{2} \times \dfrac{4}{3}$

4. Observe the relation between division and multiplication:

$$\dfrac{1}{2} \div \dfrac{1}{3} = \dfrac{1}{2} \times \dfrac{3}{1}$$

$$\dfrac{3}{4} \div \dfrac{5}{6} = \dfrac{3}{4} \times \dfrac{6}{5}$$

$$\dfrac{4}{5} \div \dfrac{3}{7} = \dfrac{4}{5} \times \dfrac{7}{3}$$

$$\dfrac{5}{2} \div \dfrac{3}{4} = \dfrac{5}{2} \times \dfrac{4}{3}$$

Now complete the pattern.

$$\dfrac{\square}{\triangle} \div \dfrac{\bigcirc}{\square\!\!\!/} = \dfrac{\ }{\ } \times \dfrac{\ }{\ }$$

CLOSURE

Suppose you have the following set of numbers $\{0, 1\}$. That is, the only numbers you have to work with are 0 and 1. Let us see how much we can do with these numbers.

Addition: $0 + 0 = 0$; $0 + 1 = 1$; $1 + 1 = ?$. We do not have the number 2 in our set, so there is no answer in our set.

Subtraction: $0 - 0 = 0$; $1 - 0 = 1$; $0 - 1 = ?$; $1 - 1 = 0$. There is no answer to $0 - 1$ in our set.

Multiplication: $0 \times 0 = 0$; $1 \times 0 = 0$; $1 \times 1 = 1$. We are able to do all multiplication combinations in the set $\{0, 1\}$.

Division: $0 \div 0 = ?$; $1 \div 0 = ?$. Soon we will show why we avoid dividing by 0.

$0 \div 1 = 0$; $1 \div 1 = 1$. So our set is all right for division if we ignore division by 0.

■ If we are able to perform all operation combinations within a given set, we say that the set is *closed* under this operation. We have *closure* for this set under this operation.

We saw that $\{0, 1\}$ was closed under multiplication. Is it closed under addition?

1. As in the example above, perform all combinations of four operations with the elements of the set $\{1, 2\}$. Are there answers to all combinations?

2. Is the set $\{1, 2\}$ closed under

   a. addition?   **c.** multiplication?

   b. subtraction?   **d.** division?

The set of whole numbers, $\{0, 1, 2, 3, 4, 5, 6, \ldots\}$, is an *infinite set*.

$3 + 7 = 10$	$36 - 15 = 21$
$0 + 25 = 25$	$17 - 1 = 16$
$100 + 78 = 178$	$15 - 36 = ?$
.	.
.	.
.	.

We can always add two whole numbers, and the answer is a whole number.

Not every subtraction problem with whole numbers has an answer among whole numbers.

The set of whole numbers is *closed under addition*.

The set of whole numbers is *not closed under subtraction*.

3. Is the set of natural numbers closed under addition?

4. Prove that the set of natural numbers is not closed under subtraction. [HINT: It is sufficient to find one case in which the difference of two natural numbers is not a natural number.]

5. Prove that the set of whole numbers is not closed under division.

To prove that the set of whole numbers is closed under multiplication is difficult. Since the set is infinite, it is impossible to display all pairs of numbers and their products.

$5 \times 6 = 30$
$35 \times 0 = 0$
$1 \times 78 = 78$
$92 \times 3 = 276$
.
.
.

It is reasonable to claim that the set of whole numbers is closed under multiplication. Anyone who disputes this claim has the burden of displaying a pair of whole numbers whose product is not a whole number. Can you find such a pair?

6. Prove that the set $\{0, 1, 2, 3\}$ is not closed under addition.

7. Prove that the set $\{4, 2\}$ is not closed under division.

8. $T =$ the set of multiples of 3. That is, $T = \{3, 6, 9, 12, 15, 18, \ldots\}$.

   a. By experimenting with addition, tell whether set T is closed under addition. [Remember that if you claim no closure, you must show an example where the sum of two multiples of 3 is a number which is not a multiple of 3.]

   b. Do the same for multiplication, subtraction, and division for the set T.

9. $A = \{0, 1, 2\}$.

   a. By checking all addition combinations, tell whether set A is closed under addition.

   b. Do the same for multiplication, subtraction, and division for the set A. [HINT: Ignore division by 0.]

10. $F =$ the set of multiples of 5. That is, $F = \{5, 10, 15, 20, 25, 30, \ldots\}$.

   a. By experimenting with addition, tell whether set F is closed under addition.

   b. Do the same for multiplication, subtraction, and division for the set F.

11. G = the set of multiples of 4. That is, $G = \{4, 8, 12, 16, 20, 24, \ldots\}$.

    a. By experimenting with addition tell whether set G is closed under addition.

    b. Do the same for multiplication, subtraction, and division for the set G.

We can draw reasonably reliable conclusions concerning the closure of infinite sets under a given operation by examining a few examples. It is also possible to *prove* that a set is closed under a given operation so that no doubt is left.

Proof   *The set of multiples of 3 is closed under addition.*

Every multiple of 3 is of the form $3 \times n$ or $3 \times m$, where n and m are natural numbers.

$$3 \times n \text{ and } 3 \times m \text{ are multiples of 3}$$

The sum of any two multiples of 3 is

$$3 \times m + 3 \times n$$

According to the Left-Distributive Property,

$$3 \times m + 3 \times n = 3 \times (m + n)$$

Since $m + n$ is a natural number, for any natural numbers m and n, $3 \times (m + n)$ is a multiple of 3. Therefore, the sum of any two multiples of 3 is a multiple of 3.

Did you understand each step in the proof? If not, be sure to ask your teacher to explain to you the parts which you do not understand.

ADDITION AND SUBTRACTION

Adding 5 to a number, then subtracting 5 from the result is the same as leaving the number alone.

$$(n + 5) - 5 = n$$

Addition and subtraction are related operations. Every subtraction statement can be changed to a corresponding addition statement.

1. Change each subtraction statement to a corresponding addition statement.

    Example $9 - 2 = 7$ means $7 + 2 = 9$.

    a. $17 - 6 = 11$ **b.** $14 - 9 = 5$ **c.** $20 - 7 = 13$

2. Replace the blank to obtain the correct pattern showing the relation between addition and subtraction.

$$\square - \triangle = \bigcirc \text{ means } \bigcirc + \underline{\quad} = \square$$

3. Using a, b, and c in place of $\square$, $\triangle$, and $\bigcirc$, write the pattern showing the relation between addition and subtraction.

The relation between addition and subtraction can be shown in a different way:

$$(7 + 2) - 2 = 7$$

Subtracting 2 undoes what adding 2 does.

4. In each example, replace $\square$ with the correct numerals to obtain true statements.

a. $(9 + 3) - \square = 9$ 　　　　d. $(15 - \square) + 5 = 15$

b. $(\square + 7) - 7 = 14$ 　　　　e. $(\square - 10) + 10 = 36$

c. $(15 + 178) - 178 = \square$ 　　f. $(150 - 100) + \square = 150$

The operations of addition and subtraction are related in a way shown in the previous examples.

■ Subtraction is called the *inverse* of addition.

It follows that addition is also the inverse of subtraction. That is, addition and subtraction are inverse operations.

5. a. Given the set of numbers $A = \{2, 5, 7, 15, 20\}$. Add 5 to each member of the set. Call the new set B.

   b. Subtract 5 from each member of the set B. Did you obtain set A?

   Subtracting 5 undoes what adding 5 does.

6. For each addition statement, write a related subtraction statement.

   Example　　$4 + 15 = 19$;　$19 - 15 = 4$

   a. $8 + 3 = 11$　　　c. $25 + 7 = 32$　　　e. $55 + 9 = 64$

   b. $123 + 88 = 211$　　d. $320 + 90 = 410$　　f. $430 + 110 = 540$

7. For each subtraction statement, write a related addition statement.

   Example　　$360 - 90 = 270$;　$270 + 90 = 360$

   a. $25 - 10 = 15$　　　c. $17 - 8 = 9$　　　e. $45 - 12 = 33$

   b. $99 - 20 = 79$　　　d. $136 - 17 = 119$　　f. $211 - 12 = 199$

8. In each example, replace □ with the correct numeral to obtain a true statement.

a. $(35 + 13) - □ = 35$
b. $(□ + 12) - 12 = 89$
c. $(37 + □) - 24 = 37$
d. $(17 + 96) - 96 = □$
e. $(127 + 36) - □ = 127$
f. $(□ + 20) - 20 = 91$

g. $(112 + □) - 13 = 112$
h. $(14 + 120) - 120 = □$
i. $(56 + 130) - □ = 56$
j. $(□ + 37) - 37 = 112$
k. $(500 + □) - 700 = 500$
l. $(52 + 96) - 96 = □$

9. a. List the members of the set which you obtain by adding 1 to each member of the set $A = \{0, 1, 2, 3, 4, 5\}$.

   b. Subtract 1 from each member of the set you obtained in part a. Did you get set A?

10. Describe the inverse of each of the following:

a. opening a door
b. traveling east
c. taking off shoes
d. assembling a radio

e. hanging up a coat
f. opening a book
g. unlocking a door
h. flying upward

11. Perform each operation and check by performing the inverse operation.

a.	2,375	d.	37,006	g.	88,368	j.	3,468
	+965		+9,379		−9,429		+2,957
b.	22,385	e.	3,006	h.	16,002	k.	5,063
	+4,890		−982		−7,004		−3,084
c.	1,004	f.	4,963	i.	34.37	l.	12,349
	+985		−897		+5.68		−3,473

12. What is the inverse operation of adding 35?

13. What is the inverse operation of subtracting 12?

14. On December 24, the temperature in Frazer, Colorado, was 40° below zero. How many degrees does the temperature have to rise before it will reach 0°?

15. If the temperature were 60° below zero, how many degrees would it have to rise to reach 0°?

16. In Holland there is a meadow whose altitude is 10 feet below sea level. How high should you make a heap for its top to reach sea level.

17. How many feet is it from 20 feet below to 400 feet above sea level?

18. How many degrees is it from 5° below zero to 37° above zero?

19. Which is a larger change: from 10° below zero to 20° above zero, or from 0° to 30°?

MULTIPLICATION AND DIVISION

Multiplying a number by 5, then dividing the result by 5 is the same as leaving the number alone.

$$(n \times 5) \div 5 = n$$

1. For each multiplication statement, give a related division statement using the pattern suggested in the example.

    Example $6 \times 5 = 30$ $30 \div 5 = 6$

    a. $3 \times 4 = 12$ **c.** $7 \times 3 = 21$

    b. $5 \times 2 = 10$ **d.** $12 \times 4 = 48$

2. On the basis of examples in exercise **1**, give the pattern involving division for $\bigcirc \times \square = \triangle$.

3. The example, $(30 \times 5) \div 5 = 30$, shows the relation between multiplication and division in a different way. Replace each $\square$ to obtain a true statement.

    a. $(12 \times \square) \div 3 = 12$ **f.** $(987 \times 67) \div \square = 987$

    b. $(7 \times 5) \div \square = 7$ **g.** $(12 \times \square) \div 706 = 12$

    c. $(\square \times 7) \div 7 = 15$ **h.** $(\square \times 7) \div 7 = 1,268$

    d. $(36 \times 5) \div 5 = \square$ **i.** $(2,000 \times 17) \div 17 = \square$

    e. $(\square \times 9) \div 9 = 73$ **j.** $(697 \times 781) \div \square = 697$

4. Replace the blank to complete the pattern.

    $$(\bigcirc \times \square) \div \square = \underline{\quad\quad}$$

5. a. Given the set $M = \{1, 2, 3, 4, 5\}$. Multiply each member of M by 3. Call the new set T.

   b. Divide each member of T by 3. Do you obtain the set M?

   c. Does dividing by 3 undo what multiplying by 3 does?

6. Replace x by the correct numerals to obtain true statements.

   a. $60 \div 15 = x$ **c.** $66 \div x = 11$ **e.** $x \div 2 = 52$ **g.** $x \cdot 6 = 48$

   b. $x \cdot 15 = 60$ **d.** $11 \cdot x = 66$ **f.** $52 \cdot 2 = x$ **h.** $48 \div 6 = x$

7. What is the inverse of multiplying by 12?

8. What is the inverse of dividing by 16?

9. Perform each operation and check by performing the inverse operation.

   a. 235
           $\times 72$

   b. $1,036$
           $\times 105$

   c. 136
           $\times 138$

   d. 125
           $\times 125$

   e. 35
           $\times 47$

   f. 127
           $\times 139$

   g. 45
           $\times 45$

   h. $37\overline{)4,625}$

   i. $12\overline{)7,476}$

   j. $235\overline{)184,710}$

   k. $19\overline{)5,795}$

   l. $3.6\overline{)1,296}$

   m. $4.2\overline{)5,250}$

   n. $3.9\overline{)4,914}$

10. Replace $\square$ with the correct numerals to obtain true statements.

   a. $(5 \times 7) \div \square = 5$

   b. $(3 \times 12) \div \square = 3$

   c. $(\square \times 6) \div 6 = 17$

   d. $(\square \times 12) \div 12 = 10$

   e. $(13 \times \square) \div 5 = 13$

   f. $(50 \times \square) \div 11 = 50$

   g. $(36 \times 2) \div 2 = \square$

   h. $(13 \times 9) \div 9 = \square$

11. a. If set $X = \{0, 2, 5, 9\}$, list the members of the set you obtain by multiplying each member of set X by 7.

   b. Divide each member of the set you obtained in part **a** by 7. What set do you get?

12. For each multiplication statement, write a related division statement.

   Example $21 \times 3 = 63$ $63 \div 3 = 21$

   a. $9 \times 3 = 27$ **b.** $11 \times 9 = 99$ **c.** $12 \times 13 = 156$

SOLVING PROBLEMS

Study the solution of the problem below. It will provide you with some help in solving problems.

Example   5 is added to a number. The result is multiplied by 4 giving the product 32. What was the original number?

How to   We use $\square$ in place of a name of the number we are after.
Solve

5 is added to a number: $\square + 5$.
The result is multiplied by 4: $(\square + 5) \times 4$.
The product is 32: $(\square + 5) \times 4 = 32$.
What number multiplied by 4 gives 32? Answer: 8.
Therefore, $\square + 5 = 8$.
5 added to what number gives 8? Answer: 3.
Therefore, $\square = 3$.

The number we are looking for is 3.

Check   5 is added to 3; the result is 8. 8 multiplied by 4 is 32.

Solve each problem.

1. A number is added to 12. The result is multiplied by 5 giving the product 105. What was the original number?

2. A number is subtracted from 23. The result is divided by 7 giving the quotient $\frac{1}{7}$. What was the original number?

3. Doubling a number and then multiplying the result by 5 gives 35. What is the number? [HINT: Doubling means multiplying by 2.]

4. Adding 6 to a number and then multiplying the result by 7 gives 56. What is the number?

5. Squaring a number and then dividing the result by 4 gives 16. What is the number? [HINT: Squaring a number means multiplying the number by itself.]

6. Square a number, multiply the result by 4, add $\frac{1}{4}$, then multiply the result by 6. The answer is 3. What was the original number?

7. Multiply a number by 6, then add 3 to the product. Divide the result by 2. The answer is $7\frac{1}{2}$. What was the original number?

KEEPING ARITHMETICALLY FIT

1. Add.

a. 1,407	**b.** 48.75	**c.** 367.8	**d.** 497.6
395	19.36	76.9	2.37
406	25.07	80.1	81.09
9,808	13.78	72.5	670.01
589	95.25	36.9	2.1

2. Subtract.

a. 22,305	**b.** 569.33	**c.** 486.06	**d.** 724.00
3,498	479.44	227.68	99.99

3. Multiply.

a. 709	**b.** 3,266	**c.** 33.05	**d.** 325.9
832	509	7.56	4.25

4. Divide.

a. $15\overline{)1,766}$ **b.** $.11\overline{)34.54}$ **c.** $.23\overline{)67.6}$ **d.** $82\overline{)218.94}$

For exercises **5–9**, numerals in parentheses refer to pages where you can find more practice in these operations.

5. Supply the missing numerators. (428)

a. $\dfrac{3}{4} = \dfrac{}{24}$ **b.** $\dfrac{5}{7} = \dfrac{}{49}$ **c.** $\dfrac{3}{11} = \dfrac{}{44}$ **d.** $\dfrac{2}{9} = \dfrac{}{72}$

6. Add. (428–430)

a. $\dfrac{4}{5} + \dfrac{3}{5}$ **b.** $\dfrac{1}{2} + \dfrac{3}{4}$ **c.** $2\dfrac{1}{3} + \dfrac{7}{8}$ **d.** $4\dfrac{2}{5} + 2\dfrac{3}{9}$

7. Subtract. (430–432)

a. $\dfrac{7}{8} - \dfrac{2}{8}$ **b.** $\dfrac{3}{4} - \dfrac{1}{2}$ **c.** $\dfrac{9}{4} - \dfrac{4}{5}$ **d.** $5\dfrac{1}{6} - 3\dfrac{3}{4}$

8. Multiply. (432–434)

a. $\dfrac{2}{5} \times \dfrac{1}{3}$ **b.** $5 \times \dfrac{7}{8}$ **c.** $4\dfrac{1}{2} \times 5$ **d.** $3\dfrac{7}{8} \times 5\dfrac{1}{2}$

9. Divide. (434–436)

a. $\dfrac{1}{2} \div \dfrac{2}{3}$ **b.** $\dfrac{3}{5} \div 6$ **c.** $\dfrac{7}{9} \div 3\dfrac{1}{2}$ **d.** $5\dfrac{1}{2} \div 3\dfrac{3}{5}$

10. Copy the examples and fill in the missing numerals to obtain true statements.

a.
$$\begin{array}{r} 5{,}691 \\ +?\ ??? \\ \hline 9{,}748 \end{array}$$

b.
$$\begin{array}{r} 79.58 \\ +?0.1? \\ \hline ?4?.?? \end{array}$$

c.
$$\begin{array}{r} 1{,}125 \\ -??? \\ \hline 589 \end{array}$$

d. $\dfrac{1}{2} - ? = \dfrac{1}{5}$

11. Compute the answers.

a.
$$\begin{array}{l} 5 \text{ ft. } 7 \text{ in.} \\ +12 \text{ ft. } 4 \text{ in.} \\ \hline \end{array}$$

b.
$$\begin{array}{l} 2 \text{ qts. } 1 \text{ pt.} \\ +1 \text{ qt. } \ 1 \text{ pt.} \\ \hline \end{array}$$

c.
$$\begin{array}{l} 12 \text{ ft. } 6 \text{ in.} \\ \times 4 \\ \hline \end{array}$$

d.
$$\begin{array}{l} 7 \text{ ft. } \ 8 \text{ in.} \\ +4 \text{ ft. } 10 \text{ in.} \\ \hline \end{array}$$

e.
$$\begin{array}{l} 6 \text{ gals. } 3 \text{ qts. } 1 \text{ pt.} \\ -3 \text{ gals. } 4 \text{ qts. } 1 \text{ pt.} \\ \hline \end{array}$$

f.
$$\begin{array}{l} 3 \text{ gals. } 3 \text{ qts. } 1 \text{ pt.} \\ \times 5 \\ \hline \end{array}$$

g.
$$\begin{array}{l} 8 \text{ yds. } 1 \text{ ft. } 10 \text{ in.} \\ -5 \text{ yds. } 2 \text{ ft. } 11 \text{ in.} \\ \hline \end{array}$$

h. $3.6 \times (1.4 + 7.9)$

i. $(3.5 + 4.7)(4.6 + 9.5)$

j. $\left(\dfrac{1}{2} + \dfrac{1}{3}\right) - \left(\dfrac{1}{5} + \dfrac{1}{6}\right)$

k. $1.5 \times 1.5 \times 1.5$

l. $(75 \div 5) \div 30$

m. $(100 \div 1{,}000) \div 10$

n. $4 \times (16.4 - 12.7)$

o. $\left(\dfrac{1}{2} + \dfrac{1}{3}\right)\left(\dfrac{1}{3} + \dfrac{1}{4}\right)$

p. $(1.25 + 4.35)(2.5 + 4.5)$

q. $(3.7 + 4.6) - (2.7 + 3.8)$

r. $\dfrac{2}{5} \times \dfrac{3}{6} \times \dfrac{1}{7}$

12. What number added to 12.5 gives 99.6?

13. What number multiplied by 12.5 gives 15,625?

14. What number subtracted from 1,776 gives 1,258?

15. What number divided by 13.5 gives 182.25?

16. An article costs $1.89. Find the cost of a dozen of these articles.

17. One gross is the same as 12 dozen. What is the cost of a gross of articles if the price of each article is $.12?

18. A man paid $84.36 for 76 yards of wire fencing. What was the price of one yard of fencing?

19. A lecture lasted 1 hr. 40 min. and ended at 3:05 P. M. At what time did the lecture begin?

VOCABULARY REVIEW

Associative Property of Addition (40)

Associative Property of Multiplication (41)

closure (54)

commutative operations (37)

Commutative Property of Addition (36)

Commutative Property of Multiplication (37)

counting numbers (31)

equal sets (32)

infinite set (31)

inverse operations (57)

is greater than (42)

is less than (42)

Left-Distributive Property of Multiplication over Addition (44)

natural numbers (31)

Property of One for Multiplication (34)

Property of Zero for Addition (34)

Property of Zero for Multiplication (34)

Right-Distributive Property of Multiplication over Addition (45)

subset (31)

A CHALLENGE TO YOU

1. For the pattern below, write the next two steps. Then study the pattern and answer the following questions. [HINT: 2^2 means 2×2 and 2^3 means $2 \times 2 \times 2$.]

$$1 + 3 = 4 = 2^2$$

$$1 + 3 + 5 = 9 = 3^2$$

$$1 + 3 + 5 + 7 = 16 = 4^2$$

$$1 + 3 + 5 + 7 + 9 = 25 = 5^2$$

   a. What is the sum of the first 20 odd whole numbers?

   b. What is the sum of the first 50 odd whole numbers?

   c. What is the sum of the first n odd whole numbers?

2. a. For the pattern below write the next two steps.

$$1^3 + 2^3 = 9 = (1 + 2)^2 = 3^2$$

$$1^3 + 2^3 + 3^3 = 36 = (1 + 2 + 3)^2 = 6^2$$

$$1^3 + 2^3 + 3^3 + 4^3 = 100 = (1 + 2 + 3 + 4)^2 = 10^2$$

$$1^3 + 2^3 + 3^3 + 4^3 + 5^3 = 225 = (1 + 2 + 3 + 4 + 5)^2 = 15^2$$

   b. What is the sum of the cubes of the first 10 natural numbers?

   c. What is the sum of the cubes of the first n natural numbers?

CHAPTER TEST

1. Is the set X a subset of the set Y?

$$X = \left\{0, \frac{1}{2}, \frac{1}{4}\right\} \qquad Y = \left\{0, \frac{1}{2}, \frac{1}{3}, \frac{1}{4}, \frac{1}{5}\right\}$$

2. If you know that $105 \times 27 = 2{,}835$, then what property tells you that $27 \times 105 = 2{,}835$?

3. If you know that $(37 \times 3) \times 55 = 6{,}105$, then what property tells you that $37 \times (3 \times 55) = 6{,}105$?

4. Write the related subtraction statement for $13 + 21 = 34$.

5. Write the related division statement for $11 \times 15 = 165$.

6. Prove that the set $\{0, 1, 2\}$ is not closed under addition.

7. What property tells you that if $5 \times (15 + 10) = 125$, then $(5 \times 15) + (5 \times 10) = 125$?

8. What property is illustrated by $2 + 7 = 7 + 2$?

9. What property is illustrated by $(3 + 6) + 5 = 3 + (6 + 5)$?

10. Multiply 375×29, then check by dividing.

11. Replace the blanks with either $=$, $<$, or $>$ to obtain true statements.

    a. $4 + 12$ _____ $12 + 4$ c. $(3 \times 11) \times 12$ _____ $3 \times (11 \times 12)$

    b. 1×37 _____ 0×37 d. $(24 \div 6) \div 2$ _____ $24 \div (6 \div 2)$

12. According to what property is $3{,}607 + 0 = 3{,}607$ true?

13. According to what property is $5{,}632 \times 1 = 5{,}632$ true?

14. According to what property is $9{,}607 \times 0 = 0$ true?

15. A jar contains $1{,}120$ nickels. How many dollars is it? *$56.00*

16. What number added to itself gives $\frac{1}{4}$?

17. The product of two numbers is 51. One of the numbers is $12\frac{1}{2}$. What is the other number?

18. A number is added to 5 and the sum multiplied by 7. The answer is 42. What was the original number?

CHAPTER THREE

Numeration Systems

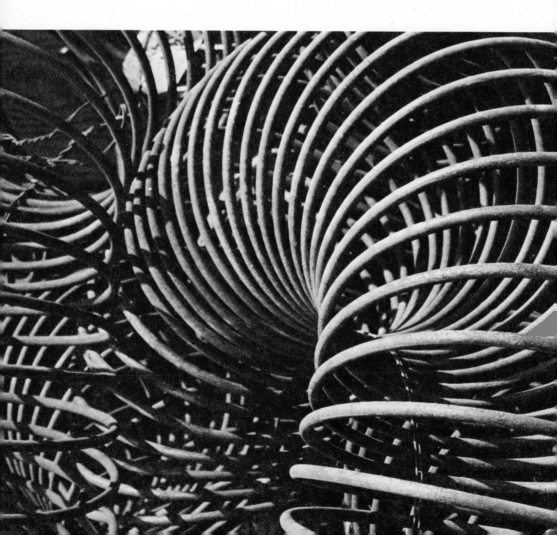

THE DECIMAL NUMERATION SYSTEM

To record work with numbers, we write number names. Number names are called *numerals*. Every numeral names some number. Every number has many different names.

1. Each group of numerals below names some number. In each group, one numeral does not fit with the group. Find it!

    a. $2\frac{1}{2} \times 2$ $\frac{10}{2}$ $100 \div 20$ $\frac{15}{5}$ V

    b. $3\frac{1}{3} \times 3$ $\frac{18}{2}$ $1 + 8$ $4\frac{1}{2} \times 2$ $\frac{81}{9}$

    c. $5 - 5$ 0 $\frac{1}{2} + \frac{1}{2}$ 3×0 $10 - 10$

2. Write five different names for the number 7.

We call our system of writing numerals the *decimal system*. The Latin word *decem* means *tenth*. The word "decimal" is suggestive of ten symbols: 0, 1, 2, 3, 4, 5, 6, 7, 8, 9.

When we write

$$785,205$$

we read it "seven hundred eighty-five thousand, two hundred five." Its meaning can be pictured as follows:

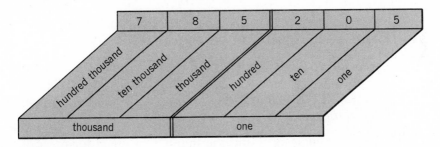

3. Write numerals in the decimal system for the following:

    a. forty-six

    b. six hundred eighty-seven

    c. five thousand, three hundred eighty-nine

    d. seventy-six thousand, nine hundred thirty-four

    e. three hundred forty-eight thousand, seven hundred nine

4. Write in words the names for the following:

a. 14	**d.** 167	**g.** 5,641	**j.** 672,503
b. 40	**e.** 305	**h.** 76,125	**k.** 908,005
c. 234	**f.** 603	**i.** 43,005	**l.** 573,075

It is easy to read names for very large numbers once we observe the regularity of our decimal system. This pattern is shown below for the numeral 205,376,174,290.

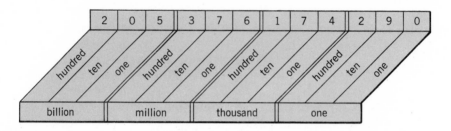

The word name for 205,376,174,290 is: two hundred five billion, three hundred seventy-six million, one hundred seventy-four thousand, two hundred ninety.

5. Write word names for the following:

a. 135,600	**c.** 35,365,105	**e.** 78,365,700,341
b. 806,705	**d.** 170,006,340	**f.** 263,109,305,700

PLACE VALUES OF BASIC NUMERALS

There are ten *basic numerals* in the decimal system of numeration. They are: 0, 1, 2, 3, 4, 5, 6, 7, 8, 9. Basic numerals are also called *digits*.

For example, 3,001 is a four-digit numeral. The *place value* of 3 in 3,001 is *three thousand*.

1. Tell the place value of 3 and the number of digits for each of the following numerals.

a. 35	**c.** 31,005	**e.** 300,000,000
b. 93	**d.** 39,100,907	**f.** 3,609

2. Tell the place value of 5 in each of the following:

a. 56	**c.** 50,007	**e.** 305,763	**g.** 151,000,000
b. 501	**d.** 567,001	**f.** 159,867	**h.** 356,001,367,900

3. How many ones make a thousand?

4. How many tens make a hundred?

5. How many tens make a thousand?

6. How many hundreds make a thousand?

7. How many thousands make a million?

8. How many millions make a billion?

POWERS OF TEN

There is another way of showing the *ten* character of our numeration system. Look at this pattern.

$$100 = 10 \times 10$$
$$1,000 = 10 \times 10 \times 10$$
$$10,000 = 10 \times 10 \times 10 \times 10$$
$$100,000 = 10 \times 10 \times 10 \times 10 \times 10$$
$$\text{and so on}$$

We can simplify writing by the use of the following abbreviation:

$$10 \times 10 = 10^2$$

Read "10^2" as "ten squared" or "the second power of ten" or "ten to the second power."

$$10 \times 10 \times 10 = 10^3$$

Read "10^3" as "ten cubed" or "the third power of ten" or "ten to the third power."

$$10 \times 10 \times 10 \times 10 = 10^4$$

Read "10^4" as "the fourth power of ten" or "ten to the fourth power."

It took man centuries to develop our present decimal system. This system was developed in India and brought to Europe by the Arabs. It is called the *Hindu-Arabic system*.

1. Write as powers of ten.

   a. $10 \times 10 \times 10 \times 10 \times 10$

   b. $10 \times 10 \times 10 \times 10 \times 10 \times 10$

   c. $10 \times 10 \times 10 \times 10 \times 10 \times 10 \times 10 \times 10$

   d. $10 \times 10 \times 10 \times 10 \times 10 \times 10 \times 10 \times 10 \times 10 \times 10$

2. Write two ways of reading each of the following:

Example 10^9 the ninth power of ten;
ten to the ninth power

a. 10^5 **b.** 10^8 **c.** 10^{10} **d.** 10^{14}

Although 10^1 and 10^0 seem to be the simplest powers of ten, their meaning is more difficult to decide upon. In mathematics, we quite often decide upon the meaning of symbols by observing patterns.

Let us build a pattern.

$$10,000 = 10^4$$
$$1,000 = 10^3$$
$$100 = 10^2$$

What is the next line in this pattern? It is $10 = 10^1$. So, now we agree that 10^1 means simply 10.

What line comes after $10 = 10^1$ in this pattern? It is $1 = 10^0$. So, in order to continue the pattern, we agree to define 10^0 to be 1.

$$10^1 = 10 \qquad\qquad\qquad 10^0 = 1$$

10 to the first power is 10.   10 to the zero power is 1.

We can show values of digits using powers of ten.

$$25 = 2 \times 10 + 5 \times 1$$
$$25 = 2 \times 10^1 + 5 \times 10^0$$

$$349 = 3 \times 10^2 + 4 \times 10^1 + 9 \times 10^0$$

$$4,801 = 4 \times 10^3 + 8 \times 10^2 + 0 \times 10^1 + 1 \times 10^0$$

3. Expand by powers of ten.

Example   346 $346 = 3 \times 10^2 + 4 \times 10^1 + 6 \times 10^0$

a. 37   **d.** 540   **g.** 37,165

b. 98   **e.** 1,394   **h.** 98,003

c. 239   **f.** 7,003   **i.** 405,301

4. Write each of the following in powers of ten form.

Example   100,000 $100,000 = 10^5$

a. 10,000   **d.** 1   **g.** 1,000,000,000

b. 1,000,000   **e.** 100,000,000   **h.** 1,000,000,000,000

c. 10   **f.** 100   **i.** 10,000,000

5. Given an expansion by powers of ten, write each numeral in the ordinary form.

   Example $4 \times 10^2 + 0 \times 10^1 + 3 \times 10^0$

   $= 4 \times 100 + 0 \times 10 + 3$
   $= 400 + 3$
   $= 403$

   a. $3 \times 10^1 + 9 \times 10^0$

   b. $5 \times 10^2 + 2 \times 10^1 + 7 \times 10^0$

   c. $9 \times 10^3 + 0 \times 10^2 + 0 \times 10^1 + 6 \times 10^0$

   d. $7 \times 10^4 + 0 \times 10^3 + 0 \times 10^2 + 0 \times 10^1 + 0 \times 10^0$

   e. $3 \times 10^5 + 4 \times 10^4 + 3 \times 10^3 + 0 \times 10^2 + 0 \times 10^1 + 0 \times 10^0$

   f. $5 \times 10^4 + 3 \times 10^0$

   g. $3 \times 10^9 + 2 \times 10^6 + 1 \times 10^3$

   h. $4 \times 10^7 + 1 \times 10^0$

   i. 9×10^6

Test in Addition (Decimal Numerals)

Find the sums.

1.	.4	.9	.8	5.	3.15	39.09	40.63
	.2	.6	.5		26.09	4.16	58.13
					7.25	9.83	9.06
2.	4.1	5.8	3.6	6.	34.63	15.18	75.13
	3.6	6.4	7.9		17.82	82.25	22.65
	1.8	8.9	5.4		49.08	46.78	59.07
3.	.35	.61	.58	7.	.306	.909	.136
	.67	.92	.73		.519	.081 ·	.806
	.75	.13	.69		.620	.107	.005
	.39	.28	.35		.364	.865	.980
4.	4.25	7.35	1.66	8.	1.136	9.983	3.265
	7.61	8.69	5.35		2.605	7.009	8.099
	3.59	2.08	7.16		4.990	6.805	7.603

If you had fewer than two problems correct in any one group, turn to pages 436–437 for practice in addition (decimal numerals).

Understanding Decimal Numerals

1. How many times as great as 0.01 is 0.1? [HINT: By what number must you multiply 0.01 to obtain 0.1?]

2. How many times as great as 0.05 is 0.1?

3. $n \times 0.02 = 0.1$. What in place of n gives a true statement?

4. How many 0.01's are there in 1?

5. How many 0.01's are there in 10?

6. How many 0.01's are there in 100?

7. How many 0.1's are there in 1?

8. How many 0.1's are there in 10?

9. How many 0.1's are there in $\frac{1}{2}$?

10. How many 0.5's are there in 1?

11. How many 0.5's are there in 10?

12. How many 0.5's are there in 100?

13. How many 0.5's are there in 1,000?

POSITIONAL SYSTEM

Recall from page 68 our explanation of the place value of a numeral. We will sometimes use merely *value* of a numeral to mean the same thing.

1. In 257, what is the value of 2?

2. In 25, what is the value of 2?

3. In 2, what is the value of 2?

4. In 200, what is the value of 2?

5. In 2,000, what is the value of 2?

The answers to the five questions above show that the same numeral can have different values. The value of a numeral depends on its *position*. These examples illustrate why our system is called a *positional system*.

In the following table, place values are shown using the powers of ten.

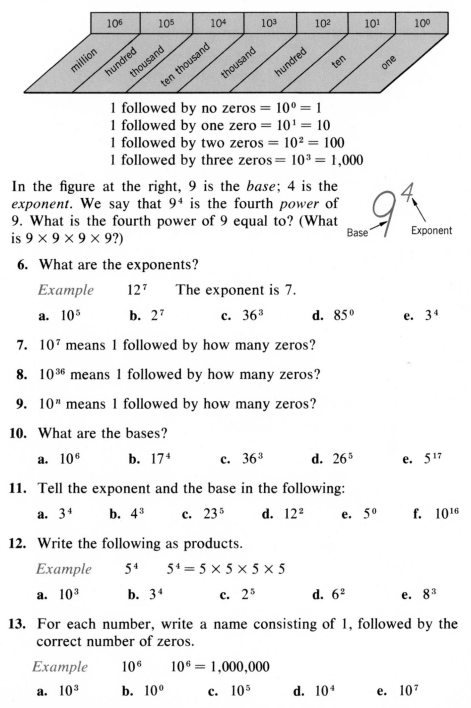

1 followed by no zeros $= 10^0 = 1$
1 followed by one zero $= 10^1 = 10$
1 followed by two zeros $= 10^2 = 100$
1 followed by three zeros $= 10^3 = 1,000$

In the figure at the right, 9 is the *base*; 4 is the *exponent*. We say that 9^4 is the fourth *power* of 9. What is the fourth power of 9 equal to? (What is $9 \times 9 \times 9 \times 9$?)

9^4

Base   Exponent

6. What are the exponents?

   Example 12^7 The exponent is 7.

   a. 10^5 **b.** 2^7 **c.** 36^3 **d.** 85^0 **e.** 3^4

7. 10^7 means 1 followed by how many zeros?

8. 10^{36} means 1 followed by how many zeros?

9. 10^n means 1 followed by how many zeros?

10. What are the bases?

   a. 10^6 **b.** 17^4 **c.** 36^3 **d.** 26^5 **e.** 5^{17}

11. Tell the exponent and the base in the following:

   a. 3^4 **b.** 4^3 **c.** 23^5 **d.** 12^2 **e.** 5^0 **f.** 10^{16}

12. Write the following as products.

   Example 5^4 $5^4 = 5 \times 5 \times 5 \times 5$

   a. 10^3 **b.** 3^4 **c.** 2^5 **d.** 6^2 **e.** 8^3

13. For each number, write a name consisting of 1, followed by the correct number of zeros.

   Example 10^6 $10^6 = 1,000,000$

   a. 10^3 **b.** 10^0 **c.** 10^5 **d.** 10^4 **e.** 10^7

14. Write the following using 10 with the correct exponent.

  a. 10,000   **b.** 1,000,000   **c.** 1   **d.** 10   **e.** 100

15. For each number, write its name in words.

  Example   125,675   one hundred twenty-five thousand, six hundred seventy-five

  a. 575   **c.** 5,375,000   **e.** 3,120,001,756

  b. 10,398   **d.** 360,000,003   **f.** 999,999,999,000

16. Write each number as a base-ten numeral.

  a. five thousand, six hundred seventy-three

  b. seventy-five thousand, one hundred nine

  c. nine million, seven hundred seventeen thousand, three hundred

  d. ten billion, three hundred

17. Tell the value of 6 in each of the following:

  Example   260,112   The value of 6 is sixty thousand.

  a. 63   **c.** 215,116   **e.** 5,060,000,318

  b. 10,672   **d.** 35,695,000   **f.** 56,000,000

EXPONENTIAL NOTATION

Every number has many different names.

The name for 256 in *expanded product form* is
$2 \times 2 \times 2 \times 2 \times 2 \times 2 \times 2 \times 2$.

The name for 256 in *exponential form* is 2^8.

$$2 \times 2 \times 2 \times 2 \times 2 \times 2 \times 2 \times 2 = 2^8$$

The work above shows that the exponential form is an economical way of naming numbers.

1. Write the following using exponential form.

  Example $7 \times 7 \times 7 \times 7 \times 7$ 7^5

  a. 3×3 **d.** $8 \times 8 \times 8 \times 8 \times 8 \times 8$

  b. $10 \times 10 \times 10 \times 10$ **e.** $100 \times 100 \times 100$

  c. $2 \times 2 \times 2 \times 2 \times 2$ **f.** $37 \times 37 \times 37 \times 37$

The decimal system has the number *ten* for its *base*. In order to write numerals in the decimal system, we need ten *basic numerals*: 0, 1, 2, 3, 4, 5, 6, 7, 8, 9. Numerals beyond that consist of two or more basic numerals. Thus in 10, 1 means one ten and 0 means no ones.

Expanding a numeral by powers of ten shows the *decimal* (ten) nature of our system.

2. Expand by powers of ten.

Example   37,498 $3 \times 10^4 + 7 \times 10^3 + 4 \times 10^2 + 9 \times 10^1 + 8 \times 10^0$

a. 465   c. 436,879   e. 5,368,972

b. 1,059   d. 100,106   f. 7,003,007

3. Given an expansion by powers of ten, write each numeral in the ordinary form.

Example $3 \times 10^5 + 2 \times 10^3 + 9 \times 10^2 + 7 \times 10^0$ 302,907

a. $1 \times 10^4 + 3 \times 10^3 + 2 \times 10^0$

b. $5 \times 10^5 + 9 \times 10^3 + 6 \times 10^1$

c. $9 \times 10^7 + 3 \times 10^6 + 8 \times 10^5 + 1 \times 10^4 + 8 \times 10^3 + 3 \times 10^0$

d. $1 \times 10^9 + 1 \times 10^6 + 1 \times 10^3 + 1 \times 10^0$

e. $6 \times 10^6 + 9 \times 10^4 + 7 \times 10^2 + 3 \times 10^0$

f. $9 \times 10^5 + 1 \times 10^3 + 8 \times 10^1$

g. $8 \times 10^6 + 9 \times 10^0$

h. $3 \times 10^7 + 5 \times 10^1$

i. $4 \times 10^8 + 3 \times 10^1 + 6 \times 10^0$

PATTERNS IN NUMERALS

We know that the ten basic numerals (digits) in the numeration system in base ten are 0, 1, 2, 3, 4, 5, 6, 7, 8, 9, and that 235 is a three-digit numeral and 5,000 is a four-digit numeral.

1. Tell the value of each basic numeral in the following numerals in the decimal system.

Example   349   The value of 3 is three hundreds.
                    The value of 4 is four tens.
                    The value of 9 is nine ones.

a. 92   b. 318,962   c. 1,234,567   d. 987,654,321

2. Write the numerals that have the following values.

    a. three hundreds, five tens, seven ones

    b. nine millions, five thousands, three hundreds, eight ones

    c. one billion, two tens, seven ones

3. Supply the missing number in each pattern based on the number 2.

    a. $?^5 = 2 \times 2 \times 2 \times 2 \times ? = 32$ **d.** $?^2 = ? \times 2 = 4$

    b. $2^? = 2 \times 2 \times 2 \times 2 = ?$ **e.** $2^? = 2$

    c. $2^? = 2 \times 2 \times 2 = ?$ **f.** $2^? = 1$

4. Supply the missing numbers in each pattern based on the number 7.

    a. $7^5 = 7 \times 7 \times 7 \times 7 \times ? = 16{,}807$ **d.** $7^? = 7 \times ? = 49$

    b. $7^? = 7 \times 7 \times 7 \times 7 = ?$ **e.** $7^? = 7$

    c. $?^3 = 7 \times 7 \times 7 = ?$ **f.** $7^? = 1$

5. Is the statement $7^0 = 2^0$ true? Prove your answer.

6. What is any number raised to the zero power equal to?

Test in Subtraction (Decimal Numerals)

1.	.9	.7	.8	6.	3.683	5.982	7.005
	.3	.4	.4		1.241	3.984	3.016

2.	7.6	3.8	4.6	7.	3.25 − 1.08
	2.3	1.9	3.8		7.63 − 2.75
					10.05 − 3.93

3. .63   .62   .87
    .42   .58   .59

8. Subtract:
    1.5 from 3.6
    3.7 from 10.5
    2.9 from 11.8

4. 9.36   2.38   4.35
    2.15   1.12   2.29

5. .327   .806   .325
    .112   .602   .116

9. Subtract:
    10.3 from 23.1
    1.26 from 3.27
    1.03 from 9.2

If you had fewer than two problems correct in any one group, turn to pages 438–439 for practice in subtraction (decimal numerals).

ABACUS FOR BASE TEN

You have seen that in the numeration system in base ten we counted
by tens. An *abacus* helps in studying the positional values of basic
numerals.

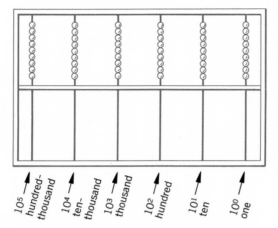

When we want to show some number on the abacus, we move beads
into the lower part. The abacus below shows the number 850,039.

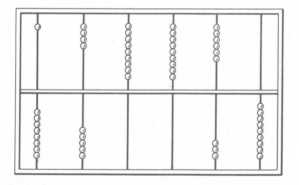

The abacus below shows the number 159,403.

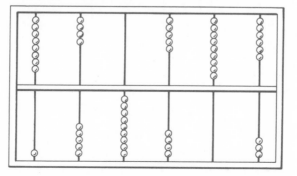

For each abacus below, write the name of the number it shows

    a. as a numeral in base ten

    b. in words

1.

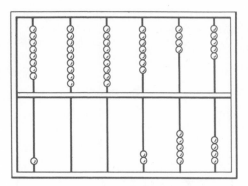

2.

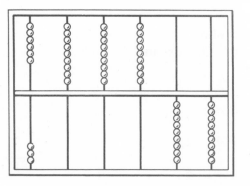

3.

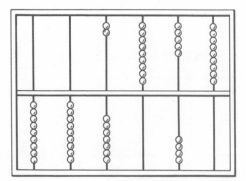

Make a picture of an abacus to show each number.

    4. 1,007,303   **5.** 27,001   **6.** 101,101

ABACUS FOR BASE SEVEN

The abacus you have been working with may be called an abacus for base ten. In this abacus each rod has nine beads. Explain why it is not necessary to have ten beads on each rod.

Let us make a picture of an abacus for base seven built on the same principle as the abacus for base ten. Let us draw a picture of a very simple abacus having only three rods (columns).

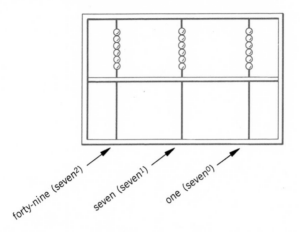

forty-nine (seven²)   seven (seven¹)   one (seven⁰)

Write in words the name of the number in base ten shown on each base-seven abacus.

Example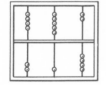

Column 1: four ones   =   4
Column 2: one seven   =   7
Column 3: two forty-nines =   98
                             ———
                             109

The number shown is one hundred nine.

1.   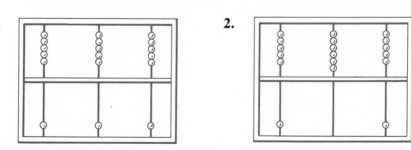   **2.**

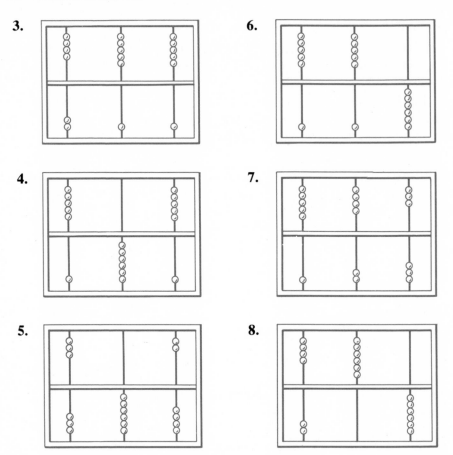

9. a. Make a picture of the abacus for base seven with three columns showing the greatest possible number.

   b. Write the name of this number in words.

   c. Write a numeral for it in the decimal system.

10. a. Make a picture of the abacus in base seven with three columns showing the smallest possible three-digit numeral.

   b. Write the name of this number in words.

   c. Write a numeral for it in the decimal system.

11. a. If you have a base-seven abacus with two columns, what is the greatest possible number you can show?

   b. If you have a base-seven abacus with two columns, what is the smallest possible two-digit numeral you can show?

12. Would your answer to exercise **9** be different if the abacus had four columns? What would be the answer?

13. Would your answer to exercise **10** be different if the abacus had four columns? What would it be?

14. Make a picture of the abacus for base seven with three columns showing the number 0.

15. For each pair of abaci below, first write in words the name of the number each abacus shows. Then add the two numbers and write in words the name of the number both abaci show together.

a.

b.

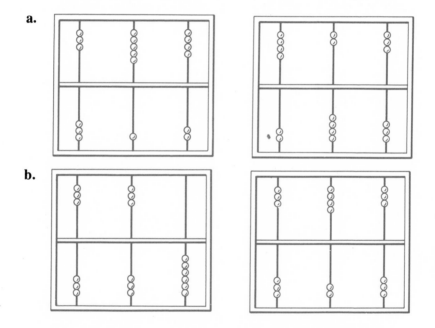

16. What is the largest number of beads you would ever have in the lower part of any one column in the abacus for base seven?

17. What number would be shown on a five-column abacus for base seven with one bead in the fifth column on the bottom and no beads at the bottom of other columns?

18. What number would a six-column abacus for base seven show with one bead in the sixth column and no beads at the bottom of other columns?

BASE-SEVEN NUMERALS

We can name all possible numbers of beads in any one column on the bottom of the abacus for base seven by the seven basic numerals: 0, 1, 2, 3, 4, 5, 6.

Read the numeral 213_{seven} as
"two-one-three, base seven."

For each picture of an abacus write:

    a. the base-seven numeral it shows

    b. the word name of the number

    c. the base-ten numeral for this number

Example 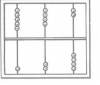   **a.** 124_{seven}
    b. sixty-seven
    c. 67_{ten}

1.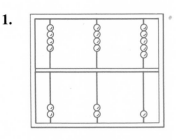

2.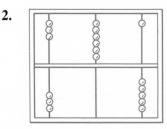

3.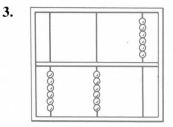

4.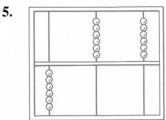

5.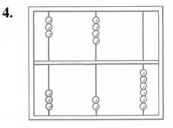

6.

FOUR-DIGIT BASE-SEVEN NUMERALS

The diagram below shows the positional pattern of a four-digit numeral in base seven.

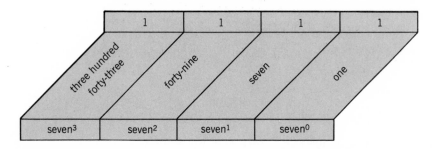

Example $1111_{seven} = (1 \times seven^3) + (1 \times seven^2) + (1 \times seven^1)$
$$+ (1 \times seven^0)$$
$$= (1 \times 343_{ten}) + (1 \times 49_{ten}) + (1 \times 7) + (1 \times 1)$$
$$= 343_{ten} + 49_{ten} + 7 + 1$$
$$= 400_{ten}$$

1. Why is it necessary to write the "ten" in "343_{ten}?"

For each base-seven numeral, write its equivalent base-ten numeral.

Example $6012_{seven} = (6 \times seven^3) + (0 \times seven^2)$
$$+ (1 \times seven^1) + (2 \times seven^0)$$
$$= (6 \times 343_{ten}) + (1 \times 7) + (2 \times 1)$$
$$= 2{,}058_{ten} + 7 + 2$$
$$= 2{,}067_{ten}$$

2. 11_{seven} **7.** 125_{seven} **12.** 5555_{seven}

3. 21_{seven} **8.** 606_{seven} **13.** 6000_{seven}

4. 32_{seven} **9.** 666_{seven} **14.** 6432_{seven}

5. 56_{seven} **10.** 1000_{seven} **15.** 6500_{seven}

6. 66_{seven} **11.** 1066_{seven} **16.** 6555_{seven}

17. What is the greatest number that can be named with a four-digit base-seven numeral?

18. Write the base-ten name for the number in exercise **17.**

19. Which is larger, 56_{seven} or 56_{ten}?

20. Which is larger, 111_{seven} or 111_{ten}?

Test in Multiplication (Decimal Numerals)

Compute the products.

1. $10 \times .3$ 100×7.35 100×4.7 $10 \times .1$

2. $100 \times .45$ $1,000 \times .109$ $10 \times .102$ $10 \times .12$

3. $10 \times .78$ 10×3.68 $100 \times .5$ $10 \times .159$

4. $.2 \times 4$ $.5 \times .1$ $.05 \times 5$ $.03 \times .6$

5. $.5 \times 7$ $.4 \times .7$ $.07 \times 9$ $.1 \times 2.7$

6.	23 .7	89 .5	316 .8	3.9 .6	17.1 .8	33.5 .9
7.	.71 .5	.83 .9	.95 .3	.306 .8	.411 .5	.109 .2
8.	3.65 .5	7.05 .9	4.11 .23	9.05 .86	32.5 .9	86.1 1.6
9.	3.9 5.3	4.5 7.6	3.16 2.3	7.09 3.8	3.116 .2	10.004 .8

If you had more than one problem incorrect in any one group, turn to pages 439–440 for practice in multiplication (decimal numerals).

FROM BASE TEN TO BASE SEVEN

In finding base-seven names for numbers, it is necessary to keep in mind the place values of the base-seven numeration system.

Example 1   Given 13_{ten}, how do we write a base-seven name for it?
First: How many sevens in 13_{ten}? Answer: 1
Second: How many ones are left? Answer: 6
Thus, $13_{ten} = 16_{seven}$.

Example 2   Given 109_{ten}, how do we write a base-seven name for it?
First: How many forty-nines in 109_{ten}? Answer: 2

$$2 \times 49 = 98 \qquad\qquad 109 - 98 = 11$$

Second: How many sevens in 11_{ten}? Answer: 1

$$1 \times 7 = 7 \qquad\qquad 11 - 7 = 4$$

Thus, $109_{ten} = 214_{seven}$.

Example 3   Given 524_{ten}, how do we write a base-seven name for it?
First: How many three hundred forty-three's in 524_{ten}?
Answer: 1

$$\begin{array}{ll} 343 & 524 \\ \underline{\times 1} & \underline{-343} \\ 343 & 181 \end{array}$$

Second: How many forty-nines in 181_{ten}? Answer: 3

$$\begin{array}{ll} 49 & 181 \\ \underline{\times 3} & \underline{-147} \\ 147 & 34 \end{array}$$

Third: How many sevens in 34_{ten}? Answer: 4

$$\begin{array}{ll} 7 & 34 \\ \underline{\times 4} & \underline{-28} \\ 28 & 6 \end{array}$$

Thus, $524_{ten} = 1346_{seven}$.

For each of the following give the base-seven numeral.

1. 10_{ten}	**4.** 42_{ten}	**7.** 89_{ten}	**10.** 455_{ten}
2. 15_{ten}	**5.** 49_{ten}	**8.** 267_{ten}	**11.** $1,535_{ten}$
3. 21_{ten}	**6.** 57_{ten}	**9.** 350_{ten}	**12.** $2,211_{ten}$

There is another way of finding the base-seven numeral for a number given in base ten. To learn this method, we shall first divide some number, say $2,365_{ten}$, by ten, and record quotients and remainders.

$$2,365 \div 10 = 236, \text{ R } 5$$
$$236 \div 10 = 23, \text{ R } 6$$
$$23 \div 10 = 2, \text{ R } 3$$

These successive divisions can be recorded in one array.

$$\begin{array}{r} 2, \text{ R } 3 \\ \overline{10\,)23, \text{ R } 6} \\ \overline{10\,)236, \text{ R } 5} \\ \overline{10\,)2,365} \end{array}$$

Now note that if we write the last quotient followed by the remainders, we have 2,365, which is the name of the number we started with in base ten. If we divide by seven, instead of by ten, we should obtain the name for this number in base seven.

Example 1 $2,365_{ten} = \underline{\quad ? \quad}_{seven}$

$$\begin{array}{r} 6,\ R\ 6 \\ 7\overline{)48,\ R\ 1} \\ 7\overline{)337,\ R\ 6} \\ 7\overline{)2,365} \end{array}$$

Check using base ten:

$$\begin{array}{cccc} 343 & 49 & 7 & 1 \\ \times 6 & \times 6 & \times 1 & \times 6 \\ \hline 2,058 & 294 & 7 & 6 \end{array}$$

$$\begin{array}{r} 2,058 \\ 294 \\ 7 \\ +\quad 6 \\ \hline 2,365 \end{array}$$

Answer: $2,365_{ten} = 6616_{seven}$

Example 2 $1,970_{ten} = \underline{\quad ? \quad}_{seven}$

$$\begin{array}{r} 5,\ R\ 5 \\ 7\overline{)40,\ R\ 1} \\ 7\overline{)281,\ R\ 3} \\ 7\overline{)1,970} \end{array}$$

Check using base ten:

$$\begin{array}{cccc} 343 & 49 & 7 & 1 \\ \times 5 & \times 5 & \times 1 & \times 3 \\ \hline 1,715 & 245 & 7 & 3 \end{array}$$

$$\begin{array}{r} 1,715 \\ 245 \\ 7 \\ +\quad 3 \\ \hline 1,970 \end{array}$$

Answer: $1,970_{ten} = 5513_{seven}$

Use the method shown in the examples to find base-seven numerals for each of the following. Then check using base ten.

13. 12_{ten} **15.** 26_{ten} **17.** 67_{ten} **19.** 156_{ten} **21.** $1,135_{ten}$

14. 19_{ten} **16.** 45_{ten} **18.** 95_{ten} **20.** 301_{ten} **22.** $2,000_{ten}$

Test in Division (Decimal Numerals)

1. $36.5 \div 10$ $376.9 \div 100$ $45.9 \div 100$ $100.1 \div 1,000$

2. $.4 \div 10$ $.05 \div 10$ $109 \div 100$ $.3 \div 100$

3. $3.6 \div 2$ $1.8 \div 3$ $2.8 \div 4$ $3.6 \div 9$

4. $3 \div .1$ $17 \div .01$ $36 \div .1$ $50 \div .01$

5. $4\overline{)5.6}$ $3\overline{)74.4}$ $9\overline{)81.9}$ $6\overline{)42.06}$

6. $.5\overline{)1.5}$ $.3\overline{)2.1}$ $.7\overline{)8.4}$ $.6\overline{)9.6}$

7. $.05\overline{)1.5}$ $.03\overline{).306}$ $.04\overline{).404}$ $.03\overline{).102}$

8. $4.02\overline{)64.32}$ $.7\overline{)47.6}$ $11.8\overline{)106.2}$ $90.6\overline{)18.12}$

If you had fewer than three problems correct in any one group, turn to pages 440–442 for practice in division (decimal numerals).

THE BINARY NUMERATION SYSTEM

All of us are familiar with the electric switch. It is always in one of the two positions, "on" or "off." It would be very convenient to "write" numerals by means of a switch if we had a system which uses only two symbols.

1. A base-ten numeration system uses ten basic numerals. Write these numerals.

2. A base-seven numeration system uses seven basic numerals. Write these numerals.

■ A *binary* numeration system uses two symbols: 0, 1.

"Bi" means "two." The binary numeration system, or *base-two* system, is used by many electronic computers.

on means 1   off means 0

To understand the base-ten, or decimal system, we study powers of ten.

3. Tell what each of the following is equal to.

Example 10^6 1,000,000

   a. 10^2 **b.** 10^4 **c.** 10^1 **d.** 10^0 **e.** 10^3

Showing numerals in expanded notation helps us to see the values of the basic numerals.

4. Show each numeral in expanded notation.

Example   3,265 $3 \times 10^3 + 2 \times 10^2 + 6 \times 10^1 + 5 \times 10^0$

   a. 17   **b.** 1,593   **c.** 367,205

5. What is the value of 2 in each of the following numerals?

   a. 1,268   **b.** 1,628   **c.** 1,682   **d.** 2,861

To understand the base-two, or binary system, we study powers of two.

6. Tell what each of the following is equal to.

   a. 2^0 **b.** 2^1 **c.** 2^2 **d.** 2^3 **e.** 2^4 **f.** 2^5 **g.** 2^6

FROM BASE TEN TO BASE TWO

1. Study the record of counting from one through sixteen in the binary system. Then continue writing on your paper through thirty-two.

Base Ten	Base Two	
1	1	1 one
2	10	(1 two) + (0 one)
3	11	(1 two) + (1 one)
4	100	(1 four) + (0 two) + (0 one)
5	101	(1 four) + (0 two) + (1 one)
6	110	(1 four) + (1 two) + (0 one)
7	111	(1 four) + (1 two) + (1 one)
8	1000	(1 eight) + (0 four) + (0 two) + (0 one)
9	1001	(1 eight) + (0 four) + (0 two) + (1 one)
10	1010	(1 eight) + (0 four) + (1 two) + (0 one)
11	1011	(1 eight) + (0 four) + (1 two) + (1 one)
12	1100	(1 eight) + (1 four) + (0 two) + (0 one)
13	1101	(1 eight) + (1 four) + (0 two) + (1 one)
14	1110	(1 eight) + (1 four) + (1 two) + (0 one)
15	1111	(1 eight) + (1 four) + (1 two) + (1 one)
16	10000	(1 sixteen) + (0 eight) + (0 four) + (0 two) + (0 one)

2. Give the value of each basic numeral. Then write the name of the number in base-ten notation.

$$1010_{two} \quad (1 \text{ eight}) + (0 \text{ four}) + (1 \text{ two}) + (0 \text{ one})$$
$$= 10_{ten}$$

a. 10_{two} c. 101_{two} e. 1000_{two}

b. 11_{two} d. 1111_{two} f. 1011_{two}

3. Write in words the value of 1 in the following:

a. 10000_{two} b. 100000_{two} c. 1000000_{two}

4. What is the greatest possible number that can be named by a three-digit binary numeral?

5. What is the least possible number that can be named by a three-digit binary numeral?

6. What is the greatest possible number that can be named by a four-digit binary numeral?

THE ELECTRONIC COMPUTER

We said that working with the binary system can be likened to a switch with "off" and "on" positions. Look at the picture of a box with light windows to see how it can record numbers in the binary system.

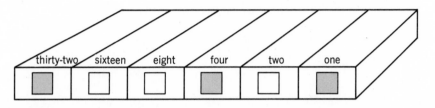

The compartments "thirty-two," "four," and "one" are lighted. Thus the machine shows 100101_{two} = thirty-seven = 37_{ten}.

1. Make pictures of a six-digit binary machine like the one above and show on it the following. Light on means 1, light off means 0.

   a. 101_{two} **c.** 11101_{two} **e.** 111011_{two}

   b. 1001_{two} **d.** 100011_{two} **f.** 100010_{two}

2. Write in words the name of each number in exercise 1.

3. Could you show the number sixty-three on the six-digit binary machine? Why or why not?

4. Could you show the number sixty-four on the six-digit binary machine? Why or why not?

5. How many digits must a machine have to show two hundred fifty-six? one thousand twenty-four?

6. Which is greater, 101_{two} or 1000_{two}?

7. What is the least possible number that can be named by a four-digit binary numeral?

8. What is the greatest possible number that can be named by a four-digit binary numeral?

It takes more digits to write a numeral in the binary system than to write it in the decimal system.

> 91_{ten} is a two-digit numeral in the decimal system.
> $91_{ten} = 1011011_{two}$
> 1011011_{two} is a seven-digit numeral in the binary system.

Each of the following numerals is in base ten. Write a binary numeral for the same number. Tell the number of digits in each system.

Example   70 1000110_{two}

2 digits in the decimal system
7 digits in the binary system

9. 2	**12.** 10	**15.** 25	**18.** 64	**21.** 200
10. 4	**13.** 15	**16.** 32	**19.** 100	**22.** 256
11. 8	**14.** 16	**17.** 59	**20.** 128	**23.** 512

POSITIONAL NUMERATION SYSTEMS

The base-ten, or decimal, numeration system uses ten basic numerals. The place value of the numeral depends on the *position* in which it is written.

1. What is the place value of the basic numeral 2 in each of the following numerals in base ten?

   Example 267_{ten} The place value of 2 is two hundred.

   a. 25_{ten} **b.** $2,001_{ten}$ **c.** $25,003_{ten}$ **d.** $200,000_{ten}$

Because the value of a numeral changes with its position, the base ten system is called a *positional system.*

2. What is the place value of the basic numeral 3 in each of the following numerals in base seven?

   a. 300_{seven} **b.** 103_{seven} **c.** 230_{seven} **d.** 3001_{seven}

3. What is the place value of the basic numeral 1 in each of the following binary numerals?

   a. 100_{two} **b.** 1000_{two} **c.** 10_{two} **d.** 100000_{two}

All positional systems have the following property.

■ For all positional systems, the base is the same as the number of basic symbols used.

4. How many symbols are used in the binary system? What are they?

5. How many symbols are used in the quinary (base-five) system? What are they?

The place value of each digit depends on the position it occupies in the numeral.

6. What is the place value of the digit 4 in each of the following quinary numerals?

   a. 40_{five} b. 4 c. 400_{five} d. 4000_{five}

We stated two properties which all positional systems have. There is one more important property.

■ The value of each succeeding *place* to the left is obtained by multiplying the value of the preceding place by the base.

In a base-ten numeral of the form $\square\,\triangle_{ten}$, the place value of $\triangle$ is $\triangle \times$ one, and the place value of $\square$ is $\square \times$ ten. In 256_{ten},

The value of the place occupied by 6 is *one*.
The value of the place occupied by 5 is one $\times$ ten, or *ten*.
The value of the place occupied by 2 is ten $\times$ ten, or *hundred*.

7. In 25_{ten}, what is the value of the place occupied by

   a. 5?   b. 2?

8. To obtain the value of the second place from the right, by what number did you multiply the value of the first place?

9. In 357_{ten}, what is the value of the place occupied by

   a. 7?   b. 5?   c. 3?

10. To obtain the value of the third place from the right, by what number did you multiply the value of the second place?

11. In 35_{seven}, what is the value of the place occupied by

   a. 5?   b. 3?

12. To obtain the value of the second place from the right, by what number did you multiply the value of the first place?

13. In 452_{seven}, what is the value of the place occupied by

   a. 2?   b. 5?   c. 4?

14. To obtain the value of the third place from the right, by what number did you multiply the value of the second place?

EXPANDED NUMERALS

The following example shows an expansion of a three-digit quinary numeral.

Example $340_{five} = (3 \times 25_{ten}) + (4 \times 5) + (0 \times 1)$
$$= 75_{ten} + 20_{ten}$$
$$= 95_{ten}$$

The following example shows an expansion of a three-digit numeral in base twelve. To write numerals in a base greater than ten, we need more than ten basic numerals.

Example $T = ten; E = eleven$

$$T2E_{twelve} = (10_{ten} \times 144_{ten}) + (2 \times 12_{ten}) + (11_{ten} \times 1)$$
$$= 1{,}440_{ten} + 24_{ten} + 11_{ten}$$
$$= 1{,}475_{ten}$$

Expand each numeral. Then write the base-ten numeral naming the same number.

1. 514_{six}
2. 344_{five}
3. $E53_{twelve}$
4. 2120_{three}
5. 716_{eight}

6. $2T9_{eleven}$
7. 385_{nine}
8. 4102_{six}
9. $12TE_{twelve}$
10. 1088_{nine}

11. 2706_{eight}
12. 12212_{three}
13. $31TT_{eleven}$
14. 10244_{five}
15. 112211_{three}

16. How many basic numerals are needed for the numeration system, base fifteen?

17. What is the value of the second place from the right in the numeration system in each of the following bases?

    a. five   b. eight   c. ten   d. twelve   e. fifteen

18. What is the value of the third place from the right in the numeration system in each of the following bases?

    a. five   b. eight   c. ten   d. twelve   e. fifteen

19. Give a base-ten numeral for each of the following:

    a. 100_{five} c. 100_{eight} e. 100_{seven} g. 100_{twelve}

    b. 100_{three} d. 100_{nine} f. 100_{eleven} h. $100_{fifteen}$

FRACTIONAL NUMERALS

1. Give a word name for each number.

   Examples 1 0.1_{ten} one-tenth

           2 0.1_{twelve} one-twelfth

   a. 0.1_{two} **b.** 0.1_{five} **c.** 0.01_{two} **d.** 0.01_{five}

Give a fractional numeral in base ten for each number.

Example $\left(\dfrac{10}{11}\right)_{\text{twelve}} = \left(\dfrac{12}{13}\right)_{\text{ten}}$

2. $\left(\dfrac{10}{11}\right)_{\text{two}}$ 5. $\left(\dfrac{10}{11}\right)_{\text{seven}}$ 8. $\left(\dfrac{10}{11}\right)_{\text{eight}}$

3. $\left(\dfrac{10}{11}\right)_{\text{three}}$ 6. $\left(\dfrac{10}{11}\right)_{\text{six}}$ 9. $\left(\dfrac{10}{11}\right)_{\text{nine}}$

4. $\left(\dfrac{10}{11}\right)_{\text{four}}$ 7. $\left(\dfrac{10}{11}\right)_{\text{eleven}}$ 10. $\left(\dfrac{10}{11}\right)_{\text{thirteen}}$

In the following base-ten numerals, place values are shown.

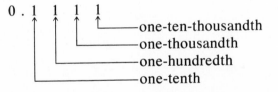

```
0 . 1  1  1  1
       └─────one-ten-thousandth
    └────────one-thousandth
 └───────────one-hundredth
└──────────────one-tenth
```

11. To obtain one-hundredth, by what number must one-tenth be multiplied?

12. To obtain one-thousandth, by what number must one-hundredth be multiplied?

13. 0.1111 is a fractional numeral in base two.
    └─one-half

   a. What is the value of 1 in the second place to the right of the point?

   b. What is the value of 1 in the third place to the right of the point?

   c. What is the value of 1 in the fourth place to the right of the point?

KEEPING ARITHMETICALLY FIT

Add.

1. 36.78
9.46

2. 105.9
96.8

3. 49.05
53.72

4. 1,365.2
489.9

Subtract.

5. 3,066
159

6. .31
.28

7. 4.62
3.79

8. 12.63
9.79

Multiply.

9. 3.6
7.9

11. 101.9
2.7

13. 378
115

15. 17.62
2.55

10. 10.6
9.5

12. 263.5
.33

14. $3\frac{1}{2}$
$4\frac{1}{4}$

16. $37\frac{1}{2}$
$5\frac{1}{4}$

Divide.

17. $17\overline{)11,376}$

19. $1.5\overline{)13.5}$

21. $0.1\overline{)13.6}$

23. $2.3\overline{)0.023}$

18. $.2\overline{)365.6}$

20. $2.25\overline{)155.25}$

22. $.5\overline{)375.6}$

24. $0.06\overline{)9.66}$

Add.

25. 378
95
1,166
469
105

26. 1.63
7.55
9.03
6.25
8.38

27. $1\frac{1}{2}$
$3\frac{1}{3}$
$6\frac{1}{2}$
$8\frac{2}{3}$

28. 375.6
38.9
117.6
35.9
17.8

Subtract.

29. 13.62
8.79

30. 135.01
49.99

31. 376.8
79.9

32. $3\frac{1}{6}$
$2\frac{2}{3}$

Multiply.

33. 3.7×0.06 **38.** $33\frac{1}{3} \times 6$ **43.** 39.5×0.01

34. 17.6×0.1 **39.** $\frac{1}{2} \times 57$ **44.** 6.7×0.01

35. 0.05×100 **40.** $\frac{3}{5} \times 98$ **45.** 0.001×135

36. 0.009×0.1 **41.** $\frac{1}{6} \times 66\frac{2}{3}$ **46.** 0.01×0.2

37. 1.09×10.5 **42.** $78 \times \frac{3}{5}$ **47.** 0.01×0.09

Divide.

48. $35 \div 0.1$ **55.** $0.1 \div 10$ **62.** $0.1 \div 100$

49. $7 \div 0.01$ **56.** $0.01 \div 10$ **63.** $0.01 \div 100$

50. $10 \div 0.01$ **57.** $0.1 \div 0.1$ **64.** $0.1 \div 1,000$

51. $100 \div 0.1$ **58.** $0.1 \div 0.01$ **65.** $0.01 \div 1,000$

52. $126 \div 0.01$ **59.** $0.01 \div 0.001$ **66.** $0.001 \div 10$

53. $3 \div 0.001$ **60.** $0.1 \div 0.001$ **67.** $0.001 \div 100$

54. $50 \div 0.001$ **61.** $0.001 \div 0.1$ **68.** $0.001 \div 1,000$

VOCABULARY REVIEW

abacus (77)
base (73)
base-seven numeration system (84)
basic numeral (68)
binary numeration system (87)
decimal numeration system (67)
digit (68)
expanded product form (74)
exponent (73)
exponential form (74)

Hindu-Arabic numeration system (69)
numeral (67)
place value (68)
position (72)
positional numeration system (90)
positional system (72)
power (73)
quinary numeral (90)
value of a place (91)

A CHALLENGE TO YOU

1. Write names for the numbers one through fifty in the base-seven system. Examine the sum of the digits for the numbers divisible by 3. State a rule for divisibility by 3 when numerals are written in the base-seven system.

Give the answers to exercises **2–5** without performing the multiplication.

2. Is $1011_{two} \times 111_{two}$ an even or an odd number?

3. Is $101_{two} \times 10000110_{two}$ an even or an odd number?

4. Is $3021_{four} \times 223_{four}$ an even or an odd number?

5. Is $64_{seven} \times 53_{seven}$ an even or an odd number?

6. Write binary fractional numerals for the following:

   a. $\left(\dfrac{1}{10}\right)_{ten}$ **b.** $\left(\dfrac{1}{16}\right)_{ten}$ **c.** $\left(\dfrac{1}{64}\right)_{ten}$ **d.** $\left(\dfrac{1}{100}\right)_{ten}$

7. Let us write names for 1, 2, 3, and 4 using exactly four 4's.

$$1 = \frac{4+4}{4+4} \qquad 2 = \frac{4}{4} + \frac{4}{4} \qquad 3 = \frac{4+4+4}{4} \qquad 4 = \frac{4 \times 4}{\sqrt{4} \times \sqrt{4}}$$

   ($\sqrt{4}$ is read "square root of 4" and is equal to 2, because $2 \times 2 = 4$.) Now keep going! See how many more you can get.

CHAPTER TEST

1. Expand by powers of ten.

   a. 10,987   **b.** 9,001   **c.** 343,107,205

2. Write 10,000 as a power of ten.

3. Give the base-seven numeral for each base-ten numeral.

   a. 10   **b.** 49   **c.** 45   **d.** 343

4. Using each of the basic numerals 0, 1, 2, and 3 once, write the base-seven four-digit numeral for the least possible number.

5. Using each of the basic numerals 3, 4, and 5 once, write the base-seven three-digit numeral for the greatest possible number.

6. Explain why 82_{seven} makes no sense.

7. In base ten, which names the greater number, 2^3 or 3^2?

8. Which is the exponent and which is the base in 4^{17}?

9. Write a four-digit base-seven numeral meeting the following conditions. In the second place from the left is 6. The other three digits are 5, 4, and 3. The numeral names the least possible number.

10. Write in words the value of 1 in the following binary numerals.

   a. 10_{two} b. 1000_{two} c. 100_{two} d. 10000_{two}

11. Tell the value of each digit.

   a. the second digit from the right in the base-four system

   b. the third digit from the right in the base-three system

   c. the second digit from the right in the base-eight system

   d. the third digit from the right in the base-four system.

12. Write names for the number *seven* in the following bases.

   a. seven   b. eight   c. four   d. five

13. What is the value of 1 in 0.01_{four}?

14. Which is greater, 0.01_{three} or 0.01_{four}?

15. Write names for the number *twelve* in the following bases.

   a. twelve   b. eleven   c. two   d. five   e. nine

16. In 689_{ten}, what is the value of

   a. 9?   b. 8?   c. 6?

17. In 135_{seven}, what is the value of

   a. 5?   b. 3?   c. 1?

18. Which is greater, 21_{ten} or 12_{twenty}?

19. Which is greater, 31_{four} or 13_{eight}?

CHAPTER FOUR

Rational and Irrational Numbers of Arithmetic

SUCCESSORS AND PREDECESSORS

The set of whole numbers is closed under addition; that is, the sum of each pair of whole numbers is a whole number. It is also closed under multiplication; that is, the product of each pair of whole numbers is a whole number.

The set of whole numbers is not closed under subtraction, however. For example, $2 - 5$ is not a whole number. This one example is sufficient to disprove the closure of the set of whole numbers under subtraction. Similarly, the set of whole numbers is not closed under division. One example, like $2 \div 7$ which is not a whole number, is sufficient to establish this.

Natural numbers are used in counting, because for every natural number, there is a next natural number. Also, for every natural number except 1, there is a natural number which precedes it.

■ A natural number which follows a given natural number is called its *successor*.

5 is the successor of 4.

■ A natural number which precedes a given natural number is called its *predecessor*.

4 is the predecessor of 5.

1. Name the successor and the predecessor of each number. (One number has neither of these. Find it!)

   a. 12   **b.** 998   **c.** $13\frac{1}{2}$ **d.** 3,425   **e.** 10,000

There is a first number in the set of natural numbers. It is the least number.

2. What is the least natural number?

Natural numbers have the qualifications which make them convenient for counting. You are familiar with numbers other than natural numbers. Some of these are $\frac{1}{2}, \frac{5}{12}$, 1.3, and .7. These numbers are not used for counting.

3. Is there a next fractional number after $\frac{1}{2}$?

4. Why are numbers such as $\frac{1}{2}$ and 1.3 not used for counting?

THE ARITHMETIC MEAN

What is the number half-way between $\frac{1}{2}$ and $\frac{1}{3}$? To find it, we multiply $\frac{1}{2}$ by the sum of $\frac{1}{2}$ and $\frac{1}{3}$. Check the computations below.

$$\frac{1}{2}\left(\frac{1}{2}+\frac{1}{3}\right)=\frac{1}{2}\left(\frac{3}{6}+\frac{2}{6}\right)$$
$$=\frac{1}{2}\cdot\frac{5}{6}$$
$$=\frac{5}{12}$$

One way to check that $\frac{5}{12}$ is half-way between $\frac{1}{2}$ and $\frac{1}{3}$ is as follows: $\frac{1}{2}=\frac{6}{12}$ and $\frac{1}{3}=\frac{4}{12}$. We know that $\frac{5}{12}$ is half-way between $\frac{4}{12}$ and $\frac{6}{12}$ because 5 is half-way between 4 and 6.

$\frac{5}{12}$ is called the *arithmetic mean,* or *average,* of $\frac{1}{2}$ and $\frac{1}{3}$.

■ To find the arithmetic mean of two numbers, multiply $\frac{1}{2}$ by their sum.

1. Find the arithmetic mean of each pair of numbers.

a. 3; 7	**e.** $\frac{2}{5}$; $\frac{4}{5}$	**i.** $\frac{1}{4}$; $\frac{1}{6}$	**m.** $2\frac{4}{5}$; 3
b. 7; 13	**f.** $\frac{1}{7}$; $\frac{1}{9}$	**j.** 1.4; 1.6	**n.** 7.25; 7.27
c. 8; 15	**g.** 0; 5	**k.** $1\frac{1}{2}$; $1\frac{1}{3}$	**o.** 3.5; 4.5
d. 2; 17	**h.** $\frac{4}{5}$; 1	**l.** 1.3; 1.4	**p.** 5.12; 5.13

Suppose someone claims that $\frac{1}{2}$ is the next number greater than $\frac{1}{3}$. To prove that this is not true, we find a number which is closer to $\frac{1}{3}$ than $\frac{1}{2}$ is and which is greater than $\frac{1}{3}$. One such number is the arithmetic mean of $\frac{1}{2}$ and $\frac{1}{3}$. We have already found it to be $\frac{5}{12}$.

$\frac{1}{3}$ is less than $\frac{5}{12}$ and $\frac{5}{12}$ is less than $\frac{1}{2}$. We write this as

$$\frac{1}{3} < \frac{5}{12} < \frac{1}{2}$$

2. **a.** Is there a number half-way between $\frac{5}{12}$ and $\frac{1}{2}$? Find it.

    b. Find the number half-way between $\frac{1}{2}$ and the number you found in part **a.**

    c. Find the number half-way between $\frac{1}{2}$ and the number you found in part **b.**

    d. How far can this process be carried on?

3. Find the number half-way between $\frac{1}{12}$ and $\frac{1}{15}$.

4. Find the number half-way between $\frac{1}{25}$ and $\frac{1}{50}$.

5. In exercises **1a–d**, subtract the smaller number from the larger. Divide the difference by 2 and add the result to the smaller number. Do you get the arithmetic mean of the two numbers in each case?

6. In exercises **1a–d**, divide the difference of the two numbers by 2 and subtract the result from the larger number. Do you get the arithmetic mean in each case?

There are several ways of finding the arithmetic mean of two numbers. Each way may be shown as a general pattern. One such pattern is the following:

■ For the numbers □ and △, the arithmetic mean is $\frac{1}{2}(\square + \triangle)$.

7. In the pattern above replace □ by 6 and △ by 1 and perform the operations. Did you get the arithmetic mean of 6 and 1?

8. If ○ is the arithmetic mean of □ and △, is the following statement true? ○ is between □ and △.

9. Illustrate your answer to exercise **8** with an example.

10. The pattern used in exercise **5** may be described as follows:

If $\square > \triangle$, then $\triangle + \dfrac{\square - \triangle}{2}$ is the arithmetic mean of $\square$ and $\triangle$.

In a similar way, show the pattern used in exercise **6**.

To find the arithmetic mean of three numbers, we multiply $\dfrac{1}{3}$ by the sum of the three numbers. The arithmetic mean of 5, 6, and 8 is

$$\frac{1}{3}(5 + 6 + 8) = \frac{1}{3} \cdot 19 = \frac{19}{3}$$

11. Find the arithmetic mean of each group of numbers.

    a. 7, 2, 15   **b.** 11, 15, 20   **c.** $5\frac{1}{2}, 3\frac{1}{3}, 10\frac{1}{4}$ **d.** 1.5, 2.7, 3.9

To find the arithmetic mean of four numbers, we multiply $\dfrac{1}{4}$ by the sum of the four numbers.

12. State the rule for finding the arithmetic mean of five numbers.

13. State the rule for finding the arithmetic mean of 75 numbers.

14. On a test six students received the following scores: 65, 92, 78, 80, 66, and 98. Compute the arithmetic mean of their scores.

15. If a student received the scores of 80 and 90 on two tests, then what score must he make on the third test in order to have the arithmetic mean of the three tests equal to 90?

16. If a student received the scores of 70, 75, and 80 on three tests, then what score must he make on the fourth test to have the arithmetic mean of the four tests equal to 80?

Numbers Between Two Given Numbers

We have learned that such numbers as $\dfrac{2}{3}$ and $\dfrac{1}{5}$ do not have numbers which are next larger or next smaller. We now want to answer the question, how many numbers are there between $\dfrac{2}{3}$ and $\dfrac{1}{5}$? [Warning: between does not mean half-way between.]

■   The number a is *between* the numbers b and c if $c < a < b$ or $b < a < c$.

Example 1   3 is between 10 and 0, because $0 < 3 < 10$.

Remember that $0 < 3 < 10$ means: 0 is less than 3 and 3 is less than 10.

Example 2   For the number pair $\frac{2}{3}$ and $\frac{1}{5}$, subtract the smaller number from the larger. Then multiply $\frac{1}{3}$ by the difference and add the result to the smaller number. Verify that the resulting number is between $\frac{2}{3}$ and $\frac{1}{5}$.

How to solve

STEP 1 $\dfrac{2}{3} - \dfrac{1}{5} = \dfrac{10}{15} - \dfrac{3}{15} = \dfrac{7}{15}$

STEP 2 $\dfrac{1}{3} \times \dfrac{7}{15} = \dfrac{7}{45}$

STEP 3 $\dfrac{1}{5} + \dfrac{7}{45} = \dfrac{9}{45} + \dfrac{7}{45} = \dfrac{16}{45}$

STEP 4   Is $\dfrac{16}{45}$ between $\dfrac{2}{3}$ and $\dfrac{1}{5}$? We prove that it is:

$\dfrac{2}{3} = \dfrac{30}{45}$ and $\dfrac{1}{5} = \dfrac{9}{45}$.

$\dfrac{9}{45} < \dfrac{16}{45} < \dfrac{30}{45}$ is true, because $9 < 16 < 30$.

Therefore, $\dfrac{1}{5} < \dfrac{16}{45} < \dfrac{2}{3}$.

1. For the number pair $\frac{2}{3}$ and $\frac{1}{5}$, multiply $\frac{1}{4}$ by their difference and add the result to the smaller number. Verify that the resulting number is between $\frac{2}{3}$ and $\frac{1}{5}$.

2. For the number pair $\frac{2}{3}$ and $\frac{1}{5}$, multiply $\frac{1}{5}$ by their difference and add the result to the smaller number. Verify that the resulting number is between $\frac{2}{3}$ and $\frac{1}{5}$.

3. For the number pair $\frac{2}{3}$ and $\frac{1}{5}$, multiply $\frac{1}{10}$ by their difference and add the result to the smaller number. Verify that the resulting number is between $\frac{2}{3}$ and $\frac{1}{5}$.

4. What is your guess—how many numbers are there between $\frac{2}{3}$ and $\frac{1}{5}$?

5. For the number pair 2 and 3, subtract the smaller number from the larger. Multiply $\frac{1}{2}$ by their difference and add the result to the smaller number. Verify that the resulting number is between 2 and 3.

6. For the number pair 2 and 3, multiply $\frac{1}{10}$ by their difference and add the result to the smaller number. Verify that the resulting number is between 2 and 3.

7. For the number pair 2 and 3, multiply $\frac{1}{50}$ by their difference and add the result to the smaller number. Verify that the resulting number is between 2 and 3.

8. What is your guess—how many numbers are there between 2 and 3?

9. For the number pair 2.5 and 2.6, multiply $\frac{1}{2}$ by their difference and add the result to the smaller number. Verify that the resulting number is between 2.5 and 2.6.

10. For the number pair 2.5 and 2.6, multiply $\frac{1}{10}$ by their difference and add the result to the smaller number. Verify that the resulting number is between 2.5 and 2.6.

11. What is your guess—how many numbers are there between 2.5 and 2.6?

12. For the number pair 3.21 and 3.22, multiply $\frac{1}{10}$ by their difference and add the result to the smaller number. Verify that the resulting number is between 3.21 and 3.22.

13. For the number pair 3.21 and 3.22, multiply $\frac{1}{100}$ by their difference and add the result to the smaller number. Verify that the resulting number is between 3.21 and 3.22.

14. How many numbers are there between 3.21 and 3.22? How would you prove your answer?

RATIONAL NUMBERS OF ARITHMETIC

Numbers such as $\frac{2}{3}, \frac{8}{5}$, 5, .25, and 3.6 are called rational numbers of

arithmetic. Each of these numbers has a name of the form $\frac{a}{b}$, where

a and b are whole numbers, and $b \neq 0$. For example, in $\frac{2}{3}$, $a = 2$ and

$b = 3$. We can express the numbers 5, .25, and 3.6 as follows:

$$5 = \frac{5}{1} \qquad .25 = \frac{1}{4} \qquad 3.6 = \frac{18}{5}$$

■ Every number which has a name of the form $\frac{a}{b}$, where a and b are
whole numbers, and $b \neq 0$, is called a *rational number of arithmetic*, or a *rational arithmetic number*.

Note that each rational arithmetic number has many names of the form
$\frac{a}{b}$. For example, we can express 5 as $\frac{5}{1}, \frac{10}{2}, \frac{15}{3}$, and so on.

Is 1 a rational number of arithmetic? Yes, because $1 = \frac{1}{1}$. Explain

why 0 is also a rational arithmetic number.

For each number, write a name of the form $\frac{a}{b}$, where a and b are whole

numbers.

1. 3

2. $1\frac{1}{2}$

3. $5\frac{1}{3}$

4. $10\frac{4}{5}$

5. .6

6. .55

7. .107

8. 3.2

9. 4.65

10. 2.176

11. 10.5

12. 125.1

From the problems you worked on pages 103–104, it is possible to
conclude that there is an infinite number of numbers between any two
rational arithmetic numbers. This means that there is no limit to how
many numbers there are between any two rational numbers. This property of rational numbers is called *density*.

■ The set of rational arithmetic numbers is a *dense set*, because
between any two rational arithmetic numbers, there is an infinite
number of rational numbers.

Give three other names of the form $\frac{a}{b}$ for each rational arithmetic number.

Example $\frac{3}{4}$ Three other names are $\frac{6}{8}$, $\frac{15}{20}$, and $\frac{30}{40}$.

13. $\frac{1}{2}$ **15.** 4   **17.** .5   **19.** .17

14. $3\frac{1}{4}$ **16.** 10   **18.** .9   **20.** 3.5

COMPARING RATIONAL NUMBERS

Because between any two rational numbers of arithmetic, there is an infinite number of rational arithmetic numbers, the set of such numbers is called a dense set. *Dense* means closely packed, or compact.

1. **a.** Is there a *whole* number between 1 and 2?

   b. Is there a *whole* number between 121 and 122?

   c. How many *whole* numbers are there between 5 and 7?

   d. Explain why the set of whole numbers is not a dense set.

2. For every pair of whole numbers, is there an arithmetic mean which is also a whole number? Give two examples to support your answer.

We will now examine ways of telling which of two given rational numbers of arithmetic is the greater. You should discover ways of doing this from the examples below. Study them thoughtfully.

Example 1 $\frac{1}{2} > \frac{1}{3}$;   also $1 \times 3 > 2 \times 1$ [3 > 2]

Example 2 $\frac{3}{4} > \frac{1}{2}$;   also $3 \times 2 > 4 \times 1$ [6 > 4]

Example 3 $\frac{5}{4} > \frac{9}{8}$;   also $5 \times 8 > 4 \times 9$ [40 > 36]

Example 4 $\frac{6}{7} > \frac{5}{6}$;   also $6 \times 6 > 7 \times 5$ [36 > 35]

3. Write a pattern involving multiplication which follows from $\frac{a}{b} > \frac{c}{d}$, and which is based on the examples above.

Replace each □ to obtain a true statement.

4. $\frac{4}{7} > \frac{1}{2}$; also □ × 2 > 7 × 1

5. $\frac{4}{9} > \frac{3}{8}$; also 4 × □ > 9 × 3

6. $\frac{5}{6} > \frac{4}{5}$; also 5 × 5 > □ × 4

7. $\frac{11}{12} > \frac{10}{11}$; also 11 × 11 > □ × 10

8. $\frac{19}{20} > \frac{18}{19}$; also □ × □ > 20 × 18

9. $\frac{4}{7} > \frac{7}{13}$; also 4 × 13 > □ × □

10. In exercises **4–9** perform the multiplication to verify the truth of the statements you obtained after replacing □.

Here is another set of examples for your study.

Example 1 $\frac{1}{2} = \frac{2}{4}$; also 1 × 4 = 2 × 2 [4 = 4]

Example 2 $\frac{2}{3} = \frac{8}{12}$; also 2 × 12 = 3 × 8 [24 = 24]

Example 3 $\frac{3}{5} = \frac{15}{25}$; also 3 × 25 = 5 × 15 [75 = 75]

Example 4 $\frac{7}{4} = \frac{28}{16}$; also 7 × 16 = 4 × 28 [112 = 112]

11. Write a pattern involving multiplication which follows from $\frac{a}{b} = \frac{c}{d}$, and which is based on Examples 1–4 above.

Replace each □ to obtain a true statement.

12. $\frac{3}{5} = \frac{9}{15}$; also 3 × 15 = □ × 9

13. $\frac{1}{7} = \frac{4}{28}$; also 1 × □ = 7 × 4

14. $\dfrac{3}{11} = \dfrac{21}{77}$;   also $3 \times 77 = 11 \times \square$

15. $\dfrac{25}{5} = \dfrac{5}{1}$;   also $\square \times 1 = 5 \times 5$

Study thoughtfully the following examples.

Example 1 $\dfrac{1}{4} < \dfrac{1}{2}$;   also $1 \times 2 < 4 \times 1$ $[2 < 4]$

Example 2 $\dfrac{3}{4} < \dfrac{4}{4}$;   also $3 \times 4 < 4 \times 4$ $[12 < 16]$

Example 3 $\dfrac{5}{6} < \dfrac{6}{7}$;   also $5 \times 7 < 6 \times 6$ $[35 < 36]$

Example 4 $\dfrac{6}{5} < \dfrac{7}{5}$;   also $6 \times 5 < 5 \times 7$ $[30 < 35]$

16. Write a pattern involving multiplication which follows from $\dfrac{a}{b} < \dfrac{c}{d}$, and which is based on Examples 1–4 above.

Replace each $\square$ and $\triangle$ to obtain a true statement.

17. $\dfrac{7}{8} < \dfrac{8}{9}$;   also $\square \times 9 < \triangle \times 8$

18. $\dfrac{1}{3} < \dfrac{1}{2}$;   also $1 \times \square < \triangle \times 1$

19. $\dfrac{7}{4} < \dfrac{5}{2}$;   also $7 \times \square < 4 \times \triangle$

Which are true and which are false?

20. $\dfrac{1}{2} > \dfrac{1}{3}$

21. $\dfrac{3}{8} < \dfrac{3}{7}$

22. $\dfrac{4}{3} < \dfrac{5}{4}$

23. $\dfrac{3}{5} > \dfrac{2}{3}$

24. $\dfrac{4}{7} = \dfrac{5}{8}$

25. $\dfrac{4}{3} = \dfrac{60}{45}$

26. $\dfrac{11}{12} < \dfrac{12}{13}$

27. $\dfrac{16}{17} > \dfrac{15}{16}$

28. $\dfrac{9}{2} = \dfrac{81}{17}$

29. $\dfrac{7}{11} = \dfrac{56}{88}$

30. $\dfrac{13}{12} > \dfrac{15}{13}$

31. $\dfrac{21}{20} < \dfrac{25}{22}$

32. $\dfrac{1}{17} > \dfrac{1}{16}$

33. $\dfrac{10}{11} < \dfrac{11}{12}$

34. $\dfrac{4}{7} = \dfrac{9}{12}$

35. $\dfrac{10}{7} = \dfrac{9}{6}$

DIFFERENT NAMES

Every rational number of arithmetic has many different names. When adding rational numbers, one name may be more convenient to use than another. For example, when adding $\frac{1}{2}$ and $\frac{1}{3}$, we choose the name $\frac{3}{6}$ for $\frac{1}{2}$ and the name $\frac{2}{6}$ for $\frac{1}{3}$.

$$\frac{1}{2} + \frac{1}{3} = \frac{3}{6} + \frac{2}{6} = \frac{5}{6}$$

There is a method for finding different names for the same number. This method is suggested by the examples below.

Replace each $\square$ and $\triangle$ to obtain a true statement.

Example $\frac{2}{5} = \frac{2 \times 3}{5 \times 3}$; $\frac{2}{5} = \frac{\square}{\triangle}$ $\frac{2}{5} = \frac{6}{15}$

1. $\frac{2}{5} = \frac{2 \times 5}{5 \times 5}$; $\frac{2}{5} = \frac{\square}{\triangle}$
3. $\frac{2}{5} = \frac{2 \times 8}{5 \times 8}$; $\frac{2}{5} = \frac{\square}{\triangle}$

2. $\frac{2}{5} = \frac{2 \times 6}{5 \times 6}$; $\frac{2}{5} = \frac{\square}{\triangle}$
4. $\frac{2}{5} = \frac{2 \times 10}{5 \times 10}$; $\frac{2}{5} = \frac{\square}{\triangle}$

Replace each $\square$ and $\triangle$ to obtain a true statement.

Example $\frac{6}{15} = \frac{6 \div 3}{15 \div 3}$; $\frac{6}{15} = \frac{\square}{\triangle}$ $\frac{6}{15} = \frac{2}{5}$

5. $\frac{15}{20} = \frac{15 \div 5}{20 \div 5}$; $\frac{15}{20} = \frac{\square}{\triangle}$
7. $\frac{9}{12} = \frac{9 \div 3}{12 \div 3}$; $\frac{9}{12} = \frac{\square}{\triangle}$

6. $\frac{18}{24} = \frac{18 \div 6}{24 \div 6}$; $\frac{18}{24} = \frac{\square}{\triangle}$
8. $\frac{21}{28} = \frac{21 \div 7}{28 \div 7}$; $\frac{21}{28} = \frac{\square}{\triangle}$

Find another name for the first number in each pair by multiplying the numerator and the denominator by the second number.

Example $\frac{3}{17}$; 5 $\frac{3}{17} = \frac{3 \times 5}{17 \times 5} = \frac{15}{85}$

9. $\frac{4}{9}$; 6   10. $\frac{2}{17}$; 3   11. $\frac{1}{6}$; 4   12. $\frac{2}{7}$; 4   13. $\frac{4}{11}$; 5

Find another name for the first number in each pair by dividing the numerator and the denominator by the second number.

14. $\frac{16}{18}$; 2   15. $\frac{12}{24}$; 6   16. $\frac{36}{56}$; 4   17. $\frac{11}{121}$; 11   18. $\frac{25}{625}$; 25

MATHEMATICAL GENERALIZATIONS

Suppose we decide to use letters of the alphabet in place of numerals. These letters will be replaced by different numerals to obtain names of numbers.

Replace the letters by the designated numerals to obtain names of numbers.

Example   In $\dfrac{a}{b}$ replace a by 3, b by 7.   Result: $\dfrac{3}{7}$.

1. In $\dfrac{x}{y}$ replace x by 4, y by 9.   **3.** In $\dfrac{c}{d}$ replace c by 9, d by 2.

2. In $\dfrac{m}{n}$ replace m by 5, n by 27.   **4.** In $\dfrac{w}{z}$ replace w by 6, z by 11.

Find the products.

Example $\dfrac{3}{4} \times \dfrac{5}{7}$ $\dfrac{3 \times 5}{4 \times 7} = \dfrac{15}{28}$

5. $\dfrac{2}{3} \times \dfrac{4}{7}$ **7.** $\dfrac{2}{5} \times \dfrac{7}{11}$ **9.** $\dfrac{4}{5} \times \dfrac{9}{7}$ **11.** $\dfrac{1}{5} \times \dfrac{4}{13}$

6. $\dfrac{4}{9} \times \dfrac{5}{11}$ **8.** $\dfrac{1}{7} \times \dfrac{2}{9}$ **10.** $\dfrac{6}{7} \times \dfrac{8}{5}$ **12.** $\dfrac{7}{3} \times \dfrac{2}{15}$

The pattern illustrated by the examples above is

$$\frac{a}{b} \times \frac{c}{d} = \frac{a \times c}{b \times d} = \frac{ac}{bd}$$

Recall that $a \times b$ is abbreviated as ab.

We know that any non-zero number divided by itself is 1.

$$\frac{x}{x} = 1 \qquad [x \neq 0]$$

In the generalization $\dfrac{x}{x} = 1$, replace x by the given numeral and write the resulting statement.

Example   5 for x $\dfrac{5}{5} = 1$

13. 10 for x **16.** 12,606 for x

14. 7 for x **17.** 999 for x

15. 125 for x **18.** 1,000 for x

RECIPROCALS

Is there a number which when multiplied by 3 gives the number 1 for the product? This number is $\frac{1}{3}$, because $3 \times \frac{1}{3} = 1$.

We call $\frac{1}{3}$ the *reciprocal* of 3

because the product of $\frac{1}{3}$ and 3 is 1.

Similarly, $\frac{3}{2}$ is the reciprocal of $\frac{2}{3}$, because $\frac{2}{3} \times \frac{3}{2} = 1$.

1. For each number, give its reciprocal. Then check to see whether the product of each number and its reciprocal is 1.

   Example $\frac{1}{2}$ The reciprocal of $\frac{1}{2}$ is 2 because $\frac{1}{2} \times 2 = \frac{2}{2} = 1$.

   a. $\frac{4}{5}$ **c.** $\frac{4}{3}$ **e.** $\frac{2}{7}$ **g.** $\frac{10}{3}$ **i.** 5

   b. $\frac{1}{3}$ **d.** $\frac{5}{4}$ **f.** $\frac{7}{2}$ **h.** 10   **j.** 1

2. What number is its own reciprocal?

3. Is the following generalization true? For all natural numbers m and n, $\frac{m}{n}$ and $\frac{n}{m}$ are reciprocals.

4. Show that the product $\frac{m}{n}$ and $\frac{n}{m}$ is equal to 1.

The number 0 does not have a reciprocal. Let us see why.
   Recall that multiplication and division are related operations.

$$\text{If } \frac{a}{b} = c, \text{ then } c \times b = a.$$

If 0 had a reciprocal, it would be $\frac{1}{0}$. What does $\frac{1}{0}$ mean? Suppose it is some number n; that is, $\frac{1}{0} = n$. Then it follows that $n \times 0 = 1$, or the number n multiplied by 0 is 1. But we know that there is no such number because any number multiplied by 0 is 0. Therefore,

$\frac{1}{0}$ does not name any number. $\frac{1}{0}$ is a meaningless symbol.

5. For each number, give a name of the form $\frac{a}{b}$, where a and b are whole numbers with no common factor other than 1.

Example   2.5 $2.5 = \frac{2.5}{1} = \frac{2.5 \times 10}{1 \times 10} = \frac{25}{10} = \frac{5}{2}$

a. 3.6   **c.** 20.7   **e.** 5.33   **g.** 25.37

b. 12.5   **d.** 1.25   **f.** 500.2   **h.** 999.999

6. For each number, find its reciprocal.

Example   2.5 $2.5 = \frac{25}{10} = \frac{5}{2}$.

Therefore, the reciprocal of 2.5 is $\frac{2}{5}$.

a. 1.2   **b.** 3.6   **c.** 10.3   **d.** 5.25   **e.** $1\frac{1}{2}$ **f.** $3\frac{3}{4}$

Which of the following natural numbers have reciprocals which are also natural numbers?

7. 5   **8.** 2   **9.** 100   **10.** 1

11. Name all natural numbers which have reciprocals which are also natural numbers.

For each set of numbers, check whether each member of the set has a reciprocal in that set. Then tell whether the set is closed under the operation *take the reciprocal of.*

Example $\left\{1, \frac{1}{3}, 3\right\}$

Reciprocal of 1 is 1; it is in the set.

Reciprocal of $\frac{1}{3}$ is 3; it is in the set.

Reciprocal of 3 is $\frac{1}{3}$; it is in the set.

Therefore, we can conclude that $\left\{1, \frac{1}{3}, 3\right\}$ is closed under the operation *take the reciprocal of.*

12. $\left\{1, \frac{1}{2}, 2\right\}$ **14.** $\left\{5, \frac{1}{5}\right\}$ **16.** $\left\{\frac{5}{4}, .8\right\}$ **18.** $\left\{1, \frac{1}{2}\right\}$

13. $\{1, .1, 10\}$ **15.** $\{1, 2\}$ **17.** $\{1.1, .9\}$ **19.** $\{10, .1\}$

TERMINATING DECIMALS

It is rather easy to find names of the form $\frac{a}{b}$ [a and b are whole numbers, $b \neq 0$] for such numbers as 1.5, 2.67, 3.906, and 159.3967.

$$1.5 = \frac{15}{10} \qquad 2.67 = \frac{267}{100} \qquad 3.906 = \frac{3,906}{1,000} \qquad 159.3967 = \frac{1,593,967}{10,000}$$

Decimals such as 1.5, 2.67, 3.906, and 159.3967 are called *terminating decimals*. What does "terminate" mean? Look it up in a dictionary.

There are decimals which are not terminating. For example,

1.666 . . . is a non-terminating decimal.

Three dots mean that 6 is repeated without end.

A non-terminating decimal like 1.666 . . .
is called a *non-terminating repeating decimal*.

Let us develop a way for finding decimal names for numbers in fractional form. We do this by performing division. Study these examples.

Example 1 $\frac{3}{4} = ?$

$$\begin{array}{r} .75 \\ 4\overline{)3.00} \\ 2\,8 \\ \hline 20 \\ 20 \\ \hline 0 \end{array}$$

$\frac{3}{4} = .75$

Example 2 $\frac{7}{8} = ?$

$$\begin{array}{r} .875 \\ 8\overline{)7.000} \\ 6\,4 \\ \hline 60 \\ 56 \\ \hline 40 \\ 40 \\ \hline 0 \end{array}$$

$\frac{7}{8} = .875$

Example 3 $\frac{3}{40} = ?$

$$\begin{array}{r} .075 \\ 40\overline{)3.000} \\ 2\,80 \\ \hline 200 \\ 200 \\ \hline 0 \end{array}$$

$\frac{3}{40} = .075$

Example 4 $\dfrac{7}{250} = ?$ $250\overline{)7.000}$ $\dfrac{7}{250} = .028$

$$\begin{array}{r} .028 \\ 250\overline{)7.000} \\ 5\ 00 \\ \hline 2\ 000 \\ 2\ 000 \\ \hline 0 \end{array}$$

CONCLUSION   Some rational numbers of arithmetic have names which are terminating decimals.

Find a decimal name for each number.

1. $\dfrac{4}{8}$ 7. $\dfrac{4}{5}$ 13. $\dfrac{3}{8}$ 19. $\dfrac{1}{16}$

2. $\dfrac{3}{2}$ 8. $\dfrac{3}{5}$ 14. $\dfrac{9}{8}$ 20. $\dfrac{5}{16}$

3. $\dfrac{7}{2}$ 9. $\dfrac{7}{5}$ 15. $\dfrac{11}{8}$ 21. $\dfrac{17}{16}$

4. $\dfrac{1}{4}$ 10. $\dfrac{12}{5}$ 16. $\dfrac{19}{8}$ 22. $\dfrac{9}{40}$

5. $\dfrac{5}{4}$ 11. $\dfrac{31}{5}$ 17. $\dfrac{21}{8}$ 23. $\dfrac{37}{40}$

6. $\dfrac{11}{4}$ 12. $\dfrac{42}{5}$ 18. $\dfrac{75}{8}$ 24. $\dfrac{49}{40}$

Copy the following and replace the blanks with either =, <, or >, to obtain true statements.

Example $\dfrac{36}{10}$ ___ 3.6 $\dfrac{36}{10} = 3.6$

25. 1.0756 ___ 1.0656   29. .6 ___ $\dfrac{2}{3}$ 33. $\dfrac{1}{3}$ ___ $\dfrac{1}{2}$

26. $\dfrac{1,075}{100}$ ___ 1.075   30. 1.5 ___ $\dfrac{3}{2}$ 34. 1.3 ___ $1\dfrac{1}{3}$

27. $\dfrac{3,763}{100}$ ___ 37.63   31. $\dfrac{21}{20}$ ___ 1.05   35. 1.01 ___ $\dfrac{101}{1,000}$

28. $\dfrac{14}{5}$ ___ 2.8   32. 2.737 ___ 2.7371   36. 1.1 ___ $1\dfrac{1}{9}$

For each number, give the simplest fractional name.

Example 1   .56 $.56 = \dfrac{56}{100} = \dfrac{14}{25}$

Example 2   3.122 $3.122 = \dfrac{3,122}{1,000} = \dfrac{1,561}{500}$

37. .2   **41.** .04   **45.** 10.32

38. .5   **42.** .95   **46.** 1.326

39. .35   **43.** 1.12   **47.** 2.008

40. .09   **44.** 5.46   **48.** 10.605

NON-TERMINATING REPEATING DECIMALS

The example below shows how to divide 1 by 6.

$$6\overline{)1.0000} = .166\overline{6}$$

```
      .1666
  6)1.0000
      6
      40
      36
      40
      36
      40
      36
      4
```

As we continue dividing, 6 will be repeated. The bar in .166$\overline{6}$ means that 6 repeats on and on. The decimal name for $\dfrac{1}{6}$ is a *non-terminating repeating decimal*.

$\dfrac{1}{6} = .166\overline{6}$

1. Divide 1 by 3. Carry out the process to four decimal places. Place a bar above the last repeating digit.

2. Divide 1 by 9. Carry out the process to four decimal places. Place a bar above the last repeating digit.

3. Divide 1 by 11. Carry out the process to six decimal places. Place a bar above the last two repeating digits.

4. Divide 1 by 7. Carry out the process to twelve decimal places. Place a bar above the last six repeating digits.

For each rational number give a decimal name. Some will have terminating, others non-terminating decimals for their names.

Example 1 $\dfrac{9}{5}$ $\dfrac{9}{5} = 1\dfrac{4}{5} = 1.8$

Example 2 $\dfrac{11}{6}$ $\dfrac{11}{6} = 1\dfrac{5}{6};$ $6\overline{)5.000}$ giving $.833\overline{3}$ $\dfrac{11}{6} = 1\dfrac{5}{6} = 1.83\overline{3}$

$$\begin{array}{r} .833\overline{} \\ 6\overline{)5.000} \\ \underline{4\,8} \\ 20 \\ \underline{18} \\ 20 \\ \underline{18} \\ 2 \end{array}$$

5. $\dfrac{4}{15}$ 8. $\dfrac{5}{6}$ 11. $\dfrac{3}{16}$ 14. $\dfrac{11}{9}$

6. $\dfrac{2}{7}$ 9. $\dfrac{4}{9}$ 12. $\dfrac{7}{5}$ 15. $\dfrac{15}{11}$

7. $\dfrac{1}{12}$ 10. $\dfrac{7}{18}$ 13. $\dfrac{8}{7}$ 16. $\dfrac{7}{2}$

Give fractional numerals for the following numbers.

17. 1.25   18. 10.45   19. 1.1076   20. 56.235   21. 100.1001

Once we know that $\dfrac{1}{6} = 0.166\overline{6}$, it is possible to find a repeating decimal name for $\dfrac{5}{6}$ using multiplication.

$$\frac{5}{6} = \frac{1}{6} \times 5$$

$$\frac{1}{6} = .1\overline{6} \text{ or } .16\overline{6} \text{ or } .166\overline{6}$$

$$\begin{array}{ccc} .1\overline{6} & .16\overline{6} & .166\overline{6} \\ \underline{\times 5} & \underline{\times 5} & \underline{\times 5} \\ .8\overline{3} & .83\overline{3} & .833\overline{3} \end{array}$$

Therefore, $\dfrac{5}{6} = .833\overline{3}$. (From the pattern do you see why we do not write 0 in the ten-thousandth's place?)

22. Given $\frac{1}{9} = .1\overline{1}$, write decimal numerals using multiplication.

a. $\frac{2}{9}$ **c.** $\frac{4}{9}$ **e.** $\frac{6}{9}$ **g.** $\frac{8}{9}$ **i.** $\frac{10}{9}$

b. $\frac{3}{9}$ **d.** $\frac{5}{9}$ **f.** $\frac{7}{9}$ **h.** $\frac{9}{9}$ **j.** $\frac{11}{9}$

23. Given $\frac{1}{11} = .09\overline{09}$, write decimal numerals for the following:

Example $\frac{25}{11}$ $\frac{25}{11} = 2\frac{3}{11}; \frac{3}{11} = .09\overline{09} \times 3 = .27\overline{27}$

Therefore, $2\frac{3}{11} = 2.27\overline{27}$.

a. $\frac{2}{11}$ **c.** $\frac{4}{11}$ **e.** $\frac{10}{11}$ **g.** $\frac{15}{11}$ **i.** $\frac{43}{11}$

b. $\frac{3}{11}$ **d.** $\frac{8}{11}$ **f.** $\frac{12}{11}$ **h.** $\frac{23}{11}$ **j.** $\frac{58}{11}$

24. Given $\frac{1}{7} = .142857\overline{142857}$, write decimal numerals for the following: [HINT: Do not forget to adjust the first digit on the right.]

a. $\frac{8}{7}$ **b.** $\frac{9}{7}$ **c.** $\frac{10}{7}$ **d.** $\frac{36}{7}$ **e.** $\frac{76}{7}$

25. Given $\frac{1}{6} = .16\overline{6}$, give a repeating decimal name for $10 \times \frac{1}{6}$.

26. Given $\frac{1}{11} = .09\overline{09}$, give a repeating decimal name for $100 \times \frac{1}{11}$.

MULTIPLYING REPEATING DECIMALS

Recall that to find a decimal name for a fractional numeral, we divide the numerator by the denominator. The process either stops, or it goes on with a repetition of one or more digits.

What about finding a fractional name for a decimal numeral? If the decimal numeral is terminating we proceed as in the examples below.

$$.1 = \frac{1}{10} \qquad .125 = \frac{125}{1,000} \qquad .00065 = \frac{65}{100,000}$$

But if the decimal numeral is repeating, our task is not so easy.

Let's try to find a fractional name for $.7\overline{7}$. First, observe the following:

$$\text{If } n = .7\overline{7}, \text{ then } 10 \times n = 7.7\overline{7}$$
$$\text{If } n = .12\overline{12}, \text{ then } 100 \times n = 12.12\overline{12}$$
$$\text{If } n = .105\overline{105}, \text{ then } 1{,}000 \times n = 105.105\overline{105}$$

1. If $n = .3\overline{3}$, what is $10 \times n$?

2. If $n = .78\overline{78}$, what is $100 \times n$?

3. If $n = .3763\overline{3763}$, what is $10{,}000 \times n$?

4. If $n = 1.3\overline{3}$, what is $10 \times n$?

5. If $n = 5.09\overline{09}$, what is $100 \times n$?

6. If $n = 17.35\overline{35}$, what is $100 \times n$?

7. If $n = 12.906\overline{906}$, what is $1{,}000 \times n$?

8. If $n = .1069\overline{1069}$, what is $10{,}000 \times n$?

9. If $n = 138.2601\overline{2601}$, what is $10{,}000 \times n$?

To find a fractional name for $.7\overline{7}$ we need another important pattern. After discovering this pattern, we shall return to this problem.

The following example suggests a pattern that may be true in general.

$$\text{If } \frac{3}{4} = .75 \text{ and } \frac{1}{4} = .25, \text{ then } \frac{3}{4} - \frac{1}{4} = .75 - .25.$$

To check whether the last statement is true, we carry out the necessary operations.

$$\frac{3}{4} - \frac{1}{4} = \frac{2}{4} = \frac{1}{2} \text{ and } .75 - .25 = .50 = \frac{1}{2}.$$

Thus, the statement, $\frac{3}{4} - \frac{1}{4} = .75 - .25$, is true.

A more convenient form of writing the example above is

$$\frac{3}{4} = .75$$
$$\frac{1}{4} = .25$$
$$\overline{\frac{3}{4} - \frac{1}{4} = .75 - .25}$$

Check: $\frac{3}{4} - \frac{1}{4} = \frac{2}{4} = \frac{1}{2}$

$.75 - .25 = .50 = \frac{5}{10} = \frac{1}{2}$

As in the preceding example, use subtraction and write the statement which follows from each pair of given statements. Carry out the necessary operations to check whether your statement is true.

10. $\dfrac{5}{4} = 1.25$

$\dfrac{2}{4} = .50$

11. $\dfrac{9}{10} = .9$

$\dfrac{4}{10} = .4$

12. $\dfrac{21}{25} = .84$

$\dfrac{4}{5} = .8$

13. $\dfrac{11}{20} = .55$

$\dfrac{9}{20} = .45$

14. Given the two statements below, write the pattern you used in exercises **10–13**.

$$a = b$$
$$c = d$$

DISTRIBUTIVE PROPERTIES

We found the pattern called the Right-Distributive Property of Multiplication over Addition to be true for all whole numbers.

$$(x + y)z = (xz) + (yz)$$

Find the answers for each pair of problems to see whether the Right-Distributive Property holds for the rational numbers of arithmetic.

Example
$$\left(\frac{2}{5} + \frac{1}{7}\right) \times \frac{1}{3}; \quad \left(\frac{2}{5} \times \frac{1}{3}\right) + \left(\frac{1}{7} \times \frac{1}{3}\right)$$

$$\left(\frac{2}{5} + \frac{1}{7}\right) \times \frac{1}{3} = \frac{14 + 5}{35} \times \frac{1}{3} = \frac{19}{35} \times \frac{1}{3} = \frac{19}{105}$$

$$\left(\frac{2}{5} \times \frac{1}{3}\right) + \left(\frac{1}{7} \times \frac{1}{3}\right) = \frac{2}{15} + \frac{1}{21} = \frac{14 + 5}{105} = \frac{19}{105}$$

The Right-Distributive Property holds.

1. $\left(\dfrac{1}{4} + \dfrac{1}{2}\right) \times \dfrac{1}{2}; \quad \left(\dfrac{1}{4} \times \dfrac{1}{2}\right) + \left(\dfrac{1}{2} \times \dfrac{1}{2}\right)$

2. $\left(\dfrac{1}{2} + \dfrac{1}{3}\right) \times \dfrac{2}{3}; \quad \left(\dfrac{1}{2} \times \dfrac{2}{3}\right) + \left(\dfrac{1}{3} \times \dfrac{2}{3}\right)$

3. $\left(\dfrac{2}{3} + \dfrac{1}{2}\right) \times \dfrac{4}{5}; \quad \left(\dfrac{2}{3} \times \dfrac{4}{5}\right) + \left(\dfrac{1}{2} \times \dfrac{4}{5}\right)$

4. $(0.1 + 0.7) \times 0.2; \quad (0.1 \times 0.2) + (0.7 \times 0.2)$

5. $(2.3 + 3.7) \times 1.5; \quad (2.3 \times 1.5) + (3.7 \times 1.5)$

6. $(3.5 + 1.6) \times 2.4; \quad (3.5 \times 2.4) + (1.6 \times 2.4)$

Let us now investigate another pattern which is like the pattern on page 119, except that subtraction takes the place of addition.

$$\left(\frac{3}{4}-\frac{1}{4}\right)\times\frac{1}{2}=\frac{2}{4}\times\frac{1}{2}=\frac{1}{2}\times\frac{1}{2}=\frac{1}{4}$$

$$\left(\frac{3}{4}\times\frac{1}{2}\right)-\left(\frac{1}{4}\times\frac{1}{2}\right)=\frac{3}{8}-\frac{1}{8}=\frac{2}{8}=\frac{1}{4}$$

It follows that $\left(\frac{3}{4}-\frac{1}{4}\right)\times\frac{1}{2}=\left(\frac{3}{4}\times\frac{1}{2}\right)-\left(\frac{1}{4}\times\frac{1}{2}\right)$

Find the answers for each pair of problems. Are the answers in each pair the same?

7. $\left(\frac{5}{6}-\frac{1}{3}\right)\times\frac{3}{5};\quad \left(\frac{5}{6}\times\frac{3}{5}\right)-\left(\frac{1}{3}\times\frac{3}{5}\right)$

8. $\left(\frac{1}{3}-\frac{1}{4}\right)\times\frac{2}{5};\quad \left(\frac{1}{3}\times\frac{2}{5}\right)-\left(\frac{1}{4}\times\frac{2}{5}\right)$

9. $\left(2-\frac{4}{5}\right)\times\frac{4}{7};\quad \left(2\times\frac{4}{7}\right)-\left(\frac{4}{5}\times\frac{4}{7}\right)$

10. $\left(\frac{5}{6}-\frac{1}{6}\right)\times 12;\quad \left(\frac{5}{6}\times 12\right)-\left(\frac{1}{6}\times 12\right)$

11. $\left(1-\frac{5}{6}\right)\times\frac{1}{6};\quad \left(1\times\frac{1}{6}\right)-\left(\frac{5}{6}\times\frac{1}{6}\right)$

12. $(15-12)\times\frac{1}{3};\quad \left(15\times\frac{1}{3}\right)-\left(12\times\frac{1}{3}\right)$

13. $(.7-.4)\times .5;\quad (.7\times .5)-(.4\times .5)$

14. $(2.5-1.9)\times 1.3;\quad (2.5\times 1.3)-(1.9\times 1.3)$

15. $(5-1)\times 1.7;\quad (5\times 1.7)-(1\times 1.7)$

16. The pattern which follows from the examples in exercises **7–15** is called the Right-Distributive Property of Multiplication over Subtraction. Write this pattern using x, y, and z.

Replace each □ to obtain a true statement.

17. $\left(7-\frac{1}{3}\right)\times\frac{1}{2}=\left(\square\times\frac{1}{2}\right)-\left(\frac{1}{3}\times\frac{1}{2}\right)$

18. $(5-1)\times\frac{4}{7}=(5\times\square)-(1\times\square)$

19. $\left(\frac{1}{2}-\frac{1}{8}\right)\times 5=\left(\frac{1}{2}\times 5\right)-\left(\frac{1}{8}\times\square\right)$

20. $\left(\square-\frac{1}{4}\right)\times 9=(3\times 9)-\left(\frac{1}{4}\times 9\right)$

21. $\left(5-\frac{4}{9}\right)\times\square=(5\times\square)-\left(\frac{4}{9}\times\frac{2}{9}\right)$

22. $(6-\square)\times\frac{4}{5}=\left(6\times\frac{4}{5}\right)-\left(\frac{9}{2}\times\frac{4}{5}\right)$

Distributive Patterns sometimes help to simplify computations.

$$(37\times 5)+(13\times 5)=(37+13)\times 5=50\times 5=250$$

Use the distributive patterns to simplify computations.

23. $(88\times 9)+(12\times 9)$

24. $\left(197\times\frac{1}{2}\right)+\left(3\times\frac{1}{2}\right)$

25. $\left(217\times\frac{3}{4}\right)-\left(17\times\frac{3}{4}\right)$

26. $\left(111\times\frac{7}{10}\right)+\left(89\times\frac{7}{10}\right)$

27. $\left(212\times\frac{3}{11}\right)-\left(102\times\frac{3}{11}\right)$

28. $\left(217\times\frac{4}{15}\right)-\left(67\times\frac{4}{15}\right)$

REPEATING DECIMALS AS FRACTIONAL NUMERALS

Let us now return to the problem we posed on page 118.

What is a fractional numeral for $.7\overline{7}$?

To answer this, we will use the following three principles.

1. $n=1\times n$ 2. $(a-b)c=(ac)-(bc)$ 3.   If $a=b$
and $c=d$
then $a-c=b-d$

Suppose we let $n=.7\overline{7}$
Then $10\times n=7.7\overline{7}$

Now we will subtract n from $10\times n$. On the right we tell which principle we have used for each step.

$$(10\times n)-n=(10\times n)-(1\times n)\qquad\text{Principle 1}$$
$$=(10-1)\times n\qquad\text{Principle 2}$$
$$=9\times n$$
$$=9n$$

Thus, we can conclude that $10n - n = 9n$. We will now use this subtraction in vertical form.

$$10n = 7.7\overline{7}$$
$$\underline{n = .7\overline{7}}$$
$$10n - n = 7.7\overline{7} - .7\overline{7} \qquad \text{Principle 3}$$
$$9n = 7$$
$$n = \frac{7}{9}$$

Therefore, $.7\overline{7} = \frac{7}{9}$.

1. Using the necessary principles, show that $10x - x = 9x$.

2. Using the necessary principles, show that $100n - n = 99n$.

3. **a.** If $n = .12\overline{12}$, what is $100n$ equal to?

   b. What is $100n - n$ equal to?

   c. What is $12.12\overline{12} - .12\overline{12}$ equal to?

   d. From the answers in parts **a–c**, find a fractional numeral for $.12\overline{12}$.

4. **a.** If $n = .206\overline{206}$, what is $1{,}000n$ equal to?

   b. What is $1{,}000n - n$ equal to?

   c. What is $206.206\overline{206} - .206\overline{206}$ equal to?

   d. From the answers in parts **a–c**, find a fractional numeral for $.206\overline{206}$.

Every repeating decimal numeral has a name in the form of a fractional numeral. The method above gives a way to find fractional names for these decimals.

Find fractional numerals for the following:

5. $.3\overline{3}$	9. $.8\overline{8}$	13. $.14\overline{14}$	17. $.101\overline{101}$
6. $.4\overline{4}$	10. $.9\overline{9}$	14. $.15\overline{15}$	18. $.216\overline{216}$
7. $.5\overline{5}$	11. $.10\overline{10}$	15. $.25\overline{25}$	19. $.987\overline{987}$
8. $.6\overline{6}$	12. $.13\overline{13}$	16. $.89\overline{89}$	20. $.1001\overline{1001}$

If we have a repeating decimal for a number larger than 1, we can temporarily "set aside" the whole number and work only with the decimal part, as shown in the example below.

Example $15.73\overline{73}$ $15.73\overline{73} = 15 + .73\overline{73}$ Let $n = .73\overline{73}$.

$$100n = 73.73\overline{73}$$
$$\underline{n = .73\overline{73}}$$
$$100n - n = 73.73\overline{73} - .73\overline{73}$$
$$99n = 73$$
$$n = \frac{73}{99}$$

Therefore, $15.73\overline{73} = 15\frac{73}{99}$.

$15\frac{73}{99}$ is sometimes called a "mixed numeral." How would you justify this name?

Find mixed numerals for the following:

21. $6.1\overline{1}$ 24. $1,002.2\overline{2}$ 27. $11.112\overline{112}$

22. $150.1\overline{1}$ 25. $27.32\overline{32}$ 28. $268.112\overline{112}$

23. $75.2\overline{2}$ 26. $126.32\overline{32}$ 29. $176.109\overline{109}$

■ Every number named by a repeating decimal has a name of the form $\frac{a}{b}$, where a and b are natural numbers. Therefore, every repeating decimal names a rational number.

There are repeating decimals in which the repetition does not start immediately to the right of the decimal point.

Example   Give a fractional numeral for $.126\overline{26}$.

$$\text{Let } n = .126\overline{26}$$
$$1,000n = 126.26\overline{26}$$
$$\underline{10n = 1.26\overline{26}}$$
$$990n = 125$$
$$n = \frac{125}{990}, \text{ or } \frac{25}{198}$$

Therefore, $.126\overline{26} = \frac{25}{198}$.

Find fractional numerals for the following:

30. $.12\overline{2}$ **34.** $.315\overline{15}$ **38.** $.216\overline{6}$

31. $.84\overline{4}$ **35.** $.426\overline{26}$ **39.** $.353\overline{3}$

32. $.57\overline{7}$ **36.** $.962\overline{62}$ **40.** $.902\overline{2}$

33. $.39\overline{9}$ **37.** $.751\overline{51}$ **41.** $.468\overline{8}$

DECIMALS AND DENOMINATORS

Below are given fractional numerals and their decimal equivalents. Supply decimal numerals wherever there is a question mark.

1. $\frac{1}{2} = .5$

12. $\frac{1}{13} = .076923\overline{076923}$

2. $\frac{1}{3} = .3\overline{3}$

13. $\frac{1}{14} = .0\overline{714285}$

3. $\frac{1}{4} = ?$

14. $\frac{1}{15} = ?$

4. $\frac{1}{5} = ?$

15. $\frac{1}{16} = ?$

5. $\frac{1}{6} = ?$

16. $\frac{1}{17} = .\overline{0588235294117647}$

6. $\frac{1}{7} = .142857\overline{142857}$

17. $\frac{1}{18} = ?$

7. $\frac{1}{8} = ?$

18. $\frac{1}{19} = .\overline{052631578947368421}$

8. $\frac{1}{9} = .1\overline{1}$

19. $\frac{1}{20} = ?$

9. $\frac{1}{10} = ?$

20. $\frac{1}{21} = ?$

10. $\frac{1}{11} = .09\overline{09}$

21. $\frac{1}{22} = ?$

11. $\frac{1}{12} = ?$

22. Refer to exercises **1–21** and write down all denominators of those fractional numerals which correspond to terminating decimals.

Since $\frac{1}{5}$ has a terminating decimal for one of its names, so do $\frac{2}{5}, \frac{3}{5}$, and $\frac{4}{5}$. Similarly, since $\frac{1}{7}$ has a non-terminating repeating decimal for one of its names, so do $\frac{2}{7}, \frac{3}{7}, \frac{4}{7}, \frac{5}{7}$, and $\frac{6}{7}$.

Refer to exercises **1–21** and tell which of the following can be expressed as terminating decimals. [HINT: Be sure fractional numerals are in simplest form.]

23. $\frac{5}{2}$	**28.** $\frac{3}{8}$	**33.** $\frac{4}{7}$	**38.** $\frac{4}{9}$
24. $\frac{7}{3}$	**29.** $\frac{8}{5}$	**34.** $\frac{5}{12}$	**39.** $\frac{2}{8}$
25. $\frac{5}{16}$	**30.** $\frac{8}{21}$	**35.** $\frac{5}{6}$	**40.** $\frac{9}{18}$
26. $\frac{7}{20}$	**31.** $\frac{7}{11}$	**36.** $\frac{9}{14}$	**41.** $\frac{75}{25}$
27. $\frac{9}{15}$	**32.** $\frac{3}{4}$	**37.** $\frac{11}{18}$	**42.** $\frac{17}{17}$

NON-REPEATING NON-TERMINATING DECIMALS

By this time you may be asking yourself whether there are any non-terminating decimals which are also non-repeating. The answer to your question is "yes, there are, and plenty of them." In fact, you will be able to make them up yourself. Here is one of them.

.35 2 35 22 35 222 35 2222 35 22222 35 222222 . . .

1. In the example above, explain how we made sure that there would be no group of digits which would repeat on and on.

2. Here is another non-repeating decimal.

.7 1 7 12 7 123 7 1234 7 12345 7 123456 7 1234567 7 12345678 7 123456789 7 12345678910 7 1234567891011 7 . . .

Explain how we made sure that there would be no repetition in this example.

3. Make up four non-repeating and non-terminating decimals.

Non-repeating non-terminating decimals are *not* names for rational numbers of arithmetic.

■ Numbers named by non-repeating non-terminating decimals are called *irrational* numbers of arithmetic.

In the two examples on page 125 we chose decimals which have patterns in them. Once we observe the pattern, we can continue writing on and on as far as we please. But a non-repeating decimal does not have to have a pattern.

Suppose we toss a die and whatever "comes up" we write down to the right of a decimal point. We may obtain a decimal that looks something like this:

$$.1625333516221164461542144 2561 \ldots$$

It is unlikely that we will get a repeating decimal. How would you argue that this is true?

4. Give an example of a non-repeating non-terminating decimal determined by drawing cards from a deck and replacing them before drawing again.

DIVISION BY ZERO

We have stated that we never divide a number by 0. Now we will show why this is the case.

First, consider dividing a non-zero number by zero, say $5 \div 0$. Suppose $5 \div 0$ is some number x.

If $5 \div 0 = x$, then it follows that $x \cdot 0 = 5$.

But we know that any number multiplied by 0 is equal to 0. So $x \cdot 0 = 5$ cannot be true for any number x. Therefore, $5 \div 0$ is a meaningless statement. By similar arguments, we can show that $n \div 0$ is meaningless for every non-zero number n.

Now consider dividing 0 by 0. Suppose $0 \div 0$ is some number y.

If $0 \div 0 = y$, then it follows that $y \cdot 0 = 0$.

But y can be replaced by 5 or 16 or any numeral, since any number multiplied by 0 is equal to 0. Thus, we can conclude that $0 \div 0 = 5$ and $0 \div 0 = 16$. But this means that $5 = 16$. Since this is obviously not true, we must conclude that $0 \div 0$ is meaningless.

Thus, $n \div 0$ is meaningless for every number n.

KEEPING ARITHMETICALLY FIT

Here is a shortcut for multiplying by 50. Consider 36×50.

$$36 \times 50 = 36 \times \left(100 \times \frac{1}{2}\right) \quad \left[\text{Replace 50 by } \left(100 \times \frac{1}{2}\right).\right]$$

$$= (36 \times 100) \times \frac{1}{2} \quad [\text{Assoc. prop. mult.}]$$

$$= 3600 \times \frac{1}{2}$$

$$= 1800$$

Thus, to multiply a number by 50, multiply it by 100; then multiply the result by $\frac{1}{2}$.

1. Use the short cut above to find the products.

   a. 78×50 c. 212×50 e. 96×50

   b. 128×50 d. 250×50 f. 121×50

Now, let's find a quick way to multiply by 25. Consider 72×25.

$$72 \times 25 = 72 \times \left(100 \times \frac{1}{4}\right) \quad \left[\text{Replace 25 by } \left(100 \times \frac{1}{4}\right).\right]$$

$$= (72 \times 100) \times \frac{1}{4} \quad [\text{Assoc. prop. mult.}]$$

$$= 7,200 \times \frac{1}{4}$$

$$= 1,800$$

Thus, to multiply a number by 25, multiply it by 100; then multiply the result by $\frac{1}{4}$.

2. Use the short cut above to find the products.

   a. 44×25 c. 444×25 e. $1,608 \times 25$

   b. 240×25 d. 880×25 f. 721×25

3. Develop a short cut of your own for multiplying by $33\frac{1}{3}$.

4. Use the short cut you developed in exercise 3 to find the products.

   a. $96 \times 33\frac{1}{3}$ b. $114 \times 33\frac{1}{3}$ c. $201 \times 33\frac{1}{3}$ d. $441 \times 33\frac{1}{3}$

For exercises **5–23**, numerals in parentheses refer to pages where you can find similar exercises.

Add. (436–437)

5. 5.406	**6.** 25.09	**7.** 118.3	**8.** 367.3	**9.** 100.3
3.711	36.17	206.9	25.9	99.7
9.212	98.26	310.4	9.8	82.9

Subtract. (438–439)

10. .409	**11.** 22.45	**12.** 9.003	**13.** 1.103	**14.** 2.063
.389	9.86	8.237	.998	.989

Multiply. (439–440)

15. 3.9	**16.** .896	**17.** 8.07	**18.** 9.07	**19.** .67
4.7	.9	.39	.41	.93

Divide. (440–441)

20. $1.5\overline{)2.25}$ **21.** $.6\overline{)9.42}$ **22.** $3.9\overline{)49.53}$ **23.** $.006\overline{)2.7}$

VOCABULARY REVIEW

arithmetic mean (100)
dense set (105)
irrational number of arithmetic (126)
non-repeating non-terminating decimal (125)
non-terminating repeating decimal (113)

predecessor (99)
rational number of arithmetic (105)
reciprocal (111)
Right-Distributive Property (119)
successor (99)
terminating decimal (113)

A CHALLENGE TO YOU

1. Given the terminating decimal $.n_1n_2n_3$, where n_1, n_2, and n_3 are the three digits, give its name of the form $\frac{a}{b}$, where a and b are whole numbers. [HINT: $\frac{n_1n_2}{100}$ is such a name, where n_1n_2 is a two-digit numeral with the digits n_1 and n_2].

2. Given the terminating decimal with k digits, $.n_1n_2 \ldots n_k$, give its name of the form $\frac{a}{b}$. [HINT: Recall that $10 \times 10 = 10^2$, $10 \times 10 \times 10 = 10^3$, and so on].

3. Given the repeating decimal $.\overline{n_1n_2}$, give its name of the form $\frac{a}{b}$.

CHAPTER TEST

Find the arithmetic mean of each pair of numbers.

1. 17, 12   **2.** $\frac{1}{2}, \frac{1}{5}$ **3.** 2.7, 13.5   **4.** 5.16, 9.24   **5.** $1\frac{1}{2}, 1\frac{1}{3}$

Find the number $\frac{1}{4}$ of the way from the smaller to the larger number.

6. 5, 9   **7.** 12, 14   **8.** 25, 26   **9.** $0, \frac{1}{2}$ **10.** $\frac{1}{3}, \frac{1}{4}$

Give a terminating or a repeating decimal name for each number.

11. $\frac{1}{2}$ **12.** $\frac{3}{4}$ **13.** $\frac{1}{32}$ **14.** $\frac{3}{11}$ **15.** $\frac{7}{8}$ **16.** $\frac{5}{12}$

Give the simplest fractional name for each number.

17. $.1\overline{1}$ **18.** $.12\overline{12}$ **19.** $.078\overline{078}$ **20.** $.251\overline{616}$

Which are true and which are false?

21. $\frac{1}{3} > \frac{1}{4}$ **23.** $\frac{3}{10} = \frac{10}{17}$ **25.** $\frac{9}{11} = \frac{5}{7}$ **27.** $\frac{3}{2} > \frac{7}{5}$

22. $\frac{4}{7} < \frac{5}{8}$ **24.** $\frac{12}{13} > \frac{4}{5}$ **26.** $\frac{3}{5} = \frac{27}{45}$ **28.** $\frac{9}{5} < \frac{3}{2}$

Give the reciprocal of each number.

29. $\frac{4}{9}$ **30.** 1   **31.** 17   **32.** 1.5   **33.** .06

Give the statements which follow from the distributive patterns.

34. $(7 + 11) \times 36$ **35.** $(31 - 17) \times 3$

Which are repeating and which are non-repeating decimals?

36. .353535 . . .   **38.** .231232233234235 . . .

37. .010010001 . . .   **39.** .11507635076350763 . . .

40. How many whole numbers are there between 30 and 76?

41. How many rational numbers are there between $\frac{1}{2}$ and $5\frac{1}{3}$?

42. Use the distributive patterns to find the answers.

   a. $(78 \times 13) + (22 \times 13)$ **b.** $(128 \times 17) - (28 \times 17)$

CHAPTER FIVE

Real Numbers of Arithmetic

SQUARE ROOT OF A NUMBER

We have seen that every rational number has a name of the form $\frac{a}{b}$, where a and b are whole numbers and $b \neq 0$.

OBSERVATION   A decimal numeral for a rational number of arithmetic is either a terminating decimal or a repeating non-terminating decimal.

We have also seen that there are non-repeating non-terminating decimals. These decimals name irrational numbers of arithmetic. To understand these irrational numbers better, let us consider the problem of multiplication of a number by itself.

2 is a *square root* of 4, because $2 \times 2 = 4$.
The symbol for square root is $\sqrt{}$.
Thus $\sqrt{4} = 2$ means a square root of 4 equals 2.

In the table below are given squares of the numbers from 1 through 25. It would be well if you could commit these to your memory. Of course, the squares of the numbers from 1 through 10 should be "old friends" to you.

Number	Square	Number	Square
1	1	14	196
2	4	15	225
3	9	16	256
4	16	17	289
5	25	18	324
6	36	19	361
7	49	20	400
8	64	21	441
9	81	22	484
10	100	23	529
11	121	24	576
12	144	25	625
13	169		

Name each of the following as a whole number.

1. $\sqrt{25}$ 4. $\sqrt{169}$ 7. $\sqrt{324}$ 10. $\sqrt{4,900}$

2. $\sqrt{64}$ 5. $\sqrt{225}$ 8. $\sqrt{576}$ 11. $\sqrt{8,100}$

3. $\sqrt{121}$ 6. $\sqrt{196}$ 9. $\sqrt{1,600}$ 12. $\sqrt{14,400}$

Name each of the following as a fractional numeral.

Example $\sqrt{\dfrac{9}{16}}$ $\sqrt{\dfrac{9}{16}} = \dfrac{3}{4}$ because $\dfrac{3}{4} \times \dfrac{3}{4} = \dfrac{9}{16}$.

13. $\sqrt{\dfrac{25}{36}}$ 14. $\sqrt{\dfrac{81}{100}}$ 15. $\sqrt{\dfrac{64}{121}}$ 16. $\sqrt{\dfrac{324}{256}}$ 17. $\sqrt{\dfrac{289}{625}}$

Square roots of *some* whole numbers are whole numbers. For example, $\sqrt{576} = 24$ and $\sqrt{841} = 29$. Square roots of *some* rational numbers are rational numbers. For example, $\sqrt{\dfrac{9}{16}} = \dfrac{3}{4}$ and $\sqrt{\dfrac{25}{64}} = \dfrac{5}{8}$.

You have seen that $\sqrt{9} = 3$ because $3 \times 3 = 9$. Thus, $\sqrt{9} \times \sqrt{9} = 9$. Similarly, $\sqrt{2}$ is a number such that the following is true.

$$\sqrt{2} \times \sqrt{2} = 2$$

Since $1 \times 1 = 1$ and $2 \times 2 = 4$, $\sqrt{2}$ is between 1 and 2.

$$1 < \sqrt{2} < 2$$

In exercises **18–26**, we examine a number of approximations to $\sqrt{2}$.

Explain why each statement is true.

Example 1 $\sqrt{2} > 1$ $\sqrt{2} \times \sqrt{2} = 2$ and $1 \times 1 = 1$. Since $2 > 1$ is true, $\sqrt{2} > 1$ is true.

Example 2 $\sqrt{2} < 1.6$ $\sqrt{2} \times \sqrt{2} = 2$ and $1.6 \times 1.6 = 2.56$. Since $2 < 2.56$ is true, $\sqrt{2} < 1.6$ is true.

18. $\sqrt{2} < 2$ 21. $\sqrt{2} > 1.41$ 24. $\sqrt{2} < 1.415$

19. $\sqrt{2} > 1.4$ 22. $\sqrt{2} < 1.42$ 25. $\sqrt{2} > 1.4142$

20. $\sqrt{2} < 1.5$ 23. $\sqrt{2} > 1.414$ 26. $\sqrt{2} < 1.4143$

From exercises **25** and **26** we can conclude the following:

$$1.4142 < \sqrt{2} < 1.4143$$

The last statement means: 1.4142 is less than $\sqrt{2}$ and $\sqrt{2}$ is less than 1.4143, or simply, $\sqrt{2}$ is between 1.4142 and 1.4143. Correct to three decimal places, $\sqrt{2} \doteq 1.414$. [Read: $\sqrt{2}$ is approximately equal to 1.414.]

There are various methods of computing approximations to square roots of numbers to as many decimal places as are necessary.

On page 421 there is a table which gives squares, square roots, cubes, and cube roots of numbers from 1 through 100. We say that

10 is the *cube root* of 1,000, because $10 \times 10 \times 10 = 1,000$.

The symbol for cube root is $\sqrt[3]{}$.

Thus $\sqrt[3]{1,000} = 10$ means the cube root of 1,000 equals 10.

Use the table and give the answers to the following:

Examples	24^2	$24^2 = 576$	$\sqrt{76}$	$\sqrt{76} \doteq 8.718$
	49^3	$49^3 = 117,649$	$\sqrt[3]{95}$	$\sqrt[3]{95} \doteq 4.563$

27. 50^2 **30.** 81^3 **33.** $\sqrt{80}$ **36.** $\sqrt{37}$

28. 50^3 **31.** 60^2 **34.** $\sqrt[3]{100}$ **37.** $\sqrt[3]{10}$

29. 81^2 **32.** 60^3 **35.** $\sqrt[3]{92}$ **38.** $\sqrt[3]{77}$

Use the table and give the answers to the following:

39. $\sqrt{9,216}$ **42.** $\sqrt{10,000}$ **45.** $\sqrt[3]{97,336}$ **48.** $\sqrt[3]{8,000}$

40. $\sqrt{7,744}$ **43.** $\sqrt{5,476}$ **46.** $\sqrt[3]{512}$ **49.** $\sqrt[3]{1,000,000}$

41. $\sqrt{2,209}$ **44.** $\sqrt{5,776}$ **47.** $\sqrt[3]{729,000}$ **50.** $\sqrt[3]{64,000}$

REAL NUMBERS OF ARITHMETIC

Recall that the set of real numbers of arithmetic consists of two disjoint subsets: the set of rational numbers and the set of irrational numbers of arithmetic.

OBSERVATION   If a square root of a whole number is not a whole number, then it is an irrational number.

1. Read the important observation above once more. Now answer these questions.

   a. Is $\sqrt{2}$ a whole number?

   b. What kind of a number is $\sqrt{2}$?

2. Tell which are irrational numbers.

   a. $\sqrt{1}$ **c.** $\sqrt{16}$ **e.** $\sqrt{25}$ **g.** $\sqrt{9}$ **i.** $\sqrt{2,705}$

   b. $\sqrt{5}$ **d.** $\sqrt{20}$ **f.** $\sqrt{30}$ **h.** $\sqrt{2,601}$ **j.** $\sqrt{29}$

3. **a.** Multiply 3.162 by itself and subtract the product from 10.

    b. Multiply 3.1622 by itself and subtract the product from 10.

    c. Is the answer in part **a** larger than the answer in part **b**?

    d. Which is a closer approximation to $\sqrt{10}$, 3.162 or 3.1622?

Now study Examples 1 and 2 carefully. Watch for a pattern.

Example 1 $\sqrt{4 \times 9} = \sqrt{36} = 6$
$\sqrt{4} \times \sqrt{9} = 2 \times 3 = 6$
Thus, $\sqrt{4 \times 9} = \sqrt{4} \times \sqrt{9}.$

Example 2 $\sqrt{25 \times 4} = \sqrt{100} = 10$
$\sqrt{25} \times \sqrt{4} = 5 \times 2 = 10$
Thus, $\sqrt{25 \times 4} = \sqrt{25} \times \sqrt{4}.$

Here is the pattern which you may have discovered.

■ For all whole numbers a and b, $\sqrt{a \times b} = \sqrt{a} \times \sqrt{b}.$

In the table on page 421 are listed the squares of whole numbers from 1 through 100. Using this table and the pattern above, we can find approximations to numbers such as $\sqrt{200}$.

Example $\sqrt{200}$ $\sqrt{200} = \sqrt{100 \times 2}$
$= \sqrt{100} \times \sqrt{2}$
$= 10 \times \sqrt{2}$
$\doteq 10 \times 1.414$ (We find in the table that $\sqrt{2} \doteq 1.414$.)
$= 14.14$
Thus, $\sqrt{200} \doteq 14.14.$

Using the table on page 421, find an approximation to a square root of each of the following:

4. $\sqrt{300}$ 9. $\sqrt{675}$ [HINT: $675 = 225 \times 3$]

5. $\sqrt{500}$ 10. $\sqrt{3,200}$ [HINT: $3,200 = 1,600 \times 2$]

6. $\sqrt{700}$ 11. $\sqrt{32,000}$ [HINT: $32,000 = 6,400 \times 5$]

7. $\sqrt{1,000}$ 12. $\sqrt{49,000}$ [HINT: $49,000 = 4,900 \times 10$]

8. $\sqrt{1,700}$ 13. $\sqrt{36,000}$ [HINT: $36,000 = 3,600 \times 10$]

RIGHT TRIANGLES

Squares of numbers have an interesting relation to right triangles. First we shall learn to *construct* a right triangle. For this you will need a straightedge (ruler used only for drawing lines) and compass.

1. Follow these directions as you construct a right triangle on your paper. Identify various parts as they are constructed in the picture.

    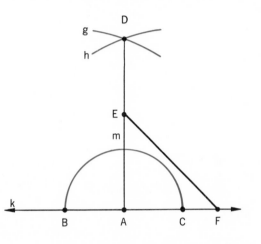

    a. Make a picture of a straight line; call it *k*.

    b. On line *k* mark *any* point; call it *A*.

    c. Put the foot of the compass at *A* and make an arc. It does not matter how much you open your compass. Call the two points in which the arc crosses line *k*, *B* and *C*.

    d. Put the foot of the compass at point *B* and make an arc *g* with an opening larger than the distance from *B* to *A*.

    e. Without changing the opening of the compass, put the foot of the compass at *C* and make another arc *h*.

    f. Call the point where arcs *g* and *h* intersect, *D*.

    g. Connect points *A* and *D* and call this line segment *m*.

    h. Angle *CAD* is a *right* angle.

    i. Pick any point on *m* different from *A*; call it *E*. Pick any point on line *k* different from *A*; call it *F*.

    j. Connect *E* and *F*. Triangle *FAE* is a right triangle, with angle *EAF* the right angle.

2. a. Construct a right angle using the procedure given above. Make one side of the angle 3 in. and the other 4 in. long.

    b. Connect the two points to make a right triangle.

    c. Measure the length of the *hypotenuse* (side opposite the right angle). How long is the hypotenuse?

INTERESTING TRIPLES OF NUMBERS

If you made the construction on page 135 correctly and made measurements with care, you found the hypotenuse to be 5 in. long. The lengths of the three sides of the triangle are then 3 in., 4 in., and 5 in.

The numbers 3, 4, and 5 have an interesting relation to each other. It is shown below.

$$3^2 = 9 \qquad 4^2 = 16 \qquad 5^2 = 25$$

$$9 + 16 = 25$$
$$3^2 + 4^2 = 5^2$$

1. **a.** Square each of the numbers 6, 8, and 10.

   b. Is the statement $6^2 + 8^2 = 10^2$ true?

   c. By what one number should you multiply each of the numbers 3, 4, and 5 to obtain the numbers 6, 8, and 10?

2. **a.** Square each of the numbers 9, 12, and 15.

   b. Is the statement $9^2 + 12^2 = 15^2$ true?

   c. By what one number should you multiply each of the numbers 3, 4, and 5 to obtain the numbers 9, 12, and 15?

3. **a.** Square each of the numbers 12, 16, and 20.

   b. Is the statement $12^2 + 16^2 = 20^2$ true?

   c. By what one number should you multiply each of the numbers 3, 4, and 5 to obtain the numbers 12, 16, and 20?

You have seen that to show patterns in mathematics, we frequently use letters which are replaced by various numerals. For example, we write $5x$ to mean $5 \cdot x$, where x can be replaced by a numeral for a whole number.

4. Give the number which is obtained when x is replaced by 6 in each of the following:

   Examples 1 $3x$ $3 \cdot 6 = 18$

            2 $4xx$ $4 \cdot 6 \cdot 6 = 144$

   a. $10x$ **c.** $4x$ **e.** $x + x$ **g.** $7x - 2x$ **i.** $3xx$

   b. $15x$ **d.** $20x$ **f.** $3x + 4x$ **h.** $9x - 5x$ **j.** $5xx$

An abbreviation commonly used for xx is x^2 (x squared). For example, if x is replaced by 7 in x^2, we obtain 7^2 which is equal to 49.

5. In the pattern $(3x)^2 + (4x)^2 = (5x)^2$, replace x by the given number name and make the necessary computations to check whether the statement you obtain is true.

> *Example*   3 $(3 \cdot 3)^2 + (4 \cdot 3)^2 = (5 \cdot 3)^2$
> $$9^2 + 12^2 = 15^2$$
> $$81 + 144 = 225$$
> $$225 = 225 \text{ is true.}$$

Therefore, the statement $9^2 + 12^2 = 15^2$ is true.

a. 2   **b.** 4   **c.** 5   **d.** 6   **e.** 10

THE PROPERTY $a^2 + b^2 = c^2$

It appears that the pattern $(3x)^2 + (4x)^2 = (5x)^2$ gives rise to triples of numbers with the property

$$a^2 + b^2 = c^2$$

All we have to do is replace x by a whole number name, and a triple with this property is created. Below are listed twenty such triples.

x	$3x$	$4x$	$5x$	$(3x)^2 + (4x)^2 = (5x)^2$		
1	3	4	5	$3^2 + 4^2 = 5^2$	$9 + 16 =$	25
2	6	8	10	$6^2 + 8^2 = 10^2$	$36 + 64 =$	100
3	9	12	15	$9^2 + 12^2 = 15^2$	$81 + 144 =$	225
4	12	16	20	$12^2 + 16^2 = 20^2$	$144 + 256 =$	400
5	15	20	25	$15^2 + 20^2 = 25^2$	$225 + 400 =$	625
6	18	24	30	$18^2 + 24^2 = 30^2$	$324 + 576 =$	900
7	21	28	35	$21^2 + 28^2 = 35^2$	$441 + 784 =$	1,225
8	24	32	40	$24^2 + 32^2 = 40^2$	$576 + 1,024 =$	1,600
9	27	36	45	$27^2 + 36^2 = 45^2$	$729 + 1,296 =$	2,025
10	30	40	50	$30^2 + 40^2 = 50^2$	$900 + 1,600 =$	2,500
11	33	44	55	$33^2 + 44^2 = 55^2$	$1,089 + 1,936 =$	3,025
12	36	48	60	$36^2 + 48^2 = 60^2$	$1,296 + 2,304 =$	3,600
13	39	52	65	$39^2 + 52^2 = 65^2$	$1,521 + 2,704 =$	4,225
14	42	56	70	$42^2 + 56^2 = 70^2$	$1,764 + 3,136 =$	4,900
15	45	60	75	$45^2 + 60^2 = 75^2$	$2,025 + 3,600 =$	5,625
16	48	64	80	$48^2 + 64^2 = 80^2$	$2,304 + 4,096 =$	6,400
17	51	68	85	$51^2 + 68^2 = 85^2$	$2,601 + 4,624 =$	7,225
18	54	72	90	$54^2 + 72^2 = 90^2$	$2,916 + 5,184 =$	8,100
19	57	76	95	$57^2 + 76^2 = 95^2$	$3,249 + 5,776 =$	9,025
20	60	80	100	$60^2 + 80^2 = 100^2$	$3,600 + 6,400 =$	10,000

1. In the pattern $(3x)^2 + (4x)^2 = (5x)^2$ replace x by the following and perform the necessary operations to check whether the resulting statements are true.

   a. 100   **b.** 1,000   **c.** 10,000

   Are there other triples of numbers, not derived from 3, 4, and 5, which have the property $a^2 + b^2 = c^2$?
   Here is one such triple: 5, 12, 13.

   $$5^2 = 25 \qquad 12^2 = 144 \qquad 13^2 = 169$$
   $$25 + 144 = 169$$
   $$5^2 + 12^2 = 13^2$$

2. In the pattern $(5y)^2 + (12y)^2 = (13y)^2$ replace y by the following and make the necessary computations to check whether the resulting statements are true.

   a. 2   **b.** 3   **c.** 4   **d.** 10   **e.** 20

3. Make a list of ten triples obtained by replacing y in $5y$, $12y$, and $13y$ by 1 through 10 consecutively.

4. Make the necessary computations to see whether the triple 7, 24, 25 has the property $a^2 + b^2 = c^2$.

5. Make the necessary computations to see whether the triple 8, 15, 17 has the property $a^2 + b^2 = c^2$.

6. Each of the triples below is derived from one of the following basic triples.

   A: 3, 4, 5   C: 7, 24, 25
   B: 5, 12, 13   D: 8, 15, 17

   Label each triple A, B, C, or D according to which basic triple it is derived from.

   a. 10, 24, 26   **f.** 30, 40, 50

   b. 30, 72, 78   **g.** 24, 32, 40

   c. 14, 48, 50   **h.** 24, 45, 51

   d. 16, 30, 34   **i.** 70, 240, 250

   e. 40, 75, 85   **j.** 800, 1500, 1700

   Do you see that there is no limit to the number of triples of whole numbers with the property $a^2 + b^2 = c^2$?

FROM PAIRS TO TRIPLES

You may have been wondering how you can discover triples of numbers with the property $a^2 + b^2 = c^2$. Actually it is not hard. First we must observe that the triple 3, 4, 5 can be obtained from two numbers, 2 and 1, as follows:

STEP 1   Square 2: $2^2 = 4$; square 1: $1^2 = 1$;
          subtract: $2^2 - 1^2 = 4 - 1 = 3$.

STEP 2   Multiply 2 by 1: $2 \times 1 = 2$;
          multiply this product by 2: $2 \times 2 = 4$.

STEP 3   Square 2: $2^2 = 4$; square 1: $1^2 = 1$;
          add: $2^2 + 1^2 = 4 + 1 = 5$.

And so, we have the numbers 3, 4, and 5:

$$3^2 + 4^2 = 5^2$$

Now, we start with another pair of numbers, 3 and 1, and do the same as we did with 2 and 1.

STEP 1   Square 3: $3^2 = 9$; square 1: $1^2 = 1$;
          subtract: $3^2 - 1^2 = 9 - 1 = 8$.

STEP 2   Multiply 3 by 1: $3 \times 1 = 3$;
          multiply this product by 2: $3 \times 2 = 6$.

STEP 3   Square 3: $3^2 = 9$; square 1: $1^2 = 1$;
          add: $3^2 + 1^2 = 9 + 1 = 10$.

And we have now obtained the triple 6, 8, 10.

Observe: $6^2 = 36$ $8^2 = 64$ $10^2 = 100$

$$36 + 64 = 100$$
$$6^2 + 8^2 = 10^2$$

1. **a.** Begin with the pairs of numbers, 3 and 2. Perform on these numbers the operations as in Steps 1, 2, and 3; that is,

   STEP 1   Subtract the square of 2 from the square of 3.

   STEP 2   Double the product of 3 and 2.

   STEP 3   Add the square of 3 to the square of 2.

   b. What triple did you obtain? Check to see whether it has the property $a^2 + b^2 = c^2$.

2. Follow the three steps in exercise **1a** and obtain triples of numbers from the following pairs.

   a. 4, 1   **b.** 4, 2   **c.** 5, 1   **d.** 5, 3   **e.** 6, 1

3. Make the necessary computations to check whether the triples you obtained in exercise **2** have the property $a^2 + b^2 = c^2$.

Let m and n be two numbers such that $m > n$. We shall now describe the pattern used in the three steps in exercise **1a**.

STEP 1 $m^2 - n^2$

STEP 2 $2(mn)$

STEP 3 $m^2 + n^2$

4. Make the following replacements for m and n in Steps 1, 2, and 3 above to obtain triples of numbers.

   a. 5 for m; 2 for n **b.** 5 for m; 4 for n **c.** 6 for m; 4 for n

5. Make the necessary computations to check whether each triple of numbers you obtained in exercise **4** has the property $a^2 + b^2 = c^2$.

THE PYTHAGOREAN RELATION

A triangle consists of three line *segments*. In the triangle on the right, the three segments are $\overline{AC}$, $\overline{BC}$, and $\overline{AB}$. [We use a bar over two letters to indicate a segment.]

The small square symbol at point C tells us that triangle ABC is a *right* triangle. Sides $\overline{AC}$ and $\overline{BC}$ are called *legs*. $\overline{AB}$ is called the *hypotenuse*.

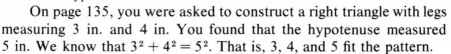

On page 135, you were asked to construct a right triangle with legs measuring 3 in. and 4 in. You found that the hypotenuse measured 5 in. We know that $3^2 + 4^2 = 5^2$. That is, 3, 4, and 5 fit the pattern.

$$a^2 + b^2 = c^2$$

If you were to examine many right triangles, you would find that the lengths of their sides all fit the pattern, $a^2 + b^2 = c^2$. The first accepted proof of this relation is credited to the Greek philospher, Pythagoras (584 B.C.–495 B.C.). It is therefore called the *Pythagorean Relation*.

■   *The Pythagorean Relation*

In a right triangle, $a^2 + b^2 = c^2$.

Note that a and b are the lengths of the legs, and c is the length of the hypotenuse.

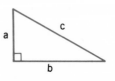

The Pythagorean Relation enables us to compute the length of the third side of a right triangle once we know the lengths of two sides.

Example 1   The lengths of two legs in a right triangle are 6 in. and 8 in. What is the length of the hypotenuse?

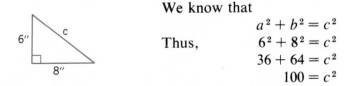

We know that

$$a^2 + b^2 = c^2$$

Thus, $$6^2 + 8^2 = c^2$$
$$36 + 64 = c^2$$
$$100 = c^2$$

Think: 100 is equal to what number squared?
Answer: 10, because $10 \times 10 = 100$.
Thus, $c = 10$, and the hypotenuse is 10 in. long.

Example 2   The lengths of two legs in a right triangle are 2 in. and 5 in. What is the length of the hypotenuse?

$$a^2 + b^2 = c^2$$
$$2^2 + 5^2 = c^2$$
$$4 + 25 = c^2$$
$$29 = c^2$$

Think: What number squared is 29?
Answer: $\sqrt{29}$, because $\sqrt{29} \times \sqrt{29} = 29$.
Thus, the hypotenuse is $\sqrt{29}$ in. long, which is approximately 5.4 in. [$\sqrt{29} \doteq 5.4$].

Example 3   The length of the hypotenuse in a right triangle is 7″ and the length of one of the legs is 3″. What is the length of the other leg?

$$a^2 + b^2 = c^2$$
$$3^2 + b^2 = 7^2$$
$$9 + b^2 = 49$$

Think: What number added to 9 is equal to 49?
Answer: 40. Therefore,

$$b^2 = 40$$

What number squared is equal to 40?
Answer: $\sqrt{40}$, because $\sqrt{40} \times \sqrt{40} = 40$.
Thus, the length of the second leg is $\sqrt{40}$ in., which is approximately 6.3 in. [$\sqrt{40} \doteq 6.3$].

1. Consider a right triangle with legs measuring a in. and b in. and hypotenuse measuring c in. Fill in the missing measures in the table. The first problem is solved for you in the example below. If the answer is an irrational number, state it as a square root.

a	3	9	?	2	?	4	?	10	1	2	?	1
b	5	?	24	2	1	1	5	24	?	?	1	2
c	$\sqrt{34}$	15	25	?	$\sqrt{2}$	?	7	?	10	10	2	?

Example   [first column in the table]

$$3^2 + 5^2 = c^2$$
$$9 + 25 = c^2$$
$$34 = c^2$$
$$\sqrt{34} = c$$

The hypotenuse is $\sqrt{34}$ in. long.

2. What is the length of the hypotenuse in a right triangle in which each leg is 1 in. long?

3. In a right triangle, which of the three sides is always the longest?

4. For the given measures, tell which can be sides of right triangles and which cannot.

Example   1 in., 4 in., 6 in. $1^2 + 4^2 = 1 + 16 = 17$
$$6^2 = 36$$
Since $17 \neq 36$ $[1^2 + 4^2 \neq 6^2]$, these measures do not form a right triangle.

a. 2 in., 3 in., 4 in.   d. $\sqrt{2}$ in., $\sqrt{3}$ in., $\sqrt{5}$ in.

b. 1 in., 2 in., 3 in.   e. $\sqrt{6}$ in., $\sqrt{7}$ in., $\sqrt{13}$ in.

c. 1 in., 3 in., $\sqrt{10}$ in.   f. $\sqrt{2}$ in., 1 in., $\sqrt{3}$ in.

5. Using the lengths marked in the picture, compute the lengths of the following:

a. $\overline{AB}$ b. $\overline{AD}$ c. $\overline{BD}$

6. If, instead of walking from A to D, then to C, you walk directly from A to C, how many feet do you save?

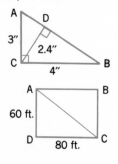

7. If a side of a square is 4 in. long, what is its area?

8. a. The Pythagorean relation can be shown in terms of areas of squares built on the sides of a right triangle. Copy the picture at the right on your paper.

   b. Build a square on the hypotenuse as one of its sides.

   c. What is the area of square *ABCD*?

   d. What is the area of square *EFGB*?

   e. What is the area of the square built on the hypotenuse?

   f. What is the sum of the areas of squares *ABCD* and *EFGB*? Is it the same as the area of the square built on the hypotenuse?

9. *EFCD* and *ABFE* are rectangles.

   a. How long is $\overline{AD}$?

   b. How long is $\overline{EF}$?

   c. How long is $\overline{DF}$?

   d. How long is $\overline{AF}$?

10. a. A steel ball rolls from *D* to *A* at the speed of 4 in. per second. How long does it take the ball to get to *A*?

    b. It now continues from *A* to *B* at the same speed. How long does it take to roll from *D* to *B* via *A*?

    c. How much time is saved by rolling the ball directly from *D* to *B*?

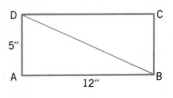

A NUMBER RAY

You are familiar with the idea of a straight line. The arrows in the picture of a line suggest that a line does not end. It extends indefinitely in two directions.

Using the idea of a ruler, we will make markings on a line and assign numbers to these points. To do this, we will consider only a *ray*. It will have a beginning but no end, as is shown in the picture.

We have marked eleven points on the ray. We can continue marking points to the right as far as we wish. There is no end to how far we can go.

The points we have marked are only those which correspond to whole numbers. But you know that between any two points we have marked, there are many other points. Let us enlarge the part of the ray between 0 and 2 and mark a few more points.

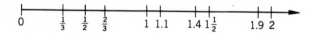

Make a picture of a part of the ray between 0 and 2 and mark on it the points corresponding to the following:

1. 1	**3.** 1.2	**5.** 1.8	**7.** $\frac{1}{5}$	**9.** $1\frac{7}{8}$
2. 1.5	**4.** $\frac{3}{4}$	**6.** $\frac{1}{4}$	**8.** .5	**10.** $1\frac{4}{5}$

Imagine a picture of a ray and describe where the points corresponding to the following numbers would be.

Example   1.3   three tenths of the distance from 1 toward 2

11. $1\frac{1}{2}$	**13.** 1.25	**15.** $\frac{8}{7}$	**17.** $\frac{3}{2}$	**19.** 1.01
12. $\frac{1}{2}$	**14.** $\frac{7}{8}$	**16.** $\frac{9}{5}$	**18.** .99	**20.** 1.99

RATIONAL NUMBERS AND A RAY

When we marked points on a ray, we chose only rational numbers for the points. Recall that the set of rational numbers is *dense*. This means that there are infinitely many rational numbers between any two rational numbers.

Find the number half-way between the two given numbers.

Example   2, 10 $\frac{1}{2}(2+10) = \frac{1}{2}(12) = 6$

6 is half-way between 2 and 10.

1. 1, 3

2. $5\frac{1}{2}$, 5

3. 3, 4

4. $\frac{1}{2}$, 0

5. 2.1, 2.2

6. 0, .5

7. $\frac{1}{3}$, 0

8. 1, $\frac{1}{8}$

9. 3.6, 3.5

10. 2.25, 2.26

11. 1.03, 1.04

12. 2.001, 2.002

Find the number one-third of the way from the smaller toward the larger number.

Example   4, 6 $\frac{1}{3}(6-4) = \frac{1}{3}(2) = \frac{2}{3}; 4 + \frac{2}{3} = 4\frac{2}{3}$

$4\frac{2}{3}$ is one-third of the way from 4 toward 6.

13. 2, 5

14. 10, 13

15. 3, 5

16. 7, 8

17. $\frac{1}{3}$, $\frac{4}{3}$

18. 1.2, 1.5

19. 2.5, 2.8

20. 6.7, 7

21. $\frac{1}{2}$, $\frac{1}{3}$

22. $\frac{1}{4}$, $\frac{1}{5}$

23. 1.12, 1.15

24. 1.113, 1.116

Find the number one-hundredth of the way from the smaller toward the larger number.

Example   3, 7 $\frac{1}{100}(7-3) = \frac{1}{100}(4) = \frac{4}{100} = \frac{1}{25}; 3 + \frac{1}{25} = 3\frac{1}{25}$

$3\frac{1}{25}$ is one-hundredth of the way from 3 toward 7.

25. 1, 2

26. 1, 3

27. 1, 4

28. $\frac{1}{2}$, 1

29. 2.2, 12.2

30. 3.1, 4.1

31. .2, .3

32. .01, .02

Find the number one-hundredth of the way from the larger toward the smaller number.

Example   7, 12 $\frac{1}{100}(12-7) = \frac{1}{100}(5) = \frac{1}{20}; \ 12 - \frac{1}{20} = 11\frac{19}{20}$

$11\frac{19}{20}$ is one-hundredth of the way from 12 toward 7.

33. 5, 6   **35.** 3, 12   **37.** 4.5, 4.6   **39.** 5.14, 5.15

34. 9, 11   **36.** 100, 200   **38.** 3.2, 3.4   **40.** 6.24, 6.34

IRRATIONAL NUMBERS AND A RAY

We think of a ray as having no "holes." That is, a ray "flows" without any break in it. As we "move" along a ray we "move" along the points with no empty spaces between them.

You may wonder whether *every point* on a ray has a rational number corresponding to it. There is nothing to stop us from imagining that between 1 and 2 on a ray we have assigned all rational numbers to the points. Now have we used up all the points?

The answer to this question is "no." There would still be some points left with no rational numbers assigned to them. That is, there are points on a number ray which cannot be located by means of rational numbers. These are the points which correspond to *irrational* numbers.

First recall that $\sqrt{2}$ is an irrational number. To show that there are points on a number ray which correspond to irrational numbers, we will prove that there is a point on a number ray which corresponds to an irrational number.

1. Using a compass and ruler, draw a picture according to the directions below.

   a. Make a picture of part of a ray and mark points corresponding to 0, 1, and 2.

   b. Label the point corresponding to 0 with the letter A and the point corresponding to 1 with the letter B.

   c. Draw $\overline{BC}$ perpendicular to $\overline{AB}$ and make $\overline{BC}$ 1 unit long.

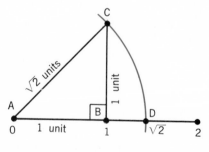

d. Connect A and C to make the right triangle ABC.

e. $\overline{AC}$ is $\sqrt{2}$ units long. Why?

f. With the foot of the compass placed at A, draw an arc from C to D.

g. Point D corresponds to $\sqrt{2}$. Why?

h. Is there a point on a number ray corresponding to an irrational number? What is it?

2. Using a construction similar to that in exercise **1**, show that there is a point on a ray which corresponds to $\sqrt{3}$. [HINT: A right triangle with one leg $\sqrt{2}$ units long and one leg 1 unit long has the hypotenuse $\sqrt{3}$ units long.]

Recall that the set of rational numbers and the set of irrational numbers of arithmetic are disjoint sets. That is, they have no common elements. If we combine both of these sets, we obtain the set of real numbers. These two ideas are expressed in concise statements below.

Q = the set of rational numbers of arithmetic
I = the set of irrational numbers of arithmetic
R = the set of real numbers of arithmetic

$$Q \cap I = \phi$$
$$Q \cup I = R$$

3. The answer to each of the following is either R, I, or Q. Give the correct answer for each case.

a. $Q \cap R =$ _____   c. $Q \cup R =$ _____   e. $Q \cap Q =$ _____

b. $I \cap R =$ _____   d. $I \cup R =$ _____   f. $I \cup I =$ _____

UNIVERSAL SET

When forming sets of things, we select the things from some specified set. For example, if the specified set is the set of natural numbers, $N = \{1, 2, 3, 4, 5, 6, \ldots\}$, we may form the following sets.

$\{1, 10, 15\}$ $\{25, 100\}$ $\{5000, 33, 17\}$ $\{1, 3\}$

We cannot obtain the set $\{0\}$ for example, because 0 is not in the set of natural numbers.

■ The set from which we select elements to form subsets is called the *universal set*.

Most of the time, when we work arithmetic problems, the universal set for answers will be the set of real numbers of arithmetic, that is, the rationals and irrationals we have just mentioned. Occasionally we may restrict our universal set to just the rationals or the irrationals, or perhaps even to the natural numbers or the whole numbers.

1. Q = the set of rational numbers of arithmetic
   I = the set of irrational numbers of arithmetic
   R = the set of real numbers of arithmetic

   Which are true and which are false? Recall that " $\subseteq$ " means "is a subset of."

   a. $Q \subseteq R$ c. $Q \subseteq I$ e. $R \subseteq Q$ g. $Q \cup I = R$

   b. $I \subseteq R$ d. $I \subseteq Q$ f. $R \subseteq I$ h. $Q \cap I = \phi$

2. N = the set of natural numbers; W = the set of whole numbers
   Which are true and which are false?

   a. $N \subseteq W$ b. $W \subseteq N$ c. $N = W$ d. $N \cap W = N$

Recall that every number which has a name of the form $\frac{a}{b}$, where a and b are whole numbers and $b \neq 0$, is a rational number.

3. For each whole number, give a name of the form $\frac{a}{b}$, where a and b are whole numbers.

   a. 5   b. 100   c. 23   d. 1,206   e. 980

4. Is every whole number a rational number? Why or why not?

5. Is every rational number a whole number? If your answer is "no," give an example of a rational number which is not a whole number.

6. Can a whole number be an irrational number?

7. N = the set of natural numbers
   W = the set of whole numbers
   Q = the set of rational numbers of arithmetic
   I = the set of irrational numbers of arithmetic
   R = the set of real numbers of arithmetic

   Which are true and which are false?

   a. $N \cap W = N$ d. $Q \cap W = Q$ g. $R \cap I = R$

   b. $N \cup W = W$ e. $I \cap W = \phi$ h. $Q \cup R = R$

   c. $Q \cup N = N$ f. $R \cap N = N$ i. $I \cap N = N$

8. For each false statement in exercise 7, change the right side of the equation to obtain a true statement.

9. Which of the five sets of numbers given in exercise 7 would you say is the most inclusive set (that is, the "richest")?

In each problem, you are given a universal set U. Which of the sets in parts a–d are formed from the elements of the universal set?

10. U = the set of all U.S. presidents

   a. {John Quincy Adams, James Buchanan, Harry S. Truman}

   b. {Martin Van Buren, Abraham Adams}

   c. {John F. Kennedy, Grover Cleveland}

   d. {Richard M. Nixon, Thomas Hayes}

11. U = the set of all U.S. presidents inaugurated before 1880

   a. {William McKinley, Lyndon B. Johnson}

   b. {James Monroe, Abraham Lincoln, John Adams}

   c. {Warren G. Harding, Calvin Coolidge}

   d. {James K. Polk, Zachary Taylor}

12. U = the set of all states bordering on Canada

   a. {Maine, Minnesota, Washington}

   b. {Michigan, North Dakota}

   c. {Vermont, Idaho, West Virginia}

   d. {New York, New Hampshire, Maryland}

13. U = the set of all rational numbers

   a. $\left\{\dfrac{1}{2}, \dfrac{1}{4}, \dfrac{1}{8}, \dfrac{1}{16}, \dfrac{1}{32}, \ldots\right\}$

   e. $\{.1, .2, .3, \ldots\}$

   b. $\{\sqrt{2}, \sqrt{3}, \sqrt{4}, \sqrt{5}, \sqrt{6}, \sqrt{7}, \ldots\}$

   f. $\left\{\dfrac{1}{3}, \dfrac{1}{9}, \dfrac{1}{27}, \dfrac{1}{81}, \dfrac{1}{243}, \ldots\right\}$

   c. $\{1^2, 2^2, 3^2, 4^2, 5^2, 6^2, \ldots\}$

   g. $\left\{0, \dfrac{1}{2}, \dfrac{1}{3}, \ldots\right\}$

   d. $\{\sqrt{1}, \sqrt{4}, \sqrt{9}, \sqrt{16}\}$

   h. $\left\{\sqrt{\dfrac{1}{4}}, \sqrt{\dfrac{2}{4}}, \sqrt{\dfrac{3}{4}}, \ldots\right\}$

THE COMPLEMENT OF A SET

Consider the set $U = \{1, 2, 3, 4, 5, 6\}$. This set may be described in several different ways. Here are three different descriptions.

U = the set of all natural numbers less than 7

U = the set of all whole numbers less than 7 and greater than 0

U = the set of all whole numbers between 0 and 7 (Whenever we say "between," we do not include the end numbers, 0 and 7 in this case.)

1. Is $A = \{1, 3, 5\}$ a subset of $U = \{1, 2, 3, 4, 5, 6\}$?

2. Give the set which consists of the elements in $U = \{1, 2, 3, 4, 5, 6\}$ which are *not* in $A = \{1, 3, 5\}$.

■ The set consisting of the elements in U which are not in A is *the complement of A in U*. The symbol for the complement of A is $\bar{A}$.

Example $U = \{5, 10, 15, 20, 25\}$ and $A = \{5, 20\}$

Then $\bar{A} = \{10, 15, 25\}$.

3. If $U = \{1, 2, 3, 4, 5, 6\}$, give the complement of each set.

a. $B = \{1, 2, 3\}$ d. $T = \{1\}$

b. $M = \{1, 4\}$ e. $H = \{1, 2, 3, 4, 5\}$

c. $S = \{1, 6\}$ f. $U = \{1, 2, 3, 4, 5, 6\}$

4. What is the complement of any universal set?

5. What is the complement of ϕ?

6. Use the sets in exercise **3** and complete each of the following:

a. $B \cup \bar{B} =$ _____   c. $S \cup \bar{S} =$ _____

b. $M \cup \bar{M} =$ _____   d. $T \cup \bar{T} =$ _____

7. For every set X, what is $X \cup \bar{X}$ equal to?

8. Use the sets in exercise **3** and complete each of the following:

a. $B \cap \bar{B} =$ _____   c. $S \cap \bar{S} =$ _____

b. $M \cap \bar{M} =$ _____   d. $T \cap \bar{T} =$ _____

9. For every set X, what is $X \cap \bar{X}$ equal to?

ONE-TO-ONE CORRESPONDENCE

Every point on a number ray has either a rational or an irrational number corresponding to it. Here are some points with numbers corresponding to them.

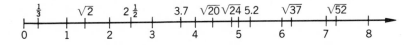

Of course, there is no limit to the number of points on a ray. Similarly, there is no limit to the number of real numbers. However, we can imagine that we have mentally assigned a real number to every point on the ray. Also, we can imagine that we have assigned a point on the ray to every real number. The correspondence between the points and the real numbers is called a one-to-one correspondence.

One-to-one correspondence:

one point for each number, one number for each point.

A number ray can be used to tell which of two given numbers is the greater. If the picture of the number ray is in a horizontal position with numbers arranged from left to right, then the following example suggests a rule for telling which of two numbers is the greater.

6 > 5 because the point corresponding to 6 is to the
right of the point corresponding to 5.

1. In each instance, insert either < or > to obtain a true statement.

   a. $\sqrt{20}$ ____ 4

   b. 3.7 ____ 3.72

   c. $\sqrt{52}$ ____ $\sqrt{51}$

   d. $\frac{1}{3}$ ____ $\frac{1}{4}$

   e. 1 ____ $\sqrt{2}$

   f. 8 ____ $\sqrt{63}$

   g. $2\frac{1}{2}$ ____ $\sqrt{7}$

   h. $\sqrt{20}$ ____ 4.5

   i. $\sqrt{65}$ ____ 8

2. Give three rational numbers which are between

   a. 1 and 2

   b. 3 and 4

   c. 10 and 12

3. Give an irrational number which is between

   a. 1 and 2

   b. 3 and 4

   c. 10 and 12

4. Make a picture of a number ray showing points from 0 to 8. Mark points corresponding to the following numbers.

   a. $\sqrt{8}$

   b. $\sqrt{25}$

   c. $\sqrt{17}$

   d. $\sqrt{63}$

   e. $\sqrt{64}$

MATCHING FINITE SETS

The arrows establish a one-to-one correspondence between the two sets below. These two finite sets are called *matching* sets.

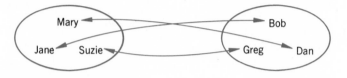

■ If it is possible to establish a one-to-one correspondence between two sets, then the sets are called *matching* sets.

It is easy to see that two finite sets with the same number of elements are matching sets. Consider sets A and B below.

$$A = \{1, 2, 3\} \qquad B = \{8, 10, 12\}$$

There are several ways in which we can establish a one-to-one correspondence between A and B.

1	2	3	Match: 1 with 8
↕	↕	↕	2 with 10
8	10	12	3 with 12

1	2	3	Match: 1 with 10
↕	↕	↕	2 with 8
10	8	12	3 with 12

1	2	3	Match: 1 with 8
↕	↕	↕	2 with 12
8	12	10	3 with 10

1	2	3	Match: 1 with 10
↕	↕	↕	2 with 12
10	12	8	3 with 8

1. Show two more ways of matching sets A and B.

2. $X = \{1, 2\}$ and $Y = \{100, 101\}$. In how many different ways is it possible to establish a one-to-one correspondence between X and Y? Show all of these ways.

3. There are four couples in a dance club. How many different sets of four dance couples can be formed? Let a, b, c, d be girls; x, y, v, w be boys. Show four different ways of forming couples. [HINT: Two sets of four dance couples are different if the sets differ in at least one couple.]

MATCHING INFINITE SETS

It is easy to decide whether two finite sets are matching by counting the elements in each set. If the number of elements in each set is the same, the sets are matching sets.

There is no end to the elements in an infinite set. Therefore, it is impossible to count all the elements in such a set. Then how can we tell whether two infinite sets are matching sets or not?

To answer this question, we try to establish a one-to-one correspondence between the sets. If we succeed, we know that the sets are matching. Let us consider two infinite sets.

$$A = \{1, 2, 3, 4, 5, 6, \ldots\}$$
$$B = \{2, 4, 6, 8, 10, 12, \ldots\}$$

A is the set of *all* natural numbers; B is the set of *even* natural numbers.

A:	1	2	3	4	5	6	$\ldots$
	$\updownarrow$	$\updownarrow$	$\updownarrow$	$\updownarrow$	$\updownarrow$	$\updownarrow$	
B:	2	4	6	8	10	12	$\ldots$

1 in A is matched with 2 in B, 2 in A with 4 in B, 3 in A with 6 in B, and so on. It is easy to see the relation between the matched elements of A and B. Every element in B is twice the element in A with which it is matched.

1. For the sets A and B given above, what element in B is matched with the following?

   a. 1,000 in A **b.** 5,000 in A **c.** 100,250,361 in A

2. What element in A is matched with the following?

   a. 500 in B **b.** 5,000 in B **c.** 250,360 in B

3. What element in B is matched with n in A?

4. What element in A is matched with m in B?

5. Is there any element in set A which is not matched with an element in set B?

6. Is there any element in set B which is not matched with an element in set A?

As we have seen, it is sometimes possible to establish a one-to-one correspondence between two infinite sets. Thus, two infinite sets can be matching sets.

Let us consider the set of all natural numbers

$$N = \{1, 2, 3, 4, 5, 6, \ldots\}$$

and the set of all natural numbers except 1

$$M = \{2, 3, 4, 5, 6, 7, \ldots\}$$

Sets N and M are matching sets. Here is one way to establish a one-to-one correspondence between these two sets.

$$
\begin{array}{ccccccc}
N: & 1 & 2 & 3 & 4 & 5 & 6 & \ldots \\
 & \updownarrow & \updownarrow & \updownarrow & \updownarrow & \updownarrow & \updownarrow & \\
M: & 2 & 3 & 4 & 5 & 6 & 7 & \ldots
\end{array}
$$

Thus, 1 in N is associated with 2 in M, 2 in N with 3 in M, 3 in N with 4 in M, and so on. Generally, if x belongs to N, then $x + 1$ in M is associated with x in N.

1. Display a one-to-one correspondence between N, the set of all natural numbers, and P, the set of all odd natural numbers.

2. For each of the following numbers in set N in exercise 1, give the corresponding number in set P.

   a. 1   d. 5   g. 255   j. 2,500

   b. 2   e. 10   h. 500   k. x

   c. 3   f. 100   i. 1,000   l. w

3. For each of the following numbers in set P in exercise 1, give the corresponding number in set N.

   a. 1   d. 7   g. 99   j. 1,001

   b. 3   e. 23   h. 499   k. y

   c. 5   f. 49   i. 901   l. m

4. Let N be the set of all natural numbers and L be the set $\{101, 102, 103, 104, 105, 106, \ldots\}$. Thus, L is the set of all natural numbers greater than 100. Display a one-to-one correspondence between N and L.

5. For each of the following numbers in set N in exercise 4, give the corresponding number in set L.

   a. 1   c. 8   e. 500   g. 10,000

   b. 2   d. 14   f. 1,002   h. a

6. For each of the following numbers in set L in exercise 4, give the corresponding number in set N.

a. 102   c. 205   e. 1,998   g. 10,450

b. 199   d. 502   f. 7,264   h. b

Below is shown a one-to-one correspondence between the set of natural numbers and a subset of the rational numbers of arithmetic.

$$X = \{1 \quad 2 \quad 3 \quad 4 \quad 5 \quad 6 \quad 7 \quad \ldots\}$$
$$\updownarrow \quad \updownarrow \quad \updownarrow \quad \updownarrow \quad \updownarrow \quad \updownarrow \quad \updownarrow$$
$$Y = \left\{\frac{1}{1} \quad \frac{1}{2} \quad \frac{1}{3} \quad \frac{1}{4} \quad \frac{1}{5} \quad \frac{1}{6} \quad \frac{1}{7} \quad \ldots\right\}$$

X and Y are infinite sets. Because there is a one-to-one correspondence between these two sets, they are matching sets.

$n \in X$; $\frac{1}{n} \in Y$; the correspondence follows the pattern: $n \leftrightarrow \frac{1}{n}$.

"$n \leftrightarrow \frac{1}{n}$" means "the number n is matched with the number $\frac{1}{n}$."

7. $A =$ the set of all multiples of 3.
   $B =$ the set of all natural numbers.
   Display a one-to-one correspondence between A and B.

8. For each of the following numbers in set B in exercise 7, give the corresponding number in set A.

a. 1   b. 2   c. 15   d. 40   e. 300   f. n

9. For each of the following numbers in set A in exercise 7, give the corresponding number in set B.

a. 3   b. 6   c. 333   d. 1,011   e. 5,274   f. m

10. $C =$ the set of all multiples of 5.
    $D =$ the set of all multiples of 10.
    Display a one-to-one correspondence between C and D.

11. For each of the following numbers in set C in exercise 10, give the corresponding number in set D.

a. 5   b. 10   c. 555   d. 205   e. 5,050   f. p

12. For each of the following numbers in set D in exercise 10, give the corresponding number in set C.

a. 10   b. 20   c. 100   d. 1,500   e. 2,610   f. r

KEEPING ARITHMETICALLY FIT

Add.

1. 2,340
985
1,362
9,088
172
1,765
349

2. .35
.78
.32

3. 3.06
5.98
7.36

4. 37.65
17.90
39.58

5. $\frac{1}{2} + \frac{1}{3} + \frac{1}{4} + \frac{1}{5}$

6. $3\frac{3}{5} + 16\frac{2}{3}$

7. .67 + 3.23 + 17.68 + 12.12

Subtract.

8. 3,115
229

9. 4,781
2,930

10. 20,362
17,895

11. 13,365
987

12. 32.75
13.89

13. 381.6
198.7

14. $25\frac{4}{7} - 13\frac{5}{6}$

15. $\frac{5}{8} - \frac{1}{3}$

Multiply.

16. 68×312

17. 1.2×37

18. 25.5×3.3

19. 36.2×12.5

20. $.37 \times 1.9$

21. $.25 \times .5$

22. $.01 \times .06$

23. $.002 \times .09$

24. $\frac{1}{3} \times \frac{17}{8}$

25. $3\frac{1}{4} \times \frac{1}{4}$

26. $2\frac{1}{2} \times 3\frac{1}{2}$

27. $5\frac{1}{3} \times 7\frac{3}{4}$

Divide.

28. $.3\overline{)78}$

29. $.2\overline{)34}$

30. $.5\overline{)215}$

31. $.03\overline{)63}$

32. $.01\overline{)782}$

33. $.01\overline{)3.175}$

34. $.3\overline{).1011}$

35. $.09\overline{).01026}$

36. $.002\overline{).26}$

37. $.23\overline{)3.91}$

38. $.87\overline{).2001}$

39. $.035\overline{)7}$

Give decimal names for the following:

40. $\frac{2}{5}$

41. $\frac{7}{10}$

42. $\frac{135}{100,000}$

43. $\frac{3}{25}$

44. $\frac{19}{50}$

45. $\frac{11}{125}$

46. $\frac{31}{32}$

47. $\frac{13}{64}$

Compute the arithmetic mean of each group of numbers.

48. 32; 43

49. 11; 23; 67

50. $\dfrac{1}{2}$; $\dfrac{3}{2}$

51. 1.3; 5.9

52. 3; 7; 11; 15; 19

53. 1; 6; 11; 16

54. 3.34; 4.34

55. 11.25; 12.25

56. $3\dfrac{1}{2}$; $4\dfrac{3}{4}$

57. $1\dfrac{1}{5}$; $3\dfrac{1}{4}$

VOCABULARY REVIEW

complement (150)
hypotenuse (135)
irrational numbers of arithmetic (147)
is approximately equal to (132)
leg (140)
matching sets (152)
number ray (144)
one-to-one correspondence (151)

Pythagorean Relation (140)
rational numbers of arithmetic (147)
real numbers of arithmetic (147)
right triangle (135)
square root (131)
triples of numbers (136)
universal set (147)

A CHALLENGE TO YOU

1. The sum of two numbers is 55. One number is 4 times the other. What are the two numbers?

2. The sum of two numbers is 33. One number is 5 more than the other. What are the two numbers?

3. The teacher calculated that if he gives each student three sheets of paper, he will have 31 sheets left. If, however, he gives each student 4 sheets of paper, he will have 8 sheets left. How many sheets of paper did he have, and how many students are there in the class?

4. A car travels 1 mile up hill at 30 mph. How fast should it travel 1 mile down hill in order to have an average speed of 60 mph over the entire 2 mile stretch?

5. How soon after 12 o'clock are the two hands of a clock together?

CHAPTER TEST

Which are true and which are false?

1. 1.414 is an irrational number of arithmetic.

2. The intersection of the set of rational numbers of arithmetic and the set of irrational numbers of arithmetic is the empty set.

3. The union of the set of rational numbers of arithmetic and the set of irrational numbers of arithmetic is the set of real numbers of arithmetic.

4. $\sqrt[3]{125}$ is an irrational number of arithmetic.

5. The Pythagorean Relation holds for the numbers 1, 2, and 3.

6. There is a finite number of rational numbers of arithmetic between any two rational numbers of arithmetic.

7. A number ray consists of only those points which have rational numbers of arithmetic assigned to them.

8. The set of real numbers of arithmetic includes the set of whole numbers.

9. It is not possible to establish a one-to-one correspondence between the set of even numbers and the set of odd numbers.

10. $\sqrt{\dfrac{4}{25}}$ is a rational number of arithmetic.

$U = \{2, 4, 6, 8\}$. List the elements of the following sets.

11. Complement of $\{2\}$ **13.** Complement of U

12. Complement of $\{2, 6, 8\}$ **14.** Complement of ϕ

15. Sets A and B are matching sets. If for every number n in A, the corresponding number in B is $n + 11$, what number in B corresponds to 25 in A?

16. What is the length of the hypotenuse in a right triangle in which the two legs are 4 in. and 6 in. long?

From the table of square roots. give an approximation for each of the following:

17. $\sqrt{21}$ **18.** $\sqrt{99}$ **19.** $\sqrt[3]{20}$ **20.** $\sqrt{80}$

21. Show how you would establish a one-to-one correspondence between the set of all natural numbers and the set of natural numbers greater than 205.

22. Is $\sqrt{156}$ a rational number? Why or why not?

23. N = the set of natural numbers
    Q = the set of rational numbers of arithmetic
    I = the set of irrational numbers of arithmetic
    R = the set of real numbers of arithmetic

    Which are true and which are false?

    a. $N = Q$ d. $Q \subseteq N$ g. $Q \cup I = R$ j. $\sqrt{2} \in Q$

    b. $I \subseteq R$ e. $Q \cap I = N$ h. $\sqrt{2} \in I$ k. $N \cap I = \phi$

    c. $N \subseteq R$ f. $N \cup Q = Q$ i. $\sqrt{2} \in R$ l. $5 \in N$

24. If $A = \{6, 12, 18, 24, \ldots\}$, which are true and which are false?

    a. $120 \in A$ c. $48 \in A$ e. $1{,}302 \in A$ g. $38{,}100 \in A$

    b. $376 \in A$ d. $966 \in A$ f. $5{,}001 \in A$ h. $38{,}106 \in A$

25. Check to see which of the following are Pythagorean triples.

    a. 1, 2, 3   c. 2, 3, $\sqrt{13}$ e. 6, 8, 10

    b. 2, 3, 13   d. 5, 6, 61   f. 5, 12, 13

26. One leg of a right triangle is 5 in. long and the hypotenuse is $\sqrt{29}$ in. long. How long is the other leg?

CHAPTER SIX

Per Cent and Its Uses

WHAT DOES PER CENT MEAN?

"Per cent" means "per hundred." For example, 35 per cent means 35 per hundred, or 35 out of one hundred.

The symbol for per cent is %.

$$9\% = \frac{9}{100} \qquad 17\% = \frac{17}{100}$$

And generally,

$$n\% = \frac{n}{100}$$

PER CENTS TO FRACTIONAL NUMERALS

For each per cent, give the simplest fractional name.

Example 1   29% $29\% = \frac{29}{100}$; $\frac{29}{100}$ is the simplest name since 29 and 100 have no common factors other than 1.

Example 2   35% $35\% = \frac{35}{100} = \frac{7}{20}$

1. 1%	**4.** 79%	**7.** 22%	**10.** 41%
2. 4%	**5.** 42%	**8.** 2%	**11.** 3%
3. 80%	**6.** 99%	**9.** 55%	**12.** 25%

In exercises **1–12**, we dealt with per cents between 1% and 99%. Let us now turn to numbers greater than 100%. First note that

$$100\% = \frac{100}{100} = 1$$

For each per cent, give the simplest whole number or mixed numeral.

Example 1   120% $120\% = \frac{120}{100} = 1\frac{20}{100} = 1\frac{1}{5}$

Example 2   300% $300\% = \frac{300}{100} = 3$

13. 110%	**16.** 320%	**19.** 1,000%	**22.** 4,013%
14. 400%	**17.** 717%	**20.** 1,237%	**23.** 10,000%
15. 560%	**18.** 950%	**21.** 5,000%	**24.** 6,172%

We know that $n\% = \dfrac{n}{100}$. Since $\dfrac{n}{100} = n \times \dfrac{1}{100}$, it follows that

$$n\% = n \times \dfrac{1}{100}$$

This relation helps us to find fractional names for per cents which are less than 1%.

For each per cent, give the simplest fractional name.

Example 1 $\dfrac{1}{2}\%$ $\dfrac{1}{2}\% = \dfrac{1}{2} \times \dfrac{1}{100} = \dfrac{1}{200}$

Example 2 $\dfrac{4}{5}\%$ $\dfrac{4}{5}\% = \dfrac{4}{5} \times \dfrac{1}{100} = \dfrac{4}{500} = \dfrac{1}{125}$

25. $\dfrac{1}{3}\%$ **27.** $\dfrac{1}{6}\%$ **29.** $\dfrac{1}{8}\%$ **31.** $\dfrac{5}{9}\%$ **33.** $\dfrac{1}{25}\%$

26. $\dfrac{2}{3}\%$ **28.** $\dfrac{5}{6}\%$ **30.** $\dfrac{5}{8}\%$ **32.** $\dfrac{3}{10}\%$ **34.** $\dfrac{3}{37}\%$

For each per cent, give the simplest fractional or mixed numeral.

Example 1   250% $250\% = \dfrac{250}{100} = 2\dfrac{1}{2}$

Example 2 $1\dfrac{2}{3}\%$ $1\dfrac{2}{3}\% = 1\dfrac{2}{3} \times \dfrac{1}{100} = \dfrac{5}{3} \times \dfrac{1}{100} = \dfrac{5}{300} = \dfrac{1}{60}$

35. 15%   **37.** 75%   **39.** 240%   **41.** $2\dfrac{1}{5}\%$ **43.** $6\dfrac{5}{8}\%$

36. 20%   **38.** 150%   **40.** 500%   **42.** $28\dfrac{3}{10}\%$ **44.** $12\dfrac{1}{20}\%$

PER CENTS TO DECIMALS

Recall the basic relation

$$n\% = n \times \dfrac{1}{100}$$

Since $\dfrac{1}{100} = .01$, we have

$$n\% = n \times .01$$

We use this relation to find decimal names for per cents.

For each per cent, give a decimal name.

Example 1 30% $30\% = 30 \times .01 = .30$

1. 45%   3. 98%   5. 33%   7. 32%   9. 2%

2. 67%   4. 3%   6. 25%   8. 88%   10. 50%

Example 2 685% $685\% = 685 \times 0.01 = 6.85$

11. 750%   13. 101%   15. 980%   17. 1,250%   19. 20,670%

12. 230%   14. 533%   16. 1,000%   18. 2,000%   20. 32,758%

Example 3 0.5% $0.5\% = 0.5 \times 0.01 = 0.005$

Example 4 0.015% $0.015\% = 0.015 \times 0.01 = 0.00015$

21. 0.1%   24. 0.03%   27. 0.105%   30. 0.125%

22. 0.26%   25. 0.016%   28. 0.001%   31. 0.0001%

23. 0.95%   26. 0.268%   29. 0.007%   32. 0.0009%

Example 5 2.5% $2.5\% = 2.5 \times 0.01 = 0.025$

33. 45%   37. 96.5%   41. 22.5%   45. 0.06%

34. 90%   38. 525%   42. 67.9%   46. 0.012%

35. 11%   39. 0.4%   43. 1,300%   47. 100.6%

36. 210%   40. 15.2%   44. 1.25%   48. 1.006%

For each per cent, give the simplest fractional or mixed numeral.

Example 6 150% $150\% = \dfrac{150}{100} = 1\dfrac{50}{100} = 1\dfrac{1}{2}$

Example 7 $37\dfrac{1}{2}\%$ $37\dfrac{1}{2}\% = 37\dfrac{1}{2} \times \dfrac{1}{100} = \dfrac{75}{2} \times \dfrac{1}{100} = \dfrac{75}{200} = \dfrac{3}{8}$

49. 65%   53. 2,000%   57. $\dfrac{1}{7}\%$ 61. 16%

50. 34%   54. $\dfrac{3}{4}\%$ 58. $\dfrac{2}{9}\%$ 62. 500%

51. 660%   55. 4%   59. $\dfrac{3}{11}\%$ 63. 10,000%

52. $\dfrac{1}{8}\%$ 56. $12\dfrac{1}{2}\%$ 60. $2\dfrac{3}{5}\%$ 64. $16\dfrac{2}{3}\%$

FRACTIONAL AND DECIMAL NUMERALS TO PER CENTS

If a fractional numeral has the denominator 100, it is easy to find its per cent name.

For each number, give its per cent name.

Example $\dfrac{17}{100}$ $\dfrac{17}{100} = 17\%$

1. $\dfrac{15}{100}$

2. $\dfrac{47}{100}$

3. $\dfrac{360}{100}$

4. $\dfrac{1,765}{100}$

5. $\dfrac{\frac{1}{3}}{100}$

6. $\dfrac{n}{100}$

7. $\dfrac{k+1}{100}$

8. $\dfrac{h-1}{100}$

9. $\dfrac{3m}{100}$

10. $\dfrac{7k-1}{100}$

11. $\dfrac{n+m}{100}$

12. $\dfrac{2c-g}{100}$

For each number, give its name in the form of a fractional numeral with the denominator 100. Then give its per cent name.

Example 1 $\dfrac{3}{5}$ $\dfrac{3}{5} = \dfrac{3 \times 20}{5 \times 20} = \dfrac{60}{100}$; $\dfrac{3}{5} = 60\%$

Example 2 $\dfrac{7}{200}$ $\dfrac{7}{200} = \dfrac{7 \times \frac{1}{2}}{200 \times \frac{1}{2}} = \dfrac{3\frac{1}{2}}{100}$; $\dfrac{7}{200} = 3\frac{1}{2}\%$

Example 3 $\dfrac{12}{30}$ $\dfrac{12}{30} = \dfrac{4}{10}$; $\dfrac{4 \times 10}{10 \times 10} = \dfrac{40}{100}$; $\dfrac{12}{30} = 40\%$

13. $\dfrac{1}{2}$

14. $\dfrac{3}{4}$

15. $\dfrac{7}{10}$

16. $\dfrac{21}{25}$

17. $\dfrac{19}{20}$

18. $\dfrac{63}{50}$

19. $\dfrac{22}{40}$

20. $\dfrac{24}{30}$

21. $\dfrac{18}{200}$

22. $\dfrac{20}{125}$

23. $\dfrac{30}{150}$

24. $\dfrac{24}{300}$

To find a per cent name for a decimal, we use the relation

$$n\% = n \times .01$$

For each decimal, find a per cent name.

Example 1 $.369 = 36.9 \times .01 = 36.9\%$

Example 2 $3 = 300 \times .01 = 300\%$

25. .26	**28.** 1.32	**31.** 2	**34.** .563
26. .70	**29.** 26.04	**32.** 98	**35.** .09
27. .04	**30.** 89.1	**33.** 430	**36.** .0058

RATIO

30 boys and 33 girls came to a party. The ratio of the number of boys to the number of girls was $\frac{30}{33}$. The ratio of the number of boys to the number of those present was $\frac{30}{63}$. Explain the last ratio.

1. In the example above, what was the ratio of the number of girls to the number of all present?

2. A mixture is in the ratio of 1 cup of orange juice to 2 cups of water.

    a. What is the ratio of the number of cups of orange juice to the number of cups of water?

    b. What is the ratio of the number of cups of orange juice to the number of cups of the entire mixture?

    c. What is the ratio of the number of cups of water to the number of cups of the entire mixture?

3. For every 5 pedestrians in downtown Chicago there are 2 drivers.

    a. What is the ratio of the number of drivers to the number of pedestrians?

    b. What is the ratio of the number of pedestrians to the number of drivers?

    c. What is the ratio of the number of pedestrians to the number of all people?

    d. What is the ratio of the number of drivers to the number of all people?

    e. What is the ratio of the number of all people to the number of drivers?

4. A mixture of 3 quarts contains $\frac{1}{2}$ quart of fertilizer. The remainder is black soil. What is the ratio of the number of quarts of fertilizer to the number of quarts of black soil? [Give the ratio as a fractional numeral containing two whole number names.]

5. The school chorus has 50 members. 22 members are girls. What is the ratio of the number of girls to the number of boys?

6. A large square is divided into 225 small squares. 5 small squares are shaded. What is the ratio of the number of shaded squares to the number of unshaded squares?

7. Jim "hits" the basket 8 times out of 11 throws. What is Jim's ratio of "hits" to "misses"?

8. Ann's collection of stamps consists of 85 U. S., 15 German, 3 French, and 12 Canadian stamps.

   a. What is the ratio of the number of German stamps to the total number of stamps?

   b. What is the ratio of the number of U. S. stamps to the number of Canadian stamps?

   c. What is the ratio of the number of French stamps to the total number of stamps?

PROPORTION

We know that the ratio of 1 to 2 is the same as the ratio of 2 to 4. To say this, we write

$$\frac{1}{2} = \frac{2}{4}$$

The statement above is called a *proportion*.

■ A statement of the form $\frac{a}{b} = \frac{c}{d}$ is called a *proportion*.

1. Write three more proportions showing other pairs of numbers which are in the ratio of 1 to 2.

2. Replace each □ to obtain a true statement.

   a. $\frac{1}{2} = \frac{2}{4}$; $1 \times 4 = 2 \times \square$ b. $\frac{2}{3} = \frac{6}{9}$; $\square \times 9 = 3 \times 6$

c. $\dfrac{3}{4} = \dfrac{15}{20}$; $3 \times \square = 4 \times 15$ **f.** $\dfrac{4}{9} = \dfrac{80}{180}$; $4 \times 180 = 9 \times \square$

d. $\dfrac{16}{28} = \dfrac{4}{7}$; $16 \times 7 = \square \times 4$ **g.** $\dfrac{16}{36} = \dfrac{4}{9}$; $\square \times 9 = 36 \times 4$

e. $\dfrac{50}{160} = \dfrac{5}{16}$; $50 \times \square = 160 \times 5$ **h.** $\dfrac{25}{1,000} = \dfrac{1}{40}$; $25 \times 40 = \square \times 1$

The examples in exercise **2** suggest the following pattern.

■ If $\dfrac{a}{b} = \dfrac{c}{d}$, then $a \times d = b \times c$.

Which are true and which are false?

Example 1 $\dfrac{8}{24} = \dfrac{20}{60}$ True, because $8 \times 60 = 24 \times 20$;

$8 \times 60 = 480$ and $24 \times 20 = 480$.

Example 2 $\dfrac{5}{12} = \dfrac{6}{13}$ False, because $5 \times 13 \neq 12 \times 6$;

$5 \times 13 = 65$ but $12 \times 6 = 72$.

3. $\dfrac{1}{2} = \dfrac{4}{8}$ **7.** $\dfrac{12}{13} = \dfrac{60}{64}$ **11.** $\dfrac{4}{16} = \dfrac{22}{88}$ **15.** $\dfrac{65}{67} = \dfrac{5}{7}$

4. $\dfrac{2}{6} = \dfrac{7}{21}$ **8.** $\dfrac{5}{7} = \dfrac{15}{17}$ **12.** $\dfrac{33}{44} = \dfrac{3}{4}$ **16.** $\dfrac{104}{105} = \dfrac{4}{5}$

5. $\dfrac{5}{2} = \dfrac{27}{9}$ **9.** $\dfrac{17}{2} = \dfrac{34}{4}$ **13.** $\dfrac{45}{2} = \dfrac{225}{10}$ **17.** $\dfrac{1.5}{2} = \dfrac{3}{4}$

6. $\dfrac{6}{32} = \dfrac{2}{11}$ **10.** $\dfrac{5}{33} = \dfrac{3}{20}$ **14.** $\dfrac{3}{60} = \dfrac{7}{120}$ **18.** $\dfrac{3.6}{3} = \dfrac{2.4}{2}$

19. Replace each $\square$ to obtain a true statement.

a. $\dfrac{1}{2} = \dfrac{2}{4}$; $\dfrac{2}{1} = \dfrac{\square}{2}$ **e.** $\dfrac{50}{160} = \dfrac{5}{16}$; $\dfrac{160}{50} = \dfrac{16}{\square}$

b. $\dfrac{2}{3} = \dfrac{6}{9}$; $\dfrac{3}{\square} = \dfrac{9}{6}$ **f.** $\dfrac{4}{9} = \dfrac{8}{18}$; $\dfrac{\square}{4} = \dfrac{18}{8}$

c. $\dfrac{3}{4} = \dfrac{15}{20}$; $\dfrac{\square}{3} = \dfrac{20}{15}$ **g.** $\dfrac{16}{36} = \dfrac{4}{9}$; $\dfrac{36}{\square} = \dfrac{9}{4}$

d. $\dfrac{4}{7} = \dfrac{16}{28}$; $\dfrac{7}{4} = \dfrac{28}{\square}$ **h.** $\dfrac{25}{1,000} = \dfrac{1}{40}$; $\dfrac{\square}{25} = \dfrac{40}{1}$

20. Using the pattern

$$\text{if } \frac{a}{b} = \frac{c}{d}, \text{ then } a \times d = b \times c$$

check whether each statement you obtained in exercise **19** is true. Part **a** is done for you below.

a. $\frac{2}{1} = \frac{4}{2}$ $2 \times 2 = 1 \times 4; 4 = 4;$ therefore $\frac{2}{1} = \frac{4}{2}$ is true.

The examples in exercise **19** suggest the following pattern.

■ If $\frac{a}{b} = \frac{c}{d}$, then $\frac{b}{a} = \frac{d}{c}$.

21. Supply the missing numbers to follow the pattern given in the example below.

Example $\frac{8}{16} = \frac{2}{4}; \quad 8 = \frac{2}{4} \times \square \qquad 8 = \frac{2}{4} \times 16$

a. $\frac{2}{3} = \frac{6}{9}; \quad 2 = \frac{6}{9} \times \square$

e. $\frac{4}{9} = \frac{80}{180}; \quad 4 = \frac{80}{180} \times \square$

b. $\frac{3}{4} = \frac{15}{20}; \quad 3 = \frac{\square}{20} \times 4$

f. $\frac{16}{36} = \frac{4}{9}; \quad 16 = \frac{4}{\square} \times 36$

c. $\frac{4}{7} = \frac{16}{28}; \quad \square = \frac{16}{28} \times 7$

g. $\frac{25}{1,000} = \frac{1}{40}; \quad 25 = \frac{\square}{40} \times 1,000$

d. $\frac{50}{160} = \frac{5}{16}; \quad 50 = \frac{\square}{16} \times 160$

h. $\frac{15}{225} = \frac{1}{15}; \quad 15 = \frac{1}{15} \times \square$

22. Check the truth of the statements you obtained in exercise **21** by doing the necessary computations.

Example $8 = \frac{2}{4} \times 16 \qquad \frac{2}{4} \times 16 = \frac{1}{2} \times 16 = 8$

The following pattern is suggested by the examples in exercise **21**.

■ If $\frac{a}{b} = \frac{c}{d}$, then $a = \frac{c}{d} \times b$.

23. In the pattern above, make the following replacements for *a*, *b*, *c*, and *d*, respectively.

Example   5, 6, 15, 18   If $\frac{5}{6} = \frac{15}{18}$, then $5 = \frac{15}{18} \times 6$.

a. 1, 2, 5, 10   **b.** 7, 3.5, 14, 7   **c.** 9, 3, 36, 12

PROPORTIONS AND PER CENTS

One way to find a per cent name for a number is to find its fractional name with the denominator 100. We can use proportions to do this.

Example 1   Find a per cent name for $\frac{3}{20}$.

We write the proportion

$$\frac{n}{100} = \frac{3}{20}$$

$$n = \frac{3}{20} \times 100 \leftarrow$$
$\begin{bmatrix} \text{Here we use} \\ \text{the pattern: If} \\ \frac{a}{b} = \frac{c}{d}, \text{ then } a = \frac{c}{d} \times b. \end{bmatrix}$

$$n = \frac{300}{20}$$

$$n = 15$$

Since $\frac{n}{100} = n\%$, we know that $\frac{3}{20} = \frac{15}{100} = 15\%$

Example 2   Find a per cent name for $\frac{4}{7}$.

$$\frac{n}{100} = \frac{4}{7}$$

$$n = \frac{4}{7} \times 100$$

$$n = \frac{400}{7}$$

$$n = 57\frac{1}{7}$$

$$\begin{array}{r} 57 \\ 7\overline{)400} \\ \underline{35} \\ 50 \\ \underline{49} \\ 1 \end{array}$$

Therefore, $\frac{4}{7} = \frac{57\frac{1}{7}}{100} = 57\frac{1}{7}\%$.

Find a per cent name for each fractional numeral.

1. $\frac{2}{5}$ **4.** $\frac{1}{3}$ **7.** $\frac{3}{8}$ **10.** $\frac{7}{8}$ **13.** $\frac{2}{18}$

2. $\frac{3}{4}$ **5.** $\frac{1}{6}$ **8.** $\frac{2}{3}$ **11.** $\frac{5}{12}$ **14.** $\frac{25}{40}$

3. $\frac{1}{8}$ **6.** $\frac{2}{9}$ **9.** $\frac{5}{6}$ **12.** $\frac{8}{15}$ **15.** $\frac{36}{57}$

16. Copy the chart below and fill in the missing numerals.

Fractional Numeral	Decimal Numeral	Per cent
$\frac{1}{2}$	.50	50%
$\frac{1}{3}$	.3$\overline{3}$	$33\frac{1}{3}$%
$\frac{2}{3}$	.6$\overline{6}$	
$\frac{1}{4}$		
	.75	75%
$\frac{1}{5}$	.20	
$\frac{2}{5}$		40%
		60%
	.80	
$\frac{1}{6}$	.16$\overline{6}$	
$\frac{5}{6}$		$83\frac{1}{3}$%
$\frac{1}{8}$	.125	
		$37\frac{1}{2}$%
	.625	
$\frac{7}{8}$		

FINDING n% OF A NUMBER

Example 1   What number is 30% of 60?

Let us estimate. The number should be somewhat less than $\frac{1}{3}$ of 60, or less than 20.

How to Solve   To solve, we let x represent the number and we write the proportion

$$\frac{x}{60} = \frac{30}{100}$$

$$x = \frac{30}{100} \times 60 \qquad \text{[What pattern did we use here?]}$$

$$x = \frac{3}{10} \times 60 \qquad \left[\frac{3}{10} \text{ is a simpler name for } \frac{30}{100}. \right]$$

$$x = \frac{180}{10}$$

$$x = 18$$

Thus, 18 is 30% of 60. (The answer agrees with our estimate.)

Note that to find 30% of 60, we multiplied $\frac{30}{100}$ by 60. Since $\frac{30}{100} = .30$, we could have multiplied .30 by 60. The answer would still be 18.

Example 2   What number is 5% of 350?

Estimate: 5% of 100 is 5, so 5% of 350 should be somewhat more than 3 times 5, or more than 15.

How to Solve   Let x represent the number.

$$\frac{x}{350} = \frac{5}{100}$$

$$x = \frac{5}{100} \times 350$$

$$x = \frac{1}{20} \times 350$$

$$x = \frac{350}{20}$$

$$x = 17\frac{1}{2}$$

Thus, $17\frac{1}{2}$ is 5% of 350. (The answer agrees with our estimate.)

Note that to find 5% of 350, we multiplied $\frac{5}{100}$ by 350. The answer would be the same if we had multiplied .05 by 350. Why?

We can generalize as follows:

■ To find n% of a number, we multiply $\frac{n}{100}$ by the number.

Example 3   What number is 32% of 35?

The answer should be close to 10. Why?

How to Solve   To find the number, we multiply $\frac{32}{100}$ by 35.

$$\frac{32}{100} \times 35 = .32 \times 35 = 11.20$$

Therefore, 11.2 is 32% of 35.

Solve as in Example 3 above. Be sure to estimate first.

1. What number is 50% of 37?
2. What number is 37% of 120?
3. What number is 1% of 15?
4. What number is 3% of 1,000?
5. What number is 10% of 1?
6. What number is 90% of 6?

Now we can solve certain problems involving per cent.

Example 4   There are 150 students in an auditorium. 40% of them are girls. How many girls are there in the auditorium?

Estimate: We know 40% is somewhat less than $\frac{1}{2}$. Therefore, the answer should be less than 75 girls.

How to Solve   To find 40% of 150, we multiply $\frac{40}{100}$ by 150. This is the same as multiplying .40 by 150.

$$.40 \times 150 = 60.00$$

Thus, there are 60 girls in the auditorium. (The answer agrees with our estimate.)

Solve each problem. Be sure to estimate first.

7. Dan receives a weekly allowance of $5.50. He spends 30% of it on lunches. How much does he spend on lunches?
8. A football team won 60% of the total of 15 games played. How many games did they win?

9. Out of the 180 school days last year Nancy was absent from school 5% of the days. How many days was she absent?

10. Jim bought a bicycle for $62.00. He sold it, after some use, at a loss of 15%. How much money did he lose?

11. The area of a square is 450 sq. in. The area of a rectangle is 120% of the area of the square. What is the area of the rectangle?

12. The speed of a jet is 180% of the speed of a conventional plane. If the conventional plane flies at 350 mph, how fast does the jet fly?

13. The traffic during the Christmas holidays is 160% of the regular traffic. If there are 24 million cars on the road during the regular traffic, how many cars are there on the road during the holidays?

14. A certain house was appraised at $26,500. An addition to the house and certain innovations raised its value by 30%. How much were the addition and innovations worth?

15. How many dollars is a raise of 15% on an allowance of $12.50?

PUTTING PROPORTION TO USE

Example 1   16 is 12% of what number?

Estimate: 16 is 10% of 160. Since 10% is less than 12%, the number is somewhat less than 160.

How to Solve   To solve, we let x represent the number and we write this proportion:

$$\frac{16}{x} = \frac{12}{100}$$

$$\frac{x}{16} = \frac{100}{12} \quad \leftarrow \quad \left[\begin{array}{l} \text{Here we use the} \\ \text{pattern: If } \dfrac{a}{b} = \dfrac{c}{d}, \\ \text{then } \dfrac{b}{a} = \dfrac{d}{c}. \end{array} \right.$$

$$x = \frac{100}{12} \times 16$$

$$x = \frac{25}{3} \times 16$$

$$x = \frac{400}{3}$$

$$x = 133\frac{1}{3}$$

Therefore, 16 is 12% of $133\frac{1}{3}$. (Compare with estimate.)

Answer the following questions. Refer to Example 1.

1. 23 is 10% of what number?

5. 10 is 80% of what number?

2. 12 is 5% of what number?

6. 5 is 1% of what number?

3. 1 is 3% of what number?

7. 50 is 125% of what number?

4. $\frac{1}{2}$ is 4% of what number?

8. 2 is $\frac{1}{2}$% of what number?

Example 2   15 is what per cent of 200?

Estimate: 15 is 10% of 150; 150 is less than 200, so the answer should be somewhat less than 10%.

How to Solve   To solve, we let x represent the number and we write this proportion: $\dfrac{x}{100} = \dfrac{15}{200}$.

$$x = \frac{15}{200} \times 100 = \frac{1,500}{200} = 7\frac{1}{2}$$

Therefore, 15 is $7\frac{1}{2}$% of 200. (Compare with estimate.)

Answer the following questions. Refer to Example 2.

9. 1 is what per cent of 25?

13. 50 is what per cent of 25?

10. 2 is what per cent of 200?

14. 50 is what per cent of 50?

11. 12 is what per cent of 60?

15. $\frac{1}{4}$ is what per cent of 5?

12. $\frac{1}{5}$ is what per cent of 10?

16. $\frac{1}{2}$ is what per cent of 32?

Give answers to the following questions without using pencil and paper.

17. If a person saves $10 out of $100, what per cent is saved?

18. If a person earns $30 and saves $10, what per cent is saved?

19. If a person earns $10 and saves $10, what per cent is saved?

20. If a person is 20 years old now, what per cent older will he be 20 years from now?

21. If a person is 10 years old now, what per cent older will he be 20 years from now?

PUTTING PER CENT TO WORK

Per cent is a very useful concept. It has many applications in business, industry, and government, as well as in an individual's daily life. The problems below illustrate some of its uses.

Example 1 15% of the students were absent from school on Monday. 527 students were absent. How many students are there in the school?

How to We reason as follows: If 15% of the students were absent,
Solve then 85% were present.

Let x represent the number of all students in the school, that is, 100% of the students. The ratio of the number of students present (527) to the total number of students (x) is the same as the ratio of 85 (85% of the students are present) to 100 (100% of the number of students is the total number of students).

$$\frac{527}{x} = \frac{85}{100}$$

$$\frac{x}{527} = \frac{100}{85}$$

$$x = \frac{100}{85} \times 527$$

$$x = \frac{20}{17} \times 527$$

$$x = \frac{10,540}{17}$$

$$x = 620$$

Therefore, there are 620 students in the school.

Example 2 After an excise tax of 10% is added to the price, a tube of shampoo costs 88 cents. What is the price of the tube before the tax is added?

How to If the price of the tube before the tax is added corresponds
Solve to 100%, then the price after 10% tax is added corresponds to 110%.

Let x represent the price before the tax is added. Then the ratio $\dfrac{88}{x}$ is the ratio of the price after tax to the price before tax. We write the proportion shown at the top of the next page.

$$\frac{88}{x} = \frac{110}{100}$$

$$\frac{x}{88} = \frac{100}{110}$$

$$x = \frac{100}{110} \times 88$$

$$x = \frac{10}{11} \times 88$$

$$x = \frac{880}{11}$$

$$x = 80$$

Therefore, the price is 80 cents before the tax is added.

Solve the following problems.

1. There were 140 questions on an examination. Bill answered 120 questions correctly. What per cent of the questions did Bill miss?

2. Susan answered 81 questions on an examination correctly and received the grade of 90%. How many questions did she miss?

3. John received a grade of 68% on an examination which contained 150 questions. How many questions did he answer correctly?

4. While on vacation, a family spent 28% of its budget of $450 for food. The rest was spent on other items. How much money was spent on other items?

5. Out of the total U.S. investment abroad of $9.7 billion, 17% is invested in chemicals. How much money is invested in chemicals?

6. Since a new junior high school was built last year, the student body of Oiltown Junior High School has decreased 40%. Oiltown Junior High now has 2,340 students. How many students were enrolled at Oiltown Junior High before the new school was built?

7. Every month, 4% of Miss Jones' salary is deducted for teachers' retirement and 3% for investment in the teachers' credit union. How much is deducted for the retirement fund and how much for the credit union, if her monthly salary is $580?

8. An assembly line produces 600 units of electronic equipment per day. The manager demands an increase of 17%. How many units does he expect to be produced?

9. 45% of 600 students in a school are girls. How many of the 600 students are boys?

10. A path 150 feet long is 80% as long as another path. How long is the other path?

11. The price of a candy bar dropped 20%. If the original price was 5¢, what is the new price?

12. An article sold during January for $5.20. The price during February dropped 10%. During March the price increased 10% of the February price. What did the article sell for during March?

13. Mr. Needy withdrew 5% from his $200 account. Then he withdrew 10% of the remainder. How much money was left in the account after the two withdrawals?

14. A driver reaches the maximum speed of 70.8 mph, which is 18% over the legal maximum speed limit. What is the legal maximum speed limit?

DISCOUNT

Discount is usually given as a per cent of the marked price. Study the following examples.

Example 1   For a clearance sale, a store offered a 20% discount on all clothing. If a sweater was originally priced at $12.00, how much less did it cost when on sale?

How to   To find the amount of the discount, we find 20% of $12.00.
Solve   Recall that to do this, we multiply $\frac{20}{100} \times 12$.

$$\frac{20}{100} \times 12 = .20 \times 12 = 2.40$$

Thus, when on sale, the sweater cost $2.40 less.

Solve each problem.

1. How much is a discount of 30% on an item regularly costing $10?

2. An item which regularly sells for $25 is on sale at a discount of 40%. How much less does it cost on sale?

3. How much is a discount of 5% on an item regularly costing $20.00?

4. How much is a discount of 5% on an item regularly costing $40.00?

5. Is it true that, given a certain fixed per cent discount, the higher the price of an item, the more dollars the discount amounts to?

6. Item A is twice as expensive as item B. The same per cent discount is allowed on each item. Is the discount in dollars on item A twice the discount on item B? Defend your answer by an example.

Example 2   Every student is entitled to a discount of 15% on every item in a store. If the regular price of shirts is $3.98, what is the price for students?

How to Solve   A 15% discount means that students pay 85% of the regular price. To find 85% of $3.98, we multiply $\frac{85}{100}$ by 3.98. This is the same as multiplying .85 by 3.98.

$$3.98 \times .85 = 3.3830$$

Thus, the price for students is $3.38.

Solve each problem.

7. The regular price of an article is $3.70. What is the price of this article after a 10% discount?

8. The list price of a fountain pen is $2.95. What is the selling price at the discount of 20%?

9. Every item in an electrical appliance store was marked down 35%. Compute the selling prices of the following items whose marked prices are as follows:

a. Iron: $24.50

b. Coffee maker: $37.98

c. Radio: $75.90

Example 3   Ted bought a used bicycle for $72. He obtained a discount of 20% on the price of the bicycle when it was new. What was the price of the bicycle when new?

How to Solve   Since Ted obtained a discount of 20%, the bicycle cost him 80% of the price of a new bicycle. Let x be the price of the new bicycle. We write the proportion shown on the next page.

$$\frac{72}{x} = \frac{80}{100}$$

$$\frac{x}{72} = \frac{100}{80}$$

$$x = \frac{100}{80} \times 72$$

$$x = \frac{5}{4} \times 72$$

$$x = 90$$

Therefore, the price of the bicycle when new was $90.

Solve each problem.

10. Jim bought a used book for $1.75. He obtained a discount of 40% on the price of the new book. What was the price of the new book?

11. In a sporting goods store, the following selling prices were posted after a discount of 30% was applied to the list prices. Compute the list prices.

a. Ping-pong set: $6.30   **c.** Football: $3.90

b. Tennis racket: $12.50

COMMISSION

Many salesmen receive a *commission*, which is usually given as a per cent of their sales. If a salesman works on the basis of a commission of 5%, he receives $5 for every $100 worth of goods he sells. The per cent commission varies from company to company and from product to product. It may be, for example, as little as 1% or as much as 40%.

■   The per cent commission received is sometimes called the *rate of commission*.

Example   A salesman sold $150,330 worth of electrical equipment in one year. His rate of commission is 8%. How much commission did he earn?

How to   The salesman's commission is 8% of $150,330. To find
Solve   this amount, we multiply $\frac{8}{100}$ by 150,330. Or we can multiply .08 by 150,330.

$$150,330 \times .08 = 12,026.40$$

Therefore, the salesman's commission is $12,026.40.

Solve each problem.

1. Mr. Commission gets 40% of his sales as his pay. Last week his sales amounted to $655. What was his commission?

2. A salesman whose rate of commission is $2\frac{1}{2}\%$ sells $120,000 worth of merchandise. What is his commission?

3. Mr. Travel sells two cars. Each car is priced at $5,400. If his rate of commission is 20%, how much commission does he receive?

4. Mr. Gethim receives commissions at the rate of 10% for up to $10,000 of sales, and 25% for sales in excess of $10,000. What is his commission on $25,000 of sales?

5. Salesman *A* works at a certain rate of commission. *B*'s rate of commission is twice *A*'s rate. If *A* and *B* sell the same dollar worth of goods, how will their commissions compare? Defend your answer with an example.

6. In exercise 5, how should the sales of *A* and *B* compare in order for them to receive the same commission? Defend your answer with an example.

BATTING AVERAGES

If a batter makes 1 hit out of 2 times at bat, his *batting average* is $\frac{1}{2}$. It is reported in the form of a decimal to three decimal places, or .500.

1. If a batter makes 1 hit out of 4 times at bat, what is his batting average? (Give it as a decimal to three decimal places.)

2. If a batter makes 3 hits out of 8 times at bat, what is his batting average? (Give it as a decimal to three decimal places.)

■ To compute a batting average, divide the number of hits by the number of times at bat. Then round off the result to 3 decimal places.

Recall that to give the result to 3 decimal places, we carry out the division to 3 decimal places. If the remainder is one-half of the divisor, or more, we add 1 to the third decimal place. If the remainder is less than one-half of the divisor, we leave the third decimal place unaltered.

Example   If a batter gets 27 hits out of 89 times at bat, what is his batting average?

How to   We divide 27 by 89, and round to 3 decimal places.
Solve

$$
\begin{array}{r}
.303 \\
89\overline{)27.000} \\
26\ 7 \\
\hline
30 \\
00 \\
\hline
300 \\
267 \\
\hline
33
\end{array}
$$

Since the remainder (33) is less than half of the divisor (89), we leave the third decimal place unaltered.

Therefore, his batting average is .303.

3. Compute batting averages to 3 decimal places. The first number is the number of hits, and the second is the number of times at bat.

   a. 12; 82   **c.** 21; 96   **e.** 56; 192

   b. 33; 95   **d.** 36; 123   **f.** 43; 203

What does a batting average of .303 mean? It means that *on the average,* a batter gets 303 hits out of 1,000 times at bat. It does not mean that he has necessarily been to bat 1,000 times.

4. Tell the meaning of each of the following batting averages.

   a. .346   **b.** .401   **c.** .200   **d.** .000

5. What does the batting average of 1.000 mean?

6. What does the batting average of .001 mean?

7. Is it possible to have a batting average which is greater than 1? Why or why not?

8. Is it possible to have a batting average which is less than .001? Why or why not?

9. Is it possible to have a batting average of 0? Why or why not?

10. If a batter has a batting average of .306, what is the ratio of the number of hits to the number of "misses" for this batter?

PER CENT CHANGE

Per cent is frequently used to describe the increase or the decrease from one number to another.

Example 1   The population of Bulgetown increased from 12,000 to 16,000. What was the per cent increase?

How to $16,000 - 12,000 = 4,000$, the amount of increase.
Solve   Let n be the per cent increase.

$$\frac{n}{100} = \frac{4,000}{12,000}$$

$$\frac{n}{100} = \frac{1}{3}$$

$$n = \frac{1}{3} \times 100$$

$$n = 33\frac{1}{3}$$

Therefore, the per cent increase was $33\frac{1}{3}\%$.

Example 2   The price of an article dropped from $4.50 to $3.60. What was the per cent decrease?

How to $4.50 - 3.60 = .90$, the amount of decrease.
Solve   Let n be the per cent decrease.

$$\frac{n}{100} = \frac{.90}{4.50}$$

$$\frac{n}{100} = \frac{1}{5}$$

$$n = \frac{1}{5} \times 100$$

$$n = 20$$

Therefore, the per cent decrease was 20%.

In general, if n is the per cent increase (or decrease), we write the proportion

$$\frac{n}{100} = \frac{\text{amount of increase (or decrease)}}{\text{original amount}}$$

Solve each problem.

1. The population of Welcome High School at the beginning of the year was 2,400. It increased to 2,600 at the end of the year. What was the per cent increase?

2. A bicycle factory turned out 15,200 bicycles in one week. The following week 14,600 bicycles were manufactured. What was the per cent decrease in the number of bicycles from one week to the next?

3. The Martins' January electricity bill was $24. Their February bill is $21.50. What is the per cent decrease from January to February?

4. If the average weekly earnings of a worker increased from $80 to $95, what is the per cent increase?

5. The following are the numbers of students aged 5 to 34 years enrolled in schools and colleges in various years.

1947	28.6 million
1950	30.3 million
1955	37.4 million
1960	46.3 million
1968	56.4 million

Compute per cent change in enrollment from

a. 1947 to 1950   d. 1950 to 1960

b. 1950 to 1955   e. 1960 to 1968

c. 1955 to 1960

6. Below are given daily averages in billions of gallons of total water used in the United States. Figures for the future are projected.*

Year	Daily Average in Billions of Gallons
1910	65
1920	90
1930	110
1940	135
1950	200
1960	320
1970	410
1980	500

Compute the per cent change of water consumption from

a. 1910 to 1920   d. 1940 to 1950   g. 1970 to 1980

b. 1920 to 1930   e. 1950 to 1960   h. 1910 to 1950

c. 1930 to 1940   f. 1960 to 1970   i. 1910 to 1980

* Source: Road Maps of Industry, No. 1304, Dec. 23, 1960.

KEEPING ARITHMETICALLY FIT

For exercises **1–36**, numerals in parentheses refer to pages where you can find similar exercises.

Add. (436–437)

1. 3.706	**2.** 37.09	**3.** 109.5	**4.** 1.26	**5.** 26.33
5.895	24.12	36.6	9.68	9.48
3.226	37.08	23.9	8.73	39.12

Subtract. (438–439)

6. 8.368	**7.** 23.68	**8.** 8.006	**9.** 1.206	**10.** 23.08
2.179	17.89	5.998	.898	9.99

Multiply. (439–440)　　　　　(432–434)

11. 2.368　　**14.** 10.65　　**17.** $\dfrac{3}{4} \times \dfrac{4}{5}$　　**20.** $2\dfrac{3}{5} \times 7\dfrac{1}{2}$
　　.12　　　　　34.5

12. 36.12　　**15.** 7.486　　**18.** $\dfrac{7}{11} \times \dfrac{8}{13}$　　**21.** $6\dfrac{5}{6} \times 7\dfrac{6}{7}$
　　7.55　　　　　.38

13. 365.5　　**16.** .5692　　**19.** $\dfrac{10}{7} \times \dfrac{8}{15}$　　**22.** $12\dfrac{2}{5} \times 7\dfrac{1}{6}$
　　35.6　　　　　52.8

Divide. (440–442)　　　　　(434–436)

23. $.2\overline{)1.6}$　　**27.** $.02\overline{)13.26}$　　**31.** $\dfrac{7}{11} \div \dfrac{4}{11}$　　**34.** $3\dfrac{1}{2} \div 7$

24. $.3\overline{)45.3}$　　**28.** $1.3\overline{)278.2}$　　**32.** $\dfrac{3}{10} \div \dfrac{6}{10}$　　**35.** $10\dfrac{1}{2} \div 31\dfrac{1}{2}$

25. $.03\overline{)100.2}$　　**29.** $.32\overline{)1,024.64}$　　**33.** $\dfrac{4}{13} \div \dfrac{2}{13}$　　**36.** $4\dfrac{1}{4} \div 17$

26. $.9\overline{)36.9}$　　**30.** $.11\overline{).3333}$

Give the simplest fractional name for each of the following.

37. $\dfrac{3}{33}$　　**40.** $\dfrac{400}{825}$　　**43.** .008　　**46.** .24

38. $\dfrac{4}{64}$　　**41.** $\dfrac{325}{725}$　　**44.** .75　　**47.** .125

39. $\dfrac{150}{375}$　　**42.** .12　　**45.** .009　　**48.** .875

VOCABULARY REVIEW

batting average (180)
commission (179)
discount (177)
per cent (161)

proportion (166)
rate of commission (179)
ratio (165)

A CHALLENGE TO YOU

1. Gregg has a certain number of boxes and marbles. If he drops 6 marbles into each box, he will lack 16 marbles. Whereas, if he drops 3 marbles into each box, he will have a surplus of 8 marbles. How many boxes and how many marbles does Gregg have?

2. The sum of two numbers is 20. If one number is doubled and the other is multiplied by 4, the sum of the two new numbers is 66. What are the two numbers?

3. Class A has 5 students more than class B. If 4 students from class A are transferred to class B, how many more students will be in class B than in class A?

4. A man is $\frac{3}{8}$ of the way across a railroad bridge when he suddenly hears a train which is traveling at 60 mph. He can run in either direction in an effort to get off the bridge and just make it. How fast does he have to run?

CHAPTER TEST

1. Give a decimal name for each per cent.

    a. 17%   **b.** 3%   **c.** 126%   **d.** $\frac{1}{4}$%

2. Give the simplest fractional name for each per cent.

    a. 36%   **b.** 6%   **c.** $\frac{1}{3}$%   **d.** $2\frac{1}{8}$%

3. Give a per cent name for each decimal numeral.

    a. .306   **b.** 9.85   **c.** .039   **d.** 50.6

4. For each per cent, give a fractional numeral with denominator 100.

    a. $\frac{3}{4}$ **b.** $\frac{7}{20}$ **c.** $\frac{18}{30}$ **d.** $\frac{32}{200}$

5. Give a per cent name for each fractional numeral.

a. $\dfrac{13}{20}$ c. $\dfrac{21}{30}$ e. $\dfrac{8}{5}$ g. $\dfrac{1}{8}$

b. $\dfrac{3}{25}$ d. $\dfrac{5}{2}$ f. $\dfrac{2}{3}$ h. $\dfrac{5}{6}$

6. Tell which of the following name the ratio of 4 to 5.

a. $\dfrac{8}{10}$ b. $\dfrac{30}{24}$ c. $\dfrac{36}{44}$ d. $\dfrac{2}{2\frac{1}{2}}$ e. $\dfrac{17}{21\frac{1}{4}}$

7. Replace each □ to obtain a true statement.

a. $\dfrac{1}{2} = \dfrac{\square}{50}$ d. $\dfrac{\square}{120} = \dfrac{4}{5}$ g. $\dfrac{3}{15} = \dfrac{\square}{50}$

b. $\dfrac{2}{3} = \dfrac{\square}{15}$ e. $\dfrac{3}{\square} = \dfrac{63}{21}$ h. $\dfrac{7}{\square} = \dfrac{15}{30}$

c. $\dfrac{15}{21} = \dfrac{5}{\square}$ f. $\dfrac{4}{12} = \dfrac{\square}{54}$ i. $\dfrac{\square}{3} = \dfrac{1}{2}$

8. What number is 15% of 60?

9. What number is 120% of 55?

10. 20 is 40% of what number?

11. 45 is 150% of what number?

12. 8 is what per cent of 25?

13. 13 is what per cent of 39?

14. What is the meaning of .125 batting average?

15. What would be the meaning of a 100% discount? Why would such a discount be unreasonable?

16. What would be the meaning of a 100% commission? Why would such a commission be unreasonable?

17. Bob bought a book for $4.80. This was 15% of his monthly allowance. What is Bob's monthly allowance?

18. Mr. Freewheel spends $10.40 on gas weekly. If his weekly wages are $208, what per cent of the wages does he spend on gas?

19. The length of a rectangle is 16 ft. The width is 35% shorter than the length. What is the width?

20. Jane spent $12 on clothing. This was 150% of her weekly allowance. What is her allowance?

21. In a class of 120 students enrolled in mathematics, 10% received the grade of A, 45% the grade of B, and the remainder the grade of C. How many students received the grade of C?

22. What is the per cent increase from

    a. 20 to 21?   **c.** 100 to 101?

    b. 50 to 51?   **d.** 1,000 to 1,001?

23. What is the per cent decrease from

    a. 20 to 19?   **c.** 100 to 99?

    b. 50 to 49?   **d.** 1,000 to 999?

24. Which per cent increase is greater?

    a. from 20 to 30 or from 30 to 40?

    b. from 100 to 200 or from 200 to 300?

25. Which per cent decrease is greater?

    a. from 50 to 40 or from 40 to 30?

    b. from 200 to 150 or from 150 to 100?

CHAPTER SEVEN

Directed Numbers— Addition and Subtraction

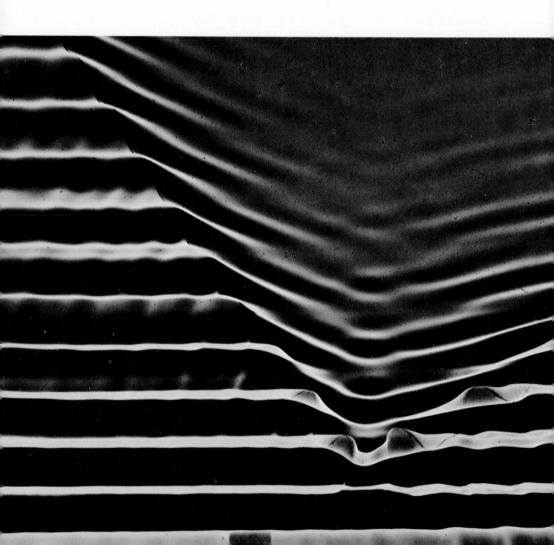

NUMBER LINE

We have learned that there is a one-to-one correspondence between the real numbers of arithmetic and the points on a number ray. We have observed that each real number of arithmetic, either rational or irrational, has one point on the number ray which corresponds to it. The picture below shows a ray. Some points and their numbers are marked in this picture.

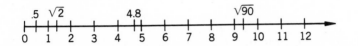

1. Make a picture like the one above on your paper, marking first only the points corresponding to the whole numbers. Then mark the points corresponding to the following numbers. Write the appropriate number name next to each point.

   a. 7.5

   b. $\sqrt{43}$

   c. $\sqrt[3]{27}$

   d. 11.7

   e. $\sqrt{15}$

   f. $\sqrt{101}$

   g. $3\frac{1}{3}$

   h. $\frac{5}{6}$

Notice that a ray has a beginning point, but it does not have an endpoint. The arrow on the right in the picture above suggests that the ray goes on and on. We know, however, that a complete line has neither a beginning nor an endpoint. This picture shows that a line continues on and on in both directions.

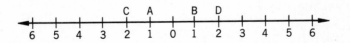

To obtain a *complete number line*, we need to mark points to the left of the point associated with the number 0 as well. We can do this in the following way.

2. From the picture, tell what number corresponds to point *B*.

3. What number corresponds to point *A*?

4. What number corresponds to point *D*?

5. What number corresponds to point *C*?

6. How many points correspond to the number 1?

7. How many points correspond to the number 2?

To have a one-to-one correspondence, there must be exactly one point for each number and exactly one number for each point. If there are two points for one number, then we do *not* have a one-to-one correspondence.

POSITIVE AND NEGATIVE NUMBERS

Perhaps you have thought of several ways of assigning numbers to the points to the left of the point which corresponds to the number 0. The accepted way of doing this is shown in the picture below. $^-1$ is read *negative one*; $^-2$, negative two, and so on.

The arrows on the picture of the line above indicate that the line does not end. It continues on and on in both directions.

To clearly differentiate between the numbers assigned to the points on the left of A and those on the right of A, we have marked the points on the right as $^+1$ (Read: *positive one*), $^+2$ (positive two), and so on.

1. What number corresponds to each of the following points on the number line above?

Examples 1   H $^+5$ (positive five)

          2   M $^-6$ (negative six)

a. *F*   **b.** *B*   **c.** *A*   **d.** *I*   **e.** *J*   **f.** *E*   **g.** *D*

2. What point corresponds to each of the following numbers on the number line above?

Examples 1 $^+3$ point *C*

          2 $^-3$ point *J*

a. $^-1$ **b.** $^+4$ **c.** $^-2$ **d.** $^+6$ **e.** $^-5$ **f.** 0   **g.** $^-4$

3. The point which corresponds to the number 0 is called the *origin*. How would you justify this name? [What does "origin" mean?]

4. What letter is assigned to the origin on the number line above?

5. a. What number corresponds to point C?

   b. What number corresponds to point J?

   c. What is the distance from C to the origin? Give the distance as the number of units marked on the picture.

6. a. What number corresponds to point K? to point G?

   b. What is the distance from K to the origin? from G to the origin?

7. a. What number corresponds to point H? to point E?

   b. What is the distance from H to the origin? from E to the origin?

INTEGERS

When we assigned numbers to points on a number line, we used only whole numbers. Some were positive numbers, others were negative numbers.

■ The set consisting of all positive whole numbers, negative whole numbers, and the number 0 is called the *set of integers*.

1. Tell which of the following are integers.

   a. $^-7$ b. $^+17{,}305$ c. $\dfrac{^+3}{4}$ d. 0 e. $^-1.6$ f. $^-1{,}065$

Each integer has an *opposite* integer. The two examples in exercise **2** give you a clue as to how to find the opposite of an integer.

2. Give the opposite of each of the following integers.

   Examples 1 $^+2$ The opposite of $^+2$ is $^-2$.

   2 $^-5$ The opposite of $^-5$ is $^+5$.

   a. $^-5$ b. $^+2$ c. $^-70$ d. $^+70$ e. $^-980$ f. $^+980$

3. Is $^-876{,}532{,}967$ the opposite of $^+876{,}532{,}967$?

4. Complete each statement.

   a. The opposite of a positive integer is a _____ integer.

   b. The opposite of a negative integer is a _____ integer.

   The opposite of 0 is 0.

   0 is the only integer which is its own opposite.

5. Make a picture of a number line. Label points as in the picture on page 190. Answer the following questions.

   a. Are $^+4$ and $^-4$ opposites of each other? Are the distances from I to A and from B to A the same?

   b. Are $^+6$ and $^-6$ opposites of each other? Are the distances from F to A and from M to A the same?

   c. Are $^+3$ and $^-4$ opposites of each other? Are the distances from C to A and from B to A the same?

6. What conclusion can you draw about the distances from the origin of points corresponding to opposites?

7. If two numbers are not opposites of each other, then what is true of the distances from the origin of the points corresponding to these two numbers?

DIRECTED REAL NUMBERS

Positive and negative numbers are called *directed* numbers. These numbers help us to answer not only the question "how many?", but also "in what direction?"

We consider the direction to the right to be positive, and the direction to the left to be negative.

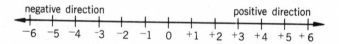

There are many more points between the points which are marked on the number line. For example, there is a point half-way between $^+1$ and $^+2$.

What number would be assigned to each of the following points.

1. $\frac{1}{3}$ of the way from 0 toward $^+1$

2. $\frac{1}{3}$ of the way from 0 toward $^+2$

3. $\frac{1}{4}$ of the way from 0 toward $^-1$

4. $\frac{1}{4}$ of the way from 0 toward $^-2$

5. $\frac{1}{5}$ of the way from $^+3$ toward $^+4$

6. $\frac{2}{3}$ of the way from $^-1$ toward $^-4$

7. $\frac{1}{5}$ of the way from $^-5$ toward $^-3$

8. $\frac{1}{8}$ of the way from $^-2$ toward 0

9. $\frac{2}{5}$ of the way from $^+4$ toward $^+1$

Below is an enlarged picture of the portion of a number line between $^-1$ and $^+1$.

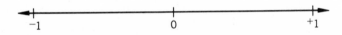

10. Copy this picture on your paper. Mark as accurately as you can the points corresponding to the following:

a. $^+.9$	**c.** $^-.9$	**e.** $\frac{^-1}{5}$
b. $\frac{^-1}{3}$	**d.** $^+.5$	**f.** $^+.1$

11. Make an enlarged picture of a number line between $^-2$ and $^+2$. Mark on it the points corresponding to the following:

a. $^-1.5$	**d.** $^+1.1$	**g.** $^+\sqrt{2}$	**j.** $\frac{^-3}{7}$
b. $^+1.5$	**e.** $\frac{^-5}{4}$	**h.** $^-\sqrt{2}$	**k.** $^+\sqrt{3}$
c. $^-1.1$	**f.** $\frac{^+5}{4}$	**i.** $\frac{^+3}{7}$	**l.** $^-\sqrt{3}$

Each of the following numbers is a *directed real number.*

$$\frac{^-3}{7} \quad ^-2 \quad ^+1.5 \quad ^-\sqrt{2} \quad ^+\sqrt{2} \quad \frac{^+3}{7} \quad ^+360 \quad ^+1,176.5$$

12. Give examples of four other directed real numbers.

USES OF DIRECTED NUMBERS

On the right is a picture of a thermometer. Directed numbers are used in telling the temperature. Thus, instead of saying "twenty below zero," we may say "negative twenty" (⁻20). Or, instead of saying "thirty above zero," we may say "positive thirty" (⁺30).

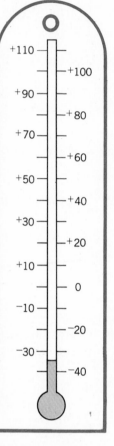

1. Give the directed number describing each of the following temperatures.

   a. fifteen below zero

   b. seventy-five above zero

   c. forty below zero

   d. twenty-one above zero

   e. six and a half above zero

Directed numbers can be used to describe the status of your basketball team as compared with the opponent. A positive number would show the number of points by which your team is *ahead* of the opponent, and a negative number the number of points by which your team is *behind* the opponent.

2. Use a directed number to show each of the following standings of your basketball team as compared with the opponent.

   a. ahead four points   d. behind two points

   b. ahead one point   e. behind five points

   c. tie   f. ahead seven points

In football, directed numbers can be used to describe *gain* or *loss* in yardage. A positive number would be a logical choice for the description of gain, and a negative number for the description of loss.

3. Use a directed number to describe each of the following outcomes in football.

   a. gain of five yards   c. loss of thirty-three yards

   b. gain of twenty-five and a   d. neither loss nor gain
      half yards

MOVES ON THE NUMBER LINE

Directed numbers can be used to describe "moves" along the number line. To make the illustrations simple, we shall use first only whole directed numbers and zero, that is, integers.

R P M E B J D G A K L C I H F Q N
−8 −7 −6 −5 −4 −3 −2 −1 0 +1 +2 +3 +4 +5 +6 +7 +8

Let us agree that for every move, the beginning point is the origin. On the picture above, trace these moves mentally.

Examples 1   from *A* to *L* $^{+}2$

        2   from *A* to *B* $^{-}4$

        3   from *A* to *A* (standstill)   0

1. For each description of a move, give the directed number.

     a. from *A* to *D*   **c.** from *A* to *C*   **e.** from *A* to *I*

     b. from *A* to *Q*   **d.** from *A* to *E*   **f.** from *A* to *R*

We do not need to restrict the beginning of our moves to the origin. We can start our moves anywhere and still use directed numbers to describe these moves. Trace these moves mentally.

Examples 4   from *C* to *H* $^{+}2$

        5   from *N* to *L* $^{-}6$

2. For each description of a move, give the directed number.

     a. from *P* to *B*   **c.** from *N* to *A*   **e.** from *N* to *R*

     b. from *R* to *E*   **d.** from *Q* to *G*   **f.** from *Q* to *Q*

Four different moves are shown on the picture below.

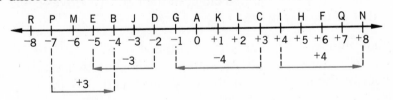

3. **a.** What number describes the longest positive move marked on the picture?

     b. What number describes the shortest positive move?

     c. What number describes the longest negative move?

     d. What number describes the shortest negative move?

4. On a number line showing points from $^-8$ to $^+8$, make pictures of four different moves each described by $^+2$.

5. On a similar number line, make pictures of four different moves each described by $^-3$.

6. What is the meaning of a move described by the number 0?

7. Think of the number line as extending without an end in both directions: positive and negative. How many different moves could you find described by $^-5$? by $^+4$? by 0?

The picture below shows two moves, one followed by another. Trace these two moves.

Move from A to L: $^+2$
Move from L to H: $^+3$

Now consider the following:

Move from A to H: $^+5$

Observe that two moves, from A to L and from L to H, are equivalent to one move from A to H. For this reason, we say that

$$^+2 + {}^+3 = {}^+5$$

8. What number describes the move from A to K? from K to H? from A to H? Make an addition statement similar to that above showing that the combined effect of the first two moves is the same as that of the last move.

9. What number describes a move from A to I? from I to F? from A to F? Make an addition statement showing that the combined effect of the first two moves is the same as that of the last move.

10. Describe moves which illustrate each of the following. Use the number line at the top of page 195.

   a. $^+1 + {}^+1 = {}^+2$ d. $^-1 + {}^-2 = {}^-3$

   b. $^+2 + {}^+4 = {}^+6$ e. $^-2 + {}^-5 = {}^-7$

   c. $^+3 + {}^+1 = {}^+4$ f. $^-3 + {}^-1 = {}^-4$

ADDING DIRECTED NUMBERS

The idea of moves on a number line can be used to good advantage in learning to add directed numbers.

Example 1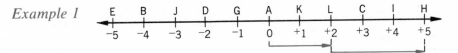

A move from *A* to *L*: $^+2$
Followed by a move from *L* to *H*: $^+3$
Result is the same as a move from *A* to *H*: $^+5$
Therefore, $^+2 + {}^+3 = {}^+5$.

Example 2

A move from *A* to *D*: $^-2$
Followed by a move from *D* to *J*: $^-1$
Result is the same as a move from *A* to *J*: $^-3$
Therefore, $^-2 + {}^-1 = {}^-3$.

For each picture, describe each pair of moves as in Examples 1 and 2. Then write the resulting addition statement.

1.

2.

3.

4.

5.

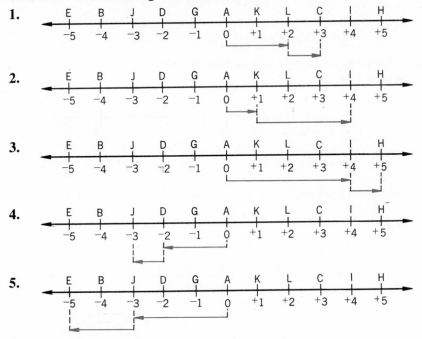

6.

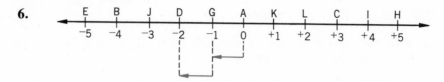

Look at your answers for exercises **1–6**. Complete the following:

7. The sum of two positive numbers is a _____ number.

8. The sum of two negative numbers is a _____ number.

Answer the following without using a number line.

9. $^+7 + {}^+20$ **13.** $^+600 + {}^+2,500$ **17.** $^-56 + {}^-8$

10. $^+11 + {}^+36$ **14.** $^+70 + {}^+1,360$ **18.** $^-200 + {}^-130$

11. $^+25 + {}^+25$ **15.** $^-1 + {}^-37$ **19.** $^-300 + {}^-740$

12. $^+125 + {}^+300$ **16.** $^-39 + {}^-12$ **20.** $^-1,260 + {}^-150$

Example

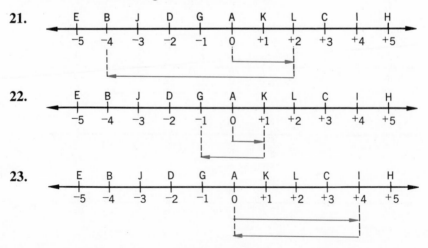

A move from *A* to *C*: $^+3$
Followed by a move from *C* to *D*: $^-5$
Result is the same as a move from *A* to *D*: $^-2$
Therefore, $^+3 + {}^-5 = {}^-2$.

For each picture, describe each pair of moves, as in the example above.
Then write the resulting addition statement.

21.

22.

23.

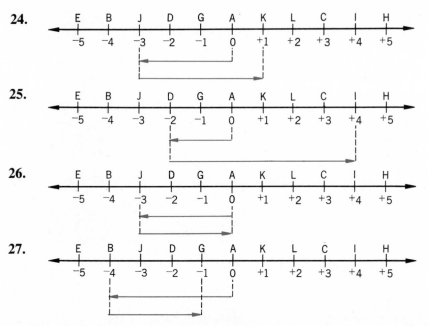

24.

25.

26.

27.

Look at your answers for exercises **21–27**. Complete the following:

28. The sum of a positive and a negative number is sometimes a _____ number, sometimes a _____ number.

29. The sum of a number and the opposite of this number is _____.

30. One of the six statements below is false. Find it!

a. $^+1 + {}^-7 = {}^-6$ c. $^+11 + {}^-11 = 0$ e. $^-17 + {}^+9 = {}^-8$

b. $^+10 + {}^-3 = {}^+7$ d. $^+30 + {}^-20 = {}^+10$ f. $^+40 + {}^-30 = {}^-10$

31. Two of the nine statements below are false. Find them!

a. $^+16 + {}^-8 = {}^+8$ d. $^+132 + {}^-132 = 0$ g. $^-38 + {}^+6 = {}^-32$

b. $^+30 + {}^-10 = {}^-20$ e. $^-20 + {}^+5 = {}^-15$ h. $^-50 + {}^+12 = {}^-38$

c. $^+40 + {}^-10 = {}^+30$ f. $^-200 + {}^+200 = 0$ i. $^-72 + {}^+72 = {}^+2$

Add.

32. $^+8 + {}^-2$

33. $^+17 + {}^-7$

34. $^+25 + {}^-9$

35. $^+59 + {}^-28$

36. $^+3 + {}^-4$

37. $^+12 + {}^-37$

38. $^+53 + {}^-67$

39. $^+78 + {}^-99$

40. $^+39 + {}^-39$

41. $^+40 + 0$

42. $0 + {}^-35$

43. $^-126 + {}^+126$

Add.

44. $\dfrac{^+3}{4} + \dfrac{^-1}{4}$

45. $\dfrac{^-5}{7} + \dfrac{^+3}{7}$

46. $\dfrac{^-4}{9} + \dfrac{^+7}{9}$

47. $^-1.6 + {}^+1.2$

48. $^-1.5 + {}^+.3$

49. $^-3.7 + {}^-4.3$

50. $^+16.2 + {}^-16.2$

51. $\dfrac{^-4}{3} + \dfrac{^+5}{6}$

52. $\dfrac{^-1}{4} + \dfrac{^+3}{8}$

53. $\dfrac{^+4}{7} + \dfrac{^-1}{14}$

54. $^-.3 + {}^+4.3$

55. $^-.7 + {}^+3.7$

56. $^-3.6 + {}^+1.8$

57. $^+4.5 + {}^-1.6$

58. $\dfrac{^-5}{2} + \dfrac{^+3}{4}$

59. $^+1\dfrac{1}{3} + {}^-1\dfrac{1}{3}$

60. $^+4\dfrac{1}{6} + {}^-2\dfrac{1}{3}$

61. $^-10.7 + {}^+11.6$

62. $^+3.6 + {}^-1.8$

63. $^-3.6 + {}^-1.8$

64. $^-10.9 + {}^+1.1$

ABSOLUTE VALUE

Every directed number has an *absolute value*. From the examples below you should be able to tell the absolute value of any number. We use the symbol | | to denote the absolute value. For example,

$$|^-3| \text{ is read: absolute value of negative three}$$
$$|^+7| \text{ is read: absolute value of positive seven}$$

Read each example.

$$|^-3| = {}^+3 \qquad \left|\dfrac{^-3}{4}\right| = \dfrac{^+3}{4} \qquad |^+3| = {}^+3 \qquad \left|\dfrac{^+7}{8}\right| = \dfrac{^+7}{8}$$
$$|^-10| = {}^+10 \qquad |^-1.5| = {}^+1.5 \qquad |^+2{,}000| = {}^+2{,}000 \qquad |0| = 0$$
$$|^-167| = {}^+167 \qquad\qquad\qquad\qquad |^+7.9| = {}^+7.9$$

Complete each statement.

1. $|^-307| = $ _____

2. $|^-2{,}506| = $ _____

3. $|0| = $ _____

4. $\left|\dfrac{^-3}{8}\right| = $ _____

5. $|^+4.5| = $ _____

6. $\left|\dfrac{^+1}{10}\right| = $ _____

Complete the following:

7. The absolute value of 0 is _____.

8. The absolute value of a positive number is a _____ number.

9. The absolute value of a negative number is a _____ number.

10. The absolute value of any non-zero number is a _____ number.

COMPARING DIRECTED NUMBERS

A number line gives us a very good way of comparing two directed numbers. To compare two directed numbers means to tell which is the greater. We will use the following method.

■   On a number line, locate the points corresponding to the two numbers. The number whose point is farther to the right is the greater of the two numbers.

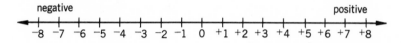

Example 1 $^+5$ is greater than $^+1$ [$^+5 > {}^+1$] because the point corresponding to $^+5$ is to the right of the point corresponding to $^+1$.

Example 2 $^-8$ is less than $^-2$ [$^-8 < {}^-2$] because the point corresponding to $^-8$ is to the left of the point corresponding to $^-2$.

Insert either ">" or "<" to obtain true statements.

Examples 1 $^+7$ ____ $^+1$ $^+7 \underline{>} {}^+1$

   2 $^-9$ ____ $^-1$ $^-9 \underline{<} {}^-1$

   3 $^-3$ ____ $^+1$ $^-3 \underline{<} {}^+1$

1. $^+12$ ____ $^+1$	5. $^-4$ ____ $^-5$	9. $^+1$ ____ $^-1$
2. $^+75$ ____ $^+74$	6. $^-7$ ____ $^-1$	10. $^+2$ ____ $^-200$
3. $^+12$ ____ $^+20$	7. $^-3$ ____ $^-150$	11. $^+99$ ____ $^-2$
4. $^+21$ ____ 0	8. 0 ____ $^-4$	12. $^-5,000$ ____ $^+3$

Insert either "greater" or "less" to obtain true statements.

13. Any positive number is _____ than any negative number.

14. Any negative number is _____ than any positive number.

15. Any positive number is _____ than 0.

16. Any negative number is _____ than 0.

17. 0 is _____ than any negative number.

18. 0 is _____ than any positive number.

19. The statements below are arranged in related pairs. Both statements in one pair are false. Find them!

a. $^+3 > {}^+1$; $|{}^+3| > |{}^+1|$ **d.** $^+8 < {}^+7$; $|{}^+8| < |{}^+7|$

b. $^+17 > {}^+3$; $|{}^+17| > |{}^+3|$ **e.** $^+1,200 > {}^+3$; $|{}^+1,200| > |{}^+3|$

c. $^+23 > {}^+9$; $|{}^+23| > |{}^+9|$ **f.** $^+8 < {}^+9$; $|{}^+8| < |{}^+9|$

20. Insert either "$<$" or "$>$" to obtain true statements.

     a. Given two *positive* numbers a and b,

$$\text{if } a < b, \text{ then } |a| \underline{\hspace{1cm}} |b|$$

     b. Given two *positive* numbers c and d,

$$\text{if } c > d, \text{ then } |c| \underline{\hspace{1cm}} |d|$$

21. The statements below are arranged in related pairs. Both statements in one pair are false. Find them!

a. $^-6 < {}^-3$; $|{}^-6| > |{}^-3|$ **d.** $^-30 < {}^-6$; $|{}^-30| > |{}^-6|$

b. $^-9 < {}^-1$; $|{}^-9| > |{}^-1|$ **e.** $^-40 < {}^-50$; $|{}^-40| > |{}^-50|$

c. $^-25 < {}^-5$; $|{}^-25| > |{}^-5|$ **f.** $^-100 < {}^-2$; $|{}^-100| > |{}^-2|$

Insert either "$<$" or "$>$" to obtain true statements.

22. Given two *negative* numbers x and y,

$$\text{if } x < y, \text{ then } |x| \underline{\hspace{1cm}} |y|$$

23. Given two *negative* numbers n and p,

$$\text{if } n > p, \text{ then } |n| \underline{\hspace{1cm}} |p|$$

Which are true and which are false?

24. $|{}^-7| < |{}^-2|$ **30.** $|{}^-200| < |{}^+1|$ **36.** $\left|\dfrac{{}^-3}{4}\right| = \left|\dfrac{{}^+3}{4}\right|$

25. $|0| \neq |{}^-1|$ **31.** $|{}^-1| < |{}^+200|$ **37.** $|{}^-.6| \neq |{}^+.6|$

26. $|{}^-200| > |0|$ **32.** $|0| > |{}^-1|$ **38.** $\left|\dfrac{{}^-1}{2}\right| < \left|\dfrac{{}^+1}{2}\right|$

27. $|0| < |{}^-1|$ **33.** $|{}^-2| \neq |{}^+2|$ **39.** $|{}^+5,000| \neq |{}^-5,000|$

28. $|{}^-3| < |{}^+2|$ **34.** $|{}^+500| = |{}^-500|$ **40.** $|{}^-1| < |{}^-3|$

29. $|{}^+200| > |{}^-1|$ **35.** $|{}^+10| < |{}^-10|$ **41.** $|{}^-2,000| \neq |{}^+2,000|$

ABSOLUTE VALUE AND ADDITION

We have observed some patterns in addition of directed numbers. These patterns are summarized below.

1. The sum of any two positive numbers is a positive number.
2. The sum of any two negative numbers is a negative number.
3. The sum of two numbers which are opposites is 0.
4. The sum of a positive number and a negative number is sometimes a positive number and sometimes a negative number.

The last statement is somewhat vague. Can we tell exactly when the sum is positive and when it is negative? The examples below suggest the answer to this question.

1. Supply the missing parts. The first example is completely done. Study all of the examples in order to discover the pattern.

   a. $^+5 + {}^-2 = {}^+3; |^+5| > |^-2|$ d. $^-1 + {}^+2 = \underline{\quad}; |\underline{\quad}| > |^-1|$

   b. $^+4 + {}^-3 = {}^+1; |^+4| \underline{\quad} |^-3|$ e. $^+5 + \underline{\quad} = {}^+4; |^+5| > |\underline{\quad}|$

   c. $^-3 + {}^+7 = \underline{\quad}; |^+7| > |^-3|$ f. $^-2 + {}^+9 = {}^+7; |^+9| > |\underline{\quad}|$

2. a. Is the sum of two numbers in each example in exercise 1 a positive or a negative number?

   b. In each example, is the absolute value of the positive number less than or greater than the absolute value of the negative number?

3. Fill in the missing words to obtain a correct description of the pattern illustrated by the examples in exercise 1.

   A positive and a _____ number are added. If the absolute value of the positive number is _____ than the absolute value of the _____ number, then the sum of the two numbers is a _____ number.

4. Supply the missing parts. The first example is completely done. Study all of the examples in order to discover the pattern.

   a. $^-3 + {}^+1 = {}^-2; |^-3| > |^+1|$ d. $^+3 + \underline{\quad} = {}^-4; |\underline{\quad}| > |^+3|$

   b. $^+4 + {}^-7 = {}^-3; |\underline{\quad}| > |^+4|$ e. $^+4 + {}^-5 = {}^-1; |\underline{\quad}| \underline{\quad} |\underline{\quad}|$

   c. $^-5 + {}^+2 = \underline{\quad}; |^-5| > |\underline{\quad}|$ f. $\underline{\quad} + {}^+1 = {}^-1; |\underline{\quad}| \underline{\quad} |\underline{\quad}|$

5. a. Is the sum of the two numbers in each example in exercise **4** a positive or a negative number?

  b. In each example, is the absolute value of the negative number less than or greater than the absolute value of the positive number?

6. Fill in the missing words to obtain a correct description of the pattern illustrated by the examples in exercise **4**.

A positive and a _____ number are added. If the absolute value of the negative number is _____ than the absolute value of the _____ number, then the sum of the two numbers is a _____ number.

Add.

Example $^+12 + {}^+16 = {}^+28$

7. $^+7 + {}^+19$

8. $^+26 + {}^+3$

9. $^+13 + {}^+38$

10. $\dfrac{^+3}{4} + \dfrac{^+5}{8}$

11. $^+3\dfrac{1}{3} + {}^+2\dfrac{1}{4}$

12. $\dfrac{^+4}{7} + {}^+9\dfrac{5}{7}$

13. $\dfrac{^+1}{2} + \dfrac{^+3}{9}$

14. $^+3\dfrac{1}{7} + \dfrac{^+1}{8}$

15. $^+9\dfrac{1}{9} + {}^+10\dfrac{1}{10}$

Example $^-13 + {}^-62 = {}^-75$

16. $^-1 + {}^-11$

17. $^-34 + {}^-12$

18. $^-45 + {}^-16$

19. $\dfrac{^-1}{2} + \dfrac{^-1}{2}$

20. $\dfrac{^-3}{4} + \dfrac{^-7}{8}$

21. $^-1\dfrac{1}{3} + \dfrac{^-2}{3}$

22. $^-6\dfrac{2}{5} + {}^-3\dfrac{1}{2}$

23. $^-8\dfrac{1}{7} + {}^-9\dfrac{5}{7}$

24. $^-4\dfrac{1}{5} + {}^-5\dfrac{1}{4}$

Example $^+12 + {}^-5 = {}^+7$

25. $^+20 + {}^-6$

26. $^-3 + {}^+25$

27. $^+32 + {}^-16$

28. $\dfrac{^+3}{4} + \dfrac{^-1}{4}$

29. $\dfrac{^-1}{8} + \dfrac{^+3}{4}$

30. $\dfrac{^+7}{9} + \dfrac{^-1}{3}$

31. $^+3\dfrac{1}{3} + \dfrac{^-2}{3}$

32. $^-10\dfrac{1}{4} + {}^+20\dfrac{3}{8}$

33. $^+32\dfrac{1}{3} + {}^-31\dfrac{1}{6}$

Example $^-12 + ^+7 = ^-5$

34. $^-10 + ^+5$

37. $\dfrac{^-4}{5} + \dfrac{^+2}{3}$

40. $^+7\dfrac{1}{9} + ^-12\dfrac{1}{3}$

35. $^+12 + ^-20$

38. $^+1\dfrac{1}{5} + ^-3\dfrac{3}{5}$

41. $^-2\dfrac{1}{7} + \dfrac{^+1}{3}$

36. $^-39 + ^+23$

39. $\dfrac{^+1}{3} + ^-12\dfrac{1}{9}$

42. $^-3\dfrac{1}{2} + ^+2\dfrac{1}{3}$

PRACTICE IN ADDITION

Now we are able to add any combination of two directed numbers. The exercises here offer practice in addition.

Add.

1. $^-1\dfrac{1}{2} + ^+3$

7. $^+3.6 + ^+7.5$

13. $\dfrac{^-4}{7} + \dfrac{^+9}{7}$

2. $^+5 + ^-13\dfrac{1}{3}$

8. $^-12\dfrac{1}{3} + ^+8\dfrac{2}{3}$

14. $^-1.6 + ^+.7$

3. $^-7\dfrac{1}{2} + ^+7\dfrac{1}{2}$

9. $^-7\dfrac{1}{2} + ^-8\dfrac{1}{2}$

15. $^-36.1 + ^+16.2$

4. $^-300 + ^-50\dfrac{1}{3}$

10. $^-20 + ^+36.7$

16. $^+1.9 + ^-3.7$

5. $^-125 + ^+80$

11. $^-99 + ^+99$

17. $^-6.9 + ^+3.1$

6. $^-1.6 + ^-3.4$

12. $^+109 + ^-109$

18. $^-5\dfrac{1}{6} + ^+4\dfrac{1}{8}$

Write down the answers as quickly as you can.

19. $^+3 + ^+2$

25. $^-1 + ^-3$

31. $^-11 + ^-9$

20. $^+7 + ^+4$

26. $^-4 + ^-7$

32. $^-9 + ^-11$

21. $^+6 + ^+12$

27. $^-3 + ^-17$

33. $^-15 + ^-12$

22. $^+12 + ^+6$

28. $^-11 + ^-12$

34. $^-12 + ^-15$

23. $^+17 + ^+4$

29. $^-4 + ^-27$

35. $^+5 + ^-2$

24. $^+4 + ^+17$

30. $^-27 + ^-4$

36. $^+4 + ^-1$

37. $^+10 + ^-3$ **47.** $^-5 + ^+2$ **57.** $^+70 + ^+40$

38. $^+15 + ^-14$ **48.** $^-4 + ^+1$ **58.** $^+40 + ^+70$

39. $^+3 + ^-4$ **49.** $^-7 + ^+3$ **59.** $^+150 + ^+61$

40. $^+4 + ^-7$ **50.** $^-20 + ^+12$ **60.** $^+61 + ^+150$

41. $^+7 + ^-12$ **51.** $^+12 + ^-17$ **61.** $^-500 + ^+250$

42. $^+10 + ^-30$ **52.** $^-17 + ^+12$ **62.** $^+250 + ^-500$

43. $^-3 + ^+5$ **53.** $^+20 + ^-3$ **63.** $^+1,000 + ^-500$

44. $^-1 + ^+4$ **54.** $^-3 + ^+20$ **64.** $^-500 + ^+1,000$

45. $^-9 + ^+12$ **55.** $^-8 + ^-13$ **65.** $^-34 + ^+13$

46. $^-15 + ^+40$ **56.** $^-13 + ^-8$ **66.** $^+13 + ^-34$

COMMUTATIVITY OF ADDITION

Give answers to the following pairs of addition problems.

1. $^-2 + ^+4;\quad ^+4 + ^-2$

2. $^-20 + ^+5;\quad ^+5 + ^-20$

3. $^-13.5 + ^-10;\quad ^-10 + ^-13.5$

4. $^-7 + ^+7;\quad ^+7 + ^-7$

5. $^+\dfrac{1}{2} + ^-\dfrac{1}{4};\quad ^-\dfrac{1}{4} + ^+\dfrac{1}{2}$

6. $^+3.6 + ^+1.6;\quad ^+1.6 + ^+3.6$

Each picture suggests an addition statement. Compare these statements.

Example   **a.**

$$^+2 + ^-5 = ^-3$$

b.

$$^-5 + ^+2 = ^-3$$

Write the addition statement suggested by each picture.

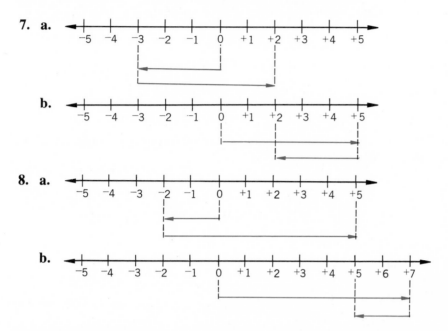

7. a.

b.

8. a.

b.

Exercises **7** and **8** confirm visually what you may have suspected about directed numbers. From exercise **7**, we see that

$$^-3 + {}^+5 = {}^+5 + {}^-3$$

Exercise **8** shows that

$$^-2 + {}^+7 = {}^+7 + {}^-2$$

In general, it appears that addition of directed numbers is commutative.

■ Commutative Property of Addition

$$x + y = y + x$$

We will be discovering many properties which hold for the set of directed real numbers. We will use letters such as x and y when stating these properties. The letters may be replaced by names of any directed numbers, and the resulting statements will be true.

9. Give answers without computing.

    a. If $^-112.63 + {}^+17.32 = {}^-95.31$, then what is $^+17.32 + {}^-112.63$ equal to?

    b. If $^+37\frac{1}{6} + {}^-2\frac{1}{7} = {}^+35\frac{1}{42}$, then what is $^-2\frac{1}{7} + {}^+37\frac{1}{6}$ equal to?

ASSOCIATIVITY OF ADDITION

You are already familiar with the use of parentheses. For example,

$$(2 + 7) + 8$$

means: add 2 and 7 first, then add 8 to the result. Thus, we have

$$(2 + 7) + 8 = 9 + 8 = 17$$

The operation indicated within parentheses is performed first.

Find the answers to the following by performing the operation within parentheses first.

1. $(^-2 + {}^+5) + {}^-7;$ $^-2 + ({}^+5 + {}^-7)$

2. $(^+3 + {}^+6) + {}^-10;$ $^+3 + ({}^+6 + {}^-10)$

3. $(^-4 + {}^-10) + {}^+20;$ $^-4 + ({}^-10 + {}^+20)$

4. $(^-1 + {}^+19) + {}^-3;$ $^-1 + ({}^+19 + {}^-3)$

5. $(^-2 + {}^+5) + {}^-30;$ $^-2 + ({}^+5 + {}^-30)$

6. $\left(\dfrac{^-1}{2} + \dfrac{^-3}{4}\right) + \dfrac{^+1}{4};$ $\dfrac{^-1}{2} + \left(\dfrac{^-3}{4} + \dfrac{^+1}{4}\right)$

7. $(^+.5 + {}^-2.5) + {}^-3.5;$ $^+.5 + ({}^-2.5 + {}^-3.5)$

8. $(^-3.6 + {}^-4.4) + {}^+10.5;$ $^-3.6 + ({}^-4.4 + {}^+10.5)$

9. $\left(\dfrac{^+1}{3} + \dfrac{^-2}{3}\right) + \dfrac{^-1}{6};$ $\dfrac{^+1}{3} + \left(\dfrac{^-2}{3} + \dfrac{^-1}{6}\right)$

10. $(^+1.55 + {}^-.55) + {}^+3.65;$ $^+1.55 + ({}^-.55 + {}^+3.65)$

11. $\left(^-3\dfrac{1}{2} + {}^+5\dfrac{1}{2}\right) + {}^-7\dfrac{1}{2};$ $^-3\dfrac{1}{2} + \left(^+5\dfrac{1}{2} + {}^-7\dfrac{1}{2}\right)$

Exercises **1–11** suggest that addition of directed numbers is associative.

■ *Associative Property of Addition*
    $(x + y) + z = x + (y + z)$

Find the answers. Use the Associative Property of Addition to make the work easier.

12. $^+130 + ({}^+70 + {}^-513)$

14. $\dfrac{^-1}{8} + \left(\dfrac{^-7}{8} + \dfrac{^+3}{5}\right)$

13. $(^+360 + {}^-49) + {}^-51$

ADDITION AND SUBTRACTION

Let us return for a minute to the addition and subtraction of numbers of ordinary arithmetic (non-directed numbers).

1. Observe the pattern in parts **a** and **b**. Complete parts **c–f** to fit this pattern.

   a. $7 - 3 = 4; 4 + 3 = 7$ **d.** $12 - 4 = 8;$ ____ $+ 4 =$ ____

   b. $10 - 4 = 6; 6 + 4 = 10$ **e.** $20 - 7 = 13;$ ____ $+ 7 =$ ____

   c. $9 - 4 = 5; 5 +$ ____ $= 9$ **f.** $16 - 9 = 7;$ ____ $+$ _9_ $=$ ____

2. Write the addition pattern which follows from $a - b = c$ as in the examples in exercise **1**.

The examples in exercise **1** show that for every subtraction statement, there is a related addition statement. We can obtain the answer to a subtraction problem by replacing it with the related addition problem.

Complete each statement as in the example.

Example $11 - 4 = \square$

   $\square + 4 = 11;$ to what number can 4 be added to obtain 11?
   Answer: 7. Therefore, $11 - 4 = 7$.

3. $25 - 8 = \square$ 5. $20 - 14 = \square$

4. $17 - 9 = \square$ 6. $32 - 18 = \square$

We wish for addition and subtraction of *directed* numbers to have the same relation. This will help us to learn to subtract one directed number from another by the use of addition. That is, we can find an answer to a subtraction problem by finding an answer to the related addition problem.

Complete each statement as in the example.

Example $^+7 - {}^+3 = \square$

   $\square + {}^+3 = {}^+7;$ to what number can $^+3$ be added to obtain $^+7$?
   Answer: $^+4$. Therefore, $^+7 - {}^+3 = {}^+4$.

7. $^+10 - {}^+4 = \square$ 10. $^+26 - {}^+12 = \square$

8. $^+5 - {}^+1 = \square$ 11. $^+32 - {}^+17 = \square$

9. $^+12 - {}^+9 = \square$ 12. $^+93 - {}^+13 = \square$

Complete each statement as in the example.

Example $^+2 - {}^+6 = \square$

$\square + {}^+6 = {}^+2$; to what number can $^+6$ be added to obtain $^+2$?
Answer: $^-4$. Therefore, $^+2 - {}^+6 = {}^-4$.

13. $^+1 - {}^+3 = \square$ 17. $^+12 - {}^+18 = \square$

14. $^+10 - {}^+23 = \square$ 18. $^+8 - {}^+9 = \square$

15. $^+2 - {}^+13 = \square$ 19. $^+10 - {}^+19 = \square$

16. $^+11 - {}^+21 = \square$ 20. $^+5 - {}^+27 = \square$

Complete each statement as in the example.

Example $^+3 - {}^-5 = \square$

$\square + {}^-5 = {}^+3$; to what number can $^-5$ be added to obtain $^+3$?
Answer: $^+8$. Therefore, $^+3 - {}^-5 = {}^+8$.

21. $^+1 - {}^-3 = \square$ 25. $^+25 - {}^-1 = \square$

22. $^+8 - {}^-4 = \square$ 26. $^+2 - {}^-15 = \square$

23. $^+6 - {}^-9 = \square$ 27. $^+9 - {}^-5 = \square$

24. $^+14 - {}^-8 = \square$ 28. $^+31 - {}^-4 = \square$

Find each answer by first writing the related addition problem.

29. $^+9 - {}^-6 = \square$ 38. $^-12 - {}^+2 = \square$

30. $^-7 - {}^+12 = \square$ 39. $^+4 - {}^-12 = \square$

31. $^+2 - {}^+12 = \square$ 40. $^+10 - {}^-3 = \square$

32. $^-5 - {}^-6 = \square$ 41. $^-8 - {}^-8 = \square$

33. $^-8 - {}^-3 = \square$ 42. $^+16 - {}^+16 = \square$

34. $^+7 - {}^+4 = \square$ 43. $^-3 - 0 = \square$

35. $^+10 - {}^+16 = \square$ 44. $^-4 - {}^-4 = \square$

36. $^-5 - {}^+8 = \square$ 45. $^+4 - {}^+4 = \square$

37. $^-11 - {}^+11 = \square$ 46. $^+13 - {}^-5 = \square$

SUBTRACTING BY ADDING

We have learned one way of subtracting one directed number from another. It involves writing a related addition problem. There is actually another (perhaps easier) way of replacing a subtraction problem by the related addition problem.

To the right of each subtraction problem, the related addition problem is given. After you have observed the pattern, replace the missing parts.

1. $^+7 - {}^+3 = {}^+4$; $^+7 + {}^-3 = {}^+4$

2. $^+10 - {}^+4 = {}^+6$; $^+10 + {}^-4 = {}^+6$

3. $^+5 - {}^+8 = {}^-3$; $^+5 + {}^-8 = {}^-3$

4. $^+9 - {}^+14 = {}^-5$; $^+9 + \square = {}^-5$

5. $^+3 - {}^-5 = \square$; $^+3 + \triangle = {}^+8$

6. $^+6 - {}^-7 = {}^+13$; $\square + \triangle = {}^+13$

7. $^-2 - {}^+5 = \square$; $^-2 + \triangle = \square$

8. $^-1 - \square = {}^+2$; $\triangle + {}^+3 = \bigcirc$

9. $^-5 - \square = {}^-3$; $\triangle + \bigcirc = \square$

10. $^-9 - {}^-3 = {}^-6$; $\triangle + \bigcirc = \square$

11. $\triangle - \bigcirc = \square$; $^+3 + {}^-7 = {}^-4$

12. $^-7 - {}^-9 = {}^+2$; $\triangle + \bigcirc = \square$

Subtracting $^+3$ from $^+7$ is the same as adding $^-3$ to $^+7$. Observe: $^-3$ is the opposite of $^+3$.

13. **a.** Complete the following statement: Subtracting $^-5$ from $^+3$ is the same as adding ____ to ____.

  b. What is the opposite of $^-5$?

■ Subtracting x from y is the same as adding the opposite of x to y.

Use the pattern above to find the answers.

Example $^+9 - {}^-15$ $^+9 - {}^-15 = {}^+9 + {}^+15 = {}^+24$

14. $^+3 - {}^-16$

15. $^+3 - {}^-1$

16. $^-14 - {}^-12$

17. $^-2 - {}^+25$

18. $^+12 - {}^+15$

19. $^-10 - {}^-10$

20. $^-1 - {}^-98$

21. $^+1 - {}^+98$

22. $^+25 - {}^-23$

23. $^-15 - {}^-3$

24. $^-4 - {}^-1$

25. $^+3 - {}^+37$

26. $^+15 - {}^+15$

27. $^+7 - {}^-45$

28. $^-3 - {}^-97$

29. $^+35 - {}^+37$

30. $^-12 - {}^+10$

31. $^-25 - {}^-30$

32. $^+49 - {}^+56$

33. $^-12 - {}^-12$

34. $^-12 - {}^+12$

OPPOSITES OF DIRECTED REAL NUMBERS

Each directed real number has an opposite. For example,

the opposite of $^+\frac{1}{3}$ is $^-\frac{1}{3}$

the opposite of $^-5.8$ is $^+5.8$

Use the pattern on page 211 to find the answers.

1. $^-\frac{1}{2} - ^-\frac{1}{2}$

2. $^-\frac{1}{2} - ^-\frac{1}{4}$

3. $^-\frac{1}{3} - ^+\frac{1}{2}$

4. $^-1\frac{1}{2} - ^+3\frac{1}{2}$

5. $^-\frac{1}{2} - ^+\frac{1}{2}$

6. $^-\frac{1}{2} - ^+\frac{1}{4}$

7. $^-\frac{3}{4} - ^-\frac{5}{6}$

8. $^+3\frac{1}{2} - ^-4\frac{3}{4}$

9. $^+\frac{1}{2} - ^-\frac{1}{2}$

10. $^+\frac{1}{4} - ^-\frac{1}{2}$

11. $^+\frac{1}{4} - ^+\frac{1}{2}$

12. $^-10\frac{1}{3} - ^+7\frac{5}{6}$

13. $^-10.5 - ^+3.7$

14. $^-10.15 - ^+3.15$

15. $^-1.15 - ^+14.45$

16. $^-3.7 - ^-10.5$

17. $^-100.1 - ^-90.1$

18. $^+4.75 - ^-3.25$

19. $^+5.9 - ^-3.8$

20. $^+3.65 - ^-3.65$

21. $^-10.0 - ^+10.1$

Find the answers.

22. $^+2 + ^-2$

23. $^+\frac{1}{3} + ^-\frac{1}{3}$

24. $^-7.6 + ^+7.6$

25. $0 + 0$

Exercises 22–25 suggest the following:

■ The sum of two opposite numbers is 0.

26. Compute the answers to each pair of problems.

a. $^+3 - ^+4$; $^+4 - ^+3$

b. $^-5 - ^+7$; $^+7 - ^-5$

c. $^-7 - ^+1$; $^+1 - ^-7$

d. $^+10 - ^+7$; $^+7 - ^+10$

e. $^-3 - ^+5$; $^+5 - ^-3$

f. $^+1 - ^+7$; $^+7 - ^+1$

g. $^+\frac{1}{2} - ^+\frac{3}{2}$; $^+\frac{3}{2} - ^+\frac{1}{2}$

h. $^-\frac{1}{3} - ^-\frac{4}{3}$; $^-\frac{4}{3} - ^-\frac{1}{3}$

27. What is true of each pair of answers to exercise **26**?

28. From the results in exercise **26**, is it true that $(a - b)$ is the opposite of $(b - a)$?

29. What is the answer to $(a - b) + (b - a)$, for all replacements of a and b?

30. Find the answers without doing any computations.

   a. $(^+8 - {}^-7) + (^-7 - {}^+8)$ **b.** $(^-6.2 - {}^+3.1) + (^+3.1 - {}^-6.2)$

CLOSURE

Recall that the set of natural numbers is closed under addition; that is, the sum of any pair of natural numbers is a natural number. But the set of natural numbers is not closed under subtraction. The same is true of the set of all non-directed real numbers of arithmetic. There is no answer to a problem of subtracting a larger number from a smaller number among the non-directed real numbers of arithmetic.

The set of all directed numbers is closed under both addition and subtraction. There is an answer to every subtraction problem among directed numbers.

1. Consider the set of all integers.

$$I = \{\ldots\, ^-5, ^-4, ^-3, ^-2, ^-1, 0, ^+1, ^+2, ^+3, ^+4, ^+5, \ldots\}$$

   a. Is I closed under addition, that is, is the sum of any two integers an integer?

   b. Is I closed under subtraction, that is, is the difference of two integers an integer?

2. Consider the set $A = \{^-1, 0, ^+1\}$.

   a. Is A closed under addition, that is, is the sum of any two numbers from A found in A?

   b. Is A closed under subtraction?

3. Consider the set of all non-negative integers.

$$N = \{0, ^+1, ^+2, ^+3, ^+4, \ldots\}$$

   a. Is N closed under addition?

   b. Is N closed under subtraction?

4. Consider the set of all non-positive integers.

$$R = \{0, {}^-1, {}^-2, {}^-3, {}^-4, \ldots\}$$

a. Is R closed under addition?

b. Is R closed under subtraction?

5. Consider the following infinite set of numbers.

$$T = \left\{0, \frac{{}^+1}{2}, \frac{{}^-1}{2}, \frac{{}^+1}{4}, \frac{{}^-1}{4}, \frac{{}^+1}{8}, \frac{{}^-1}{8}, \frac{{}^+1}{16}, \frac{{}^-1}{16}, \frac{{}^+1}{32}, \frac{{}^-1}{32}, \ldots\right\}$$

a. Is T closed under addition?

b. Is T closed under subtraction?

6. Consider the following infinite set of numbers.

$$V = \left\{0, \frac{{}^+1}{3}, \frac{{}^-1}{3}, \frac{{}^+1}{9}, \frac{{}^-1}{9}, \frac{{}^+1}{27}, \frac{{}^-1}{27}, \frac{{}^+1}{81}, \frac{{}^-1}{81}, \ldots\right\}$$

a. Is V closed under addition?

b. Is V closed under subtraction?

KEEPING ARITHMETICALLY FIT

For exercises **1–50**, numerals in parentheses refer to pages where you can find similar exercises.

Add. (436–437)   (428–430)

1. 32.75 **2.** 1.306 **3.** $\frac{1}{7} + \frac{5}{6}$ **5.** $31\frac{5}{6} + 70\frac{7}{6}$
  63.35   9.118
  17.25   7.206
  19.98   6.335 **4.** $\frac{3}{8} + \frac{5}{7}$ **6.** $12\frac{2}{3} + 13\frac{1}{8}$
  32.55   9.105
  17.69   8.379
  18.32   6.406

Subtract. (438–439)   (430–431)

7. .5774 **9.** 6.3138 **11.** $\frac{1}{7} - \frac{1}{8}$ **13.** $\frac{6}{7} - \frac{5}{6}$
  .4452   4.0108

8. 1.6003 **10.** .7193 **12.** $3\frac{1}{2} - 1\frac{1}{3}$ **14.** $10\frac{1}{2} - 9\frac{1}{3}$
  .9657   .6428

Multiply. (425)   (439–440)   (432–434)

15. 49 $\underline{67}$	**20.** 367 $\underline{\;\;17}$	**25.** 45.5 $\underline{\;\;7.6}$	**30.** $\frac{3}{7} \times \frac{4}{5}$
16. 98 $\underline{89}$	**21.** 987 $\underline{\;\;79}$	**26.** 95.6 $\underline{\;\;3.9}$	**31.** $2\frac{1}{7} \times 3\frac{1}{6}$
17. 67 $\underline{48}$	**22.** 809 $\underline{166}$	**27.** 18.9 $\underline{\;\;9.7}$	**32.** $\frac{11}{6} \times \frac{2}{7}$
18. 17 $\underline{79}$	**23.** 568 $\underline{205}$	**28.** 33.7 $\underline{\;\;5.9}$	**33.** $5\frac{2}{3} \times 6\frac{7}{8}$
19. 365 $\underline{\;\;29}$	**24.** 709 $\underline{295}$	**29.** 82.5 $\underline{\;\;8.2}$	**34.** $7\frac{1}{8} \times 5\frac{1}{9}$

Divide. (426–427)   (434–436)

35. $15\overline{)15,375}$	**39.** $6.7 \div 10$	**43.** $\frac{3}{4} \div \frac{4}{5}$	**47.** $\frac{10}{11} \div 5$
36. $198\overline{)376,398}$	**40.** $9.35 \div .01$	**44.** $\frac{1}{4} \div \frac{5}{6}$	**48.** $3\frac{1}{2} \div 1\frac{1}{4}$

(440–442)

37. $2.5\overline{)62.5}$	**41.** $8.8 \div 2$	**45.** $\frac{2}{3} \div \frac{8}{5}$	**49.** $4\frac{2}{3} \div 7\frac{1}{4}$
38. $.03\overline{)372.30}$	**42.** $3.5 \div .5$	**46.** $7 \div \frac{7}{8}$	**50.** $9\frac{1}{2} \div 3\frac{1}{3}$

51. Multiply: $25 \times .9$

Answer the questions in exercises **52–56** without multiplying.

52. Is $500 \times .999$ greater or less than 500?

53. Is 375×1.0001 greater or less than 375?

54. Is 200×2.001 greater or less than 400?

55. Is 40×1.999 greater or less than 80?

56. Is 500×3.999 greater or less than 2,000?

57. Explain why the sum of 10.98 and 36.13 must be between 46 and 48. Compute the sum.

58. What is the average of $\frac{1}{2}, \frac{1}{3}$, and $\frac{1}{4}$?

What is the reciprocal of each of the following?

59. 3   **60.** $\frac{1}{2}$ **61.** $\frac{4}{5}$ **62.** $\frac{7}{3}$ **63.** $1\frac{2}{3}$ **64.** 1.5

Give replacements for *n* to obtain true statements.

65. 60% of 120 = *n*   **68.** *n*% of 10,000 = 1   **71.** 1% of *n* = 2

66. $\frac{1}{2}$% of 1,000 = *n*   **69.** *n*% of 10,000 = $\frac{1}{4}$ **72.** .01% of *n* = 2

67. *n*% of 150 = 25   **70.** 20% of *n* = 16   **73.** $\frac{1}{2}$% of *n* = 2

Subtract.

74. 20 ft. 7 in.   **76.** 15 lb. 12 oz.   **78.** 12 gal. 2 qt.
    18 ft. 10 in.   10 lb. 15 oz.   9 gal. 3 qt.

75. 125 m. 36 cm.   **77.** 12 km. 750 m.   **79.** 1 yd. 2 ft. 8 in.
     30 m. 48 cm.   9 km. 836 m.   2 ft. 10 in.

80. The table below gives the number of citizens of voting age in ten states and the per cent of votes cast in 1960. For each state, compute the number of citizens who voted.

State	Number of Citizens of Voting Age in Millions	Per Cent Voted in 1960
New York	17.5	65
California	12.0	65
Pennsylvania	7.1	65
Illinois	6.2	71
Ohio	5.8	65
Texas	5.3	40
Michigan	4.5	67
New Jersey	3.9	70
Massachusetts	3.3	75
Florida	3.1	47

81. A man's monthly salary was increased from $720 to $800. What per cent of his lower salary was the increase?

82. The average U.S. income in 1959 was $2,166. Below are given the average incomes of six states as per cents of the average U.S. income. Compute the average income in dollars for each of these states.

State	Per Cent of Average U.S. Income
Delaware	126
Illinois	120
Michigan	103
Tennessee	70
Mississippi	47

83. Sue received the score of 71 right out of the total 75 problems. What per cent score was that?

84. Betty missed 7 points on a 125-point test. What per cent of 125 points did she miss?

85. The net income of a company increased from $12 million in one year to $13 million the next year. What per cent increase is this?

VOCABULARY REVIEW

absolute value (200)
directed real number (192)
integers (191)
negative numbers (191)

non-directed numbers (209)
opposite (191)
origin (190)
positive numbers (190)

A CHALLENGE TO YOU

1. Find a rational number equal to $\frac{2}{9}$ such that the sum of the numerator and denominator is 120.

2. Shelves contain 210 books. There are twice as many English books as French and 10 more Spanish books than English. How many French, English, and Spanish books are there?

3. Divide 310 into three numbers in the ratio $\frac{1}{2} : \frac{1}{5} : \frac{1}{3}$.

4. Add 1 to the numerator and to the denominator named in a fractional numeral. The new rational number is larger than the original rational number. Give an example of such a rational number.

5. Add 1 to the numerator and to the denominator named in a fractional numeral. The new rational number is smaller than the original rational number. Give an example of such a rational number.

6. When tossing a coin there are two possible outcomes, H (heads) and T (tails). We say that the probability of each outcome is $\frac{1}{2}$. We write

$$P(H) = \frac{1}{2} \qquad P(T) = \frac{1}{2}$$

   a. List the four possible outcomes when a coin is tossed twice. [HINT: "HH" describes the outcome of obtaining heads on the first toss and heads on the second toss.]

   b. Assuming that the probability of each of the four outcomes is the same, give the probability of each outcome.

   c. What is the sum of the four probabilities in part b?

CHAPTER TEST

Give the opposite of each number.

1. $^-6$ 3. 0 5. $^+\sqrt{17}$

2. $^+7$ 4. $^-\sqrt{5}$ 6. $^+12\frac{1}{2}$

Without performing any operations, tell whether each answer is a positive or a negative number.

7. $^-268 + {}^+1{,}032$ 9. $^-765 + {}^-323$ 11. $^-267 - {}^-198$

8. $^-789 + {}^-1{,}325$ 10. $^+105 + {}^+537$ 12. $^+1{,}268 - {}^-35$

Add.

13. $^+6 + {}^-8$ 17. $^+7 + {}^+32$ 21. $\frac{^-1}{2} + \frac{^+3}{4}$

14. $^+12 + {}^-7$ 18. $^+49 + {}^+12$ 22. $\frac{^-3}{4} + \frac{^-6}{7}$

15. $^-5 + {}^+1$ 19. $^-3 + {}^-21$ 23. $^-3\frac{1}{2} + {}^+7\frac{3}{4}$

16. $^-13 + {}^+23$ 20. $^-17 + {}^-9$ 24. $^-1.01 + {}^+2.02$

Subtract.

25. $^-3 - {^+9}$

26. $^-12 - {^+3}$

27. $^+4 - {^-15}$

28. $^+11 - {^-3}$

29. $^+11 - {^+25}$

30. $^+36 - {^+23}$

31. $^-1 - {^-15}$

32. $^-20 - {^-4}$

33. $\dfrac{^-1}{3} - \dfrac{^+2}{3}$

34. $\dfrac{^+3}{4} - \dfrac{^-1}{4}$

35. $\dfrac{^-1}{6} - \dfrac{^-1}{7}$

36. $^-2.03 - {^+3.03}$

37. Give a directed number which describes the final temperature after the following chain of changes: Start at 20 below zero, up 30, down 20, up 40, up 2, down 15, up 30, down 52.

38. $^-30$ is added to a number. The result is $^+12$. What is the number?

39. $^-2$ is subtracted from a number. The result is $^-5$. What is the number?

40. What number should be added to $^+3$ to obtain $^-7$?

41. List all pairs of positive integers such that the sum of each pair is $^+5$.

42. Explain why the set of directed real numbers is closed under subtraction.

CHAPTER EIGHT

Directed Numbers—
Multiplication and Division

MULTIPLICATION OF POSITIVE NUMBERS

You may have noticed that the positive integers "behave" just like the natural numbers under addition. For example, the statements $+2 + +3 = +5$ and $2 + 3 = 5$ are similar. We can establish a one-to-one correspondence between the natural numbers and the positive integers as shown on the right. Then if we know the sum of two natural numbers, we can find the sum of the corresponding positive integers.

Since the directed numbers are new to us, we need to decide how to operate with these new numbers. We already know how to add and subtract. Now we shall learn how to multiply directed numbers. To do this, we shall use this correspondence between the natural numbers and positive integers. We know, for example, that the product of 2 and 4 is 8. To find the product of $+2$ and $+4$, we will find the positive integer corresponding to 8. It is $+8$. Thus, $+2 \times +4 = +8$.

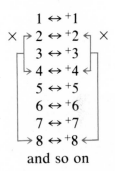

We shall assume that the same correspondence holds between the real numbers of arithmetic and the positive directed numbers and zero.

Give the answers.

1. $+3 \times +9$

2. $+11 \times +4$

3. $+4 \times +11$

4. $+12 \times +12$

5. $+13 \times 0$

6. $+22 \times +11$

7. $\frac{+1}{2} \times \frac{+1}{3}$

8. $\frac{+3}{4} \times \frac{+7}{8}$

9. $+2\frac{1}{3} \times +1\frac{1}{4}$

10. $+10\frac{1}{2} \times +5\frac{3}{4}$

11. $+3.6 \times +4.5$

12. $+10.3 \times +3.8$

13. $+3.8 \times +10.3$

14. $+.2 \times +.5$

15. $+.5 \times +.2$

16. Using the correspondence described above, write an argument establishing that the multiplication of positive real numbers is commutative.

The correspondence which we have established tells us how to find the product of any two positive real numbers.

17. Complete the following statement.

The product of two positive numbers is a _____ number.

MULTIPLICATION OF POSITIVE AND NEGATIVE NUMBERS

Many mathematical discoveries are made by observing patterns. Patterns may suggest to us which mathematical agreements are reasonable. We shall observe patterns to discover a reasonable way to multiply a positive number by a negative number.

Study the examples below with your eyes wide open! Watch for a pattern!

$$
\begin{aligned}
{}^{+}2 \times {}^{+}4 &= {}^{+}8 \\
{}^{+}2 \times {}^{+}3 &= {}^{+}6 \\
{}^{+}2 \times {}^{+}2 &= {}^{+}4 \\
{}^{+}2 \times {}^{+}1 &= {}^{+}2 \\
{}^{+}2 \times \phantom{{}^{+}}0 &= \phantom{{}^{+}}0 \\
{}^{+}2 \times {}^{-}1 &= \phantom{{}^{+}}?
\end{aligned}
$$

The question is: "What number should be the answer to ${}^{+}2 \times {}^{-}1$ in order to continue the pattern?" Answer the questions below to arrive at the solution.

1. What number appears first each time?

2. How do the numbers in the second column change as we move down the column?

3. How do the numbers in the third column change as we move down the column?

4. What answer should follow 0 in the third column?

5. Complete the statement: ${}^{+}2 \times {}^{-}1 = \square$

6. Continue the pattern by supplying the answers to the following:

$$
\begin{aligned}
{}^{+}2 \times {}^{-}1 &= \square \\
{}^{+}2 \times {}^{-}2 &= \square \\
{}^{+}2 \times {}^{-}3 &= \square \\
{}^{+}2 \times {}^{-}4 &= \square
\end{aligned}
$$

7. Complete: ${}^{+}2 \times {}^{-}50 = \square$

8. Supply the next five statements which fit into the pattern.

$$^+3 \times {}^+3 = {}^+9$$
$$^+3 \times {}^+2 = {}^+6$$
$$^+3 \times {}^+1 = {}^+3$$
$$^+3 \times 0 = 0$$
$$^+3 \times {}^-1 = {}^-3$$

9. Give the answers. Then supply the next five statements which fit into the pattern.

$$^+4 \times {}^+3 = \square$$
$$^+4 \times {}^+2 = \square$$
$$^+4 \times {}^+1 = \square$$
$$^+4 \times 0 = \square$$
$$^+4 \times {}^-1 = \square$$

10. Complete each statement.

a. $^+3 \times {}^-10 = \square$ b. $^+4 \times {}^-30 = \square$

11. Complete the following statement.

The product of a positive number and a negative number
is a _____ number.

If we want multiplication of directed numbers to be commutative, then the following must be true: $^+2 \times {}^-3 = {}^-3 \times {}^+2$.

12. On the basis of the Commutative Property of Multiplication, give a statement which follows from each of the following:

a. $^+2 \times {}^-6$ b. $^+2 \times {}^-49$ c. $^+2 \times {}^-100$

Give the answers.

13. $^+16 \times {}^-4$ **18.** $^+125 \times {}^-10$ **23.** $\dfrac{^-2}{3} \times \dfrac{^+7}{8}$

14. $^+25 \times {}^-8$ **19.** $^+500 \times \dfrac{^-1}{2}$ **24.** $\dfrac{^+4}{3} \times \dfrac{^-5}{7}$

15. $^-12 \times {}^+11$ **20.** $\dfrac{^-1}{3} \times {}^+150$ **25.** $\dfrac{^+2}{3} \times \dfrac{^-3}{2}$

16. $^+40 \times {}^-50$ **21.** $\dfrac{^-2}{3} \times {}^+300$ **26.** $\dfrac{^-4}{7} \times \dfrac{^+7}{4}$

17. $^+12 \times {}^-100$ **22.** $^-400 \times \dfrac{^+1}{4}$ **27.** $^-2\dfrac{1}{4} \times {}^+5\dfrac{3}{4}$

MULTIPLICATION OF NEGATIVE NUMBERS

The display below illustrates another interesting pattern. Try to discover it while supplying answers to the following questions.

$$^-2 \times {}^+3 = {}^-6$$
$$^-2 \times {}^+2 = {}^-4$$
$$^-2 \times {}^+1 = {}^-2$$
$$^-2 \times 0 = 0$$
$$^-2 \times {}^-1 = ?$$

1. What number appears first each time?

2. How do the numbers in the second column change as we move down the column?

3. How do the numbers in the third column change as we move down the column?

4. What answer should follow 0 in the third column?

5. Complete the statement: $^-2 \times {}^-1 = \square$

6. Continue the pattern by supplying the answers to the following:

$$^-2 \times {}^-2 = \square$$
$$^-2 \times {}^-3 = \square$$
$$^-2 \times {}^-4 = \square$$
$$^-2 \times {}^-5 = \square$$
$$^-2 \times {}^-6 = \square$$

7. Complete: $^-2 \times {}^-50 = \square$

8. Supply the next five statements which fit into the pattern.

$$^-1 \times {}^+3 = {}^-3$$
$$^-1 \times {}^+2 = {}^-2$$
$$^-1 \times {}^+1 = {}^-1$$
$$^-1 \times 0 = 0$$
$$^-1 \times {}^-1 = {}^+1$$

9. Give the answers.

   a. $^-1 \times {}^-20 = \square$

   b. $^-1 \times {}^-50 = \square$

   c. $^-1 \times {}^-3.7 = \square$

   d. $^-1 \times {}^-100 = \square$

   e. $^-1 \times {}^-250 = \square$

   f. $^-1 \times {}^-3\frac{1}{6} = \square$

10. Supply the next five statements which fit into the pattern.

$$^-3 \times {}^+3 = {}^-9$$
$$^-3 \times {}^+2 = {}^-6$$
$$^-3 \times {}^+1 = {}^-3$$
$$^-3 \times \ \ 0 = \ \ 0$$
$$^-3 \times {}^-1 = {}^+3$$

11. Give the answers.

a. $^-3 \times {}^-20 = \square$

d. $^-3 \times \dfrac{^-4}{5} = \square$

b. $^-3 \times {}^-50 = \square$

e. $^-3 \times {}^-1.1 = \square$

c. $^-3 \times {}^-120 = \square$

f. $^-3 \times {}^-5.2 = \square$

12. Complete the following statement.

The product of two negative numbers is a _____ number.

Give the answers.

13. $^-12 \times {}^-3$

17. $^-2.6 \times {}^-2$

21. $^-3.2 \times {}^-4$

14. $^-20 \times {}^-6$

18. $^-1.5 \times {}^-4$

22. $^-5 \times {}^-12$

15. $^-.5 \times {}^-.1$

19. $^-21 \times {}^-4$

23. $^-.1 \times {}^-.3$

16. $^-18 \times \dfrac{^-1}{2}$

20. $\dfrac{^-1}{4} \times {}^-20$

24. $\dfrac{^-2}{3} \times {}^-9$

Write the answers as quickly as you can.

25. $^-3 \times {}^+5$

31. $^-3 \times {}^+20$

37. $0 \times {}^-17$

26. $^-1 \times {}^-175$

32. $\dfrac{^-3}{4} \times {}^-4$

38. $^+360 \times 0$

27. $^+2 \times {}^-16$

33. $^-1.1 \times {}^+5$

39. $\dfrac{^-1}{2} \times \dfrac{^+1}{2}$

28. $^+1.5 \times {}^+2$

34. $\dfrac{^-2}{3} \times {}^+9$

40. $^+1.3 \times {}^+4$

29. $^-13 \times {}^-3$

35. $^+1.5 \times {}^+6$

41. $^+3 \times \dfrac{^-2}{3}$

30. $^-5 \times {}^+16$

36. $^+10 \times \dfrac{^-1}{5}$

42. $^-10 \times \dfrac{^+1}{20}$

PROPERTIES OF MULTIPLICATION

Give answers to each pair of problems.

1. $^-3 \times {}^+4$; $^+4 \times {}^-3$

2. $^-7 \times {}^-8$; $^-8 \times {}^-7$

3. $^-5 \times 0$; $0 \times {}^-5$

4. $^+487 \times {}^-1$; $^-1 \times {}^+487$

5. $^+11 \times {}^+3$; $^+3 \times {}^+11$

6. $\dfrac{^-1}{2} \times \dfrac{^+1}{3}$; $\dfrac{^+1}{3} \times \dfrac{^-1}{2}$

7. $^+3 \times {}^-16$; $^-16 \times {}^+3$

8. $^+1.5 \times {}^-4$; $^-4 \times {}^+1.5$

Recall that multiplication of whole numbers is commutative. Exercises **1–8** suggest that multiplication of directed numbers is also commutative.

■ *Commutative Property of Multiplication*
  $x \times y = y \times x$

Since we are dealing with directed real numbers, x and y may be replaced by names of any two such numbers, and the resulting statements will be true.

Compute the following. Recall that the operations inside parentheses are to be performed first.

9. $(^+2 \times {}^-3) \times {}^-4$; $^+2 \times ({}^-3 \times {}^-4)$

10. $(^-7 \times {}^-2) \times {}^-3$; $^-7 \times ({}^-2 \times {}^-3)$

11. $\left(\dfrac{^+1}{2} \times {}^+4 \right) \times \dfrac{^-1}{2}$; $\dfrac{^+1}{2} \times \left({}^+4 \times \dfrac{^-1}{2} \right)$

12. $(^-1 \times {}^+1) \times {}^-1$; $^-1 \times ({}^+1 \times {}^-1)$

13. $(^+387 \times 0) \times {}^-20$; $^+387 \times (0 \times {}^-20)$

14. $(0 \times {}^-20) \times {}^+4$; $0 \times ({}^-20 \times {}^+4)$

15. $\left(\dfrac{^-1}{3} \times {}^+20 \right) \times {}^-6$; $\dfrac{^-1}{3} \times ({}^+20 \times {}^-6)$

16. $^-1.1 \times ({}^+.3 \times {}^+2)$; $(^-1.1 \times {}^+.3) \times {}^+2$

Exercises **9–16** illustrate that multiplication of directed real numbers is associative.

■ *Associative Property of Multiplication*
  $(x \times y) \times z = x \times (y \times z)$

Give answers to each pair of problems.

17. $^-2 \times (^+3 + ^-2)$; $(^-2 \times ^+3) + (^-2 \times ^-2)$

18. $^-4 \times (^+3 + 0)$; $(^-4 \times ^+3) + (^-4 \times 0)$

19. $^-1 \times (^-1 + ^+1)$; $(^-1 \times ^-1) + (^-1 \times ^+1)$

20. $\frac{^-1}{2} \times (^+4 + ^-6)$; $\left(\frac{^-1}{2} \times ^+4\right) + \left(\frac{^-1}{2} \times ^-6\right)$

21. $^-8 \times \left(\frac{^-1}{4} + \frac{^-1}{2}\right)$; $\left(^-8 \times \frac{^-1}{4}\right) + \left(^-8 \times \frac{^-1}{2}\right)$

22. $^-3 \times (^+97 + ^+3)$; $(^-3 \times ^+97) + (^-3 \times ^+3)$

The following property is illustrated by the examples in exercises **17–22.**

■ *Left-Distributive Property of Multiplication over Addition*
$x(y + z) = (xy) + (xz)$

Compute the following:

23. $(^+3 + ^-12) \times ^-7$; $(^+3 \times ^-7) + (^-12 \times ^-7)$

24. $(^-1 + ^-12) \times ^+4$; $(^-1 \times ^+4) + (^-12 \times ^+4)$

25. $\left(\frac{^-1}{2} + \frac{^-1}{2}\right) \times ^-500$; $\left(\frac{^-1}{2} \times ^-500\right) + \left(\frac{^-1}{2} \times ^-500\right)$

26. $\left(\frac{^+1}{3} + \frac{^-1}{3}\right) \times ^+300$; $\left(\frac{^+1}{3} \times ^+300\right) + \left(\frac{^-1}{3} \times ^+300\right)$

27. $(^+1.2 + ^+.3) \times ^-6$; $(^+1.2 \times ^-6) + (^+.3 \times ^-6)$

28. $(^-4.6 + 0) \times ^+5.5$; $(^-4.6 \times ^+5.5) + (0 \times ^+5.5)$

29. Using x, y, and z, state the property illustrated by exercises **23–28.** What would you call this property?

Compute the following:

30. $^-2 \times (^+5 - ^+3)$; $(^-2 \times ^+5) - (^-2 \times ^+3)$

31. $^+4 \times (^-3 - ^+4)$; $(^+4 \times ^-3) - (^+4 \times ^+4)$

32. $^-6 \times (^+4 - ^-5)$; $(^-6 \times ^+4) - (^-6 \times ^-5)$

33. $^+10 \times \left(\frac{^-1}{2} - \frac{^-1}{5}\right)$; $\left(^+10 \times \frac{^-1}{2}\right) - \left(^+10 \times \frac{^-1}{5}\right)$

34. $\frac{^-1}{2} \times (^+8 - ^-6)$; $\left(\frac{^-1}{2} \times ^+8\right) - \left(\frac{^-1}{2} \times ^-6\right)$

35. $^+2.5 \times (^+5 - ^+5)$; $(^+2.5 \times ^+5) - (^+2.5 \times ^+5)$

36. Using x, y, and z, state the property illustrated by exercises **30–35**. What would you call this property?

Using the distributive properties, find the answers in the simplest way.

Example $(^-2 \times ^+98) + (^-2 \times ^+2) = ^-2 \times (^+98 + ^+2)$
$$= ^-2 \times ^+100 = ^-200$$

37. $(^+5 \times ^-205) + (^+5 \times ^+5)$

38. $(^+31 \times ^+45) + (^+31 \times ^+55)$

39. $(^-11 \times ^-115) + (^-11 \times ^+15)$

40. $\left(\frac{^-1}{2} \times ^+98\right) + \left(\frac{^-1}{2} \times ^+102\right)$

41. $(^-16 \times ^-201) - (^-16 \times ^+99)$

42. $(^-12 \times ^+155) - (^-12 \times ^+55)$

Without doing any computations, tell whether each answer is positive or negative.

43. $(^+37 \times ^-1135) \times ^-45$

44. $(^-11 \times ^+33) \times ^-107$

45. $\left(\frac{^+1}{3} \times \frac{^+1}{6}\right) \times \frac{^-21}{27}$

46. $^+37 \times (^-12 \times ^+41)$

47. $^+44 \times (^+36 \times ^+11)$

48. $^-13 \times (^+25 \times ^-60)$

49. $^-\sqrt{5} \times (^+5 \times ^+\sqrt{36})$

50. $^-10 \times (^-11 \times ^-12)$

51. $(^-55 \times ^-30) \times ^-78$

52. $(^-100 \times ^-18) \times ^-38$

Study these abbreviations.

$$(^-2)^3 = ^-2 \times ^-2 \times ^-2 \qquad (^+4)^5 = ^+4 \times ^+4 \times ^+4 \times ^+4 \times ^+4$$

Without doing any computations, tell whether each answer is positive or negative.

53. $(^-2)^3$

54. $(^+6)^3$

55. $(^-4)^5$

56. $(^-2)^2$

57. $(^-2)^4$

58. $(^-2)^5$

59. $(^-1)^2$

60. $(^-1)^3$

61. $(^-1)^4$

62. $(^-1)^5$

63. $(^-1)^6$

64. $(^-1)^7$

65. $(^-10)^{25}$

66. $(^-10)^{30}$

67. $(^-10)^{100}$

68. $(^-10)^{217}$

69. $(^+10)^{12}$

70. $(^-10)^{15}$

71. $(^+10)^{20}$

72. $(^+10)^{100}$

LEFT AND RIGHT DISTRIBUTIVE PROPERTIES

In mathematics, some statements are *taken for granted* and other statements are *derived* from them. Those statements which are taken for granted are called *axioms,* or *assumptions.* The derived, or proved, statements are called *theorems.*

To *prove* a statement means to start with something known or assumed to be true, and through a series of logically related steps, to arrive at a new statement. In a proof, it is important that every step is supported by an axiom or a previously proved theorem.

We have already agreed that for all directed real numbers, the Left-Distributive Property of Multiplication over Addition holds. That is,

$$x(y + z) = (xy) + (xz)$$

Also, multiplication of directed numbers is commutative.

$$xy = yx$$

It also seems logical that the Right-Distributive Property holds. We shall see that if we accept the two statements above as axioms, then we can actually *prove* the Right-Distributive Property as a theorem. That is, we can prove that

$$(x + y)z = (xz) + (yz)$$

Proof
$$
\begin{aligned}
(x + y)z &= z(x + y) &&\text{[by Comm. prop. mult.]} \\
&= (zx) + (zy) &&\text{[by Left-dist. prop.]} \\
&= (xz) + (yz) &&\text{[by Comm. prop. mult. used twice]}
\end{aligned}
$$

Therefore, $(x + y)z = (xz) + (yz)$, and we have *proved* the Right-Distributive Property of Multiplication over Addition.

1. We have seen that the Left-Distributive Property of Multiplication over Subtraction holds for directed numbers. State this property.

2. What properties tell us that the following statements are true?

   a. $(y - z)x = x(y - z)$ **c.** $(xy) - (xz) = (yx) - (zx)$

   b. $xy = yx$

3. Prove the Right-Distributive Property of Multiplication over Subtraction. Use the Left-Distributive Property of Multiplication over Subtraction and the Commutative Property of Multiplication as axioms. [HINT: Refer to exercises 1 and 2.]

Use the appropriate distributive property to compute each answer in the simplest possible way.

4. $(^+237 \times {}^-17) + (^-237 \times {}^-17)$ **7.** $(^-225 \times {}^-7) + (^+125 \times {}^-7)$

5. $(^-83 \times {}^+12) + (^-17 \times {}^+12)$ **8.** $(^-136 \times {}^+12) - (^-136 \times {}^+22)$

6. $(^-25 \times {}^+13) - (^-25 \times {}^+3)$ **9.** $(^+37 \times {}^+42) - (^+37 \times {}^+32)$

DIVISION OF DIRECTED NUMBERS

From studying whole numbers, we can observe a relation between the operations of multiplication and division. Observe the pattern in the examples below and replace the missing parts.

1. $6 \div 3 = 2$; $2 \times 3 = 6$ **4.** $20 \div 4 = 5$; $5 \times \square = \triangle$

2. $10 \div 2 = 5$; $5 \times 2 = 10$ **5.** $12 \div 3 = 4$; $\square \times \triangle = \bigcirc$

3. $14 \div 7 = 2$; $2 \times \square = 14$ **6.** $27 \div 9 = \square$; $\square \times \triangle = \bigcirc$

Exercises **1-6** suggest the following pattern.

■   If $a \div b = c$, then $c \times b = a$.

We shall assume that the same relation holds for directed numbers.

For each statement, give the related multiplication statement and find the answer.

Example $^+10 \div {}^+2 = \square$

$\square \times {}^+2 = {}^+10$; what number multiplied by $^+2$ is $^+10$?
Answer: $^+5$; $^+5 \times {}^+2 = {}^+10$
Therefore, $^+10 \div {}^+2 = {}^+5$.

7. $^+15 \div {}^+3 = \square$ **10.** $^+50 \div {}^+5 = \square$

8. $^+26 \div {}^+13 = \square$ **11.** $^+100 \div {}^+40 = \square$

9. $^+32 \div {}^+8 = \square$ **12.** $^+25 \div {}^+2 = \square$

Complete the following statement.

When a positive number is divided by a positive number,
        the quotient is a _____ number.

Example $^+12 \div {}^-3 = \square$

$\square \times {}^-3 = {}^+12$; what number multiplied by $^-3$ is $^+12$?
Answer: $^-4$; $^-4 \times {}^-3 = {}^+12$.
Therefore, $^+12 \div {}^-3 = {}^-4$.

13. $^+6 \div ^-2 = \square$

16. $^+16 \div ^-4 = \square$

14. $^+21 \div ^-7 = \square$

17. $^+30 \div ^-6 = \square$

15. $^+10 \div ^-5 = \square$

18. $^+40 \div ^-8 = \square$

Complete the following statement.

When a positive number is divided by a negative number, the quotient is a _____ number.

Example $^-18 \div ^+2 = \square$

$\square \times ^+2 = ^-18$; what number multiplied by $^+2$ is $^-18$?
Answer: $^-9$; $^-9 \times ^+2 = ^-18$.
Therefore, $^-18 \div ^+2 = ^-9$.

19. $^-22 \div ^+2 = \square$

22. $^-64 \div ^+4 = \square$

20. $^-56 \div ^+7 = \square$

23. $^-100 \div ^+10 = \square$

21. $^-16 \div ^+16 = \square$

24. $^-52 \div ^+4 = \square$

Complete the following statement.

When a negative number is divided by a positive number, the quotient is a _____ number.

Example $^-20 \div ^-4 = \square$

$\square \times ^-4 = ^-20$; what number multiplied by $^-4$ is $^-20$?
Answer: $^+5$; $^+5 \times ^-4 = ^-20$.
Therefore, $^-20 \div ^-4 = ^+5$.

25. $^-42 \div ^-6 = \square$

28. $^-112 \div ^-112 = \square$

26. $^-96 \div ^-16 = \square$

29. $^-20 \div ^-5 = \square$

27. $^-81 \div ^-9 = \square$

30. $^-51 \div ^-3 = \square$

Complete the following statement.

When a negative number is divided by a negative number, the quotient is a _____ number.

Write down the answers as quickly as you can.

31. $^+18 \div ^+2$

35. $^-6 \div ^-2$

39. $^+300 \div ^+150$

32. $^-84 \div ^-2$

36. $^+12 \div ^-36$

40. $^+3.7 \div ^-3.7$

33. $^+122 \div ^-2$

37. $^-20 \div ^-80$

41. $^-0.048 \div ^-0.048$

34. $^-200 \div ^-5$

38. $^+500 \div ^-100$

42. $^-16.8 \div ^+8.4$

RECIPROCALS AND DIVISION

Find the product of each pair of numbers.

1. $^+2$, $\dfrac{^+1}{2}$

4. $^+1.5$, $\dfrac{^+2}{3}$

7. $\dfrac{^-3}{5}$, $^-1\dfrac{2}{3}$

2. $\dfrac{^+1}{5}$, $^+5$

5. $^+1$, $^+1$

8. $^-1$, $^-1$

3. $\dfrac{^+3}{4}$, $\dfrac{^+4}{3}$

6. $\dfrac{^-1}{8}$, $^-8$

9. $^-.625$, $^-1.6$

The pairs of numbers in exercises **1–9** are called *reciprocals*.

■ Two numbers are *reciprocals* if their product is $^+1$.

Give the reciprocal of each number.

Example $\dfrac{^-4}{5}$ The reciprocal of $\dfrac{^-4}{5}$ is $\dfrac{^-5}{4}$, because $\dfrac{^-4}{5} \times \dfrac{^-5}{4} = {}^+1$.

10. $^+7$

13. $\dfrac{^+1}{5}$

16. $^-.1$

19. $^+3.1$

22. $^-.01$

11. $^-8$

14. $\dfrac{^-3}{4}$

17. $^+.2$

20. $^-3\dfrac{1}{2}$

23. $^+1$

12. $^+20$

15. $\dfrac{^-7}{3}$

18. $^-1.2$

21. $^+4\dfrac{1}{3}$

24. $^-1$

Complete each statement.

25. The reciprocal of a positive number is a _____ number.

26. The reciprocal of a negative number is a _____ number.

27. If the reciprocal of x is y, then the reciprocal of y is _____.

28. The only two numbers which are their own reciprocals are _____ and _____.

Note that we have not yet considered the number 0.

29. What number, if any, multiplied by 0 is $^+1$?

30. From your answer to exercise **29**, tell whether or not the reciprocal of 0 exists.

31. Do you think that there is another number, besides 0, which does not have a reciprocal?

DIVIDING BY MULTIPLYING

Let us observe something interesting:

$$^+10 \div {}^+2 = {}^+5 \qquad {}^-18 \div {}^+3 = {}^-6 \qquad {}^-20 \div {}^-5 = {}^+4$$

$$^+10 \times \frac{^+1}{2} = {}^+5 \qquad {}^-18 \times \frac{^+1}{3} = {}^-6 \qquad {}^-20 \times \frac{^-1}{5} = {}^+4$$

Compare each pair of problems above. Note that in the first pair, dividing by $^+2$ gives the same result as multiplying by $\frac{^+1}{2}$. Also note that $^+2$ and $\frac{^+1}{2}$ are reciprocals. Are the results similar in the other two pairs of problems?

■ Dividing by a number gives the same result as multiplying by its reciprocal.

Change each division problem to the related multiplication problem, as in the example, and find the answers.

Example $^-42 \div {}^+2$ $^-42 \div {}^+2 = {}^-42 \times \frac{^+1}{2} = {}^-21$

1. $^-5 \div {}^+5$

2. $^+20 \div {}^-4$

3. $^-12 \div {}^-3$

4. $^-52 \div {}^-2$

5. $^+7 \div \frac{^+1}{7}$

6. $\frac{^+2}{3} \div {}^+5$

7. $\frac{^-4}{7} \div {}^+4$

8. $\frac{^+1}{2} \div \frac{^-1}{3}$

9. $\frac{^-7}{8} \div \frac{^-9}{5}$

10. $^+3\frac{1}{2} \div {}^-5\frac{1}{6}$

11. $^-77 \div {}^-11$

12. $^+120 \div {}^-40$

13. $^+99 \div {}^-9$

14. $^-500 \div {}^-25$

15. $^-6 \div \frac{^+1}{7}$

16. $\frac{^-1}{5} \div {}^+6$

17. $\frac{^-9}{10} \div {}^-10$

18. $\frac{^-2}{7} \div \frac{^+4}{3}$

19. $\frac{^-1}{3} \div \frac{^+1}{3}$

20. $^-3\frac{3}{4} \div {}^-1\frac{1}{2}$

21. $^+600 \div {}^+15$

22. $^-160 \div {}^+40$

23. $^-121 \div {}^+11$

24. $^-450 \div {}^+30$

25. $^-4 \div \frac{^-1}{8}$

26. $\frac{^-3}{4} \div {}^-5$

27. $\frac{^-3}{5} \div {}^+6$

28. $\frac{^+3}{4} \div \frac{^+5}{6}$

29. $\frac{^-1}{2} \div \frac{^-1}{2}$

30. $^+6\frac{1}{2} \div {}^-3\frac{1}{3}$

Complete each statement.

31. The reciprocal of x is ____ , because $x \times$ ____ $= {}^+1$. $[x \neq 0]$

32. If $a \div b = c$, then $a \times \dfrac{1}{b} =$ ____ . $[b \neq 0]$

By just looking at each problem, tell whether the answer is positive or negative. Do not compute the answers.

33. $\dfrac{{}^-13}{47} \div {}^+131$

36. ${}^-1.05 \div {}^-3.78$

39. $\dfrac{{}^-1}{12} \div \dfrac{{}^-13}{47}$

34. ${}^+107 \div {}^-1,146$

37. ${}^+1,138 \div {}^-645$

40. $\dfrac{{}^+5}{17} \div \dfrac{{}^+3}{18}$

35. ${}^-1.07 \div {}^-3.68$

38. $\dfrac{{}^-11}{12} \div \dfrac{{}^+13}{67}$

41. $\dfrac{{}^+1}{13} \div \dfrac{{}^-1}{27}$

PATTERNS IN DIVISION

Find the answers to each pair of problems. Remember to do the operations within the parentheses first.

1. $({}^+4 + {}^-6) \div {}^-2$; $({}^+4 \div {}^-2) + ({}^-6 \div {}^-2)$

2. $({}^-12 + {}^-15) \div {}^+3$; $({}^-12 \div {}^+3) + ({}^-15 \div {}^+3)$

3. $({}^+16 + {}^-12) \div {}^-4$; $({}^+16 \div {}^-4) + ({}^-12 \div {}^-4)$

4. $({}^-1 + {}^-1) \div {}^+1$; $({}^-1 \div {}^+1) + ({}^-1 \div {}^+1)$

5. $({}^-12 + {}^-18) \div {}^-6$; $({}^-12 \div {}^-6) + ({}^-18 \div {}^-6)$

6. $({}^+5 + {}^-5) \div {}^-5$; $({}^+5 \div {}^-5) + ({}^-5 \div {}^-5)$

7. a. Using the letters a, b, and c, state the pattern suggested by the examples in exercises **1-6**.

  b. What name would you give to this pattern?

In exercise **1** you found that

$$({}^+4 + {}^-6) \div {}^-2 = ({}^+4 \div {}^-2) + ({}^-6 \div {}^-2)$$

This may also be written as

$$\frac{{}^+4 + {}^-6}{{}^-2} = \frac{{}^+4}{{}^-2} + \frac{{}^-6}{{}^-2}$$

Let's check to verify that the statement above is true.

$$\frac{^+4+{}^-6}{^-2}=\frac{^-2}{^-2}={}^+1 \qquad \frac{^+4}{^-2}+\frac{^-6}{^-2}={}^-2+{}^+3={}^+1$$

Thus, it is true that

$$\frac{^+4+{}^-6}{^-2}=\frac{^+4}{^-2}+\frac{^-6}{^-2}$$

8. Rewrite each problem in exercises **2–6** using bars instead of division signs. Then find the answers.

9. Using a, b, and c, state the pattern suggested by the examples in exercise **8**.

Find the answers to each pair of problems.

10. $(^-3-{}^+3)\div{}^+3; \quad (^-3\div{}^+3)-({}^+3\div{}^+3)$

11. $(^-15-{}^-45)\div{}^-5; \quad (^-15\div{}^-5)-({}^-45\div{}^-5)$

12. $(^+64-{}^+50)\div{}^-2; \quad (^+64\div{}^-2)-({}^+50\div{}^-2)$

13. $(^-100-{}^-40)\div{}^+10; \quad (^-100\div{}^+10)-({}^-40\div{}^+10)$

14. $(^-2-{}^-3)\div{}^-1; \quad (^-2\div{}^-1)-({}^-3\div{}^-1)$

15. $(^-200-{}^+100)\div{}^-20; \quad (^-200\div{}^-20)-({}^+100\div{}^-20)$

16. **a.** Using a, b, and c, state the pattern suggested by the examples in exercises **10–15**.

    b. What name would you give to this pattern?

17. **a.** Find the answer to $^-10\div(^-2-{}^+3)$.

    b. Find the answer to $(^-10\div{}^-2)-(^-10\div{}^+3)$.

    c. Are the answers to parts **a** and **b** different?

    d. Can you conclude that the statement

    $$a\div(b-c)=(a\div b)-(a\div c)$$

    is not true for some replacements of a, b, and c?

18. Give one example illustrating that this sentence is not true for some replacements of a, b, and c.

$$\frac{a}{b-c}=\frac{a}{b}-\frac{a}{c}$$

19. Give one example illustrating that this sentence is not true for some replacements of *a*, *b*, and *c*.

$$a \div (b + c) = (a \div b) + (a \div c)$$

20. Give one example illustrating that this sentence is not true for some replacements of *a*, *b*, and *c*.

$$\frac{a}{b + c} = \frac{a}{b} + \frac{a}{c}$$

21. Which are true and which are false?

a. $\dfrac{^+2 + {}^+3}{^+5} = \dfrac{^+2}{^+5} + \dfrac{^+3}{^+5}$ **d.** $\dfrac{^+5}{^-6 + {}^-7} = \dfrac{^+5}{^-6} + \dfrac{^+5}{^-7}$

b. $\dfrac{^+4 - {}^+1}{^+7} = \dfrac{^+4}{^+7} - \dfrac{^+1}{^+7}$ **e.** $(^-4 + {}^-9) \div {}^+2 = (^-4 \div {}^+2) + (^-9 \div {}^+2)$

c. $\dfrac{^+3}{^+5 - {}^+2} = \dfrac{^+3}{^+5} - \dfrac{^+3}{^+2}$ **f.** $(^-9 - {}^+3) \div {}^-3 = (^-9 \div {}^-3) - (^+3 \div {}^-3)$

KEEPING ARITHMETICALLY FIT

For exercises **1–36**, numerals in parentheses refer to the pages where you can find similar exercises.

Add. (444–445)

1. $^+34 + {}^-82$ **4.** $\dfrac{^+3}{5} + \dfrac{^+17}{5}$ **7.** $^+10\frac{1}{2} + {}^-20\frac{1}{2}$

2. $^+44 + {}^-13$ **5.** $\dfrac{^+1}{3} + \dfrac{^+4}{7}$ **8.** $^-3\frac{1}{3} + {}^+27\frac{2}{3}$

3. $^-27 + {}^-55$ **6.** $\dfrac{^-2}{5} + \dfrac{^-4}{10}$ **9.** $^-5\frac{1}{7} + {}^-10\frac{6}{7}$

Subtract. (445–446)

10. $^-13 - {}^+36$ **13.** $^+21 - {}^+69$ **16.** $\dfrac{^+1}{3} - \dfrac{^+10}{3}$

11. $^-26 - {}^+18$ **14.** $^+133 - {}^+35$ **17.** $\dfrac{^-2}{7} - \dfrac{^-12}{7}$

12. $^-14 - {}^-29$ **15.** $\dfrac{^+4}{7} - \dfrac{^+9}{7}$ **18.** $^+3\frac{1}{6} - {}^-5\frac{5}{6}$

Multiply. (447)

19. $^-6 \times {}^-12$

20. $^-13 \times {}^+10$

21. $^+12 \times {}^-5$

22. $\dfrac{^-3}{7} \times \dfrac{^+4}{3}$

23. $\dfrac{^+6}{7} \times \dfrac{^+3}{2}$

24. $\dfrac{^-4}{5} \times \dfrac{^-2}{7}$

25. $^-3\dfrac{1}{3} \times {}^+9$

26. $^+10 \times {}^+5\dfrac{1}{2}$

27. $^-4\dfrac{1}{7} \times {}^-70$

Divide. (448)

28. $^-70 \div {}^-10$

29. $^+120 \div {}^-40$

30. $^-66 \div {}^+11$

31. $\dfrac{^+2}{3} \div \dfrac{^+5}{7}$

32. $\dfrac{^-3}{4} \div \dfrac{^+3}{11}$

33. $\dfrac{^+1}{12} \div \dfrac{^-11}{4}$

34. $\dfrac{^-3}{7} \div {}^-6$

35. $\dfrac{^+3}{2} \div {}^-5$

36. $^+3\dfrac{1}{2} \div {}^+4\dfrac{1}{3}$

Compute the answers.

37. $\left(\dfrac{^-3}{4} \div \dfrac{^+3}{4} \right) + \left(\dfrac{^-1}{2} \div \dfrac{^+1}{2} \right)$

38. $(^+1.6 - {}^-1.4) \times (^-2.5 + {}^-7.5)$

39. $^-5\dfrac{1}{2} \div \left(\dfrac{^-1}{2} + \dfrac{^+3}{2} \right)$

40. $\left(^-5\dfrac{1}{2} \div \dfrac{^-1}{2} \right) + \left(^-5\dfrac{1}{2} \div \dfrac{^+3}{2} \right)$

Replace each ☐ to obtain a true statement.

41. $☐ + {}^-7 = {}^+1$

42. $^-13 \times ☐ = {}^-6\dfrac{1}{2}$

43. $☐ - {}^-8 = {}^+9$

44. $^+11 \div ☐ = {}^-121$

Give decimal names for the following:

45. 15%   **47.** 2%   **49.** 0.04%   **51.** 960%   **53.** 5,000%

46. 125%   **48.** $12\dfrac{1}{2}\%$ **50.** 0.013%   **52.** $\dfrac{1}{2}\%$ **54.** $\dfrac{1}{8}\%$

Replace each *n* to obtain a true statement.

55. 22% of 250 = *n*

56. 140% of 240 = *n*

57. *n*% of 75 = 15

58. *n*% of 150 = 60

59. 30% of *n* = 16

60. 500% of *n* = 55

Add.

61. 20 yds. 2 ft.
17 yds. 1 ft.

62. 15 mi. 1276 yds.
33 mi. 934 yds.

63. 39° 49'
15° 35'

64. 10 min. 42 sec.
36 min. 55 sec.

65. 42° 15' 55"
31° 52' 17"

66. 2 gal. 3 qt. 1 pt.
5 gal. 3 qt. 1 pt.

Subtract.

67. 30 yds. 1 ft.
21 yds. 2 ft.

68. 17 mi. 500 yds.
3 mi. 1500 yds.

69. 25° 16'
10° 25'

70. 35 min. 17 sec.
32 min. 45 sec.

71. 35° 45' 30"
14° 52' 45"

72. 5 gal. 2 qt. 1 pt.
2 gal. 3 qt. 1 pt.

Give the answers.

73. 5^2

74. 11^2

75. 20^2

76. $\left(\dfrac{1}{3}\right)^2$

77. $\left(\dfrac{1}{6}\right)^2$

78. $\left(\dfrac{2}{3}\right)^2$

79. $(.1)^2$

80. $(.01)^2$

81. $(.5)^2$

82. $(.02)^2$

83. $(.03)^2$

84. $(.001)^2$

85. If a number between 0 and 1 is squared, is the result smaller or larger than the original number?

For each ratio, give an equal ratio of two whole numbers.

86. $.1:.01$

87. $\dfrac{1}{2}:\dfrac{1}{3}$

88. $4.5:18.0$

89. $\dfrac{1}{3}:\dfrac{1}{2}$

90. $1.5:3.0$

91. $\dfrac{2}{5}:\dfrac{1}{3}$

92. $.001:.01$

93. $\dfrac{3}{7}:\dfrac{4}{9}$

Replace each x to obtain a true statement.

94. $\dfrac{x}{5}=\dfrac{20}{100}$

95. $\dfrac{5}{7}=\dfrac{x}{24.5}$

96. $\dfrac{48}{16}=\dfrac{16}{x}$

97. $\dfrac{3}{x}=\dfrac{10}{7}$

98. $\dfrac{12}{42}=\dfrac{3}{x}$

99. $\dfrac{x}{8}=\dfrac{1.4}{1.4}$

100. $\dfrac{x}{1.5}=\dfrac{.1}{15}$

101. $\dfrac{.5}{.7}=\dfrac{15}{x}$

102. $\dfrac{7.1}{x}=\dfrac{71}{10}$

VOCABULARY REVIEW

assumption (229)   reciprocal (232)
axiom (229)   Right-Distributive Property (229)
Left-Distributive Property (227)   theorem (229)

A CHALLENGE TO YOU

1. Replace each □ to obtain a true statement.

   a. $^-2 \times □ + {}^+1 = {}^+11$

   b. $^+3 - {}^+2 \div □ = {}^+5$

   c. $□ \times □ = {}^+16$

   d. $□ \times □ \times □ = \dfrac{^-1}{64}$

   e. $□ \times □ \times □ = {}^-1$

   f. $□ \times □ + □ = 0$

   g. $□ = □ \times □$

   h. $\dfrac{□}{^-2} = \dfrac{□}{^-1}$

2. Two cars 30 miles apart start toward each other traveling at 30 mph. At the time the cars are set in motion, a bee flies off one of the cars flying at 60 mph., meets the oncoming car and then continues to fly from one car to the other until the cars meet. How many miles did the bee cover?

3. Replace each letter by a numeral so that a correct addition problem will result. In each example the same letters should be replaced by the same numerals, different letters by different numerals.

SEND	AHAHA	HOCUS	MERRY	FORTY
+MORE	+ TEHE	+ POCUS	+ XMAS	TEN
MONEY	TEHAW	PRESTO	TOALL	+ TEN
				SIXTY

4. Write a ten-digit numeral so that the first digit on the left tells how many 0's there are in the entire numeral, the second digit how many 1's, the third digit how many 2's, etc.

5. For the experiment of tossing a coin twice, we say that the *sample space* is the following set: $\{HH, HT, TH, TT\}$.

   a. Give the sample space for the experiment of tossing a coin three times. How many elements does it have?

   b. What is the probability of each of the outcomes in this experiment?

   c. What is the sum of all of the probabilities in part **b**?

CHAPTER TEST

Tell whether each answer is a positive or a negative number. Do not compute the answers.

1. $^-367 \times {}^+105$

5. $^-2,685 \div \dfrac{{}^+3}{15}$

2. $^+1,206 \times \dfrac{^-1}{3}$

6. $^+35 \div {}^-3,907$

3. $^+3,685 \times {}^+107$

7. $^-2,365 \div \dfrac{^-4}{5}$

4. $\dfrac{^-5}{21} \times {}^-8231$

8. $^+2 \div {}^+198$

Give the reciprocal of each of the following numbers.

9. $^+3$ **10.** $^-8$ **11.** $\dfrac{^-1}{4}$ **12.** $^-.4$ **13.** $^+1.5$ **14.** $\dfrac{^-9}{11}$

Multiply.

15. $^-4 \times {}^+16$

19. $\dfrac{^-2}{3} \times \dfrac{^+3}{7}$

23. $^-1.2 \times {}^+5$

16. $^+22 \times {}^-5$

20. $\dfrac{^+4}{3} \times \dfrac{^-7}{2}$

24. $^-4 \times {}^-2.5$

17. $^-11 \times {}^-5$

21. $\dfrac{^-7}{4} \times \dfrac{^-10}{3}$

25. $^+2.6 \times {}^-6$

18. $^+10 \times {}^+17$

22. $\dfrac{^+2}{7} \times \dfrac{^+9}{4}$

26. $^+1.1 \times {}^+1.1$

Divide.

27. $^-26 \div {}^+2$

31. $\dfrac{^-2}{3} \div {}^+2$

35. $\dfrac{^-1}{2} \div \dfrac{^-5}{7}$

28. $^+112 \div {}^-2$

32. $\dfrac{^+4}{7} \div {}^-4$

36. $\dfrac{^+1}{9} \div \dfrac{^-3}{4}$

29. $^-64 \div {}^-8$

33. $\dfrac{^-2}{3} \div {}^-6$

37. $\dfrac{^-2}{7} \div \dfrac{^+3}{2}$

30. $^+63 \div {}^+3$

34. $\dfrac{^+4}{5} \div {}^+10$

38. $\dfrac{^+3}{4} \div \dfrac{^+1}{11}$

39. A number is multiplied by ⁻6. The result is ⁺3. What is the number?

40. A number is divided by $\frac{+1}{2}$. The result is ⁻20. What is the number?

41. Is the set of rational numbers closed under division? (Exclude division by 0.) Why or why not?

42. Give an example showing that division does not have the commutative property.

43. The example $(^{+}6 + {}^{-}5) - {}^{-}5 = {}^{+}6$ suggests that subtraction is the inverse of addition: it undoes what addition does. Give an analogous example showing that division is the inverse of multiplication.

44. Without computing, tell whether the answer is ⁻1 or ⁺1.

    a. $(^{-}1)^2$ **c.** $(^{-}1)^4$ **e.** $(^{-}1)^6$ **g.** $(^{-}1)^8$

    b. $(^{-}1)^3$ **d.** $(^{-}1)^5$ **f.** $(^{-}1)^7$ **h.** $(^{-}1)^9$

CHAPTER NINE

Variables in Equations and Inequalities

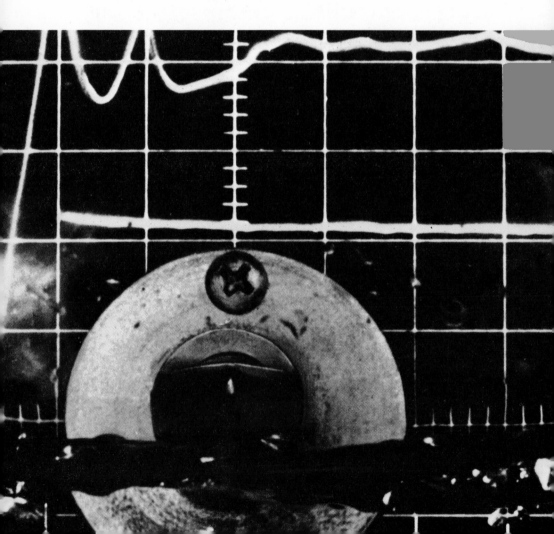

TRUE STATEMENTS

In Chapter 2 we made the following statement.

$$a + b = b + a$$

This was an abbreviation for the statement:

■ For all numbers a and b, $a + b = b + a$.

This is a short way of saying that for all replacements of a and of b by numerals, the resulting statements are true.

In each problem, replace x by 2, y by 4, and z by 5; then carry out the computations to see that the resulting statements are true.

Example $(x + y) + \dfrac{1}{z} = x + \left(y + \dfrac{1}{z}\right)$

How to Solve   We make the required replacements.

$$(2 + 4) + \frac{1}{5} = 2 + \left(4 + \frac{1}{5}\right)$$

$$6 + \frac{1}{5} = 2 + 4\frac{1}{5}$$

$$6\frac{1}{5} = 6\frac{1}{5}$$

Since the last statement, $6\frac{1}{5} = 6\frac{1}{5}$, is true, it follows that

$(2 + 4) + \dfrac{1}{5} = 2 + \left(4 + \dfrac{1}{5}\right)$ is also true.

1. $x + y = y + x$

6. $\dfrac{\frac{1}{x}}{y} = \dfrac{y}{x}$

2. $x \cdot y = y \cdot x$

7. $x \div y = x \cdot \dfrac{1}{y}$

3. $x \cdot \dfrac{1}{y} = \dfrac{x}{y}$

8. $x + (-x) = 0$
   [Read "$-x$" as "the opposite of x."]

4. $x \cdot (y \cdot z) = (x \cdot y) \cdot z$

9. $x \cdot \dfrac{1}{x} = 1$

5. $x \cdot (y + z) = (x \cdot y) + (x \cdot z)$

10. $(-x) + (-y) = -(x + y)$

We will assume that these ten sentences are true for all real number replacements.

OPPOSITES

In exercise **8** on page 243, we agreed that "$-x$" should be read as "the opposite of x." Thus, the symbol "$-$" is an abbreviation for "the opposite of."

"$-^+5$" means "the opposite of $^+5$" which is $^-5$.

$$-^+5 = {}^-5$$

"$-^-2$" means "the opposite of $^-2$" which is $^+2$.

$$-^-2 = {}^+2$$

■   The opposite of a positive number is a negative number. The opposite of a negative number is a positive number. The opposite of 0 is 0.

To simplify writing, we will no longer use "$+$" for positive numbers. For example, when we write "2," it will mean "$^+2$" (positive two). Thus, whenever a numeral is not preceded by a "$+$" or a "$-$," we will know that it names a positive number.

$$3 \text{ means } {}^+3 \qquad \frac{1}{2} \text{ means } {}^+\frac{1}{2} \qquad \sqrt{2} \text{ means } {}^+\sqrt{2}$$

Give the opposite of each of the following numbers.

1. 6   **3.** $\frac{1}{2}$ **5.** $\sqrt{5}$ **7.** 35

2. $^-10$ **4.** $^-30$ **6.** $^-\sqrt{10}$ **8.** $\frac{^-10}{13}$

Now we can write "-5" instead of "$-^+5$." This means "the opposite of positive five," which is the same as negative 5, or $^-5$.

$$-5 = {}^-5$$

The opposite of 5 and *negative 5* name the same number.

From now on we shall write -5 instead of $^-5$.

Write each of the following as the simplest possible numeral.

9. the opposite of ten

10. the opposite of negative seven

11. the opposite of one-half

12. the opposite of the opposite of six

13. the opposite of the opposite of negative twelve

14. the opposite of the opposite of the opposite of nine

15. the opposite of the opposite of the opposite of negative one

Compute the answers.

16. $9 + (-3)$ **22.** $-10 - (-3)$ **28.** $24 \div (-6)$

17. $10 + (-7)$ **23.** $20 \times (-4)$ **29.** $-100 \div 2$

18. $-12 + 5$ **24.** $-5 \times (-12)$ **30.** $-25 \div (-5)$

19. $-26 + (-10)$ **25.** -11×7 **31.** $-2 \div .1$

20. $16 - (-5)$ **26.** $-12 \times (-12)$ **32.** $-3 \div .01$

21. $26 - (-35)$ **27.** -100×4 **33.** $-.6 \div (-.6)$

NUMERICAL VARIABLES

You have already had experience in answering such questions as: To what number must 3 be added to obtain -5? You probably can answer without too much effort that this number is -8. To convince yourself that you are right you would check: $-8 + 3 = -5$.

The question above is frequently written in an abbreviated form.

$$x + 3 = 5$$

Instead of the letter x another letter can be used:

$$a + 3 = -5 \qquad m + 3 = -5 \qquad y + 3 = -5$$

Or even some other symbol may be used instead of a letter.

$$\triangle + 3 = -5 \qquad \square + 3 = -5 \qquad \bigcirc + 3 = -5$$

The important thing to know is that these symbols or letters may be replaced by numerals.

■ Letters or symbols like $\triangle$, $\square$, and $\bigcirc$ used to take the place of numerals are called *numerical variables*, or simply *variables*.

AGREEMENT   If not otherwise stated, we will agree that names for *real numbers* may be used as replacements for x, a, m, y, n, $\triangle$, $\square$, $\bigcirc$, and so on.

Sentences like those shown below are called *equations*.

$$x + 3 = -5 \qquad n - 6 = 3 \qquad 4 - \triangle = -1 \qquad \square + (-4) = 1$$

Find one replacement for each variable to obtain a true statement.

1. $x + 5 = 7$

2. $a - 3 = 5$

3. $1 + m = 10$

4. $3 - y = -2$

5. $5 - n = -15$

6. $s + (-3) = 12$

7. $\frac{1}{2} + p = 1$

8. $\square + \frac{3}{4} = \frac{1}{2}$

9. $\triangle - 4 = -4$

10. $5 \cdot x = 20$

11. $y \cdot 7 = 3\frac{1}{2}$

12. $-2 \cdot m = 5$

13. $-30 = -4 \cdot t$

14. $0 = -5 \cdot \square$

15. $16 \div n = -8$

16. $-3 = \triangle \div (-2)$

17. $2.1 \div \bigcirc = 1.05$

18. $100 \div \square = -200$

ENGLISH AND MATHEMATICAL SENTENCES

English sentences can be translated into mathematical sentences. Study each example.

Example 1   English sentence: 3 is added to some number. The sum is -10.
Mathematical sentence: $x + 3 = -10$
(We are free to choose any letter for "some number.")

Example 2   English sentence: Some number is added to -4. The sum is 8.
Mathematical sentence: $-4 + y = 8$

Example 3   English sentence: -1 is subtracted from some number. The difference is 5.
Mathematical sentence: $n - (-1) = 5$

Example 4   English sentence: Some number is subtracted from -5. The difference is 6.
Mathematical sentence: $-5 - m = 6$

Example 5   English sentence: Some number is multiplied by -3. The product is 10.
Mathematical sentence: $t \cdot (-3) = 10$

Example 6 English sentence: 7 is multiplied by some number. The product is −4.
Mathematical sentence: $7 \cdot n = -4$

Example 7 English sentence: Some number is divided by 10. The quotient is −2.
Mathematical sentence: $m \div 10 = -2$, or $\frac{m}{10} = -2$

Example 8 English sentence: 3 is divided by some number. The quotient is 12.
Mathematical sentence: $3 \div s = 12$, or $\frac{3}{s} = 12$

Translate each English sentence into a mathematical sentence. Use any letters you wish as variables.

1. Some number is added to −1. The sum is 0.

2. Some number is added to 15. The sum is −4.

3. 4 is divided by some number. The result is −2.

4. Some number is multiplied by −4. The result is 15.

5. −2 is multiplied by some number. The result is −2.

6. Some number is subtracted from 4. The result is 0.

7. −5 is subtracted from some number. The result is −1.

8. Some number is multiplied by −7. The result is −1.

9. Some number is divided by 2. The result is $\frac{1}{2}$.

10. −5 is divided by some number. The result is 9.

Sometimes we need to translate mathematical sentences into English sentences. Study each example.

Example 1 Mathematical sentence: $y + 3 = -3$
English sentence: 3 is added to some number. The sum is −3.

Example 2 Mathematical sentence: $n - 7 = -6$
English sentence: 7 is subtracted from some number. The difference is −6.

Example 3   Mathematical sentence: $-2 \cdot p = 9$
English sentence: -2 is multiplied by some number. The product is 9.

Example 4   Mathematical sentence: $n \div (-1) = 3$
English sentence: Some number is divided by -1. The quotient is 3.

Translate each mathematical sentence into an English sentence.

1. $3 + a = -2$

2. $n \div (-5) = -7$

3. $\dfrac{-4}{m} = 6$

4. $t - 16 = -1$

5. $\triangle \cdot (-10) = 100$

6. $-1.1 \div u = -2$

7. $\dfrac{y}{-5} = -15$

8. $x + (-3) = -6$

9. $s \cdot 6 = -1$

10. $10 - \square = -4$

11. $\bigcirc + 6 = -10$

12. $7 \div v = -12$

The sentence $2 + x = -6$ can be translated into English as follows: "Some number is added to 2. The sum is -6." You may ask, "Is this number 4?" To answer this question, do the following:

$$2 + x = -6$$

4 in place of x: $\qquad 2 + 4 = -6$

Now you must answer the question:

Is $2 + 4 = -6$ a true statement?

The answer is "no," because $6 \neq -6$.
We try -8 in place of x.

$$2 + (-8) = -6$$

This statement is true. Thus, the number we are seeking is -8.

Replace each variable to obtain a true statement.

13. $x + 6 = 1$

14. $7 + y = 9$

15. $9 + m = -3$

16. $\dfrac{1}{2} + z = \dfrac{1}{4}$

17. $t - 1 = 3\dfrac{1}{2}$

18. $1.6 - c = 1.2$

19. $3 - v = 7$

20. $\dfrac{1}{2} - u = \dfrac{1}{6}$

21. $a - \dfrac{2}{5} = \dfrac{4}{5}$

22. $\dfrac{1}{2} \cdot s = -2$

23. $1.5 \times t = -15$

24. $p \cdot (-3) = 1.5$

25. $m \div 6 = -12$

26. $\dfrac{n}{-3} = \dfrac{1}{2}$

27. $\dfrac{1}{2} \div g = -\dfrac{1}{4}$

PHRASES

Each of the following is a mathematical *sentence*.

$$x + 3 = -10 \qquad t \cdot (-3) = 10 \qquad n \div 10 = -2 \qquad -5 - m = 6$$

A mathematical sentence expresses a complete thought. It can be translated into an English sentence. The sentence, $x + 3 = -10$, translated into English is:

> When 3 is added to some number, the result is -10.

This is a complete thought.

A phrase is different from a sentence. Here is an example of an English phrase.

> 3 more than twice some number

Translated into a mathematical phrase, it is:

$$2 \cdot n + 3$$

Translate each English phrase into a mathematical phrase. Use any letters you wish.

Example 1   3 less than 4 times some number
$$4 \cdot a - 3$$

Example 2   5 more than one-third of a number
$$\frac{1}{3} \cdot x + 5$$

Example 3   the sum of two numbers divided by -2
$$\frac{a + b}{-2}$$

Example 4 -5 divided by the difference of two numbers
$$-5 \div (x - y)$$

1. three times some number

2. 5 less than some number

3. -2 more than twice some number

4. $\frac{1}{2}$ of some number, decreased by 7

5. 3 times some number, divided by -2

6. the sum of some number and 5, divided by 3

7. the product of -1 and some number, divided by -4

8. one-fifth of the sum of two numbers

9. the product of the difference of two numbers and -10

10. the sum of two numbers divided by the difference of these numbers

11. one-third of some number, decreased by 3

12. the sum of twice some number and -2, multiplied by 5 times the number

Translate each mathematical phrase into an English phrase.

Example 1 $\dfrac{a+b}{-4}$ the sum of two numbers divided by -4

Example 2 $(2a+c) \times 9$ the sum of twice some number and another number, multiplied by 9

13. $4 \cdot x$

14. $2n - 6$

15. $-2 \cdot m + m$

16. $3 \cdot y + \dfrac{1}{2}$

17. $3 \cdot (m + 7)$

18. $(3 \cdot n + 9) \div (-10)$

19. $(a + b)(2a - b)$

20. $\dfrac{2m + n}{5}$

21. $\dfrac{x + y + z}{-8}$

Write the mathematical phrase for each of the following:

22. the number of inches in c feet

23. the number of feet in a inches

24. the number of nickels in m dimes

25. the number of feet in t miles

26. the number of hours in u minutes

27. the number of dollars in k cents

Recall that "$5x$" means "$5 \cdot x$."

28. What does "$17y$" mean?

29. What does "xyz" mean?

30. Explain why "$3 \cdot 5$" cannot be abbreviated as "35."

SOLVING EQUATIONS

To *solve* an equation means to find a replacement for the variable which will result in a true statement.

The *solution* of the equation

$$n + 3 = -5$$

is the number -8, because

$$-8 + 3 = -5$$

is a true statement. The solution set of the equation is the set $\{-8\}$.

We can solve equations by asking ourselves certain questions.

Example 1   Solve the equation $n + 8 = -6$.

We ask: "To what number must 8 be added to obtain -6?"
Answer: -14
Since $-14 + 8 = -6$ is a true statement, -14 is the solution of $n + 8 = -6$. Thus, the solution set is $\{-14\}$.

Example 2   Solve $5x - 2 = -12$.

We cover up $5x$ like this

$$\boxed{5x}\ - 2 = -12$$

and ask: What number minus 2 is equal to -12?
Answer: -10
Therefore, $5x = -10$. Now we cover up the x

$$5\ \boxed{x}\ = -10$$

and ask: 5 multiplied by what number is equal to -10?
Answer: -2

Now we replace x by -2 in the original equation to see if the result is a true statement.

Check

$5x - 2$	-12
$5(-2) - 2$	-12
$-10 - 2$	
-12	

Since each side of the equation is -12, we know that -2 is the correct solution. Thus, $\{-2\}$ is the solution set of the equation $5x - 2 = -12$.

Find solution sets by asking yourself appropriate questions. You may find it helpful to use the "cover-up" method.

1. $2n + 3 = 5$

2. $3y - 2 = 7$

3. $5t + 3 = 4$

4. $4n + 5 = 1$

5. $1 + 4u = -3$

6. $4 - 2s = 8$

7. $1 - 6z = 0$

8. $5 - 2k = 5$

9. $2 = 1 + 10c$

10. $0 = 3 - 3a$

11. $1 = 3 - x$

12. $9 = 7 - \dfrac{1}{2}n$

Example 3   Solve $8 - \dfrac{y + 3}{2} = 7$.

$$8 - \boxed{\dfrac{y + 3}{2}} = 7$$

Consider $\dfrac{y + 3}{2}$ to be some number.

Question: What number subtracted from 8 is equal to 7?

Answer: 1; therefore, $\boxed{\dfrac{y + 3}{2}} = 1$.

Question: What number divided by 2 is equal to 1?

Answer: 2; therefore, $\boxed{y} + 3 = 2$

Question: What number plus 3 is equal to 2?

Answer: -1; therefore, $y = -1$.

Check

$8 - \dfrac{y + 3}{2}$	7
$8 - \dfrac{-1 + 3}{2}$	7
$8 - \dfrac{2}{2}$	
$8 - 1$	
7	

Therefore, the solution set of $8 - \dfrac{y + 3}{2} = 7$ is $\{-1\}$.

Find solution sets by asking yourself appropriate questions. Use the "cover-up" method whenever you find it helpful.

13. $\frac{1}{2}a + 2 = 0$

14. $5 - 10n = 0$

15. $2 - \frac{3}{4}c = 1$

16. $6 = 20x + 5$

17. $1 = 3y - 1$

18. $\frac{1}{3}m - \frac{1}{6} = 0$

19. $\frac{1}{2} = \frac{1}{4} - s$

20. $3t - 1.5 = 0$

21. $4u + 3 = 15$

22. $\frac{d}{4} - \frac{1}{2} = 0$

23. $\frac{z}{3} - \frac{1}{3} = \frac{1}{3}$

24. $5 - \frac{n}{5} = 4$

25. $\frac{p}{3} + \frac{1}{3} = 0$

26. $\frac{m + 1}{2} + 3 = 5$

27. $\frac{r - 4}{5} + 1 = 0$

28. $9 - \frac{a + 1}{2} = 8$

29. $\frac{5}{x} + \frac{1}{2} = 1$

30. $\frac{4}{y} - \frac{1}{2} = 0$

ABSOLUTE VALUE

Every directed real number has an absolute value. Recall that the symbol "$|x|$" means "the absolute value of x."

$$|-5| = 5 \quad \text{Read: The absolute value of } -5 \text{ is } 5.$$
$$|5| = 5 \quad \text{Read: The absolute value of } 5 \text{ is } 5.$$
$$|0| = 0 \quad \text{Read: The absolute value of } 0 \text{ is } 0.$$

Read aloud each of the following:

1. $|-6| = 6$

2. $|6| = 6$

3. $\left|-\frac{1}{2}\right| = \frac{1}{2}$

4. $\left|\frac{1}{2}\right| = \frac{1}{2}$

5. $|0| = 0$

6. $|-2.6| = 2.6$

7. $|2.6| = 2.6$

8. $\left|-\frac{3}{7}\right| = \frac{3}{7}$

9. $\left|\frac{3}{7}\right| = \frac{3}{7}$

■ The absolute value of a positive number is a positive number.
The absolute value of a negative number is a positive number.
The absolute value of 0 is 0.

The equation $|x| = 3$ has two solutions, 3 and -3, because $|3| = 3$ and $|-3| = 3$ are both true. The solution set of $|x| = 3$ is $\{3, -3\}$.

What is the solution set of $2 \cdot |n| = 8$? Let us ask ourselves some questions.

Example $2 \cdot \boxed{|n|} = 8$

Question: 2 multiplied by what number is equal to 8?
Answer: 4, because $2 \cdot 4 = 8$.

Thus, $| \boxed{n} | = 4$

Question: The absolute value of what number is equal to 4?
Answer: There are two such numbers, 4 and -4. Thus,

$$n = 4 \text{ or } n = -4$$

Check

$2 \cdot |n|$	8
$2 \cdot |4|$	8
$2 \cdot 4$	
8	

$2 \cdot |n|$	8
$2 \cdot |-4|$	8
$2 \cdot 4$	
8	

Thus, $\{4, -4\}$ is the solution set of $2 \cdot |n| = 8$.

Find the solution sets.

10. $|m| = 6$

11. $3 \cdot |x| = 3$

12. $-2 \cdot |u| = -10$

13. $\frac{1}{2} \cdot |n| = 2\frac{1}{2}$

14. $|a| + 2 = 3$

15. $-4 + |c| = 8$

16. $5 + |y| = 5$

17. $4 \cdot |z| - 12 = -8$

18. $1.5 \times |s| - 1.5 = 0$

19. $\frac{1}{2} \cdot |t| - 5 = 0$

20. $16 \cdot |v| - 16 = 0$

21. $\frac{1}{3} \cdot |p| - 3 = -3$

Example   Find the solution set of $|x| = -5$.

Think: The absolute value of some number is -5. But the absolute value of any number is either a positive number or 0. Therefore, no number has the absolute value -5. Therefore, the solution set of $|x| = -5$ is the empty set.

■   If no number is a solution of an equation, then the solution set of the equation is ϕ (the empty set).

GRAPHS OF SOLUTION SETS

On the picture of a number line below, the solution set of the equation $2x + 2 = 0$ is marked. The solution set of $2x + 2 = 0$ is $\{-1\}$ because $2 \cdot (-1) + 2 = 0$ is a true statement.

The solution set of $|m| = 1\frac{1}{2}$ is $\left\{1\frac{1}{2}, -1\frac{1}{2}\right\}$ because $\left|1\frac{1}{2}\right| = 1\frac{1}{2}$ and $\left|-1\frac{1}{2}\right| = 1\frac{1}{2}$ are true statements.

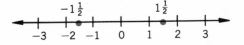

The solution set of $|t| = -4$ is ϕ. No number has the absolute value of -4.

The solution set of $2 - |u| = 2$ is $\{0\}$ because $2 - |0| = 2$ is a true statement. [NOTE: The graph of $\{0\}$ consists of one point; the graph of ϕ consists of no points.]

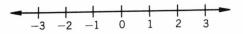

On a picture of a number line, graph the solution set of each equation.

1. $3x - 3 = -2$

2. $4a + 1 = -3$

3. $\dfrac{n}{2} = \dfrac{1}{2}$

4. $3 \cdot |c| = 3$

5. $|m| - 6 = -5$

6. $-7 + |n| = -7$

7. $-1 + 2 \cdot |y| = 0$

8. $\dfrac{|t|}{-2} = -2$

9. $\dfrac{10}{|s|} = 2.5$

10. $\dfrac{4}{|b|} + 1 = 5$

COMPARING NUMBERS

In the table below, we show different mathematical symbols which have the same meaning.

Symbol	Read	Equivalent Symbol	Read
$5 > 3$	5 is greater than 3	$5 \nleq 3$	5 is not less than and is not equal to 3
$3 < 5$	3 is less than 5	$3 \ngeq 5$	3 is not greater than and is not equal to 5
$5 \geq 3$	5 is greater than or equal to 3	$5 \nless 3$	5 is not less than 3
$3 \leq 5$	3 is less than or equal to 5	$3 \ngtr 5$	3 is not greater than 5
$3 \neq 5$	3 is not equal to 5	$3 > 5$ or $3 < 5$	3 is greater than 5 or 3 is less than 5

Note that the symbols in the left-hand column are probably easier to understand than the equivalent symbols. You may want to use the table when doing the exercises below. Any symbol used may be replaced by its equivalent symbol.

Which are true and which are false?

1. $-6 \neq -1 - 5$

2. $-7 < -2$

3. $|-1| \nless 0$

4. $-1 \ngtr 2$

5. $|1 - 4| \ngtr 3$

6. $5 \leq 10$

7. $-1 \ngeq 1$

8. $0 \geq 0$

9. $5 \leq |5 - 10|$

10. $-4 \nless -5$

11. $0 \leq |-3 + 3|$

12. $|4 - 6| \ngtr 0$

13. $3 - 1 \nless 1 - 3$

14. $|3 - 1| \neq |1 - 3|$

15. $|-1 - 6| = |6 - (-1)|$

16. $|-3 - 5| \neq |5 - (-3)|$

17. $|2 - (-7)| = |-7 - 2|$

18. $|2 \times (-3)| \neq |-2 \times (-3)|$

19. $|-2 \times (-3)| = |2 \times 3|$

20. $|0 \times (-6)| \neq |0 \times (-42)|$

UNIVERSAL SETS AND GRAPHS

What does $\{x|x > 1\}$ mean? [Read: the set of all numbers x, such that x is greater than 1] Here is the graph of this set.

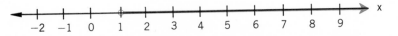

The part in color shows the points which belong to the solution set. Of course, the complete graph cannot be marked; it continues indefinitely to the right. A circle around the point corresponding to 1 indicates that this point does not belong to the set.

Here is the graph of $\{x|x \geq 1\}$.

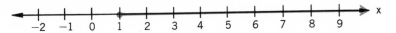

The solid dot at 1 indicates that the point corresponding to 1 also belongs to the set.

The graphs you obtain depend upon the replacement set for x.

■ The *replacement set* for a variable is the set of all numbers whose names may be used in place of the variable. The replacement set is also called the *universal set*, or simply the *universe*.

In the two graphs shown above, the replacement set is the set of *real* numbers.

Now suppose the replacement set is the set of *natural* numbers. Then the number "line" becomes a series of isolated points.

The points continue indefinitely to the right. For this universal set, the two graphs shown above would look like this:

Points which belong to the solution set are marked like this △.

In the universe of real numbers, graph each of the following sets. (Use a separate number line for each graph.)

1. $\{n|n > 3\}$ 3. $\{y|y < 0\}$ 5. $\{s|s < -1\}$ 7. $\{p|p > -3.5\}$

2. $\{m|m \geq 3\}$ 4. $\{t|t \leq 0\}$ 6. $\{a|a \leq -1\}$ 8. $\{r|r \geq -3.5\}$

GRAPHS IN THE UNIVERSE OF INTEGERS

Suppose the universal set is the set of integers. Below we show the graph of $\{s \mid s < -1\}$.

Here is the graph of $\{s \mid s \leq -1\}$.

Which point belongs to the graph of $\{s \mid s \leq -1\}$, but does not belong to the graph of $\{s \mid s < -1\}$?

1–8. Using the universal set of integers, graph each set given in exercises **1–8** on page 257.

Here is the graph of $\left\{n \mid n \geq -1\frac{1}{2}\right\}$ in the universe of integers.

9. Graph $\left\{n \mid n \geq -1\frac{3}{4}\right\}$ in the universe of integers.

10. Are the graphs of $\left\{n \mid n \geq -1\frac{1}{2}\right\}$ and $\left\{n \mid n \geq -1\frac{3}{4}\right\}$ the same?

11. Without graphing, tell whether each of the following graphs is the same as the graph of $\left\{n \mid n \geq -1\frac{1}{2}\right\}$ in the universe of integers.

a. $\{n \mid n \geq -1.9\}$ **e.** $\{n \mid n \geq -1.1\}$

b. $\{n \mid n \geq -1.6\}$ **f.** $\{n \mid n \geq -1.00000001\}$

c. $\{n \mid n \geq -1.4\}$ **g.** $\{n \mid n \geq -1\}$

d. $\{n \mid n \geq -1.3\}$ **h.** $\{n \mid n \geq -2\}$

Graph each of the following in the universe of integers.

12. $\left\{x \mid x \geq 1\frac{1}{2}\right\}$ **15.** $\{m \mid m \geq .99\}$ **18.** $\left\{s \mid s \leq -3\frac{1}{4}\right\}$

13. $\{y \mid y \geq 2.99\}$ **16.** $\{u \mid u \geq -2.1\}$ **19.** $\{t \mid t \geq -2.5\}$

14. $\{n \mid n \leq .87\}$ **17.** $\{u \mid u \leq -2.005\}$ **20.** $\{w \mid w \leq -2.99\}$

Observe how we can graph the following sets in the universe of integers without performing the addition.

Example 1 $\{x \mid x \geq 1.56 + 1.42\}$

Since $.56 + .42$ is less than 1, $1.56 + 1.42$ is less than 3; therefore, the smallest number in the solution set is 3.

Example 2 $\left\{ y \mid y \geq 2\frac{1}{2} + 1\frac{3}{4} \right\}$

Since $\frac{1}{2} + \frac{3}{4}$ is more than 1 but less than 2, $2\frac{1}{2} + 1\frac{3}{4}$ is more than 4 but less than 5; therefore, the smallest number in the solution set is 5.

Graph in the universe of integers.

21. $\left\{ a \mid a \geq 1\frac{1}{2} + \frac{1}{3} \right\}$

22. $\left\{ c \mid c \geq 1\frac{1}{4} + \frac{3}{5} \right\}$

23. $\{k \mid k \geq 1.205 + .713\}$

24. $\{p \mid p \geq 1.99 + .002\}$

25. $\{r \mid r \geq 1.5 + .5\}$

26. $\{t \mid t \geq 1.46 + .54\}$

27. $\{v \mid v \geq 1.5 + .51\}$

28. $\{w \mid w \geq 1.5 + 1.4\}$

GREATEST INTEGER

Study the following examples. The first example, $\left[1\frac{1}{2} \right] = 1$, is read "the greatest integer not greater than $1\frac{1}{2}$ is 1."

$$\left[1\frac{1}{2} \right] = 1 \qquad \left[\frac{1}{3} \right] = 0 \qquad [7] = 7$$

$$\left[1\frac{3}{4} \right] = 1 \qquad \left[\frac{24}{7} \right] = 3 \qquad \left[\frac{6}{3} \right] = 2$$

$$[3.0001] = 3 \qquad [.01] = 0 \qquad [7.9999] = 7$$

$$[4.99] = 4 \qquad [2.001] = 2 \qquad [6] = 6$$

Write out in words how you would read each of the following:

1. $\left[1\frac{3}{4}\right] = 1$ **2.** $[4.99] = 4$ **3.** $[.01] = 0$ **4.** $[7.9999] = 7$

Give integers which are the correct answers to the following:

5. $\left[10\frac{1}{3}\right]$ **9.** $[.99]$ **13.** $[.000001]$

6. $[21.8]$ **10.** $\left[\frac{20}{3}\right]$ **14.** $[3.999999]$

7. $\left[\frac{12}{3}\right]$ **11.** $\left[\frac{100}{9}\right]$ **15.** $\left[\frac{1,000}{999}\right]$

8. $\left[\frac{1}{4}\right]$ **12.** $\left[\frac{35}{7}\right]$ **16.** $\left[\frac{9,999}{10,000}\right]$

Which are true and which are false?

17. $\left[1\frac{1}{2}\right] = \left[1\frac{1}{10}\right]$ **20.** $[.99] = [1.01]$ **23.** $\left[\frac{1}{2} + \frac{1}{2}\right] = \left[\frac{1}{4} + \frac{3}{4}\right]$

18. $[3.99] = [3.01]$ **21.** $[2.5 + 2.1] = [2 + 2]$ **24.** $\left[\frac{1}{4} + \frac{1}{4}\right] = \left[\frac{1}{3} + \frac{1}{3}\right]$

19. $[2.99] = [3]$ **22.** $[.9 + .9] = [.5 + .6]$ **25.** $[.7 + .2] = [.7 + .3]$

Note that bracketed numerals like those above can be used to tell age. For example, if a person's age is 12 years 8 months, it is given as 12 years; $\left[12\frac{8}{12}\right] = 12$. Give the age indicated by each of the following:

26. $\left[7\frac{1}{12}\right]$ **27.** $\left[14\frac{11}{12}\right]$ **28.** $\left[9\frac{7}{12}\right]$ **29.** $\left[1\frac{9}{12}\right]$

Uses of Bracketed Numerals

What is the maximum number of tens we can subtract from 43? We can find the answer by doing something like this:

$$43 - 10 = 33 \quad (1 \text{ ten})$$
$$33 - 10 = 23 \quad (2 \text{ tens})$$
$$23 - 10 = 13 \quad (3 \text{ tens})$$
$$13 - 10 = 3 \quad (4 \text{ tens})$$

There are 4 tens in 43.

.But we can take a short-cut and say

$$43 \div 10 = 4, \text{ remainder } 3$$

Instead of subtracting 10 at a time, we divided by 10. The quotient told us how many times 10 can be subtracted from 43.

We can use our bracketed notation to answer the question, "How many tens in 43?"

$$\left[\frac{43}{10}\right] = 4, \text{ so there are 4 tens in 43.}$$

Using bracketed notation, answer the following questions.

1. How many tens in 98?

2. How many tens in 71?

3. How many hundreds in 195?

4. How many hundreds in 801?

5. How many hundreds in 799?

6. How many thousands in 2,001?

7. How many thousands in 7,999?

8. How many thousands in 5,555?

Consider the following:

$$\left[\frac{1}{2}+\frac{1}{2}\right] = [1] = 1 \qquad \left[\frac{1}{2}\right] + \left[\frac{1}{2}\right] = 0 + 0 = 0$$

Therefore,

$$\left[\frac{1}{2}+\frac{1}{2}\right] \neq \left[\frac{1}{2}\right] + \left[\frac{1}{2}\right]$$

Which are true and which are false?

9. $[.4 + .4] = [.4] + [.4]$

10. $\left[\frac{3}{4}+\frac{3}{4}\right] = \left[\frac{3}{4}\right] + \left[\frac{3}{4}\right]$

11. $\left[1\frac{1}{3}+1\frac{2}{3}\right] = \left[1\frac{1}{3}\right] + \left[1\frac{2}{3}\right]$

12. $[1.56 + 2.43] = [1.56] + [2.43]$

13. $\left[\frac{1}{2}+3\frac{3}{4}\right] = \left[\frac{1}{2}\right] + \left[3\frac{3}{4}\right]$

14. $\left[2\frac{1}{2}+3\frac{1}{3}\right] = \left[2\frac{1}{2}\right] + \left[3\frac{1}{3}\right]$

Bracketed numerals may be used in estimation problems.

Example   How many 10-gallon units can be obtained from two tanks, one containing 37 gal. of fuel oil and the other 45 gal.?

How to Solve $\left[\dfrac{37+45}{10}\right] = 8.$ Thus, 8 units can be obtained.

Note that it is not necessary to add 37 and 45. You are interested only in the number of tens. There are 3 tens in 37, 4 tens in 45, and 1 ten in 7 + 5.

15. A rod of length 12.7 ft. is welded to a rod of length 15.2 ft. How many 2 ft. long pieces can be obtained by cutting the entire rod?

16. Mary has 25¢, and Jane has 10¢. How many candy bars at 6¢ each can they buy by pooling their money?

17. How many 3 ft. logs can be obtained from two logs, one 112 ft. long and the other 80 ft. long? $\left[\text{HINT: } \left[\frac{112}{3}\right] + \left[\frac{80}{3}\right]\right]$

Which are true and which are false?

18. $[1.8 + 1.3] \geq [1.8] + [1.3]$　　**21.** $\left[\frac{1}{4} + \frac{1}{5}\right] < \left[\frac{1}{4}\right] + \left[\frac{1}{5}\right]$

19. $[2.1 + 3.8] \geq [2.1] + [3.8]$　　**22.** $[.9 + .9] \geq [.9] + [.9]$

20. $\left[\frac{1}{2} + \frac{3}{4}\right] < \left[\frac{1}{2}\right] + \left[\frac{3}{4}\right]$　　**23.** $[.01 + .02] \geq [.01] + [.02]$

24. On the basis of the results in exercises **18–23** do you suspect that the generalization $[x + y] \geq [x] + [y]$ is true for all non-negative numbers? Test your answer on some more specific cases.

GRAPHS OF INEQUALITIES

Let us consider the set of whole numbers

$$W = \{0, 1, 2, 3, 4, 5, 6, 7, 8, \ldots\}$$

as the universal set. Here is the graph of W.

Suppose we want to graph the set $A = \{x \mid 0 < x \text{ and } x < 5\}$. First, let us identify the members of the set A, keeping in mind that the universal set is W. Every member which belongs to A must be a whole number greater than 0 *and* less than 5. Then $A = \{1, 2, 3, 4\}$.

$0 < x$ and $x < 5$ can also be written as

$$0 < x < 5$$

and is read: "0 is less than x and x is less than 5." Here is a graph of $A = \{x \mid 0 < x < 5\} = \{1, 2, 3, 4\}$.

Example 1 Graph $\{m \mid m \le 5 \text{ or } m \le 7\}$ in the set of whole numbers.
This set is the *union* of two sets.
$\{m \le 5\}$ includes the numbers 0, 1, 2, 3, 4, 5.
$\{m \le 7\}$ includes the numbers 0, 1, 2, 3, 4, 5, 6, 7.
$\{m \le 5\}$ *or* $m \le 7$ includes all numbers in the union:

$$\{0, 1, 2, 3, 4, 5\} \cup \{0, 1, 2, 3, 4, 5, 6, 7\}$$

which is $\{0, 1, 2, 3, 4, 5, 6, 7\}$

Example 2 Graph $\{n \mid 5 < n \le 10\}$ in the set of whole numbers.
This set is the *intersection* of two sets.
$\{5 < n\}$ includes the numbers 6, 7, 8, 9, 10, ...
                                            (marked ○)

$\{n \le 10\}$ includes the numbers
          0, 1, 2, 3, 4, 5, 6, 7, 8, 9, 10.   (marked □)
$\{5 < n \le 10\}$ includes all numbers in the intersection:

$\{6, 7, 8, 9, 10, 11, 12, . . .\}$ ∩
                    $\{0, 1, 2, 3, 4, 5, 6, 7, 8, 9, 10\}$
which is $\{6, 7, 8, 9, 10\}$ (marked ⊡)

Graph each of the following inequalities using the set of whole numbers as the universal set.

1. $\{a \mid a \ge 4\}$

2. $\{b \mid b > 4\}$

3. $\{c \mid c \le 10\}$

4. $\{d \mid d < 10\}$

5. $\{e \mid e \ge 4 \text{ and } e \le 10\}$

6. $\{f \mid f > 4 \text{ and } f \le 10\}$

7. $\{g \mid g \ge 4 \text{ and } g < 10\}$

8. $\{h \mid h > 4 \text{ and } h < 10\}$

9. $\{i \mid 4 < i < 6\}$

10. $\{j \mid 4 < j < 5\}$

11. $\{k \mid 0 \le k < 1\}$

12. $\{l \mid l > 4 \text{ or } l > 2\}$

13. $\{m \mid m > 4 \text{ or } m \ge 2\}$

14. $\{n \mid n \ge 4 \text{ or } n > 2\}$

15. $\{p \mid p \ge 4 \text{ or } p \ge 2\}$

16. $\{q \mid q < 0 \text{ or } q < -5\}$

17. $\{r \mid r > 5 \text{ or } r < 5\}$

18. $\{s \mid s \ge 5 \text{ or } s \le 5\}$

Which are true and which are false? The universe is the set of whole numbers.

19. $\{t \mid t < 5 \text{ and } t < 0\} = \{t \mid t \leq 4 \text{ and } t \geq 1\}$

20. $\{u \mid u \geq 6 \text{ and } u < 6\} = $ the set of all whole numbers

21. $\{v \mid v < 0 \text{ and } v > 5\} = \phi$

22. $\{w \mid w > 1 \text{ and } w > 2\} = \{w \mid w > 1\}$

23. $\{x \mid x < 5 \text{ or } x > 7\} = $ the set of all whole numbers

24. $\{y \mid 0 < y < 3\} = \{y \mid 0 \leq y \leq 3\}$

25. $\{z \mid 5 < z < 1\} = \phi$

PATTERNS IN INEQUALITIES

The exercises below will help you to discover a new pattern.

For each inequality, there is given a number for you to use. Add that number to each member of the inequality to obtain a second inequality.

Example $-4 > -7; 3$ $-4 + 3 > -7 + 3$ $[-1 > -4]$

1. $5 > 2; 3$

2. $3 > 1; 15$

3. $-2 > -3; 5$

4. $-4 > -5; 4$

5. $7 > 6; -3$

6. $-1 > -5; -2$

The exercises above suggest the following:

■   *Addition Property for* >
     If $a > b$, then $a + c > b + c$.

The property above states that we can add the same number to each member of an inequality without changing the relation.

For each inequality, there is given a positive number for you to use. Multiply each member of the given inequality by that number to obtain a new inequality.

Example $-1 > -6; 4$ $-1 \times 4 > -6 \times 4$ $[-4 > -24]$

7. $3 > 1; 4$

8. $4 > -2; 5$

9. $1 > 0; 6$

10. $-1 > -5; 10$

11. $2 > -1; 12$

12. $0 > -3; 7$

Exercises **7–12** suggest the following:

■ *Positive Multiplication Property for >*
If $a > b$, then $a \times c > b \times c$. $[c > 0]$

For each inequality, there is given a negative number for you to use. Multiply each member of the given inequality by that number to obtain a new inequality.

Example $1 > -2; -4$ $1 \times (-4) < -2 \times (-4)$ $[-4 < 8]$

13. $4 > 1; -2$

14. $3 > -1; -5$

15. $5 > 0; -1$

16. $-2 > -3; -3$

17. $2 > -2; -7$

18. $0 > -5; -6$

The exercises above suggest the following:

■ *Negative Multiplication Property for >*
If $a > b$, then $a \times c < b \times c$. $[c < 0]$

For each inequality, there is given a number for you to use. Add that number to both members of the inequality to obtain a second inequality.

Example $3 > 1; 7$ $3 + 7 > 1 + 7$ $[10 > 8]$

19. $17 > 10; 13$

20. $-13 > -14; 14$

21. $2 > -7; -5$

22. $0 > -40; -30$

23. $5 > -5; -5$

24. $-.5 > -1; 1$

$15 > 0$ means the same as $0 < 15.$
15 is greater than 0 means the same as 0 is less than 15.

25. In exercises **19–24** change $a > b$ to $b < a$. Add the given number to each member of each inequality to obtain new inequalities.

Example $3 > 1; 7$ $1 < 3; 1 + 7 < 3 + 7$ $[8 < 10]$

For each inequality, there is given a number for you to use. Multiply each member of the inequality by that number to obtain a second inequality.

Example $7 > 2; 12$ $7 \times 12 > 2 \times 12$ $[84 > 24]$

26. $5 > 4; 7$

27. $3 > -1; 10$

28. $0 > -3; 4$

29. $-1 > -5; 3$

30. $-2 > -3; 20$

31. $-.3 > -.9; 100$

32. In exercises **26–31** change $a > b$ to $b < a$. Multiply each member of each inequality by the given number to obtain new inequalities.

Example $7 > 2; 12$ $2 < 7; 2 \times 12 < 7 \times 12$ $[24 < 84]$

For each inequality, there is given a number for you to use. Multiply each member of the inequality by that number to obtain a second inequality.

Example $6 > 4; -4$ $6 \times (-4) < 4 \times (-4)$ $[-24 < -16]$

33. $2 > 1; -5$ **36.** $0 > -\dfrac{1}{2}; -2$

34. $10 > 5; -\dfrac{1}{5}$ **37.** $-1 > -10; -1$

35. $7 > 0; -10$ **38.** $-1.5 > -3.5; -100$

39. In exercises **33–38** change $a > b$ to $b < a$. Multiply each member of each inequality by the given number to obtain new inequalities.

Example $6 > 4; -4$ $4 < 6; 4 \times (-4) > 6 \times (-4)$
$$[-16 > -24]$$

TRANSITIVITY

Supply the missing words in each conclusion below. After completing the conclusions, tell whether you agree with them.

1. Assumption: June is older than Mary and Mary is older than Kate.
   Conclusion: June is _____ than Kate.

2. Assumption: Bob is taller than Hank and Hank is taller than Jim.
   Conclusion: Bob is _____ than Jim.

3. Assumption: The area of North America is larger than the area of Australia and the area of Australia is larger than the area of Europe.
   Conclusion: The area of North America is _____ than the area of Europe.

The relation in exercise **3** above is of the following form.

> If *a is larger than b* and *b is larger than c,*
> then *a is larger than c.*

A relation which falls into this kind of a pattern is said to have the *transitive property*. Thus, the relation *is larger than* has the transitive property.

Now we will examine several relations to see if they are transitive. First consider the relation *is less than* (<).

Example 1   If $3 < 5$ and $5 < 10$, then $3 < 10$.

Example 2   If $0 < 1$ and $1 < 1\frac{1}{2}$, then $0 < 1\frac{1}{2}$.

Example 3   If $-5 < -4$ and $-4 < -3$, then $-5 < -3$.

Examples 1–3 suggest that *is less than* is a transitive relation.

$$\text{If } a < b \text{ and } b < c, \text{ then } a < c.$$

In examples 4–6, we consider the relation *is greater than* (>).

Example 4   If $5 > 4$ and $4 > 1$, then $5 > 1$.

Example 5   If $0 > -\frac{1}{2}$ and $-\frac{1}{2} > -3$, then $0 > -3$.

Example 6   If $-2 > -3$ and $-3 > -4$, then $-2 > -4$.

Thus, *is greater than* is also a transitive relation.

$$\text{If } a > b \text{ and } b > c, \text{ then } a > c.$$

Now consider the relation *is equal to* (=).

Example 7   If $5 = 4 + 1$ and $4 + 1 = 3 + 2$, then $5 = 3 + 2$.

Example 8   If $-7 = 8 + (-15)$ and $8 + (-15) = -1 + (-6)$,
$$\text{then } -7 = -1 + (-6).$$

Example 9   If $17 = 20 - 3$ and $20 - 3 = 21 - 4$, then $17 = 21 - 4$.

Thus, *is equal to* is also a transitive relation.

$$\text{If } a = b \text{ and } b = c, \text{ then } a = c.$$

Is the relation *is not equal to* a transitive relation? If we think that it is not transitive, all we need to do is find one example showing that the following pattern is not true.

$$\text{If } a \neq b \text{ and } b \neq c, \text{ then } a \neq c.$$

Here is such an example.

$$5 \neq 7 \text{ and } 7 \neq 4 + 1$$
$$\text{but}$$
$$5 = 4 + 1$$

So, *is not equal to* is *not* a transitive relation.

Jane is a daughter of mama Mary and mama Mary is a daughter of grandma Kate. Does it follow that Jane is a daughter of grandma Kate? Is *is a daughter of* a transitive relation?

Let *R* be an abbreviation for a relation. Some statements below are of the form *aRb and bRc*. If possible, state the conclusion, *aRc*. Then tell whether the conclusion follows from the given statement.

Example 1   The Pacific Ocean is deeper than the Atlantic Ocean and the Atlantic Ocean is deeper than the Gulf of Mexico.

Conclusion: The Pacific Ocean is deeper than the Gulf of Mexico.

The conclusion follows from the given statement.

Example 2   Yankees beat Dodgers and Dodgers beat Braves.

Conclusion: Yankees beat Braves.

The conclusion does not follow from the given statement. (Yankees might not have even played Braves!)

4. $5 > 0$ and $0 > -1$ **7.** $3 \neq 4$ and $4 \neq -1 + 4$

5. $-2 < 5$ and $5 < 6$ **8.** $4 \not< 3$ and $3 \not< 1$

6. $-2 < 0$ and $0 < 1$ **9.** $7 = 1 + 6$ and $1 + 6 = -7 + 14$

10. The area of New York is smaller than the area of Illinois and the area of Illinois is smaller than the area of California.

11. The Tigers beat the Rattlers and the Rattlers beat the Boilermakers.

12. Gold is harder than bronze and bronze is harder than copper.

13. Tim is taller than Bob and Jerry is taller than Bob.

14. Susan's rank in a math class is higher than that of Mary and Mary's rank is higher than that of Jean.

15. An inch is longer than a centimeter and a centimeter is longer than a millimeter.

16. A mile is longer than a meter and a meter is longer than a centimeter.

17. A meter is shorter than a yard and a yard is shorter than a mile.

18. The population of New York is greater than that of Chicago and the population of Chicago is greater than that of Miami.

KEEPING ARITHMETICALLY FIT

Compute.

1. a. $3 + (-35)$ **b.** $-17 + (-41)$ **c.** $125 + (-26)$

2. a. $-15 + 125$ **b.** $-\frac{1}{2} + \left(-\frac{1}{6}\right)$ **c.** $-\frac{1}{3} + \frac{3}{4}$

3. a. $-.17 + .35$ **b.** $-1.3 + (-3.8)$ **c.** $.2 + (-.9)$

4. a. $1 - (-32)$ **b.** $-3 - 7$ **c.** $-5 - 2$

5. a. $-4 - (-12)$ **b.** $0 - (-125.7)$ **c.** $0 - 153.99$

6. a. $-\frac{3}{2} - \frac{3}{2}$ **b.** $-\frac{7}{15} - 0$ **c.** $0 - \left(-\frac{5}{19}\right)$

7. a. $-5 \times (-16)$ **b.** -4×16 **c.** $17 \times (-11)$

8. a. $-\frac{1}{3} \times \left(-\frac{4}{7}\right)$ **b.** $\frac{5}{6} \times \left(-\frac{7}{8}\right)$ **c.** $\frac{3}{5} \times \frac{4}{9}$

9. a. $-3\frac{1}{2} \times 5\frac{1}{3}$ **b.** $10\frac{1}{3} \times \left(-6\frac{1}{4}\right)$ **c.** $\left(-5\frac{1}{5}\right) \times \left(-3\frac{1}{3}\right)$

10. a. $-30 \div (-60)$ **b.** $-125 \div 25$ **c.** $26 \div (-52)$

11. a. $-390 \div (-13)$ **b.** $2 \div (-.1)$ **c.** $-10 \div (-.01)$

12. a. $-\frac{1}{2} \div 2$ **b.** $\frac{1}{3} \div 3$ **c.** $\frac{1}{5} \div (-5)$

13. a. $-\frac{3}{2} \div \left(-\frac{2}{3}\right)$ **b.** $-\frac{5}{6} \div \left(-\frac{6}{5}\right)$ **c.** $-\frac{7}{8} \div \left(-\frac{8}{7}\right)$

14. a. $3\frac{1}{2} \div 5$ **b.** $-5\frac{1}{3} \div (-7)$ **c.** $5\frac{2}{7} \div (-9)$

15. a. $-5 \div \frac{1}{5}$ **b.** $-7 \div \frac{1}{7}$ **c.** $15 \div \left(-\frac{1}{15}\right)$

16. a. 16% of 34 **b.** 75% of 12 **c.** 125% of 30

17. a. 11% of $5,000$ **b.** 325% of $1,000$ **c.** $\frac{1}{2}\%$ of $10,000$

18. a. 78 is what per cent of 200?   **b.** 15 is 30% of what number?

To each problem **19** through **27** there is only one correct answer. Choose "none of these" only if none of the preceding answers is correct.

19. Which of the following in place of n in $\frac{3}{7}=\frac{10}{n}$ will give a true statement?

    a. $3\frac{1}{3}$ **b.** $23\frac{1}{3}$ **c.** 30   **d.** 70   **e.** none of these

20. Which pair of numbers is in the same ratio as 4 to 5?

    a. 6, 10   **b.** 8, 10   **c.** 10, 8   **d.** 1, 2   **e.** 2, 1

21. $\frac{74}{83}=\frac{444}{498}$ is a true statement, because

    a. $74 \times 444 = 83 \times 498$ **d.** $83 \times 444 = 498 \times 83$

    b. $74 \times 498 = 83 \times 444$ **e.** none of these

    c. $444 \times 498 = 74 \times 83$

22. What is the Greatest Common Factor of 12 and 44?

    a. 1   **b.** 2   **c.** 3   **d.** 4   **e.** none of these

23. What is the Greatest Common Factor of 17 and 31?

    a. 1   **b.** 2   **c.** 3   **d.** 4   **e.** none of these

24. What is the Lowest Common Multiple of 8 and 12?

    a. 12   **b.** 24   **c.** 48   **d.** 96   **e.** none of these

25. What is the Lowest Common Multiple of 7 and 11?

    a. 18   **b.** 22   **c.** 77   **d.** 55   **e.** none of these

26. Which fractional numeral is in simplest form?

    a. $\frac{18}{262}$ **b.** $\frac{21}{93}$ **c.** $\frac{17}{42}$ **d.** $\frac{405}{972}$ **e.** none of these

27. Which numeral does not name the number $\frac{1}{4}$?

    a. $\frac{1}{16} \times 4$ **b.** $\frac{\frac{1}{2}}{2}$ **c.** $\left(\frac{1}{2}\right)^2$ **d.** $\frac{1}{8} \times 2$ **e.** none of these

28. Find replacements for n to obtain true statements.

a. 35% of 160 $= n$ **d.** 110% of $n = 220$

b. 145% of 2,000 $= n$ **e.** $10.8 = n\%$ of 72

c. 60% of $n = 54$ **f.** $360 = n\%$ of 240

29. a. What is the per cent increase from 10 to 11?

b. What is the percent decrease from 11 to 10?

30. For each number give its reciprocal.

a. -1 **b.** 1   **c.** $-\dfrac{2}{5}$ **d.** 1.6   **e.** $-2\dfrac{1}{2}$

VOCABULARY REVIEW

absolute value (‖) (253)
equation (245)
graph of a solution set (255)
greatest integer (259)
inequality (256)
is greater than (>) (256)
is greater than or equal to (≥) (256)
is less than (<) (256)

is less than or equal to (≤) (256)
is not equal to (≠) (256)
mathematical sentence (249)
numerical variable (245)
solution set (251)
transitivity (266)
universal set (257)

A CHALLENGE TO YOU

We defined $[a]$ to mean the greatest integer not greater than a. Compute each of the following:

1. a. $[5.01 \times 6.01]$ **c.** $[-5.01 \times 6.01]$

b. $[5.01] \times [6.01]$ **d.** $[-5.01] \times [6.01]$

2. a. $[1.8 \times 3.9]$ **c.** $[-1.8 \times 3.9]$

b. $[1.8] \times [3.9]$ **d.** $[-1.8] \times [3.9]$

3. a. $[6.1 \times 8.1]$ **c.** $[-6.1 \times (-8.1)]$

b. $[6.1] \times [8.1]$ **d.** $[-6.1] \times [-8.1]$

4. a. $[1.9 \times 3.7]$ **c.** $[-1.9 \times (-3.7)]$

b. $[1.9] \times [3.7]$ **d.** $[-1.9] \times [-3.7]$

5. **a.** Give the sample space for the experiment of rolling a die once. [HINT: One of the outcomes is, for example, 6.]

   b. What is the probability of each outcome when rolling a die once?

6. **a.** If a die is rolled twice, (2, 5) describes the outcome of obtaining 2 on the first roll and 5 on the second. Give the sample space for the experiment of rolling a die twice. [HINT: There are 36 elements.]

   b. What is the probability of each outcome?

CHAPTER TEST

1. Translate each English sentence into a mathematical sentence.

   a. The result of multiplying a number by -7 is 5.

   b. Some number is divided by 3; -4 is added to the quotient; the result is 6.

   c. The result of doubling a number and subtracting -6 from the product is $-\dfrac{1}{2}$.

2. Find the solution sets of the following equations.

   a. $3x + 1 = -2$ **c.** $4|n| = 8$

   b. $1 + m = -6$ **d.** $-2t + 5 = 5$

3. Graph the solution sets of the following on the number line. Use the set of all real numbers as the universal set.

   a. $\{a \mid |a| = 1\}$ **c.** $\{x \mid -2 \le x \le 1\}$

   b. $\{n \mid |n| - 3 = 0\}$ **d.** $\left\{y \mid |y| \ge 2\tfrac{1}{2}\right\}$

4. For each statement, tell whether it is true or false.

   a. $-7 \not< -5$ **d.** $|5 - 7| \ne |7 - 5|$

   b. $1 \ge 1$ **e.** $0 - \dfrac{1}{2} > \dfrac{1}{2} - 0$

   c. $|-3 - 5| = |5 - (-3)|$ **f.** $1 - 8 \not\ge 7$

5. Write out in words the meaning of
$$a + b = b + a$$

6. Tell which of the following are true for all replacements of the variables.

   a. $|x| \geq 0$ **c.** $|a - b| = |b - a|$

   b. $y - y = 0$ **d.** $|-x| \leq 0$

7. Write an equation to fit each problem.

   a. A number is multiplied by 4; 2 is added to the product. The result is 0. What is the number?

   b. Multiplying a number by 3 and adding 1 to the product results in 0. What is the number?

8. What is $|0|$ equal to?

9. What is the meaning of "the solution set of a sentence is ϕ"?

10. What does each of the following symbols mean?

    a. $<$ **c.** $>$ **e.** $=$ **g.** $\not<$ **i.** $\not\leq$

    b. $\leq$ **d.** $\geq$ **f.** $\neq$ **h.** $\not>$ **j.** $\not\geq$

11. Give an example of an equation whose solution set is ϕ, if the universal set is the set of natural numbers, and it has a solution if the universal set is a set of integers.

12. Explain why $[.5 + .6] = [.5] + [.6]$ is false.

13. Give an example of an inequality whose solution set in the universe of natural numbers is ϕ and in the universe of integers the solution set is an infinite set.

14. In each statement the conclusion is underlined. Tell whether this conclusion follows from the preceding assumptions.

    a. If a is harder than b and b is harder than c, then *a is harder than c*.

    b. If $a > b$ and $c > b$, then $a > c$.

    c. If $a \neq b$ and $b \neq c$, then $a \neq c$.

15. Give an example illustrating the transitivity of the relation $>$.

16. Give an example illustrating the transitivity of the relation *is younger than*.

17. Give an example showing that the relation $\neq$ is not transitive.

CHAPTER TEN

Coordinate Geometry

A 5-BY-5 ARRAY

Let us consider an array of 25 dots. It has 5 rows and 5 columns, as marked in the picture.

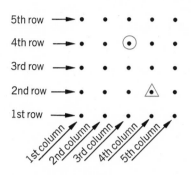

The point marked like this △ is in the 4th column and in the 2nd row. To describe it briefly, we shall use a pair of numbers (4, 2).

(4, 2)
4th column, 2nd row

1. **a.** In what column and in what row is the point described by (3, 4)?

 b. How is this point marked in the array above?

2. In the number pair (5, 2), which number tells the column and which number tells the row?

3. Make a 5-by-5 array of dots like the one above. Mark like this △ the points corresponding to the following:

 a. (1, 5)   **b.** (5, 5)   **c.** (2, 4)   **d.** (4, 3)   **e.** (5, 1)

LOCATING POINTS

In the array at the right, the columns are numbered at the bottom and the rows at the left.

△ corresponds to (4, 2)

1. To what number pair does the point marked like this ○ correspond?

NOTE: △ and ⊙ are two different points. (4, 2) and (2, 4) describe different points.

The *order* of listing numbers is important: (2, 4) is not the same as (4, 2). We call such pairs of numbers *ordered* pairs. Each ordered pair of numbers has a first member and a second member. In (2, 4), 2 is the first member, 4 is the second member.

2. In (4, 2), what is the first member and what is the second?

3. Explain why (1, 5) and (5, 1) are different.

4. Explain why (1 + 2, 4) and (3, 3 + 1) are the same.

Examples 1–4 show conditions which may be placed on the members of ordered pairs. Study these examples carefully.

Example 1   The second member is 2 more than the first member.

All such ordered pairs are $(1, 3), (2, 4), (3, 5)$.

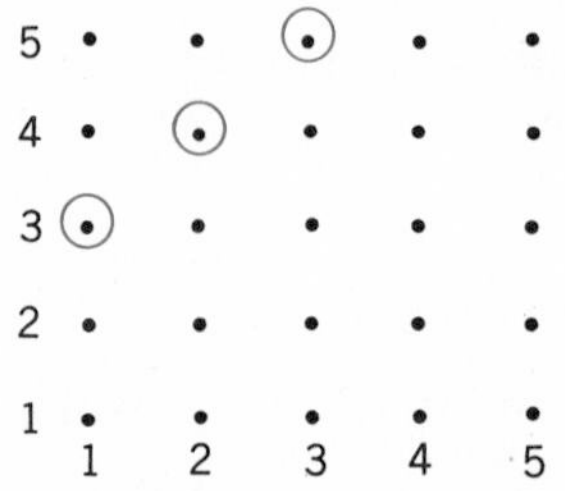

```
5 •   •   ⊙   •   •

4 •   ⊙   •   •   •

3 ⊙   •   •   •   •

2 •   •   •   •   •

1 •   •   •   •   •
  1   2   3   4   5
```

Example 2   The first member is 4. (We shall agree that if the other member is not mentioned, then it can be each of the numbers.)

All ordered pairs in which the first member is 4 are $(4, 1)$, $(4, 2)$, $(4, 3)$, $(4, 4)$, $(4, 5)$.

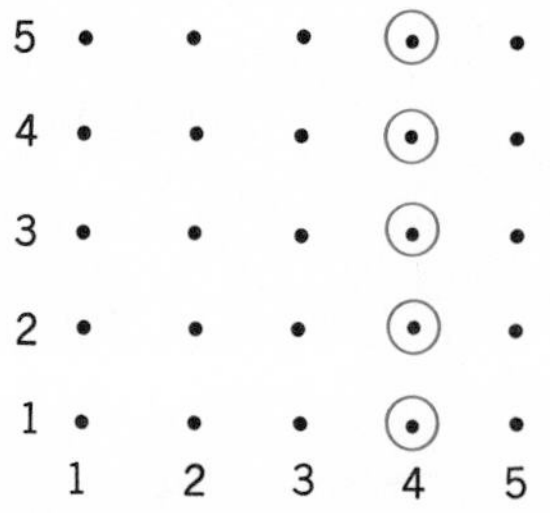

```
5 •   •   •   ⊙   •

4 •   •   •   ⊙   •

3 •   •   •   ⊙   •

2 •   •   •   ⊙   •

1 •   •   •   ⊙   •
  1   2   3   4   5
```

Example 3   The first member is greater than or equal to 2 and the second member is greater than or equal to 4.

All such ordered pairs are $(2, 4)$, $(2, 5)$, $(3, 4)$, $(3, 5)$, $(4, 4)$, $(4, 5)$, $(5, 4)$, $(5, 5)$.

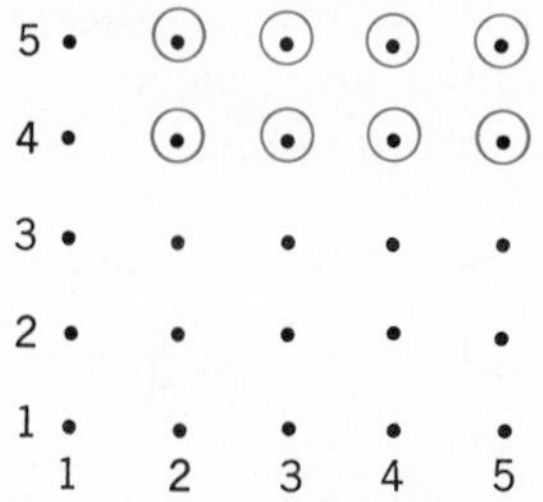

```
5 •   ⊙   ⊙   ⊙   ⊙

4 •   ⊙   ⊙   ⊙   ⊙

3 •   •   •   •   •

2 •   •   •   •   •

1 •   •   •   •   •
  1   2   3   4   5
```

Example 4   The first member is less than 3. (Since the second member is not mentioned, it can be each of the numbers.)

All such ordered pairs are $(2, 1)$, $(2, 2)$, $(2, 3)$, $(2, 4)$, $(2, 5)$, $(1, 1)$, $(1, 2)$, $(1, 3)$, $(1, 4)$, $(1, 5)$.

For exercises **5–28**, list the ordered pairs of a 5-by-5 array which meet each set of conditions. Then mark these points like this ○ on a 5-by-5 array.

 5. The first member is the same as the second member.

 6. The first member is twice the second member.

 7. The second member is twice the first member.

 8. The first member is three times the second member.

 9. The second member is three times the first member.

10. The first member is 1 less than the second member.

11. The first member is 1 more than the second member.

12. The second member is 3 more than the first member.

13. The second member is 4 less than the first member.

14. The first member is 5 less than the second member.

15. The first member is 2.

16. The second member is 2.

17. The first member is 5.

18. The second member is 5.

19. The first member is greater than or equal to 3 and the second member is greater than or equal to 3.

20. The first member is less than 6 and the second is less than 6.

21. The first member is less than 2 and the second is less than 2.

22. The first member is greater than or equal to 5 and the second is greater than or equal to 5.

23. The first member is greater than 5.

24. The second member is greater than 5.

25. The first member is less than or equal to 1.

26. The second member is less than or equal to 1.

27. The first member is greater than 4.

28. The second member is greater than 4.

SQUARE AND RECTANGULAR ARRAYS

An array of points like the 5-by-5 array is called a *finite lattice of points*. A finite lattice can have any finite number of rows and any finite number of columns.

If the number of columns and rows is the same, the lattice is a *square lattice*. If the number of rows is different from the number of columns, the lattice is a *rectangular lattice*.

5-by-5 lattice has	3-by-7 lattice has
5 columns and 5 rows.	3 columns and 7 rows.
It is a square lattice.	It is a rectangular lattice.

An x-by-y lattice has
x columns and y rows.

1. If $x = y$, then what kind of lattice is an x-by-y lattice?

2. If $x \neq y$, then what kind of lattice is an x-by-y lattice?

3. a. Make a picture of a 5-by-6 lattice. How many points does it have?

 b. How many rows are there in this lattice?

 c. How many columns are there in this lattice?

 d. What is an easy way to tell how many points a 5-by-6 lattice has?

For each lattice, tell how many columns, rows, and points it has.

4. 2-by-2   **7.** 10-by-10   **10.** 15-by-7

5. 6-by-1   **8.** 100-by-1   **11.** 7-by-15

6. 3-by-3   **9.** 1-by-100   **12.** 100-by-100

Make a picture of a 10-by-10 lattice of points. On it mark like this $\bigcirc$ the following points.

13. (1, 10)   **14.** (10, 1)   **15.** (5, 5)   **16.** (7, 4)   **17.** (10, 10)

We can use letters, such as x and y, to refer to ordered pairs of numbers. For example, in Example 1 below we shall refer to all points (x, y) such that $x < 3$ and $y > 8$. This means that we wish to locate all points for which the first member (x) is less than 3, and the second member (y) is greater than 8. We will use a 10-by-10 lattice.

Example 1 $x < 3$ and $y > 8$

All ordered pairs which meet these conditions are $(1, 9)$, $(1, 10)$, $(2, 9)$, $(2, 10)$. Do you see that for each of the four points marked on the lattice the first member (x) is less than 3 and the second member (y) is greater than 8?

Example 2 $3x = y$

All ordered pairs which meet the given conditions are $(1, 3)$, $(2, 6)$, $(3, 9)$. Do you see that for each ordered pair the second member (y) is 3 times the first member (x)? Refer to the lattice at the top of the next page.

For exercises **18–29**, list the ordered pairs of a 10-by-10 lattice which meet each set of conditions. Then mark these points like this ○ on a 10-by-10 lattice.

18. $x < 4$ and $y < 2$ **22.** $2y = x$ **26.** $x > y$

19. $x \leq 3$ and $y \leq 1$ **23.** $x \leq y$ **27.** $x \leq 2$

20. $x = y$ **24.** $x < y$ **28.** $y < 3$

21. $2x = y$ **25.** $x \geq y$ **29.** $4x = y$

COORDINATES OF POINTS

Each point of a lattice has an ordered pair of numbers corresponding to it. These numbers are called the *coordinates* of the point.

Point A in the lattice on the right corresponds to the ordered pair $(2, 4)$. 2 is the *first* coordinate and 4 is the *second* coordinate of point A.

The *first* coordinate tells the *column*.
The *second* coordinate tells the *row*.

$(2, 4)$
2nd column, 4th row

1. For each point named by a letter in the lattice on page 280, give the ordered number pair corresponding to it. For point A, the answer is $(2, 4)$.

2. What is true of the first coordinate of points which are in the same column?

3. What is true of the second coordinate of points which are in the same row?

4. What is true of the coordinates of points which are in the diagonal from K to H?

5. Name all pairs of points whose first and second coordinates are reversed.

To indicate the *set* of all points in which the first coordinate is the same as the second coordinate, we write

$$\{(x, y) \mid x = y\}$$

Read: the set of all ordered pairs (x, y) such that $x = y$.

We shall agree that x is the first coordinate, and y is the second coordinate.

Mark the following sets of points on 10-by-10 lattices.

6. $\{(x, y) \mid x = y\}$

7. $\{(x, y) \mid x \leq y\}$

8. $\{(x, y) \mid x \geq y\}$

9. $\{(x, y) \mid x < y\}$

10. $\{(x, y) \mid x > y\}$

11. $\{(x, y) \mid x = 2\}$

12. $\{(x, y) \mid y = 10\}$

13. $\{(x, y) \mid 1 \leq x \leq 3 \text{ and } 1 \leq y \leq 3\}$

14. $\{(x, y) \mid x \leq 5 \text{ and } y \leq 5\}$

15. $\{(x, y) \mid 1 < x < 3 \text{ and } y > 6\}$

GRAPHS OF SETS

By now you have probably noticed that in any lattice, to each ordered pair of numbers chosen from the given universal set, there corresponds exactly one point. Also to each point there corresponds exactly one ordered pair of numbers.

■ There is a one-to-one correspondence between ordered pairs of numbers (x, y) and the points of an x-by-y lattice.

We will now locate points which belong to various sets.

Example 1   On a 10-by-10 lattice, graph the set

$$\{(x, y) \mid 1 \le x \le 3 \text{ and } 7 \le y \le 10\}$$

We first locate the set

$$\{(x, y) \mid 1 \le x \le 3\}$$

The points of this set are marked like this ○ on the lattice. Then we locate the set

$$\{(x, y) \mid 7 \le y \le 10\}$$

The points of this set are marked like this □.

Since we want the set $\{(x, y) \mid 1 \le x \le 3 \text{ and } 7 \le y \le 10\}$, we seek the points which are in *both* sets. That is, we want the *intersection* of the two sets. This is the set of points marked ⊡. How many points are there in this set?

Example 2   On a 10-by-10 lattice, graph the set

$$\{(x, y) \mid x = y \text{ and } x + y = 11\}$$

First, we graph the set

$$\{(x, y) \mid x = y\}$$

The points which belong to this set are marked like this ○. Then we graph the set

$$\{(x, y) \mid x + y = 11\}$$

These points are marked like this □.

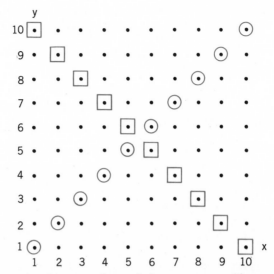

We want the intersection of the two sets. Since no point is marked like this ▣, there are no points which belong to both sets. Therefore, their intersection is the empty set.

$$\{(x, y)\,|\,x = y \text{ and } x + y = 11\} = \phi$$

Example 3   Graph the set $\{(x, y)\,|\,x = 2 \text{ and } y = 10\}$.

The points which belong to the set $\{(x, y)\,|\,x = 2\}$ are marked like this ○. Note that since no restriction is made on y in this set, y may assume all values, 1 through 10. The points which belong to the set $\{(x, y)\,|\,y = 10\}$ are marked like this ▢.

We want the intersection of the two sets. There is one point which belongs to both sets, namely, the point corresponding to (2, 10). Therefore,

$$\{(x, y) \,|\, x = 2 \text{ and } y = 10\} = \{(2, 10)\}$$

Graph each set as in Examples 1-3. Then list the number pairs which belong to the intersection.

1. $\{(x, y) \,|\, 9 \le x \le 10 \text{ and } 1 \le y \le 2\}$

2. $\{(x, y) \,|\, 4 < x < 5 \text{ and } 4 < y < 5\}$

3. $\{(x, y) \,|\, 1 < x \le 2 \text{ and } 1 \le y < 5\}$

4. $\{(x, y) \,|\, 1 \le x \le 5 \text{ and } 2 < y < 3\}$

5. $\{(x, y) \,|\, 1 \le x \le 10 \text{ and } 1 \le y \le 10\}$

6. $\{(x, y) \,|\, x = y \text{ and } y = 3\}$

7. $\{(x, y) \,|\, x = y \text{ and } x = 10\}$

8. $\{(x, y) \,|\, x + y = 11 \text{ and } x = 1\}$

9. $\{(x, y) \,|\, x + y = 11 \text{ and } y = 3\}$

10. $\{(x, y) \,|\, x + y = 4 \text{ and } x = y\}$

11. $\{(x, y) \,|\, x + y = 12 \text{ and } x = y\}$

12. $\{(x, y) \,|\, x + y = 7 \text{ and } x = y\}$

13. $\{(x, y) \,|\, x = 5 \text{ and } y = 5\}$

14. $\{(x, y) \,|\, x - y = 6 \text{ and } x + y = 6\}$

15. $\{(x, y) \,|\, x - y = 8 \text{ and } x + y = 2\}$

INTERSECTION AND UNION

We can find the intersection or the union of two sets by graphing both sets on the same lattice. Consider these two sets:

$$\{(x, y) \,|\, x + y \le 7\} \qquad \{(x, y) \,|\, x \le 3\}$$

Before graphing $\{(x, y) \,|\, x + y \le 7\}$, we list the ordered pairs which belong to the set. (See top of next page.)

(6, 1),
(5, 1), (5, 2),
(4, 1), (4, 2), (4, 3),
(3, 1), (3, 2), (3, 3), (3, 4),
(2, 1), (2, 2), (2, 3), (2, 4), (2, 5),
(1, 1), (1, 2), (1, 3), (1, 4), (1, 5), (1, 6)

Then we mark them like this $\bigcirc$ on a 10-by-10 lattice. We mark the points belonging to $\{(x, y) \mid x \le 3\}$ like this $\square$.

The intersection of the two sets is

$$\{(x, y) \mid x + y \le 7\} \cap \{(x, y) \mid x \le 3\}$$

which is the same as $\{(x, y) \mid x + y \le 7 \text{ and } x \le 3\}$.

The points of the intersection are marked like this $\boxed{\bigcirc}$. The coordinates of these points meet both conditions:

    1. The sum of the two coordinates is at most 7, that is, $x + y \le 7$.

    2. The first coordinate is at most 3, that is, $x \le 3$.

The union of the two sets is

$$\{(x, y) \mid x + y \le 7\} \cup \{(x, y) \mid x \le 3\}$$

which is the same as $\{(x, y) \mid x + y \le 7 \text{ or } x \le 3\}$.

The graph of the union consists of all marked points — $\bigcirc$, $\square$, and $\boxed{\bigcirc}$. The coordinates of each marked point satisfy at least one of the two conditions.

In each problem, there are given two sets. Do the following:

   a. Mark the points which belong to the *first* set like this ○.

   b. Mark the points which belong to the *second* set like this □.

   c. Tell which points belong to the *intersection* of the two sets.

   d. Tell which points belong to the *union* of the two sets.

1. $\{(x, y) \mid x + y \leq 5\}$; $\{(x, y) \mid x < 3\}$

2. $\{(x, y) \mid x + y > 7\}$; $\{(x, y) \mid y > 4\}$

3. $\{(x, y) \mid 2x > 7\}$; $\{(x, y) \mid x \leq 2y\}$

4. $\{(x, y) \mid x - y > 4\}$; $\{(x, y) \mid x + y \leq 4\}$

5. $\{(x, y) \mid x + 3 > y\}$; $\{(x, y) \mid 2y \leq 5\}$

6. $\{(x, y) \mid 2x \geq 3y\}$; $\{(x, y) \mid x \leq y\}$

7. $\{(x, y) \mid x \leq 4\}$; $\{(x, y) \mid y \geq 7\}$

8. $\{(x, y) \mid x \geq 10\}$; $\{(x, y) \mid y \geq 10\}$

9. $\{(x, y) \mid x + y \leq 2\}$; $\{(x, y) \mid x + y \leq 3\}$

10. $\{(x, y) \mid x + y \leq 20\}$; $\{(x, y) \mid x + y > 20\}$

Describe each of the following sets in set notation. Then list the ordered pairs of a 10-by-10 lattice which belong to each set.

11. The first member is twice the second member.

12. The first member is equal to the second member.

13. The second member is five times the first member.

14. The second member is one-half of the first member.

15. The second member is six more than the first member.

16. The first member is four less than the second member.

17. Three subtracted from the first member equals the second.

18. Three multiplied by the second member equals twice the first.

19. The first member is greater than three times the second.

NEGATIVE AND POSITIVE COORDINATES

We will make a different lattice of points now. Note how the rows and columns are numbered in this lattice.

We locate points in this lattice the same way as we did on the 10-by-10 lattice. Check the points listed below to see whether you agree that their coordinates are given correctly. Coordinates for one point are stated incorrectly. Find it!

$$A(2,1), B(4,3), C(0,0), D(-2,3),$$
$$E(-5,5), F(-4,-1), G(-1,-4), H(0,3),$$
$$I(5,0), J(-1,0), K(0,-2), L(-3,4)$$

On your paper make a lattice like the one above. Label the following points on it.

1. $A(1,3), B(4,1), C(5,5), D(2,5)$

2. $E(-1,5), F(-4,1), G(-5,2), H(-1,1)$

3. $I(-2,-5), J(-1,-2), K(-4,-4), L(-5,-2)$

4. $M(4,-5), N(5,-3), O(1,-1), P(3,-3)$

5. $Q(0,4), R(0,-4), S(0,1), T(0,-1)$

6. $U(4,0), V(-2,0), W(5,0), X(0,0)$

QUADRANTS

Examine the picture of the lattice below. Notice that there are six distinct sets of points in this lattice. In Exercises **1–6** below you will identify some properties of the coordinates of these sets of points in relation to their position on the lattice. Once you observe the patterns, you will be able to predict to which of the six sets a point belongs by just glancing at its coordinates.

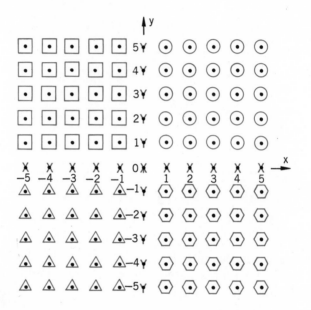

1. Each point in the *first quadrant* is marked like this ○. If "Q_1" means "first quadrant," then for each (x, y) which belongs to Q_1, which of the following is true?

    a. $x > 0$ and $y > 0$

    b. $x < 0$ and $y > 0$

    c. $x < 0$ and $y < 0$

    d. $x > 0$ and $y < 0$

    e. $x = 0$ and $y \neq 0$

    f. $x \neq 0$ and $y = 0$

2. Each point in the *second quadrant* is marked like this □. If "Q_2" means "second quadrant," then for each (x, y) which belongs to Q_2, which of the following is true?

    a. $x > 0$ and $y > 0$

    b. $x < 0$ and $y > 0$

    c. $x < 0$ and $y < 0$

    d. $x > 0$ and $y < 0$

    e. $x = 0$ and $y \neq 0$

    f. $x \neq 0$ and $y = 0$

3. Each point in the *third quadrant* is marked like this $\triangle$. If "Q_3" means "third quadrant," then for each (x, y) which belongs to Q_3, which of the following is true?

   a. $x > 0$ and $y > 0$ **d.** $x > 0$ and $y < 0$

   b. $x < 0$ and $y > 0$ **e.** $x = 0$ and $y \neq 0$

   c. $x < 0$ and $y < 0$ **f.** $x \neq 0$ and $y = 0$

4. Each point in the *fourth quadrant* is marked like this $\bigcirc$. If "Q_4" means "fourth quadrant," then for each (x, y) which belongs to Q_4, which of the following is true?

   a. $x > 0$ and $y > 0$ **d.** $x > 0$ and $y < 0$

   b. $x < 0$ and $y > 0$ **e.** $x = 0$ and $y \neq 0$

   c. $x < 0$ and $y < 0$ **f.** $x \neq 0$ and $y = 0$

5. Each point which belongs to the *x-axis* is marked like this x. For each (x, y) which belongs to the *x*-axis, which of the following is true?

   a. $x > 0$ and $y > 0$ **d.** $x > 0$ and $y < 0$

   b. $x < 0$ and $y > 0$ **e.** $x = 0$ and $y \neq 0$

   c. $x < 0$ and $y < 0$ **f.** $y = 0$

6. Each point which belongs to the *y-axis* is marked like this Y. For each (x, y) which belongs to the *y*-axis, which of the following is true?

   a. $x > 0$ and $y > 0$ **d.** $x > 0$ and $y < 0$

   b. $x < 0$ and $y > 0$ **e.** $x = 0$

   c. $x < 0$ and $y < 0$ **f.** $x \neq 0$ and $y = 0$

7. Imagine that our lattice of points extends indefinitely in all directions. For each pair of coordinates, tell where its point is found: Q_1, Q_2, Q_3, Q_4, *x*-axis, or *y*-axis.

   a. $(-25, -78)$ **f.** $(298, 0)$ **k.** $(258, -1139)$

   b. $(126, -306)$ **g.** $(-1005, -1)$ **l.** $(2005, 3678)$

   c. $(154, 360)$ **h.** $(256, 1342)$ **m.** $(0, 507)$

   d. $(-1125, 3)$ **i.** $(-99, 256)$ **n.** $(-11, 0)$

   e. $(0, -368)$ **j.** $(706, -365)$ **o.** $(0, 0)$

INFINITE LATTICES

In the lattice below, the arrows indicate that the number of points is unlimited. Even though the arrows point only in the positive directions, we consider the points to continue on and on in all four directions.

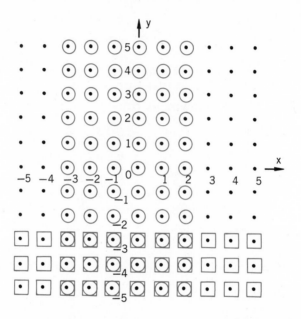

The points in the graph of the set $\{(x, y) \mid -3 \leq x \leq 2\}$ are marked like this ○. Remember, however, that it is impossible to mark all the points in this set. Infinitely many points above and below also belong to the graph.

The points in the graph of the set $\{(x, y) \mid y \leq -3\}$ are marked like this □. In this case, infinitely more points to the right, left, and below belong to this set.

The points marked like this ◙ belong to the intersection of the two sets

$$\{(x, y) \mid -3 \leq x \leq 2\} \cap \{(x, y) \mid y \leq -3\}$$

which is the same as

$$\{(x, y) \mid -3 \leq x \leq 2 \text{ and } y \leq -3\}$$

Note that infinitely many more points below those marked like this ◙ belong to the intersection of the two sets. But no points above, to the right, and to the left of those marked like this ◙ belong to the intersection.

To answer exercises **1–3** which follow, refer to the graph above.

1. Tell which ordered pairs belong to $\{(x, y)\,|-3 \le x \le 2\}$.

   a. $(1, 27)$ c. $(3, 1)$ e. $(-4, -2)$

   b. $(-2, 160)$ d. $(-3, -298)$ f. $(-4, 2)$

2. Tell which ordered pairs belong to $\{(x, y)\,|y \le -3\}$.

   a. $(-3, -17)$ c. $(-1, 3)$ e. $(-100, -200)$

   b. $(167, -255)$ d. $(5, -15)$ f. $(-5, -3)$

3. Tell which ordered pairs belong to
   $\{(x, y)\,|-3 \le x \le 2\} \cap \{(x, y)\,|y \le -3\}$.

   a. $(0, -215)$ c. $(3, -198)$ e. $(2, 56)$

   b. $(-4, -200)$ d. $(-3, -1000)$ f. $(-3, -3)$

4. Graph $\{(x, y)\,|x \ge 3\}$ and $\{(x, y)\,|y < 0\}$ on an infinite lattice like that on the previous page.

5. Tell which ordered pairs belong to $\{(x, y)\,|x \ge 3\}$.

   a. $(1, 25)$ c. $(4, -250)$ e. $(-3, -250)$

   b. $(3, 25)$ d. $(3, 178)$ f. $(3, 3)$

6. Tell which ordered pairs belong to $\{(x, y)\,|y < 0\}$.

   a. $(37, -2)$ c. $(-189, -189)$ e. $(0, 0)$

   b. $(37, 0)$ d. $(0, -1)$ f. $(-200, 200)$

7. Tell which ordered pairs belong to
   $\{(x, y)\,|x \ge 3\} \cap \{(x, y)\,|y < 0\}$.

   a. $(3, 0)$ c. $(157, -105)$ e. $(0, 0)$

   b. $(3, -1)$ d. $(2, -1)$ f. $(2.99, -1)$

8. Graph $\{(x, y)\,|-5 < x \le 1\}$ and $\{(x, y)\,|-2 < y \le 0\}$.

9. Tell which ordered pairs belong to $\{(x, y)\,|-5 < x \le 1\}$.

   a. $(-4, 265)$ c. $(1, 38)$ e. $(-12, -13)$

   b. $(2, -3)$ d. $(0, 0)$ f. $(-5, -5)$

10. Tell which ordered pairs belong to $\{(x, y)\,|-2 < y \le 0\}$.

    a. $(12, 0)$ c. $(-6, -1)$ e. $(-1265, -1)$

    b. $(-2, -2)$ d. $(376, 1)$ f. $(-5, 15)$

11. Tell which ordered pairs belong to
$\{(x, y) | -5 < x \le 1\} \cap \{(x, y) | -2 < y \le 0\}$.

a. $(1, 0)$ **c.** $(0, 0)$ **e.** $(-2, 0)$

b. $(-5, -1)$ **d.** $(-12, -12)$ **f.** $(1, -2)$

RECTANGULAR COORDINATE SYSTEM

In making graphs on lattices, we have considered only those points whose coordinates are *integers*, that is, positive and negative whole numbers and 0. We will now consider ordered pairs of *real* numbers and their graphs in a plane. A *plane* is a set of points which resembles a flat surface. A flat sheet of paper is a model of a plane.

Below we show a *rectangular coordinate system*, or a *Cartesian coordinate system*. "Cartesian" comes from the name of a French mathematician, René Descartes, who invented coordinate geometry.

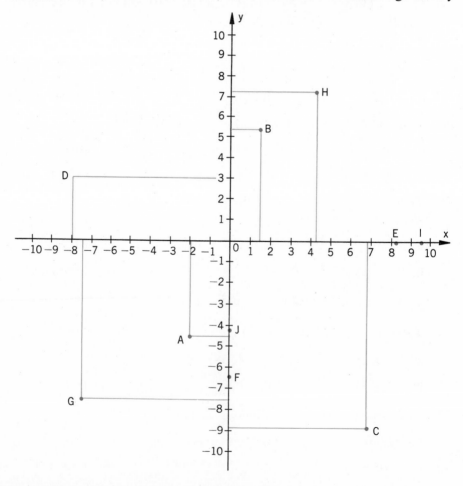

Identify the following points in the graph on page 292. As you identify the points, check to see that the coordinates are correctly placed.

$A\left(-2,-4\frac{1}{2}\right)$

$B\left(\sqrt{2},5\frac{1}{3}\right)$

$C\ (6.8,-8.9)$

$D\ (-8,3)$

$E\ (8.1,0)$

$F\left(0,-6\frac{1}{2}\right)$

$G\ (-7.5,-7.5)$

$H\ (\sqrt{18},7.2)$

$I\ (9.5,0)$

$J\ (0,-\sqrt{17})$

On your paper, make a coordinate system like the one on page 292. Plot the following points.

1. $A\ (-1,3)$

2. $B\ (-.3,-8.4)$

3. $C\left(\frac{1}{2},9\frac{1}{2}\right)$

4. $D\ (\sqrt{5},-3.4)$

5. $E\ (8.5,2.5)$

6. $F\left(0,-5\frac{1}{3}\right)$

7. $G\ (-1.6,-8.5)$

8. $H\ (-\sqrt{26},\sqrt{30})$

9. $I\left(3\frac{1}{4},0\right)$

THE PLANE AND FOUR QUADRANTS

We can think of the quadrants of a coordinate system in a plane as sets of points. We will use the following abbreviations.

Quadrant I $= Q_1$
Quadrant II $= Q_2$
Quadrant III $= Q_3$
Quadrant IV $= Q_4$
x-axis $= X$
y-axis $= Y$

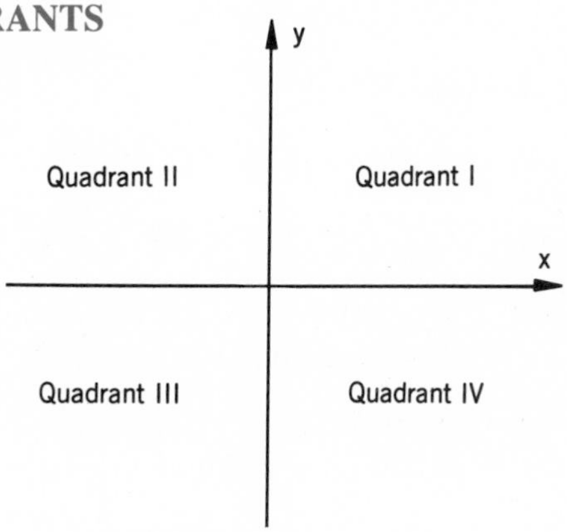

Both coordinates of the points in Quadrant I are positive. To say this, we write

$$Q_1 = \{(x,y)\,|\,x > 0 \text{ and } y > 0\}$$

That is, Quadrant I is the set of all points such that the first and second coordinates are positive.

1. Give the word description for Quadrant II, like the description given above for Quadrant I.

$$Q_2 = \{(x,y)\,|\,x < 0 \text{ and } y > 0\}$$

2. Give the word description for Quadrant III.

$$Q_3 = \{(x,y)\,|\,x < 0 \text{ and } y < 0\}$$

3. Give the word description for Quadrant IV.
$$Q_4 = \{(x, y) \mid x > 0 \text{ and } y < 0\}$$

4. Give the word description for the x-axis.
$$X = \{(x, y) \mid y = 0\}$$

5. Give the word description for the y-axis.
$$Y = \{(x, y) \mid x = 0\}$$

Give a simpler name for each of the following:

Example $Q_1 \cap Q_2$

$Q_1 \cap Q_2 = \phi$, since the intersection of Quadrant I and Quadrant II is the empty set. Recall that the axes do not belong to any quadrants.

6. $Q_2 \cap Q_3$

7. $Q_3 \cap Q_4$

8. $Q_1 \cap Q_4$

9. $(Q_1 \cup Q_2) \cap (Q_3 \cup Q_4)$

10. $(Q_1 \cup Q_4) \cup (Q_2 \cup Q_3)$

11. $X \cap Y$

12. $X \cap (Q_1 \cup Q_2)$

13. $Y \cap (Q_1 \cup Q_4)$

14. $X \cap (Q_1 \cup Q_4)$

15. $Y \cap (Q_1 \cup Q_2)$

■ The point in which the x and y-axes intersect is called the *origin*. It has the coordinates $(0, 0)$.

On a coordinate system, graph each pair of points. Then connect each pair with a straight line segment.

16. $(2, 5)$; $(2, -5)$

17. $(-4, 3)$; $(-4, -3)$

18. $\left(0, 4\frac{1}{2}\right)$; $\left(0, -4\frac{1}{2}\right)$

19. $\left(1, 6\frac{1}{3}\right)$; $\left(1, -6\frac{1}{3}\right)$

20. $(-7, 1)$; $(-7, -1)$

21. $(3, 4)$; $(-3, 4)$

22. $(1, 7)$; $(-1, 7)$

23. $(5, 0)$; $(-5, 0)$

24. $(-1, -5)$; $(1, -5)$

25. $\left(-2, -6\frac{1}{2}\right)$; $\left(2, -6\frac{1}{2}\right)$

In the next section, we will study the relationship between the pairs of points given in the exercises above.

SYMMETRY

The two curved objects shown at the right are *symmetric* with respect to line k.

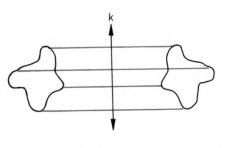

   Examine the pictures you obtained for exercises **16–20** on page 294. Note how the positions of the pairs of points are related. Are the points symmetric with respect to the x-axis?

AGREEMENT We shall abbreviate "the point with coordinates (x, y)" as "the point (x, y)."

■ Point (x, y) and point $(x, -y)$ are symmetric with respect to the x-axis.

1. For two points symmetric with respect to the x-axis,

   a. how are their first coordinates related?

   b. how are their second coordinates related?

2. See how the positions of pairs of points in exercises **21–25** are related. With respect to what axis are these pairs of points symmetric?

■ Point (x, y) and point $(-x, y)$ are symmetric with respect to the y-axis.

3. For two points symmetric with respect to the y-axis,

   a. how are their first coordinates related?

   b. how are their second coordinates related?

We can say that each point in exercises **16–20** is the *mirror reflection* of the other point in the pair through x-axis.

4. Make a similar statement about points in exercises **21–25**.

On a coordinate system, graph each pair of points. Then connect each pair with a straight line segment.

5. $(3, 3)$; $(-3, -3)$	**9.** $(-4, -8)$; $(4, 8)$	**13.** $(-4, 5)$; $(4, -5)$
6. $(2, 5)$; $(-2, -5)$	**10.** $(-9, -2)$; $(9, 2)$	**14.** $(6, -6)$; $(-6, 6)$
7. $(4, 1)$; $(-4, -1)$	**11.** $(-2, 2)$; $(2, -2)$	**15.** $(4, -10)$; $(-4, 10)$
8. $(-3, -6)$; $(3, 6)$	**12.** $(-1, 7)$; $(1, -7)$	**16.** $(1, -9)$; $(-1, 9)$

The pairs of points in exercises **5–16** are symmetric with respect to the origin.

◾ Point (x, y) and point $(-x, -y)$ are symmetric with respect to the origin.

17. For two points symmetric with respect to the origin,

    a. how are their first coordinates related?

    b. how are their second coordinates related?

STRAIGHT LINES

For each point, give the coordinates of the point which is symmetric with respect to

    a. the x-axis   **b.** the y-axis   **c.** the origin

Example $(2, 3)$ **a.** $(2, -3)$ **b.** $(-2, 3)$ **c.** $(-2, -3)$

1. $(1, 4)$ **3.** $\left(-1\frac{1}{2}, -3\frac{1}{3}\right)$ **5.** $(0, 5)$ **7.** $(0, -6)$

2. $(-3, 5)$ **4.** $(4, -2.6)$ **6.** $(-1, 0)$ **8.** $(0, 0)$

9. For exercises **1–8**, graph each point and the three related points on a coordinate system. Connect the given point with each of the three related points, In the graph on the right, we do this for the point $(2, 3)$.

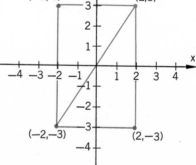

10. On a coordinate system, graph the following points.

    a. $(-2, -7)$ **c.** $(-2, 0)$ **e.** $(-2, 8.3)$

    b. $\left(-2, 3\frac{1}{2}\right)$ **d.** $\left(-2, -4\frac{1}{2}\right)$ **f.** $(-2, -2)$

11. Draw a picture of a straight line through the points you graphed in exercise **10.**

12. Note that all the points in exercise **10** are contained in the same line. Does this line contain all points whose first coordinate is -2, no matter what the second coordinate is?

The line in exercise **11** is perpendicular to the x-axis and parallel to the y-axis. It is the set of points described by

$$\{(x, y)\,|\,x = -2\}$$

13. On a coordinate system, plot the following points.

a. $\left(3\frac{1}{2}, -4\right)$ c. $\left(3\frac{1}{2}, 0\right)$ e. $\left(3\frac{1}{2}, -1\right)$

b. $\left(3\frac{1}{2}, 8\right)$ d. $\left(3\frac{1}{2}, 1\right)$ f. $\left(3\frac{1}{2}, -3\frac{1}{2}\right)$

14. Draw a picture of a straight line through the points you plotted in exercise **13**.

15. Using braces, describe the set of points which make up the line in exercise **14**.

16. On a coordinate system, plot the following points.

a. $(1, 5)$ c. $(0, 5)$ e. $(-1, 5)$

b. $(-3, 5)$ d. $\left(-6\frac{1}{2}, 5\right)$ f. $(7, 5)$

17. Draw a picture of a straight line through the points you plotted in exercise **16**.

18. Is the line in exercise **17** perpendicular to the y-axis?

19. Since the second coordinate of every point on the line in exercise **17** is 5, this set of points can be described as $\{(x, y)\,|\,y = 5\}$. Is every point whose second coordinate is 5 contained in this line?

20. On a coordinate system, plot the following points.

a. $(0, -2)$ c. $(-4, -2)$ e. $\left(8\frac{1}{2}, -2\right)$

b. $(5, -2)$ d. $\left(-5\frac{1}{2}, -2\right)$ f. $(-2, -2)$

21. Draw a picture of a straight line through the points you plotted in exercise **20**.

22. Using braces, describe the set of points which make up the line in exercise **21**.

23. On a coordinate system, plot the following points.

    a. (2, 2)   c. $\left(7\frac{1}{2}, 7\frac{1}{2}\right)$ e. (−4.6, −4.6)

    b. (−3, −3)   d. (0, 0)   f. (−1, −1)

24. Draw a picture of a straight line through the points you plotted in exercise **23**.

25. Does every point which belongs to the line in exercise **24** have the same x and y-coordinate? Is $\{(x, y) \mid x = y\}$ a correct description for this set of points?

26. On a coordinate system, plot the following points.

    a. (−3, 0)   c. (0, 0)   e. (6, 0)

    b. (−1, 0)   d. (5, 0)   f. (1, 1)

27. Is each point in exercise **26** contained in the x-axis?

28. Is $\{(x, y) \mid y = 0\}$ a correct description of the x-axis?

29. On a coordinate system, plot the following points.

    a. (0, 4)   c. (0, 0)   e. (0, −4)

    b. $\left(0, 2\frac{1}{2}\right)$ d. (0, −1)   f. (0, 1)

30. Is each point in exercise **29** contained in the y-axis?

31. Is $\{(x, y) \mid x = 0\}$ a correct description of the y-axis?

32. On a coordinate system, plot the following points.

    a. (2, 1)   c. (−4, −2)   e. (6, 3)

    b. $\left(1, \frac{1}{2}\right)$ d. $\left(-7, -3\frac{1}{2}\right)$ f. (−2, −1)

33. Will a picture of a line fit the points in exercise **32**? Try to draw a line through all of these points.

34. Do you see that for each point in exercise **32**, the x-coordinate is 2 times the second coordinate? Using braces, describe the set of points which makes up this line.

35. On a coordinate system, plot the following points.

a. $(1, 3)$ c. $(-1, -3)$ e. $(0, 0)$

b. $(2, 6)$ d. $\left(\frac{1}{2}, 1\frac{1}{2}\right)$ f. $\left(-1\frac{1}{2}, -4\frac{1}{2}\right)$

36. Will a picture of a line fit these points? Try to draw one.

37. What is the relation between the x and y-coordinates of the points in exercise **35**?

38. Using braces, describe the set of points, which makes up the line in exercise **36**.

NUMBER PATTERNS AND SETS

In each table, the first coordinates of points are listed in the left-hand column; the second coordinates are listed in the right-hand column. Discover each pattern and describe the set.

Example

x	y
-4	-7
-3	-5
-2	-3
-1	-1
0	1
1	3
2	5
3	7
4	9

Pattern: The y-coordinate is twice the x-coordinate, plus 1.

Set: $\{(x, y) \mid y = 2x + 1\}$

1.

x	y
-4	-8
-3	-6
-2	-4
-1	-2
0	0
1	2
2	4
3	6
4	8

2.

x	y
-4	-5
-3	-4
-2	-3
-1	-2
0	-1
1	0
2	1
3	2
4	3

3.

x	y
-4	-3
-3	-2
-2	-1
-1	0
0	1
1	2
2	3
3	4
4	5

4.

x	y
-4	-12
-3	-9
-2	-6
-1	-3
0	0
1	3
2	6
3	9
4	12

5.	x	y	6.	x	y	7.	x	y	8.	x	y
	-4	-9		-4	-5		-4	-1		-4	$-\frac{1}{2}$
	-3	-7		-3	-3		-3	$-\frac{1}{2}$		-3	0
	-2	-5		-2	-1		-2	0		-2	$\frac{1}{2}$
	-1	-3		-1	1		-1	$\frac{1}{2}$		-1	1
	0	-1		0	3		0	1		0	$1\frac{1}{2}$
	1	1		1	5		1	$1\frac{1}{2}$		1	2
	2	3		2	7		2	2		2	$2\frac{1}{2}$
	3	5		3	9		3	$2\frac{1}{2}$		3	3
	4	7		4	11		4	3		4	$3\frac{1}{2}$

SET DESCRIPTIONS OF STRAIGHT LINES

Turn back to the example on page 299. The set described was

$$\{(x, y) \mid y = 2x + 1\}$$

The following points were listed in the table.

$$(-4, -7), (-3, -5), (-2, -3), (-1, -1),$$
$$(0, 1), (1, 3), (2, 5), (3, 7), (4, 9)$$

On the next page, these points are plotted, and a picture of a line containing them is drawn.

1–8. For exercises **1–8** on pages 299–300, plot the points listed in each table and draw a picture of a line containing these points. Use a separate coordinate system for each exercise.

Examine the descriptions of sets you gave for exercises **1–8**. Note that they are all of the form $y = mx + b$, that is, of the form y equals some number m multiplied by x, plus some number b.

■ The graph of each set of points $\{(x, y) \mid y = mx + b\}$ is a straight line.

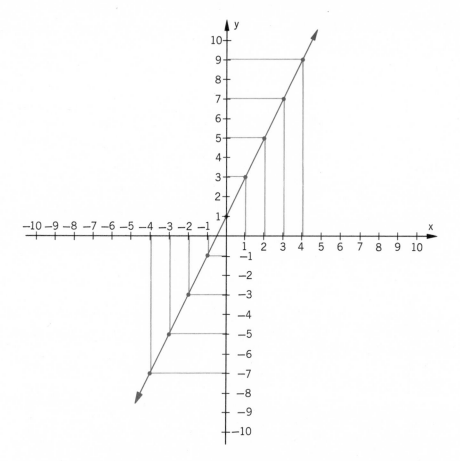

By experimenting with points and lines, we can see that for each pair of points there is exactly one line which contains them. For this reason we say that two points *determine* a line. Thus, it is sufficient to locate just two points in order to determine a line. Since, however, we might make an error and choose a wrong point, it is always a good idea to select a third point and check to see whether it belongs to the line.

For each set, plot two points on a coordinate system and draw a picture of a straight line containing these points.

9. $\{(x, y) | y = x + 5\}$

10. $\{(x, y) | y = 2x - 3\}$

11. $\{(x, y) | y = 3x - 4\}$

12. $\{(x, y) | y = -x + 4\}$

13. $\{(x, y) | y = -2x + 1\}$

14. $\{(x, y) | y = -3x - 2\}$

OTHER PATTERNS

For each table below, discover the pattern and describe the set. Do not give up too easily! Keep trying!

Example

x	y
−4	32
−3	18
−2	8
−1	2
0	0
1	2
2	8
3	18
4	32

Pattern: The y-coordinate is equal to 2 multiplied by the square of the x-coordinate.

Set: $\{(x, y) \mid y = 2x^2\}$

Verify this pattern for each pair (x, y) given in the table.

1.

x	y
−4	16
−3	9
−2	4
−1	1
0	0
1	1
2	4
3	9
4	16

2.

x	y
−4	8
−3	4.5
−2	2
−1	.5
0	0
1	.5
2	2
3	4.5
4	8

3.

x	y
−4	4
−3	2.25
−2	1
−1	.25
0	0
1	.25
2	1
3	2.25
4	4

4.

x	y
−4	48
−3	27
−2	12
−1	3
0	0
1	3
2	12
3	27
4	48

5.

x	y
−4	−16
−3	−9
−2	−4
−1	−1
0	0
1	−1
2	−4
3	−9
4	−16

6.

x	y
−4	−32
−3	−18
−2	−8
−1	−2
0	0
1	−2
2	−8
3	−18
4	−32

7.

x	y
−4	−48
−3	−27
−2	−12
−1	−3
0	0
1	−3
2	−12
3	−27
4	−48

8.

x	y
−4	−8
−3	−4.5
−2	−2
−1	−.5
0	0
1	−.5
2	−2
3	−4.5
4	−8

PARABOLAS

In the example on page 302, the following points are listed.

$(-4, 32)$, $(-3, 18)$, $(-2, 8)$,
$(-1, 2)$, $(0, 0)$, $(1, 2)$,
$(2, 8)$, $(3, 18)$, $(4, 32)$

These points are plotted on the coordinate system at the right. It is clear that a straight line would not fit through these points. A picture of a smooth curve is drawn through them.

The picture is part of the graph of

$$\{(x, y) \mid y = 2x^2\}.$$

It is impossible to show the entire graph because it does not end.

For each of the following x-coordinates, compute the y-coordinate of $\{(x, y) \mid y = 2x^2\}$.

1. 0

4. $2\frac{1}{2}$

7. $-1\frac{1}{2}$

2. $\frac{1}{2}$

5. $3\frac{1}{2}$

8. $-2\frac{1}{2}$

3. $1\frac{1}{2}$

6. $-\frac{1}{2}$

9. $-3\frac{1}{2}$

10. Examine the coordinates you found in exercises **1–9**. Does it appear that these points lie on the curve?

Since we have agreed to use the set of real numbers as our universal set, the curve pictured on the right is an infinite set of points.

■ A curve like the one at the right is called a *parabola*.

11–18. For exercises **1–8** on page 302, plot the points listed in each table. Connect the points with a smooth curve.

19. Compare the graphs of $\{(x, y) \mid y = x^2\}$, $\{(x, y) \mid y = 2x^2\}$ and $\{(x, y) \mid y = 3x^2\}$. From the shapes of these graphs, predict the shapes of the graphs of $\{(x, y) \mid y = 4x^2\}$ and $\{(x, y) \mid y = 100x^2\}$.

20. Compare the graphs of $\{(x, y) \mid y = x^2\}$, $\left\{(x, y) \mid y = \frac{1}{2}x^2\right\}$, and $\left\{(x, y) \mid y = \frac{1}{4}x^2\right\}$. From the shapes of these graphs, predict the shapes of the graphs of $\left\{(x, y) \mid y = \frac{1}{10}x^2\right\}$ and $\left\{(x, y) \mid y = \frac{1}{100}x^2\right\}$.

21. Compare the graphs of $\{(x, y) \mid y = x^2\}$ and $\{(x, y) \mid y = -x^2\}$. How are they similar and how do they differ?

22. Do the same for the graphs of $\{(x, y) \mid y = 2x^2\}$ and $\{(x, y) \mid y = -2x^2\}$.

23. Do the same for the graphs of $\{(x, y) \mid y = 3x^2\}$ and $\{(x, y) \mid y = -3x^2\}$.

24. Make a statement of comparison between the graphs of $\{(x, y) \mid y = ax^2\}$ and $\{(x, y) \mid y = -ax^2\}$, where a is positive.

INTERIORS AND EXTERIORS

On the right we show the graph of

$$\{(x, y) \mid y = x^2\}$$

The following points lie in the shaded portion of the parabola.

$$(1, 9), \quad \left(-1, 1\frac{1}{2}\right), \quad (2, 4.001),$$

and many others. For each point in the *interior* of the parabola, the following relation between the first and second coordinates is true.

$$y > x^2$$

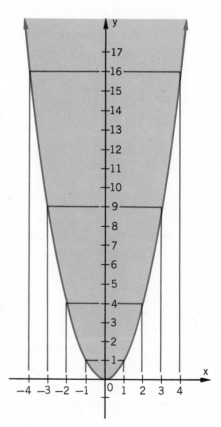

The interior of the parabola on page 304 may be described as

$$\{(x, y) \mid y > x^2\}$$

Test the following points in the inequality $y > x^2$.

1. $(1, 9)$ 2. $\left(-1, 1\frac{1}{2}\right)$ 3. $(2, 4.001)$

The set of points on the outside of a parabola is called the *exterior* of the parabola. A description for the exterior of the parabola shown on page 304 is

$$\{(x, y) \mid y < x^2\}$$

4. Locate two points which are in the exterior of the parabola and test their coordinates in the inequality $y < x^2$.

Describe in words each of the following sets of points.

Example $\{(x, y) \mid y \geq x^2\}$ the parabola $\{(x, y) \mid y = x^2\}$ and its interior

5. $\{(x, y) \mid y \leq x^2\}$ 8. $\{(x, y) \mid y < 2x^2\}$

6. $\{(x, y) \mid y > 2x^2\}$ 9. $\{(x, y) \mid y \leq 2x^2\}$

7. $\{(x, y) \mid y \geq 2x^2\}$ 10. $\{(x, y) \mid y > 3x^2\}$

MORE PATTERNS WITH NUMBERS

In the example below, there is a pattern connecting the first and second coordinates of the points listed in the table. See if you can discover the pattern and describe the set. Do not give up too easily if you do not see the pattern immediately.

Example

x	y
16	-4
9	-3
4	-2
1	-1
0	0
1	1
4	2
9	3
16	4

Pattern: The x-coordinate is the square of the y-coordinate.

Set: $\{(x, y) \mid y^2 = x\}$

For each table below, discover the pattern and describe the set.

1. x	y
32	−4
18	−3
8	−2
2	−1
0	0
2	1
8	2
18	3
32	4

2. x	y
48	−4
27	−3
12	−2
3	−1
0	0
3	1
12	2
27	3
48	4

3. x	y
8	−4
$4\frac{1}{2}$	−3
2	−2
$\frac{1}{2}$	−1
0	0
$\frac{1}{2}$	1
2	2
$4\frac{1}{2}$	3
8	4

4. x	y
4	−4
$2\frac{1}{4}$	−3
1	−2
$\frac{1}{4}$	−1
0	0
$\frac{1}{4}$	1
1	2
$2\frac{1}{4}$	3
4	4

5. x	y
−16	−4
−9	−3
−4	−2
−1	−1
0	0
−1	1
−4	2
−9	3
−16	4

6. x	y
−32	−4
−18	−3
−8	−2
−2	−1
0	0
−2	1
−8	2
−18	3
−32	4

7. x	y
−8	−4
$-4\frac{1}{2}$	−3
−2	−2
$-\frac{1}{2}$	−1
0	0
$-\frac{1}{2}$	1
−2	2
$-4\frac{1}{2}$	3
−8	4

8. x	y
−4	−4
$-2\frac{1}{4}$	−3
−1	−2
$-\frac{1}{4}$	−1
0	0
$-\frac{1}{4}$	1
−1	2
$-2\frac{1}{4}$	3
−4	4

In the example on page 305, the points listed in the table are

$$(16, -4), (9, -3), (4, -2), (1, -1),$$
$$(0, 0), (1, 1), (4, 2), (9, 3), (16, 4)$$

These points are plotted on the coordinate system on the next page. Do you see that a straight line would not fit through these points? A picture of a smooth curve is drawn through the points.

The picture below is a part of the graph of

$$\{(x, y) \mid y^2 = x\}$$

It would not be possible to show the entire parabola. Explain why. How does this parabola differ from the parabolas you studied before?

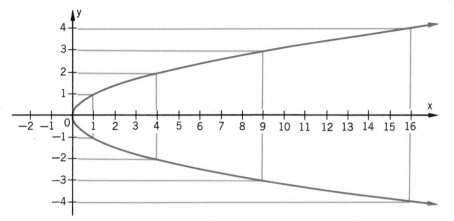

For the parabola $\{(x, y) \mid y^2 = x\}$, compute the values of y to one decimal place for the following values of x. Use the table for square roots on page 421. [HINT: Note that for one value of x, there are two values of y; for example, $(4, 2)$ and $(4, -2)$ are on the parabola, because $2^2 = 4$ and $(-2)^2 = 4$.]

1. 2   **2.** 3   **3.** 7   **4.** 13   **5.** 20   **6.** 25

7–14. For exercises **1–8** on page 306, plot the listed points on a coordinate system. Connect the points by making a picture of a smooth curve.

15. Compare the shapes of the parabolas $\{(x, y) \mid y^2 = x\}$, $\{(x, y) \mid 2y^2 = x\}$, and $\{(x, y) \mid 3y^2 = x\}$. On the basis of your observation, predict the shapes of the parabolas $\{(x, y) \mid 10y^2 = x\}$ and $\{(x, y) \mid 100y^2 = x\}$.

16. Compare the shapes of the parabolas $\{(x, y) \mid y^2 = x\}$, $\left\{(x, y) \mid \frac{1}{2}y^2 = x\right\}$ and $\left\{(x, y) \mid \frac{1}{4}y^2 = x\right\}$. On the basis of your observation, predict the shapes of the parabolas $\left\{(x, y) \mid \frac{1}{10}y^2 = x\right\}$ and $\left\{(x, y) \mid \frac{1}{100}y^2 = x\right\}$.

17. How is the graph of $\{(x, y) \mid ay^2 = x\}$ affected as larger and larger positive numbers are used for a?

18. Compare the graphs of $\{(x, y) \mid y^2 = x\}$ and $\{(x, y) \mid -y^2 = x\}$. In what ways are they similar and in what ways do they differ?

19. Do the same for the graphs of $\{(x, y) \mid 2y^2 = x\}$ and $\{(x, y) \mid -2y^2 = x\}$.

20. Do the same for the graphs of $\left\{(x, y) \mid \frac{1}{2}y^2 = x\right\}$ and $\left\{(x, y) \mid -\frac{1}{2}y^2 = x\right\}$.

21. Make a statement comparing the graphs of $\{(x, y) \mid ay^2 = x\}$ and $\{(x, y) \mid -ay^2 = x\}$, where a is a positive number.

22. Draw the graph of $\{(x, y) \mid y^2 = x\}$. Shade the interior of the parabola.

   a. Locate the point $(4, 1.9)$. Check the coordinates $(4, 1.9)$ in the inequality $y^2 < x$.

   b. Locate the point $(9, -2.5)$. Check the coordinates $(9, -2.5)$ in the inequality $y^2 < x$.

The set of points which are in the interior of the parabola

$$\{(x, y) \mid y^2 = x\}$$

is described by $\{(x, y) \mid y^2 < x\}$

23. Explain why $(4, 1.9)$ and $(9, -2.5)$ are in the interior of the parabola $\{(x, y) \mid y^2 = x\}$.

24. Describe the set of points which are in the exterior of the parabola $\{(x, y) \mid y^2 = x\}$.

Describe in words each set of points.

25. $\{(x, y) \mid y^2 \leq x\}$

26. $\{(x, y) \mid y^2 \geq x\}$

27. $\{(x, y) \mid y^2 < x\} \cup \{(x, y) \mid y^2 > x\}$

28. $\{(x, y) \mid y^2 \leq x\} \cup \{(x, y) \mid y^2 > x\}$

29. $\{(x, y) \mid y^2 \leq x\} \cap \{(x, y) \mid y^2 > x\}$

SUBSETS OF A PLANE

You have seen that equations and inequalities can be used to describe sets of points in a plane.

■ $\{(x, y) \mid y = mx + b\}$ is a set of points making up a line.

■ $\{(x, y) \mid y = ax^2\}$ is a set of points making up a parabola $[a \neq 0]$.

Now we will graph the set of points

$$\{(x, y) \mid y > 3\}$$

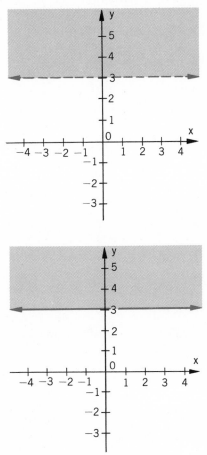

Remember that the plane extends indefinitely in all directions. The set of points $\{(x, y) \mid y > 3\}$ is shaded in color in the graph on the right. Note that the *boundary* of this set is marked with a dashed line to show that it does not belong to the set. The set $\{(x, y) \mid y > 3\}$ is the *half-plane* above the line described by the equation $y = 3$.

On the right is a graph of the set

$$\{(x, y) \mid y \geq 3\}$$

The boundary of this set is marked with a solid line to show that it does belong to the set. The set $\{(x, y) \mid y \geq 3\}$ is the union of the line described by $y = 3$ and the half-plane above this line.

Describe in words the following sets of points.

1. $\{(x, y) \mid y \geq 3\} \cap \{(x, y) \mid y = 3\}$

2. $\{(x, y) \mid y > 3\} \cup \{(x, y) \mid y \geq 3\}$

3. $\{(x, y) \mid y > 3\} \cap \{(x, y) \mid y < 3\}$

4. $\{(x, y) \mid y \geq 3\} \cap \{(x, y) \mid y < 3\}$

5. $\{(x, y) \mid y \geq 3\} \cup \{(x, y) \mid y < 3\}$

6. $\{(x, y) \mid y > 3\} \cup \{(x, y) \mid y < 3\}$

Graph each set of points.

7. $\{(x, y) \mid x > 3\}$

8. $\{(x, y) \mid x \geq 3\}$

9. $\{(x, y) \mid x < 3\}$

10. $\{(x, y) \mid x \leq 3\}$

11. $\{(x, y) \mid y > 0\}$

12. $\{(x, y) \mid y \geq 0\}$

13. $\{(x, y) \mid y < 0\}$

14. $\{(x, y) \mid y \leq 0\}$

15. $\{(x, y) \mid x > 0\}$

16. $\{(x, y) \mid x \geq 0\}$

17. $\{(x, y) \mid x < 0\}$

18. $\{(x, y) \mid x \leq 0\}$

19. $\{(x, y) \mid y < -4\}$

20. $\{(x, y) \mid y \leq -4\}$

21. $\{(x, y) \mid y > -4\}$

22. $\{(x, y) \mid y \geq -4\}$

Describe in words each set of points.

23. $\{(x, y) \mid x > 3\} \cap \{(x, y) \mid x < 3\}$

24. $\{(x, y) \mid x \geq 3\} \cap \{(x, y) \mid x < 3\}$

25. $\{(x, y) \mid x > 3\} \cup \{(x, y) \mid x < 3\}$

26. $\{(x, y) \mid x \geq 3\} \cup \{(x, y) \mid y < 3\}$

27. $\{(x, y) \mid y > 0\} \cup \{(x, y) \mid y < 0\}$

28. $\{(x, y) \mid y \geq 0\} \cup \{(x, y) \mid y < 0\}$

Recall these abbreviations:

$$Q_1 = \text{Quadrant I}$$
$$Q_2 = \text{Quadrant II}$$
$$Q_3 = \text{Quadrant III}$$
$$Q_4 = \text{Quadrant IV}$$

Which are true and which are false?

29. $\{(x, y) \mid y > 0\} = Q_1 \cup Q_2$

30. $\{(x, y) \mid x < 0\} = Q_2 \cup Q_3$

31. $\{(x, y) \mid x \geq 0\} \cup \{(x, y) \mid x < 0\} =$
$$Q_1 \cup Q_2 \cup Q_3 \cup Q_4 \cup \text{x-axis} \cup \text{y-axis}$$

32. $\{(x, y) \mid x = 0\} \cup \{(x, y) \mid y = 0\} = \text{x-axis} \cup \text{y-axis}$

33. $\{(x, y) \mid x = 0\} \cap \{(x, y) \mid y = 0\} = \{(0, 0)\}$

INTERSECTION AND UNION

Let us graph the set

$$\{(x, y) \mid x \geq 3 \text{ and } y < -2\}$$

We shall graph it in two parts:

$$A = \{(x, y) \mid x \geq 3\}$$
$$B = \{(x, y) \mid y < -2\}$$

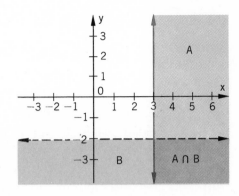

Set A is shaded in color. Set B is shaded in gray. Note that the boundary of set A is marked with a solid line because it belongs to the set. The boundary of set B is marked with a dashed line because it does not belong to the set.

The set we are seeking is the intersection of sets A and B:

$$\{(x, y) \mid x \geq 3\} \cap \{(x, y) \mid y < -2\}$$

The graph of $A \cap B$ is that part of the plane which is marked with both shadings. Of course, it extends indefinitely. All points whose first coordinates are greater than or equal to 3 *and* whose second coordinates are less than -2 belong to the graph of $A \cap B$.

Tell which points belong to $\{(x, y) \mid x \geq 3 \text{ and } y < -2\}$.

1. $\left(175, -15\frac{1}{2}\right)$ **2.** $(3, -2)$ **3.** $(3, -2.0001)$ **4.** $(2.99, -6)$

Now we change the word *and* to *or* in our set description.

$$\{(x, y) \mid x \geq 3 \text{ or } y < -2\}$$

This set is the same as the union of sets A and B:

$$\{(x, y) \mid x \geq 3\} \cup \{(x, y) \mid y < -2\}$$

The graph of $A \cup B$ consists of all points in the shaded areas in the graph above. The portions of the plane shaded in color, in gray, and in color and gray are all part of the set.

Tell which points belong to $\{(x, y) \mid x \geq 3 \text{ or } y < -2\}$.

5. $(5, -368)$ **8.** $(0, -100)$ **11.** $(1, -2)$

6. $(-5, 37)$ **9.** $(17, 35)$ **12.** $(1, -2.00001)$

7. $(-189, -189)$ **10.** $(17, -35)$ **13.** $(3, 9768)$

Let us now graph the set

$$\{(x, y)\,|-1 < x \le 3 \text{ and } 0 \le y < 4\}$$

As before, we will graph the set in two separate parts.

$$A = \{(x, y)\,|-1 < x \le 3\}$$
$$B = \{(x, y)\,|\,0 \le y < 4\}$$

Set *A* is shaded in color. Set *B* is shaded in gray. Since the descriptions of the sets are linked with the word *and*, we are looking for the intersection of the two sets, *A* ∩ *B*.

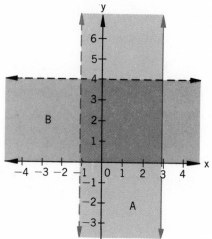

A ∩ *B* consists of points in the interior of a square, including two sides of the square. Which two sides belong to *A* ∩ *B*?

Tell which points belong to $\{(x, y)\,|-1 < x \le 3 \text{ and } 0 \le y < 4\}$

14. (3, 4)   **17.** (−.9999, 4)   **20.** (.01, 3.99)

15. (3, 3.9999)   **18.** (−.9999, 3.999)   **21.** (0, 0)

16. (−1, 2)   **19.** (2, 4)   **22.** (0, 0.00001)

By changing the word *and* to *or*, we obtain the set

$$\{(x, y)\,|-1 < x \le 3 \text{ or } 0 \le y < 4\}$$

This is the same as the union of the two sets, *A* ∪ *B*.

$$\{(x, y)\,|-1 < x \le 3\} \cup \{(x, y)\,|\,0 \le y < 4\}$$

Every point which is shaded in color, in gray, and in color and gray belongs to this set.

Tell which points belong to $\{(x, y)\,|-1 < x \le 3 \text{ or } 0 \le y < 4\}$.

23. (0, 1765)   **26.** (3, 4)   **29.** (909, 0)

24. (−365, 0)   **27.** (3, 1165)   **30.** (0, −2064)

25. (596, 4)   **28.** (3, −9071)   **31.** (2.1, 998365)

For each exercise, graph sets *A* and *B* on a coordinate system. Identify the two sets.

32. $A = \{(x, y)\,|\,x \le -2 \text{ and } y \le -2\}$; $B = \{(x, y)\,|\,x \le -2 \text{ or } y \le -2\}$

33. $A = \{(x, y)\,|\,x \ge 0 \text{ and } y < -3.5\}$; $B = \{(x, y)\,|\,x \ge 0 \text{ or } y < -3.5\}$

34. $A = \{(x, y) \mid x > -1 \text{ and } y > -1\}$; $B = \{(x, y) \mid x > -1 \text{ or } y > -1\}$

35. $A = \{(x, y) \mid x \geq -1 \text{ and } y \geq -1\}$; $B = \{(x, y) \mid x \geq -1 \text{ or } y \geq -1\}$

36. $A = \{(x, y) \mid x > 0 \text{ and } y > 0\}$; $B = \{(x, y) \mid x > 0 \text{ or } y > 0\}$

37. $A = \{(x, y) \mid x < 0 \text{ and } y > 0\}$; $B = \{(x, y) \mid x < 0 \text{ or } y > 0\}$

38. $A = \{(x, y) \mid x < 0 \text{ and } y < 0\}$; $B = \{(x, y) \mid x < 0 \text{ or } y < 0\}$

39. $A = \{(x, y) \mid x > 0 \text{ and } y < 0\}$; $B = \{(x, y) \mid x > 0 \text{ or } y < 0\}$

RECALL $\{(0, 0)\}$ means the set consisting of the origin.
$$x\text{-axis} = \{(x, y) \mid y = 0\}$$
$$y\text{-axis} = \{(x, y) \mid x = 0\}$$

Tell which of the following describe the empty set.

40. $\{(0, 0)\} \cap \{(x, y) \mid y = 0\}$

41. $\{(0, 0)\} \cap \{(x, y) \mid x = 0\}$

42. $Q_1 \cap Q_2$

43. $\{(x, y) \mid x < 0\} \cap \{(x, y) \mid x \geq 0\}$

44. $\{(x, y) \mid x = 0\} \cap \{(x, y) \mid y = 0\}$

45. $\{(x, y) \mid x < 2\} \cap \{(x, y) \mid x \geq 2\}$

46. $\{(x, y) \mid x < -1\} \cap \{(x, y) \mid y > -1\}$

Which are true and which are false?

47. $(1, 3) \in Q_1$

48. $(0, 0) \in x\text{-axis}$

49. $(0, -1) \in x\text{-axis}$

50. $(-2, -37) \in Q_4$

51. $(-255, 0) \in y\text{-axis}$

52. $(0, 398) \in y\text{-axis}$

53. $(-4, -301) \in Q_3$

54. $(-12, 37) \in Q_2$

55. $(0, 1237) \in y\text{-axis}$

56. $(0, 0) \in Q_1$

57. $(0, .00001) \in y\text{-axis}$

58. $(-367109, 0) \in x\text{-axis}$

59. $(-17109, -41286) \in Q_3$

60. $(4301, -16001) \in Q_4$

61. $(-.0001, -.0001) \in Q_3$

62. $\left(\dfrac{1}{8}, \dfrac{1}{9}\right) \in Q_1$

KEEPING ARITHMETICALLY FIT

For exercises **1–28**, numerals in parentheses refer to pages where you can find similar exercises.

For each per cent, give its decimal name. (442–443)

1. 15%	**3.** 110%	**5.** 560%	**7.** .3%	**9.** 2.5%
2. 48%	**4.** 2%	**6.** $\frac{1}{4}$%	**8.** .09%	**10.** 12.6%

Find replacements for n to obtain true statements. (442–443)

11. 30% of $100 = n$ **14.** .5% of $3,000 = n$

12. 15% of $120 = n$ **15.** $\frac{1}{3}$% of $9,000 = n$

13. 68% of $500 = n$ **16.** 150% of $12 = n$

Find replacements for n to obtain true statements. (442–443)

17. $5 = n$% of 20   **20.** $.01 = n$% of 1

18. $1 = n$% of 150   **21.** $100 = n$% of 20

19. $.5 = n$% of 4   **22.** $2 = n$% of .5

Find replacements for n to obtain true statements. (442–443)

23. $3 = 1$% of n **26.** $35 = 2.5$% of n

24. $1 = 200$% of n **27.** $12 = 120$% of n

25. $.5 = 1$% of n **28.** $33 = 60$% of n

Compute 12% of each of the following numbers.

29. 100	**30.** 10	**31.** 1	**32.** 1	**33.** .01

Classify each number into one of the following three categories.

       T: divisible by 3 and not divisible by 9
       N: divisible by 9
       D: not divisible by 3

34. 8,883	**36.** 504	**38.** 5,007	**40.** 563	**42.** 31,986
35. 10,011	**37.** 986	**39.** 23,112	**41.** 31,503	**43.** 98,303

Factor completely.

44. 72	**45.** 146	**46.** 225	**47.** 950

48. What is the Least Common Multiple of 12 and 9?

49. What is the Greatest Common Divisor of 51 and 34?

Give the set of all factors of:

50. 36   **51.** 50   **52.** 23

Classify each number into one of the following five categories.

        E: even   PE: prime and even
        O: odd   PO: prime and odd
        P: prime

53. 100   **54.** 2   **55.** 41   **56.** 51   **57.** 65   **58.** 101

Give the opposite of each number.

59. -7 **60.** $-3\frac{1}{3}$ **61.** -1.8 **62.** 8   **63.** 0   **64.** $\frac{5}{7}$

Give the reciprocal of each number.

65. 5   **66.** $-\frac{1}{3}$ **67.** $\frac{3}{7}$ **68.** -1.5 **69.** $-.6$ **70.** 2.7

Classify each number into one of the following categories.

           R: rational   I: irrational

71. $\frac{3}{4}$ **73.** $\sqrt{10}$ **75.** $.2020020002\ldots$ **77.** $\frac{3.7}{12.6}$

72. 1.6   **74.** $1.9\overline{9}$ **76.** $26.3567\overline{878}$ **78.** $\sqrt{225}$

Add.

79. 6 yd. 2 ft.   **80.** 12 hrs. 32 min. 54 sec.   **81.** 3 lb. 7 oz.
     8 yd. 1 ft.   15 hrs. 48 min. 14 sec.   8 lb. 12 oz.
     <u>9 yd. 2 ft.</u>   <u>19 hrs. 35 min. 59 sec.</u>   <u>1 lb. 15 oz.</u>

Subtract.

82. 17 ft. 8 in.   **83.** 9 gal. 1 qt.   **84.** 7 min. 31 sec.
     <u>12 ft. 11 in.</u>   <u>2 gal. 3 qt.</u>   <u>3 min. 48 sec.</u>

Multiply.

85. 376   **86.** 89   **87.** 37.6   **88.** .88   **89.** 1.05
    <u>17</u>   <u>9</u>   <u>1.8</u>   <u>.16</u>   <u>.3</u>

Divide each number by .01 mentally.

90. 17 **91.** 106 **92.** 1.3 **93.** .1 **94.** .01

Give the answers.

95. $20 + (-131)$ **105.** $-11 - (-4)$ **115.** $-\frac{2}{3} \times 15$

96. $-31 + (-72)$ **106.** $-\frac{1}{3} - \left(-\frac{1}{2}\right)$ **116.** $\frac{4}{7} \times \left(-\frac{2}{4}\right)$

97. $-98 + 52$ **107.** $\frac{1}{4} - \left(-\frac{1}{7}\right)$ **117.** $-64 \div 8$

98. $-132 + 264$ **108.** $-3\frac{1}{4} - \left(-5\frac{1}{5}\right)$ **118.** $-125 \div (-5)$

99. $-\frac{1}{2} + \left(-\frac{1}{2}\right)$ **109.** $-1.7 - 13.7$ **119.** $22 \div \left(-\frac{1}{2}\right)$

100. $\frac{1}{3} + \left(-\frac{2}{5}\right)$ **110.** $-7 \times (-14)$ **120.** $11 \div \left(-\frac{1}{3}\right)$

101. $-\frac{3}{7} + \frac{10}{7}$ **111.** -12×12 **121.** $-34 \div .1$

102. $13 - (-29)$ **112.** $-140 \times .01$ **122.** $\frac{2}{7} \div \left(-\frac{1}{4}\right)$

103. $-25 - (-67)$ **113.** $-1.6 \times (-5)$ **123.** $-\frac{1}{3} \div (-12)$

104. $23 - 68$ **114.** $-\frac{1}{7} \times 42$ **124.** $67 \div (-.01)$

Give replacements for x to obtain true statements.

125. $\frac{x}{5} = \frac{2}{10}$ **129.** $\frac{.7}{.4} = \frac{x}{-1.2}$

132. $\frac{\frac{4}{3}}{x} = \frac{\frac{4}{9}}{\frac{2}{5}}$

126. $\frac{x}{-6} = \frac{3}{2}$ **130.** $\frac{1.5}{-3.6} = \frac{4.5}{x}$

127. $\frac{-3}{-10} = \frac{x}{50}$

131. $\frac{\frac{1}{2}}{\frac{2}{3}} = \frac{3}{x}$ **133.** $\frac{x}{\frac{1}{2}} = \frac{\frac{3}{2}}{-\frac{3}{2}}$

128. $\frac{4}{x} = \frac{-10}{5}$

VOCABULARY REVIEW

array of points (275)
Cartesian coordinate system (292)
coordinates (280)
exterior of a parabola (305)
finite lattice of points (278)
infinite lattice (290)
interior of a parabola (304)
ordered pair of numbers (275)
origin (294)

parabola (303)
plane (292)
quadrant (288)
rectangular coordinate system
   (292)
rectangular lattice (278)
symmetry (295)
x-axis (289)
y-axis (289)

A CHALLENGE TO YOU

1. For how many years should $1,000 be invested at the rate of 4% simple interest to obtain $100 in interest?

2. On a checkerboard two diagonally opposite squares are removed. Can you cover the remaining 62 squares using domino pieces each covering two squares? Prove your answer.

3. A man usually comes home from work on the 5 o'clock train. He is met by his wife at the station and driven home. One day he takes the 4 o'clock train. Upon arrival at the station, he starts walking toward home. He is met by his wife on the way, and they arrive at home 20 minutes earlier than usual. For how long did the man walk?

4. "Are those your children whom I hear playing in the garden?" asked the visitor.
   "There are really four families of children," replied the host. "Mine is the largest, my brother's family is smaller, my sister's is smaller still, and my cousin's is the smallest of all. They are playing drop the handkerchief," he went on; "they prefer baseball, but there are not enough children to make two teams. Curiously enough," he mused, "the product of the four numbers each telling the size of one of the four groups is my house number, which you saw when you came in."
   "I am something of a mathematician," said the visitor, "let me see whether I can find the numbers of children in the various families." After figuring for a time he said, "I need more information. Does your cousin's family consist of a single child?" The host answered his question, whereupon the visitor said, "Knowing your house number and knowing the answer to my question, I can now deduce the exact number of children in each family."
   How many children were there in each of the four families?

5. Given a sample space for a particular experiment, each subset of the sample space is called an *event*. When rolling a die twice, the sample space consists of 36 elements. The event in which 1 comes up on the first roll is $\{(1, 1), (1, 2), (1, 3), (1, 4), (1, 5), (1, 6)\}$.

   a. Give the event in which 1 comes up on the second roll.

   b. Give the event in which the same number comes up on the second roll as on the first roll.

   c. Give the event in which the sum of the outcomes on the first and on the second rolls is 10.

CHAPTER TEST

1. Form the 9 possible ordered number pairs using the numbers 1, 2, and 3. Then label these points on a 3-by-3 array.

2. In the 3-by-3 array in problem **1**, mark all points for which the first coordinate is greater than the second coordinate.

3. Explain why the intersection of any two quadrants in a coordinate system is the empty set.

4. Using the concept of the union of sets, write an expression for the entire plane in terms of the four quadrants and the two axes.

5. What points belong to the set $\{(x, y) \,|\, x = 0 \text{ and } y = 0\}$?

Graph each set on a rectangular coordinate system.

6. $A = \{(x, y) \,|\, x \geq 2 \text{ and } y < -3\}$

7. $B = \{(x, y) \,|\, -4 < x \leq 0 \text{ and } -3 \leq y < -1\}$

8. $C = \{(x, y) \,|\, x = y\}$

9. $D = \{(x, y) \,|\, x < 5 \text{ or } y \geq -6\}$

10. $E = \{(x, y) \,|\, -3 \leq x \leq 0 \text{ or } -3 \leq y \leq -1\}$

Tell which of the following sets of points are straight lines.

11. $\{(x, y) \,|\, x = 3\}$

12. $\{(x, y) \,|\, y = x^2\}$

13. $\{(x, y) \,|\, y = 2x + 7\}$

14. $\{(x, y) \,|\, y = -2.5\}$

15. $\{(x, y) \,|\, 2y^2 = x\}$

16. $\{(x, y) \,|\, x + y = 1\}$

For each point, give the coordinates of the point which is symmetric
with respect to

    a. the x-axis   **b.** the y-axis   **c.** the origin

17. $(1, \sqrt{3})$ **20.** $(-6, 3)$ **23.** $(1, 0)$

18. $\left(2\frac{1}{2}, -1\right)$ **21.** $(0, 3)$ **24.** $(-\sqrt{5}, 0)$

19. $(-5, -1.6)$ **22.** $(0, -4)$ **25.** $(0, 0)$

In which quadrant or on which axis is each point found?

26. $(0, 847)$ **30.** $(-\sqrt{39}, 0)$ **34.** $(-3, -3)$

27. $(-117, -368)$ **31.** $(0, -13.1)$ **35.** $(1261, -9072)$

28. $(305, -39.7)$ **32.** $(0, 0)$ **36.** $\left(.000001, -\frac{1}{17}\right)$

29. $\left(-\sqrt{3}, \frac{1}{2}\right)$ **33.** $(\sqrt{126}, 0)$ **37.** $\left(-\frac{1}{13}, -\frac{1}{127}\right)$

Each of the following describes a parabola.

    a. Write a description of the interior of each parabola.

    b. Write a description of the exterior of each parabola.

38. $\{(x, y) | y = 3x^2\}$ **40.** $\{(x, y) | 4y^2 = x\}$

39. $\{(x, y) | y = -2x^2\}$ **41.** $\{(x, y) | -3y^2 = x\}$

Which ordered number pairs belong to the set $\left\{ (x, y) \left| \frac{1}{2}y = 2x^2 \right. \right\}$?

42. $(2, 16)$ **44.** $\left(\frac{1}{2}, 2\right)$ **46.** $(.1, .04)$

43. $(-2, 16)$ **45.** $\left(-\frac{1}{2}, 2\right)$ **47.** $(.1, -.04)$

CHAPTER ELEVEN

Basic Geometric Figures

POINTS AND SEGMENTS

A *point* is the simplest geometric figure. On paper we make dots to suggest points. We will use capital letters as names for points.

A

•   ⟵   This is *point A*.

Another simple geometric figure is a segment.

On the right is a picture of a segment, $\overline{AB}$. It is made up of points A and B and all points *between* A and B. The points A and B are called the *endpoints* of $\overline{AB}$. Note that we make a bar over AB to refer to the segment.

1. **a.** There are four segments shown in the figure on the right. Name them.

   b. Four pairs of segments share a common endpoint. Name these pairs of segments and name the endpoints each pair shares.

   c. How many pairs of segments do not have any common endpoints? Name them.

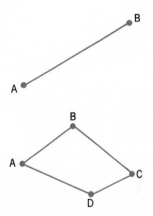

2. **a.** There are seven segments shown in the figure on the right. Name them.

   b. Name the endpoint(s) shared by four segments.

   c. Name the endpoint(s) shared by three segments.

   d. Name the endpoint(s) shared by two segments.

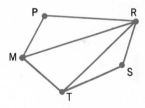

Recall the meaning of the term *segment*.

■   Segment $\overline{AB}$ is the set of points consisting of points A and B and all points between A and B.

3. **a.** In the picture on the right, explain why point Y belongs to both $\overline{XY}$ and $\overline{YZ}$.

   b. Why does point X not belong to $\overline{YZ}$?

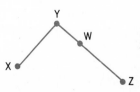

POLYGONS

"Poly" means "many," "gon" means "angle." Hence, a *polygon* is a figure having a number of angles. Below are pictures of several polygons.

1. Is it possible to have a polygon with two sides? Why or why not?

2. What is the smallest number of sides that a polygon may have?

A *triangle* is a polygon with the smallest number of *sides*. The sides of a polygon are segments.

3. **a.** Name the three segments which are sides of the triangle pictured on the right.

   b. What two sides share the point *P*?

   c. What two sides share the point *Q*?

   d. What two sides share the point *R*?

4. Can a triangle have two sides that do not have a common point?

■ A *triangle* is the union of three segments. Each pair of segments has one common endpoint.

$$\triangle ABC = \overline{AB} \cup \overline{BC} \cup \overline{AC}$$

5. Name the sets of points which will correctly complete the following:

   a. $\overline{AB} \cap \overline{BC} = $ _____

   c. $\overline{CA} \cap \overline{AB} = $ _____

   b. $\overline{BC} \cap \overline{CA} = $ _____

6. According to the definition of a triangle, does the picture on the right show a triangle? Why or why not?

Each triangle has three *vertices*. Point *A* is one *vertex of* $\triangle ABC$.

7. Name two other vertices of $\triangle ABC$.

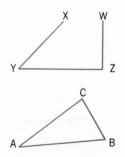

8. **a.** On your paper make a picture of a triangle. Name the vertices of this triangle X, Y, and Z.

b. Name $\triangle XYZ$ as a union of three segments.

c. In your picture, label a point A anywhere on $\overline{XY}$. Is the statement $A \in \triangle XYZ$ true? Why or why not?

■ A polygon with four sides is called a *quadrilateral*.

9. Name the four vertices of the quadrilateral pictured on the right.

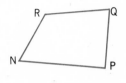

10. Name the four sides of the quadrilateral on the right.

11. In the quadrilateral $NPQR$, name two pairs of sides which have the following common points.

a. N **b.** P **c.** Q **d.** R

12. In the quadrilateral $NPQR$, name two pairs of sides which do not have common points.

In $NPQR$, $\overline{NP}$ and $\overline{PQ}$ are one pair of *adjacent sides* because they have a common point.

13. In quadrilateral $NPQR$, name three other pairs of adjacent sides.

14. In quadrilateral $NPQR$ on the right, two *diagonals* are shown. One diagonal is $\overline{PR}$. Name the other diagonal.

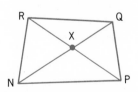

15. In what point do the two diagonals intersect?

16. For the picture above, is the following statement true?

$$\overline{PR} \cap \overline{NQ} = X$$

Why or why not?

■ A polygon with five sides is called a *pentagon*.

17. A pentagon has five diagonals. Copy the pentagon on the right and show its diagonals. Name the diagonals as segments.

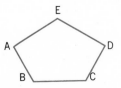

HALF-LINES AND RAYS

Below is a picture of a line.

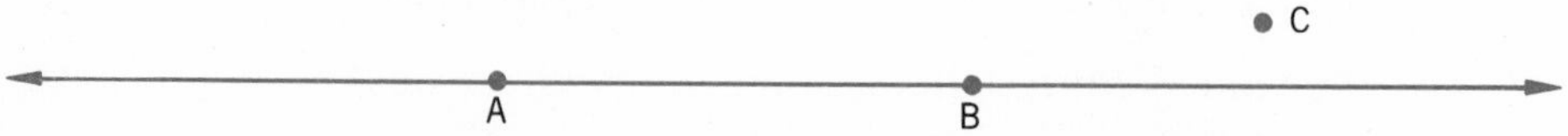

Unlike a segment, a line does not end. It extends without end in both directions. This is indicated by arrows in the picture.

1. Does point *A* belong to the line? Does point *B*? Does point *C*?

We will use the following symbol to name the line shown.

$$\overleftrightarrow{AB}$$

2. Give a name for the line pictured on the right.

Point *M* separates the line on the right into two sets of points:

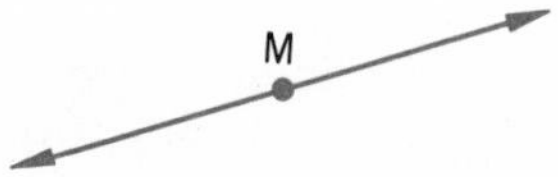

> the set of points to the left of *M*
>   and
> the set of points to the right of *M*

Note that the point *M* (the separator) does not belong to either of these sets.

Here is a picture of a portion of that line. It is called a *half-line* and is named by the symbol

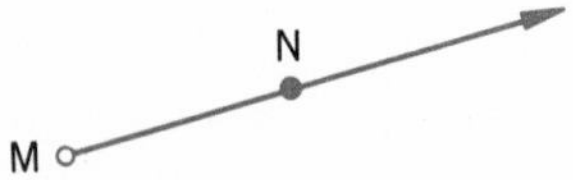

$$\overset{\circ}{M}\overset{\;}{\overrightarrow{N}}$$

This half-line consists of all points on $\overleftrightarrow{MN}$ which are to the right of *M*. Notice that we draw a small circle at one end to show that *M* is not a part of the half-line.

If point *M* is included with the half-line, the resulting set is called a *ray*. Thus, the ray, named by the symbol

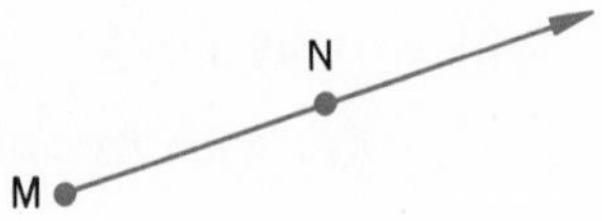

$$\overrightarrow{MN}$$

consists of *M* and the half-line on the right of *M*. Notice that we draw a dot at one end to show that *M* is part of the ray.

3. Describe ray $\overrightarrow{ST}$ pictured on the right as the union of two sets of points.

Remember, we agree that

$\overline{AB}$ means a segment. It is the same as $\overline{BA}$.

$\overleftrightarrow{AB}$ means a line. It is the same as $\overleftrightarrow{BA}$.

$\overset{\circ}{\overrightarrow{AB}}$ means a half-line. Why is $\overset{\circ}{\overrightarrow{AB}}$ not the same as $\overset{\circ}{\overrightarrow{BA}}$?

$\overrightarrow{AB}$ means a ray. Why is $\overrightarrow{AB}$ *not* the same as $\overrightarrow{BA}$?

4. Which are true and which are false? (Refer to the picture on the right.)

a. $\overrightarrow{QR} \cup \overrightarrow{QT} = \overrightarrow{QR}$

b. $\overrightarrow{QR} \cap \overrightarrow{QT} = \{Q\}$

c. $\overrightarrow{RQ} = \overrightarrow{QT}$

d. $\overrightarrow{TQ} \cup \overrightarrow{QR} = \overleftrightarrow{RT}$

e. $\overrightarrow{QT} = \overrightarrow{TQ}$

f. $\overrightarrow{RQ} = \overrightarrow{RT}$

ANGLES

Each ray has one endpoint. The endpoint of $\overrightarrow{AB}$ is A.

1. Look at the picture on the right and give the endpoint of each of the following:

a. $\overrightarrow{XY}$ b. $\overrightarrow{YC}$ c. $\overrightarrow{CW}$ d. $\overrightarrow{WY}$

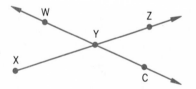

2. Refer to the picture on the right and name two rays which have a common endpoint.

$\overrightarrow{YC}$ and $\overrightarrow{YW}$ are called *collinear* rays because their union is a line.

3. Explain why $\overrightarrow{YW}$ and $\overrightarrow{YZ}$ are *non-collinear*.

4. In the picture on the right, name two pairs of collinear rays and two pairs of non-collinear rays.

■ An *angle* is the union of two non-collinear rays having a common endpoint. The rays are called the *sides* of the angle.

5. In the picture given above, why is the union of $\overrightarrow{AE}$ and $\overrightarrow{AC}$ not an angle?

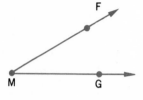

6. Name the two rays pictured on the right.

7. What is the common point of the two rays?

Since the geometric figure pictured on the right is the union of two non-collinear rays with a common endpoint, it is an angle. This angle may be named in three different ways.

	∠M	∠FMG	∠GMF
Read:	angle M	angle FMG	angle GMF

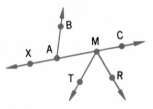

8. Using three letters in each case, name seven different angles shown in the picture on the right.

9. Explain why the following statements are true.

   a. ∠BAM = ∠BAC

   b. ∠RMA = ∠RMX

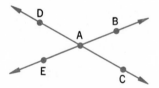

10. ∠DAE is *vertical* to ∠BAC, because $\overrightarrow{AD}$ and $\overrightarrow{AC}$ form a line and $\overrightarrow{AB}$ and $\overrightarrow{AE}$ form a line. Why is ∠BAD not vertical to ∠BAC?

11. Name another pair of angles in the picture on the right such that one angle is vertical to the other.

12. Explain why this statement is true.

$$\overrightarrow{AD} \cup \overrightarrow{AB} = \angle BAD$$

MEASURES OF SEGMENTS AND ANGLES

1. Draw a picture showing that $\overline{AB}$ is a subset of $\overleftrightarrow{AB}$.

2. Using the same line $\overleftrightarrow{AB}$ as in exercise **1**, label a point C not on $\overleftrightarrow{AB}$. Draw a picture showing that $\overline{AC}$ is a subset of $\overleftrightarrow{AC}$. Connect B and C.

     △ABC has three sides: $\overline{AB}$, $\overline{BC}$, and $\overline{AC}$.

3. Explain the following:

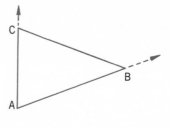

$\overline{AB} \cup \overline{AC}$ is a subset of $\angle A$.

We will say that triangle ABC has three angles: $\angle A$, $\angle B$, and $\angle C$. You must remember, however, that the sides of $\angle A$ are rays, $\overrightarrow{AB}$ and $\overrightarrow{AC}$. Therefore, the sides of $\angle A$ are *not* subsets of $\triangle ABC$.

Each side of a triangle has a measure. It is the number of units of length, such as inches, or centimeters, or feet, or any other unit of length we may choose. Similarly, each angle has a measure. It is the number of degrees, or radians, or any other angular measure we may choose.

■ Two line segments which have the same measure are said to be *congruent*. Similarly, two angles which have the same measure are said to be congruent.

4. Name two pairs of congruent line segments in the picture on the right.

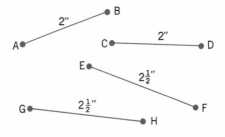

To indicate that the measure of $\overline{AB}$ is 2 inches, we write

$$AB = 2$$

Read: The measure of $\overline{AB}$ is 2.

NOTE: $\overline{AB}$ means a segment;
             AB means the measure of a segment.

5. Name two pairs of congruent angles in the picture below.

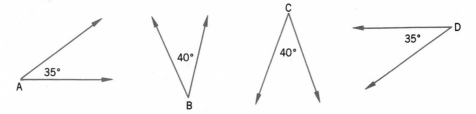

To indicate that the measure of angle A is 35°, we write

$$m \angle A = 35°$$

Read: The measure of angle A is 35 degrees.

CLASSIFICATION OF TRIANGLES – MEASURES OF SIDES

Triangles can be classified according to the measures of their sides.

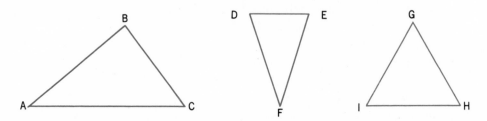

In △*ABC* pictured above no two sides have the same measure.

■ A triangle in which the measures of no two sides are the same is called a *scalene* triangle.

In △*DEF* above, *DF* = *EF*; that is, the measures of two sides are the same.

■ A triangle in which the measures of at least two sides are the same is called an *isosceles* triangle.

In △ *GHI* above, *GH* = *HI* = *IG*; that is, the measures of all three sides are the same.

■ An isosceles triangle in which the measures of all three sides are the same is called an *equilateral* triangle.

Tell whether each triangle is scalene, isosceles, or equilateral.

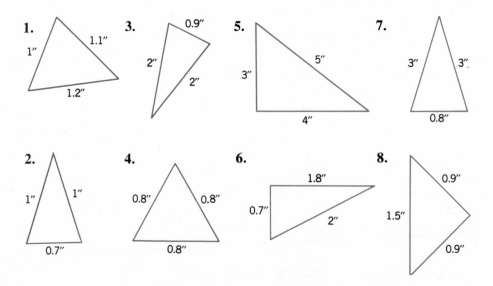

In $\triangle XYZ$, $\overline{XY}$ is opposite vertex Z.

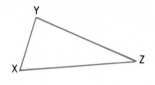

9. What side is opposite vertex X?

10. What side is opposite vertex Y?

11. What vertex is opposite $\overline{XY}$?

12. **a.** Draw pictures of three isosceles triangles. Measure their sides and angles and record these measures.

   b. What conclusion can be stated about the measure of the angles opposite the congruent sides in an isosceles triangle?

13. **a.** Draw pictures of three equilateral triangles. Measure their sides and angles and record these measures.

   b. What conclusion can be stated about the measure of the angles in an equilateral triangle?

14. For each of the six triangles you drew for exercises **12** and **13**, add the measures of the three angles. What is the sum in each case?

CLASSIFICATION OF TRIANGLES – MEASURES OF ANGLES

Triangles can also be classified according to the measures of their angles.

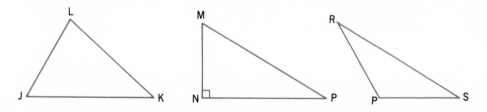

Every angle of $\triangle JKL$ above has a measure less than 90°.

■ A triangle in which the measure of each angle is less than 90° is called an *acute* triangle. (An angle whose measure is less than 90° is called an *acute* angle.)

The measure of $\angle N$ in $\triangle MNP$ above is 90°. We use the small square symbol to indicate that the angle measures 90°.

■ A triangle in which the measure of one angle is 90° is called a *right* triangle.

1. Can a triangle have more than one angle whose measure is 90°? Why?

   In △*RPS* on page 329, the measure of ∠*P* is greater than 90°.

   ■ A triangle in which the measure of one angle is greater than 90° is called an *obtuse* triangle. (An angle whose measure is greater than 90° and less than 180° is called an *obtuse* angle.)

2. Can a triangle have more than one obtuse angle? Why?

In exercises **3–10** whenever your answer is "yes," draw a picture to illustrate the triangle described in the problem.

3. Can an acute triangle be a scalene triangle?

4. Must an equilateral triangle be an acute triangle?

5. Can a right triangle be a scalene triangle?

6. Can a right triangle be an isosceles triangle?

7. Can an obtuse triangle be a scalene triangle?

8. Can an obtuse triangle be an isosceles triangle?

9. Can an obtuse triangle be an equilateral triangle?

10. Can an obtuse triangle be a right triangle?

INTERIORS OF ANGLES

Each line in a plane separates the plane into two subsets called *half-planes*. A line extends indefinitely in both directions. The line which is the separator does not belong to either of the two half-planes. Thus, $\overleftrightarrow{AB}$ on the right separates the plane into two half-planes. However, $\overleftrightarrow{AB}$ belongs to neither set. One half-plane contains point C. We will call this half-plane h_C. Point D belongs to the other half-plane.

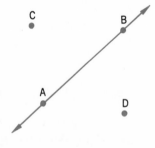

1. What do we call the half-plane containing point D?

2. Let p be the plane. Explain the meaning of the following statement.

$$h_C \cup h_D \cup \overleftrightarrow{AB} = p$$

An angle in a plane also separates the plane into two subsets. Recall that $\overrightarrow{XY}$ and $\overrightarrow{XZ}$, which are the sides of $\angle X$, each extend indefinitely in some direction. Some of the points of the plane are "inside" the angle. Point K is such a point.

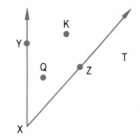

3. Is point Q such a point? Is point T?

To decide which points are "inside" an angle, let us look at the picture below.

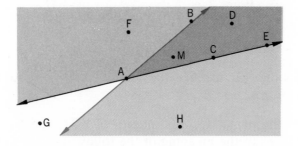

$\overleftrightarrow{AC}$ separates the plane into two half-planes. The half-plane which is shaded gray contains points M, D, B, and F. We call this half-plane h_B.

But $\overleftrightarrow{AB}$ also separates the plane into two half-planes. The half-plane which contains points D, M, C, and H is shaded in color; we call this half-plane h_C.

That part of the plane which is doubly shaded is the intersection of h_B and h_C.

4. For the picture above, which of the following points belong to $h_B \cap h_C$?

    a. M b. G c. H d. D e. F f. E

5. $\overleftrightarrow{AC}$ does not belong to h_B. Does point C belong to h_B?

6. a. Does point B belong to $h_B \cap h_C$?

    b. Does point C belong to $h_B \cap h_C$?

    c. Does point A belong to $h_B \cap h_C$?

■   The set of points $h_B \cap h_C$ is called the *interior* of $\angle BAC$.

7. On your paper, draw a picture like the one on the right. Shade the interior of $\angle M$.

An angle in a plane separates the plane into two subsets: the interior and the exterior of the angle. Remember the separator "stands between" the two sets and is not a subset of either set. The exterior of an angle consists of all points which are not in the interior and not on the angle.

Point R is in the interior of $\angle M$.
Point T is in the exterior of $\angle M$.
Point Q is on $\angle M$.

8. Is point Q either in the interior or the exterior of $\angle M$?

9. Make another picture like the one on the right above. Shade the exterior of $\angle M$.

10. Let p be the plane, $I_{\angle M}$ the interior of $\angle M$, and $E_{\angle M}$ the exterior of $\angle M$. Explain the meaning of the following statement.

$$(I_{\angle M}) \cup (\angle M) \cup (E_{\angle M}) = p$$

11. On your paper, make a picture like the one on the right. Shade the portion which is the intersection of the interiors of $\angle BAC$ and $\angle EAD$.

12. a. In the picture you made for exercise 11, connect E and B with a segment. Describe the points of $\overline{EB}$ which belong to the interior of $\angle EAB$.

b. Which points of $\overline{EB}$ do not belong to the interior of $\angle EAB$?

13. On your paper, draw a picture like the one on the right. Shade the portion which is the intersection of the interiors of $\angle XYZ$ and $\angle YXZ$. Which of the following points belong to this intersection?

a. W b. V c. Z d. T

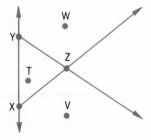

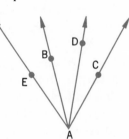

INTERIORS OF TRIANGLES

1. Name the three lines shown in the picture on the right.

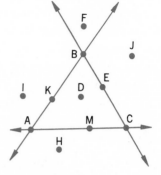

2. Complete each statement.

   a. $\overleftrightarrow{AB} \cap \overleftrightarrow{BC} = $ _____

   b. $\overleftrightarrow{BC} \cap \overleftrightarrow{AC} = $ _____

   c. $\overleftrightarrow{AC} \cap \overleftrightarrow{AB} = $ _____

3. $\overleftrightarrow{AC}$ separates the plane into two half-planes; h_B is the half-plane determined by $\overleftrightarrow{AC}$ and containing point B.

   a. Describe h_A similarly. [HINT: Consider $\overleftrightarrow{BC}$.]

   b. Describe h_C similarly. [HINT: Consider $\overleftrightarrow{AB}$.]

4. a. Draw a picture like the one above. Shade the half-plane h_B.

   b. Shade the half-plane h_C.

On your picture for exercise 4, mark all points which are in the picture above. Which are true and which are false?

5. $H \in (h_B \cap h_C)$ 10. $K \in (h_B \cap h_C)$

6. $B \in (h_B \cap h_C)$ 11. $J \in (h_B \cap h_C)$

7. $D \in (h_B \cap h_C)$ 12. $I \in (h_B \cap h_C)$

8. $F \in (h_B \cap h_C)$ 13. $M \in (h_B \cap h_C)$

9. $E \in (h_B \cap h_C)$ 14. $A \in (h_B \cap h_C)$

The shaded portion in the picture below is the *interior* of $\triangle ABC$. The sides of the triangle do not belong to the interior of the triangle.

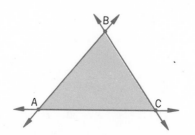

15. **a.** Make a picture like the one on the right. Shade h_X (that half-plane determined by $\overleftrightarrow{YZ}$ and containing point X).

   b. Shade h_Y.

   c. Shade h_Z.

   d. Is the following statement true?

   $h_X \cap h_Y \cap h_Z =$ interior of $\triangle XYZ$

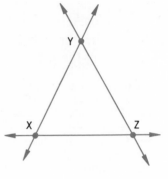

16. **a.** Does X belong to the interior of $\triangle XYZ$? Why or why not?

   b. Do any of the three vertices of a triangle belong to the interior of the triangle?

SIMPLE CLOSED CURVES

You are familiar with many geometric figures which have applications in our every-day activities. Some of these are triangles, squares, rectangles, parallelograms, and circles. All of these belong to the set of *simple closed curves*. Below are pictures of some simple closed curves.

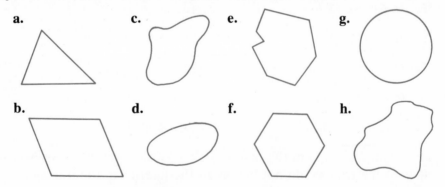

Each of the pictures below shows a figure which is *not* a simple closed curve.

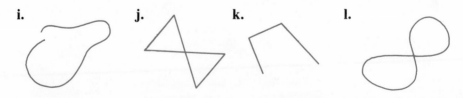

We can use the following test to determine whether or not a figure is a simple closed curve.

TEST   If you are able to trace a figure by starting at a certain point and returning to the same point without lifting your pencil or crossing any points, then the figure is a simple closed curve.

1. Using the test, tell why each of the figures **i–l** on page 334 fails to be a simple closed curve.

Although each of the curves **a–h** on page 334 is a simple closed curve, there are basically two kinds of curves represented. We will sort these curves into two kinds.

2. Copy each picture **a–h** on a sheet of paper.

3. For each picture, choose 5 pairs of points in the interior.

4. Connect each pair of points with a segment.

5. Does every point of every segment lie in the interior of the curve?

6. **a.** Can you find two points in the interior of curve **d** such that the segment connecting these two points has some points outside the interior of the curve?

   b. Answer the same question for curve **c**.

   c. Answer the same question for curve **e**.

■ Simple closed curves are either *convex* or *concave*. If for every two points in the interior of a curve, the segment connecting these points lies entirely in the interior, then the curve is *convex*. If there is one such segment which is not entirely in the interior, then the curve is *concave*.

BUILDING GEOMETRIC FIGURES

The simplest geometric figure is a point. The next simplest figure is a segment. The segment pictured below, $\overline{AB}$, consists of points A and B and all points between A and B.

1. Below are pictured four sets of points. For each set, tell whether the three labeled points are on *one* segment or not.

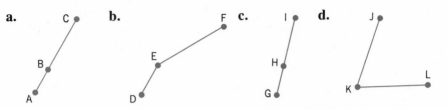

There is *one* line which contains all three points in part **a** above. There is no one line which contains all three points in part **b**.

■ Points which lie on the same line are called *collinear* points.

2. Explain why the following statement is true.

Every two points are collinear.

3. On your paper, copy three sets of points like those below. In each set, connect the three points to obtain triangles *ABC*, *DEF*, and *GHI*.

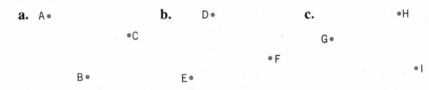

■ Every set of three non-collinear points determines a triangle.

4. Explain the following statement.

Every set of three non-collinear points determines not only a triangle, but an entire plane.

So far we have considered three simple figures.

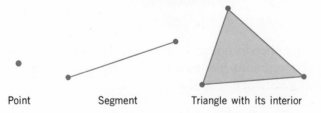

Point   Segment   Triangle with its interior

Consider four points in space. They can be arranged so that they determine *one* plane.

■ Points which lie in the same plane are called *coplanar* points.

It is possible for four points to be arranged so that they cannot lie in *one* plane. Such points are *non-coplanar*.

Suppose we have four points not all of which are in the same plane. The four non-coplanar points are in space. They form a figure called a *tetrahedron*. So, the fourth simplest figure, which is determined by four points, is a tetrahedron. Four is the smallest number of points required to determine a solid figure.

REGULAR TETRAHEDRONS

The most complex of the four basic figures we have considered so far is the tetrahedron. Polygons can be classified into regular polygons (all sides have the same measure and all angles have the same measure) and all others. We may also classify tetrahedra into regular tetrahedra and all others.

The directions below tell how to make a model of a regular tetrahedron. Refer to the picture as you read these directions.

1. On a piece of paper, construct a picture of an equilateral triangle. To do this, start with a segment, $\overline{AB}$. Then with a compass make arcs AC and BC. Draw pictures of $\overline{AC}$ and $\overline{BC}$.

2. Bisect each side of $\triangle ABC$. (Divide each side into two parts of the same length.) Here are the directions for bisecting $\overline{AB}$.

    a. Put the foot of a compass at the point A and open the compass to more than half the distance from A to B.

    b. Make an arc $X'YX$.

    c. With the same opening of the compass and with the foot at the point B, make another arc $X'ZX$. The two arcs intersect in X and X'.

    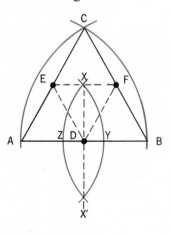

    d. Connect X and X'.

    e. Point D bisects $\overline{AB}$, so $AD = DB$.

3. Using a compass, mark off $\overline{AE}$ and $\overline{BF}$ equal in length to $\overline{AD}$. (Why do E and F bisect $\overline{AC}$ and $\overline{BC}$, respectively?)

4. Draw $\overline{ED}$, $\overline{DF}$, and $\overline{FE}$.

5. Cut out $\triangle ABC$, and fold along $\overline{ED}$, $\overline{DF}$, and $\overline{FE}$. Fasten edges with adhesive tape. You now have a model of a regular tetrahedron.

KEEPING ARITHMETICALLY FIT

For exercises **1–32**, numerals in parentheses refer to pages where you can find similar exercises.

Add.

(423–424)

1. 1,478
    333
    488
  9,007
  6,005
  5,363
  4,071
    309

(436–437)

2. 125.3
  366.2
    7.8
  632.1
  500.9
   63.6
   75.4
  115.5

(428–430)

3. $\dfrac{3}{7} + \dfrac{4}{6} + \dfrac{1}{3}$

4. $3\dfrac{2}{3} + 6\dfrac{1}{4} + 10\dfrac{2}{3}$

5. $10\dfrac{1}{2} + 11\dfrac{1}{3} + 12\dfrac{1}{4}$

Subtract.

(424)

6. 442,305
  $-$ 59,476

(438–439)

7. 40.26
  $-$ 9.38

(430–432)

8. $\dfrac{4}{7} - \dfrac{1}{9}$

9. $3\dfrac{1}{2} - 1\dfrac{5}{7}$

Multiply.

(425)

10. 309
  $\times 258$

(439–440)

11. 13.7
  $\times 9.8$

(432–434)

12. $\dfrac{3}{7} \times \dfrac{5}{9}$

13. $3\dfrac{1}{2} \times 5\dfrac{3}{5}$

Divide.

(425–427)

14. $305\overline{)365,211}$

(440–442)

15. $2.7\overline{)365.2}$

(434–435)

16. $\dfrac{1}{2} \div 23$

17. $3\dfrac{1}{4} \div 5\dfrac{1}{6}$

Give names in the form of per cent for the following: (442–443)

18. .37   **19.** .87   **20.** 2.36   **21.** 12.4   **22.** 100

Give replacements for n to obtain true statements. (442–443)

23. 30% of 120 = n

24. .5% of 200 = n

25. 120% of 120 = n

26. 5 = n% of 100

27. $\frac{1}{2}$ = n% of $\frac{1}{2}$

28. 2 = n% of .5

29. 3 = 20% of n

30. $\frac{1}{2}$ = 200% of n

31. 56 = .5% of n

32. $\frac{1}{n}$ = 50% of 1

Do exercises **33–40** mentally.

33. Take 15, divide by 3, multiply by 5, subtract 25. Result?

34. Take square root of 100, divide by 10, subtract 1, multiply by 250, add 5, multiply by 13, subtract 16. Result?

35. Take 75, multiply by 2, add 150, multiply by 5, add 500, divide by 200, subtract 9. Result?

36. Take 3, multiply by 4, multiply by 12, divide by 2, divide by 4. Result?

37. Take 5, square it, divide by 2, multiply by 3, subtract 9, subtract $3\frac{1}{2}$. Result?

38. Take $\frac{1}{3}$, multiply by $\frac{1}{2}$, multiply by 12, divide by 6, multiply by 10. Result?

39. Take .1, multiply by 100, divide by 20, subtract $\frac{1}{2}$. Result?

40. Take $\frac{1}{4}$, multiply by 16, subtract 2, square, add 16, multiply by 100, divide by 2, subtract 1, take square root. Result?

Find the numbers called for in exercises **41–44**.

41. Multiplying a number by 2 and adding 7 results in 15. What is the number?

42. One-half of a number increased by 2 is $9\frac{1}{2}$. What is the number?

43. Adding 25 to a number and multiplying the result by 4 results in 148. What is the number?

44. What is the arithmetic mean of 1.5, 2.5, and .5?

Use this table for exercises **45–48**.

1 kilometer ≐ .6 mile	1 inch ≐ 2.54 centimeters
1 meter ≐ 39.4 inches	1 foot ≐ 30.48 centimeters
1 centimeter ≐ .4 inches	1 yard ≐ .91 meter

45. A car traveling at the speed of 85 kilometers per hour is traveling how many miles per hour? How many yards per minute? How many feet per second?

46. A 100 meter dash is how many feet?

47. 400 yards is how many meters?

48. A train traveling at 80 miles per hour travels at how many kilometers per hour? How many feet per second?

49. 100 feet per second is how many miles per hour?

VOCABULARY REVIEW

acute triangle (329)
adjacent sides (323)
angle (325)
between (321)
collinear points (336)
collinear rays (325)
concave curves (335)
convex curves (335)
congruent (327)
coplanar points (337)
diagonal (323)
endpoint (321)
equilateral triangle (328)
exterior of an angle (332)
half-line (324)
half-plane (330)
interior of an angle (331)
interior of a triangle (333)
isosceles triangle (328)

measure (327)
non-collinear points (336)
non-coplanar points (337)
obtuse triangle (330)
pentagon (323)
point (321)
polygon (322)
quadrilateral (323)
ray (324)
regular polygon (337)
regular tetrahedron (337)
right triangle (329)
scalene triangle (328)
segment (321)
simple closed curve (334)
tetrahedron (337)
triangle (322)
vertex (322)
vertical angles (326)

A CHALLENGE TO YOU

1. In the base-ten numeration system .1 means one-tenth, .01 means one-hundredth, and so on. In the base-five numeration system .1 means one-fifth, .01 means one twenty-fifth, and so on. Write in words the name for each of the following:

   a. $.3_{\text{five}}$ **c.** $.001_{\text{five}}$ **e.** $.11_{\text{five}}$ **g.** $.213_{\text{five}}$

   b. $.04_{\text{five}}$ **d.** $.23_{\text{five}}$ **f.** $.111_{\text{five}}$ **h.** $.0001_{\text{five}}$

2. For the numerals in exercise **1**, write fractional names.

3. For the numerals in exercise **1**, write decimal names.

4. For the experiment of rolling a die twice, the sample space S consists of 36 elements. To say that the number of elements in S is 36, we write

$$n(S) = 36$$

   The event E of obtaining 1 on the first roll contains 6 elements. That is,

$$n(E) = 6$$

   The probability of E, denoted by $P(E)$, is computed as follows:

$$p(E) = \frac{n(E)}{n(S)} = \frac{6}{36} = \frac{1}{6}$$

   a. Compute the probability of the event in which the sum of the outcomes on the first and on the second rolls is 10.

   b. Compute the probability of the event in which the sum of the outcomes on the first and on the second rolls is 6.

   c. Compute the probability of the event in which the sum of the outcomes on the first and on the second rolls is 12.

   d. When it is *impossible* for an event to occur, we say that its probability is 0. What is the probability of the event in which the sum of the outcomes on the first and on the second rolls is 13?

   e. When it is *certain* that an event will occur, we say that its probability is 1. What is the probability of the event in which the sum of the outcomes on the first and on the second rolls is less than 13 and greater than 1?

CHAPTER TEST

Match each picture with the letter of the correct name chosen from the list below.

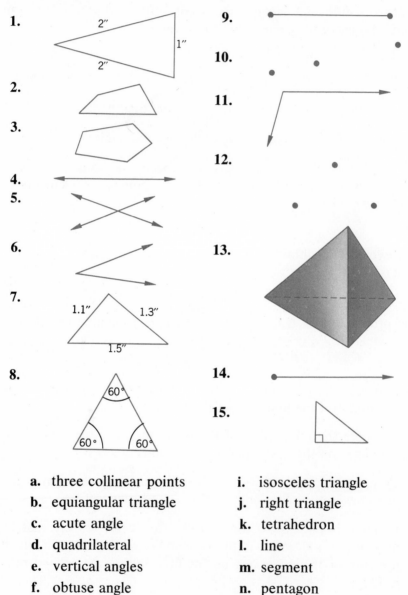

1. 2″ 2″ 1″

2.

3.

4.

5.

6.

7. 1.1″ 1.3″ 1.5″

8. 60° 60° 60°

9.

10.

11.

12.

13.

14.

15.

a. three collinear points
b. equiangular triangle
c. acute angle
d. quadrilateral
e. vertical angles
f. obtuse angle
g. ray
h. scalene triangle

i. isosceles triangle
j. right triangle
k. tetrahedron
l. line
m. segment
n. pentagon
o. three non-collinear points

16. Describe $\triangle ABC$ as the union of three segments.

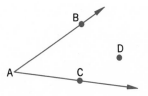

17. Name three kinds of triangles classified according to measures of their sides.

18. Name three kinds of triangles classified according to measures of their angles.

19. a. On your paper, draw a picture like the one on the right. Shade the interior of A.

   b. Does point B belong to the interior?

   c. Does point D belong to the interior?

20. Which simple closed curves are *convex*?

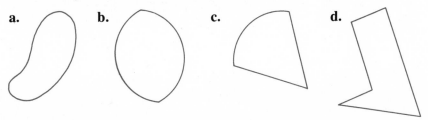

a. **b.** **c.** **d.**

21. Explain why it is not possible to have more than one obtuse angle in a triangle.

Which are true and which are false? For each false statement, introduce the necessary correction(s) to change it to a true statement.

22. It is not possible for 3 points to be non-collinear.

23. A triangle is a set of points.

24. Not every ray is a set of points.

25. A segment may be a subset of a ray.

26. A ray may be a subset of a segment.

27. The two simplest geometric figures are a point and a segment.

28. A triangle may have two right angles.

29. A right triangle may be isosceles.

30. Two lines may intersect in more than one point.

CHAPTER TWELVE

Areas and Volumes

AREAS OF RECTANGLES AND RIGHT TRIANGLES

A *rectangle* is a quadrilateral in which opposite sides are parallel and all angles are right angles. To abbreviate "rectangle *ABCD*," we write "□ *ABCD*."

The shaded region on the right is the interior of rectangle *ABCD*. Strictly speaking, the area of rectangle *ABCD* is 0, because rectangle *ABCD* is the union of four segments:

$$\overline{AB} \cup \overline{BC} \cup \overline{CD} \cup \overline{DA}$$

That is, the boundary itself has an area of 0 square units. However, the area which the boundary encloses is not 0.

To simplify matters, we shall agree that whenever we say "area of a rectangle," we shall mean "area of the interior of a rectangle."

■ If the length of a rectangle is *l* units and the width is *w* units, then the area of this rectangle is *lw* square units.

$$\text{Area}_\square = lw$$

1. Explain why the area of the rectangle pictured on the right is 21 square inches.

2. What is true of the measures of the opposite sides of a rectangle?

Find the area of each rectangle with the given length and width. The first number gives length, the second width.

3. 4 in., 2 in.

4. 1.5 in., .6 in.

5. 2 in., 1 in.

6. 12 in., $\frac{3}{4}$ ft.   [HINT: Change feet to inches or inches to feet before computing the area.]

7. 2 ft., 7 in.

8. 3 yd., 2 ft.

9. Make a picture of three different rectangles. Connect two opposite vertices with a segment. This segment is a diagonal which divides the rectangle into two triangles. Do the pairs of triangles in each rectangle have the same area?

10. **a.** If the area of □*MPRS* is *lw* square units, what is the area of △*MPS*?

    b. What is the area of △*PRS*?

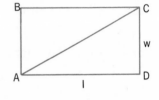

MATHEMATICAL DERIVATION

If we know that a diagonal of a rectangle divides the rectangle into two right triangles having the same area, then we can determine the formula for the area of a right triangle.

1. Area of □*ABCD* = *lw* square units

2. $\text{Area}_{\triangle ABC} = \text{Area}_{\triangle ACD}$

3. Therefore, $\text{Area}_{\square ABCD} = 2 \times \text{Area}_{\triangle ABC}$

4. Therefore, $lw = 2 \times \text{Area}_{\triangle ABC}$

5. Therefore, $\text{Area}_{\triangle ABC} = \frac{1}{2}lw$

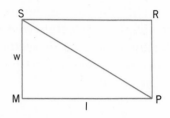

The conclusion is that the area of triangle *ABC* is one-half of the area of rectangle *ABCD*. Of course, this would be true in *any* rectangle, since we did not choose any special rectangle.

Find the following areas.

1. $\text{Area}_{\square ABCD}$

2. $\text{Area}_{\triangle ABC}$

3. $\text{Area}_{\triangle ACD}$

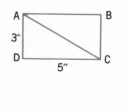

Find the following areas.

4. $\text{Area}_{\square MPRS}$

5. $\text{Area}_{\triangle MPT}$ [*T* divides $\overline{PR}$ into two congruent segments.]

6. $\text{Area}_{\triangle TRS}$

7. $\text{Area}_{\triangle MTS}$

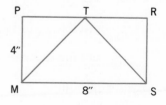

Find the following areas if $YV = VW = WU$, and $XT = TZ$.

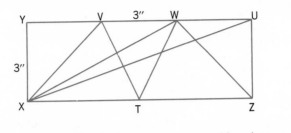

8. Area$_{\square XYUZ}$ **9.** Area$_{\triangle XYV}$ **10.** Area$_{\triangle WUZ}$

11. Lines $\overleftrightarrow{AB}$ and $\overleftrightarrow{CD}$ are parallel. $\overline{XA}$ is an altitude upon $\overline{CD}$ in $\triangle CDA$, and $\overline{BY}$ is an altitude upon $\overline{CD}$ in $\triangle CDB$. Name all pairs of segments which appear to have the same measure.

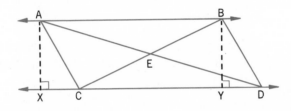

PARALLELOGRAMS

A *parallelogram* is a special kind of a quadrilateral. Its opposite sides are parallel, but its angles do not have to be right angles. Below is a picture of a parallelogram. To abbreviate "parallelogram $ABCD$," we write "$\square ABCD$."

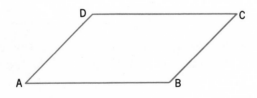

Which are true and which are false?

1. Every parallelogram is a rectangle.

2. Every rectangle is a parallelogram.

3. Every parallelogram is a quadrilateral.

4. Every quadrilateral is a parallelogram.

5. Every square is a quadrilateral.

6. No triangle is a quadrilateral.

7. Some rectangles have no right angles.

8. Every parallelogram has two diagonals.

9. Every square is a parallelogram.

Let us use the pictures of the three parallelograms below to make some conclusions about the measures of their sides and angles.

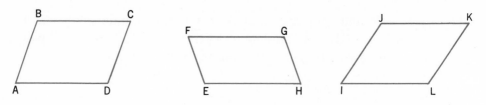

10. Use a ruler and a protractor to measure the sides and the angles of each parallelogram. Record the measures of the four sides and four angles of each parallelogram on a piece of paper.

On the basis of these measures, answer the following questions.

11. What seems to be true about the measures of opposite sides?

12. What seems to be true about the measures of opposite angles?

In the picture, $\overline{PT}$ is perpendicular to $\overline{RT}$ and $\overline{SU}$ is perpendicular to $\overline{QR}$. We abbreviate this as follows:

$$\overline{PT} \perp \overline{RT} \qquad \overline{SU} \perp \overline{QR}$$

13. Draw pictures of two more parallelograms. Draw pictures of line segments like $\overline{PT}$ and $\overline{SU}$ above, and shade the corresponding triangles.

14. What do you suspect to be true about the areas of triangles PTQ and SUR? What about the areas of the pairs of corresponding triangles in your pictures?

15. Draw a picture of two parallel lines. Choose three points on one of the lines. Draw perpendiculars from these points to the other line. Measure the lengths of the three perpendiculars between the two lines. What appears to be true about these measures?

AREAS OF PARALLELOGRAMS AND TRIANGLES

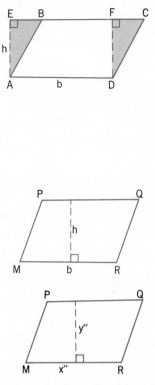

Let us assume that the area of $\triangle AEB$ is the same as the area of $\triangle DFC$. From this assumption, we can draw a conclusion about the area of a parallelogram. We know that $AEFD$ is a rectangle. Its area is bh square units. Since $\triangle AEB$ and $\triangle DFC$ have the same area, the area of $\square ABCD$ is the same as the area of $\square AEFD$. Explain why this is true. The area of the parallelogram, therefore, is also bh square units.

■ The area of a parallelogram is equal to the product of the measures of the base and the altitude.

$$\text{Area}_\square = bh$$

1. Compute the area of $\square EFGH$. The measures of the base and altitude are as shown in the picture.

2. The area of $\square IJKL$ is 24 sq. in. Determine the length of its altitude $\overline{JM}$, if $IL = 8$ in.

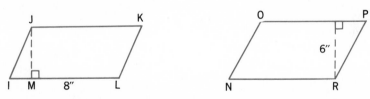

3. The area of $\square NOPR$ is 48 sq. in. Determine the length of $\overline{NR}$.

4. Determine the area of the parallelogram on the left below.

5. $SV = 5$ in., $VW = 1$ in. The area of $\triangle VUW = 1.5$ sq. in. Determine the area of $\square STUV$.

Diagonal $\overline{BD}$ divides $\square\, ABCD$ into two triangles. These two triangles have the same area, that is

$$\text{Area}_{\triangle ABD} = \text{Area}_{\triangle BCD}$$

If the length of $\overline{AD}$, the base of the parallelogram, is b, and the altitude of the parallelogram is h, then the area of the parallelogram is bh.

$$\text{Area}_{\square ABCD} = bh$$

The area of each of the two triangles ABD and BCD is, therefore, $\frac{1}{2}bh$.

■ If the base of a triangle is b units and the height is h units, then the area of the triangle is $\frac{1}{2}bh$ square units.

$$\text{Area}_{\triangle} = \frac{1}{2}bh$$

Determine the area of each triangle with the given base and altitude.

6. $b = 5$ in., $h = 15$ in.

9. $b = \frac{1}{2}$ ft., $h = \frac{1}{3}$ ft.

7. $b = 1$ ft., $h = 5\frac{1}{2}$ in.

10. $b = \frac{3}{4}$ ft., $h = 8$ in. *36 sq. in. or*

8. $b = 3.6$ in., $h = 2.8$ in.

11. $b = 1$ yd., $h = 2$ ft.

12. What is the altitude of $\triangle XYZ$?

13. Find the area of $\triangle XYZ$.

Find the following areas.

14. Area$_{\triangle ADB}$

15. Area$_{\triangle BCD}$

16. Area$_{\triangle ABC}$

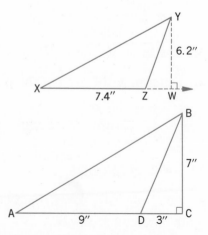

REGULAR POLYGONS

■ A *regular polygon* is a polygon in which all sides have the same measure and all angles have the same measure.

1. Without measuring, tell which polygons appear to be regular polygons.

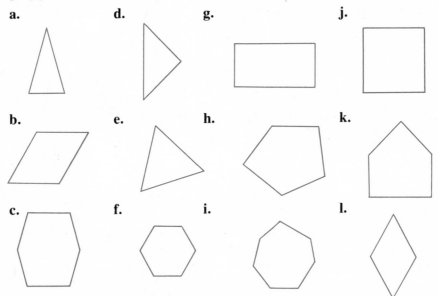

a.   **d.**   **g.**   **j.**

b.   **e.**   **h.**   **k.**

c.   **f.**   **i.**   **l.**

2. In order for a polygon to be a regular polygon, what two conditions must it meet?

3. Do all sides of an equilateral triangle have the same measure?

4. Do all angles of an equilateral triangle have the same measure? What is that measure? Is it the same for all equilateral triangles?

5. Is an equilateral triangle a regular polygon? Why or why not?

EQUILATERAL TRIANGLES

To compute the area of a triangle, you need to know the measure of one side and the measure of the altitude to that side.

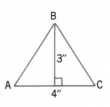

1. Compute the area of △*ABC*.

2. What is true about the measure of each side in an equilateral triangle?

We want to explore whether it is possible to determine the area of an equilateral triangle once we know the measure of its sides.

First, observe that an altitude in an equilateral triangle divides the base into two congruent segments.

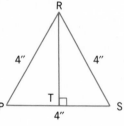

3. What is the measure of $\overline{PT}$?

4. Is $\triangle PTR$ a right triangle? Why?

5. What relation holds between the measures of the sides of $\triangle PTR$?

According to the Pythagorean Relation, we know that in $\triangle PTR$,

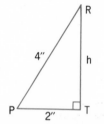

$$2^2 + h^2 = 4^2$$
$$4 + h^2 = 16$$
$$h^2 = 12$$
$$h = \sqrt{12} \doteq 3.5 \text{ in.}$$

If we know the measure of a side of an equilateral triangle, we can compute the measure of an altitude. In a triangle with sides 4 in., the altitude is about 3.5 in. Now we can compute the area of the triangle.

$$\text{Area}_{\triangle PRS} \doteq \frac{1}{2} \times 4 \times 3.5 = 7.0 \text{ sq. in.}$$

If we wanted to know the exact area, we would use $\sqrt{12}$ for the measure of the altitude. Note that $\sqrt{12} = \sqrt{4 \times 3} = \sqrt{4} \times \sqrt{3} = 2\sqrt{3}$.

$$\text{Area}_{\triangle PRS} = \frac{1}{2} \times 4 \times 2\sqrt{3} = 4\sqrt{3} \text{ sq. in.}$$

We can use the procedure above to find the length of an altitude and the area of any equilateral triangle. This is possible because each altitude of an equilateral triangle bisects a side of the triangle. ["Bisects" means "divides into two segments of the same length."]

Compute the area of each equilateral triangle. [HINT: Compute the measure of an altitude first.]

6.   7.   8.   9.

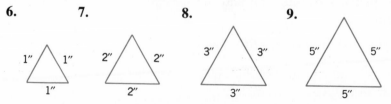

Knowing that an altitude upon the base of an isosceles triangle bisects the base, compute the area of each isosceles triangle.

10.   **11.**   **12.**

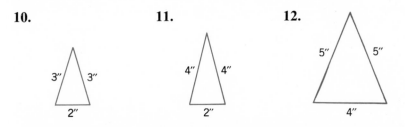

AREAS OF EQUILATERAL TRIANGLES

When you were computing areas of equilateral triangles, perhaps you noticed a pattern which shows a relation between the area and the measure of a side of the triangle. Examine this table.

Measure of side in inches	Area in square inches
1	$\dfrac{\sqrt{3}}{4} = \dfrac{1^2\sqrt{3}}{4}$
2	$\dfrac{\sqrt{3}}{4} = \dfrac{2^2\sqrt{3}}{4}$
3	$\dfrac{9\sqrt{3}}{4} = \dfrac{3^2\sqrt{3}}{4}$
4	$\dfrac{16\sqrt{3}}{4} = \dfrac{4^2\sqrt{3}}{4}$
5	$\dfrac{25\sqrt{3}}{4} = \dfrac{5^2\sqrt{3}}{4}$

It should not be difficult to generalize:

side: s

Area: $\dfrac{s^2\sqrt{3}}{4}$

We can prove that the formula below gives the area of an equilateral triangle.

$$\text{Area} = \frac{s^2\sqrt{3}}{4}$$

The proof is based on the Pythagorean Relation. First, we determine the length of the altitude (BD), in terms of the length of each side (s).

$$(BD)^2 + \left(\frac{s^2}{2}\right) = s^2; \qquad (BD)^2 + \frac{s^2}{4} = s^2$$

$$(BD)^2 = s^2 - \frac{s^2}{4} = \frac{4s^2}{4} - \frac{s^2}{4} = \frac{4s^2 - s^2}{4} = \frac{3s^2}{4}$$

$$BD = \sqrt{\frac{3s^2}{4}} = \frac{\sqrt{3}\sqrt{s^2}}{\sqrt{4}} = \frac{s\sqrt{3}}{2}$$

Area of $\triangle ABC = \frac{1}{2} \cdot s \cdot \frac{s\sqrt{3}}{2} = \frac{s \cdot s\sqrt{3}}{2 \cdot 2} = \frac{s^2\sqrt{3}}{4}$

To compute the area of an equilateral triangle, replace s in $\frac{s^2\sqrt{3}}{4}$ by a numeral giving the measure of the side of the triangle.

Using the formula, determine the area of each equilateral triangle whose sides have the following measures.

1. 6 in.   2. 4 in.   3. $\sqrt{2}$ 4. $\sqrt{3}$

5. If the area of an equilateral triangle is $\frac{7^2\sqrt{3}}{4}$ sq. in., how long is its side?

6. If the area of an equilateral triangle is $\frac{3\sqrt{3}}{4}$ sq. in., how long is its side?

REGULAR POLYGONS AND CIRCLES

In the picture of the circle with the center at P, every point of the circle is the same distance from the point P. This distance is 2 in. $\overline{PA}$ is one of many radii (singular: radius) of this circle. The measure of each radius of this circle is 2 in. $\overline{AB}$ is one of many diameters of this circle. The length of a circle is called its circumference.

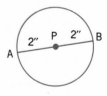

1. What is the measure of diameter $\overline{AB}$?

2. In any circle, how does the measure of a diameter compare with the measure of a radius?

3. Make a picture of a circle. Using a protractor, make an angle of 60° whose vertex is at the center of the circle and whose sides contain two radii. Keep making such angles next to each other. How many 60° angles can you make?

4. There are four angles in the picture on the right, each of which measures 90°. What is the sum of the measures of the four angles?

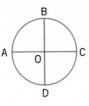

5. Suppose we make 360 angles with the vertices at the center of a circle, each of the same measure. What would be the measure of each angle?

6. Suppose we have a circle with angles at the center.

    a. Each angle at the center measures 120°. Each pair of angles shares one side. How many such angles are there in a circle?

    b. Each angle measures 30°. How many such angles are there in a circle?

    c. Each angle measures 15°. How many such angles are there in a circle?

    d. Each angle measures 5°. How many such angles?

    e. Each angle measures 2°. How many such angles?

    f. Each angle measures 1°. How many such angles?

    g. Each angle measures $\frac{1}{2}^{\circ}$. How many such angles?

7. In exercise **6**, as the measure of angles gets smaller, what happens to the number of angles? Dividing the measure of angles by 2, multiplies the number of angles by what number?

INSCRIBED HEXAGONS

Six angles each measuring 60° will "fit" at the center of a circle, as shown in the picture.

    Let us connect the consecutive points at which the six radii cut the circle. This gives us the hexagon (six-sided polygon) $ABCDEF$. Each vertex of the hexagon is on the circle. We say that the hexagon is *inscribed* in the circle, or the circle is *circumscribed* about the hexagon.

    Let us take a closer look at one of the triangles, say $\triangle OAB$. We can immediately observe that it is an isosceles triangle, because $AO = BO$. Also $m\angle OBA = m\angle OAB$.

1. **a.** In $\triangle AOB$, what is the sum of the measures of $\angle OBA$ and $\angle OAB$?

   b. If $m \angle OBA = m \angle OAB$, then what is the measure of each of these angles?

RECALL   A triangle in which all angles have the same measure is called an *equiangular* triangle.

2. Explain why an equilateral triangle is also equiangular.

3. If $\triangle OAB$ in the picture on page 355 is an equilateral triangle, prove that $\overline{AB}$ has the same length as any radius of the circle.

4. Is the area of hexagon $ABCDEF$ in the picture on page 355 greater or less than the area of the circle.

5. **a.** Draw a picture of a circle having a radius of any length you choose. Inscribe a regular hexagon in it by measuring off six angles of 60° each at the center of the circle.

   b. Divide each angle into two 30° angles, obtaining 12 angles, each having measure of 30°. Connect the points on the circle to form a dodecagon (twelve-sided polygon).

   c. Is the area of the dodecagon greater than or less than the area of the circle?

   d. Is the area of the dodecagon greater than or less than the area of the hexagon?

   e. Recall that the *perimeter* of a polygon is the sum of the lengths of its sides. Is the perimeter of the dodecagon greater or less than the perimeter of the hexagon?

6. **a.** If you would divide each 30° angle in your picture into two angles of the same size, how many angles would you obtain?

   b. What would be the size of each angle?

   c. How many sides would there be in the polygon obtained by connecting the new points on the circle?

7. A radius of a circle measures 4 in. What is the area of a regular hexagon inscribed in this circle?

8. A radius of a circle measures 6 in. What is the area of a regular hexagon inscribed in this circle?

INSCRIBED REGULAR POLYGONS

1. What kind of a polygon is *CGKOSW* pictured below?

2. What kind of a polygon is *ACEGIKMOQSUW*?

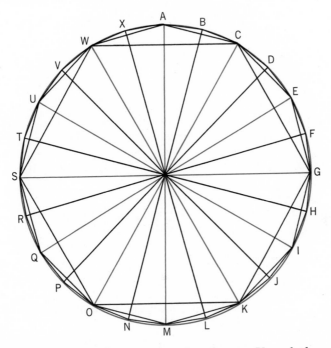

Let us call the polygon in exercise **1** polygon *X* and the polygon in exercise **2** polygon *Y*.

3. Which polygon has a greater area, *X* or *Y*?

4. Which polygon has a greater perimeter, *X* or *Y*?

5. How many sides does the polygon *ABCDEFGHIJKLMNOPQRSTUVWX* have?

Let us call the polygon in exercise **5** polygon *Z*.

6. Of the three polygons *X*, *Y*, and *Z*, which has the greatest area?

7. Which has the greatest perimeter?

8. How do the areas of the polygons compare with the area of the circle as the number of sides increases?

9. How do the perimeters compare with the circumference of the circle?

10. Inscribe a square in a circle as shown in the picture below.

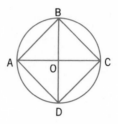

Using a compass, bisect each of the angles AOB, COB, DOC, and AOD. Draw a regular inscribed octagon (8 sides).

11. How does the area of the octagon compare with the area of the square?

12. How does the perimeter of the octagon compare with the perimeter of the square?

13. How does the area of the octagon compare with the area of the circle?

14. How does the perimeter of the octagon compare with the circumference of the circle?

15. Using a compass, bisect the appropriate angles to obtain a regular inscribed 16-sided polygon.

16. Is the area of the 16-sided polygon greater or less than the area of the octagon?

17. Is the area of the 16-sided polygon greater or less than the area of the circle?

18. Is the perimeter of the 16-sided polygon greater or less than the perimeter of the octagon?

19. Is the perimeter of the 16-sided polygon greater or less than the circumference of the circle?

■   As the number of sides of regular inscribed polygons increases, the limit of the areas of the polygons is the area of the circle.

20. Make a statement similar to that above about the circumference of the circle in relation to the perimeters of regular inscribed polygons.

AREAS OF CIRCLES

The ratio of the circumference of any circle to the length of a diameter is the same number for every circle. This number is π [Read: pi], which is approximately equal to 3.14.

$$\frac{c}{d} = \pi \qquad \text{or} \qquad \frac{c}{d} \doteq 3.14$$

Thus, the circumference of any circle is a little more than 3 times as long as a diameter of that circle.

■ If the measure of a diameter of a circle is d units, then the circumference of the circle is $d\pi$ units.

$$\text{circumference} = d\pi$$

The circumference could also be found by multiplying $2r$ and π, where r is the measure of a radius of the circle.

$$\text{circumference} = 2r \cdot \pi$$

This is illustrated in the picture below.

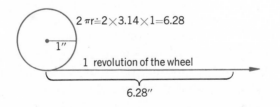

$2\,\pi r \doteq 2 \times 3.14 \times 1 = 6.28$

1 revolution of the wheel

6.28″

Look at the picture below. It shows a regular polygon inscribed in a circle.

1. If the altitude of the triangle shown in the picture is h units and the base is a units, what is the area of the triangle in terms of h and a?

2. If the number of sides in the polygon inscribed in the circle is n, how many triangles make up the area of the entire polygon?

3. What is the area of the polygon in terms of n, h, and a?

4. What is the perimeter of the polygon?

5. What is the limit of the perimeters of inscribed polygons as the number of sides of the polygons becomes indefinitely larger?

6. What is the limit of the length of the altitudes of the triangles as the number of sides of the inscribed polygons becomes indefinitely large?

We show the conclusions in exercises **5** and **6** as follows:

$$\text{perimeter of polygon} \longrightarrow \text{circumference of circle}$$
$$p \longrightarrow c$$

[Read: perimeter of polygon *approaches* circumference of circle]

$$\text{altitude of triangle} \longrightarrow \text{radius of circle}$$
$$h \longrightarrow r$$

If you had a correct answer to exercise **3**, it was,

$$\text{area of polygon} = \frac{1}{2}(ah)n.$$

But (an) is the perimeter of the polygon.

$$an = p$$

Therefore,

$$\text{area of polygon} = \frac{1}{2}(ah)n = \frac{1}{2}(an)h = \frac{1}{2}ph$$

As the number of sides of the polygons increases, the areas of the polygons approach the area of the circle. Since the perimeters of the polygons (p) approach the circumference of the circle (c) and the altitudes of the triangles (h) approach the radius (r), we have

$$\frac{1}{2}ph \longrightarrow \frac{1}{2}cr$$

We know, however, that the circumference of the circle c is equal to $2\pi r$.

$$\text{area of circle} = \frac{1}{2}cr = \frac{1}{2}(2\pi r)r = \pi r^2$$

This formula enables us to find the area of a circle. The only thing we need to know is the measure of a radius of the circle.

■   If the measure of a radius of a circle is r units, then the area of the circle is πr^2 square units.

$$\text{Area} = \pi r^2$$

7. What is the circumference of a circle with a radius of 2 in.? Give answer in terms of π; then compute the approximate answer using 3.14 for π.

8. What is the area of a circle with a radius of 5 in.? Give two answers as in exercise **7**.

9. Determine the circumference and the area of each circle having the following measures of radii. Give two answers as in exercise **7**.

    a. $\frac{1}{2}$ in.   **b.** 3 in.   **c.** 10 in.   **d.** 1 in.   **e.** 6 in.

10. A diameter of a circle measures 20 in.

    a. What is the area of the circle? (Give an answer in terms of π.)

    b. What is the area of a square inscribed in this circle?

    c. Find the difference between the area of the circle and the area of the inscribed square. (Give the answer in terms of π; then compute an approximate answer using 3.14 for π.)

11. a. Compute the area of a regular hexagon inscribed in the circle of exercise **10**.

    b. Find the difference between the areas of the circle and the inscribed hexagon. Compute two answers as in exercise **10c**.

    c. Which difference is larger, that in exercise **10c** or that in exercise **11b**?

    d. Is your answer in part **c** consistent with what you have learned?

12. Compute to two decimal places the circumference and area of each circle with the following measures of radii. (Use 3.14 for π.)

    a. 7 in.   **b.** 3 ft.   **c.** 2.5 in.   **d.** $5\frac{1}{2}$ ft.   **e.** 10 mi.

13. What distance does a wheel with a diameter of 2 in. cover when making 100 revolutions?

14. To the nearest whole number, how many revolutions does a wheel with a radius of 10 in. make, when traveling 1 mi.?

15. A diameter of a wheel measures 32 in. If the wheel moves along the road with a speed of 65 mph, how many revolutions, to the nearest whole number, does it make in one hour?

16. Approximately how many revolutions does a wheel in exercise **15** make in one hour when traveling at 130 mph?

VOLUMES OF SOLIDS

We shall now deal with geometric objects called *solids*. Examples of solids are rectangular solids, pyramids, cylinders, cones, and spheres.

In measuring areas of plane geometric objects, we use a square unit of measure. A square with a side of length 1 in. is such a unit. In measuring *volumes* of solid objects, we use a cubic unit of measure. For example, a cube with an edge of length 1 in. is such a unit.

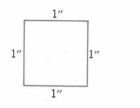
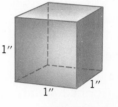

Solids whose *faces* are rectangles are called *rectangular solids*. Consider a rectangular solid like the one pictured at the right. The dimensions of the solid are: length 5 in., width 2 in., and height 3 in. One layer of cubes, shown in the picture, has a volume equal to

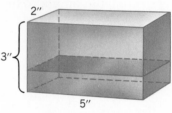

5 × 2 × 1, or 10 cubic inches

Since the height is 3 in., there are three such layers. Thus the volume of the rectangular solid is

5 × 2 × 3, or 30 cubic inches

This suggests the following formula.

■ The volume of a rectangular solid with length l units, width w units, and height h units is lwh cubic units.

$$\text{Volume} = lwh$$

When you use this formula to compute volumes of rectangular solids, be sure that all of the dimensions of the solid are given in terms of the same unit.

Recall our agreement that whenever we said "area of a rectangle" we meant "area of the interior of a rectangle." We shall make the same agreement about volume here. Whenever we say "volume of a rectangular solid" we shall mean "volume of the interior enclosed by the rectangular solid."

Compute the volume of each rectangular solid with the following dimensions.

1. 1 in., 2 in., 3 in.

2. 3.2 in., 2.5 in., 6.0 in.

3. $\frac{1}{2}$ ft., $\frac{1}{3}$ ft., 2 ft.

4. 12 cm., 20 cm., 30 cm.

5. 25 m., 2 m., 4 m.

6. $2\frac{1}{2}$ in., $4\frac{1}{2}$ in., $6\frac{1}{2}$ in.

7. Given a piece of metal in the shape of a rectangular solid with dimensions 4 in., 7 in., and 12 in., compute its weight, if 1 cu. in. of the metal weighs .25 lb.

Compute the ratio of the volumes of the first rectangular solid to the second rectangular solid if their dimensions are as follows:

8. 2 in., 3 in., 5 in.;   4 in., 3 in., 5 in.

9. 2 in., 3 in., 5 in.;   4 in., 6 in., 5 in.

10. 2 in., 3 in., 5 in.;   4 in., 6 in., 10 in.

11. 2 in., 3 in., 5 in.;   6 in., 9 in., 15 in.

Look at your answers for exercises 8–11 and answer the following:

12. If one of the three dimensions of a rectangular solid is doubled while the other two are unchanged, how is the volume changed?

13. If each of two dimensions of a rectangular solid is doubled while the third is unchanged, how is the volume changed?

14. If each of the three dimensions of a rectangular solid is doubled, how is the volume changed?

15. If each of the three dimensions of a rectangular solid is tripled, how is the volume changed?

16. In seven hours a laborer dug a hole in the form of a rectangular solid 4 ft. by 4 ft. by 6 ft. How many cubic yards of dirt did he remove per hour? Give your answer to the nearest tenth.

17. A cube with an edge of 2 ft. is filled with water. What does the water weigh? [HINT: One cubic foot of water weighs 62.5 lbs.]

18. 1 cu. yd. of black soil is called "one load." A truck has the dimensions 6 ft. by 4 ft. by 2 ft. How many loads does it carry when it is filled? Give your answer to the nearest tenth of the load.

CYLINDERS

Suppose we are given two parallel lines, k and l, as shown in the picture at the right. Imagine that line l "moves" at the constant distance d from line k. The resulting set of points is a *circular cylindrical surface*. The line k is called the *axis* of the surface.

Now imagine two planes, which are perpendicular to the axis of the cylinder, intersecting the surface in two circles. Then the union of the two circular regions and the subset of the cylindrical surface between the two planes is called a *right circular cylinder*, or simply a *cylinder*. The two circular regions are called the *bases* of the cylinder, as is shown in the picture at the right. The part of the axis between the bases is called the *altitude*.

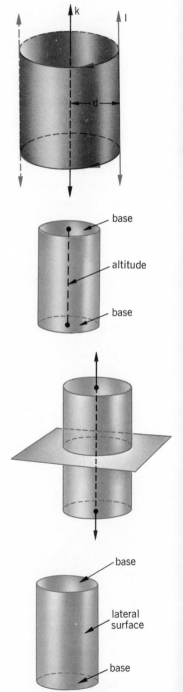

1. Suppose a cylinder is cut by a plane perpendicular to the altitude. What geometric figure is formed by the intersection of the plane and the cylinder?

2. If the length of a radius of the base of a cylinder is r in., what is the distance of any point on the outer surface of the cylinder from the altitude? [To find such a distance, imagine a perpendicular segment from a point on the surface to the altitude.]

The entire surface of the cylinder consists of two bases (circular regions) and the *lateral surface*.

3. **a.** Imagine the lateral surface of a cylinder unfolded. What geometric figure is formed?

   b. What is the length of one side of this figure in relation to the base of the cylinder?

   c. What is the length of the other side of this figure in relation to the cylinder?

4. What is the formula for the circumference of a circle in terms of π?

AREAS AND VOLUMES OF CYLINDERS

Cut a rectangle out of a piece of paper and roll it into a cylinder. In the picture at the right $\overline{BC}$ measures h in. and is the altitude of the cylinder. $\overline{CD}$ is $2\pi r$ in., where r is the length of a radius of a base of the cylinder.

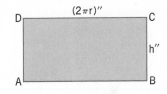

1. What is the area of the lateral surface of the cylinder in terms of π, r, and h?

2. What is the combined area of the two bases?

3. What is the entire area? [HINT: Add the areas of the two bases and the lateral area.]

4. In each pair, the first number gives the length of a radius of a base of a cylinder and the second number gives the altitude of the cylinder. Compute the lateral surface area for each cylinder. Leave the answers in terms of π.

   a. 3 in., 7 in.   **b.** 5 in., 1 ft.   **c.** 2 ft., 8 in.

5. Compute the entire area for each cylinder in exercise **4**. Leave the answers in terms of π.

Since the bases of a cylinder are circles, the area of a base is πr^2. We use the area of a base in finding the volume of a cylinder.

■   The volume of a cylinder is equal to the product of the area of its base and the measure of its altitude.

$$\text{Volume} = \pi r^2 h$$

6. Find the volume of each cylinder in exercise **4**. Leave the answers in terms of π.

7. A cylindrical water tank has the following dimensions: radius of a base 2 ft., altitude 8 ft. Compute the approximate weight of the water if the tank is half filled. Use 3.14 for π. [HINT: One cubic foot of water weighs 62.5 pounds.]

8. In the picture on the right, a cylinder fits exactly into the rectangular solid. The length of a radius of a base of the cylinder is 5 in., the altitude of the cylinder measures 20 in. Compute the volumes of the cylinder and rectangular solid. By how many cubic feet does the volume of the rectangular solid exceed the volume of the cylinder?

9. A radius of the base of a cylindrical tank has the measure of 12 ft. Its altitude is 25 ft. What is the weight of gasoline filling the tank, if a cubic foot of gasoline weighs 44.2 pounds?

PYRAMIDS

On the right is a picture of a pyramid. The base of this pyramid is a square region and the four triangular faces are exactly alike. This pyramid is a *regular pyramid.*

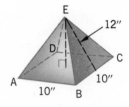

It is easy to find the total surface area of this pyramid. Compute the area of the base and add to it four times the area of one of the triangles.

Here are computations for the area of the pyramid shown in the picture.

$$10^2 + 4 \times \left(\frac{1}{2} \times 10 \times 12\right) = 100 + 4 \times 60$$
$$= 100 + 240$$
$$= 340 \text{ sq. in.}$$

1. a. What is the meaning of 10^2 in relation to the pyramid in the computations above?

   b. What is the meaning of $\frac{1}{2} \times 10 \times 12$?

   c. What is the meaning of $4 \times \left(\frac{1}{2} \times 10 \times 12\right)$?

2. Perform the following experiment. Out of cardboard make a rectangular solid like the one shown in the picture. Choose your own dimensions. Leave an opening at the top. Then make a model of a pyramid whose base and altitude are the same size as those of the rectangular solid. Remove the base of the pyramid in order to be able to fill it up with sand. Now fill up the model of the pyramid with sand and empty it into the rectangular solid. Repeat the process. How many pyramids does the rectangular solid contain?

Volume of a Rectangular Solid is (area of base) × (altitude)

Volume of a Pyramid is $\frac{1}{3}$ × (area of base) × (altitude)

■ The volume of a pyramid is equal to $\frac{1}{3}$ the product of the area of the base and the measure of the altitude.

$$\text{Volume} = \frac{1}{3}Bh$$

3. A pyramid has a square with a side of 15 in. for its base. The altitude of the pyramid is 12 in. What is the volume of the pyramid?

4. a. Sketch a picture showing a pyramid whose base is a regular pentagon.

   b. How many faces, counting the base, does this pyramid have?

5. Suppose a plane parallel to the square base of a regular pyramid intersects the pyramid. Tell what geometric figures may be obtained as a result of this intersection.

6. What is the intersection of a plane with a pyramid if the plane passes through the top vertex of the regular pyramid which has a square for its base?

CONES

As in the case of a cylinder, a cone is part of a more general object generated by a line. To imagine this object, consider the line l rotating as shown in the picture. The resulting set of points is a conical surface.

On the left below is a picture of a *cone*. Its lateral surface is part of a circle with its interior, and the base is a circle with its interior.

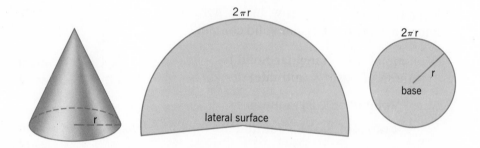

1. Explain why, as shown in the pictures above, the circumference of the base is the same as the length of the arc of the lateral surface.

To find out how the volumes of a cylinder and a cone with bases and altitudes of the same size compare, we need to have models of these. If your teacher has such models, you may want to experiment to see how many times the contents of the cone will fit into the cylinder. You will find that it is 3 times.

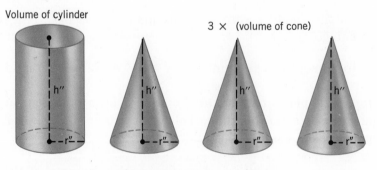

$$\text{Volume of cylinder} = \pi r^2 h$$
$$\text{Volume of cone} = \frac{1}{3}\pi r^2 h$$

■ The volume of a cone is equal to $\frac{1}{3}$ the product of the area of its base and the measure of its altitude.

$$\text{Volume} = \frac{1}{3}\pi r^2 h$$

Compute the volume of each cone with the given lengths of a radius of the base (first number) and the height (second number). Leave answers in terms of π.

2. 2 in., 5 in.   **5.** 2 in., 10 in.   **8.** 6 in., 10 in.

3. 4 in., 5 in.   **6.** 2 in., 15 in.   **9.** 6 in., 15 in.

4. 6 in., 5 in.   **7.** 4 in., 10 in.   **10.** 4 in., 15 in.

For exercises **11–20**, refer to your answers for exercises **2–10**.

11. Two cones have bases with radii of the same length. The height of cone A is twice the height of cone B. How do the volumes of cones A and B compare?

12. Two cones have bases with radii of the same length. The height of cone A is 3 times the height of cone B. How do the volumes of cones A and B compare?

13. Two cones have bases with radii of the same length. The height of cone A is *n* times the height of cone B. How do the volumes of cones A and B compare?

14. Two cones have the same height. A radius of the base of cone A is twice as long as a radius of the base of cone B. How do the volumes of cones A and B compare?

15. Two cones have the same height. A radius of the base of cone A is three times as long as a radius of the base of cone B. How do the volumes of cones A and B compare?

16. Two cones have the same height. A radius of the base of cone A is *n* times as long as a radius of the base of cone B. How do the volumes of cones A and B compare?

17. The height and radius of cone A are each twice the height and radius of cone B. How do the volumes of cones A and B compare?

18. The height and radius of cone A are each three times the height and radius of cone B. How do the volumes of cones A and B compare?

19. The height and radius of cone A are each n times the height and radius of cone B. How do the volumes of cones A and B compare?

20. The height of cone A is k times the height of cone B. The radius of cone A is n times the radius of cone B. How do the volumes of cones A and B compare?

KEEPING ARITHMETICALLY FIT

Add.

1. 36.75	**2.** 425.25	**3.** 11,362	**4.** $1\frac{1}{2} + 3\frac{1}{3}$
72.30	36.16	5,609	
4.65	117.26	3,006	
34.90	463.50	95	**5.** $10\frac{2}{3} + 23\frac{7}{8}$
12.86	32.95	126	
13.93	11.16	13	**6.** $11.05 + 38.36$

Subtract.

7. $\begin{array}{r} 10,365 \\ \underline{879} \end{array}$ **11.** $\frac{5}{6} - \frac{1}{3}$ **15.** $5\frac{1}{2} - 3\frac{3}{4}$

8. $\begin{array}{r} 375,005 \\ \underline{36,896} \end{array}$ **12.** $\frac{7}{8} - \frac{2}{3}$ **16.** $16\frac{5}{6} - 4\frac{7}{8}$

9. $\begin{array}{r} 995.37 \\ \underline{99.49} \end{array}$ **13.** $\frac{12}{15} - \frac{2}{5}$ **17.** $12\frac{3}{4} - 9$

10. $\begin{array}{r} 8,375.12 \\ \underline{7,469.48} \end{array}$ **14.** $\frac{2}{25} - \frac{3}{50}$ **18.** $15 - 12\frac{7}{8}$

Multiply.

19. $\begin{array}{r} 305 \\ \underline{99} \end{array}$ **23.** $\frac{7}{6} \times \frac{2}{3}$ **27.** 6.05×6.05

20. $\begin{array}{r} 1,196 \\ \underline{323} \end{array}$ **24.** $\frac{2}{7} \times \frac{4}{9}$ **28.** 9.3×9.3

21. $\begin{array}{r} 9,006 \\ \underline{709} \end{array}$ **25.** $1\frac{1}{2} \times 4\frac{7}{8}$ **29.** 21.2×6.7

22. $\begin{array}{r} 37.66 \\ \underline{8.5} \end{array}$ **26.** $3\frac{4}{5} \times 5\frac{1}{3}$ **30.** 3.5×3.5

Divide.

31. $34\overline{)2{,}652}$

32. $112\overline{)6{,}832}$

33. $10.01\overline{)980.98}$

34. $3 \div \dfrac{1}{2}$

35. $17 \div \dfrac{1}{2}$

36. $\dfrac{1}{6} \div 15$

37. $\dfrac{1}{8} \div 5$

38. $\dfrac{9}{11} \div \dfrac{3}{2}$

39. $\dfrac{2}{7} \div \dfrac{2}{7}$

40. $\dfrac{2}{5} \div \dfrac{5}{2}$

41. $7\dfrac{1}{2} \div 2$

42. $9\dfrac{1}{6} \div 4$

43. $7\dfrac{1}{8} \div 2\dfrac{1}{2}$

44. $10\dfrac{1}{2} \div 21$

45. $5\dfrac{3}{4} \div 11\dfrac{1}{2}$

Find the answers.

46. $37 + (-67)$

47. $12 + (-44)$

48. $45 + (-22)$

49. $-100 + (-11)$

50. $-44 + 55$

51. $-32 + 65$

52. $-50 - (-150)$

53. $-20 - (-370)$

54. $-120 - (-15)$

55. $-250 - (-13)$

56. $11 - (-23)$

57. -44×6

58. $-27 \times (-5)$

59. $12 \times (-13)$

60. $-144 \div 12$

61. $-60 \div (-5)$

62. $20 \div \left(-\dfrac{1}{2}\right)$

63. $\dfrac{1}{4} \div (-10)$

Find the answers.

64. What is 15% of 150?

65. What is 165% of 700?

66. What is $\dfrac{1}{2}$% of 1,200?

67. What is .03% of 2,000?

68. 120 is what per cent of 80?

69. $\dfrac{1}{2}$ is what per cent of 100?

70. $\dfrac{1}{2}$ is what per cent of 10,000?

71. 60 is 1% of what number?

72. 75 is 200% of what number?

73. .1 is .1% of what number?

Expand by powers of ten.

74. 369   **75.** 3,608   **76.** 10,250   **77.** 125,002

Tell what is the base and what is the exponent.

78. 17^{10} **79.** 35^0 **80.** 0^{38} **81.** 7^{10}

Give a base *ten* numeral for each of the following:

82. 73_{eight} **83.** 104_{five} **84.** 101101_{two} **85.** 203_{four}

Which are odd and which are even?

86. 451_{seven} **87.** 623_{eight} **88.** 101011_{two}

89. Give a repeating decimal name for $\frac{5}{6}$.

90. If a square root of a whole number is not a whole number, then what kind of a number is it?

Find fractional numerals for the following:

91. $.2\overline{2}$ **92.** $.25\overline{25}$ **93.** $.106\overline{106}$ **94.** $.345\overline{345}$

95. Which are irrational numbers?

    a. $\sqrt{7}$ **e.** $.3\overline{3}$ **i.** $\sqrt{15}$

    b. $\sqrt{81}$ **f.** $\frac{3}{17}$ **j.** $.010010001\ldots$

    c. $\sqrt{25}$ **g.** $\sqrt{17}$ **k.** $\sqrt{325}$

    d. $\sqrt{1}$ **h.** $\sqrt{225}$ **l.** $.625$

96. Name one property of rational numbers which the natural numbers do not have.

97. What is the meaning of the phrase: the set of rational numbers is dense?

98. Which numbers are divisible by 9?

    a. 3,689   **b.** 21,888   **c.** 1,008   **d.** 13,490

99. Which are prime numbers?

    a. 19   **c.** 49   **e.** 89   **g.** 117

    b. 27   **d.** 53   **f.** 101   **h.** 211

100. What is the Greatest Common Factor of 14 and 77?

101. What is the Least Common Multiple of 6 and 21?

Give a complete factorization of each number.

102. 35   **103.** 52   **104.** 106   **105.** 1,268

106. State two properties of the number 0 which no other numbers have.

107. State one property of the number 1 which no other numbers have.

Tell what property each exercise illustrates.

108. $(2 + 7) \times 5 = (2 \times 5) + (7 \times 5)$

109. $136 \times \frac{1}{2} = \frac{1}{2} \times 136$

110. $(17 + \sqrt{5}) + 9\frac{1}{2} = 17 + \left(\sqrt{5} + 9\frac{1}{2}\right)$

111. $(-1.5) + 17 = 17 + (-1.5)$

112. $\left(\frac{1}{2} \times \frac{1}{3}\right) \times \frac{1}{4} = \frac{1}{2} \times \left(\frac{1}{3} \times \frac{1}{4}\right)$

113. Give one example which illustrates that division is the inverse of multiplication.

In each case, give the replacement for x which will result in a true statement.

114. $\frac{x}{2} = \frac{12}{8}$ **115.** $\frac{1}{x} = \frac{6}{15}$ **116.** $\frac{2}{3} = \frac{x}{10.5}$ **117.** $\frac{4}{7} = \frac{5}{x}$

118. A number is added to 16. The result is 194. What number was added to 16?

119. In a basket with the total number of 120 oranges, 6 oranges were found to be spoiled. What per cent of oranges were spoiled?

120. Every time Jane deposits $5 to her account, her father adds 20% of what is in the account at that time. How much money did her father add to her account after Jane made two $5 deposits?

121. Mr. Ambitious is a salesman receiving pay exclusively on commission basis. He receives 20% commission on all sales. One week he received a commission of $175. What were his sales?

VOCABULARY REVIEW

altitude (349)
area (345)
axis (364)
base (349)
circumference (354)
circumscribed (355)
cone (368)
cylinder (364)
diameter (354)
dodecagon (356)
equiangular triangle (356)
equilateral triangle (351)
hexagon (355)
inscribed (355)

interior (345)
lateral surface (364)
limit (358)
octagon (358)
parallelogram (347)
perimeter (356)
pyramid (366)
quadrilateral (345)
radius (354)
rectangle (345)
rectangular solid (362)
regular polygon (351)
regular pyramid (366)
volume (362)

A CHALLENGE TO YOU

1. If each dimension of a rectangular solid is doubled, how is its lateral surface area changed?

2. The volume enclosed by a sphere is computed by the formula $V = \frac{4}{3}\pi r^3$, where r is the measure of a radius of the sphere. Compute the volume of a sphere if the measure of a radius is 2 ft. (Use 3.14 for π.)

3. The measure of a radius of a sphere is tripled. What is the ratio of the volume of the new sphere to the volume of the original sphere?

4. The surface area of a sphere is computed by the formula $A = 4\pi r^2$. If the measure of a radius of a sphere is tripled, what is the ratio of the new surface area to the original surface area?

5. Consider the experiment of rolling a die once. What is the sample space for this experiment?

6. For the experiment of rolling a die once, what is the probability that the face landing up will have the following?

   a. an even number of dots   e. more than 0 dots

   b. fewer than 3 dots   f. less than 1 dot

   c. more than 5 dots   g. more than 6 dots

   d. more than 1 dot

CHAPTER TEST

1. Rectangle *ABCD* has the dimensions 7 in. and 5 in. It is divided into two triangles by the diagonal $\overline{AC}$. What is the area of one of the triangles thus formed?

2. Assume that the sum of the measures of three angles in any triangle is 180°. Prove that the sum of the measures of the four angles in any parallelogram is 360°.

3. Define a regular polygon.

Give the formula for each of the following:

4. area of a triangle

6. volume of a cylinder

5. area of a parallelogram

7. volume of a pyramid

8. Explain why an equilateral triangle is also equiangular.

9. Explain why every square is a regular polygon.

10. Tell why no equilateral triangle may be a right triangle.

11. The area of a triangle is 36 sq. in. One of the sides measures 2 inches. Compute the length of the altitude upon that side.

12. Give the circumference in terms of π for a circle in which the length of a radius is 4 inches.

13. Give the circumference in terms of π for a circle in which the length of a radius is 3π inches.

14. Using 3.14 for π, compute the area of a circle with a radius of 2.5 in.

15. Explain why it is not possible to have two right angles in a triangle.

16. Compute the volume of a rectangular solid with the following dimensions: 3 ft., 4.5 ft., 6 ft.

17. Compute the total area and the volume of a cylinder with the following dimensions: radius of base 7 in., altitude 12 in.

18. Compute the volume of a cone with the following dimensions: radius of base 2 in., altitude 12 in.

19. Compute the volume of a pyramid whose base is a square with a side 5 in. and whose altitude is 15 in.

CHAPTER THIRTEEN

Line and Circle Constructions

MIDPOINTS

A line is a set of points which has no beginning point and no endpoint.
A line segment is a set of points which has two endpoints.

    C is called the *midpoint* of $\overline{AB}$, because *C* is the same distance from
A as it is from *B*. That is, $AC = CB$.

A   C   B

1. If *F* is the midpoint of $\overline{DE}$, what is the measure of $\overline{DF}$?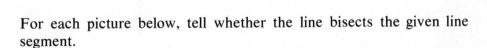

2. If *T* is the midpoint of $\overline{XY}$ and *V* is the midpoint of $\overline{XT}$, what is the measure of $\overline{XV}$?

M is the midpoint of $\overline{AC}$, *N* is the midpoint of $\overline{BC}$, and *P* is the midpoint of $\overline{AB}$. What is the measure of the following?

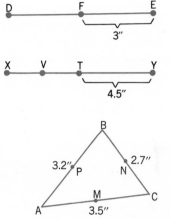

3. $\overline{AM}$

4. $\overline{BN}$

5. $\overline{AP}$

The line *l bisects* $\overline{RS}$ because the point *W* is the midpoint of $\overline{RS}$.

For each picture below, tell whether the line bisects the given line segment.

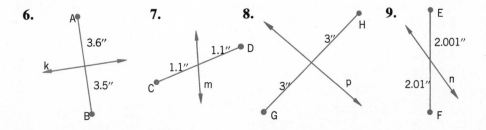

6.   7.   8.   9.

LOCATING MIDPOINTS

You are already familiar with two important tools used in geometry — a compass and a straightedge. We use a compass to draw pictures of circles and a straightedge to draw pictures of straight lines. A straightedge is a ruler which has no markings on it. Thus, we cannot use a straightedge for measuring. Making constructions in geometry is a game with its own rules. We are allowed to use *only* two tools: a straightedge and a compass. We shall illustrate the use of these tools in making various constructions.

Our first problem will be to locate the midpoint of a line segment without measuring with a ruler. On your paper, make a picture of a line segment $\overline{AB}$ and follow the steps described below. Refer to the picture as you read the directions.

1. Place the foot of the compass at point A and open the compass to more than one-half the distance from A to B.

2. Make a picture of an arc; call it m.

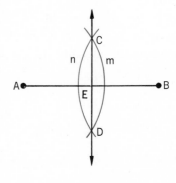

3. Keep the compass open to the same distance and transfer the foot to point B.

4. Make a picture of another arc; call it n. The two arcs, m and n, intersect in two points, C and D.

5. Make a picture of a line through points C and D. It intersects $\overline{AB}$ in point E. Point E is the midpoint of $\overline{AB}$. That is, $AE = EB$. (Recall that $\overline{AB}$ refers to a segment, whereas AB refers to the measure of the segment.)

Now let's practice.

6. Make a picture of a segment 3 inches long. Locate the midpoint of the segment using the construction described above. How long is each of the two segments formed?

7. Make a picture of a triangle like $\triangle ABC$. Using the construction described above, locate the midpoints of $\overline{AB}$, $\overline{BC}$, and $\overline{AC}$.

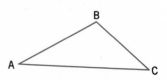

MIDPOINTS OF SIDES OF TRIANGLES

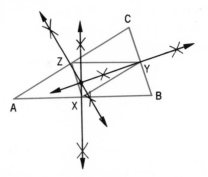

1. Make a picture of a triangle like the one on the right. Make the picture quite a bit larger on your paper.

2. Measure each side with a ruler and record the results with accuracy to one millimeter. (You need a ruler which has millimeter markings.)

3. By construction, locate the midpoint of each side of the triangle and label the midpoints X, Y, and Z, as shown in the picture.

4. Draw pictures of $\overline{XY}$, $\overline{YZ}$, and $\overline{ZX}$.

5. Measure $\overline{XY}$, $\overline{YZ}$, and $\overline{ZX}$ with a ruler and record the results with accuracy to one millimeter.

6. a. $\overline{AB}$ is how many times longer than $\overline{ZY}$?

   b. $\overline{BC}$ is how many times longer than $\overline{XZ}$?

   c. $\overline{AC}$ is how many times longer than $\overline{YX}$?

7. Make a picture of another triangle. Repeat exercises **2–6** for this triangle.

8. In the picture on the right, MN = 5 cm., $NP = 2.5$ cm., and MP = 5 cm. H is the midpoint of $\overline{MN}$, G is the midpoint of $\overline{NP}$, and K is the midpoint of $\overline{MP}$. If what you observed in exercises **6** and **7** is true for every triangle, tell the measures of $\overline{HK}$, $\overline{KG}$, and $\overline{GH}$ without measuring.

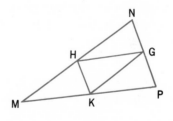

9. In $\triangle PQR$, the three sides have the following measures: $PQ = 3$ in., $QR = 6$ in., and $RP = 7$ in. Point A is the midpoint of $\overline{PQ}$, point B is the midpoint of $\overline{QR}$, and point C is the midpoint of $\overline{PR}$. Tell the measures of $\overline{AB}$, $\overline{BC}$, and $\overline{CA}$.

10. a. In exercise **9**, what is the perimeter of $\triangle PQR$?

    b. What is the perimeter of $\triangle ABC$?

DISTANCE FROM A POINT TO A LINE

On the left below is a picture of line k and point A. How do we decide how far point A is from line k? In other words, what is the *distance* from A to k?

To determine the distance from point A to line k, we construct a perpendicular from A to k. $\overline{AB}$ is perpendicular to line k.

The distance from point A to line k is the measure of $\overline{AB}$.

For exercises **1–7**, see the picture on the right.

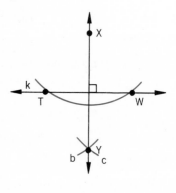

1. Make a picture of a line k on your paper. Pick a point X not on line k.

2. Place the foot of the compass at X and open the compass to reach beyond the closest point on line k.

3. Make an arc crossing k at T and W.

4. Place the foot of the compass at T and open the compass to more than one-half the distance from T to W.

5. Make an arc b.

6. Do not change the opening of the compass. Place the foot of the compass at W and make an arc c.

7. Arcs b and c intersect at Y. Make a picture of a line through X and Y. $\overline{XY}$ is perpendicular to line k.

Now let's practice.

8. Make a picture of a line n on your paper.

9. Choose a point K not on the line.

10. Construct a perpendicular from K to n.

11. Measure the distance from K to n and record it in millimeters.

CONSTRUCTING ANGLES

Now we shall construct an angle having the same measure as a given angle. We will use a straightedge and a compass. See the picture on the right.

1. On a sheet of paper, make a picture of an angle; call it ∠A.

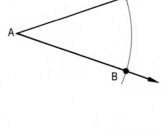

2. Make a picture of a ray; call it $\overrightarrow{A'B'}$. [Read: ray A prime B prime]

3. Put the foot of the compass at point A and open it to any length you wish. Make $\overparen{BC}$. [Read: arc BC.]

4. Do not change the opening of the compass and place the foot at point A'. Make $\overparen{B'C'}$.

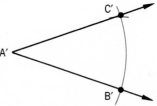

5. Put the foot of the compass at B and open it to the distance from B to C.

6. Do not change the opening of the compass and place the foot of the compass at B'. Mark off the distance from B' to C' equal to the distance from B to C.

7. Using your straightedge, draw a picture of a ray beginning with A' through C'. On the basis of this construction, ∠A' has the same measure as ∠A.

Now let's practice.

8. Using a protractor, make a picture of an angle which measures 85°. Construct an angle with the same measure following the procedure given above.

9. a. Copy the picture of △ABC on your paper. Draw a picture of $\overline{A'B'}$ twice as long as $\overline{AB}$.

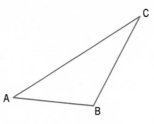

   b. At A' construct an angle of the same size as angle A, and at B' construct an angle of the same size as angle B.

   c. How would you convince someone that the third angle C' is the same size as angle C? Write out your argument.

ANGLE BISECTORS

Examine the picture at the right to answer
the following questions.

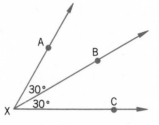

1. What is the measure of ∠CXB?

2. What is the measure of ∠BXA?

3. Do angles CXB and BXA have the
   same measure?

Since $\overrightarrow{XB}$ divides ∠AXC into two angles of equal size,
we say that $\overrightarrow{XB}$ bisects ∠AXC.

$\overrightarrow{XB}$ is an *angle bisector*.

For each picture below, tell whether $\overrightarrow{XB}$ is the bisector of ∠CXA.

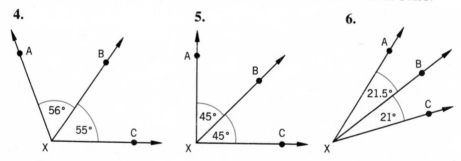

4.

5.

6.

We will now construct an angle bisector using a straightedge and
compass. As you read the directions, refer to the picture on the right.

7. On your paper, make a picture of an
   angle *TMR*. It does not have to be
   the same size as the angle in the picture on the right.

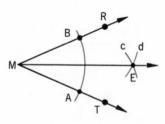

8. Place the foot of the compass at *M*,
   open the compass to any length, and
   make an arc, $\overset{\frown}{AB}$.

9. Place the foot of the compass at *A*, open the compass to any length,
   and mark an arc *c*.

10. Do not change the opening of the compass and put the foot of the
    compass at *B*. Make an arc *d*.

11. Arcs c and d intersect at the point E. With a straightedge, make a picture of a ray from M through E. $\overrightarrow{ME}$ is the bisector of $\angle TMR$.

$$m \angle TME = m \angle EMR$$

12. Using a straightedge and protractor, make a picture of an angle which measures 82°. Using a straightedge and compass, construct the bisector of this angle.

13. Make a picture of an angle which measures 90°. Construct the bisector of this angle.

14. Repeat exercise **13** for an angle which measures 120°.

POINTS ON AN ANGLE BISECTOR

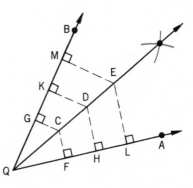

1. Make a picture of an angle AQB.

2. Construct the bisector of $\angle AQB$.

3. Choose any three points C, D, and E on the angle bisector.

4. From C, construct a perpendicular to $\overrightarrow{QA}$ and another perpendicular to $\overrightarrow{QB}$.

5. Measure the length of $\overline{CF}$ and of $\overline{CG}$. Record the measures in millimeters.

6. From D, construct a perpendicular to $\overrightarrow{QA}$ and another perpendicular to $\overrightarrow{QB}$.

7. Measure the length of $\overline{DH}$ and of $\overline{DK}$. Record the measures in millimeters.

8. From E, construct a perpendicular to $\overrightarrow{QA}$ and another perpendicular to $\overrightarrow{QB}$.

9. Measure the length of $\overline{EL}$ and of $\overline{EM}$. Record the measures in millimeters.

You should have found the following to be true.

$$CF = CG \qquad DH = DK \qquad EL = EM$$

10. What conclusion do you draw about the distances of any point on an angle bisector to the two sides of the angle?

From our experience with angle bisectors, we can assume two things.

    1. An angle has exactly one bisector.

    2. For each point on the angle bisector, its distance to each of the two sides of the angle is the same.

$\overrightarrow{AD}$ is the bisector of $\angle A$.

11. If $EF = 1.5$ in., how long is $\overline{EG}$?

12. If $HK = 3$ in., how long is $\overline{HL}$?

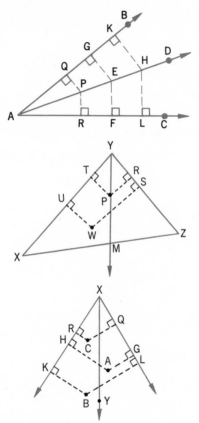

In $\triangle XYZ$, $\overrightarrow{YM}$ is the bisector of $\angle Y$.

13. Point P is on the angle bisector $\overrightarrow{YM}$. Is it true that $PT = PR$?

14. Point W is not on the angle bisector $\overrightarrow{YM}$. Is it true that $WS \neq UW$?

15. Draw a picture of $\angle X$. Construct the angle bisector $\overrightarrow{XY}$.

16. Choose a point A not on $\overrightarrow{XY}$. Construct the perpendiculars $\overline{AG}$ and $\overline{AH}$ to the sides of $\angle X$. Measure the lengths of $\overline{AG}$ and $\overline{AH}$. Are they different?

17. Choose a point B not on $\overrightarrow{XY}$. Repeat exercise **17** for point B.

18. Choose point C not on $\overrightarrow{XY}$. Repeat exercise **16** for point C.

19. Would you conclude that any point which is not on the angle bisector has different distances from the two sides of the angle?

We can now draw the following conclusions about points in relation to an angle bisector.

■   Each point on the bisector of an angle is the same distance from each of the two sides of the angle. Each point not on the bisector is a different distance from each of the two sides of the angle.

ANGLE BISECTORS IN A TRIANGLE

Study the following four observations.

1. An angle has exactly one bisector.
2. For each point on the angle bisector, its distance to each of the two sides of the angle is the same.
3. A point in the interior of an angle which is not on the bisector has different distances from the two sides of the angle.
4. If the distance of a point in the interior of an angle to each of its two sides is the same, then the point is on the angle bisector.

We now present an argument which is based on the four statements above. Read this argument thoughtfully one step at a time. Refer to the picture below on the right.

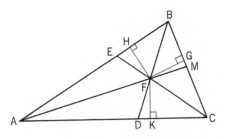

1. $\overline{BD}$ is the angle bisector of $\angle ABC$. [NOTE: We use "angle bisector" sometimes to mean a ray and sometimes a segment. You can tell from the context which meaning is intended.]

2. Therefore, $FH = FG$. Which statement above justifies this conclusion?

3. $\overline{CE}$ is the bisector of $\angle ACB$.

4. Therefore, $FG = FK$.

5. Therefore, $FH = FG = FK$.

6. Since point F is the same distance from $\overline{AB}$ as it is from $\overline{AC}$, it is on the bisector of $\angle A$. Which statement above justifies this conclusion?

7. Therefore, the bisector of $\angle A$ passes through point F. $\overline{AM}$ in the picture is this bisector.

8. Therefore, the three bisectors of three angles of a triangle pass through the same point.

▪ Three or more lines passing through the same point are called *concurrent* lines.

9. Make a picture of a right triangle. Construct the three angle bisectors.

10. Make a picture of an obtuse triangle (one obtuse angle). Construct the three angle bisectors.

11. Make a picture of an isosceles triangle (two sides the same length). Construct the three angle bisectors.

CONSTRUCTING ANGLES OF A GIVEN MEASURE

Suppose you are presented with the following problem:

> Without the use of a protractor,
> construct an angle whose measure is 45°.

Recall that the rules of construction do not permit the use of a protractor. This means that this problem cannot be solved by just measuring with a protractor and drawing a picture of an angle which measures 45°.

Following the rules for constructing sets of points, you may think along the following lines:

> If I had a 90° angle, then it would be easy. I would just bisect that angle. So, the problem is to get a 90° angle. But a 90° angle is formed by two perpendicular lines, and I know how to construct two perpendicular lines.

Now follow these steps to obtain a 45° angle.

1. Make a picture of a line; call it k.

2. Pick a point A not on k.

3. Construct a line from A perpendicular to k. Call the point where this line meets k, B.

4. $\overline{AB}$ makes two right angles with k.

5. Bisect one of these angles. Each of the two angles you now have measures 45°.

6. Now construct an angle which measures $22\frac{1}{2}^{\circ}$.

How would you construct a 30° angle? You might think like this.

> In an equilateral triangle, each angle measures 60°. If I could construct an equilateral triangle, I would have a 60° angle. Then I would bisect this angle and obtain two angles, each measuring 30°. So the problem is to construct an equilateral triangle. The picture on the right suggests how this construction can be done. Examine the picture and construct an equilateral triangle on your paper. Bisect one of its angles to obtain two 30° angles.

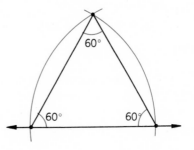

7. Without the use of a protractor, construct an angle which measures 15°. [HINT: What size angle must you bisect?]

8. Construct a $7\frac{1}{2}^\circ$ angle.

You have learned how to construct an angle which has the same measure as a given angle. Having this knowledge, we shall construct an angle which measures 75°. Read the description of this construction. Refer to the picture to identify all parts.

9. First, we construct an equilateral triangle ABC.

10. Each angle in this triangle measures 60°.

11. We bisect $\angle CAB$; $\overrightarrow{AD}$ is the bisector.

12. $m\angle CAD = 30°$.

13. We bisect $\angle CAD$; $\overrightarrow{AE}$ is the bisector.

14. $m\angle CAE = 15°$

15. We construct $\angle CAG$ to measure 15° by making it of the same measure as $\angle CAE$.

16. $m\angle BAG = 60° + 15° = 75°$

So, we have constructed an angle whose measure is 75°. It is $\angle BAG$.

Construct an angle whose measure is

17. 105° **18.** 135° **19.** 120° **20.** $67\frac{1}{2}°$

21. If we start with an angle measuring 90° and bisect it, we will have an angle of measure 45°. If we continue the process three more times, what size angle will we obtain?

PERPENDICULARS

When we constructed a right angle, we chose a point not on a line and constructed a perpendicular from that point to the line. Suppose we are asked to construct a right angle using a given point on a line as its vertex. Here is a description of this construction.

1. Make a picture of a line. Call it *k*.

2. Choose a point *A* on *k*. This point is to be the vertex of a right angle.

3. Place the foot of the compass at *A*.

4. Open the compass to any length and make an arc which meets *k* at *B* and *C*.

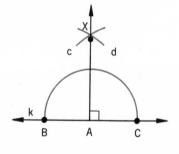

5. Place the foot of the compass at *B*.

6. Open the compass to any length and make an arc *d*.

7. Do not change the opening of the compass. Move the foot to point *C* and make an arc *c* intersecting arc *d* at point *X*.

8. Draw a picture of a ray from *A* through *X*. Angles *CAX* and *BAX* are right angles.

Now do the following:

9. On your paper, make a picture of a line; call it *k*.

10. Choose a point *A* not on *k* and construct a perpendicular to *k* passing through point *A*; call this perpendicular *m*.

11. Choose a point *B* on line *m*. Construct a perpendicular to line *m* passing through point *B*; call it *s*.

12. Is line *s* parallel to line *k*?

CENTRAL ANGLES

There is another interesting way to construct a right angle. It is done with the help of circles. First, we need to know something about angles in relation to circles. We shall agree that a circle can be measured in degrees just as an angle is measured. The entire circle will be assigned the measure of 360°.

1. What is the measure of half of a circle?

∠BAC is called a *central* angle, because its vertex is the center of a circle. $\overset{\frown}{BC}$ is *intercepted* by ∠BAC. We also say that ∠BAC intercepts $\overset{\frown}{BC}$.

■ A central angle has the same degree-measure as its intercepted arc.

For each picture, give the measure in degrees of the central angle A or $\overset{\frown}{BC}$, whichever is missing.

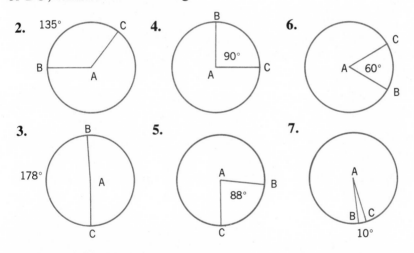

2. 135°

4. 90°

6. 60°

3. 178°

5. 88°

7. 10°

INSCRIBED ANGLES

Below we show another special kind of angle. Note that each angle has its vertex on the circle. In this case, the sides of each angle are called *chords*.

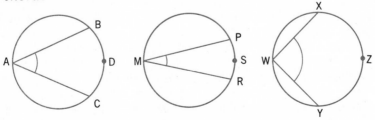

■ A *chord* is a line segment whose endpoints are on the circle.

■ An *inscribed angle* is an angle whose sides are chords of a circle.

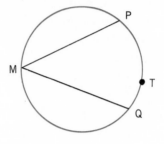

1. Is $\overline{MP}$ a chord? Why or why not?

2. Is $\overline{MQ}$ a chord? Why or why not?

3. Is *M* on the circle?

4. Is *M* a vertex of $\angle PMQ$?

5. Is $\angle PMQ$ an inscribed angle? Why or why not?

    $\angle PMQ$ intercepts $\overarc{PTQ}$ or $\overarc{PTQ}$ is intercepted by $\angle PMQ$.

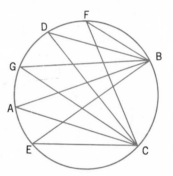

6. In the picture on the right, what arc is intercepted by $\angle E$? by $\angle A$? by $\angle G$? by $\angle D$? by $\angle F$?

7. Measure each of the angles named in exercise **6** with a protractor and record the measures.

You should have discovered the following:

■ Inscribed angles which intercept the same arc have the same measure.

Each picture below shows two angles, one a central angle and the other an inscribed angle. Both intercept the same arc.

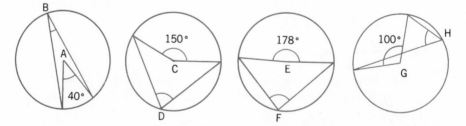

8. Measure $\angle B$. How do the measures of angles *B* and *A* compare?

9. Measure $\angle D$. How do the measures of angles *D* and *C* compare?

10. Measure $\angle F$. How do the measures of angles *F* and *E* compare?

11. Measure $\angle H$. How do the measures of angles *H* and *G* compare?

12. Examine your answers to exercises **8–11**. Now answer the following question.

> What is the relation between the measure of a central angle and the measures of inscribed angles which intercept the same arc?

13. Recall the relation between the measure of a central angle and the degree-measure of its intercepted arc. What is it?

14. Combine the answers to exercises **12** and **13** and answer the following question.

> What is the relation between the measure of an inscribed angle and the degree-measure of its intercepted arc?

SEMICIRCLES AND RIGHT ANGLES

For exercise **14** in the section above, you should have drawn the following conclusion.

■ The measure of an inscribed angle is equal to one-half the degree-measure of its intercepted arc.

Now we will consider another method of constructing a right angle. First we introduce a new word.

■ A *semicircle* is an arc of measure 180°. The prefix "semi" means "half."

1. Make a picture of a circle. Draw a diameter. Do the endpoints of the diameter divide the circle into two semicircles?

2. In the picture you made for exercise **1**, make an inscribed angle which intercepts one of the two semicircles.

3. What is the measure of the inscribed angle in exercise **2**?

4. In the picture on the right, what arc is intercepted by ∠A? (Use three letters to name the arc.) by ∠B? by ∠C?

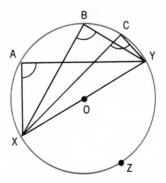

5. Explain why each of the angles A, B, and C in the picture on the right is a right angle.

6. In the picture on the right, what arc is intercepted by ∠F? (Use three letters to name the arc.) by ∠D?

7. Is it true that $m \angle F = m \angle D$? What is the measure of each?

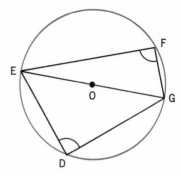

RATIO AND GEOMETRY

Ratio has many uses. If we say that the ratio of the number of boys to the number of girls in a class is 1 to 2, we mean that there are twice as many girls as there are boys. We write this as $1:2$, or $\frac{1}{2}$. We know that the ratio of 1 to 2 is the same as the ratio of 2 to 4. To show this we write $\frac{1}{2} = \frac{2}{4}$. Recall that a statement of this form is called a *proportion*.

In each proportion, find a replacement for x to make a true statement.

1. $\frac{x}{5} = \frac{8}{10}$

2. $\frac{3}{x} = \frac{12}{20}$

3. $\frac{1}{3} = \frac{x}{1.5}$

4. $\frac{4}{7} = \frac{x}{10.5}$

5. $\frac{3}{17} = \frac{5}{x}$

6. $\frac{\frac{1}{2}}{3} = \frac{x}{9}$

7. $\frac{4}{9} = \frac{16}{x}$

8. $\frac{x}{1.5} = \frac{4}{9}$

9. $\frac{\frac{1}{1}}{\frac{1}{2}} = \frac{x}{\frac{1}{4}}$

AB is the length of $\overline{AB}$, that is, a *number* telling us how many units of length are contained in $\overline{AB}$. For the picture on the right, $AB = 2$ in.

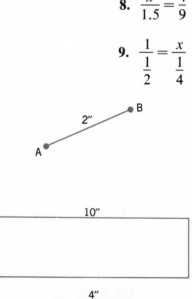

10. $AB = 2$ in. If the ratio of AB to CD is $2:3$, how long is $\overline{CD}$?

11. For the rectangles pictured on the right, the following proportion holds: $\frac{4}{10} = \frac{x}{3}$. What is the width of the smaller rectangle?

12. In the two pentagons pictured on the right, the lengths of corresponding sides have the same ratio. $\overline{AB}$ corresponds to $\overline{A'B'}$, $\overline{BC}$ corresponds to $\overline{B'C'}$, and so on. If $A'B'$ is .8 in., compute the length of each side of the smaller pentagon.

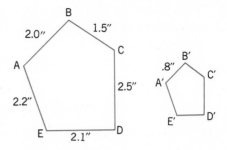

13. $\overline{AB}$ and $\overline{A'B'}$, $\overline{BC}$ and $\overline{B'C'}$ and $\overline{CA}$ and $\overline{C'A'}$ are pairs of corresponding sides in the two triangles. The ratio of measures of each pair of corresponding sides is the same. Compute the lengths of $\overline{A'B'}$ and $\overline{B'C'}$.

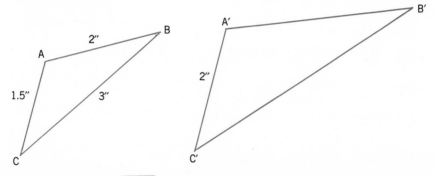

14. If the length of $\overline{A'C'}$ in exercise 13 is 4 in. and the remaining sides are as marked, compute the lengths of $\overline{A'B'}$ and $\overline{B'C'}$.

SIMILAR POLYGONS

When we say that $\triangle ABC$ corresponds to $\triangle A'B'C'$, then we also mean that $\overline{AB}$ corresponds to $\overline{A'B'}$, $\overline{BC}$ to $\overline{B'C'}$, and $\overline{CA}$ to $\overline{C'A'}$.

1. $\triangle ABC$ corresponds to $\triangle XYZ$. Name the three pairs of corresponding sides.

When we say that $\triangle ABC$ corresponds to $\triangle A'B'C'$, then we automatically mean that $\angle A$ corresponds to $\angle A'$, $\angle B$ to $\angle B'$, and $\angle C$ to $\angle C'$.

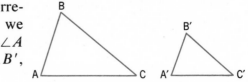

2. $\triangle ABC$ corresponds to $\triangle XYZ$. Name the three pairs of corresponding angles.

■ Two polygons are *similar* if the measures of pairs of corresponding sides have the same ratio and the measures of their corresponding angles are equal.

We will write $\triangle ABC \sim \triangle A'B'C'$

to mean

$\triangle ABC$ is similar to $\triangle A'B'C'$

By definition of similarity the following are true.

$$\frac{AB}{A'B'} = \frac{BC}{B'C'} = \frac{CA}{C'A'};$$

$$m\angle A = m\angle A'$$
$$m\angle B = m\angle B'$$
$$m\angle C = m\angle C'$$

3. $\triangle ABC \sim \triangle DEF$. $AB = 5$ in., $BC = 3$ in., and $CA = 3$ in. If $DE = 7$ in., compute EF and FD.

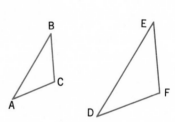

4. Prove that any two squares are similar. [HINT: See definition of similarity.]

5. $\triangle ABC \sim \triangle XYZ$. The lengths of sides are as shown in the picture on the right. Compute AC and CB.

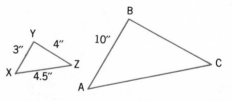

6. $\triangle MRS$ is a right triangle. How long is $\overline{RS}$?

7. $\triangle MRS \sim \triangle TWX$. If $WX = 2$ in., compute TW and TX.

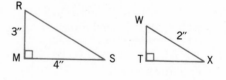

8. Name the three pairs of angles having the same measure in triangles MRS and TWX.

9. Given right triangle ABC with legs 5 in. and 12 in. and hypotenuse 13 in., compute the measures of the legs of a similar triangle if its hypotenuse is 19.5 in.

10. $\triangle EGK \sim \triangle MQT$. The two triangles are isosceles with bases $\overline{EK}$ and $\overline{MT}$. If the measures of the sides are as shown in the picture on the right, compute the measures of the remaining three sides.

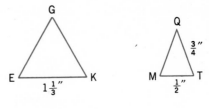

11. Prove that any two equilateral triangles are similar.

12. Prove that any two regular polygons with the same number of sides are similar.

SIMILAR TRIANGLES

In geometry it is possible to prove the following:

■ If the measures of the corresponding pairs of angles of two triangles are equal, then the triangles are similar.

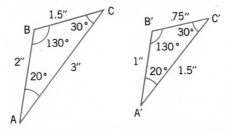

We know that the two triangles above are similar, since

$$m \angle A = m \angle A' = 20°$$
$$m \angle B = m \angle B' = 130°$$
$$m \angle C = m \angle C' = 30°$$

Then it follows from the definition of similar polygons that

$$\frac{AB}{A'B'} = \frac{BC}{B'C'} = \frac{CA}{C'A'}$$

The two triangles shown below are right triangles.

1. What is $m \angle R$?

2. What is $m \angle R'$?

3. Are the triangles similar? Why or why not?

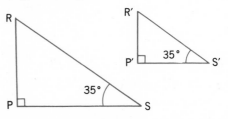

Recall that the sum of the measures of the angles of a triangle is 180°.

4. In two right triangles, if the measures of two corresponding acute angles are the same, then the measures of the other acute angles are the same. Justify this statement.

The following conclusion results.

■ If two right triangles have a pair of acute angles of the same measure, then they are similar.

Tell which pairs of right triangles are similar.

5.

7.

6.

8.

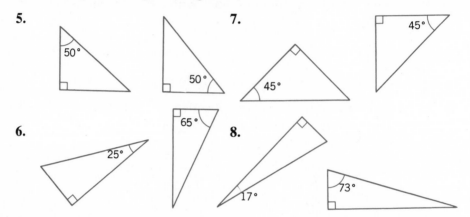

DIVIDING RIGHT TRIANGLES

Triangle ABC pictured on the right is a right triangle. $\overline{CD}$ is perpendicular to $\overline{AB}$.

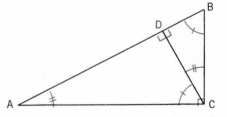

1. $\overline{CD}$ divides $\triangle ABC$ into two triangles. Name the two triangles.

2. Explain why $\triangle ACD$ and $\triangle BCD$ are right triangles.

3. Explain each statement.

a. $m\angle A + m\angle B = 90°$

b. $m\angle DCB + m\angle B = 90°$

c. $m\angle A = 90° - m\angle B$

d. $m\angle DCB = 90° - m\angle B$

e. $m\angle A = m\angle DCB$ ← conclusion which follows from steps **c** and **d**

f. $m \angle B + m \angle A = 90°$

g. $m \angle DCA + m \angle A = 90°$

h. $m \angle B = 90° - m \angle A$

i. $m \angle DCA = 90° - m \angle A$

j. $m \angle B = m \angle DCA$ ← conclusion which follows from steps **h** and **i**

k. $\triangle BCD \sim \triangle CAD$ [Look at statements **e** and **j**; do they justify this conclusion?]

4. In triangle ACD, tell which side is opposite

   a. $\angle A$ **b.** $\angle ACD$ **c.** $\angle ADC$

5. In triangle ACD, tell which angle is opposite

   a. $\overline{CD}$ **b.** $\overline{AD}$ **c.** $\overline{AC}$

6. In triangle BCD, tell which side is opposite

   a. $\angle BCD$ **b.** $\angle B$ **c.** $\angle CDB$

7. In triangle BCD, tell which angle is opposite

   a. $\overline{BC}$ **b.** $\overline{CD}$ **c.** $\overline{BD}$

8. In triangle ABC, tell which side is opposite

   a. $\angle ACB$ **b.** $\angle A$ **c.** $\angle B$

$\triangle XYZ$ is a right triangle. $\overline{ZW} \perp \overline{XY}$.

9. Why are triangles XWZ and YWZ right triangles?

10. Which angle in $\triangle YWZ$ has the same measure as $\angle X$?

11. Which angle in $\triangle YWZ$ has the same measure as $\angle XZW$?

12. Which side is opposite $\angle XWZ$?

13. Which side is opposite $\angle YWZ$?

14. Which side is opposite $\angle XZW$?

15. Which side is opposite $\angle ZYW$?

RATIOS IN SIMILAR TRIANGLES

Concentrate your attention on triangles *MPT* and *PRT*.

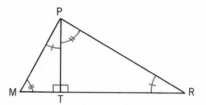

$m \angle M = m \angle TPR$ In $\triangle MPT$, $\overline{PT}$ is opposite $\angle M$.
                        In $\triangle PRT$, $\overline{RT}$ is opposite $\angle TPR$.

       $\overline{PT}$ and $\overline{RT}$ are a pair of corresponding sides.

$m \angle MPT = m \angle R$ In $\triangle MPT$, $\overline{MT}$ is opposite $\angle MPT$.
                        In $\triangle RPT$, $\overline{PT}$ is opposite $\angle R$.

       $\overline{MT}$ and $\overline{PT}$ are a pair of corresponding sides.

$m \angle MTP = m \angle RTP$ In $\triangle MPT$, $\overline{MP}$ is opposite $\angle MTP$.
                          In $\triangle PRT$, $\overline{PR}$ is opposite $\angle RTP$.

       $\overline{MP}$ and $\overline{PR}$ are a pair of corresponding sides.

1. Why is the following true? $\triangle MPT \sim \triangle PRT$

RECALL   In similar triangles, the ratios of measures of corresponding sides are equal.

What are these ratios in triangles *MPT* and *PRT*? Check the ratios below against the picture above.

$$\frac{PT}{RT} = \frac{MT}{PT} = \frac{MP}{PR}$$

For exercises **2–6**, refer to the picture at the top of the page. Use the proportion displayed above.

2. If $PT = 4$ in. and $RT = 8$ in., find MT.

3. If $RT = 6$ cm., $MP = 4$ cm., and $PR = 5$ cm., find PT.

4. If $MT = 12$ ft., $MP = 18$ ft., and $PR = 24$ ft., find PT.

5. If $MT = 3$ yd. and $PT = 6$ yd., find RT.

6. If $PT = 4$ in., $MP = 5$ in., and $PR = 6\frac{2}{3}$ in., find MT.

SQUARE ROOT AND A RIGHT TRIANGLE

In the picture at the right,

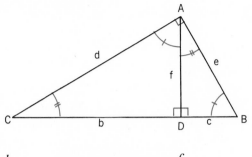

$$\triangle CDA \sim \triangle ADB$$
$$m\angle C = m\angle DAB$$
$$m\angle CAD = m\angle B$$

For $\triangle CDA$ and $\triangle ADB$, the following pairs of sides are corresponding sides.

$\overline{CD}$ and $\overline{AD}$: ratio $\dfrac{b}{f}$ $\overline{AD}$ and $\overline{BD}$: ratio $\dfrac{f}{c}$

1. $\dfrac{b}{f} = \dfrac{f}{c}$ is a true statement. Show that $f^2 = bc$.

2. $f^2 = bc$ is a true statement. Show that $f = \sqrt{bc}$.

Given $f = \sqrt{bc}$, compute f for the following replacements of b and c.

3. 4 for b, 9 for c **7.** 5 for b, 5 for c

4. 1 for b, 4 for c **8.** 11 for b, 11 for c

5. 4.5 for b, 2 for c **9.** 32 for b, 2 for c

6. 4.9 for b, 10 for c **10.** 6.05 for b, 20 for c

Given $f = \sqrt{bc}$, compute f to one decimal place for the following replacements of b and c. Use the table of square roots on page 421.

11. 1 for b, 2 for c **15.** 4 for b, 2 for c

12. 2 for b, 3 for c **16.** 4.5 for b, 4 for c

13. 5 for b, 2 for c **17.** 30 for b, $\dfrac{1}{2}$ for c

14. 3 for b, 7 for c **18.** 13 for b, 2 for c

For each picture below, compute the measure of the side marked x to one decimal place. [HINT: $x = \sqrt{yz}$.]

19.   **20.**   **21.**

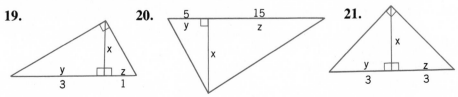

ANGLES INSCRIBED IN SEMICIRCLES

1. In the picture on the right, why is ∠B a right angle?

2. Is ∠X a right angle? Why or why not?

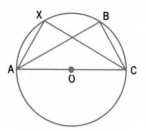

3. What is true of every angle which is inscribed in a semicircle?

In the picture on the right, ∠GKL is a right angle because it is inscribed in a semicircle. $\overline{KR} \perp \overline{GL}$. Let $KR = a$ in., $GR = b$ in., and $RL = c$ in. Then we know that the following is true.

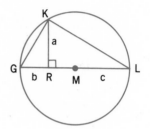

$$a = \sqrt{bc}$$

Which are true and which are false? [Refer to the figure above.]

4. If $b = 2$ in. and $c = 5$ in., then $a = \sqrt{10}$ in.

5. If $b = 1$ in. and $c = 3$ in., then $a = 2$ in.

6. If $b = 4$ in. and $c = 10$ in., then $a = \sqrt{14}$ in.

7. If $b = 5$ in. and $c = 15$ in., then $a = \sqrt{75}$ in.

8. If $b = 12$ in. and $c = 12$ in., then $a = 12$ in.

9. If $b = 7$ in. and $c = 15$ in., then $a = \sqrt{105}$ in.

10. If $b = 3$ in. and $c = 27$ in., then $a = 81$ in.

In the picture below, O and O' are the centers of the two circles.

11. Name all angles in the picture which you know to be right angles. Do no measuring.

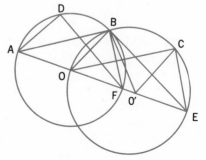

12. ∠CO'E is a central angle intercepting the same arc as does the inscribed angle COE. How do the measures of these two angles compare?

CONSTRUCTING LINE SEGMENTS

Let us consider the following problem.

> Given a line segment 1 unit long, construct a line
> segment which measures $\sqrt{3}$ of these units.

There are two things which you have learned that will enable you to solve this problem. To help you recall these two things, answer the following questions.

1. Is $\angle ABC$ a right angle? Why or why not?

2. Is this statement true?

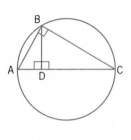

$$BD = \sqrt{AD \times CD}$$

Let us analyze our problem in terms of the picture on the right. If we make $\overline{AD}$ 1 unit long and $\overline{CD}$ 3 units long, then $\overline{BD}$ would be $\sqrt{1 \times 3}$, or $\sqrt{3}$ units long.

Take a ruler and compass and make the following construction on your paper. Refer to the figure below.

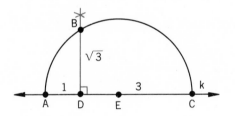

3. Make a picture of a line k.

4. Choose a unit of length on k. We chose AD to be that unit.

5. Mark off 3 of these units to the right of D. $\overline{DC}$ is 3 units long.

6. We need now to construct a semicircle passing through points A and C. This is easy. We choose point E to be the same distance from A as it is from C; it is the center of our semicircle. Construct the semicircle.

7. At D construct a perpendicular to $\overline{AC}$.

8. Why is the measure of BD $\sqrt{3}$ units?

Example   Construct a line segment which is √6 units long.

How to   Consider 6 as the product of 2 and 3. Let us agree that
solve   this line segment —— will serve as 1 unit. Follow the
steps and make the same construction on your paper.

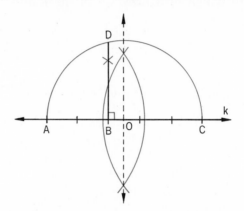

a. On a line *k*, mark off with a compass $\overline{AB}$ 2 units long
and $\overline{BC}$ 3 units long.

b. Locate the midpoint of $\overline{AC}$; call it *O*.

c. Using $\overline{OA}$ for a radius, construct a semicircle.

d. At *B* construct the perpendicular $\overline{BD}$.

e. Explain why the measure of $\overline{BD}$ is √6 units.

For the construction above, we could have considered 6 as the product
of 1 and 6.

9. The construction at the
right is based on the fact
that $6 = 1 \times 6$. Examine
the picture. Then make
this construction on your
paper. Use the same unit
length as given for the
construction above.

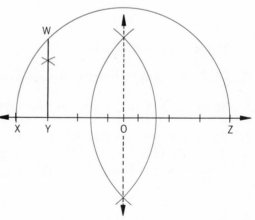

10. Explain why $\overline{WY}$ is √6
units long.

11. In your pictures, does
$\overline{WY}$ have the same measure as $\overline{BD}$?

For each picture below, tell the length of $\overline{AB}$.

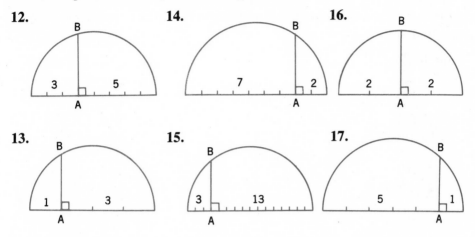

12. 3 ... 5 (A, B)

14. 7 ... 2 (A, B)

16. 2 ... 2 (A, B)

13. 1 ... 3 (A, B)

15. 3 ... 13 (A, B)

17. 5 ... 1 (A, B)

18. 8 can be viewed as the product of 2 and 4, and as the product of 1 and 8. Construct a line segment $\sqrt{8}$ units long in two ways. One way based on $8 = 2 \times 4$ and the other on $8 = 1 \times 8$. [Choose a unit of length.]

19. Construct a line segment $\sqrt{12}$ units long based on two facts: $12 = 3 \times 4$ and $12 = 6 \times 2$.

For the picture below, determine the measure of each segment. Assume that the diameter of the semicircle is 9 in. The segments along the diameter are of equal measure; that is, $SA = AC = CE$, etc.

20. $\overline{AB}$ **25.** $\overline{KL}$

21. $\overline{CD}$ **26.** $\overline{MN}$

22. $\overline{EF}$ **27.** $\overline{OP}$

23. $\overline{GH}$ **28.** $\overline{QR}$

24. $\overline{IJ}$

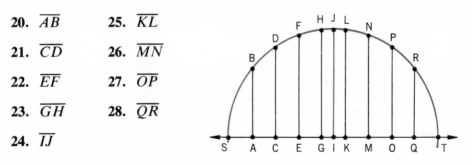

For each number, name all pairs of whole numbers whose product is that number. Do not use the number 1 in any of the pairs.

29. 32   **32.** 24   **35.** 125

30. 50   **33.** 16   **36.** 49

31. 40   **34.** 100   **37.** 25

KEEPING ARITHMETICALLY FIT

For exercises **1–62**, numerals in parentheses refer to pages where you can find similar exercises.

Add. (423–424)   (436–437)

1.	17,065	2.	.176	3.	3.75
	3,795		.905		9.31
	28,008		.367		8.66
	97,106		.405		3.05
	5,007		.196		7.12
	29,076		.805		8.93
	48,118		.107		5.66

(428–430)

4. $\dfrac{1}{2} + \dfrac{1}{3} + \dfrac{1}{4}$ **6.** $\dfrac{2}{9} + \dfrac{7}{11}$ **8.** $1\dfrac{3}{4} + 12\dfrac{4}{5}$

5. $\dfrac{1}{7} + \dfrac{1}{5} + \dfrac{1}{3}$ **7.** $1\dfrac{2}{3} + 7\dfrac{5}{7}$ **9.** $1\dfrac{1}{2} + 1\dfrac{1}{3} +$

Subtract. (424)   (430–432)

10. 387,196
        89,298   **13.** $\dfrac{4}{9} - \dfrac{2}{12}$ **16.** $5\dfrac{3}{8} - 4\dfrac{6}{7}$

(438–439)

11. .862
        .589   **14.** $\dfrac{11}{3} - \dfrac{2}{7}$ **17.** $\dfrac{7}{8} - \dfrac{5}{6}$

12. 36.89
        29.99   **15.** $3\dfrac{1}{7} - 2\dfrac{1}{11}$ **18.** $2\dfrac{1}{4} - 1\dfrac{2}{3}$

Multiply. (425)   (432–434)

19. 368
        906   **22.** $\dfrac{2}{3} \times \dfrac{2}{5}$ **25.** $3\dfrac{3}{4} \times 1\dfrac{1}{2}$

(439–440)

20. 35.7
        3.6   **23.** $\dfrac{11}{2} \times \dfrac{4}{11}$ **26.** $1\dfrac{1}{2} \times 6\dfrac{1}{3} \times 2\dfrac{3}{4}$

21. .36
        .09   **24.** $\dfrac{1}{2} \times 5\dfrac{1}{2}$ **27.** $2\dfrac{1}{3} \times 3\dfrac{1}{2} \times 4$

Divide.

(426)

28. $22\overline{)3{,}938}$ **31.** $.05\overline{)13.7}$ **34.** $4\frac{4}{5} \div 3\frac{1}{2}$

(434–436)

29. $16\overline{)1{,}709}$ **32.** $\frac{3}{5} \div \frac{7}{8}$ **35.** $\frac{2}{3} \div 9\frac{1}{2}$

(440–442)

30. $1.6\overline{)22.4}$ **33.** $\frac{11}{4} \div \frac{5}{12}$ **36.** $1\frac{1}{3} \div \frac{1}{4}$

Replace each n to obtain a true statement.

(442–443)

37. 30% of $120 = n$ **42.** $30 = n\%$ of 6

38. 200% of $17 = n$ **43.** $\frac{1}{2} = n\%$ of 50

39. .1% of $500 = n$ **44.** $5 = 10\%$ of n

40. $5 = n\%$ of 100   **45.** $.3 = 200\%$ of n

41. $1 = n\%$ of 50   **46.** $\frac{1}{10} = 33\frac{1}{3}\%$ of n

Compute the answers.

(444–448)

47. $-7 + 35$ **51.** $-26 + 10$ **55.** $12 + (-16)$ **59.** $-25 + (-36)$

48. $36 - 12$ **52.** $12 - 35$ **56.** $-2 - 7$ **60.** $-9 - (-12)$

49. -5×9 **53.** 12×10 **57.** $7 \times (-8)$ **61.** $-4 \times (-12)$

50. $-12 \div 6$ **54.** $20 \div 4$ **58.** $36 \div (-6)$ **62.** $-38 \div (-2)$

Which of the following is a subset of $\left\{\frac{1}{2}, \frac{1}{3}, \frac{1}{4}\right\}$?

63. $\left\{\frac{1}{2}, \frac{1}{3}, \frac{1}{4}\right\}$ **64.** $\{2, 3, 4\}$ **65.** $\left\{\frac{1}{2}, \frac{1}{3}\right\}$ **66.** $\{1\}$

Which of the following is the empty set?

67. $\{1, 2\} \cap \{1\}$ **68.** $\{1, 2\} \cap \{3\}$ **69.** $\{1, 2\} \cap \{1, 2\}$

Which are true and which are false?

70. $\dfrac{4}{3} < \dfrac{5}{4}$

84. 20,502 is divisible by 9.

71. $|-5| > |1|$

85. 77 is a prime number.

72. $1.23\overline{7237}$ is a rational number.

86. G.C.F. $(12, 24) = 12$

73. $1.515515551\ldots$ is a rational number.

87. 31 is a composite number.

74. $.1\% = 10$

88. L.C.M. $(3, 8) = 16$

75. $10\% = .1$

89. For each set A, $A \cup \phi = \phi$.

76. $\dfrac{3}{7} = \dfrac{5}{9}$

90. For each set A, $A \cap \phi = \phi$.

77. 20,502 is divisible by 3.

91. For each set A, $A \cap A = \phi$.

78. 20,502 is an even number.

92. For each set A, $A \cup A = A$.

79. $7^0 = 0^7$

93. $(1.1)^2 > (.9)^{100}$

80. $2^4 = 4^2$

94. $25_{\text{four}} < 13_{\text{ten}}$

81. $0 \times 25 = 167 \times 0$

95. $6^4 = 6 \times 4$

82. $4 \times \dfrac{1}{2} > 4 \times \dfrac{1}{3}$

96. $\dfrac{4}{5} \div \dfrac{2}{3} = \dfrac{4}{5} \times \dfrac{3}{2}$

83. $53_{\text{ten}} < 53_{\text{seven}}$

97. $3^2 = 2 \times 2 \times 2$

98. Show a one-to-one correspondence between the set of natural numbers and the set of negative integers.

99. If $U = \{1, 3, 5, 7, 9, 11\}$ and $A = \{1, 5, 9\}$, what is $\bar{A}$ equal to?

100. Give an example of a non-repeating non-terminating decimal.

101. Sets X and Y are matching. If for every number n in X, the corresponding number in Y is $\dfrac{1}{12}n$, what number in Y corresponds to 144 in X?

102. Is the set $\{-1, 0, 1\}$ closed under multiplication? Why or why not?

103. Is the set $\{-1, 1\}$ closed under addition? Why or why not?

104. What is the L.C.M. of 22 and 36?

105. What is the G.C.F. of 60 and 84?

106. $250 invested at $\frac{1}{2}$% simple interest rate for 5 years produces how much interest?

107. A certain amount of money invested for 3 years at 3.75% interest rate produced $2,250 interest. How much money was invested?

108. Adding 3 to some number, then multiplying the result by 7 gives 28. What was the original number?

109. Multiplying some number by 7 and subtracting from the answer the product of 3 and 2 gives 8. What was the original number?

110. The sum of some number and 10 is divided by 2. The result is 2. What is the number?

111. Some number is added to itself. The result is multiplied by 5 and the product is 15. What was the number?

112. John missed 10 out of 65 points on a test. What per cent of the work did John do correctly?

113. When milling the wheat, flour is obtained which weighs 75% of the weight of wheat. How many pounds of flour is obtained from 1,500 lb. of wheat?

114. Find the perimeter of a rectangle in which each side is 25% longer than each side of rectangle *ABCD*.

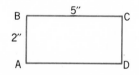

VOCABULARY REVIEW

angle bisector (382)
bisect (377)
central angle (389)
chord (390)
concurrent (386)
construction (378)
corresponding sides (393)
distance (380)

inscribed angle (390)
intercept (389)
midpoint (377)
perpendicular (380)
semicircle (391)
similar polygons (394)
similar triangles (395)

A CHALLENGE TO YOU

1. Two women sold 30 apples each. One woman charged 5¢ for 2 apples, the other 5¢ for 3 apples. What is their combined intake? The next day they decided to combine the 60 apples and have one woman sell them at 10¢ per five apples (2 apples for 5¢ and 3 apples for 5¢ is 5 apples for 10¢). What was the intake this time? What happened to the nickel?

2. A car travels for two hours at the average speed of 45 mph. The return trip is made at the average speed of 50 mph. Compute the average speed for the entire trip.

3. $\frac{3}{11}$ of the length of a pole is underground. 9 ft. of it is above the ground. What is the total length of the pole?

4. To what number should you add $2\frac{1}{2}$ to obtain four times that number?

5. A box contains 20 large paper clips and 10 small ones. One clip is drawn at random from the box. What is the probability that

   a. a small clip will be drawn?   **b.** a large clip will be drawn?

6. What is the sum of the probabilities in exercise **5**.

CHAPTER TEST

1. On your paper, make a picture of a line segment, $\overline{AB}$, like the one on the right. By construction, locate the midpoint of $\overline{AB}$.

   A •————————————• B

2. On your paper, make a picture of $\angle A$ like the one on the right.

   a. Construct an angle of the same measure as that of $\angle A$.

   b. Construct the bisector of $\angle A$.

3. On your paper, make a picture of a line k and a point P like in the picture on the right. Construct a perpendicular from point P to line k.

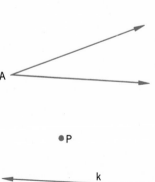

Choose a unit of length. Construct a line segment measuring

4. $\sqrt{5}$ units   **5.** $\sqrt{2}$ units   **6.** $\sqrt{7}$ units

Without using a protractor construct an angle measuring

7. 15°   **8.** 75°   **9.** 45°   **10.** 135°

Without using a protractor, tell the measure of each inscribed angle below.

11.   **12.**   **13.**   **14.**

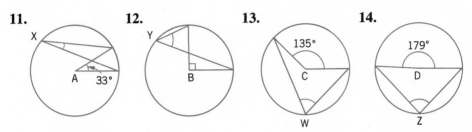

For each triangle, compute the length of the altitude, h. Your answer may contain a square root sign.

15.   **16.**   **17.**

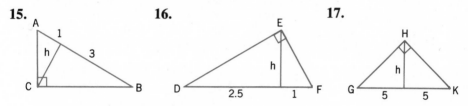

18. $\triangle ABC \sim \triangle A'B'C'$. Compute $A'B'$ and $B'C'$.

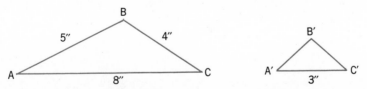

19. What is true of the distances from a point on the angle bisector to the sides of the angle?

20. How do the measures of a central angle and its intercepted arc compare?

21. How do the measures of an inscribed angle and its intercepted arc compare?

22. What is the measure of an inscribed angle which intercepts a semicircle?

CHAPTER FOURTEEN

The Metric System

METRIC UNITS OF LENGTH

METRIC UNITS OF LENGTH

There are two basic systems of measure which are in popular use. One of these is the *English system*, with which you are well familiar. The inch, the foot, the yard, and the mile are units of length in this system. The pint, the quart, and the gallon are units of capacity. The ounce and the pound are the most commonly used units of weight in the English system. The unit for measuring temperature is the Fahrenheit degree.

The relationships between the units in the English system do not follow one pattern. For example, there are 12 inches in 1 foot, but there are 3 feet in one yard. There are 16 ounces in 1 pound. Hence, in converting from one unit to another, different multipliers must be used, depending on the unit.

The *metric system*, which is quite popular in Europe and Canada, is based on the number ten. First let us examine the units of length in the metric system. A very short unit is the millimeter. Other longer units are as follows:

$$1 \text{ centimeter} = 10 \text{ millimeters}$$
$$1 \text{ decimeter} = 10 \text{ centimeters}$$
$$1 \text{ meter} = 100 \text{ centimeters}$$
$$1 \text{ kilometer} = 1,000 \text{ meters}$$

It is clear that a knowledge of the powers of ten is essential when working with relationships between the metric units of measure.

1. **a.** How many millimeters are there in a meter?

   b. Write it as a power of ten.

2. **a.** How many decimeters are there in a meter? *10*

   b. Write it as a power of ten.

3. **a.** How many centimeters are there in a kilometer?

   b. Write it as a power of ten.

Complete the following:

4. 1 millimeter = __?__ centimeter

5. 1 decimeter = __?__ meter

6. 1 centimeter = __?__ meter

7. 1 meter = __?__ kilometer

It is awkward to write out in full the names of the units. To simplify writing, we shall use the following abbreviations.

mm. for millimeter

cm. for centimeter

dm. for decimeter

m. for meter

km. for kilometer

8. Use the abbreviations above and restate the relationships displayed in the middle of page 411.

Which are true and which are false?

9. 1 cm. = .1 dm.

10. 1 cm. = .001 m.

11. 1 km. = 10^4 cm.

12. 1 m. = .001 km.

13. 1 mm. = .01 m.

14. 1 mm. = .001 m.

We use square units to express areas. For example, the area of a square with each side 1 cm. long is 1 sq. cm.

Given a square with each side 1 m. long, what is its area in square centimeters? Since 1 m. = 100 cm., its area is

$$100 \times 100, \text{ or } 10,000 \text{ sq. cm.}$$

Therefore, 1 sq. m. = 10,000 sq. cm., or 10^4 sq. cm.

15. What is the area in sq. mm. of a square with each side 1 cm. long?

16. What is the area in sq. m. of a square with each side 1 km. long?

17. What is the area of a rectangle with length 12 cm. and width 9 cm.?

18. What is the area of a rectangle with length 10 cm. and width 60 mm.? Give the answers in sq. mm.

19. What is the area of a rectangle with length 15 cm. and width 95 mm.? Give the answer in sq. mm.

20. What is the area of a rectangle with length 3 m. and width 80 cm.? Give the answer in sq. m.

21. What is the area of a rectangle with length 5 m. and width 90 cm.? Give the answer in sq. cm.

ENGLISH AND METRIC UNITS OF LENGTH

Since both the English and the metric systems are in frequent use, it is necessary to be able to change from one system to the other. Below we give some relationships between basic units, given to two decimal places. Recall that $\doteq$ means "is approximately equal to."

1 cm. $\doteq$ .39 in.	1 in. $\doteq$ 2.54 cm.
1 m. $\doteq$ 39.37 in.	1 in. $\doteq$ .03 m.
1 m. $\doteq$ 3.28 ft.	1 ft. $\doteq$ .30 m.
1 m. $\doteq$ 1.09 yds.	1 yd. $\doteq$ .91 m.
1 km. $\doteq$ .62 mi.	1 mi. $\doteq$ 1.61 km.

In the exercises which will follow, you will be asked to convert measures from one unit to another. We shall agree to give answers with accuracy to one decimal place, unless otherwise indicated. You should do the following:

1. Compute using the appropriate relationship correct to two decimal places.
2. Round the answer to one decimal place.

In rounding, if the first digit which is dropped is 5 through 9, the preceding digit is increased by 1. If the first digit which is dropped is 0 through 4, the preceding digit is left alone.

Convert each measure.

1. 10 cm. to in.

6. 5 in. to cm.

2. 58 m. to in.

7. 68 in. to m.

3. 500 m. to ft.

8. 10 ft. to m.

4. 1,000 m. to yds.

9. 220 yds. to m.

5. 7 km. to mi.

10. 4 mi. to km.

1 sq. cm. is about .39 × .39, or .2 sq. in.

11. 1 sq. m. is about how many sq. in.?

12. 1 sq. m. is about how many sq. ft.?

13. 1 sq. m. is about how many sq. yds.?

14. 1 sq. km. is about how many sq. mi.?

15. 1 sq. in. is about how many sq. cm.?

16. 1 sq. ft. is about how many sq. m.?

17. 1 sq. yd. is about how many sq. m.?

18. 1 sq. mi. is about how many sq. km.?

19. A cube with each edge of length of 1 cm. has the volume of $1 \times 1 \times 1$, or 1 cu. cm. How many cubic inches is that? [HINT: Round the first product to two decimal places before multiplying again. Then round the answer to one decimal place.]

20. Compute the volume in cu. cm. of a rectangular box with dimensions 1 in., 2 in., and 3 in.

21. What is the volume in cu. ft. of a rectangular box with the dimensions 1 m., 2 m., 3 m.?

22. Diving boards in Olympic size swimming pools are usually 1 m., 2 m., and 10 m. above the water level. Give these measures in terms of ft.

23. Jerry runs 220 yards in 29 seconds. Assuming the same rate, how long would it take him to run 100 meters?

UNITS FOR MEASURING CAPACITY

The units for measuring capacity in common use in the United States and England are the fluid ounce, the pint, the quart, and the gallon. The British and the U.S. units are not exactly the same. We shall give conversions involving the U.S. units.

The most commonly used metric units for measuring capacity are the milliliter (ml.) and the liter (l.).

$$1 \text{ liter} = 1,000 \text{ milliliters}$$

The following are approximate relationships between the non-metric and metric capacity units.

$$1 \text{ U.S. fluid ounce} \doteq 29.57 \text{ milliliters}$$
$$1 \text{ U.S. liquid quart} \doteq .95 \text{ liters}$$
$$1 \text{ U.S. gallon} \doteq 3.79 \text{ liters}$$
$$1 \text{ milliliter} \doteq .03 \text{ U.S. fluid ounces}$$
$$1 \text{ liter} \doteq 1.06 \text{ U.S. liquid quarts}$$
$$1 \text{ liter} \doteq .26 \text{ U.S. gallon}$$

1. If a gas tank holds 20 U.S. gallons of gas, how many liters does it hold?

2. An oil tank has the capacity of 100 U.S. gallons. How many liters is it?

3. A cup is equivalent to 8 fluid ounces. How many milliliters is it?

4. A pint is equivalent to $\frac{1}{2}$ quart. How many milliliters is it?

5. A container with the capacity of 2 quarts is equivalent to how many liters?

6. A container with the capacity of 2 liters is equivalent to how many fluid ounces?

7. A container with the capacity of 15 liters is equivalent to how many fluid ounces?

UNITS OF WEIGHT

The ounce and the pound are the most commonly used units of weight in the United States. One pound (lb.) is equivalent to 16 ounces (oz.).

The most commonly used metric units of weight are the gram (g.) and the kilogram (kg.).

$$1 \text{ kilogram} = 1{,}000 \text{ grams}$$

Below we show the relationships between different units of weight.

1 gram $\doteq$ .04 ounces	1 ounce $\doteq$ 28.35 grams
1 kilogram $\doteq$ 2.20 pounds	1 pound $\doteq$ .45 kilogram

1. One gram is equivalent to 1,000 milligrams. What is 1 milligram equivalent to in terms of grams?

2. a. How many milligrams is one kilogram equivalent to?

   b. Show this as a power of ten.

3. A can contains 12 oz. of orange juice. How many grams is that?

4. A store manager ordered 2,500 lbs. of butter. How many kilograms is that?

5. Which is greater, 100 lbs. or 40 kg.?

6. John weighs 95 lbs. How many kilograms is that?

7. Sally weighs 41 kg. How many pounds is that?

8. On certain international flights a passenger is allowed a maximum of 60 lbs. of baggage. Approximately how many kilograms is that?

9. If there are 7 calories in 1 g. of butter, how many calories are there in 1 lb. of butter?

MEASURING TEMPERATURE

In the English system, the *Fahrenheit* degree is used for recording temperature. In the metric system, the *Celsius* (centigrade) degree is used. The freezing point of water is 32 degrees Fahrenheit ($32°\,F.$) or 0 degrees Celsius ($0°\,C.$). The boiling point of water is $212°\,F.$ or $100°\,C.$ Below we give the relationships between these units.

$$F = \frac{9}{5}C + 32 \qquad C = \frac{5}{9}(F - 32)$$

Given a temperature in the Celsius scale, we can use the formula on the left above and compute the corresponding number of degrees in the Fahrenheit scale. In converting from the Fahrenheit scale to the Celsius scale, we use the formula on the right above.

Example 1   Compute the Fahrenheit equivalent of $40°\,C.$

$$F = \frac{9}{5}C + 32$$
$$= \frac{9}{5} \times 40 + 32$$
$$= 72 + 32$$
$$= 104$$

Thus, $40°\,C.$ is equivalent to $104°\,F.$

Example 2   Compute the Celsius equivalent of $59°\,F.$

$$C = \frac{5}{9}(F - 32)$$
$$= \frac{5}{9}(59 - 32)$$
$$= \frac{5}{9} \times 27$$
$$= 15$$

Thus, $59°\,F.$ is equivalent to $15°\,C.$

Compute the Fahrenheit equivalent of

1. $30°\,C.$ **2.** $80°\,C.$ **3.** $0°\,C.$ **4.** $-10°\,C.$

Compute the Celsius equivalent of

5. $41°\,F.$ **6.** $23°\,F.$ **7.** $-4°\,F.$ **8.** $-22°\,F.$

VOCABULARY REVIEW

Celsius (416)
centigrade (416)
centimeter (411)
decimeter (411)
Fahrenheit (416)
fluid ounce (414)
foot (413)
gallon (414)
gram (415)
inch (413)
kilogram (415)
kilometer (411)

liter (414)
meter (411)
metric system (411)
mile (413)
milliliter (414)
millimeter (411)
ounce (415)
pint (414)
pound (415)
quart (414)
yard (413)

A CHALLENGE TO YOU

1. a. Using a string, determine in millimeters the circumference of a 1 cent coin and of a quarter.

b. What is the difference of these circumferences?

c. Compute the diameter of each of these two coins in mm. to one decimal place. (Use 3.1 for π.)

d. Compute the area of each coin to one decimal place.

2. a. One meter is one-ten-millionth of one-fourth of the earth's circumference at the equator. If a one-dollar bill is about 16 cm. long, approximately how many dollar bills would it take, placed end to end lengthwise, to reach around the earth at the equator?

b. If one dollar bill is placed each second, approximately how many years would it take to get around the earth? (Compute the answer with accuracy to one year.)

3. What temperature is given as the same number of degrees in both scales, Fahrenheit and Celsius?

CHAPTER TEST

1. Show each of the following as a power of ten.

    a. The number of centimeters in a kilometer.

    b. The number of millimeters in a kilometer.

2. a. Compute the area of a rectangle with the length of 20 cm. and the width of 9 cm.

    b. Express this area in square inches.

3. a. Compute the area of a rectangle with the length of 30 in. and the width of 14 in.

    b. Express this area in square centimeters.

4. If a tank holds 24 U.S. gallons, how many liters does it hold?

5. If a tank holds 60 liters, how many U.S. gallons does it hold?

6. Which is greater, 1 U.S. gallon or 4 liters?

7. Which is greater, 1 liter or 1 quart?

8. Express 100 kg. in terms of milligrams, showing it as a power of ten.

9. A car weighs 750 kg. How many pounds is that?

10. A car weighs 2,250 lbs. How many kilograms is that? (Give the answer with accuracy to 10 kg.)

11. A can of peaches weighs 30 oz. How many grams is that? (Give the answer with accuracy to 1 gram.)

12. There are 40 calories in 6 ounces of tomato juice. How many calories are there in 1 kg. of tomato juice? (Give the answer with accuracy to 1 calorie.)

13. A bottle contains 567 grams of catsup. Express this in terms of pounds and ounces with accuracy to 1 ounce.

14. Compute the Fahrenheit equivalent of

    a. $50°\,C$.   b. $25°\,C$.   c. $-40°\,C$.

15. Compute the Celsius equivalent of

    a. $95°\,F$.   b. $50°\,F$.   c. $0°\,F$.

BIBLIOGRAPHY

ABBOTT, EDWIN A. *Flatland*. New York: Dover Publications, 1952.

ADLER, IRVING. *Thinking Machines*. New York: The John Day Company, 1961.

BAKST, AARON. *Mathematics: Its Magic and Mastery*. New York: D. Van Nostrand Co., Inc., 1967.

BARNETT, I. A. *Some Ideas About Number Theory*. Washington: National Council of Teachers of Mathematics, 1961.

BERGAMINI, DAVID. *Mathematics*. (Time-Life Library Series.) Morristown, N. J.: Silver Burdett Company, 1963.

BOEHM, GEORGE A. W., and Fortune Magazine Editors. *The New World of Math*. New York: The Dial Press, 1959.

FREITAG, H. T. and A. H. FREITAG. *The Number Story*. Washington: National Council of Teachers of Mathematics, 1960.

GARDNER, MARTIN. *Mathematics, Magic and Mystery*. New York: Dover Publications, Inc., 1955.

JOHNSON, DONOVAN A. *Paper Folding*. Washington: National Council of Teachers of Mathematics, 1957.

———, and WILLIAM H. GLENN. *Computing Devices*. St. Louis: Webster Division, McGraw-Hill Book Company, 1961.

———. *Invitation to Mathematics*. St. Louis: Webster Division, McGraw-Hill Book Company, 1960.

LIEBER, LILLIAN R. *Infinity*. New York: Holt, Rinehart and Winston, Inc., 1953.

MEYER, JEROME S. *Fun with Mathematics*. Greenwich: Fawcett Publications, Inc., 1961.

NICHOLS, EUGENE D., ROBERT KALIN, and E. HENRY GARLAND. *Arithmetic of Directed Numbers* (A Programed Unit). New York: Holt, Rinehart and Winston, Inc., 1962.

———. *Equations and Inequalities* (A Programed Unit). New York: Holt, Rinehart and Winston, Inc., 1963.

———. *Introduction to Coordinate Geometry* (A Programed Unit). New York: Holt, Rinehart and Winston, Inc., 1965.

———. *Introduction to Sets* (A Programed Unit). New York: Holt, Rinehart and Winston, Inc., 1962.

ODOM, MARY MARGARET and EUGENE D. NICHOLS. *Introduction to Exponents* (A Programed Unit). New York: Holt, Rinehart and Winston, Inc., 1964.

SMITH, DAVID EUGENE, and JEKUTHIEL GINSBURG. *Numbers and Numerals*. Washington: National Council of Teachers of Mathematics, 1961.

SMITH, EUGENE. *Number Stories of Long Ago*. Washington: National Council of Teachers of Mathematics, 1955.

STRADER, WILLIAM W. *Little Stories*. Washington: National Council of Teachers of Mathematics, 1960.

CONVERSION TABLES
Length

12 inches = 1 foot
3 feet = 1 yard
1 rod = 16.5 feet
5,280 feet = 1 mile

1 centimeter = 10 millimeters
1 decimeter = 10 centimeters
1 meter = 100 centimeters
1 kilometer = 1,000 meters

1 inch ≐ 2.54 centimeters
1 inch ≐ .03 meter
1 foot ≐ .30 meter
1 yard ≐ .91 meter
1 mile ≐ 1.61 kilometers

1 centimeter ≐ .39 inch
1 meter ≐ 39.37 inches
1 meter ≐ 3.28 feet
1 meter ≐ 1.09 yards
1 kilometer ≐ .62 mile

U.S. Liquid Measure

1 gallon = 4 quarts
1 quart = 2 pints
1 pint = 16 ounces

1 liter = 1,000 milliliters

1 fluid ounce ≐ 29.57 milliliters
1 liquid quart ≐ .95 liter
1 gallon ≐ 3.79 liters

1 milliliter ≐ .03 fluid ounce
1 liter ≐ 1.06 liquid quarts
1 liter ≐ .26 gallon

Weight

1 pound = 16 ounces
1 ton = 2,000 pounds

1 kilogram = 1,000 grams

1 ounce ≐ 28.35 grams
1 pound ≐ .45 kilogram

1 gram ≐ .04 ounce
1 kilogram ≐ 2.20 pounds

TABLE 421

TABLE OF ROOTS AND POWERS

No.	Sq.	Sq. Root	Cube	Cu. Root	No.	Sq.	Sq. Root	Cube	Cu. Root
1	1	1.000	1	1.000	51	2,601	7.141	132,651	3.708
2	4	1.414	8	1.260	52	2,704	7.211	140,608	3.733
3	9	1.732	27	1.442	53	2,809	7.280	148,877	3.756
4	16	2.000	64	1.587	54	2,916	7.348	157,564	3.780
5	25	2.236	125	1.710	55	3,025	7.416	166,375	3.803
6	36	2.449	216	1.817	56	3,136	7.483	175,616	3.826
7	49	2.646	343	1.913	57	3,249	7.550	185,193	3.849
8	64	2.828	512	2.000	58	3,364	7.616	195,112	3.871
9	81	3.000	729	2.080	59	3,481	7.681	205,379	3.893
10	100	3.162	1,000	2.154	60	3,600	7.746	216,000	3.915
11	121	3.317	1,331	2.224	61	3,721	7.810	226,981	3.936
12	144	3.464	1,728	2.289	62	3,844	7.874	238,328	3.958
13	169	3.606	2,197	2.351	63	3,969	7.937	250,047	3.979
14	196	3.742	2,744	2.410	64	4,096	8.000	262,144	4.000
15	225	3.875	3,375	2.466	65	4,225	8.062	274,625	4.021
16	256	4.000	4,096	2.520	66	4,356	8.124	287,496	4.041
17	289	4.123	4,913	2.571	67	4,489	8.185	300,763	4.062
18	324	4.243	5,832	2.621	68	4,624	8.246	314,432	4.082
19	361	4.359	6,859	2.668	69	4,761	8.307	328,509	4.102
20	400	4.472	8,000	2.714	70	4,900	8.357	343,000	4.121
21	441	4.583	9,261	2.759	71	5,041	8.426	357,911	4.141
22	484	4.690	10,648	2.802	72	5,184	8.485	373,248	4.160
23	529	4.796	12,167	2.844	73	5,329	8.544	389,017	4.179
24	576	4.899	13,824	2.884	74	5,476	8.602	405,224	4.198
25	625	5.000	15,625	2.924	75	5,625	8.660	421,875	4.217
26	676	5.099	17,576	2.962	76	5,776	8.718	438,976	4.236
27	729	5.196	19,683	3.000	77	5,929	8.775	456,533	4.254
28	784	5.292	21,952	3.037	78	6,084	8.832	474,552	4.273
29	841	5.385	24,389	3.072	79	6,241	8.888	493,039	4.291
30	900	5.477	27,000	3.107	80	6,400	8.944	512,000	4.309
31	961	5.568	29,791	3.141	81	6,561	9.000	531,441	4.327
32	1,024	5.657	32,768	3.175	82	6,724	9.055	551,368	4.344
33	1,089	5.745	35,937	3.208	83	6,889	9.110	571,787	4.362
34	1,156	5.831	39,304	3.240	84	7,056	9.165	592,704	4.380
35	1,225	5.916	42,875	3.271	85	7,225	9.220	614,125	4.397
36	1,296	6.000	46,656	3.302	86	7,396	9.274	636,056	4.414
37	1,369	6.083	50,653	3.332	87	7,569	9.327	658,503	4.431
38	1,444	6.164	54,872	3.362	88	7,744	9.381	681,472	4.448
39	1,521	6.245	59,319	3.391	89	7,921	9.434	704,969	4.465
40	1,600	6.325	64,000	3.420	90	8,100	9.487	729,000	4.481
41	1,681	6.403	68,921	3.448	91	8,281	9.539	753,571	4.498
42	1,764	6.481	74,088	3.476	92	8,464	9.592	778,688	4.514
43	1,849	6.557	79,507	3.503	93	8,649	9.644	804,357	4.531
44	1,936	6.633	85,184	3.530	94	8,836	9.695	830,584	4.547
45	2,025	6.708	91,125	3.557	95	9,025	9.747	857,375	4.563
46	2,116	6.782	97,336	3.583	96	9,216	9.798	884,736	4.579
47	2,209	6.856	103,823	3.609	97	9,409	9.849	912,673	4.595
48	2,304	6.928	110,592	3.634	98	9,604	9.899	941,192	4.610
49	2,401	7.000	117,649	3.659	99	9,801	9.950	970,299	4.626
50	2,500	7.071	125,000	3.684	100	10,000	10.000	1,000,000	4.642

Practice Exercises

Addition of whole numbers

1.

3	4	3	9	3	4	3	4	9	7	3	4	7
7	8	6	5	6	5	7	8	8	4	4	9	4
6	5	8	9	7	8	9	8	3	8	8	7	5
				4	2	6	9	8	5	6	5	8
						7	4	2	6	9	3	9
								8	7	1	8	3
									4	8	5	6
									9	7	6	8

2.

36	45	47	34	10	79	84	17	45	12	99
44	67	64	56	45	86	56	95	82	45	88
			78	37	58	79	36	17	64	62
				83	39	32	45	63	75	45
					46	76	67	42	39	39
						98	81	84	49	75
							94	66	85	18
								94	37	93

3.

376	178	395	370	446	389	440	406
424	236	496	980	378	276	671	990
	564	544	420	262	869	983	307
		367	140	878	349	365	483
			570	609	760	461	555
				786	805	372	609
					271	458	700
						761	635

4.

3,075	446	1,586	1,762	3,682	4,405	1,763
366	32	302	4,478	485	790	25
	1,362	96	3,685	37	3,681	405
		3,600	8,005	4,467	99	34,506
			3,067	321	405	4,079
				9,862	1,762	980
					5,044	17

Answers

1. 16; 17; 17; 23; 20; 19; 32; 33; 38; 50; 46; 47; 50 **2.** 80; 112; 111; 168; 175; 308; 425; 435; 493; 406; 519 **3.** 800; 978; 1,802; 2,480; 3,359; 3,719; 4,511; 4,685 **4.** 3,441; 1,840; 5,584; 20,997; 18,854; 16,186; 41,775

Subtraction of whole numbers

1.

50	39	96	175	643	825	598	247	478
30	26	91	34	13	21	117	240	265

2.

6,879	4,963	9,521	8,263	3,495	5,748	79,561
817	702	500	4,061	3,052	3,333	4,541

3.

25,837	94,686	21,438	375,280	967,587
4,603	53,265	21,406	52,130	237,024

4.

81	96	73	494	671	254	790	562	904
18	69	37	35	92	86	281	179	537

5.

4,822	9,153	2,340	5,208	3,622	7,503	63,431
735	368	592	4,859	1,847	2,786	9,847

6.

49,017	71,029	80,106	430,481	892,653
3,658	64,760	59,647	73,509	356,298

Answers

1. 20; 13; 5; 141; 630; 804; 481; 7; 213 **2.** 6,062; 4,261; 9,021; 4,202; 443; 2,415; 75,020 **3.** 21,234; 41,421; 32; 323,150; 730,563 **4.** 63; 27; 36; 459; 579; 168; 509; 383; 367 **5.** 4,087; 8,785; 1,748; 349; 1,775; 4,717; 53,584 **6.** 45,359; 6,269; 20,459; 356,972; 536,355

Multiplication of whole numbers

1.
6	6	7	8	9	7	9	8	9
8	9	6	7	7	7	9	8	8

2.
73	95	64	28	66	49	65	79
6	8	9	7	8	7	6	9

3.
267	359	816	462	754	349	579
8	7	9	7	9	8	6

4.
561	824	790	135	618	473	286
47	58	62	93	50	86	17

5.
408	613	295	734	841	396	404
217	504	631	357	462	693	202

Answers

1. 48; 54; 42; 56; 63; 49; 81; 64; 72 **2.** 438; 760; 576; 196; 528; 343; 390; 711
3. 2,136; 2,513; 7,344; 3,234; 6,786; 2,792; 3,474 **4.** 26,367; 47,792; 48,980;
12,555; 30,900; 40,678; 4,862 **5.** 88,536; 308,952; 186,145; 262,038; 388,542;
274,428; 81,608

Division of whole numbers — divisors less than 10

1. 3)957   4)1,644   5)1,675   2)8,738   6)3,358   7)3,495

2. 8)256   6)5,484   9)7,587   7)3,992   5)5,435   3)1,469

3. 4)349   3)6,148   7)6,585   8)2,164   9)6,954   5)6,120

4. 7)625   9)8,562   2)9,974   4)8,824   3)6,954   6)4,218

5. 2)538   5)1,594   8)6,281   6)4,638   7)4,963   4)6,664

6. 6)726   7)3,542   3)2,612   9)22,689   4)16,363   8)40,952

7. 5)490   8)6,768   4)3,807   3)99,636   2)80,504   9)65,031

8. 9)371   2)5,417   6)7,062   5)35,006   8)17,530   2)50,302

9. 4)276   3)3,510   9)3,307   7)83,915   3)39,001   5)90,718

10. 6)307   5)3,510   2)7,562   4)46,544   5)19,275   4)11,206

11. 2)869   7)6,619   8)9,806   6)18,424   9)28,009   7)28,637

Answers

Division of whole numbers—divisors 10 through 99

1. $71\overline{)765}$ $36\overline{)3,370}$ $12\overline{)3,162}$ $89\overline{)36,009}$ $43\overline{)29,000}$

2. $27\overline{)305}$ $11\overline{)9,067}$ $32\overline{)2,705}$ $35\overline{)47,865}$ $19\overline{)33,700}$

3. $69\overline{)650}$ $54\overline{)6,530}$ $85\overline{)5,500}$ $99\overline{)98,063}$ $14\overline{)58,990}$

4. $25\overline{)907}$ $49\overline{)2,200}$ $50\overline{)8,906}$ $13\overline{)12,276}$ $70\overline{)24,069}$

5. $30\overline{)458}$ $51\overline{)1,198}$ $37\overline{)3,125}$ $92\overline{)49,065}$ $74\overline{)35,066}$

6. $16\overline{)176}$ $29\overline{)9,609}$ $42\overline{)6,766}$ $82\overline{)69,221}$ $46\overline{)67,058}$

7. $20\overline{)200}$ $15\overline{)8,805}$ $90\overline{)3,709}$ $17\overline{)98,065}$ $67\overline{)82,639}$

8. $22\overline{)179}$ $34\overline{)4,470}$ $28\overline{)2,005}$ $45\overline{)31,207}$ $24\overline{)39,915}$

9. $10\overline{)968}$ $13\overline{)2,963}$ $21\overline{)7,009}$ $18\overline{)36,998}$ $94\overline{)49,671}$

10. $71\overline{)870}$ $55\overline{)4,579}$ $77\overline{)5,476}$ $44\overline{)11,907}$ $26\overline{)91,801}$

11. $88\overline{)999}$ $41\overline{)6,070}$ $33\overline{)3,250}$ $23\overline{)31,500}$ $31\overline{)42,666}$

Answers

Division of whole numbers — divisors 100 through 999

1. $115\overline{)7,609}$ $269\overline{)1,125}$ $309\overline{)36,298}$ $420\overline{)82,369}$

2. $255\overline{)2,659}$ $772\overline{)8,096}$ $895\overline{)98,300}$ $906\overline{)35,467}$

3. $905\overline{)9,192}$ $670\overline{)3,595}$ $325\overline{)65,034}$ $811\overline{)26,309}$

4. $618\overline{)7,265}$ $109\overline{)2,186}$ $308\overline{)31,506}$ $596\overline{)60,600}$

5. $309\overline{)3,005}$ $411\overline{)4,120}$ $751\overline{)76,333}$ $809\overline{)39,888}$

6. $226\overline{)3,760}$ $317\overline{)3,255}$ $108\overline{)98,458}$ $298\overline{)30,309}$

7. $179\overline{)2,805}$ $291\overline{)2,932}$ $609\overline{)75,301}$ $700\overline{)80,001}$

8. $333\overline{)4,444}$ $246\overline{)4,812}$ $987\overline{)78,910}$ $371\overline{)40,070}$

9. $777\overline{)8,501}$ $396\overline{)3,950}$ $176\overline{)28,300}$ $211\overline{)41,260}$

10. $645\overline{)6,442}$ $720\overline{)9,200}$ $360\overline{)76,000}$ $210\overline{)41,000}$

11. $711\overline{)1,446}$ $812\overline{)9,120}$ $395\overline{)45,450}$ $909\overline{)18,018}$

12. $390\overline{)7,800}$ $460\overline{)4,700}$ $902\overline{)18,400}$ $809\overline{)12,686}$

13. $456\overline{)1,762}$ $505\overline{)1,261}$ $652\overline{)17,303}$ $769\overline{)22,222}$

14. $842\overline{)1,235}$ $746\overline{)8,452}$ $444\overline{)13,906}$ $901\overline{)32,117}$

15. $333\overline{)9,200}$ $434\overline{)8,100}$ $909\overline{)10,600}$ $369\overline{)96,316}$

16. $111\overline{)2,233}$ $555\overline{)1,010}$ $707\overline{)14,006}$ $404\overline{)88,800}$

Answers

1. 66,R19; 4,R49; 117,R145; 196,R49 **2.** 10,R109; 10,R376; 109,R745; 39,R133
3. 10,R142; 5,R245; 200,R34; 32,R357 **4.** 11,R467; 20,R6; 102,R90; 101,R404
5. 9,R224; 10,R10; 101,R482; 49,R247 **6.** 16,R144; 10,R85; 911,R70; 101,R211
7. 15,R120; 10,R22; 123,R394; 114,R201 **8.** 13,R115; 19,R138; 79,R937;
108,R2 **9.** 10,R731; 9,R386; 160,R140; 195,R115 **10.** 9,R637; 12,R560;
211,R40; 195,R50 **11.** 2,R24; 11,R188; 115,R25; 19,R747 **12.** 20; 10,R100;
20,R360; 15,R551 **13.** 3,R394; 2,R251; 26,R351; 28,R690 **14.** 1,R393;
11,R246; 31,R142; 35,R582 **15.** 27,R209; 18,R288; 11,R601; 261,R7 **16.** 20,R13;
1,R455; 19,R573; 219,R324

Supply the missing numerators.

1. $\dfrac{1}{2} = \dfrac{}{6}$ $\dfrac{1}{2} = \dfrac{}{8}$ $\dfrac{1}{2} = \dfrac{}{10}$ $\dfrac{1}{2} = \dfrac{}{4}$

2. $\dfrac{2}{3} = \dfrac{}{12}$ $\dfrac{4}{7} = \dfrac{}{14}$ $\dfrac{5}{6} = \dfrac{}{30}$ $\dfrac{3}{4} = \dfrac{}{20}$

3. $\dfrac{3}{8} = \dfrac{}{16}$ $\dfrac{3}{8} = \dfrac{}{40}$ $\dfrac{4}{3} = \dfrac{}{12}$ $\dfrac{5}{2} = \dfrac{}{20}$

4. $\dfrac{3}{10} = \dfrac{}{30}$ $\dfrac{1}{4} = \dfrac{}{44}$ $\dfrac{5}{12} = \dfrac{}{36}$ $\dfrac{4}{9} = \dfrac{}{72}$

5. $\dfrac{8}{20} = \dfrac{}{5}$ $\dfrac{10}{15} = \dfrac{}{3}$ $\dfrac{9}{27} = \dfrac{}{3}$ $\dfrac{27}{36} = \dfrac{}{4}$

6. $\dfrac{4}{12} = \dfrac{}{6}$ $\dfrac{24}{32} = \dfrac{}{4}$ $\dfrac{11}{44} = \dfrac{}{4}$ $\dfrac{12}{8} = \dfrac{}{2}$

7. $\dfrac{14}{28} = \dfrac{}{2}$ $\dfrac{22}{33} = \dfrac{}{3}$ $\dfrac{24}{60} = \dfrac{}{5}$ $\dfrac{14}{21} = \dfrac{}{3}$

8. $\dfrac{16}{48} = \dfrac{}{3}$ $\dfrac{11}{55} = \dfrac{}{5}$ $\dfrac{36}{18} = \dfrac{}{9}$ $\dfrac{42}{8} = \dfrac{}{4}$

9. $\dfrac{24}{8} = \dfrac{}{1}$ $\dfrac{34}{17} = \dfrac{}{1}$ $\dfrac{39}{13} = \dfrac{}{1}$ $\dfrac{48}{6} = \dfrac{}{1}$

Answers

1. 3; 4; 5; 2 **2.** 8; 8; 25; 15 **3.** 6; 15; 16; 50 **4.** 9; 11; 15; 32 **5.** 2; 2; 1; 3
6. 2; 3; 1; 3 **7.** 1; 2; 2; 2 **8.** 1; 1; 18; 21 **9.** 3; 2; 3; 8

Addition (fractional numerals). Give the simplest names.

1. $\dfrac{1}{2} + \dfrac{3}{2}$ $\dfrac{2}{3} + \dfrac{1}{6}$ $\dfrac{1}{4} + \dfrac{7}{12}$ $\dfrac{5}{6} + \dfrac{1}{12}$ $\dfrac{2}{5} + \dfrac{7}{10}$

2. $\dfrac{2}{5} + \dfrac{4}{15}$ $\dfrac{1}{7} + \dfrac{4}{21}$ $\dfrac{1}{8} + \dfrac{5}{24}$ $\dfrac{2}{5} + \dfrac{4}{25}$ $\dfrac{2}{5} + \dfrac{7}{25}$

3. $2\dfrac{1}{2} + 3\dfrac{1}{4}$ $5\dfrac{1}{3} + 3\dfrac{5}{6}$ $1\dfrac{1}{4} + 3\dfrac{7}{12}$ $5\dfrac{2}{7} + 3\dfrac{1}{14}$ $4\dfrac{2}{5} + 7\dfrac{1}{15}$

4. $\dfrac{1}{2} + \dfrac{1}{3}$ $\dfrac{1}{3} + \dfrac{2}{5}$ $\dfrac{3}{4} + \dfrac{5}{6}$ $\dfrac{2}{5} + \dfrac{1}{7}$ $\dfrac{4}{9} + \dfrac{1}{2}$

5. $\dfrac{5}{8}+\dfrac{9}{10}$ $\dfrac{2}{7}+\dfrac{1}{3}$ $\dfrac{5}{8}+\dfrac{2}{3}$ $\dfrac{5}{4}+\dfrac{3}{10}$ $\dfrac{5}{8}+\dfrac{7}{12}$

6. $\dfrac{3}{5}+\dfrac{5}{6}$ $\dfrac{2}{7}+\dfrac{5}{24}$ $\dfrac{4}{11}+\dfrac{5}{7}$ $2\dfrac{1}{3}+5\dfrac{1}{5}$ $4\dfrac{2}{5}+2\dfrac{1}{7}$

7. $5+3\dfrac{1}{8}$ $2\dfrac{1}{11}+6$ $\dfrac{3}{7}+2$ $1+\dfrac{4}{3}$ $5+\dfrac{7}{2}$

8. $3\dfrac{1}{3}+4\dfrac{1}{2}$ $5\dfrac{1}{4}+1\dfrac{3}{7}$ $3\dfrac{1}{11}+1\dfrac{2}{3}$ $4\dfrac{1}{5}+6\dfrac{1}{7}$ $9\dfrac{2}{9}+6\dfrac{3}{11}$

9. $5\dfrac{1}{6}+3\dfrac{2}{7}$ $4\dfrac{1}{9}+3\dfrac{1}{8}$ $1\dfrac{1}{10}+3\dfrac{1}{3}$ $5\dfrac{2}{7}+1\dfrac{6}{11}$ $3\dfrac{1}{6}+2\dfrac{7}{9}$

10. $\dfrac{9}{7}+\dfrac{1}{6}$ $\dfrac{10}{9}+\dfrac{1}{2}$ $\dfrac{13}{6}+\dfrac{5}{7}$ $\dfrac{12}{5}+\dfrac{4}{7}$ $\dfrac{17}{11}+\dfrac{2}{3}$

11. $\dfrac{4}{3}+\dfrac{5}{4}$ $\dfrac{3}{2}+\dfrac{7}{6}$ $\dfrac{5}{3}+\dfrac{7}{2}$ $\dfrac{11}{9}+\dfrac{10}{7}$ $\dfrac{13}{6}+\dfrac{12}{5}$

12. $\dfrac{7}{2}+\dfrac{11}{9}$ $\dfrac{11}{3}+\dfrac{3}{2}$ $\dfrac{12}{11}+\dfrac{10}{3}$ $\dfrac{11}{7}+\dfrac{7}{6}$ $\dfrac{13}{9}+\dfrac{7}{6}$

13. $3\dfrac{1}{7}+9\dfrac{1}{6}$ $4\dfrac{3}{10}+1\dfrac{1}{11}$ $6\dfrac{1}{6}+2\dfrac{3}{8}$ $5\dfrac{4}{5}+7\dfrac{6}{7}$ $1\dfrac{1}{11}+2\dfrac{1}{9}$

14. $\dfrac{16}{9}+\dfrac{5}{4}$ $\dfrac{9}{2}+\dfrac{7}{5}$ $\dfrac{12}{5}+\dfrac{13}{7}$ $\dfrac{17}{12}+\dfrac{13}{11}$ $\dfrac{12}{9}+\dfrac{13}{8}$

15. $\dfrac{2}{7}+\dfrac{12}{5}$ $\dfrac{3}{10}+\dfrac{11}{3}$ $\dfrac{7}{8}+\dfrac{13}{9}$ $\dfrac{3}{5}+\dfrac{16}{9}$ $\dfrac{7}{8}+\dfrac{14}{9}$

Answers

1. $2;\ \dfrac{5}{6};\ \dfrac{5}{6};\ \dfrac{11}{12};\ 1\dfrac{1}{10}$ **2.** $\dfrac{2}{3};\ \dfrac{1}{3};\ \dfrac{1}{3};\ \dfrac{14}{25};\ \dfrac{17}{25}$ **3.** $5\dfrac{3}{4};\ 9\dfrac{1}{6};\ 4\dfrac{5}{6};\ 8\dfrac{5}{14};\ 11\dfrac{7}{15}$ **4.** $\dfrac{5}{6};\ \dfrac{11}{15};$ $1\dfrac{7}{12};\ \dfrac{19}{35};\ \dfrac{17}{18}$ **5.** $1\dfrac{21}{40};\ \dfrac{13}{21};\ 1\dfrac{7}{24};\ 1\dfrac{11}{20};\ 1\dfrac{5}{24}$ **6.** $1\dfrac{13}{30};\ \dfrac{83}{168};\ 1\dfrac{6}{77};\ 7\dfrac{8}{15};\ 6\dfrac{19}{35}$ **7.** $8\dfrac{1}{8};$ $8\dfrac{1}{11};\ 2\dfrac{3}{7};\ 2\dfrac{1}{3};\ 8\dfrac{1}{2}$ **8.** $7\dfrac{5}{6};\ 6\dfrac{19}{28};\ 4\dfrac{25}{33};\ 10\dfrac{12}{35};\ 15\dfrac{49}{99}$ **9.** $8\dfrac{19}{42};\ 7\dfrac{17}{72};\ 4\dfrac{13}{30};\ 6\dfrac{64}{77};\ 5\dfrac{17}{18}$ **10.** $1\dfrac{19}{42};\ 1\dfrac{11}{18};\ 2\dfrac{37}{42};\ 2\dfrac{34}{35};\ 2\dfrac{7}{33}$ **11.** $2\dfrac{7}{12};\ 2\dfrac{2}{3};\ 5\dfrac{1}{6};\ 2\dfrac{41}{63};\ 4\dfrac{17}{30}$ **12.** $4\dfrac{13}{18};\ 5\dfrac{1}{6};\ 4\dfrac{14}{33};$ $2\dfrac{31}{42};\ 2\dfrac{11}{18}$ **13.** $12\dfrac{13}{42};\ 5\dfrac{43}{110};\ 8\dfrac{13}{24};\ 13\dfrac{23}{35};\ 3\dfrac{20}{99}$ **14.** $3\dfrac{1}{36};\ 5\dfrac{9}{10};\ 4\dfrac{9}{35};\ 2\dfrac{79}{132};\ 2\dfrac{23}{24}$ **15.** $2\dfrac{24}{35};\ 3\dfrac{29}{30};\ 2\dfrac{23}{72};\ 2\dfrac{17}{45};\ 2\dfrac{31}{72}$

Addition (fractional numerals). Give the simplest names.

1. $3\frac{1}{3}+4\frac{1}{4}$ $5\frac{2}{7}+3\frac{6}{10}$ $1\frac{1}{6}+4\frac{4}{7}$ $3\frac{4}{7}+1\frac{5}{6}$ $4\frac{4}{7}+3\frac{7}{8}$

2. $\frac{14}{3}+\frac{5}{2}$ $\frac{16}{7}+\frac{4}{3}$ $\frac{7}{2}+\frac{4}{3}$ $\frac{11}{5}+\frac{7}{6}$ $\frac{3}{2}+\frac{17}{3}$

3. $4\frac{1}{7}+\frac{1}{2}$ $3\frac{4}{7}+\frac{3}{4}$ $9\frac{1}{6}+\frac{3}{5}$ $10\frac{3}{7}+\frac{4}{5}$ $1\frac{1}{9}+\frac{4}{5}$

4. $\frac{1}{2}+\frac{1}{3}$ $\frac{1}{3}+\frac{1}{4}$ $\frac{1}{4}+\frac{1}{5}$ $\frac{1}{5}+\frac{1}{6}$ $\frac{1}{6}+\frac{1}{7}$

5. $7+4\frac{1}{4}$ $3+6\frac{3}{5}$ $9+5\frac{6}{7}$ $3\frac{1}{9}+4$ $8\frac{3}{10}+5$

6. $3\frac{1}{6}+\frac{5}{2}$ $5\frac{1}{7}+\frac{15}{14}$ $16\frac{1}{3}+\frac{11}{6}$ $12\frac{1}{4}+\frac{11}{8}$ $7\frac{3}{7}+\frac{22}{21}$

7. $\frac{7}{2}+\frac{8}{3}$ $\frac{9}{4}+\frac{6}{5}$ $\frac{17}{3}+\frac{9}{4}$ $\frac{7}{3}+\frac{12}{5}$ $\frac{12}{11}+\frac{11}{10}$

8. $4\frac{1}{8}+5\frac{2}{7}$ $6\frac{3}{7}+5\frac{1}{6}$ $1\frac{1}{9}+2\frac{3}{8}$ $5\frac{1}{4}+1\frac{4}{5}$ $3\frac{7}{10}+4\frac{7}{9}$

Answers

1. $7\frac{7}{12}$; $8\frac{31}{35}$; $5\frac{31}{42}$; $5\frac{17}{42}$; $8\frac{25}{56}$ 2. $7\frac{1}{6}$; $3\frac{13}{21}$; $4\frac{5}{6}$; $3\frac{11}{30}$; $7\frac{1}{6}$ 3. $4\frac{9}{14}$; $4\frac{9}{28}$; $9\frac{23}{30}$; $11\frac{8}{35}$; $1\frac{41}{45}$ 4. $\frac{5}{6}$; $\frac{7}{12}$; $\frac{9}{20}$; $\frac{11}{30}$; $\frac{13}{42}$ 5. $11\frac{1}{4}$; $9\frac{3}{5}$; $14\frac{6}{7}$; $7\frac{1}{9}$; $13\frac{3}{10}$ 6. $5\frac{2}{3}$; $6\frac{3}{14}$; $18\frac{1}{6}$; $13\frac{5}{8}$; $8\frac{10}{21}$ 7. $6\frac{1}{6}$; $3\frac{9}{20}$; $7\frac{11}{12}$; $4\frac{11}{15}$; $2\frac{21}{110}$ 8. $9\frac{23}{56}$; $11\frac{25}{42}$; $3\frac{35}{72}$; $7\frac{1}{20}$; $8\frac{43}{90}$

Subtraction (fractional numerals). Give the simplest names.

1. $\frac{3}{4}-\frac{1}{2}$ $\frac{2}{3}-\frac{1}{6}$ $\frac{4}{5}-\frac{5}{10}$ $\frac{7}{8}-\frac{3}{4}$ $\frac{4}{9}-\frac{1}{3}$

2. $\frac{4}{5}-\frac{1}{10}$ $\frac{2}{3}-\frac{5}{12}$ $\frac{7}{16}-\frac{1}{4}$ $\frac{17}{20}-\frac{3}{5}$ $\frac{5}{21}-\frac{1}{7}$

3. $4\frac{1}{2}-3\frac{1}{4}$ $5\frac{1}{6}-3\frac{1}{12}$ $4\frac{3}{4}-1\frac{1}{2}$ $6\frac{1}{7}-3\frac{1}{14}$ $3\frac{3}{10}-1\frac{1}{5}$

4. $\frac{3}{5}-\frac{1}{2}$ $\frac{4}{7}-\frac{1}{2}$ $\frac{6}{7}-\frac{3}{4}$ $\frac{2}{3}-\frac{1}{5}$ $\frac{3}{4}-\frac{2}{5}$

5. $\dfrac{1}{2} - \dfrac{1}{3}$ $\dfrac{1}{3} - \dfrac{1}{4}$ $\dfrac{2}{5} - \dfrac{1}{6}$ $\dfrac{3}{4} - \dfrac{3}{5}$ $\dfrac{3}{7} - \dfrac{3}{8}$

6. $3\dfrac{1}{3} - 1\dfrac{1}{4}$ $4\dfrac{5}{6} - 3\dfrac{5}{7}$ $6\dfrac{1}{6} - 2\dfrac{1}{7}$ $5\dfrac{3}{4} - 2\dfrac{3}{5}$ $6\dfrac{1}{8} - 5\dfrac{1}{10}$

7. $\dfrac{3}{10} - \dfrac{1}{11}$ $\dfrac{7}{13} - \dfrac{1}{2}$ $\dfrac{5}{8} - \dfrac{3}{7}$ $\dfrac{5}{12} - \dfrac{2}{5}$ $\dfrac{11}{12} - \dfrac{7}{8}$

8. $\dfrac{4}{9} - \dfrac{1}{7}$ $\dfrac{5}{12} - \dfrac{2}{11}$ $\dfrac{4}{13} - \dfrac{1}{12}$ $\dfrac{7}{15} - \dfrac{2}{45}$ $\dfrac{7}{16} - \dfrac{1}{3}$

9. $6\dfrac{3}{7} - 3\dfrac{2}{9}$ $4\dfrac{3}{4} - 3\dfrac{1}{2}$ $5\dfrac{2}{3} - 2\dfrac{1}{4}$ $7\dfrac{1}{2} - 2\dfrac{2}{5}$ $9\dfrac{6}{7} - 5\dfrac{7}{10}$

10. $\dfrac{6}{11} - \dfrac{1}{9}$ $\dfrac{7}{12} - \dfrac{1}{5}$ $\dfrac{3}{13} - \dfrac{1}{6}$ $\dfrac{3}{20} - \dfrac{1}{9}$ $\dfrac{10}{17} - \dfrac{1}{3}$

11. $4\dfrac{2}{11} - 2\dfrac{1}{10}$ $3\dfrac{1}{5} - 1\dfrac{1}{6}$ $8\dfrac{2}{3} - 2\dfrac{2}{7}$ $7\dfrac{5}{8} - 4\dfrac{2}{7}$ $3\dfrac{8}{9} - 1\dfrac{6}{7}$

Answers

1. $\dfrac{1}{4}; \dfrac{1}{2}; \dfrac{3}{10}; \dfrac{1}{8}; \dfrac{1}{9}$ **2.** $\dfrac{7}{10}; \dfrac{1}{4}; \dfrac{3}{16}; \dfrac{1}{4}; \dfrac{2}{21}$ **3.** $1\dfrac{1}{4}; 2\dfrac{1}{12}; 3\dfrac{1}{4}; 3\dfrac{1}{14}; 2\dfrac{1}{10}$ **4.** $\dfrac{1}{10}; \dfrac{1}{14};$ $\dfrac{3}{28}; \dfrac{7}{15}; \dfrac{7}{20}$ **5.** $\dfrac{1}{6}; \dfrac{1}{12}; \dfrac{7}{30}; \dfrac{3}{20}; \dfrac{3}{56}$ **6.** $2\dfrac{1}{12}; 1\dfrac{5}{42}; 4\dfrac{1}{42}; 3\dfrac{3}{20}; 1\dfrac{1}{40}$ **7.** $\dfrac{23}{110}; \dfrac{1}{26}; \dfrac{11}{56};$ $\dfrac{1}{60}; \dfrac{1}{24}$ **8.** $\dfrac{19}{63}; \dfrac{31}{132}; \dfrac{35}{156}; \dfrac{19}{45}; \dfrac{5}{48}$ **9.** $3\dfrac{13}{63}; 1\dfrac{1}{4}; 3\dfrac{5}{12}; 5\dfrac{1}{10}; 4\dfrac{11}{70}$ **10.** $\dfrac{43}{99}; \dfrac{23}{60}; \dfrac{5}{78};$ $\dfrac{7}{180}; \dfrac{13}{51}$ **11.** $2\dfrac{9}{110}; 2\dfrac{1}{30}; 6\dfrac{8}{21}; 3\dfrac{19}{56}; 2\dfrac{2}{63}$

Subtraction (fractional numerals). Give the simplest names.

1. $\dfrac{3}{4} - \dfrac{1}{7}$ $\dfrac{3}{10} - \dfrac{1}{4}$ $\dfrac{4}{7} - \dfrac{1}{2}$ $\dfrac{3}{13} - \dfrac{1}{12}$ $\dfrac{6}{7} - \dfrac{1}{2}$

2. $8\dfrac{1}{4} - 5\dfrac{1}{5}$ $10\dfrac{3}{7} - 3\dfrac{1}{8}$ $17\dfrac{1}{3} - 12\dfrac{4}{5}$ $11\dfrac{1}{11} - 9\dfrac{3}{10}$ $12\dfrac{3}{7} - 8\dfrac{3}{5}$

3. $\dfrac{13}{7} - \dfrac{4}{5}$ $\dfrac{17}{3} - \dfrac{3}{2}$ $\dfrac{16}{9} - \dfrac{2}{3}$ $\dfrac{14}{5} - \dfrac{7}{6}$ $\dfrac{10}{3} - \dfrac{5}{2}$

4. $13\dfrac{1}{3} - \dfrac{2}{3}$ $9\dfrac{1}{7} - \dfrac{3}{8}$ $6\dfrac{2}{5} - \dfrac{5}{6}$ $8\dfrac{7}{9} - \dfrac{9}{10}$ $3\dfrac{3}{10} - \dfrac{10}{13}$

5. $\dfrac{8}{3} - 2$ $\qquad$ $\dfrac{11}{4} - 1$ $\qquad$ $\dfrac{17}{2} - \dfrac{3}{2}$ $\qquad$ $\dfrac{21}{4} - 4$ $\qquad$ $\dfrac{36}{7} - 5$

6. $\dfrac{1}{2} - \dfrac{3}{7}$ $\qquad$ $\dfrac{4}{9} - \dfrac{1}{3}$ $\qquad$ $\dfrac{5}{9} - \dfrac{3}{10}$ $\qquad$ $\dfrac{9}{14} - \dfrac{3}{10}$ $\qquad$ $\dfrac{3}{5} - \dfrac{14}{25}$

7. $5 - 3\dfrac{1}{6}$ $\qquad$ $13 - 8\dfrac{2}{7}$ $\qquad$ $9 - 2\dfrac{4}{9}$ $\qquad$ $11 - 6\dfrac{3}{11}$ $\qquad$ $12 - 8\dfrac{4}{17}$

8. $5\dfrac{1}{2} - \dfrac{4}{3}$ $\qquad$ $13\dfrac{1}{3} - \dfrac{5}{4}$ $\qquad$ $16\dfrac{1}{7} - \dfrac{7}{6}$ $\qquad$ $14\dfrac{1}{2} - \dfrac{9}{4}$ $\qquad$ $13\dfrac{2}{9} - \dfrac{7}{3}$

9. $16\dfrac{1}{3} - 9\dfrac{4}{5}$ $\qquad$ $12\dfrac{4}{17} - 8\dfrac{5}{6}$ $\qquad$ $9\dfrac{1}{4} - 3\dfrac{1}{7}$ $\qquad$ $17\dfrac{2}{5} - 4\dfrac{1}{6}$ $\qquad$ $13\dfrac{3}{7} - 2\dfrac{1}{8}$

Answers

1. $\dfrac{17}{28}; \dfrac{1}{20}; \dfrac{1}{14}; \dfrac{23}{156}; \dfrac{5}{14}$ **2.** $3\dfrac{1}{20}; 7\dfrac{17}{56}; 4\dfrac{8}{15}; 1\dfrac{87}{110}; 3\dfrac{29}{35}$ **3.** $1\dfrac{2}{35}; 4\dfrac{1}{6}; 1\dfrac{1}{9}; 1\dfrac{19}{30};$ $\dfrac{5}{6}$ **4.** $12\dfrac{2}{3}; 8\dfrac{43}{56}; 5\dfrac{17}{30}; 7\dfrac{79}{90}; 2\dfrac{69}{130}$ **5.** $\dfrac{2}{3}; 1\dfrac{3}{4}; 7; 1\dfrac{1}{4}; \dfrac{1}{7}$ **6.** $\dfrac{1}{14}; \dfrac{1}{9}; \dfrac{23}{90}; \dfrac{24}{70}; \dfrac{1}{25}$ **7.** $1\dfrac{5}{6};$ $4\dfrac{5}{7}; 6\dfrac{5}{9}; 4\dfrac{8}{11}; 3\dfrac{13}{17}$ **8.** $4\dfrac{1}{6}; 12\dfrac{1}{12}; 14\dfrac{41}{42}; 12\dfrac{1}{4}; 10\dfrac{8}{9}$ **9.** $6\dfrac{8}{15}; 3\dfrac{41}{102}; 6\dfrac{3}{28}; 13\dfrac{7}{30};$ $11\dfrac{17}{56}$

Multiplication (fractional numerals). Give the simplest names.

1. $6 \times \dfrac{1}{2}$ $\qquad$ $9 \times \dfrac{2}{3}$ $\qquad$ $7 \times \dfrac{4}{7}$ $\qquad$ $16 \times \dfrac{3}{8}$ $\qquad$ $15 \times \dfrac{1}{5}$

2. $\dfrac{4}{5} \times 10$ $\qquad$ $\dfrac{3}{4} \times 20$ $\qquad$ $\dfrac{1}{7} \times 21$ $\qquad$ $\dfrac{3}{5} \times 15$ $\qquad$ $\dfrac{1}{6} \times 18$

3. $5 \times \dfrac{2}{3}$ $\qquad$ $12 \times \dfrac{2}{5}$ $\qquad$ $4 \times \dfrac{6}{7}$ $\qquad$ $\dfrac{3}{8} \times 9$ $\qquad$ $\dfrac{4}{7} \times 15$

4. $\dfrac{1}{2} \times \dfrac{3}{4}$ $\qquad$ $\dfrac{3}{4} \times \dfrac{1}{8}$ $\qquad$ $\dfrac{5}{6} \times \dfrac{5}{7}$ $\qquad$ $\dfrac{3}{7} \times \dfrac{1}{7}$ $\qquad$ $\dfrac{5}{8} \times \dfrac{1}{9}$

5. $\dfrac{5}{6} \times \dfrac{2}{3}$ $\qquad$ $\dfrac{6}{7} \times \dfrac{5}{8}$ $\qquad$ $\dfrac{1}{9} \times \dfrac{3}{4}$ $\qquad$ $\dfrac{4}{9} \times \dfrac{3}{5}$ $\qquad$ $\dfrac{4}{7} \times \dfrac{5}{12}$

6. $\dfrac{3}{4} \times \dfrac{2}{3}$ $\qquad$ $\dfrac{5}{9} \times \dfrac{3}{10}$ $\qquad$ $\dfrac{4}{9} \times \dfrac{3}{8}$ $\qquad$ $\dfrac{5}{12} \times \dfrac{4}{15}$ $\qquad$ $\dfrac{4}{21} \times \dfrac{7}{16}$

7. $\dfrac{4}{9} \times \dfrac{9}{4}$ $\dfrac{2}{3} \times \dfrac{3}{2}$ $\dfrac{5}{8} \times \dfrac{8}{5}$ $\dfrac{11}{12} \times \dfrac{12}{11}$ $\dfrac{6}{13} \times \dfrac{13}{6}$

8. $2\dfrac{1}{2} \times \dfrac{2}{5}$ $4\dfrac{1}{3} \times \dfrac{3}{13}$ $1\dfrac{1}{7} \times \dfrac{7}{8}$ $3\dfrac{1}{6} \times \dfrac{6}{19}$ $5\dfrac{1}{2} \times \dfrac{2}{11}$

9. $4\dfrac{1}{2} \times 4$ $5\dfrac{1}{3} \times 6$ $3\dfrac{2}{5} \times 5$ $5\dfrac{3}{7} \times 14$ $2\dfrac{1}{6} \times 12$

10. $1\dfrac{1}{2} \times 3$ $3\dfrac{4}{7} \times 5$ $5\dfrac{1}{2} \times 5$ $3\dfrac{1}{6} \times 5$ $4\dfrac{1}{6} \times 5$

11. $9 \times 1\dfrac{1}{2}$ $10 \times 2\dfrac{2}{3}$ $3 \times 5\dfrac{1}{4}$ $6 \times 2\dfrac{1}{4}$ $5 \times 4\dfrac{4}{7}$

12. $1\dfrac{1}{2} \times 1\dfrac{1}{2}$ $2\dfrac{1}{2} \times 2\dfrac{1}{2}$ $1\dfrac{1}{3} \times 1\dfrac{1}{3}$ $2\dfrac{1}{3} \times 2\dfrac{1}{3}$ $2\dfrac{1}{4} \times 2\dfrac{1}{4}$

Answers

1. 3; 6; 4; 6; 3   2. 8; 15; 3; 9; 3   3. $3\dfrac{1}{3}$; $4\dfrac{4}{5}$; $3\dfrac{3}{7}$; $3\dfrac{3}{8}$; $8\dfrac{4}{7}$ 4. $\dfrac{3}{8}$; $\dfrac{3}{32}$; $\dfrac{25}{42}$; $\dfrac{3}{49}$; $\dfrac{5}{72}$

5. $\dfrac{5}{9}$; $\dfrac{15}{28}$; $\dfrac{1}{12}$; $\dfrac{4}{15}$; $\dfrac{5}{21}$ 6. $\dfrac{1}{2}$; $\dfrac{1}{6}$; $\dfrac{1}{6}$; $\dfrac{1}{9}$; $\dfrac{1}{12}$ 7. 1; 1; 1; 1; 1   8. 1; 1; 1; 1; 1   9. 18; 32; 17; 76; 26   10. $4\dfrac{1}{2}$; $17\dfrac{6}{7}$; $27\dfrac{1}{2}$; $15\dfrac{5}{6}$; $20\dfrac{5}{6}$ 11. $13\dfrac{1}{2}$; $26\dfrac{2}{3}$; $15\dfrac{3}{4}$; $13\dfrac{1}{2}$; $22\dfrac{6}{7}$

12. $2\dfrac{1}{4}$; $6\dfrac{1}{4}$; $1\dfrac{7}{9}$; $5\dfrac{4}{9}$; $5\dfrac{1}{16}$

Multiplication (fractional numerals). Give the simplest names.

1. $\dfrac{4}{7} \times \dfrac{2}{5}$ $\dfrac{3}{7} \times \dfrac{5}{9}$ $\dfrac{4}{7} \times \dfrac{3}{5}$ $\dfrac{1}{6} \times \dfrac{5}{7}$ $\dfrac{2}{7} \times \dfrac{5}{6}$

2. $2\dfrac{1}{2} \times \dfrac{1}{4}$ $5\dfrac{1}{3} \times \dfrac{3}{4}$ $6\dfrac{1}{7} \times \dfrac{2}{3}$ $5\dfrac{1}{2} \times \dfrac{1}{3}$ $6\dfrac{3}{7} \times \dfrac{4}{5}$

3. $\dfrac{2}{5} \times 1\dfrac{1}{2}$ $\dfrac{3}{7} \times 1\dfrac{3}{8}$ $\dfrac{4}{5} \times 3\dfrac{1}{2}$ $\dfrac{3}{7} \times 5\dfrac{1}{2}$ $\dfrac{4}{9} \times 2\dfrac{1}{6}$

4. $\dfrac{5}{3} \times \dfrac{1}{2}$ $\dfrac{7}{2} \times \dfrac{3}{4}$ $\dfrac{10}{7} \times \dfrac{1}{2}$ $\dfrac{11}{3} \times \dfrac{4}{5}$ $\dfrac{12}{7} \times \dfrac{2}{5}$

5. $\dfrac{3}{4} \times \dfrac{5}{2}$ $\dfrac{2}{5} \times \dfrac{4}{3}$ $\dfrac{1}{6} \times \dfrac{9}{2}$ $\dfrac{1}{7} \times \dfrac{10}{3}$ $\dfrac{4}{5} \times \dfrac{7}{3}$

6. $1\frac{1}{2} \times 2\frac{1}{3}$ $3\frac{1}{4} \times 1\frac{1}{3}$ $5\frac{1}{2} \times 1\frac{1}{2}$ $6\frac{1}{3} \times 5\frac{1}{3}$ $2\frac{1}{4} \times 1\frac{1}{5}$

7. $2\frac{1}{3} \times 4\frac{2}{5}$ $6\frac{2}{3} \times 7\frac{1}{5}$ $1\frac{3}{7} \times 2\frac{2}{5}$ $4\frac{3}{8} \times 2\frac{2}{7}$ $5\frac{5}{6} \times 3\frac{3}{7}$

8. $4\frac{1}{5} \times 2\frac{2}{7}$ $3\frac{6}{7} \times 1\frac{1}{6}$ $5\frac{3}{10} \times 1\frac{1}{10}$ $6\frac{3}{8} \times 2\frac{1}{10}$ $4\frac{4}{7} \times 2\frac{3}{8}$

9. $5\frac{1}{2} \times 4$ $3\frac{2}{3} \times 9$ $1\frac{1}{6} \times 12$ $4\frac{1}{7} \times 7$ $9\frac{2}{3} \times 6$

10. $5\frac{1}{6} \times 4$ $3\frac{1}{9} \times 12$ $4\frac{2}{7} \times 14$ $2\frac{3}{8} \times 16$ $4\frac{3}{4} \times 12$

11. $\frac{4}{7} \times 28$ $\frac{3}{7} \times 13$ $\frac{4}{9} \times 10$ $14 \times \frac{3}{7}$ $54 \times \frac{5}{9}$

12. $5\frac{1}{3} \times 3\frac{7}{8}$ $3\frac{1}{5} \times 5\frac{3}{4}$ $6\frac{2}{3} \times 3\frac{3}{5}$ $7\frac{1}{2} \times 6\frac{1}{3}$ $3\frac{3}{5} \times 5\frac{1}{6}$

Answers

1. $\frac{8}{35}$; $\frac{15}{63}$; $\frac{12}{35}$; $\frac{5}{42}$; $\frac{5}{21}$ **2.** $\frac{5}{8}$; 4; $4\frac{2}{21}$; $1\frac{5}{6}$; $5\frac{1}{7}$ **3.** $\frac{3}{5}$; $\frac{33}{56}$; $2\frac{4}{5}$; $2\frac{5}{14}$; $\frac{26}{27}$ **4.** $\frac{5}{6}$; $2\frac{5}{8}$; $\frac{5}{7}$; $2\frac{14}{15}$; $\frac{24}{35}$ **5.** $1\frac{7}{8}$; $\frac{8}{15}$; $\frac{3}{4}$; $\frac{10}{21}$; $1\frac{13}{15}$ **6.** $3\frac{1}{2}$; $4\frac{1}{3}$; $8\frac{1}{4}$; $33\frac{7}{9}$; $2\frac{7}{10}$ **7.** $10\frac{4}{15}$; 48; $3\frac{3}{7}$; 10; 20 **8.** $9\frac{3}{5}$; $4\frac{1}{2}$; $5\frac{83}{100}$; $13\frac{31}{80}$; $10\frac{6}{7}$ **9.** 22; 33; 14; 29; 58 **10.** $20\frac{2}{3}$; $37\frac{1}{3}$; 60; 38; 57 **11.** 16; $5\frac{4}{7}$; $4\frac{4}{9}$; 6; 30 **12.** $20\frac{2}{3}$; $18\frac{2}{5}$; 24; $47\frac{1}{2}$; $18\frac{3}{5}$

Division (fractional numerals). Give the simplest names.

1. $\frac{1}{2} \div 2$ $\frac{1}{3} \div 5$ $\frac{2}{5} \div 3$ $\frac{1}{4} \div 9$ $\frac{4}{7} \div 3$ $\frac{4}{5} \div 3$

2. $\frac{2}{3} \div 4$ $\frac{4}{5} \div 8$ $\frac{2}{7} \div 6$ $\frac{3}{7} \div 9$ $\frac{5}{6} \div 25$ $\frac{4}{9} \div 16$

3. $\frac{5}{4} \div 3$ $\frac{7}{2} \div 5$ $\frac{8}{3} \div 5$ $\frac{9}{7} \div 4$ $\frac{8}{5} \div 7$ $\frac{9}{4} \div 5$

4. $3 \div \frac{1}{2}$ $5 \div \frac{1}{3}$ $7 \div \frac{1}{4}$ $6 \div \frac{1}{5}$ $9 \div \frac{1}{3}$ $2 \div \frac{1}{9}$

5. $5 \div \dfrac{2}{3}$ $4 \div \dfrac{3}{7}$ $1 \div \dfrac{4}{5}$ $9 \div \dfrac{2}{5}$ $8 \div \dfrac{3}{4}$ $3 \div \dfrac{5}{9}$

6. $4 \div \dfrac{2}{5}$ $8 \div \dfrac{4}{7}$ $9 \div \dfrac{3}{4}$ $7 \div \dfrac{7}{9}$ $8 \div \dfrac{2}{11}$ $5 \div \dfrac{5}{7}$

7. $\dfrac{1}{2} \div \dfrac{1}{3}$ $\dfrac{1}{7} \div \dfrac{1}{2}$ $\dfrac{1}{9} \div \dfrac{1}{4}$ $\dfrac{1}{10} \div \dfrac{1}{7}$ $\dfrac{1}{4} \div \dfrac{1}{9}$ $\dfrac{1}{7} \div \dfrac{1}{10}$

8. $\dfrac{2}{3} \div \dfrac{5}{4}$ $\dfrac{4}{7} \div \dfrac{5}{3}$ $\dfrac{3}{7} \div \dfrac{4}{10}$ $\dfrac{2}{5} \div \dfrac{3}{7}$ $\dfrac{4}{9} \div \dfrac{3}{4}$ $\dfrac{5}{6} \div \dfrac{7}{11}$

9. $\dfrac{4}{7} \div \dfrac{2}{3}$ $\dfrac{5}{4} \div \dfrac{1}{8}$ $\dfrac{3}{4} \div \dfrac{6}{7}$ $\dfrac{4}{9} \div \dfrac{2}{3}$ $\dfrac{3}{8} \div \dfrac{9}{16}$ $\dfrac{4}{15} \div \dfrac{8}{5}$

10. $2\dfrac{1}{3} \div 2$ $5\dfrac{1}{2} \div 4$ $9\dfrac{2}{3} \div 3$ $4\dfrac{1}{5} \div 2$ $7\dfrac{1}{6} \div 4$ $3\dfrac{1}{7} \div 7$

11. $5\dfrac{1}{6} \div 3$ $4\dfrac{5}{7} \div 9$ $6\dfrac{1}{3} \div 5$ $7\dfrac{1}{2} \div 6$ $8\dfrac{2}{3} \div 2$ $10\dfrac{1}{6} \div 5$

12. $3\dfrac{1}{3} \div 10$ $4\dfrac{1}{6} \div 12$ $9\dfrac{2}{3} \div 3$ $12\dfrac{4}{7} \div 12$ $1\dfrac{1}{5} \div 10$ $2\dfrac{1}{2} \div 15$

Answers

1. $\dfrac{1}{4}; \dfrac{1}{15}; \dfrac{2}{15}; \dfrac{1}{36}; \dfrac{4}{21}; \dfrac{4}{15}$ **2.** $\dfrac{1}{6}; \dfrac{1}{10}; \dfrac{1}{21}; \dfrac{1}{21}; \dfrac{1}{30}; \dfrac{1}{36}$ **3.** $\dfrac{5}{12}; \dfrac{7}{10}; \dfrac{8}{15}; \dfrac{9}{28}; \dfrac{8}{35}; \dfrac{9}{20}$

4. 6; 15; 28; 30; 27; 18 **5.** $7\dfrac{1}{2}; 9\dfrac{1}{3}; 1\dfrac{1}{4}; 22\dfrac{1}{2}; 10\dfrac{2}{3}; 5\dfrac{2}{5}$ **6.** 10; 14; 12; 9; 44; 7

7. $1\dfrac{1}{2}; \dfrac{2}{7}; \dfrac{4}{9}; \dfrac{7}{10}; 2\dfrac{1}{4}; 1\dfrac{3}{7}$ **8.** $\dfrac{8}{15}; \dfrac{12}{35}; 1\dfrac{1}{14}; \dfrac{14}{15}; \dfrac{16}{27}; 1\dfrac{13}{42}$ **9.** $\dfrac{6}{7}; 10; \dfrac{7}{8}; \dfrac{2}{3}; \dfrac{2}{3}; \dfrac{1}{6}$

10. $1\dfrac{1}{6}; 1\dfrac{3}{8}; 3\dfrac{2}{9}; 2\dfrac{1}{10}; 1\dfrac{19}{24}; \dfrac{22}{49}$ **11.** $1\dfrac{13}{18}; \dfrac{11}{21}; 1\dfrac{4}{15}; 1\dfrac{1}{4}; 4\dfrac{1}{3}; 2\dfrac{1}{30}$ **12.** $\dfrac{1}{3}; \dfrac{25}{72}; 3\dfrac{2}{9};$

$1\dfrac{1}{21}; \dfrac{3}{25}; \dfrac{1}{6}$

Division (fractional numerals). Give the simplest names.

1. $5\dfrac{1}{2} \div \dfrac{1}{3}$ $6\dfrac{2}{3} \div \dfrac{2}{5}$ $1\dfrac{1}{7} \div \dfrac{4}{7}$ $2\dfrac{2}{9} \div \dfrac{4}{5}$ $6\dfrac{1}{2} \div \dfrac{1}{3}$

2. $4\dfrac{1}{6} \div \dfrac{5}{8}$ $5\dfrac{1}{3} \div \dfrac{4}{7}$ $8\dfrac{1}{4} \div \dfrac{3}{7}$ $9\dfrac{1}{2} \div \dfrac{1}{5}$ $1\dfrac{3}{11} \div \dfrac{1}{2}$

3. $2\dfrac{1}{6} \div \dfrac{2}{3}$ $5\dfrac{5}{9} \div \dfrac{2}{3}$ $4\dfrac{8}{11} \div \dfrac{2}{11}$ $5\dfrac{5}{6} \div \dfrac{5}{18}$ $1\dfrac{7}{17} \div \dfrac{2}{3}$

4. $\dfrac{1}{2} \div 2\dfrac{1}{2}$ $\qquad$ $\dfrac{2}{3} \div 5\dfrac{1}{3}$ $\qquad$ $\dfrac{4}{7} \div 1\dfrac{1}{7}$ $\qquad$ $\dfrac{3}{5} \div 4\dfrac{2}{9}$ $\qquad$ $\dfrac{1}{9} \div 1\dfrac{3}{4}$

5. $\dfrac{4}{5} \div 3\dfrac{1}{3}$ $\qquad$ $\dfrac{7}{10} \div 4\dfrac{1}{5}$ $\qquad$ $\dfrac{9}{14} \div 2\dfrac{4}{7}$ $\qquad$ $\dfrac{3}{4} \div 4\dfrac{1}{8}$ $\qquad$ $\dfrac{5}{7} \div 6\dfrac{3}{7}$

6. $\dfrac{1}{2} \div 10\dfrac{1}{2}$ $\qquad$ $\dfrac{3}{2} \div 1\dfrac{1}{4}$ $\qquad$ $\dfrac{4}{3} \div 2\dfrac{1}{6}$ $\qquad$ $\dfrac{5}{2} \div 7\dfrac{1}{2}$ $\qquad$ $\dfrac{4}{3} \div 2\dfrac{1}{8}$

7. $1\dfrac{1}{2} \div 3\dfrac{1}{2}$ $\qquad$ $4\dfrac{1}{3} \div 2\dfrac{1}{2}$ $\qquad$ $5\dfrac{1}{4} \div 1\dfrac{1}{2}$ $\qquad$ $7\dfrac{1}{3} \div 3\dfrac{1}{4}$ $\qquad$ $7\dfrac{1}{3} \div 2\dfrac{3}{4}$

8. $8\dfrac{4}{7} \div 2\dfrac{1}{2}$ $\qquad$ $7\dfrac{5}{7} \div 2\dfrac{4}{7}$ $\qquad$ $7\dfrac{1}{6} \div 4\dfrac{2}{5}$ $\qquad$ $8\dfrac{4}{9} \div 1\dfrac{1}{3}$ $\qquad$ $10\dfrac{1}{2} \div 3\dfrac{1}{2}$

9. $4\dfrac{1}{4} \div 5\dfrac{1}{5}$ $\qquad$ $7\dfrac{1}{2} \div 8\dfrac{3}{4}$ $\qquad$ $3\dfrac{1}{6} \div 7\dfrac{1}{3}$ $\qquad$ $4\dfrac{1}{8} \div 2\dfrac{1}{4}$ $\qquad$ $8\dfrac{3}{4} \div 1\dfrac{2}{3}$

10. $\dfrac{11}{2} \div \dfrac{2}{3}$ $\qquad$ $\dfrac{14}{7} \div \dfrac{4}{5}$ $\qquad$ $\dfrac{17}{2} \div \dfrac{1}{2}$ $\qquad$ $\dfrac{9}{4} \div \dfrac{2}{5}$ $\qquad$ $\dfrac{11}{7} \div \dfrac{3}{7}$

11. $\dfrac{1}{2} \div \dfrac{17}{4}$ $\qquad$ $\dfrac{3}{4} \div \dfrac{13}{2}$ $\qquad$ $\dfrac{1}{7} \div \dfrac{4}{3}$ $\qquad$ $\dfrac{1}{4} \div \dfrac{13}{6}$ $\qquad$ $\dfrac{2}{7} \div \dfrac{16}{5}$

Answers

1. $16\dfrac{1}{2}$; $16\dfrac{2}{3}$; 2; $2\dfrac{7}{9}$; $19\dfrac{1}{2}$ **2.** $6\dfrac{2}{3}$; $9\dfrac{1}{3}$; $19\dfrac{1}{4}$; $47\dfrac{1}{2}$; $2\dfrac{6}{11}$ **3.** $3\dfrac{1}{4}$; $8\dfrac{1}{3}$; 26; 21; $2\dfrac{2}{17}$

4. $\dfrac{1}{5}$; $\dfrac{1}{8}$; $\dfrac{1}{2}$; $\dfrac{27}{190}$; $\dfrac{4}{63}$ **5.** $\dfrac{6}{25}$; $\dfrac{1}{6}$; $\dfrac{1}{4}$; $\dfrac{2}{11}$; $\dfrac{1}{9}$ **6.** $\dfrac{1}{21}$; $1\dfrac{1}{5}$; $\dfrac{8}{13}$; $\dfrac{1}{3}$; $\dfrac{32}{51}$ **7.** $\dfrac{3}{7}$; $1\dfrac{11}{15}$; $3\dfrac{1}{2}$;

$2\dfrac{10}{39}$; $2\dfrac{2}{3}$ **8.** $3\dfrac{3}{7}$; 3; $1\dfrac{83}{132}$; $6\dfrac{1}{3}$; 3 **9.** $\dfrac{85}{104}$; $\dfrac{6}{7}$; $\dfrac{19}{44}$; $1\dfrac{5}{6}$; $5\dfrac{1}{4}$ **10.** $8\dfrac{1}{4}$; $2\dfrac{1}{2}$; 17; $5\dfrac{5}{8}$;

$3\dfrac{2}{3}$ **11.** $\dfrac{2}{17}$; $\dfrac{3}{26}$; $\dfrac{3}{28}$; $\dfrac{3}{26}$; $\dfrac{5}{56}$

Addition (decimal numerals)

1.

.5	.8	.4	.9	.8	.5	.4	.3
.4	.1	.6	.3	.7	.8	.9	.8

2.

.5	.6	.8	.7	.6	.3	.2	.3
.3	.8	.1	.4	.3	.9	.4	.7
.7	.5	.9	.6	.7	.1	.8	.9

3.

9.2	3.6	7.8	1.8	8.8	3.6	6.4	9.7
5.7	4.9	3.1	9.1	7.9	5.2	5.9	7.9
1.8	2.1	2.0	3.4	6.4	7.7	1.8	6.8

4. .05   .12   .18   .63   .18   .28   .06   .66
       .04   .26   .30   .72   .29   .36   .94   .77
       .07   .32   .72   .19   .87   .84   .85   .99

5. .45   .06   .31   .45   .09   .44   .08   .18
       .67   .98   .68   .68   .32   .82   .19   .81
       .82   .33   .72   .39   .67   .15   .59   .92
       .95   .82   .19   .49   .80   .63   .74   .29

Answers

1. .9; .9; 1.0; 1.2; 1.5; 1.3; 1.3; 1.1 **2.** 1.5; 1.9; 1.8; 1.7; 1.6; 1.3; 1.4; 1.9 **3.** 16.7; 10.6; 12.9; 14.3; 23.1; 16.5; 14.1; 24.4 **4.** .16; .70; 1.20; 1.54; 1.34; 1.48; 1.85; 2.42 **5.** 2.89; 2.19; 1.90; 2.01; 1.88; 2.04; 1.60; 2.20

Addition (decimal numerals)

1. 1.45   2.19   3.62   1.99   3.30   4.11   6.78
       2.67   5.06   4.09   2.03   4.91   9.12   8.23
       4.09   7.29   9.11   7.26   9.62   3.14   4.63

2. .009   .092   .123   .905   .882   .409   .776
       .025   .018   .205   .116   .673   .515   .805
       .016   .034   .362   .256   .905   .639   .992

3. 13.25   24.16   18.65   23.18   45.35   95.15   17.01
       27.65   38.62   13.23   50.09   63.06   36.19   18.95
       19.98   17.49   29.67   62.36   70.32   40.25   59.12

4. 3.127   8.505   1.309   9.005   8.116   7.053   3.009
       5.306   4.312   6.429   6.252   3.252   1.936   4.986
       9.117   7.298   7.008   4.309   5.098   2.005   3.115

5. 3.25   9.03   32.16   19.13   25.66   59.06   3.09
       17.68   8.12   1.85   2.56   6.78   19.72   4.59
       23.25   92.13   3.75   4.38   17.26   5.88   59.05
       9.06   89.98   42.49   26.45   4.35   4.13   8.78

Answers

1. 8.21; 14.54; 16.82; 11.28; 17.83; 16.37; 19.64 **2.** .050; .144; .690; 1.277; 2.460; 1.563; 2.573 **3.** 60.88; 80.27; 61.55; 135.63; 178.73; 171.59; 95.08 **4.** 17.550; 20.115; 14.746; 19.566; 16.466; 10.994; 11.110 **5.** 53.24; 199.26; 80.25; 52.52; 54.05; 88.79; 75.51

Subtraction (decimal numerals)

1.	.7	.9	.8	.7	1.9	1.6	1.2	1.8	1.5	1.4	1.9
	.4	.5	.4	.6	.6	.7	.6	.9	.7	.8	.9

2.	2.7	5.9	6.3	7.6	3.5	6.2	5.0	9.1	2.0	4.1	3.6
	1.4	3.7	3.2	1.7	.9	3.5	1.2	3.9	1.8	2.8	2.9

3.	.93	.37	.63	.30	.25	.98	.23	.90	.63
	.31	.28	.45	.17	.08	.89	.17	.67	.39

4.	7.5	9.3	2.8	19.9	13.0	16.1	20.2	19.8	41.6
	1.3	2.6	1.9	6.8	10.1	3.0	10.2	8.9	29.8

Answers

1. .3; .4; .4; .1; 1.3; .9; .6; .9; .8; .6; 1.0 **2.** 1.3; 2.2; 3.1; 5.9; 2.6; 2.7; 3.8; 5.2; .2; 1.3; .7 **3.** .62; .09; .18; .13; .17; .09; .06; .23; .24 **4.** 6.2; 6.7; .9; 13.1; 2.9; 13.1; 10.0; 10.9; 11.8

Subtraction (decimal numerals)

1.	3.68	4.58	7.32	2.12	7.05	8.69	3.68
	1.22	3.27	6.18	1.29	3.15	2.70	1.99

2.	9.06	3.29	4.11	7.65	5.01	7.00	8.01
	8.17	1.67	3.12	3.98	3.89	3.67	2.68

3.	.983	.372	.669	.906	.720	.300	.900
	.051	.161	.578	.315	.395	.172	.835

4.	.072	.036	.123	.206	.407	.506	.100
	.031	.019	.089	.185	.395	.398	.093

5. $5 - 3.7$ $7 - 4.5$ $16 - 8.9$ $12 - 7.4$ $9 - 4.9$

6. $1.8 - .9$ $2.6 - .7$ $3.5 - .6$ $7.1 - .4$ $6.2 - .5$

7. $3 - 1.25$ $4 - 3.76$ $7 - 1.27$ $9 - 3.25$ $1 - .68$

8. $10.6 - 7.3$ $15.5 - 2.3$ $13.6 - 1.2$ $14.5 - 3.1$ $19.8 - 6.7$

9. $10.8 - 7.9$ $12.6 - 3.8$ $14.6 - 9.8$ $17.1 - 2.4$ $16.2 - 3.7$

Answers

Multiplication (decimal numerals)

1. $10 \times .2$	10×1.7	10×3.05	5.19×10
2. $10 \times .9$	10×9.6	10×4.01	6.35×10
3. $10 \times .7$	10×8.5	10×5.09	7.98×10
4. $100 \times .37$	100×8.92	100×5.6	$1.03 \times 1,000$
5. $100 \times .95$	100×7.63	100×3.9	$12.5 \times 1,000$
6. $100 \times .67$	100×5.81	100×1.8	$.76 \times 1,000$
7. $.9 \times 8$	6×1.2	$.3 \times .4$	$.11 \times 5$
8. $.7 \times 4$	7×1.1	$.1 \times .5$	$.21 \times 4$
9. $.5 \times 7$	3×3.3	$.6 \times .9$	$.13 \times 6$
10. $5.6 \times .1$	$3.76 \times .1$	$367 \times .01$	$.01 \times 36$
11. $3.9 \times .1$	$9.07 \times .1$	$409 \times .01$	$.01 \times 75$
12. $4.5 \times .1$	$4.13 \times .1$	$513 \times .01$	$.01 \times 55$
13. $.03 \times 5$	7×1.1	$.11 \times 6$	$367 \times .001$
14. $.07 \times 6$	8×1.2	$.11 \times 8$	$409 \times .001$
15. $.09 \times 3$	6×1.3	$.11 \times 9$	$568 \times .001$

Answers

Multiplication (decimal numerals)

1.	45	68	39	315	608	910	395
	.4	.8	.7	.5	.6	.9	.3

2.	4.7	3.9	9.7	6.8	3.17	4.18	9.06
	.5	.8	.6	.7	.4	.3	.2

3.	3.68	4.98	1.76	3.45	5.61	8.06	7.14
	8	5	8	12	25	39	85

4.	.35	.84	.73	.39	.107	.365	.118
	.7	.4	.8	.2	.5	.3	.9

5.	9.68	7.05	3.32	2.06	1.25	6.72	3.39
	3.5	1.8	4.1	9.2	3.5	8.5	6.2

6.	39.8	92.1	40.2	68.8	92.1	36.2	82.4
	.8	.4	1.6	2.3	4.5	3.9	4.8

Answers

1. 18.0; 54.4; 27.3; 157.5; 364.8; 819.0; 118.5 **2.** 2.35; 3.12; 5.82; 4.76; 1.268; 1.254; 1.812 **3.** 29.44; 24.90; 14.08; 41.40; 140.25; 314.34; 606.90 **4.** .245; .336; .584; .078; .0535; .1095; .1062 **5.** 33.880; 12.690; 13.612; 18.952; 4.375; 57.120; 21.018 **6.** 31.84; 36.84; 64.32; 158.24; 414.45; 141.18; 395.52

Division (decimal numerals)

1.	$3.6 \div 10$	$9.8 \div 10$	$.4 \div 10$	$.05 \div 10$	$13.78 \div 10$
2.	$45.9 \div 100$	$3.8 \div 100$	$.07 \div 100$	$.1 \div 100$	$136.33 \div 100$
3.	$366.1 \div 1,000$	$45.6 \div 1,000$	$.3 \div 1,000$	$1.4 \div 1,000$	$.701 \div 1,000$
4.	$4.2 \div 2$	$9.9 \div 3$	$10.5 \div 5$	$25.5 \div 5$	$36.8 \div 4$
5.	$42.6 \div 6$	$77.7 \div 7$	$64.8 \div 8$	$81.9 \div 9$	$49.7 \div 7$
6.	$3.6 \div .6$	$1.6 \div .4$	$4.9 \div .7$	$6.4 \div .8$	$2.5 \div .5$
7.	$3\overline{)4.8}$	$11\overline{)13.2}$	$13\overline{)16.9}$	$25\overline{)62.5}$	$14\overline{)19.6}$
8.	$.4\overline{)32}$	$.2\overline{)16}$	$.3\overline{)39}$	$.5\overline{)25}$	$.6\overline{)42}$
9.	$.04\overline{)32}$	$.02\overline{)16}$	$.03\overline{)39}$	$.05\overline{)25}$	$.06\overline{)42}$

10. $.4\overline{)3.2}$ $.2\overline{)1.6}$ $.3\overline{)3.9}$ $.5\overline{)2.5}$ $.6\overline{)4.2}$

11. $.04\overline{)3.2}$ $.02\overline{)1.6}$ $.03\overline{)3.9}$ $.05\overline{)2.5}$ $.06\overline{)4.2}$

12. $.4\overline{).32}$ $.2\overline{).16}$ $.3\overline{).39}$ $.5\overline{).25}$ $.6\overline{).42}$

13. $4 \div .1$ $12 \div .1$ $5 \div .01$ $19 \div .01$ $13.6 \div .01$

14. $2.1\overline{)4.2}$ $3.6\overline{)10.8}$ $5.6\overline{)33.6}$ $6.3\overline{)44.1}$ $4.9\overline{)19.6}$

15. $4\overline{)1.40}$ $5\overline{)2.80}$ $5\overline{)3.80}$ $8\overline{)4.40}$ $5\overline{)5.30}$

16. $5\overline{).230}$ $4\overline{).170}$ $5\overline{).410}$ $8\overline{).920}$ $8\overline{).880}$

17. $2.6\overline{)3.64}$ $4.7\overline{)18.33}$ $7.1\overline{)17.75}$ $4.2\overline{)13.02}$ $4.5\overline{)30.15}$

Answers

1. .36; .98; .04; .005; 1.378 **2.** .459; .038; .0007; .001; 1.3633 **3.** .3661; .0456; .0003; .0014; .000701 **4.** 2.1; 3.3; 2.1; 5.1; 9.2 **5.** 7.1; 11.1; 8.1; 9.1; 7.1 **6.** 6; 4; 7; 8; 5 **7.** 1.6; 1.2; 1.3; 2.5; 1.4 **8.** 80; 80; 130; 50; 70 **9.** 800; 800; 1,300; 500; 700 **10.** 8; 8; 13; 5; 7 **11.** 80; 80; 130; 50; 70 **12.** .8; .8; 1.3; .5; .7 **13.** 40; 120; 500; 1,900; 1,360 **14.** 2; 3; 6; 7; 4 **15.** .35; .56; .76; .55; 1.06 **16.** .046; .0425; .082; .115; .110 **17.** 1.4; 3.9; 2.5; 3.1; 6.7

Division (decimal numerals)

1. $7\overline{)25.34}$ $9\overline{)10.17}$ $5\overline{)35.30}$ $6\overline{)37.50}$ $4\overline{)13.80}$

2. $4\overline{).12}$ $.4\overline{).12}$ $.04\overline{).12}$ $.004\overline{).12}$ $40\overline{).12}$

3. $7\overline{)3.5}$ $7\overline{).35}$ $7\overline{).035}$ $7\overline{).0035}$ $7\overline{).00035}$

4. $3\overline{)1.8}$ $.3\overline{).18}$ $30\overline{).18}$ $.03\overline{).018}$ $.003\overline{).0018}$

5. $16 \div 4$ $16 \div .4$ $16 \div .04$ $16 \div .004$ $16 \div .0004$

6. $21 \div 3$ $2.1 \div 3$ $.21 \div 3$ $.021 \div 3$ $.0021 \div 3$

7. $16\overline{)243.2}$ $18\overline{)316.8}$ $17\overline{)241.4}$ $13\overline{)183.3}$ $19.2\overline{)288}$

8. $5.1\overline{)24.99}$ $4.6\overline{)35.88}$ $6.2\overline{)7.44}$ $1.3\overline{)7.15}$ $4.2\overline{)38.22}$

9. $4.5\overline{)108.90}$ $6.5\overline{)96.20}$ $2.8\overline{)169.96}$ $1.5\overline{)109.65}$ $2.1\overline{)190.89}$

10. $.38\overline{)9.88}$ $3.1\overline{)2.232}$ $4.9\overline{)4.459}$ $.62\overline{)29.76}$ $3.7\overline{)40.7}$

11. $4.8\overline{)4.512}$ $1.7\overline{)13.77}$ $.45\overline{)4.275}$ $7.2\overline{)8.64}$ $8.2\overline{)2.378}$

Answers

Per cent

For each per cent give its decimal name.

Examples $20\% = 20 \times .01 = .20$; $\frac{1}{4}\% = .25 \times .01 = .0025$

1. 10%   30%   70%   45%   79%   61%   12%   50%

2. 420%   270%   365%   510%   605%   101%   999%   500%

3. 1% $\frac{3}{4}\%$ $\frac{1}{2}\%$ $\frac{1}{5}\%$ $\frac{2}{5}\%$ $\frac{4}{5}\%$ $\frac{1}{10}\%$ $\frac{3}{10}\%$

4. .1%   .2%   .6%   .9%   .01%   .07%   .06%   .001%

5.–8. For each per cent above give its simplest fractional name.

Examples $20\% = 20 \times \frac{1}{100} = \frac{20}{100} = \frac{1}{5}$; $\frac{1}{2}\% = \frac{1}{2} \times \frac{1}{100} = \frac{1}{200}$

For each number give its per cent name.

Example $\frac{1}{8} = (.125 \times 100)\% = 12.5\%$

9. .07   .35   .19   .99   2   3.5   9.6   10

10. 1.06   3.96   5.11   6.35   1.01   9.01   9.99   10.1

11. $\frac{1}{2}$ $\frac{1}{4}$ $\frac{3}{8}$ $\frac{1}{10}$ $\frac{9}{10}$ $\frac{1}{20}$ $\frac{7}{20}$ $\frac{1}{3}$

12. 50% of 150 = n 25% of 32 = n 30% of 600 = n

13. 10% of 11 = n 12% of 120 = n 1% of 52 = n

14. 2% of 17 = n $33\frac{1}{3}\%$ of 1,500 = n $66\frac{2}{3}\%$ of 300 = n

15. 200% of 1 = n 150% of 6 = n 500% of 9 = n

16. 1,000% of 3 = n 125% of 4 = n 225% of 8 = n

17. $10 = n\%$ of 100 $5 = n\%$ of 10 $1 = n\%$ of 3

18. $1 = n\%$ of 8 $3 = n\%$ of 10 $6 = n\%$ of 15

19. $2 = n\%$ of 16 $1 = n\%$ of 50 $4 = n\%$ of 22

20. $100 = n\%$ of 50 $500 = n\%$ of 100 $40 = n\%$ of 4

21. $200 = n\%$ of 60 $90 = n\%$ of 40 $1 = n\%$ of $\dfrac{1}{3}$

22. $1 = n\%$ of 200 $.5 = n\%$ of 100 $1 = n\%$ of 300

23. $\dfrac{1}{4} = n\%$ of 100 $1 = n\%$ of 1,000 $\dfrac{1}{2} = n\%$ of 1,000

24. $10 = 5\%$ of n $1 = 1\%$ of n $2 = 4\%$ of n

25. $7 = 100\%$ of n $17 = 3\%$ of n $50 = 1\%$ of n

26. $4 = 125\%$ of n $100 = 200\%$ of n $70 = 700\%$ of n

27. $\dfrac{1}{4} = 50\%$ of n $\dfrac{1}{3} = 1\%$ of n $\dfrac{1}{10} = 25\%$ of n

28. $\dfrac{3}{7} = 1\%$ of n $\dfrac{1}{2} = \dfrac{1}{2}\%$ of n $\dfrac{1}{3} = \dfrac{1}{4}\%$ of n

Answers

1. .10; .30; .70; .45; .79; .61; .12; .50 **2.** 4.20; 2.70; 3.65; 5.10; 6.05; 1.01; 9.99; 5.00 **3.** .01; .0075; .005; .002; .004; .008; .001; .003 **4.** .001; .002; .006; .009; .0001; .0007; .0006; .00001 **5.** $\dfrac{1}{10}; \dfrac{3}{10}; \dfrac{7}{10}; \dfrac{9}{20}; \dfrac{79}{100}; \dfrac{61}{100}; \dfrac{3}{25}; \dfrac{1}{2}$ **6.** $\dfrac{21}{5}; \dfrac{27}{10}; \dfrac{73}{20};$ $\dfrac{51}{10}; \dfrac{121}{20}; \dfrac{101}{100}; \dfrac{999}{100}; 5$ **7.** $\dfrac{1}{100}; \dfrac{3}{400}; \dfrac{1}{200}; \dfrac{1}{500}; \dfrac{1}{250}; \dfrac{1}{125}; \dfrac{1}{1,000}; \dfrac{3}{1,000}$ **8.** $\dfrac{1}{1,000};$ $\dfrac{1}{500}; \dfrac{3}{500}; \dfrac{9}{1,000}; \dfrac{1}{10,000}; \dfrac{7}{10,000}; \dfrac{3}{5,000}; \dfrac{1}{100,000}$ **9.** 7%; 35%; 19%; 99%; 200%; 350%; 960%; 1,000% **10.** 106%; 396%; 511%; 635%; 101%; 901%; 999%; 1,010% **11.** 50%; 25%; 37.5%; 10%; 90%; 5%; 35%; $33\dfrac{1}{3}\%$ **12.** 75; 8; 180 **13.** 1.1; 14.4; .52 **14.** 3.4; 500; 200 **15.** 2; 9; 45 **16.** 30; 5; 18 **17.** 10; 50; $33\dfrac{1}{3}$ **18.** $12\dfrac{1}{2}$; 30; 40 **19.** $12\dfrac{1}{2}$; 2; $18\dfrac{2}{11}$ **20.** 200; 500; 1,000 **21.** $333\dfrac{1}{3}$; 225; 300 **22.** $\dfrac{1}{2}$; .5; $\dfrac{1}{3}$ **23.** $\dfrac{1}{4}$; .1; $\dfrac{1}{20}$ **24.** 200; 100; 50 **25.** 7; $566\dfrac{2}{3}$; 5,000 **26.** 3.2; 50; 10 **27.** $\dfrac{1}{2}$; $33\dfrac{1}{3}$; $\dfrac{2}{5}$ **28.** $42\dfrac{6}{7}$; 100; $133\dfrac{1}{3}$

Conversion of some measurements and rates

The following relations between units of length are important to know.

1 ft. = 12 in.	1 mile = 5,280 ft.
1 yd. = 3 ft.	1 mile = 320 rods

1. The speed of 60 mph is how many miles per minute?

2. The speed of 600 mph is how many miles per minute?

3. The speed of 1 mph is how many feet per hour?

4. The speed of 1 mph is how many yards per hour?

5. The speed of 1 mph is how many miles per minute?

6. The speed of 1 mph is how many miles per second?

7. The speed of 100 mph is how many feet per second?

8. The speed of 6,000 mph is how many feet per second?

9. Producing 60 pieces per hour is producing how many pieces per minute?

10. Producing 3,600 pieces per hour is producing how many pieces per second?

11. Producing 4 pieces per second is producing how many pieces per hour?

12. Producing 10 pieces per second is producing how many pieces per 8 hours?

Answers

1. 1 **2.** 10 **3.** 5,280 **4.** 1,760 **5.** $\frac{1}{60}$ **6.** $\frac{1}{3,600}$ **7.** $146\frac{2}{3}$ **8.** 8,800 **9.** 1 **10.** 1
11. 14,400 **12.** 288,000

Addition of directed numbers

1. $^+78 + {}^+21$	$^+36 + {}^+25$	$^+500 + {}^+700$	$^+17 + {}^+317$
2. $^+10 + {}^-17$	$^+11 + {}^-29$	$^+30 + {}^-210$	$^+25 + {}^-375$
3. $^+98 + {}^-9$	$^+102 + {}^-4$	$^+217 + {}^-19$	$^+318 + {}^-30$
4. $^-5 + {}^+8$	$^-2 + {}^+12$	$^-25 + {}^+50$	$^-75 + {}^+225$

5. $^-36 + {}^+6$ $\qquad$ $^-47 + {}^+7$ $\qquad$ $^-100 + {}^+43$ $\qquad$ $^-200 +$

6. $^-22 + {}^-8$ $\qquad$ $^-45 + {}^-15$ $\qquad$ $^-31 + {}^-62$ $\qquad$ $^-50 + {}^-130$

7. $\dfrac{{}^+1}{3} + \dfrac{{}^+2}{3}$ $\qquad$ $\dfrac{{}^+1}{3} + \dfrac{{}^-2}{3}$ $\qquad$ $\dfrac{{}^-1}{3} + \dfrac{{}^+2}{3}$ $\qquad$ $\dfrac{{}^-1}{3} + \dfrac{{}^-2}{3}$

8. $\dfrac{{}^+3}{4} + \dfrac{{}^+1}{2}$ $\qquad$ $\dfrac{{}^+3}{4} + \dfrac{{}^-1}{2}$ $\qquad$ $\dfrac{{}^-3}{4} + \dfrac{{}^-1}{2}$ $\qquad$ $\dfrac{{}^-3}{4} + \dfrac{{}^+1}{2}$

9. $\dfrac{{}^+1}{2} + \dfrac{{}^-1}{3}$ $\qquad$ $\dfrac{{}^+2}{5} + \dfrac{{}^-1}{4}$ $\qquad$ $\dfrac{{}^+3}{10} + \dfrac{{}^-1}{5}$ $\qquad$ $\dfrac{{}^+4}{11} + \dfrac{{}^-1}{8}$

10. $\dfrac{{}^+1}{3} + \dfrac{{}^-2}{3}$ $\qquad$ $\dfrac{{}^+1}{4} + \dfrac{{}^-7}{8}$ $\qquad$ $\dfrac{{}^+2}{3} + \dfrac{{}^-6}{7}$ $\qquad$ $\dfrac{{}^-1}{4} + \dfrac{{}^-2}{9}$

11. $\dfrac{{}^-3}{2} + \dfrac{{}^-5}{8}$ $\qquad$ $^-3\frac{1}{2} + {}^+5\frac{1}{2}$ $\qquad$ $^-7\frac{1}{8} + {}^+3\frac{1}{2}$ $\qquad$ $^-5\frac{1}{3} + {}^-6\frac{1}{2}$

12. $^+1.5 + {}^+1.7$ $\qquad$ $^+1.5 + {}^-1.7$ $\qquad$ $^-1.5 + {}^-1.7$ $\qquad$ $^-1.5 + {}^+1.7$

13. $^-2.5 + {}^-2.5$ $\qquad$ $^-2.5 + {}^+2.5$ $\qquad$ $^+2.5 + {}^+2.5$ $\qquad$ $^+2.5 + {}^-2.5$

14. $^+1.08 + {}^-2.08$ $\qquad$ $^+2.5 + {}^-7.6$ $\qquad$ $^+1.6 + {}^-3.2$ $\qquad$ $^-3.8 + {}^+4.2$

15. $^-3.65 + {}^+12.35$ $\qquad$ $^+100.5 + {}^-99.5$ $\qquad$ $^-3.6 + {}^-9.5$ $\qquad$ $^+12.9 + {}^+13.2$

Answers

1. $^+99$; $^+61$; $^+1{,}200$; $^+334$ **2.** $^-7$; $^-18$; $^-180$; $^-350$ **3.** $^+89$; $^+98$; $^+198$; $^+288$ **4.** $^+3$; $^+10$; $^+25$; $^+150$ **5.** $^-30$; $^-40$; $^-57$; $^-1$ **6.** $^-30$; $^-60$; $^-93$; $^-180$; **7.** $^+1$; $\dfrac{{}^-1}{3}$; $\dfrac{{}^+1}{3}$; $^-1$ **8.** $^+1\frac{1}{4}$; $\dfrac{{}^+1}{4}$; $^-1\frac{1}{4}$; $\dfrac{{}^-1}{4}$ **9.** $\dfrac{{}^+1}{6}$; $\dfrac{{}^+3}{20}$; $\dfrac{{}^+1}{10}$; $\dfrac{{}^+21}{88}$ **10.** $\dfrac{{}^-1}{3}$; $\dfrac{{}^-5}{8}$; $\dfrac{{}^-4}{21}$; $\dfrac{{}^-17}{36}$ **11.** $^-2\frac{1}{8}$; $^+2$; $^-3\frac{5}{8}$; $^-11\frac{5}{6}$ **12.** $^+3.2$; $^-.2$; $^-3.2$; $^+.2$ **13.** $^-5.0$; 0; $^+5.0$; 0 **14.** $^-1.0$; $^-5.1$; $^-1.6$; $^+.4$ **15.** $^+8.7$; $^+1.0$; $^-13.1$; $^+26.1$

Subtraction of directed numbers

1. $^+7 - {}^+5$ $\qquad$ $^+12 - {}^+3$ $\qquad$ $^+36 - {}^+20$ $\qquad$ $^+56 - {}^+33$

2. $^+2 - {}^+4$ $\qquad$ $^+7 - {}^+13$ $\qquad$ $^+20 - {}^+70$ $\qquad$ $^+12 - {}^+43$

3. $^+5 - {}^-3$ $\qquad$ $^+12 - {}^-18$ $\qquad$ $^+30 - {}^-30$ $\qquad$ $^+48 - {}^-36$

4. $^-2 - {}^+7$ $\qquad$ $^-10 - {}^+25$ $\qquad$ $^-12 - {}^+50$ $\qquad$ $^-15 - {}^+80$

5. $^-1 - {}^-4$ $\qquad$ $^-6 - {}^-10$ $\qquad$ $^-2 - {}^-7$ $\qquad$ $^-5 - {}^-20$

$^-1 + 4$

6. $^-2 - {}^-2$ $^-5 - {}^-5$ $^-12 - {}^-2$ $^-20 - {}^-5$

7. $\dfrac{^+3}{4} - \dfrac{^+1}{4}$ $\dfrac{^+5}{6} - \dfrac{^+1}{6}$ $\dfrac{^+4}{7} - \dfrac{^+1}{7}$ $\dfrac{^+6}{11} - \dfrac{^+3}{11}$

8. $\dfrac{^+1}{2} - \dfrac{^+1}{3}$ $\dfrac{^+3}{5} - \dfrac{^+1}{10}$ $\dfrac{^+8}{9} - \dfrac{^+2}{3}$ $\dfrac{^+4}{5} - \dfrac{^+2}{3}$

9. $\dfrac{^+1}{3} - \dfrac{^+1}{2}$ $\dfrac{^+1}{10} - \dfrac{^+3}{5}$ $\dfrac{^+2}{3} - \dfrac{^+8}{9}$ $\dfrac{^+2}{3} - \dfrac{^+4}{5}$

10. $\dfrac{^+3}{4} - \dfrac{^-1}{4}$ $\dfrac{^+2}{5} - \dfrac{^-3}{5}$ $\dfrac{^+4}{7} - \dfrac{^-5}{7}$ $\dfrac{^+1}{9} - \dfrac{^-7}{9}$

11. $\dfrac{^+1}{3} - \dfrac{^-2}{5}$ $\dfrac{^+2}{5} - \dfrac{^-7}{10}$ $\dfrac{^+4}{3} - \dfrac{^-5}{6}$ $\dfrac{^+1}{7} - \dfrac{^-1}{8}$

12. $\dfrac{^-1}{2} - \dfrac{^-1}{2}$ $\dfrac{^-2}{3} - \dfrac{^-2}{3}$ $\dfrac{^-1}{4} - \dfrac{^-3}{4}$ $\dfrac{^-3}{5} - \dfrac{^-4}{5}$

13. $\dfrac{^-1}{2} - \dfrac{^+5}{2}$ $\dfrac{^-3}{4} - \dfrac{^+1}{3}$ $\dfrac{^-5}{6} - \dfrac{^-1}{12}$ $\dfrac{^-3}{5} - \dfrac{^-3}{4}$

14. $^+1.5 - {}^+.5$ $^+2.7 - {}^+2.3$ $^+8.9 - {}^+2.9$ $^+6.9 - {}^+3.4$

15. $^+2.3 - {}^+3.6$ $^+.5 - {}^+3.5$ $^+1.3 - {}^+9.6$ $^+7.6 - {}^+10.5$

16. $^+156.2 - {}^+156.2$ $^-12.7 - {}^-12.7$ $^+.5 - {}^+.5$ $^-11.9 - {}^-11.9$

17. $^-3.6 - {}^+2.4$ $^-1.8 - {}^+3.1$ $^-9.6 - {}^+2.1$ $^-11.3 - {}^-1.7$

18. $^-.2 - {}^+.8$ $^-.1 - {}^+.1$ $^-.9 - {}^+.9$ $^-.2 - {}^-.8$

19. $^+1.5 - {}^-1.5$ $^+3.6 - {}^-7.4$ $^+1.5 - {}^-3.5$ $^+6.9 - {}^-7.5$

20. $^-2.5 - {}^-.5$ $^-7.9 - {}^-1.9$ $^-12.4 - {}^-2.3$ $^-9.5 - {}^-3.8$

Answers

1. $^+2$; $^+9$; $^+16$; $^+23$ **2.** $^-2$; $^-6$; $^-50$; $^-31$ **3.** $^+8$; $^+30$; $^+60$; $^+84$ **4.** $^-9$; $^-35$; $^-62$; $^-95$ **5.** $^+3$; $^+4$; $^+5$; $^+15$ **6.** 0; 0; $^-10$; $^-15$ **7.** $\dfrac{^+1}{2}$; $\dfrac{^+2}{3}$; $\dfrac{^+3}{7}$; $\dfrac{^+3}{11}$ **8.** $\dfrac{^+1}{6}$; $\dfrac{^+1}{2}$; $\dfrac{^+2}{9}$; $\dfrac{^+2}{15}$ **9.** $\dfrac{^-1}{6}$; $\dfrac{^-1}{2}$; $\dfrac{^-2}{9}$; $\dfrac{^-2}{15}$ **10.** $^+1$; $^+1$; $^+1\dfrac{2}{7}$; $\dfrac{^+8}{9}$ **11.** $\dfrac{^+11}{15}$; $^+1\dfrac{1}{10}$; $^+2\dfrac{1}{6}$; $\dfrac{^+15}{56}$ **12.** 0; 0; $\dfrac{^+1}{2}$; $\dfrac{^+1}{5}$ **13.** $^-3$; $^-1\dfrac{1}{12}$; $\dfrac{^-3}{4}$; $\dfrac{^+3}{20}$ **14.** $^+1$; $^+.4$; $^+6$; $^+3.5$ **15.** $^-1.3$; $^-3$; $^-8.3$; $^-2.9$ **16.** 0; 0; 0; 0 **17.** $^-6$; $^-4.9$; $^-11.7$; $^-9.6$ **18.** $^-1$; $^-.2$; $^-1.8$; $^+.6$ **19.** $^+3$; $^+11$; $^+5$; $^+14.4$ **20.** $^-2$; $^+6$; $^-10.1$; $^-5.7$

Multiplication of directed numbers

1. $^+3 \times ^+7$ $\qquad$ $^+12 \times ^+9$ $\qquad$ $^+11 \times ^+10$ $\qquad$ $^+25 \times ^+11$

2. $^+2 \times ^-8$ $\qquad$ $^+9 \times ^-6$ $\qquad$ $^+7 \times ^-9$ $\qquad$ $^+5 \times ^-12$

3. $^-6 \times ^+7$ $\qquad$ $^-9 \times ^+5$ $\qquad$ $^-4 \times ^+12$ $\qquad$ $^-8 \times ^+7$

4. $^-4 \times ^-9$ $\qquad$ $^-7 \times ^-6$ $\qquad$ $^-13 \times ^-9$ $\qquad$ $^-12 \times ^-11$

5. $^+\frac{1}{2} \times ^+\frac{1}{3}$ $\qquad$ $^+\frac{2}{5} \times ^+\frac{4}{7}$ $\qquad$ $^+\frac{3}{4} \times ^+\frac{5}{6}$ $\qquad$ $^+\frac{1}{3} \times ^+\frac{7}{8}$

6. $^+\frac{2}{5} \times ^-\frac{1}{4}$ $\qquad$ $^+\frac{3}{7} \times ^-\frac{3}{5}$ $\qquad$ $^+\frac{1}{9} \times ^-\frac{3}{5}$ $\qquad$ $^+\frac{2}{7} \times ^-\frac{7}{8}$

7. $^-\frac{1}{9} \times ^+\frac{1}{9}$ $\qquad$ $^-\frac{2}{3} \times ^+\frac{3}{4}$ $\qquad$ $^-\frac{5}{6} \times ^+\frac{3}{7}$ $\qquad$ $^-\frac{4}{9} \times ^+\frac{4}{5}$.

8. $^-\frac{1}{2} \times ^-\frac{1}{2}$ $\qquad$ $^-\frac{2}{5} \times ^-\frac{3}{7}$ $\qquad$ $^-\frac{4}{5} \times ^-\frac{2}{7}$ $\qquad$ $^-\frac{4}{5} \times ^-\frac{3}{8}$

9. $^+2.1 \times ^+.7$ $\qquad$ $^+3.6 \times ^+.5$ $\qquad$ $^+.4 \times ^+8.1$ $\qquad$ $^+.9 \times ^+9.2$

10. $^+3.5 \times ^-2$ $\qquad$ $^+4.7 \times ^-5$ $\qquad$ $^+5.6 \times ^-9$ $\qquad$ $^+9.1 \times ^-8$

11. $^-5 \times ^-1.6$ $\qquad$ $^-7 \times ^-2.2$ $\qquad$ $^-3.1 \times ^-8$ $\qquad$ $^-5.6 \times ^-4$

12. $^+2\frac{1}{2} \times ^+3\frac{1}{2}$ $\qquad$ $^+4\frac{1}{3} \times ^+5\frac{1}{4}$ $\qquad$ $^+2\frac{1}{4} \times ^+8\frac{1}{2}$ $\qquad$ $^+5\frac{1}{3} \times ^+6\frac{1}{4}$

13. $^-3\frac{1}{3} \times ^+3\frac{1}{3}$ $\qquad$ $^-5\frac{1}{4} \times ^+6\frac{2}{3}$ $\qquad$ $^+7\frac{1}{2} \times ^-4\frac{1}{4}$ $\qquad$ $^+6\frac{2}{7} \times ^-2\frac{1}{3}$

14. $^-4\frac{1}{5} \times ^-5\frac{1}{6}$ $\qquad$ $^-9\frac{2}{3} \times ^-2\frac{1}{4}$ $\qquad$ $^-1\frac{1}{4} \times ^-1\frac{1}{4}$ $\qquad$ $^-2\frac{1}{2} \times ^-2\frac{1}{2}$

Answers

1. $^+21$; $^+108$; $^+110$; $^+275$ **2.** $^-16$; $^-54$; $^-63$; $^-60$ **3.** $^-42$; $^-45$; $^-48$; $^-56$ **4.** $^+36$; $^+42$; $^+117$; $^+132$ **5.** $^+\frac{1}{6}$; $^+\frac{8}{35}$; $^+\frac{5}{8}$; $^+\frac{7}{24}$ **6.** $^-\frac{1}{10}$; $^-\frac{9}{35}$; $^-\frac{1}{15}$; $^-\frac{1}{4}$ **7.** $^-\frac{1}{81}$; $^-\frac{1}{2}$; $^-\frac{5}{14}$; $^-\frac{16}{45}$ **8.** $^+\frac{1}{4}$; $^+\frac{6}{35}$; $^+\frac{8}{35}$; $^+\frac{3}{10}$ **9.** $^+1.47$; $^+1.80$; $^+3.24$; $^+8.28$ **10.** $^-7.0$; $^-23.5$; $^-50.4$; $^-72.8$ **11.** $^+8.0$; $^+15.4$; $^+24.8$; $^+22.4$ **12.** $^+8\frac{3}{4}$; $^+22\frac{3}{4}$; $^+19\frac{1}{8}$; $^+33\frac{1}{3}$ **13.** $^-11\frac{1}{9}$; $^-35$; $^-31\frac{7}{8}$; $^-14\frac{2}{3}$ **14.** $^+21\frac{7}{10}$; $^+21\frac{3}{4}$; $^+1\frac{9}{16}$; $^+6\frac{1}{4}$

Division of directed numbers

1. $^+24 \div {}^+6$ $\quad {}^+49 \div {}^+7$ $\quad {}^+128 \div {}^+4$ $\quad {}^+360 \div {}^+6$

2. $^+121 \div {}^-11$ $\quad {}^+440 \div {}^-110$ $\quad {}^+625 \div {}^-25$ $\quad {}^+900 \div {}^-30$

3. $^-1{,}200 \div {}^+40$ $\quad {}^-99 \div {}^+11$ $\quad {}^-144 \div {}^+12$ $\quad {}^+169 \div {}^-13$

4. $^-196 \div {}^-14$ $\quad {}^-484 \div {}^-22$ $\quad {}^-256 \div {}^-16$ $\quad {}^-99 \div {}^-11$

5. $^+\frac{1}{2} \div {}^+\frac{1}{2}$ $\quad {}^-\frac{2}{3} \div {}^-\frac{2}{3}$ $\quad {}^+7\frac{8}{9} \div {}^-7\frac{8}{9}$ $\quad {}^-11\frac{3}{8} \div {}^+11\frac{3}{8}$

6. $^+\frac{1}{2} \div {}^-\frac{2}{3}$ $\quad {}^+\frac{4}{5} \div {}^-\frac{2}{5}$ $\quad {}^+\frac{1}{6} \div {}^-\frac{4}{3}$ $\quad {}^+\frac{4}{3} \div {}^-\frac{2}{5}$

7. $^-\frac{1}{3} \div {}^+\frac{1}{2}$ $\quad {}^-\frac{2}{7} \div {}^+\frac{2}{3}$ $\quad {}^-\frac{4}{3} \div {}^+\frac{1}{6}$ $\quad {}^-\frac{5}{9} \div {}^+\frac{3}{5}$

8. $^-\frac{2}{3} \div {}^-\frac{1}{7}$ $\quad {}^-\frac{4}{7} \div {}^-\frac{2}{5}$ $\quad {}^-\frac{16}{5} \div {}^-\frac{4}{9}$ $\quad {}^-\frac{2}{7} \div {}^-\frac{12}{5}$

9. $^+3 \div {}^+0.5$ $\quad {}^+10 \div {}^+0.2$ $\quad {}^+9 \div {}^+0.3$ $\quad {}^+12 \div {}^+0.4$

10. $^+4.6 \div {}^-2$ $\quad {}^+9.8 \div {}^-2$ $\quad {}^-10.8 \div {}^+3$ $\quad {}^+15.3 \div {}^-3$

11. $^-2.5 \div {}^-1.25$ $\quad {}^-9.3 \div {}^-3.1$ $\quad {}^-36.6 \div {}^-6.1$ $\quad {}^-81.9 \div {}^-9.1$

12. $^+3\frac{1}{2} \div {}^+2\frac{1}{4}$ $\quad {}^+8\frac{1}{4} \div {}^+3\frac{1}{2}$ $\quad {}^+4\frac{3}{4} \div {}^+5\frac{2}{3}$ $\quad {}^+7\frac{1}{2} \div {}^+2\frac{1}{4}$

13. $^+2\frac{1}{2} \div {}^-\frac{1}{4}$ $\quad {}^+5\frac{7}{8} \div {}^-\frac{3}{4}$ $\quad {}^-2\frac{1}{2} \div {}^+\frac{1}{8}$ $\quad {}^-3\frac{1}{4} \div {}^+\frac{1}{6}$

14. $^-1\frac{1}{2} \div {}^-5\frac{1}{2}$ $\quad {}^-2\frac{1}{3} \div {}^-10\frac{1}{2}$ $\quad {}^-4\frac{1}{4} \div {}^-20\frac{1}{2}$ $\quad {}^-10\frac{1}{2} \div {}^-2\frac{1}{2}$

Answers

1. $^+4$; $^+7$; $^+32$; $^+60$ **2.** $^-11$; $^-4$; $^-25$; $^-30$ **3.** $^-30$; $^-9$; $^-12$; $^-13$ **4.** $^+14$; $^+22$; $^+16$; $^+9$ **5.** $^+1$; $^-1$; $^-1$; $^-1$ **6.** $\frac{^-3}{4}$; $^-2$; $\frac{^-1}{8}$; $^-3\frac{1}{3}$ **7.** $\frac{^-2}{3}$; $\frac{^-3}{7}$; $^-8$; $\frac{^-25}{27}$ **8.** $^+4\frac{2}{3}$; $^+1\frac{3}{7}$; $^+7\frac{1}{5}$; $\frac{^+5}{42}$ **9.** $^+6$; $^+50$; $^+30$; $^+30$ **10.** $^-2.3$; $^-4.9$; $^-3.6$; $^-5.1$ **11.** $^+2$; $^+3$; $^+6$; $^+9$ **12.** $^+1\frac{5}{9}$; $^+2\frac{5}{14}$; $\frac{^+57}{68}$; $^+3\frac{1}{3}$ **13.** $^-10$; $^-7\frac{5}{6}$; $^-20$; $^-19\frac{1}{2}$ **14.** $\frac{^+3}{11}$; $\frac{^+2}{9}$; $\frac{^+17}{82}$; $^+4\frac{1}{5}$

Glossary

The explanations given in this glossary are intended to be brief descriptions of the terms listed. They are not necessarily definitions.

abacus   a counting device which can be adjusted to do arithmetic in any base.

absolute value   The absolute value of a non-negative number is that number, and the absolute value of a negative number is the opposite of that number.

acute triangle   a triangle in which each angle has a measure of less than 90°.

adjacent sides (in a polygon)   two sides which share a common vertex.

altitude (of a parallelogram)   a segment which is perpendicular to two opposite sides of the parallelogram.

altitude (of a triangle)   a segment from a vertex of the triangle perpendicular to the line containing the opposite side.

angle   the union of two non-collinear rays which have the same endpoint.

angle bisector   a ray or a segment which divides an angle into two angles each having the same measure.

arithmetic mean (average)   The sum of n numbers multiplied by $\frac{1}{n}$.

Associative Property of Addition $(x + y) + z = x + (y + z)$.

Associative Property of Multiplication $(xy)z = x(yz)$.

assumption   a statement which is accepted as true.

axiom   a statement which is accepted as true.

base   1. In 2^3, 2 is the base.
       2. 215_{seven} is a numeral in base seven.
       3. Each side of a triangle may be considered to be the base.

basic numeral   In base ten there are ten basic numerals: 0, 1, 2, 3, 4, 5, 6, 7, 8, 9.

binary numeration system   numeration system in base two.

bisect   to divide something into two parts of equal measure.

Cartesian coordinate system   rectangular coordinate system.

Celsius   the metric scale for measuring temperature.

central angle   an angle whose vertex is the center of a circle and whose sides are radii of the circle.

chord   a line segment whose endpoints are on a circle.

circumference   the length of a circle.

closure   A set is closed under a given operation if the result of operating on any members of the set also belongs to the set.

collinear points   points which lie on the same line.

collinear rays   rays which are subsets of the same line.

commission   the percentage of his sales which a salesman receives for selling a product.

Commutative Property of Addition $x + y = y + x$.

Commutative Property of Multiplication $xy = yx$.

complement (of a set)   Set A is the complement of set B if A consists of all elements in the universal set which are not is B. The symbol for the complement of B is $\overline{B}$.

complete factorization   a number shown as a product of prime numbers only.

composite number   a natural number greater than 1 which is not a prime number.

concave curve   a non-convex curve.

concurrent lines   three or more lines passing through the same point.

convex curve   A curve in which the beginning and the endpoint are the same, and a segment connecting any two points in the interior is a subset of the interior.

coordinate   one of the numbers in an ordered pair assigned to a point.

coplanar   belonging to the same plane.

counting numbers   natural numbers: 1, 2, 3, 4, 5, . . .

decimal numeration system   numeration system in base ten.

density   the property of a set of numbers in which there is a third number between any two given numbers.

diagonal   a segment connecting two non-adjacent vertices of a polygon.

diameter (of a circle)   a chord containing the center of the circle.

digit   a basic numeral.

directed real number   a positive or a negative real number.

discount   per cent reduction applied to the price of an article.

disjoint sets   sets which have no common elements.

divisor   3 is a divisor of 15 because $15 \div 3 = 5$; that is, the quotient is a whole number and the remainder is 0.

element   a member of a set.

empty set   a set which has no members.

equal sets   sets having the same members.

equiangular triangle   a triangle in which each angle measures 60°.

equilateral triangle   a triangle in which each side has the same measure.

expanded product form   The name for 2^4 in expanded product form is $2 \times 2 \times 2 \times 2$.

expansion by powers of ten   The expansion by powers of ten of 3,457 is $3 \times 10^3 + 4 \times 10^2 + 5 \times 10^1 + 7 \times 10^0$.

exponent   In 2^3, 3 is the exponent. It tells how many times 2 is used as a factor in the product $2 \times 2 \times 2$.

exponential form   The name for 16 in exponential form is 2^4.

exterior of an angle   the set of all points which are not in the interior of an angle and not on the angle.

exterior of a triangle   the set of all points which are not in the interior of a triangle and not on the triangle.

factor   one of the numbers used in a product.

Fahrenheit   the English scale for measuring temperature.

finite set   A set is finite if the number of its elements can be expressed as a whole number.

Greatest Common Factor, G.C.F.   The largest number by which each of a given set of two or more numbers is divisible.

greatest integer $[x]$ is the greatest integer not greater than x.

hypotenuse   the side in a right triangle which is opposite the right angle.

infinite set   a set which is not finite.

inscribed angle   an angle with its vertex on a circle and with chords of the circle as sides.

integer   a directed whole number or 0.

interior of an angle   the set of all points "inside" the angle.

interior of a triangle   the set of all points "inside" the triangle.

intersection   the set which consists of only those elements which belong to both of two given sets.

inverse   Example: addition and subtraction are inverse operations, because $(x + y) - y = x$; or if $x + y = z$, then $z - y = x$.

irrational number   a number which has no name of the form $\frac{a}{b}$, a and b integers $[b \neq 0]$. Example: $\sqrt{5}$.

isosceles triangle   a triangle in which two sides have the same measure.

Least Common Multiple, L.C.M.   the smallest number of which each of two or more given numbers is a factor.

Left-Distributive Property of Multiplication over Addition
   $x(y + z) = xy + xz.$

leg   a side in a right triangle which is adjacent to the right angle.

matching sets   two sets between which there exists a one-to-one correspondence.

member   a number or any other thing which belongs to a set.

midpoint   a point which divides a segment into two segments each of the same measure.

multiplicative inverse   reciprocal.

natural numbers   counting numbers: 1, 2, 3, 4, 5, . . .

non-repeating non-terminating decimal   Example: .25225222522225 . . .

non-terminating repeating decimal   Example: .56$\overline{56}$.

null set   empty set.

number ray   a ray for which there is established a one-to-one correspondence between every point on the ray and the non-negative real numbers.

numeral   a name of a number.

numeration system   a system of writing names of numbers.

numerical variable   a letter which can be replaced by a numeral.

obtuse triangle   a triangle with one obtuse angle.

one-to-one correspondence   a matching between two sets so that to each element of one set there is assigned exactly one element of the second set and vice versa.

opposite   The opposite of a number is the number which if added to the original number gives the sum 0.

origin   the point on the number line assigned to the number 0, or the point in the coordinate plane assigned to the number pair $(0, 0)$.

per cent $n\% = \dfrac{n}{100}.$

perimeter   the sum of the measures of all sides of a polygon.

perpendicular lines   two lines intersecting each other so that right angles are formed.

place value The place value of 3 in 3,001 is three thousand.

positional system a numeration system in which the place value of a basic numeral depends on the position it occupies in the numeral. For example, in 235_{seven}, the value of 2 is 2 forty-nines.

power a number shown by means of a base and an exponent. For example, 9 is the second power of 3, because $9 = 3^2$.

predecessor (of a number) the whole number immediately preceding the given whole number. Example: 4 is the predecessor of 5.

prime factor a factor which is a prime number.

prime number a natural number which has exactly two factors, 1 and the number itself.

Property of One for Multiplication $x \cdot 1 = x$.

Property of Zero for Addition $x + 0 = x$.

Property of Zero for Multiplication $x \cdot 0 = 0$.

proportion a sentence of the form $\dfrac{a}{b} = \dfrac{c}{d}$ $[b \neq 0,\, d \neq 0]$.

Pythagorean Relation In a right triangle, if a and b are measures of the legs and c is the measure of the hypotenuse, then $a^2 + b^2 = c^2$.

Pythagorean triple The set of three numbers a, b, and c, such that $a^2 + b^2 = c^2$.

quadrant one of the four subsets of the coordinate plane into which the two axes separate the plane.

quadrilateral a polygon with four sides.

quinary numeral a numeral in base five.

radius a segment connecting any point of a circle with its center; also, the measure of this segment.

rate of commission per cent of commission received.

ratio the quotient of a pair of numbers.

rational number a number which has a name of the form $\dfrac{a}{b}$, a and b integers $[b \neq 0]$.

ray a part of a line having one endpoint and extending indefinitely in one direction.

real numbers the union of the set of rational numbers and the set of irrational numbers.

reciprocal $\dfrac{1}{3}$ is the reciprocal of 3 because $\dfrac{1}{3} \times 3 = 1$.

rectangular coordinate system a rectangular system which establishes a one-to-one correspondence between ordered pairs of real numbers and the points of a plane.

regular polygon   a polygon with all sides of the same measure and all angles of the same measure.

Right-Distributive Property of Multiplication over Addition
$(x + y)z = xz + yz$.

right triangle   a triangle which has one right angle.

scalene triangle   a triangle in which no two sides have the same measure.

segment   Segment $\overline{AB}$ is the set of points consisting of points A and B and all points between A and B.

set   a collection of things.

similar polygons   polygons in which pairs of corresponding angles have the same measure and the ratio of the measures of corresponding sides is the same.

simple closed curve   a closed curve which does not intersect itself.

solution set   the set of all numbers from a given universe which result in true statements when their names replace variables in a sentence.

square root   a number which multiplied by itself results in the given number.

subset A is a subset of $B [A \subseteq B]$ if every member of A is also a member of B.

successor (of a number)   the whole number immediately following the given whole number. Example: 5 is the successor of 4.

terminating decimal   a decimal which can be written with a finite number of digits.

theorem   a statement proved true.

Transitive Property of Equality   If $x = y$ and $y = z$, then $x = z$.

union   the set consisting of the members which belong to either of two given sets including members belonging to both sets.

universal set   the set of all things which are chosen for a particular study.

vertex (of an angle)   the point of intersection of the two rays which form an angle.

vertex (of a polygon)   the point of intersection of two adjacent sides.

vertical angles   a pair of non-adjacent angles formed by intersecting lines.

whole numbers   The set of whole numbers is $\{0, 1, 2, 3, 4, 5, \ldots\}$.

Index

decimal numeral(s), 67–76; changing to base-seven numerals, 84–86; changing to base-two numerals, 88–90; changing per cents to, 162–163; changing to per cent, 164–165, 169–170; finding fractional numerals for, 117–125; non-repeating, non-terminating, 125–126; non-terminating repeating, 113, 115–117, 128; place value in, 68–76, 90; for rational numbers of arithmetic, 113–117, 131; terminating, 113–114, 128

decrease, per cent of, 182–183

degree, 327

dense set, 105–106

Descartes, René, 292

diagonal(s), of a parallelogram, 349–350; of a polygon, 323; of a quadrilateral, 323; of a rectangle, 346–347

diameter of a circle, 354

digit, 68, 75, 90–91

directed number(s), absolute value of, 200–202, 253–254; addition of, 195–200, 203–210, 213; closure under addition and subtraction, 213–214; comparing, 201–202; division of, 230–236; multiplication of, 221–230; on the number line, 189–193; opposite of, 212–213, 244–245; subtraction of, 209–213; uses of, 194

discount, 177–179

disjoint sets, 21, 133

distance, between parallel lines, 348; from angle bisector to side of the angle, 383–384; from a point to a line, 380

distributive property, of multiplication over addition, 43–46, 50, 227–229; of multiplication over subtraction, 120–121, 228–229, 235–236

divisibility of whole numbers, 1–2, 26; by 9, 7; by the number itself, 2; by 1, 2; by 3, 6, 96; by 2, 1

division, 17–18, 37, 42; of directed numbers, 230–236; as inverse of multiplication, 16, 59–60, 230–236; of a natural number by itself, 35, 50; of negative numbers, 231; by one, 35, 50; of positive and negative numbers, 231; of positive numbers, 230; property of one for, 109; reciprocals and, 232–233; zero in, 2, 34, 50, 111, 126

divisor, 1; of whole numbers, 1–7, 26

dodecagon, 356–357

electronic computer, 87–90

element of a set, 11-12

empty set, 15, 32; complement of, 150; as an intersection of sets, 283; as a solution set, 254–255

endpoints(s), of a ray, 325; of a segment, 321

English system of measurement, 411–417

equal sets, 19, 32

equation(s), 245; graph of solution set of, 255; for a parabola, 302–308, 309; solving, 251–254; for a straight line, 296–301, 309

equiangular triangle, 356

equilateral triangle, 328–329, 351–354; area of, 351–354; construction of, 387

even number(s), 1; zero as, 33

event, 318; certain, 341; impossible, 341; probability of, 218, 239, 272, 318, 341, 374

expanded numeral(s), 69–71, 87, 92

expanded product form of a numeral, 74–75, 87, 92

exponent(s), 73–76

exponential notation, 73–76

exterior, of an angle, 332; of a parabola, 305, 308

Selected Answers

Page 1   **2. b.** No; $R \neq 0$ **3.** Yes; $R = 0$ **4. b.** no **f.** yes **l.** no **7.** no

Page 2   **1. a.** even **e.** even **j.** odd **2. d.** 143 **5. a.** 1

Page 3   **1.** one **2. b.** no **i.** yes **4.** 1, 2, 5, 10 **5. c.** 1, 17 **e.** 1, 7, 49 **7.** 0, 9, 18, 27, 36 **11.** no

Page 6   **2. c.** no **e.** yes **f.** yes **h.** no **j.** yes **3. c.** 4; 8; 24

Pages 7–8   **1.** 0, 9, 18, 27, 36, 45, 54, 63, 72, 81 **2. b.** no **5. a.** yes **e.** no

Pages 8–9   **3.** 17, 19, 23, 29, 31 **5. a.** composite **h.** prime **6. e.** 7 **h.** 7 **7. c.** 37 **h.** 71 **8. b.** 1, 3, 11, 33 **g.** 1, 3, 9, 27, 81, 243 **9. d.** odd **12.** 531

Pages 10–11   **2.** 3 **4. c.** 2, 3 **j.** 2, 7 **5. b.** 3×3 **i.** $2 \times 3 \times 5 \times 5$ **6. c.** 5 **h.** 12 **7. b.** $7 + 3$ **g.** $79 + 5$

Pages 11–12   **1.** 12 **4.** 3, 5 **7.** yes **9.** 1, 3, 7, 21 **13. c.** zero belongs to set T; zero is an element of set T; zero is a member of set T **14. a.** ten does not belong to set Q; ten is not a member (element) of set Q **15. b.** false **e.** true

Pages 13–14   **1.** yes; we can finish counting them. **5. a.** 1, 3, 5, 7, 9 **9.** No; we cannot finish counting them. **12.** 0, 5, 10, 15, 20, 25, 30, 35, 40, 45 **16. a.** true **c.** false **i.** false **17. f.** false **g.** true **l.** true **r.** false

Page 15   **1.** empty set **4.** $\{0, 5\}$ **9.** $\{2\}$

Pages 17–18   **2. d.** 35 **f.** 80 **5. a.** 0 **7. b.** 12 **h.** 0 **9. c.** $\frac{1}{2}$ **e.** 4

Page 19   **2. a.** 4, 6 **3. c.** 7 **f.** Yes; $3 + 4 = 7$ **5. a.** $\{2, 3, 4, 5, 6, 7\}$ **6.** They are equal.

Pages 20–21   **1. c.** $\left\{\frac{1}{2}, \frac{1}{3}, \frac{1}{4}\right\}$ **e.** ϕ **3. b.** $\left\{\frac{1}{4}\right\}$ **c.** $\{0\}$ **4. c.** A **6. g.** Union: $\{3, 6, 9, 12, 15, \ldots\}$; Intersection: $\{9, 18, 27, 36, 45, 54, \ldots\}$ **8. b.** $\{1, 17\}$

Pages 22–23   **4. b.** $\{1, 31\}$ **5. c.** $\{1\}$ **9. b.** Yes; 2 is a factor of 26.

Pages 23–24   **1. c.** 6 **h.** 10 **m.** 1 **3.** 1 **7.** Yes; G.C.F. $(3, 9) = 3$

Pages 25–26   **1. e.** $\{11, 22, 33, 44, 55, 66, 77, 88, 99\}$ **2. c.** $\{56\}$ **f.** $\{14, 28, 42, 56, 70, 84, 98\}$ **k.** ϕ **4.** 48, 60, 72, 84 **6. d.** 40 **7. a.** 3 **9. e.** 143

Pages 26–27   **1. c.** 6×49 **3. b.** Yes; 30×4 **4. a.** no **6. a.** 707 **8. b.** 1,001 $\times$ 507

Pages 27–28   **1. a.** 3,279 **c.** 95,679 **2. b.** 126,958 **c.** 4,005 **3. c.** 7,245 **e.** 76,362 **f.** 673,299 **h.** 1,666,225 **4. a.** 1,154 **c.** 167, R1 **f.** 11,573, R24 **h.** 2,329, R135 **5. a.** $147 = 147$ **d.** $294 = 294$ **6. b.** $196 = 196$ **d.** $490 = 490$

Page 31   **1.** 1 **5.** No; 0 is a whole number but not a natural number.

Pages 32–33   **2.** 0 **3. a.** yes **c.** no **e.** yes **4.** yes **7.** Yes; every prime number is a natural number.

Page 34   **1.** the number itself **6. b.** 0 **g.** 0

Pages 34–35   **1.** the number itself **3.** the number itself **7. a.** 1 **i.** 0

Pages 36–39   **1. b.** $12 + 36 = 48$; $36 + 12 = 48$; $12 + 36 = 36 + 12$ **c.** $30 + 17 = 47$; $17 + 30 = 47$; $30 + 17 = 17 + 30$ **4.** yes **6.** $2 \times 5 = 5 \times 2$ **8.** $2 - 5 \neq 5 - 2$ **9. a.** No answer; The results are different. **c.** No answer; The results are different. **h.** $10 = 10$; The results are the same. **i.** $51 = 51$; The results are the same. **10. b.** 27 **e.** 37 **11. c.** 20 **e.** 132 **12. d.** 36 **13. a.** 3 **14. b.** 100 **15. c.** 22 **16. e.** 1 **17. f.** 13 **18. b.** 512

Page 40   **2.** Yes; $276 \neq 1$ **5. c.** 10 **e.** 12; 12

Pages 41–42   **1. a.** 7 **4. b.** $(99 + 1) + 48 = 100 + 48 = 148$; $99 + (1 + 48) = 99 + 49 = 148$ **6. a.** 148 **j.** 810 **8.** no **11. a.** $<$ **d.** $>$

Page 44   **1. c.** $30 = 30$ **e.** $180 = 180$ **f.** $8,100 = 8,100$ **4.** two **5.** multiplication and addition

Pages 45–46   **3.** $200 = 200$ **6.** $210 = 210$ **8.** $1,800 = 1,800$

Page 46   **2.** $126 = 126$

Page 49   **2.** First $2 \times 10 = 20$; then $20 \div 2 = 10$ **3.** First $2 + 25 = 27$; then $27 - 7 = 20$; then $20 + 3 = 23$; and, finally, $23 - 4 = 19$ **6.** 6 **11.** 80 **18.** 15 **22.** 54 **25.** 159 **32.** 109 **34.** 22 **37.** 0

Pages 50–52   **2.** Prop. of zero for add.   **3.** Rt.-dist. mult. over add.   **5.** Comm. prop. mult.   **8.** Comm. prop. mult. and Prop. of one for mult.   **9.** Assoc. prop. mult.   **11.** Prop. of zero for mult. and Comm. prop. add.   **18.** 1; Prop. of number and itself for div.   **23.** $11.72 = 11.72$; Assoc. prop. add.   **26.** $5.94 = 5.94$; Comm. prop. add.

Pages 54–56   **2. a.** no   **d.** no   **6.** $1 + 3 = ?$ The sum is not in the set $\{0, 1, 2, 3\}$. **9. b.** Set A is not closed under multiplication.

Pages 56–59   **1.** $13 + 7 = 20$ **4. b.** 14   **e.** 36   **6. d.** $410 - 90 = 320$ **7. c.** 9 $+ 8 = 17$ **8. b.** 89   **i.** 130   **10. f.** closing a book   **11. g.** 78,939; $78,939 + 9,429 = 88,368$ **17.** 420

Pages 59–60   **1. d.** $48 \div 4 = 12$ **3. a.** 3   **5. b.** yes   **6. b.** 4   **e.** 104   **9. e.** 1,645; $1,645 \div 47 = 35$ **j.** 786; $235 \times 786 = 184,710$ **10. c.** 17   **12. a.** $27 \div 3 = 9$

Page 61   **1.** 9   **6.** $\frac{1}{4}$ **7.** 2

Pages 62–63   **1. b.** 202.21   **d.** 1,253.17   **2. a.** 18,807   **c.** 258.38   **3. a.** 589,888 **d.** 1,385.075   **5. a.** 18   **c.** 12   **6. b.** $1\frac{1}{4}$ **c.** $3\frac{5}{24}$ **7. b.** $\frac{1}{4}$ **d.** $1\frac{5}{12}$ **8. a.** $\frac{2}{15}$ **b.** $4\frac{3}{8}$ **9. c.** $\frac{2}{9}$ **d.** $1\frac{19}{36}$ **10. c.** 536   **d.** $\frac{3}{10}$ **11. b.** 4 qts.   **e.** 2 gals. 3 qts.   **g.** 2 yds. 1 ft. 11 in. **h.** 33.48   **j.** $\frac{7}{15}$ **m.** .01   **p.** 39.2000   **r.** $\frac{1}{35}$ **13.** 1,250   **16.** $22.68   **19.** 1:25 P.M.

Pages 67–68   **1. b.** $3\frac{1}{3} \times 3$ **3. d.** 76,934   **4. i.** forty-three thousand, five **5. d.** one hundred seventy million, six thousand, three hundred forty

Pages 68–69   **1. a.** thirty; two-digit numeral   **2. c.** fifty thousand   **5.** 100 **8.** 1,000

Pages 69–71   **1. c.** 10^8 **2. a.** the fifth power of ten; ten to the fifth power **3. d.** $5 \times 10^2 + 4 \times 10^1 + 0 \times 10^0$ **4. b.** 10^6 **5. c.** 9,006   **g.** 3,002,001,000

Pages 72–74   **4.** 200   **6. b.** 7   **8.** 36   **10. e.** 5   **12. c.** $2 \times 2 \times 2 \times 2 \times 2$ **13. d.** 10,000   **14. b.** 10^6 **15. b.** ten thousand, three hundred ninety-eight **16. a.** 5,673   **17. f.** six million

Pages 74–75   **1. d.** 86   **2. a.** $4 \times 10^2 + 6 \times 10^1 + 10^0$ **3. e.** 6,090,703

Pages 75–76   **1. a.** 9: nine tens; 2: two ones   **2. c.** 1,000,000,027   **3. c.** 3; 8 **e.** 1   **4. b.** 4; 2,401   **f.** 0

Page 78   **2. a.** 300,099 **b.** three hundred thousand, ninety-nine

4.

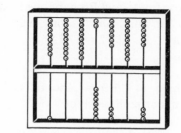

Pages 79–81   **2.** The number is fifty. **10. b.** forty-nine **12.** Yes; two thousand four hundred; 2,400 **15. a.** one hundred fifty-six; one hundred twenty-nine; two hundred eighty-five **17.** two thousand, four hundred one; 2,401

Page 82   **1. a.** 221_{seven} **b.** one hundred thirteen **c.** 113_{ten} **5. a.** 600_{seven} **b.** two hundred ninety-four **c.** 294_{ten}

Page 83   **3.** 15_{ten} **10.** 343_{ten} **14.** $2{,}277_{\text{ten}}$ **19.** 56_{ten}

Pages 85–86   **1.** 13_{seven} **3.** 30_{seven} **11.** 4322_{seven} **15.** 35_{seven} **20.** 610_{seven}

Page 87   **2.** 0, 1, 2, 3, 4, 5, 6 **3. a.** 100 **4. a.** $1 \times 10^1 + 7 \times 10^0$ **5. b.** twenty **6. e.** 16

Page 88   **2. a.** 2 **d.** 15_{ten} **6.** fifteen

Pages 89–90   **1. d.**

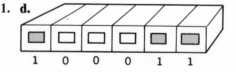

2. d. thirty-five **5.** nine; eleven **8.** fifteen **10.** $4 = 100_{\text{two}}$; 1 digit in the decimal system; 3 digits in the binary system **15.** $25_{\text{ten}} = 11{,}001_{\text{two}}$; 2 digits in the decimal system; 5 digits in the binary system

Pages 90–91   **1. c.** twenty thousand **2. b.** three **3.** thirty-two **5.** five; 0, 1, 2, 3, 4 **6. a.** 4 fives, or twenty **9. a.** one **10.** ten **13. b.** seven

Page 92   **1.** $514_{\text{six}} = (5 \times 36_{\text{ten}}) + (1 \times 6) + (4 \times 1) = 180_{\text{ten}} + 6 + 4 = 190_{\text{ten}}$ **3.** $\text{E}53_{\text{twelve}} = (11_{\text{ten}} \times 144_{\text{ten}}) + (5 \times 12_{\text{ten}}) + (3 \times 1) = 1{,}584_{\text{ten}} + 60_{\text{ten}} + 3 = 1{,}647_{\text{ten}}$ **5.** $716_{\text{eight}} = (7 \times 64_{\text{ten}}) + (1 \times 8) + (6 \times 1) = 448_{\text{ten}} + 8 + 6 = 462_{\text{ten}}$ **17. b.** eight **18. a.** twenty-five **19. d.** 81_{ten} **f.** 121_{ten}

Page 93   **1. b.** one-fifth **2.** $\dfrac{2}{3}$ **3.** $\dfrac{3}{4}$ **5.** $\dfrac{7}{8}$ **8.** $\dfrac{8}{9}$ **10.** $\left(\dfrac{13}{14}\right)_{\text{ten}}$ **13. b.** one-eighth

Pages 94–95   **2.** 202.7   **3.** 102.77   **5.** 2,907   **7.** .83   **10.** 100.7   **11.** 275.13   **13.** 43,470   **16.** $196\frac{7}{8}$ **18.** 1,828   **19.** 9   **23.** .01   **24.** 161   **25.** 2,213   **27.** 20   **30.** 85.02   **32.** $\frac{1}{2}$ **34.** 1.76   **35.** 5   **37.** 11.445   **39.** $28\frac{1}{2}$ **41.** $11\frac{1}{9}$ **43.** .395   **45.** .135   **47.** .0009   **48.** 350   **50.** 1,000   **51.** 1,000   **53.** 3,000   **56.** .001   **59.** 10   **61.** .01   **62.** .001   **65.** .00001   **68.** .000001

Page 99   **1. a.** successor: 13; predecessor: 11   **e.** successor: 10,001; predecessor: 9,999   **3.** no

Pages 100–102   **1. b.** 10   **c.** $11\frac{1}{2}$ **e.** $\frac{3}{5}$ **h.** $\frac{9}{10}$ **i.** $\frac{5}{24}$ **k.** $1\frac{5}{12}$ **m.** $2\frac{9}{10}$ **n.** 7.26   **2. b.** $\frac{23}{48}$ **3.** $\frac{3}{40}$ **4.** $\frac{3}{100}$ **8.** yes   **11. b.** $15\frac{1}{3}$ **d.** 2.7   **12.** Multiply $\frac{1}{5}$ by the sum of the five numbers.   **15.** 100

Pages 103–104   **1.** $\frac{12}{60} < \frac{19}{60} < \frac{40}{60}$ is true, so $\frac{19}{60}$ is between $\frac{1}{5}$ and $\frac{2}{3}$.   **4.** an infinite number   **5.** $2 < 2\frac{1}{2} < 3$, so $2\frac{1}{2}$ is between 2 and 3.   **7.** $2 < 2\frac{1}{50} < 3$, so $2\frac{1}{50}$ is between 2 and 3.   **10.** $2.50 < 2.51 < 2.60$, so 2.51 is between 2.5 and 2.6.   **13.** $3.2100 < 3.2101 < 3.2200$, so 3.2101 is between 3.21 and 3.22.

Pages 105–106   **2.** $\frac{3}{2}$ **4.** $\frac{54}{5}$ **6.** $\frac{55}{100}$ **8.** $\frac{32}{10}$ **10.** $\frac{2,176}{1,000}$ **12.** $\frac{1,251}{10}$ **13.** $\frac{5}{10}$, $\frac{3}{6}$, $\frac{4}{8}$ **15.** $\frac{4}{1}$, $\frac{8}{2}$, $\frac{12}{3}$ **18.** $\frac{9}{10}$, $\frac{18}{20}$, $\frac{27}{30}$ **19.** $\frac{17}{100}$, $\frac{34}{200}$, $\frac{51}{300}$

Pages 106–108   **1. b.** no   **5.** 8   **8.** 19; 19   **9.** 7; 7   **12.** 5   **14.** 21   **17.** 7; 8   **18.** 2; 3   **20.** true   **23.** false   **25.** true   **26.** true   **28.** false   **33.** true   **34.** false

Page 109   **2.** $\frac{12}{30}$ **4.** $\frac{20}{50}$ **5.** $\frac{3}{4}$ **7.** $\frac{3}{4}$ **10.** $\frac{6}{51}$ **13.** $\frac{20}{55}$ **15.** $\frac{2}{4}$ **18.** $\frac{1}{25}$

Page 110   **2.** $\frac{5}{27}$ **6.** $\frac{20}{99}$ **7.** $\frac{14}{55}$ **11.** $\frac{4}{65}$ **12.** $\frac{14}{45}$ **13.** $\frac{10}{10} = 1$ **15.** $\frac{125}{125} = 1$ **17.** $\frac{999}{999} = 1$

Pages 111–112   **1. a.** $\frac{5}{4}$ **d.** $\frac{4}{5}$ **e.** $\frac{7}{2}$ **h.** $\frac{1}{10}$ **3.** yes   **5. b.** $\frac{25}{2}$ **c.** $\frac{207}{10}$ **f.** $\frac{2,501}{5}$ **g.** $\frac{2,537}{100}$ **6. a.** $\frac{5}{6}$ **c.** $\frac{10}{103}$ **7.** no   **9.** no   **12.** yes   **15.** no   **16.** yes   **19.** yes

Pages 114–115   **1.** .5   **4.** .25   **5.** 1.25   **8.** .6   **9.** 1.4   **12.** 8.4   **13.** .375
15. 1.375   **16.** 2.375   **17.** 2.625   **18.** 9.375   **20.** .3125   **25.** >   **26.** >   **28.** =
30. =   **31.** =   **32.** <   **33.** <   **35.** >   **37.** $\frac{1}{5}$ **39.** $\frac{7}{20}$ **42.** $\frac{19}{20}$ **44.** $\frac{273}{50}$ **45.** $\frac{258}{25}$

Pages 115–117   **2.** .111$\bar{1}$ **4.** .142857$\overline{142857}$ **6.** .285714$\overline{285714}$ **8.** .833
10. .388   **13.** 1.142857$\overline{142857}$ **14.** 1.2$\bar{2}$ **15.** 1.36$\overline{36}$ **17.** $\frac{125}{100}$ **19.** $\frac{11,076}{10,000}$
22. a. .2$\bar{2}$ **e.** 66   **f.** .7$\bar{7}$ **i.** 1.1$\bar{1}$ **j.** 1.2$\bar{2}$ **23. a.** .18$\overline{18}$ **d.** .72$\overline{72}$ **g.** 1.36$\overline{36}$ **h.** 2.09$\overline{09}$
j. 5.27$\overline{27}$ **24. a.** 1.142857$\overline{142857}$ **c.** 1.428571$\overline{428571}$ **25.** 1.66

Pages 118–119   **1.** 3.3$\bar{3}$ **4.** 13.3$\bar{3}$ **6.** 1,735.35$\overline{35}$ **8.** 1,069.1069$\overline{1069}$ **11.** $\frac{9}{10}$
$-\frac{4}{10} = .9 - .4; \frac{5}{10} = .5$; true   **13.** $\frac{11}{20} - \frac{9}{20} = .55 - .45; \frac{2}{20} = .10; \frac{1}{10} = \frac{10}{100}$; true

Pages 119–121   **2.** $\frac{10}{18}; \frac{10}{18}$; Rt. dist. prop. holds   **3.** $\frac{28}{30}; \frac{28}{30}$; Rt. dist. prop.
holds   **5.** 9; 9; Rt. dist. prop. holds   **8.** $\frac{2}{60}; \frac{2}{60}$; yes   **9.** $\frac{24}{35}; \frac{24}{35}$; yes   **11.** $\frac{1}{36}; \frac{1}{36}$;
yes   **13.** .15; .15; yes   **18.** $\frac{4}{7}; \frac{4}{7}$;   **20.** 3   **22.** $\frac{9}{2}$ **23.** 900   **25.** 150   **28.** 40

Pages 122–124   **3. a.** 12.12$\overline{12}$ **c.** 12   **5.** $\frac{1}{3}$ **7.** $\frac{5}{9}$ **10.** 1   **11.** $\frac{10}{99}$ **13.** $\frac{14}{99}$
16. $\frac{89}{99}$ **18.** $\frac{8}{37}$ **20.** $\frac{1,001}{9,999}$ **21.** 6$\frac{1}{9}$ **23.** 75$\frac{2}{9}$ **25.** 27$\frac{32}{99}$ **28.** 268$\frac{112}{999}$ **29.** 176$\frac{109}{999}$
30. $\frac{11}{99}$ **32.** $\frac{26}{45}$ **35.** $\frac{211}{495}$ **38.** $\frac{13}{60}$ **39.** $\frac{53}{150}$ **41.** $\frac{203}{225}$

Pages 124–125   **4.** .2   **11.** .08$\overline{33}$ **15.** .0625   **17.** .055   **19.** .05   **23.** termi-
nating   **25.** terminating   **27.** terminating   **29.** terminating   **30.** non-terminating   **33.** non-terminating   **34.** non-terminating   **36.** non-terminating   **37.** non-
terminating   **41.** terminating

Pages 125–126   **1.** Each time we write one more 2 before writing the next 35.

Pages 127–128   **1. b.** 6,400   **e.** 4,800   **f.** 6,050   **2. a.** 1,100   **c.** 11,100   **d.** 22,000
4. a. 3,200   **c.** 6,700   **6.** 159.52   **8.** 403.0   **11.** 12.59   **13.** .105   **15.** 18.33
17. 3.1473   **18.** 3.7187   **20.** 1.5   **22.** 12.7

Pages 131–133   **2.** 8   **5.** 25   **8.** 24   **9.** 40   **11.** 90   **14.** $\frac{9}{10}$ **17.** $\frac{17}{25}$ **18.** true
21. true   **23.** true   **25.** true   **27.** 2,500   **29.** 6,561   **30.** 531,441   **34.** 4.642
36. 6.083   **40.** 88   **41.** 47   **42.** 100   **47.** 90   **50.** 40

Pages 133–134   **2. a.** no **e.** no **f.** yes **i.** yes   **3. a.** $3.162 \times 3.162 = 9.998244$; $10.000000 - 9.998244 = 0.001756$ **5.** 22.36   **7.** 31.62   **8.** 41.23   **10.** 56.56

Pages 136–137   **2. a.** $9^2 = 81$; $12^2 = 144$; $15^2 = 225$ **c.** 3 **3. c.** 4 **4. b.** 90 **d.** 120 **e.** 12 **g.** 30 **h.** 24 **5. b.** $400 = 400$; true **d.** $900 = 900$; true

Page 138   **1. a.** $250,000 = 250,000$; true **2. b.** $1,521 = 1,521$; true **d.** $16,900 = 16,900$; true **6. b.** B **c.** C **e.** D **g.** A **i.** C

Pages 139–140   **2. b.** 12, 16, 20 **d.** 16, 30, 34 **3. b.** $400 = 400$; yes **4. a.** 20, 21, 29

Pages 142–143   **2.** $\sqrt{2}$ in.   **4. a.** cannot **b.** cannot **f.** can **5. b.** 1.8 in. **8. c.** 9 sq. in. **d.** 16 sq. in. **9. c.** about 8.1 in. **10. a.** $1\frac{1}{4}$ sec. **b.** $4\frac{1}{4}$ sec.

11. a. $1\frac{1}{3}$ sec.

Page 144   **11.** one-half the distance from 1 toward 2 **12.** one-half the distance from 0 toward 1 **15.** one-seventh the distance from 1 toward 2 **18.** ninety-nine hundredths the distance from 0 toward 1 **20.** ninety-nine hundredths the distance from 1 toward 2

Pages 145–146   **1.** 2 **3.** $3\frac{1}{2}$ **4.** $\frac{1}{4}$ **5.** 2.15 **9.** 3.55 **10.** 2.255 **13.** 3 **14.** 11

18. 1.13 **19.** 2.6 **21.** $\frac{7}{18}$ **24.** 1.114 **26.** $\frac{1}{50}$ **27.** $1\frac{3}{100}$ **30.** 3.11 **31.** .201

34. $10\frac{49}{50}$ **35.** $11\frac{91}{100}$ **37.** 4.599 **40.** 6.339

Pages 146–147   **1. e.** $(AC)^2 = 1^2 + 1^2$; $AC = \sqrt{2}$ **h.** Yes; $\sqrt{2}$ **3. b.** I **c.** R

Pages 148–149   **1. a.** true **d.** false **e.** false **h.** true **2. a.** true **c.** false **3. c.** $\frac{23}{1}$ **e.** $\frac{980}{1}$ **6.** no **7. b.** true **c.** false **d.** false **f.** true **g.** false **8. g.** $R \cap I = I$ **11. a.** no **b.** yes **12. a.** yes **d.** no **13. a.** yes **e.** yes

Page 150   **2.** $\{2, 4, 6\}$ **3. b.** $\overline{M} = \{2, 3, 5, 6\}$ **d.** $\overline{T} = \{2, 3, 4, 5, 6\}$ **f.** $\overline{U} = \phi$ **6. a.** $\cup$ **c.** $\cup$ **8. a.** ϕ **d.** ϕ

Page 151   **1. b.** $<$ **d.** $>$ **f.** $>$ **h.** $<$ **2. b.** 3.3, $3\frac{1}{4}$, $3\frac{5}{6}$ **3. a.** $\sqrt{2}$ **c.** $\sqrt{101}$

4. a.–e

Page 152   **1.** 1   2   3   Match 1 with 12
     $\updownarrow$ $\updownarrow$ $\updownarrow$ 2 with 8
     12   8   10   3 with 10
     1   2   3   Match 1 with 12
     $\updownarrow$ $\updownarrow$ $\updownarrow$ 2 with 10
     12   10   8   3 with 8

Page 153   **1. b.** 10,000 **2. a.** 250 **3.** $2n$ **6.** no

Pages 154–155   **2. b.** 3 **d.** 9 **f.** 199 **h.** 999 **j.** 4,999 **1.** $2w - 1$ **3. a.** 1 **e.** 12
f. 25 **g.** 50 **j.** 501 **l.** $\frac{1}{2}(m + 1)$ **4.** $N = \{\ 1\ ,\ 2\ ,\ 3\ ,\ 4\ ,\ 5\ , \ldots\}$
                $\updownarrow$ $\updownarrow$ $\updownarrow$ $\updownarrow$ $\updownarrow$
          $L = \{101, 102, 103, 104, 105, \ldots\}$
5. a. 101 **b.** 102 **e.** 600 **h.** $100 + a$ **6. a.** 2 **d.** 402 **e.** 1,898 **g.** 10,350 **8. a.** 3
b. 6 **e.** 900 **9. a.** 1 **c.** 111 **e.** 1,758 **11. a.** 10 **c.** 1,110 **e.** 10,100 **12. b.** 10
d. 750 **e.** 1,305

Pages 156–157   **2.** 1.45   **4.** 95.13   **5.** $1\frac{17}{60}$ **7.** 33.70   **8.** 2,886   **9.** 1,851
12. 18.86 **14.** $11\frac{31}{42}$ **17.** 44.4 **20.** .703 **21.** .125 **22.** .0006 **26.** $8\frac{3}{4}$ **27.** $41\frac{1}{3}$
28. 260 **30.** 430 **32.** 78,200 **34.** .337 **35.** .114 **36.** 130 **41.** .7 **43.** .00135
44. .12 **45.** .85 **49.** .96875 **51.** .9375 **52.** $37\frac{1}{2}$ **55.** 3.6 **58.** 3.84 **60.** $4\frac{1}{8}$
61. $2\frac{9}{40}$ **63.** 12 hrs. 2 min. 22 sec.

Pages 161–162   **2.** $\frac{1}{25}$ **4.** $\frac{79}{100}$ **5.** $\frac{21}{50}$ **9.** $\frac{11}{20}$ **10.** $\frac{41}{100}$ **12.** $\frac{1}{4}$ **13.** $1\frac{1}{10}$
16. $3\frac{1}{5}$ **17.** $7\frac{17}{100}$ **19.** 10 **23.** 100 **24.** $61\frac{18}{25}$ **26.** $\frac{1}{150}$ **27.** $\frac{1}{600}$ **30.** $\frac{1}{160}$
31. $\frac{1}{180}$ **34.** $\frac{3}{3,700}$ **35.** $\frac{3}{20}$ **36.** $\frac{1}{5}$ **39.** $2\frac{2}{5}$ **40.** 5 **44.** $\frac{241}{2,000}$

Page 163   **1.** .45   **4.** .03   **5.** .33   **9.** .02   **10.** .50   **12.** 2.30   **14.** 5.33
15. 9.80 **18.** 20.00 **19.** 206.70 **21.** .001 **23.** .0095 **24.** .0003 **28.** .00001
30. .00125 **32.** .000009 **34.** .9 **36.** 2.1 **37.** .965 **39.** .004 **42.** .679
44. .0125 **47.** 1.006 **49.** $\frac{13}{20}$ **51.** $6\frac{3}{5}$ **54.** $\frac{3}{400}$ **56.** $\frac{1}{8}$ **57.** $\frac{1}{700}$ **59.** $\frac{3}{1,100}$ **62.** 5

Pages 164–165   **1.** 15%   **3.** 360%   **6.** $n\%$ **8.** $(h - 1)\%$ **9.** $(3m)\%$
12. $(2c - g)\%$ **13.** $\frac{50}{100}$; 50% **16.** $\frac{84}{100}$; 84% **18.** $\frac{126}{100}$; 126% **21.** $\frac{9}{100}$; 9%
23. $\frac{20}{100}$; 20% **25.** 26% **27.** 4% **29.** 2,604% **32.** 9,800% **34.** 56.3%

Pages 165–166   1. $\dfrac{33}{63}$ 2. b. $\dfrac{1}{3}$ 3. a. $\dfrac{2}{5}$ d. $\dfrac{2}{7}$ e. $\dfrac{7}{2}$ 5. $\dfrac{22}{88}$, or $\dfrac{11}{14}$ 7. $\dfrac{8}{3}$ 8. b. $\dfrac{85}{12}$

Pages 166–168   2. a. 2 c. 20 f. 80 h. 1,000 3. true 5. false 8. false 10. false 11. true 16. false 17. true 18. true 19. a. 4 c. 4 f. 9 g. 16 21. b. 15 e. 9 g. 1 h. 225 23. b. If $\dfrac{7}{3.5} = \dfrac{14}{7}$, then $7 = \dfrac{14}{7} \times 3.5$.

Pages 169–170   2. 75% 5. $16\dfrac{2}{3}\%$ 8. $66\dfrac{2}{3}\%$ 9. $83\dfrac{1}{3}\%$ 10. $87\dfrac{1}{2}\%$ 13. $11\dfrac{1}{11}\%$ 15. $63\dfrac{9}{57}\%$ 16. $\dfrac{1}{4} = .25 = 25\%$; $\dfrac{3}{5} = .60 = 60\%$; $\dfrac{1}{8} = .125 = 12\dfrac{1}{2}\%$

Pages 172–173   2. 44.4 3. .15 5. .1 8. 9 10. $9.30 12. 630 mph 15. $1.88

Page 174   2. 240 4. $12\dfrac{1}{2}$ 5. $12\dfrac{1}{2}$ 7. 40 9. 4% 12. 2% 13. 200% 14. 100% 15. 5% 18. $33\dfrac{1}{3}\%$ 21. 200%

Pages 176–177   1. $14\dfrac{2}{7}\%$ 4. $324 6. 3,900 9. 330 11. $828 14. $171 15. 60 mph

Pages 177–179   2. $10 4. $2.00 5. yes 7. $3.33 8. a. $15.93 c. $49.34 10. b. $17.86 c. $5.57

Page 180   2. $3,000 3. $2,160 4. $4,750

Pages 180–181   1. $\dfrac{1}{4}$, or .250 3. b. .347 d. .293 f. .212 4. a. On the average, a batter gets 346 hits out of 1,000 times at bat. d. no hits out of 1,000 times at bat 8. Yes; if you get one hit out of more than 1,000 times at bat, your average would be less than .001. 10. $\dfrac{153}{347}$

Pages 182–183   1. $8\dfrac{1}{3}\%$ 5. a. 5.94% b. 23.43% e. 21.81% 6. b. $22\dfrac{2}{9}\%$ c. $22\dfrac{8}{11}\%$ d. $48\dfrac{4}{27}\%$ g. $21\dfrac{39}{41}\%$ h. $207\dfrac{9}{13}$

Page 184   2. 98.29 5. 74.93 6. 6.189 8. 2.008 9. .308 11. .28416 12. 272.7060 15. 2.84468 17. $\dfrac{3}{5}$ 20. $19\dfrac{1}{2}$ 22. $88\dfrac{13}{15}$ 23. 8 25. 3,340

28. 214   **29.** 3,202   **31.** $1\frac{3}{4}$ **33.** 2   **35.** $\frac{1}{3}$ **38.** $\frac{1}{16}$ **40.** $\frac{16}{33}$ **41.** $\frac{13}{29}$ **43.** $\frac{1}{125}$
45. $\frac{9}{1,000}$ **48.** $\frac{7}{8}$

Pages 189–190   **2.** 1   **5.** 2   **6.** two

Pages 190–191   **1. b.** $^-4$ **d.** $^+4$ **g.** $^-2$ **2. a.** G **d.** F **g.** B **4.** A **5. c.** 3
6. a. $^+1$; $^-1$

Pages 191–192   **1. a.** yes   **c.** no   **f.** yes   **2. b.** $^-2$ **e.** $^+980$ **4. a.** negative
5. a. yes; yes   **c.** no; no   **7.** They are different.

Pages 192–193   **1.** $\frac{^+1}{3}$ **4.** $\frac{^-1}{2}$ **5.** $^+3\frac{1}{5}$ **8.** $^-1\frac{3}{4}$

10. a.–f.

Page 194   **1. c.** $^-40$ **d.** $^+21$ **2. b.** $^+1$ **d.** $^-2$ **f.** $^+7$ **3. a.** $^+5$ **c.** $^-33$

Pages 195–196   **1. b.** $^+7$ **c.** $^+3$ **f.** $^-8$ **2. a.** $^+3$ **d.** $^-8$ **e.** $^-16$ **3. b.** $^+3$ (from
P to B)   **d.** $^-3$ (from D to E)   **6.** no move at all   **7.** an infinite number
10. b. from G to K, then from K to H **d.** from F to I, then from I to G

Pages 197–200   **1.** A move from A to L: $^+2$; followed by a move from L to C:
$^+1$; result is the same as the move from A to C: $^+3$; therefore: $^+2 + {^+1} = {^+3}$
3. A move from A to I: $^+4$; followed by a move from I to H: $^+1$; result is the
same as the move from A to H: $^+5$; therefore: $^+4 + {^+1} = {^+5}$ **7.** positive   **9.** $^+27$
12. $^+425$ **14.** $^+1,430$ **15.** $^-38$ **17.** $^-64$ **19.** $^-1,040$ **21.** A move from A to L:
$^+2$; followed by a move from L to B: $^-6$; result is the same as the move from
A to B: $^-4$; therefore: $^+2 + {^-6} = {^-4}$ **24.** A move from A to J: $^-3$; followed by
a move from J to K: $^+4$; result is the same as the move from A to K: $^+1$; therefore: $^-3 + {^+4} = {^+1}$ **26.** A move from A to J: $^-3$; followed by a move from J
to A: $^+3$; result is the same as the move from A to A (standing still): 0;
therefore: $^-3 + {^+3} = 0$ **29.** 0   **31. b.** false   **d.** true   **f.** true   **h.** true   **32.** $^+6$
34. $^+16$ **37.** $^-25$ **39.** $^-21$ **40.** 0   **42.** $^-35$ **44.** $\frac{^+1}{2}$ **46.** $\frac{^+1}{3}$ **48.** $^-1.2$ **50.** 0
51. $\frac{^-1}{2}$ **53.** $\frac{^+1}{2}$ **55.** $^+3.0$ **57.** $^+2.9$ **59.** 0   **63.** $^-5.4$

Page 200   **2.** $^+2,506$ **3.** 0   **6.** $\frac{^+1}{10}$ **8.** positive   **10.** positive

Pages 201–202   **3.** < **4.** > **6.** < **9.** > **11.** > **12.** < **14.** less **17.** greater **19. d.** false **24.** false **27.** true **29.** true **31.** true **33.** false **37.** false **40.** true

Pages 203–205   **1. b.** > **c.** $^{+}4$ **e.** $^{-}1$; $^{-}1$ **3.** negative; greater; negative; positive **4. b.** $^{-}7$ **d.** $^{-}7$; $^{-}7$ **f.** $^{-}2$; $^{-}2$; >; $^{+}1$ **5. b.** greater **7.** $^{+}26$ **9.** $^{+}51$ **10.** $^{+}1\frac{3}{8}$ **12.** $^{+}10\frac{2}{7}$ **14.** $^{+}3\frac{15}{56}$ **16.** $^{-}12$ **18.** $^{-}61$ **19.** $^{-}1$ **21.** $^{-}2$ **23.** $^{-}17\frac{6}{7}$ **26.** $^{+}22$ **28.** $\frac{^{-}1}{2}$ **29.** $\frac{^{+}5}{8}$ **33.** $^{+}1\frac{1}{6}$ **35.** $^{-}8$ **37.** $\frac{^{-}2}{15}$ **39.** $^{-}11\frac{7}{9}$ **41.** $^{-}1\frac{17}{21}$

Pages 205–206   **2.** $^{-}8\frac{1}{3}$ **4.** $^{-}350\frac{1}{3}$ **6.** $^{-}5.0$ **7.** $^{+}11.1$ **9.** $^{-}16$ **11.** 0 **14.** $^{-}.9$ **16.** $^{-}1.8$ **18.** $^{-}1\frac{1}{24}$ **20.** $^{+}11$ **23.** $^{+}21$ **25.** $^{-}4$ **27.** $^{-}20$ **30.** $^{-}31$ **32.** $^{-}20$ **34.** $^{-}27$ **36.** $^{+}3$ **37.** $^{+}7$ **39.** $^{-}1$ **41.** $^{-}5$ **43.** $^{+}2$ **45.** $^{+}3$ **48.** $^{-}3$ **50.** $^{-}8$ **52.** $^{-}5$ **54.** -17 **56.** $^{-}21$ **59.** $^{+}211$ **61.** $^{-}250$ **63.** $^{+}500$ **65.** $^{-}21$

Pages 206–207   **2.** $^{-}15$; $^{-}15$ **4.** 0; 0 **6.** $^{+}5.2$; $^{+}5.2$ **7. a.** $^{-}3 + {}^{+}5 = {}^{+}2$ **b.** $^{+}5 + {}^{-}3 = {}^{+}2$ **9. a.** $^{-}95.31$

Page 208   **1.** $^{-}4$; $^{-}4$ **3.** $^{+}6$; $^{+}6$ **6.** $^{-}1$; $^{-}1$ **8.** $^{+}2.5$; $^{+}2.5$ **10.** $^{+}4.65$; $^{+}4.65$ **12.** $^{-}313$

Pages 209–210   **1. c.** 4 **e.** 13; 20 **3.** 17 **6.** 14 **7.** $^{+}6$ **8.** $^{+}4$ **11.** $^{+}15$ **14.** $^{-}13$ **16.** $^{-}10$ **17.** $^{-}6$ **20.** $^{-}22$ **22.** $^{+}12$ **24.** $^{+}22$ **25.** $^{+}26$ **27.** $^{+}14$ **29.** $^{+}15$ **30.** $^{-}19$ **33.** $^{-}5$ **35.** $^{-}6$ **37.** $^{-}22$ **40.** $^{+}13$ **42.** 0 **46.** $^{+}18$

Page 211   **4.** $^{-}14$ **6.** $^{+}6$; $^{+}7$ **7.** $^{-}7$; $^{-}5$; $^{-}7$ **10.** $^{-}9$; $^{+}3$; $^{-}6$ **12.** $^{-}7$; $^{+}9$; $^{+}2$ **14.** $^{+}19$ **16.** $^{-}2$ **18.** $^{-}3$ **20.** $^{+}97$ **23.** $^{-}12$ **25.** $^{-}34$ **28.** $^{+}94$ **31.** $^{+}5$ **33.** 0 **34.** $^{-}24$

Pages 212–213   **1.** 0 **2.** $\frac{^{-}1}{4}$ **4.** $^{-}5$ **7.** $\frac{^{+}1}{12}$ **9.** $^{+}1$ **10.** $\frac{^{+}3}{4}$ **12.** $^{-}18\frac{1}{6}$ **15.** $^{-}15.60$ **17.** $^{-}10.0$ **20.** $^{+}7.30$ **23.** 0 **25.** 0 **26. a.** $^{-}1$; $^{+}1$ **c.** $^{-}8$; $^{+}8$ **d.** $^{+}3$; $^{-}3$ **g.** $^{-}1$; $^{+}1$ **28.** yes **30. b.** 0

Pages 213–214   **2. a.** no **b.** no **4. a.** yes **b.** no **6. a.** no **b.** no

Pages 214–217   **2.** 47.855 **3.** $\frac{41}{42}$ **6.** $25\frac{19}{24}$ **9.** 2.3030 **10.** .0765 **13.** $\frac{1}{42}$ **14.** $1\frac{1}{6}$ **16.** 8,722 **18.** 1,343 **20.** 6,239 **23.** 116,440 **26.** 372.84 **27.** 183.33 **31.** $6\frac{33}{42}$ **33.** $38\frac{23}{24}$ **34.** $36\frac{5}{12}$ **35.** 1,025 **37.** 25 **39.** .67 **41.** 4.4 **42.** 7

44. $\frac{3}{10}$ **48.** $2\frac{4}{5}$ **50.** $2\frac{17}{20}$ **52.** less **54.** greater **55.** less **58.** $\frac{13}{36}$ **60.** 2 **63.** $\frac{3}{5}$

65. 72 **71.** 200 **69.** $\frac{1}{400}$ **74.** 1 ft. 9 in. **76.** 4 lb. 13 oz. **79.** 2 ft. 10 in.

80. New York: 11.375; Pennsylvania: 4.615; Ohio: 3.770; Michigan: 3.015;

Florida: 1.457 **82.** Delaware: $2,729.16; Michigan: $2,230.98 **83.** $94\frac{2}{3}\%$

Pages 221–222 **1.** $^+27$ **3.** $^+44$ **5.** 0 **8.** $\frac{^+21}{32}$ **10.** $^+60\frac{3}{8}$ **11.** $^+16.2$ **14.** $^+.1$
17. positive

Pages 222–223 **2.** decrease by $^+1$ **4.** 2 **5.** $^-2$ **7.** $^-100$ **8.** $^+3 \times ^-2 = ^-6$;
$^+3 \times ^-3 = ^-9$; $^+3 \times ^-4 = ^-12$; $^+3 \times ^-5 = ^-15$; $^+3 \times ^-6 = ^-18$ **10. b.** $^-120$
12. c. $^+2 \times ^-100 = ^-100 \times ^+2$ **13.** $^-64$ **15.** $^-132$ **17.** $^-1,200$ **18.** $^-1,250$
20. $^-50$ **22.** $^-100$ **24.** $\frac{^-20}{21}$ **27.** $\frac{^-207}{16}$

Pages 224–225 **2.** decrease by $^+1$ **4.** $^+2$ **7.** $^+100$ **9. b.** $^+50$ **e.** $^+250$
f. $^+3\frac{1}{6}$ **11. a.** $^+60$ **c.** $^+360$ **d.** $\frac{^+12}{5}$ **14.** $^+120$ **16.** $^+9$ **17.** $^+5.2$ **19.** $^+84$ **23.** $^+.03$
24. $^+6$ **25.** $^-15$ **27.** $^-32$ **28.** $^+3$ **30.** $^-80$ **32.** $^+3$ **34.** $^+6$ **37.** 0 **39.** $\frac{^-1}{4}$

Pages 226–228 **2.** $^+56$; $^+56$ **4.** $^-487$; $^-487$ **5.** $^+33$; $^-33$ **8.** $^-6$; $^-6$ **9.** $^+24$;
$^+24$ **11.** $^-1$; $^-1$ **13.** 0; 0 **16.** $^-.66$; $^-.66$ **18.** $^-12$; $^-12$ **21.** $^+6$; $^+6$ **22.** $^-300$;
$^-300$ **24.** $^-52$; $^-52$ **25.** $^+500$; $^+500$ **27.** $^-9.0$; $^-9.0$ **30.** $^-4$; $^-4$ **32.** -54; $^-54$
34. $^-7$; $^-7$ **37.** $^-1,000$ **39.** $^+1,100$ **41.** $^+4,800$ **44.** positive **46.** negative
47. positive **49.** negative **51.** negative **53.** negative **55.** negative **56.** positive **59.** positive **61.** positive **64.** negative **67.** positive **68.** negative
70. negative **72.** positive

Pages 229–230 **2. a.** Comm. prop. mult. **c.** Comm. prop. mult. used twice
4. 0 **5.** $^-1,200$ **8.** $^+1,360$

Pages 230–231 **3.** 7 **5.** 4; 3; 12 **8.** $^+2$ **10.** $^+10$ **11.** $^+2.5$ **13.** $^-3$ **15.** $^-2$
18. $^-5$ **20.** $^-8$ **23.** $^-10$ **24.** $^-13$ **25.** $^+7$ **27.** $^+9$ **29.** $^+4$ **31.** $^+9$ **33.** $^-61$
36. $\frac{^-1}{3}$ **38.** $^-5$ **39.** $^+2$ **41.** $^+1$

Page 232 **1.** $^+1$ **3.** $^+1$ **6.** $^+1$ **8.** $^+1$ **10.** $\frac{^+1}{7}$ **11.** $\frac{^-1}{8}$ **14.** $\frac{^-4}{3}$ **17.** $^+5$
20. $\frac{^-2}{7}$ **24.** $^-1$ **26.** negative **28.** $^+1$; $^-1$ **29.** none

Pages 233–234   **1.** $^-1$ **3.** $^+4$ **6.** $\dfrac{^+2}{15}$ **8.** $\dfrac{^-3}{2}$ **10.** $\dfrac{^-21}{31}$ **11.** $^+7$ **13.** $^-11$ **15.** $^-42$ **17.** $\dfrac{^+9}{100}$ **20.** $\dfrac{^+5}{2}$ **22.** $^-4$ **24.** $^-15$ **26.** $\dfrac{^+3}{20}$ **28.** $\dfrac{^+9}{10}$ **30.** $\dfrac{^-39}{20}$ **33.** negative **35.** positive **36.** positive **41.** negative

Pages 234–236   **2.** $^-9$; $^-9$ **5.** $^+5$; $^+5$ **6.** 0; 0   **10.** $^-2$; $^-2$ **12.** $^-7$; $^-7$ **14.** $^-1$; $^-1$ **15.** $^+15$; $^+15$ **17. a.** $^-10 \div (^-5) = {}^+2$ **c.** yes   **21. a.** true   **c.** false   **e.** true

Pages 236–238   **1.** $^-48$ **2.** $^+31$ **5.** $\dfrac{^+19}{21}$ **7.** $^-10$ **9.** $^-16$ **11.** $^-44$ **12.** $^+15$ **14.** $^+98$ **17.** $\dfrac{^+10}{7}$ **20.** $^-130$ **22.** $\dfrac{^-4}{7}$ **24.** $\dfrac{^+8}{35}$ **26.** $^+55$ **28.** $^+7$ **31.** $\dfrac{^+14}{15}$ **33.** $\dfrac{^-1}{33}$ **34.** $\dfrac{^+1}{14}$ **37.** $^-2$ **39.** $\dfrac{^-11}{2}$ **41.** $^+8$ **44.** $\dfrac{^-1}{11}$ **47.** .02   **50.** .00013   **53.** 50.00   **54.** .00125   **56.** 336   **58.** 40   **59.** $53\dfrac{1}{3}$ **62.** 49 mi. 450 yds.   **63.** 55° 24′   **66.** 8 gal. 3 qt. 0 pt.   **67.** 8 yds. 2 ft.   **70.** 2 min. 32 sec.   **71.** 20° 52′ 45″   **73.** 25   **77.** $\dfrac{1}{36}$ **78.** $\dfrac{4}{9}$ **81.** .25   **82.** .0004   **84.** .000001   **86.** 10:1   **89.** 2:3   **90.** 1:2   **93.** 27:28   **94.** 1   **7.** 10.5   **98.** .01

Page 243   **1.** $6 = 6$ **3.** $\dfrac{1}{2} = \dfrac{1}{2}$ **5.** $18 = 18$ **6.** $2 = 2$ **8.** $0 = 0$

Pages 244–245   **1.** $^-6$ **3.** $\dfrac{^-1}{2}$ **6.** $\sqrt{10}$ **8.** $\dfrac{10}{13}$ **9.** -10 **11.** $-\dfrac{1}{2}$ **14.** -9 **17.** 3   **19.** -36 **20.** 21   **24.** 60   **27.** -400 **28.** -4 **29.** -50 **32.** -300 **33.** 1

Page 246   **1.** 2   **4.** 5   **5.** 20   **7.** $\dfrac{1}{2}$ **9.** 0   **12.** $-2\dfrac{1}{2}$ **14.** 0   **15.** -2 **17.** 2

Page 247   **2.** $15 + n = -4$ **5.** $-2 \cdot p = -2$ **6.** $4 - b = 0$ **8.** $r \cdot (-7) = -1$ **9.** $v \div 2 = \dfrac{1}{2}$

Page 248   **2.** Some number is divided by -5. The quotient is -7.   **4.** 16 is subtracted from some number. The difference is -1.   **5.** Some number is multiplied by -10. The product is 100.   **7.** Some number is divided by -5. The quotient is -15.   **8.** -3 is added to some number. The sum is -6.   **11.** 6 is added to some number. The sum is -10.   **13.** -5 **16.** $-\dfrac{1}{4}$ **17.** $4\dfrac{1}{2}$ **20.** $\dfrac{1}{3}$ **23.** -10 **26.** $-1\dfrac{1}{2}$ **27.** -2

Pages 249–250   **2.** $d-5$ **4.** $\frac{1}{2} \cdot w - 7$ **5.** $\frac{3 \cdot m}{-2}$ **7.** $\frac{(-1) \cdot n}{-4}$ **9.** $(x-y) \cdot$ (-10) **12.** $[2a + (-2)] \cdot (5a)$ **14.** two times some number, decreased by 6   **16.** the sum of three times a number and $\frac{1}{2}$ **18.** the sum of three times a number and 9, divided by -10 **20.** 2 times some number added to a second number, the sum divided by 5   **23.** $\frac{1}{12} \cdot a$, or $\frac{a}{12}$ **25.** $5{,}280 \cdot t$ **26.** $\frac{u}{60}$ **28.** $17 \cdot y$ **30.** $3 \cdot 5 = 15$ and $15 \ne 35$

Pages 252–253   **1.** $\{1\}$ **3.** $\left\{\frac{1}{5}\right\}$ **5.** $\{-1\}$ **8.** $\{0\}$ **10.** $\{1\}$ **12.** $\{-4\}$ **14.** $\left\{\frac{1}{2}\right\}$ **17.** $\left\{\frac{2}{3}\right\}$ **18.** $\left\{\frac{1}{2}\right\}$ **19.** $\left\{-\frac{1}{4}\right\}$ **21.** $\{3\}$ **23.** $\{2\}$ **26.** $\{3\}$ **28.** $\{1\}$ **30.** $\{8\}$

Pages 253–254   **1.** The absolute value of negative six is six.   **2.** The absolute value of six is six.   **5.** The absolute value of zero is zero.   **9.** The absolute value of three-sevenths is three-sevenths.   **10.** $\{6, -6\}$ **12.** $\{5, -5\}$ **13.** $\{5, -5\}$ **15.** $\{12, -12\}$ **18.** $\{1, -1\}$ **21.** $\{0\}$

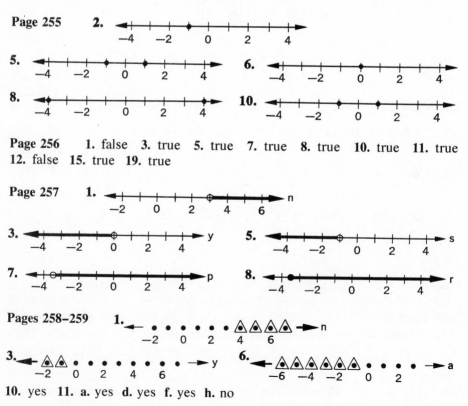

Page 255   **2.**

5.   **6.**

8.   **10.**

Page 256   **1.** false   **3.** true   **5.** true   **7.** true   **8.** true   **10.** true   **11.** true   **12.** false   **15.** true   **19.** true

Page 257   **1.**

3.   **5.**

7.   **8.**

Pages 258–259   **1.**

3.   **6.**

10. yes   **11.** a. yes   d. yes   f. yes   h. no

12. number line: −2 0 2 4 6 → x

14. number line: −2 0 2 4 6 → n

16. number line: −4 −2 0 2 4 → u

18. number line: −6 −4 −2 0 2 → s

20. number line: −6 −4 −2 0 2 → w

21. number line: 0 2 4 6 8 → a

24. number line: 0 2 4 6 8 → p

26. number line: 0 2 4 6 8 → t

Page 260   **1.** The greatest integer not greater than $1\frac{3}{4}$ is 1.   **4.** The greatest integer not greater than 7.9999 is 7.   **6.** 21   **7.** 4   **10.** 6   **13.** 0   **15.** 1   **16.** 0   **17.** true   **19.** false   **21.** true   **24.** true   **26.** 7   **28.** 9

Pages 261–262   **1.** 9   **4.** 8   **5.** 7   **7.** 7   **9.** true   **11.** false   **13.** false   **15.** 13   **16.** 5   **19.** true   **20.** false   **23.** true

Pages 263–264   **2.** number line: 0 2 4 6 8 10 → b

4. number line: 0 2 4 6 8 10 12 → d

5. number line: 0 2 4 6 8 10 12 → e

7. number line: 0 2 4 6 8 10 12 → g

9. number line: 0 2 4 6 8 10 → i

11. number line: 0 2 4 6 8 10 → k

15. number line: 0 2 4 6 8 10 → p

17. number line: 0 2 4 6 8 10 → r

18. number line: 0 2 4 6 8 10 → s

19. false   **21.** true   **23.** false   **25.** true

Pages 264–266   **2.** $[18 > 16]$ **5.** $[4 > 3]$ **6.** $[-3 > -7]$ **7.** $[12 > 4]$ **9.** $[6 > 0]$ **12.** $[0 > -21]$ **13.** $[-8 < -2]$ **15.** $[-5 < 0]$ **17.** $[-14 < 14]$ **20.** $[1 > 0]$ **22.** $[-30 > -70]$ **24.** $[.5 > 0]$ **25. 19.** $[23 < 30]$ **25. 21.** $[-12 < -3]$ **25. 23.** $[-10 < 0]$ **26.** $[35 > 28]$ **29.** $[-3 > -15]$ **31.** $[-30 > -90]$ **32. 27.** $[-10 < 30]$ **32. 29.** $[-15 < -3]$ **32. 31.** $[-90 < -30]$ **33.** $[-10 < -5]$ **35.** $[-70 < 0]$ **37.** $[1 < 10]$

Pages 266–268   **2.** taller   **3.** larger   **4.** $5 > -1$. The conclusion follows.   **6.** $-2 < 1$. The conclusion follows.   **7.** $3 \neq -1 + 4$. The conclusion does not follow. **11.** Conclusion: the Tigers beat the Boilermakers. The conclusion does not follow. **14.** Conclusion: Susan's rank in math is higher than that of Jean. The conclusion follows. **16.** Conclusion: a mile is longer than a centimeter. The conclusion follows.

Pages 269–271   **1. b.** -58 **2. a.** 110   **c.** $\dfrac{5}{12}$ **3. b.** -5.1 **c.** $-.7$ **4. a.** 33

5. c. -153.99 **6. a.** -3 **b.** $-\dfrac{7}{15}$ **7. b.** -64 **8. a.** $\dfrac{4}{21}$ **c.** $\dfrac{4}{15}$ **9. b.** $-64\dfrac{7}{12}$

c. $17\dfrac{1}{3}$ **10. a.** $\dfrac{1}{2}$ **c.** $-\dfrac{1}{2}$ **11. a.** 30   **b.** -20 **12. b.** $\dfrac{1}{9}$ **13. c.** $\dfrac{49}{64}$ **14. a.** $\dfrac{7}{10}$

15. b. -49 **16. a.** 5.44   **c.** $37\dfrac{1}{2}$ **17. b.** 3,250   **18. b.** 50   **20.** b **22.** d **24.** b

27. e **28. b.** 2,900   **d.** 200   **f.** 150   **29. b.** $9\dfrac{1}{11}\%$ **30. a.** -1 **c.** $-\dfrac{5}{2}$

Page 275   **2.** column: 5; row: 2

Pages 275–278   **1.** $(2,4)$ **2.** first member: 4; second member: 2   **5.** $(1,1)$, $(2,2)$, $(3,3)$, $(4,4)$, $(5,5)$ **8.** $(3,1)$ **10.** $(1,2)$, $(2,3)$, $(3,4)$, $(4,5)$ **12.** $(1,4)$, $(2,5)$ **14.** none   **17.** $(5,1),(5,2),(5,3),(5,4),(5,5)$ **19.** $(3,3)$, $(3,4)$, $(3,5)$, $(4,3)$, $(4,4)$, $(4,5)$, $(5,3)$, $(5,4)$, $(5,5)$ **21.** $(1,1)$ **24.** none   **26.** $(1,1)$, $(2,1)$, $(3,1)$, $(4,1)$, $(5,1)$ **28.** $(1,5)$, $(2,5)$, $(3,5)$, $(4,5)$, $(5,5)$

Pages 278–280   **1.** square lattice   **3. a.** 30   **d.** Multiply 5 by 6.   **4.** 2; 2; 4   **6.** 3; 3; 9   **9.** 1; 100; 100   **11.** 7; 15; 105

13.–17.

19. $(1,1)$, $(2,1)$, $(3,1)$ **21.** $(1,2)$, $(2,4)$, $(3,6)$, $(4,8)$, $(5,10)$ **24.** $(1,2)$, $(1,3)$, $(1,4)$, $(1,5)$, $(1,6)$, $(1,7)$, $(1,8)$, $(1,9)$, $(1,10)$, $(2,3)$, $(2,4)$, $(2,5)$, $(2,6)$, $(2,7)$, $(2,8)$, $(2,9)$, $(2,10)$, $(3,4)$, $(3,5)$, $(3,6)$, $(3,7)$, $(3,8)$, $(3,9)$, $(3,10)$, $(4,5)$, $(4,6)$, $(4,7)$, $(4,8)$, $(4,9)$, $(4,10)$, $(5,6)$, $(5,7)$, $(5,8)$, $(5,9)$, $(5,10)$, $(6,7)$, $(6,8)$, $(6,9)$, $(6,10)$, $(7,8)$, $(7,9)$, $(7,10)$, $(8,9)$,

$(8, 10)$, $(9, 10)$ **25.** $(1, 1)$, $(2, 1)$, $(3, 1)$, $(4, 1)$, $(5, 1)$, $(6, 1)$, $(7, 1)$, $(8, 1)$, $(9, 1)$, $(10, 1)$, $(2, 2)$, $(3, 2)$, $(4, 2)$, $(5, 2)$, $(6, 2)$, $(7, 2)$, $(8, 2)$, $(9, 2)$, $(10, 2)$, $(3, 3)$, $(4, 3)$, $(5, 3)$, $(6, 3)$, $(7, 3)$, $(8, 3)$, $(9, 3)$, $(10, 3)$, $(4, 4)$, $(5, 4)$, $(6, 4)$, $(7, 4)$, $(8, 4)$, $(9, 4)$, $(10, 4)$, $(5, 5)$, $(6, 5)$, $(7, 5)$, $(8, 5)$, $(9, 5)$, $(10, 5)$, $(6, 6)$, $(7, 6)$, $(8, 6)$, $(9, 6)$, $(10, 6)$, $(7, 7)$, $(8, 7)$, $(9, 7)$, $(10, 7)$, $(8, 8)$, $(9, 8)$, $(10, 8)$, $(9, 9)$, $(10, 9)$, $(10, 10)$ **26.** $(2, 1)$, $(3, 1)$, $(4, 1)$, $(5, 1)$, $(6, 1)$, $(7, 1)$, $(8, 1)$, $(9, 1)$, $(10, 1)$, $(3, 2)$, $(4, 2)$, $(5, 2)$, $(6, 2)$, $(7, 2)$, $(8, 2)$, $(9, 2)$, $(10, 2)$, $(4, 3)$, $(5, 3)$, $(6, 3)$, $(7, 3)$, $(8, 3)$, $(9, 3)$, $(10, 3)$, $(5, 4)$, $(6, 4)$, $(7, 4)$, $(8, 4)$, $(9, 4)$, $(10, 4)$, $(6, 5)$, $(7, 5)$, $(8, 5)$, $(9, 5)$, $(10, 5)$, $(7, 6)$, $(8, 6)$, $(9, 6)$, $(10, 6)$, $(8, 7)$, $(9, 7)$, $(10, 7)$, $(9, 8)$, $(10, 8)$, $(10, 9)$ **28.** $(1, 1)$, $(2, 1)$, $(3, 1)$, $(4, 1)$, $(5, 1)$, $(6, 1)$, $(7, 1)$, $(8, 1)$, $(9, 1)$, $(10, 1)$, $(1, 2)$, $(2, 2)$, $(3, 2)$, $(4, 2)$, $(5, 2)$, $(6, 2)$, $(7, 2)$, $(8, 2)$, $(9, 2)$, $(10, 2)$

Page 281   **2.** same first coordinate   **4.** Each first coordinate is equal to its second coordinate.

6.

8.

9.

13.

Page 284

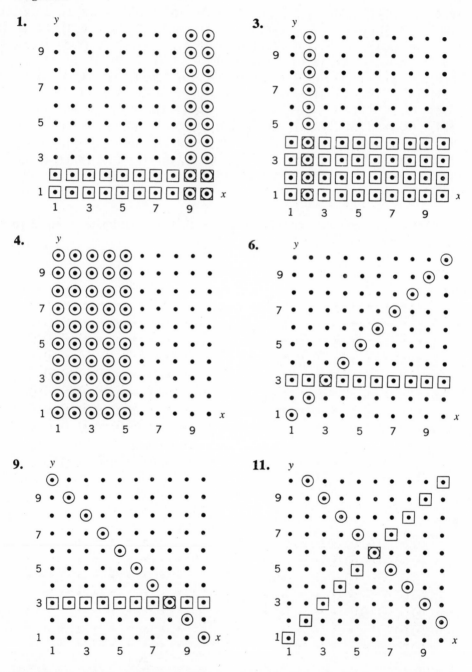

Page 286 **2., 4., 6., 9.** For parts **c**, the points belonging to the intersection are marked by ◙ . For parts **d**, the points belonging to the union are marked by ○ or □ or ◙ .

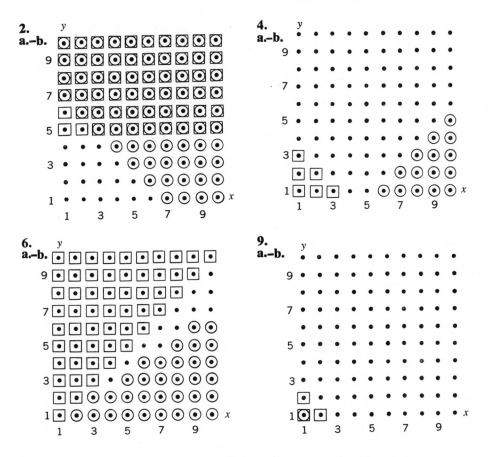

2.
a.-b.

4.
a.-b.

6.
a.-b.

9.
a.-b.

11. $\{(x, y) \mid x = 2y\} = \{(2, 1), (4, 2), (6, 3), (8, 4), (10, 5)\}$

15. $\{(x, y) \mid x + 6 = y\} = \{(1, 7), (2, 8), (3, 9), (4, 10)\}$

19. $\{(x, y) \mid x > 3y\} = \{(4, 1) \ (5, 1), \ (6, 1), \ (7, 1), \ (8, 1), \ (9, 1), \ (10, 1),$
$(7, 2), \ (8, 2), \ (9, 2), \ (10, 2), \ (10, 3)\}$ **20.** $\{(x, y) \mid x + 5 = y + 6\} = \{(2, 1),$
$(3, 2), \ (4, 3), \ (5, 4), \ (6, 5), \ (7, 6), \ (8, 7), \ (9, 8), \ (10, 9)\}$

Page 287 **1.-6.**

Pages 288–289   1. *a*   4. *d*   6. *e*   7. b. Q_4 d. Q_2 g. Q_3 i. Q_2 l. Q_1 n. *x*-axis

Pages 291–292   2. a, b, d, e, f   3. a, d, f   7. b, c   8. $\{(x,y)\,|\,-5 < x \le 1\}$ shown by $\bigcirc$; $\{(x,y)\,|\,-2 < y \le 0\}$ shown by $\square$

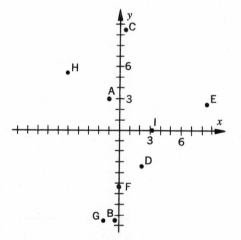

Page 293   **1.–9.**

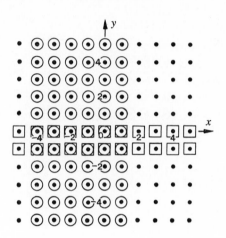

Pages 293–294   2. Quadrant III is the set of all points such that the first and second coordinates are negative.   5. The *y*-axis is the set of all points such that the first coordinate is equal to 0.   7. ϕ 9. ϕ 11. $\{(0,0)\}$ 12. ϕ 14. ϕ

Pages 295–296   1. b. The second coordinates are additive inverses. 3. a. The first coordinates are additive inverses.

5.–10.

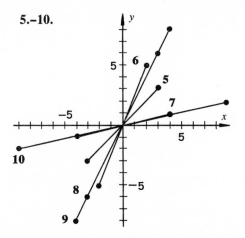

17. b. The second coordinates are additive inverses.

Pages 296–299   **1. a.** $(1,-4)$ **b.** $(-1,4)$ **c.** $(-1,-4)$ **3. a.** $\left(-1\frac{1}{2},\,3\frac{1}{3}\right)$
b. $\left(1\frac{1}{2},\,-3\frac{1}{3}\right)$ **c.** $\left(1\frac{1}{2},\,3\frac{1}{3}\right)$ **6. a.** $(-1,0)$ **b.** $1,0)$ **c.** $(1,0)$ **8. a.** $(0,0)$
b. $(0,0)$ **c.** $(0,0)$

9.1.   **3.**   **6.**   **8.**

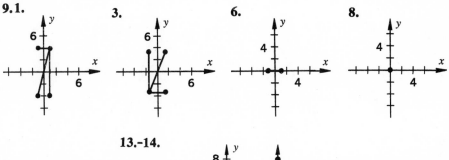

13.–14.

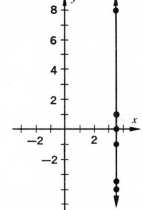

18. yes **19.** yes **22.** $\{(x, y) \,|\, y = -2\}$

23.-24.

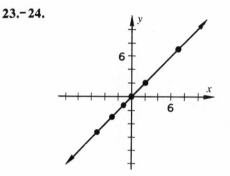

27. no **30.** yes **34.** $\{(x, y) \,|\, x = 2y\}$ **37.** The y-coordinate is 3 times the x-coordinate.

Pages 299–300 **2.** Pattern: The y-coordinate is one less than the x-coordinate. Set: $\{(x, y) \,|\, y = x - 1\}$ **4.** Pattern: The y-coordinate is 3 times the x-coordinate. Set: $\{(x, y) \,|\, y = 3x\}$ **5.** Pattern: The y-coordinate is 1 less than twice the x-coordinate. Set: $\{(x, y) \,|\, y = 2x - 1\}$ **8.** Pattern: The y-coordinate is $1\frac{1}{2}$ more than $\frac{1}{2}$ the x-coordinate. Set: $\left\{ (x, y) \,|\, y = \frac{1}{2}x + 1\frac{1}{2} \right\}$

Pages 300–301

1.-2.

12.-14.

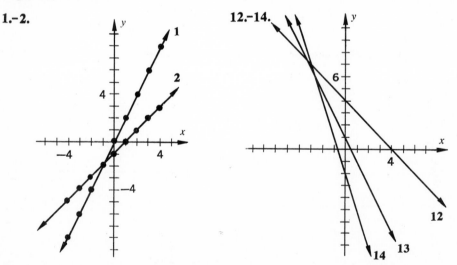

Page 302 **2.** Pattern: The y-coordinate is equal to $\frac{1}{2}$ the square of the x-coordinate. Set $\left\{ (x, y) \,|\, y = \frac{1}{2}x^2 \right\}$ **4.** Pattern: The y-coordinate is equal to 3 times the square of the x-coordinate. Set: $\{(x, y) \,|\, y = 3x^2\}$ **5.** Pattern: The

y-coordinate is equal to -1 times the square of the x-coordinate. Set: $\{(x, y) \mid y = -1(x^2)\}$ or $\{(x, y) \mid y = -x^2\}$ **8.** Pattern: The y-coordinate is equal to $-\dfrac{1}{2}$ times the square of the x-coordinate. Set: $\left\{(x, y) \mid y = -\dfrac{1}{2}x^2\right\}$

Pages 303–304 **1.** 0 **4.** $12\dfrac{1}{2}$ **7.** $4\dfrac{1}{2}$ **9.** $24\dfrac{1}{2}$ **21.** The two parabolas have the same shape. Both contain the point $(0, 0)$. They differ in that one opens upward and the other opens downward. **23.** Same description of comparison as in exercise **21**.

Page 305 **2.** $\dfrac{3}{2} > (-1)^2$; $\dfrac{3}{2} > 1$ **5.** the parabola $\{(x, y) \mid y = x^2\}$ and its exterior **7.** the parabola $\{(x, y) \mid y = 2x^2\}$ and its interior **8.** the exterior of the parabola $\{(x, y) \mid y = 2x^2\}$ **10.** the interior of the parabola $\{(x, y) \mid y = 3x^2\}$

Page 306 **1.** Pattern: The x-coordinate is 2 times the square of the y-coordinate. Set: $\{(x, y) \mid x = 2y^2\}$ **4.** Pattern: The x-coordinate is $\dfrac{1}{4}$ the square of the y-coordinate. Set: $\left\{(x, y) \mid x = \dfrac{1}{4}y^2\right\}$ **6.** Pattern: The x-coordinate is -2 times the square of the y-coordinate. Set: $\{(x, y) \mid x = -2y^2\}$ **8.** Pattern: The x-coordinate is $-\dfrac{1}{4}$ times the square of the y-coordinate. Set: $\Big\{(x, y) \mid x = -\dfrac{1}{4}y^2\Big\}$

Pages 307–308 **2.** $1.7, -1.7$ **4.** $3.6, -3.6$ **5.** $4.5, -4.5$

9.–10. **11.–12.**

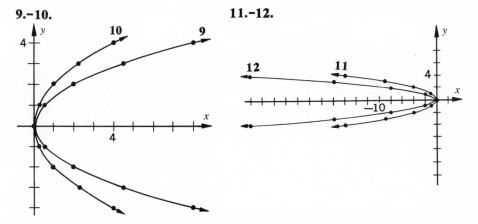

17. The parabolas get "narrower." **18.** The two parabolas have the same shape. The first one opens to the right, the second one to the left. Both contain the point $(0, 0)$.

20. Same type of comparison as in exercise **18.**   **24.** $\{(x, y) \mid y^2 > x\}$ **25.** the parabola and its interior   **27.** all points of the plane except the parabola **30.** the empty set

Pages 309–310   **1.** the line described by $y = 3$ **4.** the empty set   **6.** the entire plane except the line described by $y = 3$

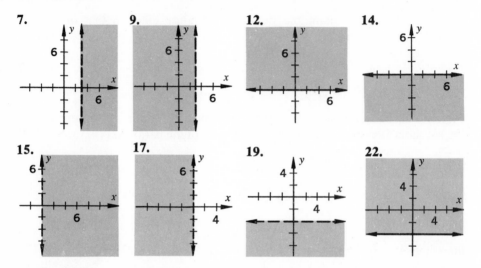

7.   **9.**   **12.**   **14.**

15.   **17.**   **19.**   **22.**

23. the empty set   **26.** the set of all points either whose first coordinate is greater than or equal to 3 or whose second coordinate is less than 3   **28.** the set of all points of the plane   **29.** false   **31.** true   **3.** true

Pages 311–313   **1.** yes   **2.** no   **6.** no   **8.** yes   **10.** yes   **12.** yes   **14.** no   **15.** yes **19.** no   **21.** yes   **24.** yes   **25.** no   **28.** yes   **29.** yes

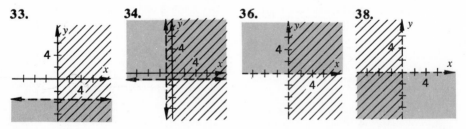

33.   **34.**   **36.**   **38.**

41. no   **42.** yes   **44.** no   **45.** yes   **47.** true   **49.** false   **51.** false   **53.** true   **56.** false **58.** true   **60.** true   **62.** true.

Pages 314–316   **1.** .15   **2.** .48   **5.** 5.6   **6.** .0025   **9.** .025   **11.** 30   **14.** 15   **15.** 30 **17.** 25   **19.** 12.5   **21.** 500   **24.** $\frac{1}{2}$ **26.** 1,400   **27.** 10   **30.** 1.2   **32.** .012   **34.** N **37.** D **38.** T **40.** D **43.** D **44.** $2 \times 2 \times 2 \times 3 \times 3$ **46.** $3 \times 3 \times 5 \times 5$ **49.** 17

51. {1, 2, 5, 10, 25, 50} **53.** *E* **55.** *PO* **58.** *PO* **59.** 7 **62.** −8 **63.** 0 **65.** $\frac{1}{5}$

67. $\frac{7}{3}$ **68.** −$\frac{2}{3}$ **71.** *R* **73.** *I* **76.** *R* **78.** *R* **79.** 24 yd. 2 ft. **83.** 6 gal. 2 qt. **86.** 801

88. .1408 **91.** 10,600 **93.** 10 **95.** −111 **97.** −46 **99.** −1 **101.** 1 **104.** −45

106. $\frac{1}{6}$ **108.** 1$\frac{19}{20}$ **110.** 98 **112.** −1.4 **114.** −6 **117.** −8 **119.** −44 **121.** −340

123. $\frac{1}{36}$ **125.** 1 **127.** 15 **130.** −10.8 **131.** 4 **133.** −$\frac{1}{2}$

Page 321   1. a. $\overline{AB}, \overline{BC}, \overline{CD}, \overline{DA}$ **2. a.** $\overline{MP}, \overline{PR}, \overline{RS}, \overline{ST}, \overline{TM}, \overline{MR}, \overline{TR}$
c. *M*, *T* **3. b.** *X* is not an endpoint of $\overline{YZ}$ and *X* is not between *Y* and *Z*.

Pages 322–323   2. 3 **3. c.** $\overline{RQ}$ and $\overline{QP}$ **5. b.** {*C*} **6.** No; $\overline{WZ}$ and $\overline{YX}$ do
not have a common endpoint. **8. b.** $\overline{XY} \cup \overline{YZ} \cup \overline{ZX}$ **10.** $\overline{NR}, \overline{RQ}, \overline{QP}, \overline{PN}$
11. a. $\overline{NR}$ and $\overline{NP}$ **d.** $\overline{RN}$ and $\overline{RQ}$ **13.** $\overline{RN}$ and $\overline{NP}, \overline{QR}$ and $\overline{RN}, \overline{RN}$ and
$\overline{NP}$ **14.** $\overline{QN}$

Pages 324–325   2. $\overleftrightarrow{XY}$ **4. a.** true **d.** true **e.** false

Pages 325–326   1. a. *X* **d.** *W* **3.** Their union is not a line. **5.** The two rays
are collinear. **7.** *M* **9. a.** ∠*BAM* and ∠*BAC* are two names for the same
set of points. **11.** ∠*DAB* is vertical ∠*EAC*.

Pages 326–327   1.

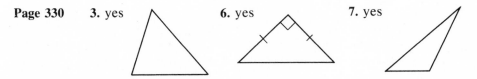

4. $\overline{AB}$ and $\overline{CD}, \overline{EF}$ and $\overline{GH}$ **5.** ∠*A* and ∠*D*, ∠*B* and ∠*C*

Pages 328–329   1. scalene **4.** isoceles; equilateral **5.** scalene **7.** isoceles
10. $\overline{XZ}$ **13. b.** Each angle in an equilateral triangle has a measure of 60°.

Page 330   3. yes   **6.** yes   **7.** yes

Pages 330–332   1. h_D **3.** yes; no **4. a.** yes **b.** no **6. b.** no **c.** no

7.

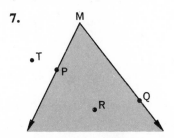

8. no   **10.** The union of the interior of $\angle M$, the $\angle M$, and the exterior of $\angle M$ is equal to the entire plane.

13.

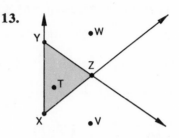

13. a. no   **c.** no

Pages 333–334   **1.** $\overleftrightarrow{AB}, \overleftrightarrow{BC}, \overleftrightarrow{AC}$ **2. b.** $\{C\}$ **3. a.** h_A is the half-plane determined by $\overleftrightarrow{BC}$ and containing point A.   **5.** false   **7.** true   **8.** false   **11.** true **14.** false   **15. d.** yes   **16. b.** no

Page 335   **1. i.** We cannot return to the point from which we start, tracing the entire curve.   **6. a.** no   **b.** yes   **c.** yes

Page 336   **1. a.** yes   **b.** no   **2.** Given any two points there is some line which contains both of them.

Pages 337–338   **3.** $\triangle ABC$ is an equilateral triangle. Thus, any segment which is half the length of one side will also be half the length of the other two sides.

Pages 338–340   **1.** 27,054   **4.** $20\frac{7}{12}$ **6.** 382,829   **8.** $\frac{29}{63}$ **10.** 79,722   **13.** $19\frac{3}{5}$ **15.** $135.259\overline{259}$ **17.** $\frac{39}{62}$ **18.** 37%   **20.** 236%   **22.** 10,000%   **24.** 1   **26.** 5   **29.** 15 **30.** $\frac{1}{4}$ **32.** 2   **33.** 0   **36.** 18   **38.** $3\frac{1}{3}$ **40.** $\sqrt{999}$ **41.** 4   **44.** 1.5   **46.** about $328\frac{1}{3}$

Pages 345–346   **2.** They are the same.   **3.** 8 sq. in.   **6.** $\frac{3}{4}$ sq. ft., or 108 sq. in. **8.** 18 sq. ft., or 2 sq. yd.   **10. b.** $\frac{1}{2}lw$

Pages 346–347   **1.** 15 sq. in.   **3.** $7\frac{1}{2}$ sq. in.   **5.** 8 sq. in.   **6.** 8 sq. in.   **8.** 27 sq. in.   **10.** $4\frac{1}{2}$ sq. in.

Pages 347–348   **2.** true   **4.** false   **5.** true   **7.** false   **9.** true   **11.** They are equal.   **12.** They are equal.

15.

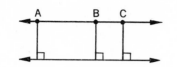

They are equal.

Pages 349–350   **1.** 9.45 sq. in.   **3.** 8 in.   **4.** 18 sq. in.   **6.** $37\frac{1}{2}$ sq. in.   **9.** $\frac{1}{12}$ sq. ft.   **10.** 36 sq. in. or $\frac{1}{4}$ sq. ft.   **13.** 22.94 sq. in.   **15.** $10\frac{1}{2}$ sq. in.

Page 351   **1. a.** no   **c.** no   **e.** yes   **g.** no   **i.** no   **j.** yes   **3.** yes   **4.** yes; 60°; yes

Pages 351–352   **1.** 6 sq. in.   **4.** Yes; $\overline{PT}$ is perpendicular to $\overline{RT}$.   **6.** $\frac{1}{4}\sqrt{3}$ sq. in.   **8.** $\frac{9}{4}\sqrt{3}$ sq. in.   **11.** $\sqrt{15}$ sq. in.

Page 354   **2.** $4\sqrt{3}$ sq. in.   **3.** $\frac{1}{2}\sqrt{3}$ sq. in.   **6.** $\sqrt{3}$ in.

Pages 354–355   **1.** 4 in.   **3.** 6   **5.** 1°   **6. b.** 12   **d.** 72   **g.** 720

Page 356   **1. a.** 120°   **4.** less   **5. c.** less   **e.** greater   **6. a.** 24   **c.** 24   **8.** $54\sqrt{3}$ sq. in.

Pages 357–358   **2.** dodecagon   **3.** Y **5.** 24   **7.** Z **9.** The perimeters of the polygons get closer to the circumference of the circle.   **11.** greater   **13.** less   **14.** less   **16.** greater   **18.** greater   **19.** less

Pages 359–361   **2.** n **4.** (an) units   **7.** 4π; 12.56 in.   **9. a.** Circumference $= \pi$ in. $\doteq 3.14$ in; Area $= \frac{1}{4}\pi$ sq. in. $\doteq .79$ sq. in.   **d.** Circumference $= 2\pi$ in. $\doteq 6.28$ in; Area $= \pi$ sq. in. $\doteq 3.14$ sq. in.   **10. b.** 200 sq. in.   **11. a.** 255 sq. in.   **c.** that in **10c.**   **12. b.** Circumference $= 6\pi \doteq 18.84$ ft.; Area $= 9\pi \doteq 28.26$ sq. ft.   **d.** Circumference $= 11\pi \doteq 34.54$ ft.; Area $= 30.25\pi \doteq 94.99$ sq. ft.   **14.** 101   **16.** 820

Page 363   **1.** 6 cu. in.   **3.** $\frac{1}{.3}$ cu. ft.   **5.** 200 cu. m.   **7.** 84 lb.   **8.** $\frac{1}{2}$ **11.** $\frac{1}{27}$ **13.** four times greater   **16.** .5 cu. yds. per hr.   **18.** 1.8 loads

Pages 364–365   **1.** circle   **3. a.** rectangle   **c.** length of the altitude

Pages 365–366   **2.** $2\pi r^2$ sq. in.   **4. a.** 42π sq. in.   **5. a.** 60π sq. in.   **c.** $1,536\pi$ sq. in.   **6. b.** 300π cu. in.   **7.** 3,140 lb.   **9.** 499,636.8 lb.

Pages 366–367   **1. b.** the area of each triangle   **3.** 900 cu. in.

4.a.    **b.** 6

Pages 368–370   **2.** $6\frac{2}{3}\pi$ cu. in.   **4.** 60π cu. in.   **6.** 20π cu. in.   **9.** 180π cu. in.
11. A's is twice B's.   **13.** A's is n times B's.   **16.** A's is n^2 times B's.   **18.** A's is 27 times B's.   **20.** A's is kn^2 times B's.

Pages 370–373   **1.** 175.39   **3.** 20,211   **5.** $24\frac{13}{24}$ **7.** 9,486   **10.** 905.64   **12.** $\frac{5}{24}$
16. $11\frac{23}{24}$ **18.** $2\frac{1}{8}$ **19.** 30,195   **21.** 6,385,254   **24.** $\frac{8}{63}$ **26.** $20\frac{4}{15}$ **27.** 36.6025
29. 142.04   **32.** 61   **34.** 6   **36.** $\frac{1}{90}$ **38.** $\frac{6}{11}$ **41.** $3\frac{3}{4}$ **43.** $2\frac{17}{20}$ **45.** $\frac{1}{2}$ **46.** -30
49. -111 **51.** 33   **52.** 100   **56.** 34   **57.** -264 **59.** -156 **61.** 12   **63.** $-\frac{1}{40}$ **64.** $22\frac{1}{2}$
67. .6   **69.** $\frac{1}{2}$ **71.** 6,000   **73.** 100   **74.** $3 \times 10^2 + 6 \times 10^1 + 9 \times 10^0$
77. $1 \times 10^5 + 2 \times 10^4 + 5 \times 10^3 + 0 \times 10^2 + 0 \times 10^1 + 2 \times 10^0$ **78.** base: 17; exponent: 10   **80.** base: 0; exponent: 38   **82.** 59   **85.** 35   **86.** even   **87.** odd
90. irrational   **91.** $\frac{2}{9}$ **93.** $\frac{106}{999}$ **95. a.** yes   **b.** no   **d.** no   **g.** yes   **i.** yes   **k.** yes
96. closure under division   **98. a.** no   **b.** yes   **99. a.** yes   **c.** no   **f.** yes   **100.** 7
102. $5 \cdot 7$ **104.** $2 \cdot 53$ **108.** Rt. dist. mult. over add.   **110.** Assoc. prop. add.
111. Comm. prop. add.   **114.** 3   **116.** 7   **119.** 5%   **121.** $875

Page 377   **1.** 3 in.   **3.** 1.75 in.   **6.** no   **8.** yes

Page 378   **7. b.**

B

A

C

Page 379   **6. a.** twice as long   **c.** twice as long   **9.** $AB = 3.5$ in.; $BC = 1.5$ in.; $CA = 3$ in.   **10. a.** 16 in.

Page 381   8.

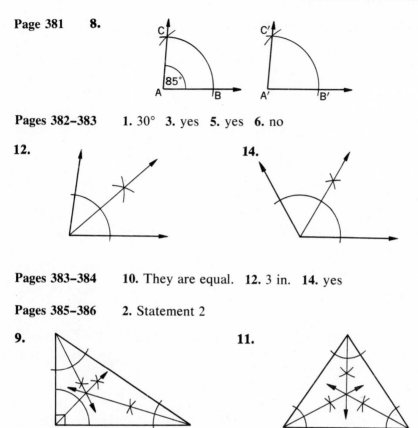

Pages 382–383   1. 30° **3.** yes **5.** yes **6.** no

12.

14.

Pages 383–384   10. They are equal. **12.** 3 in. **14.** yes

Pages 385–386   2. Statement 2

9.

11.

Page 389   2. $m\angle A = 135°$ **5.** $m\widehat{BC} = 88°$ **6.** $m\widehat{BC} = 60°$

Pages 390–391   1. Yes; the endpoints, M and P, are on the circle. **3.** yes
6. $\widehat{BC}$ in each case **8.** 20°; $m(<B) = \frac{1}{2} \cdot m(<A)$ **11.** 54°; $m(<H) = \frac{1}{2} \cdot$
$m(<G)$ **13.** They are equal.

Pages 391–392   4. $\widehat{XZY}$ in each case **5.** Each intercepts an arc of 180° and
is $\frac{1}{2}$ this measure, or 90° **7.** Yes; both intercept a semicircle.

Pages 392–393   1. 4 **3.** .5 **4.** 6 **8.** $\frac{2}{3}$ **9.** $\frac{1}{2}$ **11.** $1\frac{1}{5}$ in. **14.** $A'B' = 5.3\overline{3}$ in.;
$B'C' = 8$ in.

Pages 393–395   1. $\overline{AB}$ and $\overline{XY}$; $\overline{BC}$ and $\overline{YZ}$; $\overline{CA}$ and $\overline{ZX}$ **3.** $EF = FD = 4\frac{1}{5}$
in. **6.** 5 in. **9.** 18 in. and 7.5 in. **10.** $QM = \frac{3}{4}$ in.; $EG = GK = 2$ in.

Pages 395–396   **1.** 55°   **2.** 55°   **5.** similar   **8.** similar

Pages 396–397   **2.** They have a right angle at D.   **3. a.** $m\angle A + m\angle B + m\angle C = 180$. (Sum of the measures of the angles in a triangle is 180°.) $m\angle A + m\angle B + 90 = 180$. $m\angle A + m\angle B = 90$.   **3. d.** From b, $m\angle DCB + m\angle B = 90$; therefore it follows that $m\angle DCB = 90 - m\angle B$.   **3. g.** $m\angle DCA + m\angle A + m\angle ADC = 180$ **3. k.** If two right triangles have a pair of acute angles of the same measure, then they are similar.   **4. b.** $\overline{DA}$ **6. a.** $\overline{BD}$ **7. c.** $\angle BCD$ **9.** Both have a right angle at W.   **11.** $\angle Y$ **14.** $\overline{XW}$ **16.** $\overline{XY}$

Page 398   **2.** 2 in.   **5.** 12 yd.   **7.** 3 in.

Page 399   **1.** If $\dfrac{b}{f} = \dfrac{f}{c}$, then $b \times c = f \times f$. Thus, $bc = f^2$, or $f^2 = bc$.   **3.** 6   **6.** 7   **9.** 8   **11.** 1.4   **14.** 4.6   **16.** 4.2   **19.** 1.7   **21.** 3

Page 400   **2.** Yes; it is inscribed in a semicircle.   **4.** true   **7.** true   **10.** false   **12.** $m\angle CO'E = 2 \times m\angle COE$

Pages 402–403   **10.** $BD = \sqrt{1 \times 6} = \sqrt{6}$ units   **13.** $AB = \sqrt{7 \times 2} = \sqrt{14} \doteq 3.7$ **16.** $AB = \sqrt{3 \times 13} = \sqrt{39} \doteq 6.2$ **20.** $\sqrt{8}$ in.   **23.** $\sqrt{20}$ in.   **25.** $\sqrt{20}$ in.   **28.** $\sqrt{8}$ in.   **29.** 2×16; 4×8 **32.** 2×12; 4×6; 3×8 **35.** 5×25

Pages 404–407   **2.** 2.961   **4.** $1\dfrac{1}{12}$ **7.** $9\dfrac{8}{21}$ **10.** 297,898   **13.** $\dfrac{5}{18}$ **16.** $\dfrac{29}{56}$ **19.** 333,408   **22.** $\dfrac{4}{15}$ **25.** $5\dfrac{5}{8}$ **27.** $32\dfrac{2}{3}$ **29.** 106, R13   **32.** $\dfrac{24}{35}$ **36.** $5\dfrac{1}{3}$ **38.** 34   **41.** 2   **43.** 1   **46.** $\dfrac{3}{10}$ **48.** -16 **51.** 24   **54.** 3   **56.** 120   **59.** -2 **62.** -6 **64.** no   **65.** yes   **67.** no   **69.** no   **71.** true   **74.** false   **77.** true   **80.** true   **83.** false   **86.** true   **89.** false   **92.** true   **95.** false   **97.** false   **99.** $\{3, 7, 11\}$ **101.** 12   **103.** No; $-1 + (-1) = -2$, which is not an element of the set.

Pages 411–412   **1. b.** 10^3 **3. a.** 100,000   **6.** .01   **9.** true   **11.** false   **13.** false   **16.** 1,000,000 sq. m.   **19.** 14,250 sq. mm.   **21.** 45,000 sq. cm.

Pages 413–414   **1.** 3.9 in.   **4.** 1,090 yds.   **7.** 2.0 m.   **10.** 6.4 km.   **12.** 10.8 sq. ft.   **14.** .4 sq. mi.   **17.** .8 sq. m.   **19.** .1 cu. in.   **21.** 211.8 cu. ft.   **23.** 14.5 seconds

Pages 414–415   **2.** 379 l.   **4.** 475 ml.   **7.** 450.0 oz.

Pages 415–416   **1.** .001   **3.** 340.2 g.   **6.** 42.8 kg.   **9.** 3,150 calories

Page 417   **1.** 86° F.   **3.** 32° F.   **6.** $-5°$ C.   **8.** $-30°$ C.

radious of 3.14